ECONOMICS

Theory & Practice

NINTH EDITION

ECONOMICS

Theory & Practice

NINTH EDITION

Patrick J. Welch

St. Louis University

Gerry F. Welch

*St. Louis Community College
at Meramec*

WILEY

John Wiley & Sons, Inc.

VP & PUBLISHER   George Hoffman

ASSOCIATE PUBLISHER   Judith Joseph

ASSOCIATE EDITOR   Jennifer Manias

ASSOCIATE DIRECTOR OF MARKETING   Amy Scholz

ASSISTANT MARKETING MANAGER   Diane Mars

EXECUTIVE MEDIA EDITOR   Allie K. Morris

SENIOR PRODUCTION EDITOR   Nicole Repasky

COVER DESIGNER   Madelyn Lesure

PRODUCTION MANAGEMENT SERVICES   Ingrao Associates

EDITORIAL ASSISTANT   Emily McGee

COVER ART   © Hyacinth Manning/SUPERSTOCK

Application, Up For Debate, Test Your Understanding, and Critical Thinking icons ©istockphotos.com.

This book was set in Times Roman by Aptara®, Inc. and printed and bound by Quebecor/Versailles. The cover was printed by Phoenix Color.

This book is printed on acid free paper.   ∞

To order books or for customer service, please call 1-800-CALL WILEY (225-5945).

ISBN-13   978-0470-45009-3

Printed in the United States of America

10 9 8 7 6 5 4 3

Dear Student,

Welcome to the study of economics and to the ninth edition of *Economics: Theory & Practice*. This course may well be among the most valuable you will take for application to and enrichment of your everyday life. We are excited to join you in this learning experience.

What can you expect from this textbook and your course?

♦ Economic topics are given a great deal of attention in daily news reports. Unemployment numbers, banking issues, government stimulus programs, gasoline price changes, contamination of imported food products, and so much more are frequently featured. This textbook will provide basic information that helps you to understand economic topics in a knowledge-based context.

♦ In the first few pages of Chapter 1, you will learn that economics is rooted in scarcity and choice: Scarcity of resources, time, and money forces everyone, including businesses and governments, into making choices, or decisions, about how to use these limited resources, or deal with scarcity. Economics introduces you to tools used in decision making, and to thought processes that are valuable in problem solving and thinking through issues.

♦ Other than mathematics and parts of the natural sciences, little in these fields of study is indisputable. Instead, in most areas like economics, the subject matter is gray and lends itself to varied points of view. Every chapter in this textbook has an "Up for Debate" feature, where issues are viewed from different perspectives. For example, the issue of banning the use of cell phones while driving (the Up for Debate in Chapter 11) has both pro and con arguments.

♦ Today's focus on environmental issues is an example of the basic economic problem, and the decisions that surround these issues are perfect examples of the application of the study and tools of economics in our everyday world. Throughout this edition, you will find environmental applications and debates in almost every chapter. This text will make you smarter about thinking through global warming, carbon emissions, recycling, and a host of other "green" concerns and issues.

We have worked to maintain and improve the reputation of this textbook for its student-friendly style. For the student who needs extra support, there is a Study Guide and online help. We know that economics has a reputation as a difficult and dense subject area, but we ask that you put this notion aside as you work through this accessible textbook—you will find it most readable and interesting. We are always open to your ideas and questions.

Enjoy!
Patrick Welch
Gerry Welch

PREFACE

The study of basic economics is relevant and important. It provides information about fundamental institutions and relationships that affect everyone's quality of life and provides a framework for thinking through and understanding the process of decision making. Economic issues are reported extensively in the news media; economic policies from local government ordinances to global agreements influence jobs, the environment, and much more; and our daily lives are permeated by decision making at every level.

Since economics touches life in so many ways, a course that focuses on fundamental economic concepts and institutions is a valuable part of a person's education. *Economics: Theory & Practice* is written to provide a basic foundation in the study of economics. The book is designed as a primary text for a one-term course, whether it is an introduction to basic economics or principles of economics course, and offers a balanced presentation of macroeconomics and microeconomics.

Economics: Theory & Practice, Ninth Edition, builds on its success through eight editions by ensuring that the textbook's reputation for balanced coverage, flexibility, readability, student friendliness, applications that connect the everyday world to economic concepts, and outstanding learning aids continue to be the very foundation of the text. New to the ninth edition is an emphasis on the environment. From the first chapter's discussion of scarcity and choice and the chapter's Up for Debate on mandatory recycling, and through every chapter in the text, examples, applications, and debates focus on environmental and "green" issues. We believe that currently there is no better area to illustrate the basic problem of scarcity and choice, to connect economic concepts to the world around us, and to understand the process of decision making and its consequences.

OBJECTIVES OF THE BOOK

There are three primary objectives of this book. The first is to introduce and survey basic economic concepts and institutions in a way that provides students with a solid understanding of key economic relationships and terms. The second is to give students exposure to economic thinking that will enable them to understand some fundamental processes used in decision making that can be applied to their own decision making as well as an evaluation of opinions, news reports, and other economic information. The third objective is to engage students through a writing style, applications, and examples that connect economics to everyday life.

Economic Concepts and Institutions

Economics: Theory and Practice, Ninth Edition, includes a broad overview of what economists label the principles of macroeconomics and microeconomics. A scan through the Table of Contents provides information about topics that range from supply and demand, to total spending and economic fluctuations, to the behavior of firms in different market settings, to comparative advantage in international trade.

The text also introduces data and institutions with which students should be familiar to understand the operation of the economy. These range from measures of unemployment and GDP, to the Federal Reserve, to poverty guidelines, to foreign exchange markets. This institutional information helps to link the conceptual world to the real world and allows economics to be viewed in a broader perspective.

FEATURES OF THE BOOK

Several key features of *Economics, Theory and Practice* contribute to the successful teaching and learning of introductory economics.

Balance of Macroeconomic and Microeconomic Coverage

Economics: Theory and Practice offers a balanced presentation of macroeconomic and microeconomic topics. The book is divided into four parts: Part 1 covers basic concepts and definitions, economic systems, and supply and demand. Part 2 covers macroeconomics in six chapters. Part 3 covers microeconomics in six chapters. Part 4 covers international economics.

Flexibility in Sequencing of Macroeconomics and Microeconomics

The text can be used in a macroeconomics–microeconomics sequence by going directly through the chapters, or in a microeconomic–macroeconomic sequence by reversing the order of Parts 2 and 3. Basic tools and definitions are covered in Part 1, and extreme care has been taken to ensure that Parts 2 and 3 are independent units and can stand alone. In fact, one author has taught using the text's micro–macro sequence, and the other with the text's macro–micro sequence.

Flexibility to Shorten Course Coverage

Instructors who want to shorten material coverage will find it easy to do with *Economics: Theory and Practice*. Entire chapters, such as Chapter 9 on macroeconomic viewpoints and models, Chapter 14 on government and the markets, or Chapter 17 on internal finance, can be eliminated because they stand alone. Instructors can also easily eliminate portions of chapters such as the section on the historical development of the U.S. economy in Chapter 2 or the discussion of unionism and collective bargaining in Chapter 15. The authors are also available to work with text users in fine-tuning coverage.

Flexibility to Lengthen or Deepen Course Coverage

Instructors who want to add to course coverage, perhaps for usage in a graduate level survey course, can do so in several ways. They may want to work through all of the chapters in the text, ensuring, for example, that students have complete coverage of antitrust and government regulation by covering Chapter 14. In addition, several appendices have been added to extend coverage. For example, the appendices in chapters 12 and 13 deepen coverage of costs and market structures. Finally, there are several lengthy footnotes that explain material such as the marginal utility/price rule for maximizing utility that can be included.

Flexibility in Course Level and Content

Economics: Theory and Practice has been used in a variety of courses and course levels over the years. Its flexibility allows the text to be used effectively in basic introductory survey courses, more rigorous one-term principles courses, and even in basic graduate level MBA coursework. The range of up-to-date topics combined with traditional core topics, friendly reading style, flexibility of course coverage, and student aids have contributed to the success of this text for a wide variety of student audiences for over two decades.

Student Engagement and Learning

Economics: Theory & Practice, Ninth Edition, provides examples, applications, issue debates, and critical thinking cases to enable students to connect economic concepts to everyday life: from decision making about a wedding, to driving while using a cell phone, to exploring demand for Jonas Brothers' recordings, to evaluating economic growth and the environment. In addition to these connections to everyday life, there are a number of learning aids in each chapter to foster active student learning.

APPLICATIONS, UP FOR DEBATES, TEST YOUR UNDERSTANDINGS, CRITICAL THINKING CASES, AND OTHER LEARNING AIDS

Each chapter in *Economics: Theory and Practice,* Ninth Edition, provides tools to tie the text to real-world examples, background information, and opinions concerning topics and issues. The applications included with each chapter are lively, relevant, and up-to-date. For example, the issue of the future funding of the Social Security system comes through Application 6.2, "How Much Do We Love Granny?," and the reality for a farmer operating in a purely competitive market comes through Application 13.2, "The Farmer's Almanac: It's a Necessity."

Each chapter includes an Up for Debate that shows students the gray areas of policy and issue decisions. For example, the Up for Debate in Chapter 11, "Should Drivers Be Banned from Using Cell Phones While Operating a Vehicle?," includes arguments on both the yes and no sides of the issue. Several of the Up for Debates focus on environmental issues: mandatory recycling, nonprice competition and resource waste, banning international trade that may harm the environment, and a possible relationship between environmental damage and economic growth.

The Critical Thinking Case at the end of each chapter concentrates on a problem or situation designed to strengthen the understanding of an economic concept in the chapter and to develop some critical thinking skills. Questions are included with each case. The cases cover a wide range of issues including the delivery of health care, costly haircuts, and Frederic Bastiat's famous *Petition* that a law be passed to protect French industry from ruinous competition from the sun.

Each chapter helps students organize their studies and reinforces student learning through a variety of learning aids. These include objectives for each chapter, margin definitions, a carefully constructed chapter summary, a list of key definitions and concepts, review questions, discussion questions, and a Test Your Understanding.

The Test Your Understanding in each chapter provides a review of some typically difficult material in the chapter and usually requires some calculations or graphic analysis. For example, in Chapter 3 students tackle a set of events that allows them to strengthen their understanding of supply and demand, and in Chapter 15, students calculate marginal revenue product and graph a labor demand curve.

NEW TO THE NINTH EDITION

Economics: Theory and Practice, Ninth Edition, has been thoroughly updated. All data, both macroeconomic and microeconomic, are the latest available at the time of publication. In addition, students can locate even newer data by referring to the source of the information.

Many changes have occurred recently in the macroeconomy, and we have added these changes throughout the text, working through the latest possible print opportunities to include them. In Chapter 7, Money and Banking, we have rewritten the trends in financial institutions to emphasize legislative changes in the financial institutions industry and to include information about the recent bank bailouts, among other changes such as the inclusion of electronic payments. A section on the economic stimulus package of 2008 and 2009 has been added to Chapter 6, and an application of the multiplier principle to the auto industry issues of Spring 2009 has been added in Chapter 5.

New and updated applications, debates, and critical thinking cases have been included to retain the text's reputation for connections to a student's life. The Jonas Brothers, money and happiness, updated profiles of Starbuck's and Kraft, a Gap labor issue, and homeless families with children are just some of the new additions.

The Ninth Edition has been written with an emphasis on the environment: environmental examples, issues, and policies are woven throughout the text. Chapter 1, for example, now includes recycling, concerns over global warming, the ozone layer, greenhouse gas emissions, sustainability, carbon emissions, energy efficient appliances, and fuel efficiency requirements in the language of the chapter. Other chapters include topics and examples such as environmental damage in planned economies, toxic waste, landfills, hybrids, and more.

Several Up for Debates provide weighty looks at current environmental debates. Among the questions are: Should trade be restricted if it results in environmental damage? Does nonprice competition waste resources? Should St. Louis County, Missouri, impose mandatory trash pickup and recycling?

SUPPLEMENTARY MATERIALS

A dedicated Companion Web site with extensive resources for both students and professors can be found at http://www.wiley.com/college/welch. This Web site includes all of the resources listed here.

The student Study Guide revised by Veronica Horton, includes for each chapter, a listing of objectives and terms from the textbook, a study organizer identifying important concepts, a self-test review, computational exercises, and practice examination questions. Answers to the exercises and practice questions are included at the end of the Study Guide.

The Test Bank, authored by Pat and Gerry Welch and several contributors, contains approximately 3,000 multiple-choice, true/false, and short essay questions, many requiring students to make computations. A Computerized Test Bank containing all test questions from the test bank is also available. This version of the test bank allows instructors to customize exams for their courses.

The Instructor's Manual provides a teaching overview which is particularly useful to new instructors, and a sample syllabus giving information about topic coverage, assignments, examinations, and such. Also included for each chapter is a restatement of objectives, teaching suggestions, and recommendations on incorporating the discussion and review questions and critical thinking cases into a course. Suggested answers for the discussion and review questions are also provided.

A set of PowerPoint Presentations, which consists of chapter outlines and enlarged versions of all the figures and tables contained in the text was prepared by David Ashley. This set can be used to create overhead transparencies for viewing in the classroom or they can be copied and used as handouts for students.

ACKNOWLEDGMENTS

There are many people who have contributed to this project and to whom we owe our gratitude. We have been fortunate to receive valuable, constructive reviewers' comments in earlier editions from Steve Anderson, Fox Valley Technical College; Frederick Arnold, Madison Area Technical College; William Askwig, University of Southern Colorado; Joseph H. Atallah, DeVry Institute of Technology, Los Angeles; Mark Berger, University of Kentucky; Gordon Blake, Kearney State College; Ronald Brandolini, Valencia Community College; G. E. Breger, University of South Carolina; William Brown, California State University, Northridge; Lee Button, Fox Valley Technical Institute; Gerald Carlino, The Federal Reserve Bank of Philadelphia; Kristin Carrico, Umpqua Community College; Howard Chernick, Hunter College; James Clark, Wichita State University; Joy L. Clark, Auburn University at Montgomery; David Cooper, DeVry Institute of Technology, Los Angeles; Richard Crain, Strayer College; Jim Craven, Clark College; Philip M. DeMoss, West Chester University; Ronald Dulaney, University of Montana; Donald Fell, Ohio State University; Mary Ann Ferber, University of Illinois; Russell Flora, Pikes Peak Community College; Arthur Friedberg, Mohawk Valley Community College; David Green, Tidewater Community College; Roberta Greene, Central Piedmont Community College; Chris Greveson, DeVry Technical Institute; Fatemeh Hajiha, Strayer College; Gail Hawks, Miami-Dade Community College; Bryce Hinsch, Fox Valley Technical College; George E. Hoffer, Virgina Commonwealth University; Arthur Jansse, Emporia State University; Laura Johnson, University of Akron; Sol Kaufler, Los Angeles Pierce College; Stephen King, Midstate Technical Institute; Shephen Kyereme, South Carolina State University; John Lafky, California State University, Fullerton; Charles Lave, University of California, Irvine; Don Leet, California State University, Fresno; Carole Lundeberg, Hartford State Technical College; Michael Marlow, California Polytechnic State University; Beth Matta, New Mexico State University; Bernard McCarney, Illinois State University; Cynthia S. McCarty, Jacksonville State University; Debra L. McCracken, Lakeshore Technical College; Kenneth McKnight, Spokane Community College; Green Miller, Morehead State University; Phillip Moery, Shephard College; Todd Munson, West Wisconsin Technical College; Muhammad Mustafa, South Carolina State University; Hong Nguyen, University of Scranton; Knowles Parker, Wake Technical Community College; Terry Riddle, Central Virginia Community College; Christine Rider, St. John's University; Roger Riefler, University of Nebraska; Louis Sage, University of Akron; Rolando A. Santos, Lakeland Community College; Connie Sanzo, Pima Community College; Ted Scheinman, Mt. Hood Community College; M. K. Schrettenbrunner, Strayer College; Patricia A. Serrano, Clark College; Hushang Shahidi, Wright State University; Virginia Shingleton, Valparaiso University; William Small, Spokane Community College; Evert Van Der Heide, Calvin College; Richard Watson, University of California, Santa Barbara; Sidney Wilson, Rockland Community College; and John Young, Riverside Community College.

We are especially grateful to the following people who reviewed the manuscript for the Ninth Edition, and provided many helpful suggestions: Hans Czap, St. Lawrence University; Jahn K. Hakes, Albion College; George Hoffer, Virginia Commonwealth University; Natalia V. Ovchinnikova, St. Lawrence University; and Connie Sanzo, Pima Community College.

Over the years many editors, book reps, and design staff have worked with creating this textbook that has been a part of the economics textbook publishing world for many years. It began with encouragement from Russ Boersma, a sales representative from Dryden Press that became the initial publisher, and through mergers and other decisions moved to Harcourt, Brace Jovanovich, and then to John Wiley & Sons. We are grateful to the individuals and the companies for their support, good advice, and commitment to this text.

It has been our good fortune to work with a wonderful Wiley staff. Not only are they talented and committed to professional excellence, but they view us as part of a team. We have appreciated this effort. We are grateful for the direction provided by Judith Joseph, Associate Publisher; Emily McGee, Editorial Assistant; and Diane Mars, Associate Marketing Manager. On another level, Jennifer Manias, Associate Editor, has been an important part of creating this text and we thank her for all of her wisdom, commitment, and work.

At the production level, we would like to thank Production Manager, Dorothy Sinclair; Production Editors, Nicole Repasky and Valerie Vargas; Senior Designer, Madelyn Lesure; and Photo Editor, Hilary Newman.

In addition, over the past few editions, Suzanne Ingrao has provided outstanding, careful, professional editing, copywriting, and proofreading services. We asked this year that Suzanne be part of our team; we can't imagine working with anyone else. Thank you, Suzanne.

We have also benefited from the support of many colleagues at St. Louis University and St. Louis Community College who have been generous in their helpful comments and informal reviews. So many students at these two institutions gave us the passion to strive for a textbook that would put basic economics into a context and language that would reach them. Without a doubt, end-of-the-semester comments about really enjoying the text or wanting to take more economics or no longer believing that economics is irrelevant continue to be the impetus to produce this textbook.

Patrick Welch
Gerry Welch
August 2009

BRIEF CONTENTS

CONTENTS

PART *1*

Introduction to Economics

1

Introduction to Economics

CHAPTER OBJECTIVES

To define economics and introduce the scarcity and choice problem which underlies economics.

To explore opportunity cost, efficiency, and equity and their relationships to scarcity.

To identify the four factors of production and the income return to each type of factor.

To differentiate between economic theory and economic policy, and introduce the tools economists use to express theories and policies.

To use the production possibilities model to illustrate and explain the basic problem of scarcity.

To explain (in an appendix) how to construct a graph and interpret the illustrated relationship.

WHAT IS ECONOMICS?

We are always making choices. We constantly choose how to spend our time and our money. We make simple choices like whether to take the time to eat lunch rather than work or whether to spend money for bottled water rather than drink from a water fountain. We make complex choices about careers, where to live, and colleges. And, as members of society, we make choices about voting, supporting public policy issues, recycling, and volunteering to clean up the local park.

Choices are a part of everyday life because our wants exceed our ability to satisfy them. You may want to achieve a high grade point average (GPA) and maintain a job that gives you enough money for clothes, a car, and decent housing during a semester that does not provide enough time for both. People in a community may want a recreation complex, street repairs, an ambulance, and other services but don't have enough tax dollars to pay for it all. It is this scarcity of time and things and the resulting choices that must be made that bring us to the study of economics.

Economics is the study of how scarce, or limited, resources are used to satisfy people's unlimited wants and needs. In other words, economics is concerned with how people make decisions in a world of scarcity. Much of the study of economics is focused on satisfying people's wants and needs for material "things"—shoes, cars, medical services, entertainment, and the like. And, while happiness, sorrow, beauty, and virtue are not direct concerns of the discipline of economics, we know that often these values underlie the economic decisions that people make. Many of us have given our time and money to a person or cause rather than spend it on ourselves because it gives us greater happiness.

The field of economics is extensive and it is always growing. While you may hear economists voicing opinions about unemployment, inflation, interest rates, poverty, energy, the environment, and international trade, this just scratches the surface. This textbook will introduce you to some of the major areas of study in economics, some key institutions and relationships, and some controversial policy issues. A quick glance through the table of contents will give you an idea of the breadth of topics included in the discipline of economics.

Why study economics? What can it do for you? Economics permeates our lives. Many of our own personal decisions are obviously rooted in economics: how we pay next semester's tuition or whether we should take a job halfway across the country. But economics is also at the root of decisions made with far-reaching impacts: what items to fund in a congressional budget or how much support to provide for concerns over global warming.

A course in economics provides valuable information, but it also develops reasoning and analytical skills that allow you to think smarter. Through the study of economics, you will be introduced to important institutions, such as the Federal Reserve and foreign exchange markets, that play a key role in the unfolding of economic events. You will also be introduced to analytical techniques that develop your critical thinking and reasoning skills, enabling you to understand, for example, why the price of a product you want keeps rising, why the benefits of a job move outweigh its costs, or why you support the position of a candidate for public office.

Once you are armed with economic institutional information and skills—skills you will be developing for the rest of your life—you will be better prepared to evaluate and respond to news reports, promises of aspiring politicians, crises at work, personal decisions, and other daily situations. In short, an understanding of economics

Economics

The study of how scarce, or limited, resources are used to satisfy unlimited wants and needs; the study of decision making in a world of scarcity.

helps make you a better-informed citizen and decision maker and is important for success in your career—be it law, health care, journalism, or anything else.

Economics and Scarcity

Scarcity
Too few goods and services to satisfy all wants and needs.

Without scarcity there would be no reason to study economics. **Scarcity** means that there are not enough, nor can there ever be enough, goods and services to satisfy the wants and needs of all individuals, families, and societies. Look at your own situation. Do you own the car you would most like to have? Do you have enough money for the DVDs, concerts, textbooks, and boots you want? Does the recent car insurance bill mean ramen and peanut butter this month? Societies face the same scarcity problem on a larger scale. Money spent for roads is money not available for hospitals or schools. Gasoline and oil used now will not be available in the future.

The root of the scarcity problem is in the definition of economics—that people have limited resources to satisfy their unlimited wants and needs. People seem to continually require more goods and services and to become dissatisfied with what they have. When this psychological drive for more is considered for all members of society, wants and needs become so great in number that they can be viewed as virtually unlimited. For example, your instructor could devote one class period to listing everything everyone in the class wanted both for themselves and for society in general. By the next class period, and in all later periods, the list would increase as students added goods and services originally forgotten or introduced to them throughout the semester. The list would never be completed! One might recall that 10 years ago the average American did not need an iPod, wireless Internet, low-carb ice cream, a GPS system, or a hybrid car.

All of these unlimited wants and needs cannot be satisfied because the resources available to produce goods and services are limited. These resources include all the people, materials, machinery, and other items that contribute to the production of goods and services. For example, to provide takeout pizzas, a business needs cheese and other ingredients, people to cook and take orders, electricity, water, ovens, refrigerators, a manager, boxes, a building, and so on. Every resource available for production is limited in amount: There is not an infinite supply of labor, energy, or any other resource.

The problem of limited resources also occurs for individuals. We never seem to have enough money to purchase everything we want and need, and never have enough time to accomplish everything we want to do. Limited resources keep many students from taking a trip over spring break, upgrading a computer, or buying a new car instead of repairing an old one. Many students would like to produce a high grade point average, work at a part-time job, and enjoy an active social life but cannot achieve all of these due to time constraints.

In recent years we have become more conscious than ever of our limited resources as we face worldwide environmental issues. We are keenly aware of the limits of air, water, energy, and the ability of the earth to sustain itself. Global warming, holes in the ozone layer, greenhouse gas emissions, and water shortages throughout the world have become topics of regular discussion and concern.

Scarcity and Choice

Since it is impossible to satisfy all of the wants and needs of individuals, businesses, nonprofits, government units, and societies, decisions must be made about what to satisfy and how to use limited resources. A student, for example, who is pressed by the demands of a job and the need to study for an exam must make a decision about how to use limited available time. A state university that is facing a reduction in funds

TABLE 1.1	*Values Exercise*

Each of us has several core values that drive us. They are at the heart of our decisions and the actions that we take. Sometimes it is helpful to identify these core values so that we understand what is at the root of our actions. The following lists some possible values. Circle the five that best represent your core values.

Love	Happiness	Money	Respect
Security	Freedom	Truth	Power
Peace	Health	Learning	Thrift
Honesty	Responsibility	Change	Dependability
Safety	Family	Stability	Artistry
Religion	Friendship	Independence	Creativity
Success	Faith	Cleanliness	Knowledge
Work	Individualism	Authority	Intelligence
Integrity	Education	Community	Analysis

must make choices about what programs, staff, and services to cut. And, as a society, we must choose the degree to which we will pollute our air and water.

Tradeoff
Giving up one thing for something else.

Anytime we make a choice, there are **tradeoffs** and consequences. Suppose that a student has $100 (a limited sum) and wants to use the money for either a textbook or a weekend visit with an old friend. The visit is the tradeoff for the textbook, and the textbook is the tradeoff for the visit. In choosing between these, the student will evaluate the consequences of each alternative. The textbook purchase might result in a good grade in a course; the visit might mean renewing a friendship.

In making choices, a decision maker's values play a very important role and underlie most choices. Values are those principles and standards that a person considers to be worthwhile and are the ideals that drive people and organizations. Try the exercise in Table 1.1 to determine your own core values.

Value Judgment
The relative importance one assigns to an action or alternative.

Decisions usually involve a **value judgment,** which is the relative importance that a person assigns to an action or alternative. If the student faced with the choice of a book or a weekend with a friend decides that a good grade is more important, the book will be purchased with the $100; if friendship is valued more than a good grade, the student will choose the visit.

Scarcity also forces business owners and managers to make decisions based on value judgments. Companies often have to decide between raises for employees and equipment updates, or whether or not to continue an outstanding, yet costly, health insurance program at the expense of another business need, such as a building renovation. The choices made will reflect the value judgments of the business owners and managers. In some cases, employees are highly valued and wage increases and benefits are important; in other cases, stockholder profit or expansion needs may be the primary value.

Society faces the same scarcity-related tradeoff problem. Take a look around your community to see the value judgments of its residents. Public decisions about how well schools, parks, roads, fire and police, and other services are funded—or not funded—reflect the values of the community. Through the ballot process, choices are made about representatives who make public decisions and about the level of taxation for education and public services.

We are also aware of tradeoffs at the national level. If society chooses to balance a federal budget and increase defense spending, it may need to reduce government

| FIGURE 1.1 | *Scarcity, Choice, and Influences on Decision Makers* |

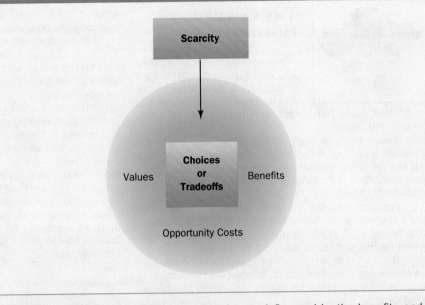

Scarcity imposes choices on decision makers who are influenced by the benefits and opportunity costs of the alternatives, as well as by their own values.

spending on other areas. If we choose to permit trucks and SUVs that guzzle gas or buses that emit large amounts of carbon, we stand to face future environmental consequences.

Each tradeoff made is necessary, because we cannot have everything, and each tradeoff reflects the value judgments of the decision makers.

Opportunity Cost   In making choices, people evaluate both the benefits and the costs of their choices. Because of scarcity, every decision to acquire a good or service or to spend time or money in a certain way has a cost attached to it. Economists call this **opportunity cost.** An opportunity cost is the cost of a purchase or a decision measured in terms of a forgone alternative—that is, what was given up to make the purchase or carry out the decision. Once time or money is devoted to one thing, the opportunity to use that time or money for other things is lost.

Everything that someone can purchase or do has an opportunity cost attached to it. If you spend $40 to put gas in your car, the opportunity cost of that gas is what was given up to buy it—perhaps a few decent meals. What was the opportunity cost of the last purchase you made? What is the opportunity cost of cutting a class in this course?

The opportunity cost of choosing to acquire more shoes or food, rather than supporting an increase in a school tax, could be an inferior education for children in a community. The opportunity cost of balancing a government budget could be forgone educational and health benefits due to reduced spending. Because of scarcity, individuals, families, businesses, and societies make choices based on both the benefits and the opportunity costs of their decisions. Figure 1.1 shows the relationship between scarcity and choice, and the influences on a decision maker.

Opportunity Cost
The cost of a purchase or decision measured in terms of a forgone alternative; what was given up to make a purchase or carry out a decision.

THE COST OF HOLDING A JOB

Some weekdays, Alicia Gunther, 17, works past midnight as a waitress at a New Jersey mall, and she readily admits that her work often hurts her grades and causes her to sleep through first period.

Jason Ferry, a high school junior, loves working 30 hours a week as a cashier at a Connecticut supermarket, but he acknowledges that when he gets home from work at 9:30 P.M. he usually does not have enough time to study for big tests.

For decades, the conventional wisdom has been that it is great for teenagers like these to hold after-school jobs because it teaches them responsibility, provides pocket money and keeps them out of trouble.

But . . . a growing body of research is challenging the conventional wisdom and concluding that working long hours often undermines teenagers' education and overall development.

[A study by] the National Academy of Sciences . . . found that when teenagers work more than 20 hours a week, it often leads to lower grades, higher alcohol use and too little time with their parents and families.

[Several other] studies . . . concluded that students who work long hours often do not have enough time or energy for homework and miss out on social and intellectual development gained from participating in school clubs and athletic teams. . . .

But many child development experts, teachers and parents said working a modest amount could be valuable for teenagers, teaching responsibility and how to work with others, as well as contributing money to households. . . .

"There are a lot of benefits to students' working in moderation," said Jeylan T. Mortimer, a sociology professor at the University of Minnesota. "But most sociologists and psychologists would say that it's an excessive load for full-time students to work 25 or 30 hours a week if you think it's important for young people to participate in extracurricular activities, develop friendships and spend time with their families." . . .

Application 1.1, "The Cost of Holding a Job," deals with the opportunity costs faced by teenagers who work long hours while going to school. Can you identify what these students are trading off to work more and earn more income?

Efficiency and Equity

In dealing with the basic problem of scarcity—not enough goods and services to satisfy everyone's wants and needs—there are two important concepts to consider: efficiency, and equity.

Efficiency is concerned with using resources effectively, or getting the most from scarce resources. **Efficiency** occurs when goods and services of a desired quality are produced at the lowest possible cost. If all goods and services were produced efficiently, society would experience the greatest possible lessening of the scarcity problem. Producing efficiently does not eliminate scarcity, but it does allow for the production of the maximum amount of goods and services to satisfy unlimited material wants and needs. This is important in a world of scarcity and is a major economic goal.

When is a student efficient? Most students set a goal for a grade, and then need to commit the time to achieve that grade. (While most instructors think this should be an A, in reality it might just be a C!) A student is efficient when this targeted grade is earned using the least amount of time possible. This could result from effective note taking, good study habits, reading a textbook, and the like. Students who study efficiently have more time for other activities and get the most from their limited resource of time.

Likewise, a society gets the most from its limited resources when efficient techniques of production allow those resources to be used to the fullest. With the aid of computers and good software, for example, professionals like architects, accountants,

Efficiency
Producing the largest attainable output of a desired quality with a given set of resources; producing at the lowest possible cost.

and others can be very efficient. As more household appliances are manufactured to operate with less energy usage, society can stretch its energy resources. Inefficient students waste their time, and an inefficient use of a society's resources wastes those resources. In both cases the scarcity problem is worsened.

In a world of scarcity, where there are not enough goods and services to satisfy everyone's wants and needs, there is the issue of what is a fair, just, or equitable distribution of goods and services among the members of a society. **Equity,** or justice and fairness, raises two basic questions: Should a fair distribution of goods and services be an economic goal for a society? If it is, how is a fair distribution defined and achieved?

The concept of what constitutes an equitable distribution of goods and services is controversial because it is based on people's value judgments. To some people, equity occurs when goods and services are divided equally: Every person receives as much as every other person. To others, the distribution of goods and services should be made according to people's needs: People who are ill or have large families should receive the goods and services they need. And to some, equity results when people are rewarded according to what they contribute to production: Those who contribute more or better resources should receive more. This last view—that people should be rewarded for their contribution to production—is the philosophical basis of a market system. Market and other economic systems will be discussed in Chapter 2.

The issue of how to define and achieve equity is not easily resolved because there are so many diverse viewpoints. In the United States, for example, there is a continuing debate over how much the government should provide for those who are in need. This debate has received extensive media coverage in recent years: We have heard or read about restructuring the health care payment system, tax breaks for specific groups, welfare payment policies, and unemployment compensation.

FACTORS OF PRODUCTION

Think about all of the thousands of different types of **resources,** or **factors of production,** that are used to produce goods and services, from the lighting fixtures in a mall to the skilled hands of a neurosurgeon to the air filters on a plane. To bring order and manageability to any discussion about resources, economists classify them into four groups: labor, capital, land, and entrepreneurship.

- ◆ **Labor** includes all human effort, both physical and mental, going into the production of goods and services. It encompasses the efforts of everyone from lawyers to lifeguards—all who work to produce goods and services.
- ◆ **Capital** includes warehouses, machinery and equipment, computers, office furniture, and all other goods that are used in the production of goods and services.
- ◆ **Land** includes all inputs into production that originate in nature and are not human-made—oil, iron ore, and fertile soil to name a few.
- ◆ **Entrepreneurship** is the function of organizing or bringing other factors together and taking the risk of success or failure. Without this function economic activity would not occur. A small business owner usually performs this function and is called an entrepreneur, and in corporations, managers organize and stockholders take the risk.

The relationship between productive resources and society's material wants and needs is summarized in Figure 1.2.

Equity
Justice or fairness in the distribution of goods and services.

Resources (Factors of Production)
Persons and things used to produce goods and services; limited in amount; categorized as labor, capital, land, and entrepreneurship.

Labor
Physical and mental human effort used to produce goods and services.

Capital
Items, such as machinery and equipment, used in the production of goods and services.

Land
Productive inputs that originate in nature, such as coal and fertile soil.

Entrepreneurship
The function of organizing resources for production and taking the risk of success or failure in a productive enterprise.

FIGURE 1.2 *Relationship between Resources and Wants and Needs*

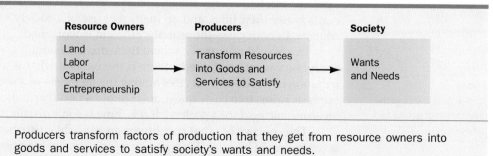

Producers transform factors of production that they get from resource owners into goods and services to satisfy society's wants and needs.

Factors and Income

People who own resources provide them for production because they expect a return. Although the return may be personal satisfaction, such as a positive feeling from community service, most often people expect to be paid, or to receive an income. While money is money, and $100 received by a worker is no different from $100 received by the owner of a machine, it is helpful to label the incomes received from selling different types of resources. There are

Wages
Income return to labor.

Interest
Income return to owners of capital.

Rent
Income return to owners of land resources.

Profit
Income return to those performing the entrepreneurial function.

♦   **wages**—income for labor,
♦   **interest**—income for capital,
♦   **rent**—income for land resources, and
♦   **profit**—income for carrying out the entrepreneurial function.

While it might appear trivial to give a separate name to the income received by each of the different groups of resources, the distinction can be significant. For example, various legislative and public policy initiatives are aimed at particular income groups. Take the Social Security program. Payments into this program come from wages as well as income, or profit, earned by the individual entrepreneur. Rent, interest, and corporate profit are incomes that are not part of the Social Security system.

The classification of people into different earning groups has also had interesting social connotations. As the economist Robert Heilbroner put it, "It is not just Labor on the one hand and Land or Capital on the other; it is the Bronx on the one hand and Park Avenue on the other."[1] In addition, Marxian theory, which has been the most persistent and powerful critique of capitalism, is based on the premise that a conflict exists between wage and profit earners that is inherent in, and ultimately fatal to, capitalistic systems.

Scarce Resources

Resources, or factors of production, are scarce, or limited. How scarce are they? Table 1.2 suggests that there is an abundance of people and things with which to produce goods and services. In the U.S. economy alone, there are over 150 million people working or looking for work, almost a billion acres of farmland, and billions of barrels of petroleum reserves. The list of available resources goes on and on.

[1]R. L. Heilbroner, *The Limits of American Capitalism*, Harper Torchbook ed. (New York: Harper & Row, 1967), p. 71.

TABLE 1.2	*Availability of Selected Resources in the U.S. Economy*

Although the U.S. economy has a large number of resources, there are not enough to satisfy all material wants and needs.

Resource	Amount in 2006[a]
Total civilian labor force	151 million people
Total farm land	932 million acres
Crude oil reserves	21.8 billion barrels
Electric generating capacity	4.05 trillion kilowatt hours
Manufacturing establishments	7.4 million

[a]Crude oil reserves and electric generating capacity are for 2005 and reported manufacturing establishments are for 2004.

Source: U.S. Bureau of the Census, *Statistical Abstract of the United States: 2008,* 127th ed. (Washington, DC: U.S. Government Printing Office, 2008), pp. 373, 532, 566, 586, 624.

Although large numbers of resources may be available in an *absolute* sense, they are scarce *relative* to the wants and needs their use attempts to satisfy. People's wants always continue to outrun the economy's ability to satisfy them.

If we cannot solve the scarcity problem, can we at least ease it? Over the last few decades, there has been debate over whether the scarcity problem has eased or worsened. On the positive side, we have made much progress: Life expectancies have increased with improved medicines; technological changes in transportation allow us to travel rapidly; fashionable clothing is available to buyers of all income levels; and we can prepare food, process information, and communicate faster than ever before. In addition, the amount of "stuff" owned by the average person has increased.

But there is evidence to suggest that, in some respects, the scarcity problem has worsened. Today we worry about the availability of clean air and water, while earlier generations thought of these as free and abundant. There is growing concern about our current rates of production and disposal of goods, and the resulting effects on our quality of life, our health, and the earth's forests, open spaces, and ozone layer. Some people argue that today we are more acutely aware of the limits of our productive capability than we have ever been.

Application 1.2, "Does Money Buy Happiness?," takes a look at some research on the ties between money and happiness. Many people think that a larger income lessens scarcity by providing more personal opportunities to satisfy wants and, therefore, makes people happier. This may not be the case. After reading this application, how would you answer the question "Does money buy happiness?"

ECONOMIC THEORY AND POLICY

As households, businesses, and governments go about conducting their economic affairs, it is helpful to have an understanding of some basic economic cause-and-effect relationships. Knowing about the drivers behind consumer behavior and spending and the causes of changing interest rates, income levels, and job growth fosters better decision making. Some economic relationships are complex, and gaining an appreciation for them is important. This task of sorting out and understanding cause-and-effect relationships falls to economic theory.

APPLICATION 1.2

DOES MONEY BUY HAPPINESS?

In recent decades much research in the fields of economics and psychology has focused on the ties between money and happiness. And the answer to the question "Does money buy happiness?" is maybe yes, maybe no.

Money allows people to buy more, and better-quality, goods and services. On the surface it appears that the basic economic problem of scarcity is lessened by having more money, and that this should lead to higher levels of happiness. We might think that people who drive new luxury cars and live in big homes are happier than people who ride a bus and live in a small apartment. A few researchers might say yes, the richer are happier, but many say the opposite, and a few say that happiness is increased very slightly with more money.

Psychologist Richard E. Lucas of Michigan State University thinks there is evidence to answer yes to three interesting happiness questions: Does money make you happier? Does being happier in the first place allow someone to earn more, perhaps through increased creativity or energy? Is there another factor that brings more of both money and happiness?

Happiness is certainly a subjective state of mind influenced by a person's values, experiences, future prospects, and a host of other factors. There is also a difference between short, even momentary, periods of happiness and a longer-term level of sustained satisfaction.

Winning the lottery or receiving a year-end bonus can provide immediate happiness, but whether or not it will have a sustained impact is another consideration.

There is also some thought that extra money for someone who is very poor might account for higher levels of happiness because it has a greater positive effect on negative circumstances. News stories of families who receive homes built through volunteer efforts or children who attend a summer camp that they could not afford without donors often focus on the intense happiness of the recipients.

So, if there is no evidence to suggest that people who live in Virginia are happier than those who live in Oregon because their average household income is greater ($54,250 for Virginia and $42,944 for Oregon in 2005), what does make us happier? A clear answer to this question would certainly land us on *Oprah* and might even challenge Dr. Phil. Professor George Lowenstein of Carnegie Mellon University suggests that people aren't good at figuring out what to do with their money and might overestimate the pleasure from something they buy. Professor Daniel Gilbert suggests that human relationships, time with family and friends, and experiences are the key to happiness. And others suggest that altruistic spending is the answer.

Sources: Malcolm Ritter, "Study: Money-Happiness Link Is Complex," Associated Press, November 26, 2006, www.sfgate.com; Matthew Herper, "Now It's a Fact: Money Doesn't Buy Happiness," *Forbes*, moneycentral.msn.com; "The Smiling Professor," *The New York Times*, April 22, 2008, www.nytimes.com; U. S. Census Bureau, *The 2008 Statistical Abstract*, Table 684, "Income—Distribution by Income Level and State: 2005," www.census.gov.

While theory tells us about relationships, economic policy deals with guidelines and actions. Policy decisions are made at many levels—from an instructor setting a grading policy, to a corporation setting policy about executive salaries, to a city setting its annual budget. When a decision maker sets parameters for actions, policy is made.

When the media speak of an economic policy for dealing with rising prices or unemployment, they are referring to the course of action that has been chosen to deal with the economic problem. Ideally, theories and policies are related. Before committing to a particular course of action, a person should make an effort to order and understand the basic relationships with which he or she is dealing.

Economic Theory

Economic Theory
A formal explanation of the relationship between economic variables.

An **economic theory** is a formal explanation of the relationship between economic variables.[2] A theory gives a reason why something happens, offers a cause-and-effect interpretation for a set of events, or shows the effect on one variable when another

---

[2]A dictionary definition of a theory is "systematically organized knowledge applicable in a relatively wide variety of circumstances; especially, a system of assumptions, accepted principles, and rules of procedure devised to analyze, predict, or otherwise explain the nature or behavior of a specified set of phenomena." From *The American Heritage Dictionary of the English Language*, ed. William Morris (New York: American Heritage Publishing Co., 1973), p. 1335.

changes. There are economic theories to explain unemployment, inflation, price movements in the soybean market, wage rates paid to teenagers, changes in foreign exchange rates, and almost any other economic condition. For example, one important economic theory deals with the relationship between changes in the price of an item and the quantity of the item demanded by consumers.

In order to obtain a valid and predictable relationship between economic variables, theories are explored within the framework of a **model.** This model framework includes several elements:

Model
The setting within which an economic theory is presented.

◆ variables to be explored,
◆ assumptions concerning the model,
◆ data collection and analysis, and
◆ conclusions.

Variables   A theory is created to provide an explanation for something. This is why the first step in developing a model is the selection of two variables that have a potential cause-and-effect relationship to explore. For example, suppose that students in a class agree that it was unusually hard to find a job last summer and are interested enough in the problem to explore it further. One student theorizes that it was hard to find a job because a major employer left the area, another student thinks that the number of 16- through 22-year-olds wanting summer jobs increased, and another says that the economy in general had weakened. From this discussion, three separate sets of variables have been identified, and each set could be selected for exploration within the context of a model: the change in the number of employers and the number of summer jobs, the changing demographics of the student population and the number of summer jobs, and the state of the economy in general and the number of summer jobs.

In developing theories, disputes may occur because a variety of factors can be considered in analyzing a problem, and only one or a few of those factors are chosen as variables when developing a theory to explain the problem. In exploring reasons for a slow-growing economy, for example, some economists focus on the relationship between the money supply and growth, some on spending and growth, and some on the price level.

Assumptions
Conditions held to be true within a model.

Assumptions   **Assumptions** are the conditions held to be true while exploring the relationship between variables. For example, if our students were to develop an economic theory about the relationship between changes in the number of employers and the number of available summer jobs, assumptions could be made about demographics, the economy in general, the number of students wanting to enroll in summer school, and so on.

Frequently an assumption is made to hold constant everything other than the variables under consideration. For example, if we were exploring the relationship between the price of coffee and the quantity demanded by consumers, an assumption to hold constant everything that affects the demand for coffee other than its price could be made. That is, it would be assumed that there would be no newly published health report extolling the virtues of coffee drinking, no shift in people's taste toward tea, and no change in income earned while the effect of a change in the price of coffee on the quantity demanded was explored.

Whether an assumption is "true" is not absolutely necessary within the context of a theory. For purposes of developing the theory, it is treated as if it were true. For example, in examining the effect of a change in the number of employers on available summer jobs, one could assume an annual growth rate in the 16- through 22-year-old population group of 0 percent, 3 percent, 12 percent, or any other rate. Whatever rate was assumed would be held constant while the theory was developed.

Data Collection and Analysis   When developing a theory, researchers collect and analyze data to determine how the variables are related. This is easy to understand with medical theories: Someone proposes a cause of a disease and then data are collected and analyzed to support or deny that cause-and-effect relationship. In other words, a theory can be supported by showing that the relationship between the variables is logically or statistically valid.

In economics, theories are often demonstrated to be statistically valid by examining real-world numbers concerning the variables. For example, if we wanted to evaluate the relationship between changes in the price of coffee and the amount consumers buy, statistics regarding coffee prices and sales could be used. When data are not readily available, a model builder might conduct a study to gain the necessary information. Offices of institutional research at colleges often conduct studies to determine levels of student satisfaction, completion rates, and such. The federal government, private research groups, and others collect and provide valuable information and extensive data on many facets of economic life, and the computer has made possible speedier and more sophisticated testing of ideas. **Econometrics,** which is the use of statistical techniques to describe the relationships between economic variables, is an important subfield in economics.

One of the most valuable sources of data for the United States is the U.S. Census Bureau's annual publication of the *Statistical Abstract of the United States*, which is available in libraries as well as online. This source provides access to information about thousands of topic areas from population to disease to government budgets—information that is valuable in many more courses than economics. Just put the *Statistical Abstract of the United States* in your search engine to locate it. You will have access to the latest copy as well as earlier editions.

Conclusions   The conclusion in a model gives the resulting relationship between the variables based on the assumptions, logic, and data analysis that went into the model. For example, by assuming buyers' tastes and incomes to be constant, and by examining past sales records, an economist could statistically show that consumers will decrease the quantity of coffee demanded as the price rises. The variables—price of coffee and quantity demanded—have an inverse relationship.

It is important to understand that different assumptions, data collection methods, or statistical techniques can cause the conclusions of studies to vary. Over the past two decades we have become obsessed with coffee: drinking lattes and cappuccinos, scheduling visits with friends and meetings in coffee shops, and conversing about coffee brands and brews. As this interest grows, so do the studies on the effects of caffeine on our health. And, these studies come with a wide variation in their conclusions.

Some studies say that caffeine causes dehydration; other studies indicate little or no evidence that it serves as a diuretic. Some studies suggest that it holds off baldness, lowers the risk of Parkinson's, and may be beneficial in type 2 diabetes prevention. Other studies have shown that caffeine raises blood pressure and that boiled unfiltered coffee (like French-pressed) may raise cholesterol levels.[3] So, what is a person to believe?

Econometrics

The use of statistical techniques to describe the relationships between economic variables.

---

[3]Anahad O'Connor, "The Claim: Caffeine Causes Dehydration," *The New York Times*, March 4, 2008, www.nytimes.com; Anna Jane Grossman, "Black for Me, Light for My Hips," *The New York Times*, July 12, 2007, www.nytimes.com; Jane E. Brody, "Personal Health: You Are Also What You Drink," *The New York Times*, March 27, 2007, www.nytimes.com.

APPLICATION 1.3

Ok, What Are They?

For most of us, our only contact with UFOs—unidentified flying objects—is watching films like Steven Spielberg's hit, *Close Encounters of the Third Kind.* Do you know that the movie's title is actually a technical term—CE-3—used by people, called "ufologists," who study UFOs?

Unidentified flying objects may have caught people's attention since ancient times. But it is only since the late 1940s that serious investigation and efforts to document the phenomenon have occurred.

Someone who wants to understand exactly what a UFO is will have to be ready to work through a not-too-short list of competing theories. One theory is that UFOs are objects flown by aliens from outer space or by some type of being who is smart enough to move back and forth in time and space. Another theory is that UFOs are simply images in the atmosphere caused by things like "ball lightning," glowing ionized gas, or light refraction.

A further theory says that UFOs are highly advanced military aircraft undergoing testing in absolute secrecy. And yet another theory claims that people who have "seen" UFOs are simply not seeing clearly enough to recognize that they are actually looking at conventional aircraft or natural atmospheric conditions. Finally, there is speculation that people "seeing a UFO" might be searching for something to save them from today's world.

If building arguments to support an economic theory seems difficult, imagine what it must be like building supporting arguments for a UFO theory! Just think, what data would you use? There is nothing comparable to the widely accessible numbers available to explain the effect of a tax increase on spending or a drop in business sales on unemployment rates. Also, like economics, for every argument there could be a counterargument. The argument that Einstein's theory of relativity raises serious doubts about whether aliens from outer space could make it to earth can be countered by the argument that his theory, while brilliant, may not capture something we have yet to learn.

So, just like someone who pulls an economic theory apart to decide whether it is realistic, a person looking into a UFO theory should want to know about the credibility of the person making the argument, the reliability of the evidence (for example, whether the photograph of the UFO has been doctored), the consistency of the arguments, and other details. In other words, we should not be surprised by a relatively large similarity in the rules to evaluate theories across fields of inquiry.

Based on: "Frequently Asked Questions about UFOs," http://www.cufos.org/Faq_English_P1.html; "Frequently Asked Questions about UFOs Part II," http://www.cufos.org/Faq_English_P2.html; "BBC—Science & Nature—Space—UFOs," http://www.bbc.co.uk/science/space/life/aliens/ufos/index.shtml; "Northern UFOs—Theories," http://www.ssimicro.com/~ufoinfo/theories.html.

Why are there so many conflicting results on the pros and cons of caffeine? As one delves into these studies, there are obvious differences in the assumptions and data collection methods. The number of observations, the conditions held constant in the study, and the choice of analytical techniques all contribute to the conclusion.

Serious controversy has always existed among economists concerning their theories. Scholarly publications sometimes devote many pages to running disputes among practitioners in the field. Questions arise as to the assumptions underlying a theory, the significance and appropriateness of the variables studied, the data collection and analysis, and the possibility that a more influential factor has not yet been tested. Controversies such as these are not limited to economics and are a healthy sign. They are found in all serious inquiry—be it in the social sciences, natural sciences, or humanities—where people are not satisfied with what they now know. Application 1.3, "OK, What Are They?", further explores problems and controversies surrounding theories by looking at an area of inquiry where alternative points of view are likely more hotly contested than in economics: explaining UFOs (unidentified flying objects).

In summary, economic theories explain the relationships between economic variables. By focusing on one or a few key relationships, economic theories simplify reality so that it can be better understood. Figure 1.3 summarizes the components of a model.

FIGURE 1.3   *Economic Theory and Models*

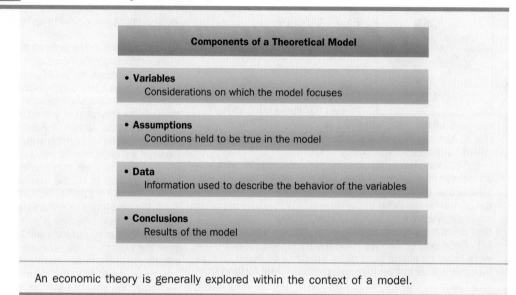

Components of a Theoretical Model

- **Variables**
  Considerations on which the model focuses

- **Assumptions**
  Conditions held to be true in the model

- **Data**
  Information used to describe the behavior of the variables

- **Conclusions**
  Results of the model

An economic theory is generally explored within the context of a model.

Economic Policy

Economic Policy
A guide for a course of
action.

An **economic policy** sets a guide for a course of action. Usually an economic policy is created to address an economic problem or change an economic condition. A legislated tax decrease to speed up the economy, mandatory clean air measures, and restrictions on imports of foreign-produced food are all examples of economic policies.

Economic policy is the result of a decision by a policymaker, whether a business manager, a local city council, the Congress, voters, or the president. Usually policymakers can choose among several courses of action and may even have several available policy tools. For example, board members of a university that is facing a serious budget crisis could put policies in place that raise tuition, hire fewer faculty members and increase class size, or postpone maintenance or new building construction.

Making policy is not always easy because of the need to weigh the consequences of various courses of action. Take the problem of rising gasoline prices due to an increased usage of gasoline coupled with a supply of gasoline that is not increasing as quickly. There are several possible policies to keep gas prices from rising. These include adopting fuel efficiency requirements for trucks and SUVs, banning all vehicles that do not get a recommended mileage per gallon of gas, funding mass transit projects, and opening up oil reserves in the Alaskan wilderness, among other things. Each of these policies carries significant consequences ranging from a loss of truck and SUV sales and jobs in that industry, to an expenditure of tax monies in rail systems, to environmental issues.

Policy decisions are heavily influenced by the values of the policymaker. Someone who values the environment would likely not support destruction of the Alaskan wilderness, while a Congressperson from a state that depends on the production of trucks and SUVs for significant employment would likely not support policies that negatively affect that industry. Take the question of granting tax credits for college tuition. Families who are facing financial difficulties sending their children to college

UP FOR DEBATE

SHOULD ST. LOUIS COUNTY, MISSOURI, IMPOSE MANDATORY TRASH PICKUP AND RECYCLING?

Issue   *In 2008, St. Louis County, Missouri, established trash districts in its unincorporated, nonmunicipal areas and mandated a subscription service that would provide trash pickup and curbside single-stream recycling. Every household was required to participate and pay a monthly fee for the service. The program sparked substantial public support, but also created a great deal of opposition. Should the program have been approved?*

Yes   Recycling should not be optional. It is the right thing to do to address growing environmental issues. Every citizen needs to participate. Furthermore, curbside pickup with wheeled carts encourages recycling by making it easy. Communities with mandatory recycling and large wheeled carts have experienced significant increases in the volume of recycled materials and decreases in items going to landfills.

There are substantial economic benefits for a district from using one trash hauling company, rather than many private haulers. With one company there is less trash traffic. Rather than many trash trucks using residential streets every day, there is just one service in the neighborhood on pickup day. This saves on street pavement conditions, noise, and gas. Typically, bills are also less for each household.

No   The government should not mess with people's garbage. It is another example of government interference with private property and the right of property owners to make their own decisions. People have a right to choose what to throw away, where to throw it, and who to haul it away. Also, by going with a government contracted trash hauler, smaller trash companies may be put out of business.

Many people produce little trash, especially single-person households. Why should these people pay the same price as all other households? Sometimes people find other means to dispose of their trash. These include taking it to work, using a neighborhood business's dumpster, or placing it in a public trash can. Why should these people be forced to now pay a monthly trash bill?

will likely favor this type of tax break, and those who think that existing programs for tuition relief are adequate may oppose it.

Because economic theories explain how economic variables interact, and because economic policies involve the manipulation of those economic variables, it is crucial that policymakers have some knowledge of these theories and their complexities. If policymakers do not understand basic economic principles, the consequences of their policy decisions could be disastrous. One benefit of a course in economics is that it enables you to better evaluate the consequences of policies and to judge how well or how poorly policymakers are informed.

Up for Debate, "Should St. Louis County, Missouri, Impose Mandatory Trash Pickup and Recycling?," provides a real-world example of an economic policy decision before a county council. Arguments that St. Louis County Council members heard in support of and against this mandated service are given. Can you identify the economic analysis in the arguments as well as the value judgments of those supporting and those opposing this program?[4]

TOOLS OF THE ECONOMIST

Words, Graphs, and Mathematical Equations

There are several ways to express economic theories and policies. The first and most basic method is a verbal presentation, or descriptive statement. Earlier we noted that

---

[4]In St. Louis County some areas are organized as cities, or municipalities, and some are unincorporated. In the unincorporated areas the county provides municipal services.

FIGURE 1.4   *Relationship between Coffee Prices and the Amount of Coffee Demanded*

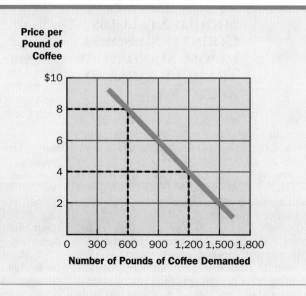

The downward-sloping line in this graph illustrates the various amounts of coffee demanded at different coffee prices.

the quantity of coffee demanded falls as its price increases. This is a simple verbal statement about buyer demand. The advantage of using such verbal statements to express theories is the ease with which concepts can be conveyed. But simple verbal statements with no information about actual numbers can be imprecise. As numbers are added, verbal descriptions can become lengthy and clumsy.

Graph

An illustration showing the relationship between two variables that are measured on the vertical and horizontal axes.

A second method for expressing theories and policies is graphing. A **graph** is a picture illustrating the relationship between two variables, one shown on the horizontal axis and the other on the vertical axis. For instance, returning to our coffee example, the graph in Figure 1.4 shows a relationship between the price of a pound of coffee and the number of pounds of coffee demanded by consumers over a certain period of time.

We frequently use graphs because numbers can easily be incorporated and relationships are visualized. For example, the graph in Figure 1.4 tells us that at a price of $8 per pound 600 pounds of coffee are demanded, and at a price of $4 the quantity demanded increases to 1,200 pounds. Or, if the price is $8 and you lower it by 50 percent, you will increase the quantity of coffee demanded by 100 percent. Or, if you are interested in selling 900 pounds of coffee, the price will need to be $6 per pound.

Direct Relationship

Two variables move in the same direction: when one increases, so does the other; graphs as an upward-sloping line.

Inverse Relationship

Two variables move in opposite directions: when one increases, the other decreases; graphs as a downward-sloping line.

Once you have had some practice in reading graphs, you will discover that a line or curve illustrates at a glance the relationship between the variables. In a **direct relationship** the variables move in the same direction and the line slopes upward. In an **inverse relationship** the variables move in opposite directions and the line slopes downward. If you are uncomfortable working with graphs, you should stop at this point and read the appendix to this chapter. In it, direct and inverse relationships and other information on constructing and interpreting graphs are presented.

A third way to express economic theories is through mathematical equations. While a major drawback with using equations is fear and lack of confidence in using mathematics, equations have an important advantage. They are very specific about how economic variables are related. Let us return to our coffee example.

Suppose we find that the relationship between the price of coffee and the amount demanded is shown by the equation

$$Qc = 1{,}800 - 150Pc.$$

Here Qc represents the quantity of coffee demanded, and Pc represents the price of coffee. By putting different prices in place of the Pc term, you can see how much coffee buyers would want. For example, if the price were $6 per pound, buyers would want 900 pounds of coffee [900 = 1,800 − 150(6)]. If the price fell to $4, they would want 1,200 pounds [1,200 = 1,800 − 150(4)]. If coffee were given away, people would want 1,800 pounds; and if coffee were $12 per pound, people would stop buying it.

SCARCITY, MODEL BUILDING, AND GRAPHS

Because economists frequently illustrate concepts and theories through models and graphs, we will use these tools to explore scarcity in greater detail.

Modeling Scarcity

As we know, theories are explored within the context of a model that includes variables, assumptions, data, and conclusions. Here we will develop a model to explore scarcity in an economy by examining the production of two goods using that economy's resources. Although this hypothetical economy has the potential for producing a large assortment of goods and services, in this model all the economy's resources will be diverted to the production of only two goods: cell phones and garden tractors. These two goods are the variables in our model.

In the example that follows, the hypothetical economy will be viewed over a short period of time using the following assumptions.

1. All resources, or factors of production, are held constant. There are no changes in the available amounts of the economy's labor, machinery, trucks, or other factors.
2. All resources are fully employed. Everyone who wants a job has one, and all other resources (such as factories and transportation equipment) available for use are being used. There is no involuntary unemployment of resources.
3. The existing technology is held fixed; no new inventions or innovations occur.

Production Possibilities Table (or Curve)
Gives the various amounts of two goods that an economy can produce with full employment and fixed resources and technology.

The data for this model are provided in Table 1.3, which lists some possible combinations of cell phones and garden tractors that could be produced in the economy given the assumptions made. Because the table provides possible levels of production, it is termed a **production possibilities table.** The data show that if all resources are fully employed in the production of cell phones, then 25 million cell phones can be made, but no garden tractors. If some garden tractors are manufactured (for example, 200,000), then some resources employed in the production of cell phones must be diverted to making tractors, and fewer cell phones will be

TABLE 1.3   *Possible Combinations of Cell Phones and Garden Tractors*

This production possibilities table illustrates various combinations of cell phones and garden tractors that a hypothetical economy could produce with full employment and fixed resources and technology.

Cell Phones (Millions)	Garden Tractors (Hundreds of Thousands)
25	0
24	2
20	4
15	6
9	8
0	10

produced. If all factors are used in the manufacture of garden tractors, no cell phones can be made.

The production possibilities listed in Table 1.3 can be graphed to illustrate the same relationship. In Figure 1.5, the different cell phone and garden tractor combinations from the table are plotted on a graph and the points are connected with a line to form a **production possibilities curve.**

FIGURE 1.5   *Possible Combinations of Cell Phones and Garden Tractors*

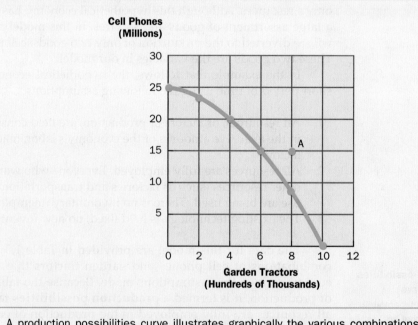

A production possibilities curve illustrates graphically the various combinations of two goods that an economy could produce with full employment and fixed resources and technology. Under these conditions, more of one good can be produced only by giving up some of the other.

Interpreting the Model

The basic conclusion of the production possibilities model is a restatement of the scarcity problem: Even with full employment, limited resources allow only limited production of goods and services. In our hypothetical economy, it would be impossible to produce 15 million cell phones and 800,000 garden tractors (shown by point A in Figure 1.5) in the time allowed, even if desired, because there are not enough factors of production to do so. In other words, scarce resources impose a boundary, or limit, on an economy that is illustrated by a production possibilities curve. Our hypothetical economy cannot produce beyond (to the right of) the curve in Figure 1.5.

The production possibilities model also emphasizes the concepts of tradeoff and opportunity cost. When an economy operates at full employment, more of one good can be produced only by giving up some amount of another good. If this economy were producing 20 million cell phones and 400,000 garden tractors, and households demanded 600,000 tractors, then households could have the additional tractors only by giving up some cell phones. This tradeoff concept is a restatement of the principle of opportunity cost, which was introduced earlier: The cost of additional garden tractors can be measured by the number of cell phones given up, and vice versa. The opportunity cost of going from 400,000 to 600,000 tractors is 5 million cell phones. What is the opportunity cost of going from 800,000 to 1,000,000 tractors?[5]

Several other economic concepts can be illustrated with the production possibilities model by changing the model's assumptions. If the assumption of full employment is dropped and it is assumed that some resources available for production are not used, or there is **unemployment,** then the economy cannot produce as much as it does under the condition of full employment. With full employment, one production combination was 15 million cell phones and 600,000 garden tractors. If some labor, machinery, or other resource is idle, then less will be produced—perhaps only 10 million cell phones and 400,000 tractors. The result of unemployment is illustrated graphically by a point inside, or to the left of, the production possibilities curve, such as point B in Figure 1.6.

When we drop the assumptions of fixed resources and fixed technology, this model can also be used to illustrate **economic growth,** which is an increase in an economy's full employment level of output over time. Economic growth can result from additional resources and/or better methods of production (technology). In this case, more labor and other resources or a newly automated manufacturing process would allow an increase in cell phone and garden tractor production. Economic growth can be illustrated graphically by a shift of the production possibilities curve to the right, as shown in Figure 1.7. Point A, which was unattainable under the original assumptions, is now within reach of the economy.

Test Your Understanding, "Production Possibilities," provides an opportunity to examine your command of the concepts illustrated by the production possibilities model. Here the model is used to evaluate the choices an economy can make between producing **capital goods,** such as machinery and equipment, which are used to produce other goods and services, and **consumer goods,** such as food and household furniture, which are produced for final buyers.

Unemployment
Resources available for production are not being used.

Economic Growth
An increase in an economy's full employment level of output over time.

Capital Goods
Goods, such as machinery and equipment, that are used to produce other goods and services.

Consumer Goods
Goods, such as food and household furniture, that are produced for final buyers.

---

[5]The production possibilities table and curve show that this economy is producing 9 million cell phones when it produces 800,000 tractors, and no cell phones when it produces 1 million tractors. Therefore, the opportunity cost of moving from 800,000 to 1 million tractors is 9 million cell phones because cell phone production goes from 9 million to zero.

FIGURE 1.6   *Unemployment in a Production Possibilities Model*

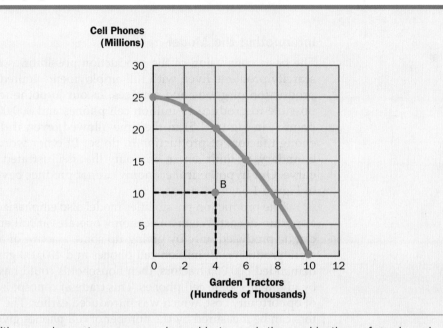

With unemployment, an economy is unable to reach the combinations of goods and services that it could produce if resources were fully employed. Point B represents production with unemployment.

FIGURE 1.7   *Economic Growth in a Production Possibilities Model*

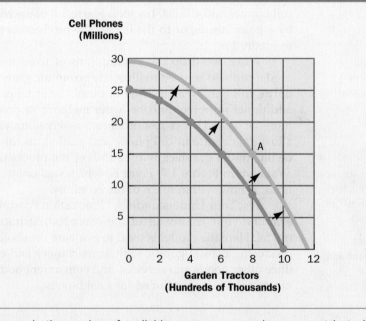

An increase in the number of available resources or an improvement in technology allows the production of goods and services to increase, and the economy's production possibilities curve shifts to the right.

TEST YOUR UNDERSTANDING

PRODUCTION POSSIBILITIES

All economies are subject to a tradeoff between the production of capital goods, which are used to produce other goods and services, and consumer goods, which are produced for final buyers. Assume that in a hypothetical economy with full employment and fixed resources and technology, the following amounts of consumer and capital goods can be produced.

Consumer Goods (Millions of Units)	Capital Goods (Millions of Units)
0	45
10	40
20	32
30	20
40	0

Create a production possibilities curve from this table on the accompanying graph and answer the following questions.

1. What is the opportunity cost of increasing the production of consumer goods from 20 million to 30 million units? What is the opportunity cost of increasing the production of capital goods from 40 million to 45 million units?
2. On the accompanying graph, illustrate the effect of a small amount of unemployment with a point labeled A, and a large amount of unemployment with a point labeled B.

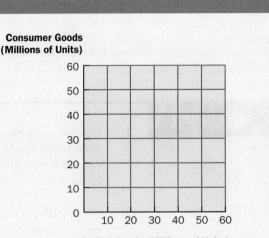

Consumer Goods (Millions of Units)

Capital Goods (Millions of Units)

3. Where, in your opinion, is the ideal point on the production possibilities curve for this economy to operate? Label this as point C. On what value judgment about the importance of capital goods and consumer goods did you base your location of point C? What would cause another student to locate point C elsewhere on the production possibilities curve?
4. What would life be like in this economy 10 years from now if today it produced only consumer goods? What would life be like in the economy today if it produced only capital goods?
5. Demonstrate graphically what would happen if new technology were created for producing both capital goods and consumer goods.

Answers can be found at the back of the book.

MACROECONOMICS AND MICROECONOMICS

Macroeconomics

The study of the operation of the economy as a whole.

Microeconomics

The study of individual decision making units and markets within the economy.

The study of economics is organized under two major headings: macroeconomics and microeconomics. **Macroeconomics** focuses on the operation of the economy as a whole and the interactions of the major groups (called the household, business, government, and foreign sectors) in the economy. It includes such topics as inflation, unemployment, taxes and government spending, and money and banking. Part 2 of this textbook deals with "The Macroeconomy."

Microeconomics focuses on the behavior of individual businesses and households and on specific product and resource markets. It includes such topics as consumer behavior, cost-benefit analysis, the determination of business profits, and pricing in specific markets. Part 3 of this textbook, "The Microeconomy," is concerned with understanding the behavior of these individual decision making units in the economy.

Both macroeconomic and microeconomic concepts have global applications and are relevant to international topics. Part 4 of this textbook, "The International Economy," which deals with international trade and finance, uses both macroeconomics and microeconomics.

Summary

1. Economics is the study of how limited resources are used to satisfy unlimited wants and needs. The basis of economics is a scarcity of goods and services caused by people's insatiable wants for goods and services coupled with a limited amount of resources to produce them.

2. Since individuals and societies cannot have everything they want, they must make choices, or tradeoffs. These tradeoffs are influenced by the decision maker's value judgments. Tradeoffs carry an opportunity cost, which measures the cost of a decision or purchase in terms of a forgone alternative.

3. Efficiency and equity are important considerations when dealing with the problem of scarcity. Efficiency results when a good or service of a desired quality is produced at the lowest resource cost. It allows the greatest attainable lessening of scarcity because resources are used to their fullest. Equity refers to fairness in the distribution of goods and services. The determination of equity differs according to people's value judgments.

4. Resources, or factors of production, are those things used in the production of goods and services. All resources are scarce, or limited, in amount. Economists classify these limited factors into four categories: land, labor, capital, and entrepreneurship. When sold, they generate incomes termed, respectively: rent, wages, interest, and profit.

5. There is a distinction between economic theory and policy. Economic theory explains why an event occurs, or gives a generalized interpretation of the relationship between economic variables. Economic theories are explored within the framework of a model that includes variables, assumptions or conditions held to be true, data, and conclusions. Economic policy is a guideline for a course of action. Value judgments are important in the selection of economic policies.

6. In expressing theories and policies, economists use verbal statements, graphs, and mathematical equations. An upward-sloping line in a graph illustrates a direct relationship between variables, and a downward-sloping line indicates an inverse relationship.

7. A production possibilities table and curve can be used to illustrate scarcity. These show that, with assumptions of full employment and constant resources and technology, more of one good can be obtained only by giving up some of another good, making tradeoffs necessary. The effect of unemployment, which causes an economy to produce fewer goods and services than with full employment, is shown by a point inside, or to the

left of, the production possibilities curve. Increases in technology and/or resources allow for economic growth, permitting a shift of the curve to the right.

8. Macroeconomics is concerned with the operation of the economy as a whole and with the interactions of its major sectors. Microeconomics deals with individual operating units and markets within the economy.

Key Terms and Concepts

Economics	Economic theory
Scarcity	Model
Tradeoff	Assumptions
Value judgment	Econometrics
Opportunity cost	Economic policy
Efficiency	Graph
Equity	Direct relationship
Resources (factors of production)	Inverse relationship
Labor	Production possibilities table (or curve)
Capital	Unemployment
Land	Economic growth
Entrepreneurship	Capital goods
Wages	Consumer goods
Interest	Macroeconomics
Rent	Microeconomics
Profit	

Review Questions

1. What are the definition of and the root of the study of economics? How does a combination of scarce resources and unlimited wants force people to make economic decisions? How are value judgments and opportunity costs important in the making of these decisions?

2. Classify each of the following factors of production into one of the four resource categories used in economics, and identify the income return to the owners of each factor.
   a. The scanner used to check out groceries in a supermarket
   b. The instructor of this course

   c. A pasture used for grazing a herd of cattle
   d. A coffee urn used by a catering service
   e. The person who just started her own lawn service company
   f. The manager of a restaurant that is part of a national chain

3.   What is meant by a direct and an inverse relationship between economic
     variables? Illustrate, using the accompanying graphs, how you think each of
     the following relationships would appear, and indicate whether each
     relationship is direct or inverse.
     a. Inches of rain and sales of umbrellas
     b. Tuition and students demanding to enroll in a university
     c. Consumers purchasing the same amount of gasoline regardless of its price
     d. Salaries and years of education

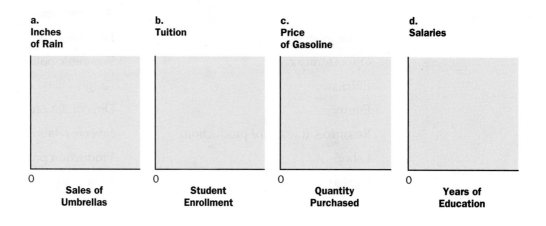

4.   Distinguish between economic theory and economic policy. What are some
     reasons for economic theory controversies and economic policy controversies?
     Give a recent example of economic policy.

5.   Identify and briefly explain the four elements of a model used to explore an
     economic theory. How can the choice of assumptions and data used affect the
     conclusions?

6.   Draw a production possibilities curve and explain how it illustrates the
     tradeoffs, or choices, that must be made when an economy is operating at
     full employment. How can unemployment and economic growth be shown
     on this graph?

7.   What is a capital good and what is a consumer good? How does an
     economy's choice about how many of its resources to devote to capital goods
     production as compared to consumer goods production affect its current
     standard of living and its future standard of living?

8.   The following production possibilities table gives the various combinations of
     hours that can be worked and GPAs that can be earned by a college student
     who holds a job and takes 12 credit hours of courses a semester. Draw a

production possibilities curve based on the information in this table on the graph provided and answer the following questions.

a. What is the opportunity cost for this student of increasing the hours worked per week from 10 to 20?

b. What factors could cause this curve to shift to the right?

c. What factors could cause this student to operate inside, or to the left, of this production possibilities curve?

d. What would determine the student's best location on this curve?

e. Are there any similarities between the choices that this student makes concerning hours worked and GPA and the choices an economy makes between the production of consumer goods and capital goods?

Hours Worked per Week	GPA
50	0.00
40	1.00
30	1.90
20	2.60
10	3.25
0	3.75

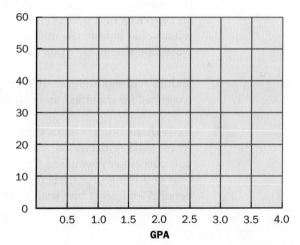

9. (appendix) Think about the relationship between driving at higher speeds and the likelihood of injury in an automobile accident. How can this relationship be illustrated in one graph to make it appear that the likelihood of injury increases relatively little at higher speeds, and in another graph to make it appear that the likelihood of injury increases dramatically at higher speeds? What warning does this sound about basing a decision on a quick scan of the appearance of a line in a graph?

10. Distinguish between macroeconomics and microeconomics, and identify some topics relevant to each.

Discussion Questions

1.   If resources are scarce and if people are always wanting more than the economy can provide, how is it possible that we would have unemployment?

2.   Suppose that you are an advisor to a health team working in a poor country. In that country, 20 percent of the children below the age of five die of a particular disease each year. If the health team were to inoculate the population, the disease would cease to be a problem. However, with more people surviving, the country's food supply would become grossly inadequate, and it is estimated that about 20 percent of the children below the age of five would die of starvation each year. Which policy would you follow: inoculation or no inoculation? What are the tradeoffs with each policy? Why would you follow your chosen policy, and how are your values important in reaching a decision?

3.   How do the popular expressions "you can't have your cake and eat it, too" and "there is no such thing as a free lunch" relate to the basic economic problems of scarcity, choice, and opportunity costs?

4.   Is there a tradeoff between efficiency and equity, or are these two goals mutually compatible for an economy? Why?

5.   In your opinion, what would be an equitable, or fair, distribution of goods and services in a society? Why would this be an equitable distribution and what value judgments underlie your opinion? Do you think your opinion would be shared by your friends and family? Why?

6.   Should national defense–related goods, such as submarines and nuclear weapons, be classified as capital goods or consumer goods? Why?

7.   Individuals and societies evaluate both the benefits and costs of their choices when making decisions. Can you think of a recent decision you made where you consciously weighed the benefits and costs of possible courses of action? Can you think of a decision where you did not consciously weigh the benefits and costs but wish now that you had?

Critical Thinking Case 1

RETHINKING MEDICAL CARE[a]

Critical Thinking Skills

Defining a problem

Determining criteria for evaluating problem solutions

Identifying reasonable solutions to a problem

Economic Concepts

Scarcity

Choice

Most Americans would identify the soaring cost of health care as a primary economic concern. It is estimated that in the year 2008 over $2.4 trillion was spent on health care in the United States. That number is projected to rise by more than $1.7 trillion, to over $4.1 trillion, by the year 2016.[b]

Advanced technology that keeps critically ill people alive, the increasing incidence of expensive diseases such as cancer and AIDS, the aging of the population, and overtreatment for fear of malpractice suits have contributed to the escalation in costs. The rising cost of health care also underlies other problems in the United States, such as some stagnation in the creation of new full-time jobs. Employers increasingly rely on part-time labor rather than hire full-time workers who might be eligible for expensive health care insurance benefits.

The philosophy in the United States has long been to pursue all medical procedures necessary to prolong life. These include life-support equipment for all persons regardless of their prognoses, organ transplants, and expensive medications. Some of these procedures have pushed the overall cost of medical care so high that people are forgoing preventive care, including routine examinations,

X rays, and blood tests. Although this saves money in the short run, it can become very costly in the long run when more expensive treatment is required because of lack of early detection. This further complicates the problem of escalating costs.

Health care reform has been an important topic for years. Proposals to provide basic preventive care for every American, to regulate hospitals and doctors, and to put ceilings on prices and malpractice awards have frequently been presented to government. Lurking behind these proposals for reform is a major, unavoidable decision imposed by scarcity: when to deny medical treatment. If we are to reallocate scarce resources to preventive and basic care and extend health insurance coverage to all Americans, then we must question whether we can continue to operate under the premises that if the technology to prolong life exists, it must be used, and if a medical procedure exists, it must be made available.

Many economic decisions are influenced by social, ethical, and other values. The decision to deny medical treatment is such an issue. What should Americans consider when making hard choices about health care?

[a]At the end of each chapter, a Critical Thinking Case will be presented. These cases have two objectives: the development of critical thinking skills and the application of economic concepts. The specific critical thinking skills and economic concepts associated with each case are identified. A few suggested questions for dealing with each case are also included. If your instructor makes no specific assignment regarding a case, you may want to try answering the questions on your own.
[b]U.S. Department of Commerce, *Statistical Abstract of the United States, 2008*, 127th ed., p. 96.

Questions

1. What is the basic economic problem in this case?
2. What reasonable solutions are available for alleviating the problem, and why are they reasonable? What solutions are unreasonable? Why? What, in your opinion, is the best solution to the problem?
3. What economic and noneconomic values underlie your appraisal of these solutions? Which values are so deeply rooted that they must not be compromised when determining solutions to the problem?

CHAPTER 1
APPENDIX

GRAPHING

Constructing a Graph

A graph is a picture of a relationship between two variables. The variables are given on the vertical and horizontal axes of the graph, and the line in the graph provides a visual image of how those variables are related. Table 1A.1 provides data about two variables that will be used to construct a graph in Figure 1A.1: various hourly wage rates in a market for day camp assistants and the numbers of teenagers applying for a job at each rate.

The first step in constructing or reading a graph is to identify the variables on the vertical and horizontal axes. In Figure 1A.1, wage rates are represented on the vertical axis and applicants for jobs on the horizontal axis. (It is conventional in economics to put money data on the vertical axis.)

The second step in graphing is to assign numbers along the axes. The numbers assigned to the axes of a graph are important for proper interpretation of the graph. In assigning numbers to a graph, several rules need to be remembered: (1) Always use zero at the origin (the point where the horizontal and vertical axes meet); (2) work up the number scale as you go out on each axis; and (3) when moving along an axis, use equal spaces for equal amounts.[1] Notice the application of these rules in Figure 1A.1. Zero is used at the origin, numbers along each axis move up the number scale, the vertical axis is labeled in equal series of $1.50, and the horizontal axis is labeled in equal series of 50 applicants.

The third step in constructing a graphic relationship is to plot data points. Each data point gives a specific combination of the two variables observed. Each point in Figure 1A.1a, for example, indicates a wage rate–applicant combination given in Table 1A.1. Point A shows that when the wage rate is $6, the number of applicants is 150, and point B shows that at a wage rate of $12, 350 teenagers apply.

TABLE 1A.1	*Hourly Wage Rates and Numbers of Applicants for a Job*

This table illustrates a relationship between hourly wage rates and the number of teenagers applying for a job.

Hourly Wage Rate	Number of Teenagers Applying for a Job
$ 3.00	50
4.50	100
6.00	150
7.50	200
9.00	250
10.50	300
12.00	350

[1]For those students who are familiar with graphing techniques, we might point out that only the first, or northeast, quadrant of a graph is used in most examples in this text.

FIGURE 1A.1   *Hourly Wage Rates and Numbers of Applicants for a Job*

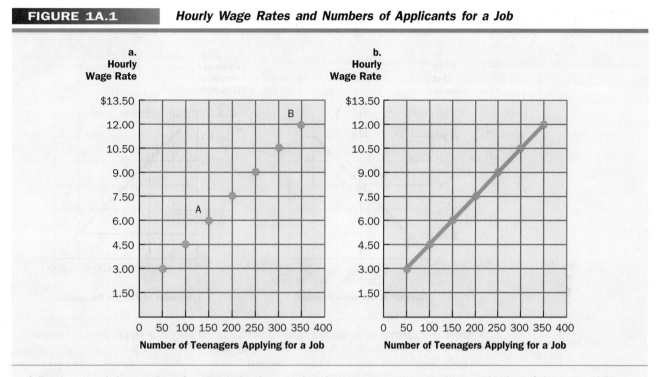

A line in a graph is a series of connected points; each point represents a particular combination of the two variables.

Finally, a line in a graph is nothing more than a series of connected data points. In Figure 1A.1b, the wage rate–applicant combinations from Figure 1A.1a are connected. Joining these points allows us to visualize the relationship between the variables and to "read between" the points. For example, we could conclude that if the wage offered were $6.75, the number of applicants would be approximately 175.

Direct and Inverse Relationships

Earlier in the chapter, it was pointed out that the slope of a line in a graph indicates whether a direct or an inverse relationship exists between the variables. A direct relationship exists when both variables move in the same direction; that is, as one gets larger or smaller, so does the other. We can conclude that the relationship between wage rates and the number of job applicants just discussed is direct. Graphically, a direct relationship is illustrated by a line that slopes upward. An inverse relationship exists when the variables move in opposite directions; that is, as one becomes larger, the other becomes smaller, and vice versa. Graphically, an inverse relationship is illustrated by a line that slopes downward.

The upward-sloping line in Figure 1A.2a illustrates a direct relationship between the price of hot fudge sundaes and the number of sundaes some ice cream stores would be willing to sell at different prices. At a price of $3.75 per sundae, the number supplied would be 1,500, and if the price fell to $1.25, they would like to sell only 500 (preferring instead to sell other, perhaps more profitable, items).

The downward-sloping line in Figure 1A.2b illustrates an inverse relationship between the price of pistachios and the number of pounds of pistachios demanded at

Direct and Inverse Relationships

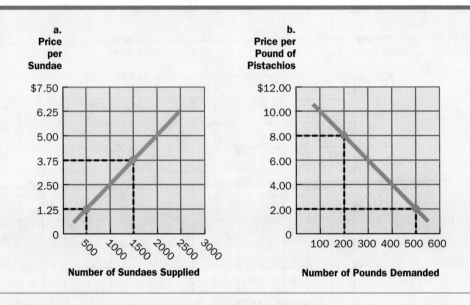

A direct relationship is illustrated by an upward-sloping line in a graph, and an inverse relationship is illustrated by a downward-sloping line.

each price. At a price of $8 a pound, consumers would demand 200 pounds, and when the price fell to $2, they would demand 500 pounds.

Students often have trouble reading a graph when there are no numbers given on the axes. If this occurs with you, just put a few hypothetical numbers along each axis and try reading it again. (Remember the rules for numbering when you do this.) After you have some practice in reading graphs, this problem should disappear. Figure 1A.3

Examples of Direct and Inverse Relationships

What type of relationship (direct or inverse) is illustrated in each of these graphs?

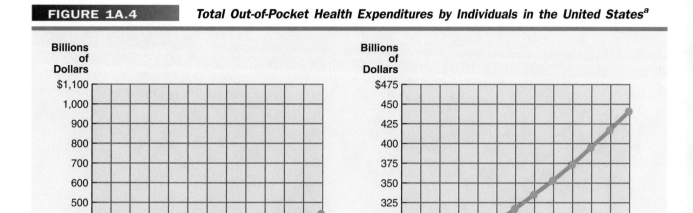

FIGURE 1A.4   *Total Out-of-Pocket Health Expenditures by Individuals in the United States[a]*

The appearance of data in a graph and the impression created for the reader can be affected by how the axes of the graph are numbered.

[a]Numbers for 2006–2016 are projections.
Source: U.S. Bureau of the Census, *Statistical Abstract of the United States: 2008*, 127th ed. (Washington, DC: U.S. Government Printing Office, 2008), p. 96.

gives you an opportunity to test your ability to recognize graphic relationships. What does each graph say about the relationship between the variables identified?

In interpreting information given in graphs, one should be aware that graphs can be used to present a point of view in a way that is often not apparent to the reader. For example, the two graphs in Figure 1A.4 give exactly the same information, yet they do not look the same. What is the difference between them? Why would someone choose to use a figure such as the one on the left rather than the one on the right?[2] Information about manipulating statistics to present a point of view is available in many books and articles.

[2]The difference between the two graphs in Figure 1A.4 is the spacing used for the numbers on the vertical axes. The graph on the left uses each vertical mark to represent $100 billion, and the graph on the right uses each vertical mark to represent $25 billion. When the unit of measure of the variable on the vertical axis is given a wider space, the resulting line appears to be more steeply sloped than the line that results when a narrower space is used. If one wanted to create the impression of a dramatic increase in the variable measured on the vertical axis, then one would use more exaggerated spacing. To create the impression of a relatively small increase, narrower spacing would be used.

Economic Decision Making and Economic Systems

CHAPTER OBJECTIVES

To introduce the basic economic choices that must be made in every society because of scarcity.

To describe differences among traditional, market, and planned economies, and how the basic economic choices are made in each of these systems.

To understand basic economic decision making in traditional, or agrarian, economies.

To explain how market economies are structured and how they operate.

To explain why, where, and how government intervenes in mixed economies, chiefly the U.S. economy.

To explore decision making in and to evaluate planned economies.

To distinguish between capitalism and socialism and to describe how these two systems relate to individual and collective economic decisions.

To explore the British foundations and the historical highlights of the U.S. economy.

Chapter 1 introduced the basic concept of scarcity that underlies the study of economics. No economy, no matter how large or sophisticated, can provide all the goods and services to satisfy every member's wants and needs. Thus, people in every economy must make decisions about what goods and services to produce, how to produce them, and who will receive the goods and services that are produced. In this chapter we focus on these decisions and how they are made in different economies.

SCARCITY AND SOCIETY'S BASIC ECONOMIC DECISIONS

All economies continually produce goods and services, whether they are simple agricultural and mineral commodities or complex surgical equipment and computer programs. The U.S. economy, for example, currently produces in excess of $14.4 trillion of cars, new construction, health care, and other goods and services over the course of a year. Unfortunately, even this seemingly huge output satisfies only part of people's wants and needs; the U.S. economy cannot satisfy everyone's material wants.

How do we decide what collection of goods and services the economy will produce? How do we decide who gets what and how much they get? Why can some households buy steak while others can afford only hamburger? This economic predicament resembles the dilemma that Santa Claus faces—millions of cherubic boys and girls dreaming of endless toys but only one workshop, a few elves, and just one sleigh to carry the goodies. What does Santa put in his bag?

Every society, regardless of its wealth and power, must make certain choices about production and distribution. Specifically, every society faces three **basic economic decisions.**

Basic Economic Decisions
The choices that must be made in any society regarding what to produce, how to produce, and to whom production is distributed.

♦ What goods and services to produce and in what quantities?
♦ How to produce goods and services, or how to use the economy's resources?
♦ Who gets the goods and services?

The first economic decision, what to produce, addresses the dilemma that every society's members voice endless wants but economies can produce only limited varieties and amounts of goods and services. As a result, in every society choices must be made about the types and quantities of goods and services to produce: Are cars or SUVs or trucks to be produced? How many? What models?

The second economic decision, how to produce goods and services, or how to use an economy's resources, reflects the reality that products can be made in any number of different ways, and different methods require different resources and processes. In producing cars, a company must decide what technology to use, how many workers to hire, whether to use sheet metal or plastic, and whether to add GIS systems and leather seats.

The third decision is a distribution issue: Who will get the goods and services produced? Who will receive the hybrid SUVs, running shoes, medical services, homes, and premium ice cream?

| FIGURE 2.1 | *Scarcity, the Basic Economic Decisions, and Economic Systems* |

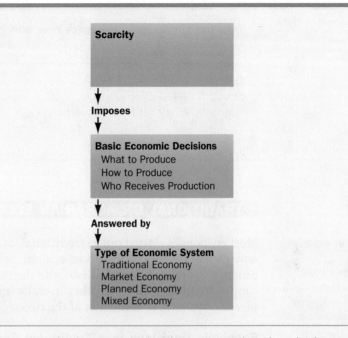

Scarcity imposes three basic economic decisions on a society. A society's economic system determines how the decisions are made.

ECONOMIC SYSTEMS AND THE THREE BASIC ECONOMIC DECISIONS

Economic System

The way in which an economy is organized to make the basic economic decisions.

The way that a society makes the three basic economic decisions depends on its **economic system.** An economic system is a particular way of organizing the relationships among businesses, households, and the government to make basic choices about what goods and services to produce, how to produce them, and who will get them. Economists often classify economic systems into four types or models:

♦ agrarian/traditional economies,
♦ market economies,
♦ planned or command economies, and
♦ mixed economies.

While today all economies are mixed economies, it is helpful to understand the basic model that underlies a particular mixed economy. Figure 2.1 summarizes the relationship among scarcity, the basic economic choices, and economic systems.

In traditional economies, decision making is based on custom or tradition. Market economies emphasize the role of individuals and businesses in decision making: Individual buyers and sellers make the basic economic decisions as they communicate through prices in marketplaces. Planned, or command, economies emphasize collective decision making: Government planners represent economic participants. A mixed economy is one that combines elements of planned and market economies.

TABLE 2.1	*Strengths and Weaknesses of Traditional Economies*

Traditional, or agrarian, economies have strengths and weaknesses.

Strengths	Weaknesses
Economic security/stability	Lack of innovation or change
Strong family/community ties	Few economic opportunities for individuals
Economic safety net for most members	Reinforcement of social hierarchies
	Low levels of production

TRADITIONAL OR AGRARIAN ECONOMIES

Traditional, or Agrarian, Economy

An economy that relies largely on tradition, custom, or ritual when making the basic economic decisions.

Most economies started out as **traditional, or agrarian, economies.** A traditional economy generally relies on tradition, custom, or ritual to decide what to produce, how to produce it, and to whom to distribute the results. As traditional economies outgrow simple traditional systems, they usually move toward market systems, centrally planned systems, or some mix of the two.

Economic Decisions in a Traditional Economy

Traditional economies rely on historical, social, political, or religious arrangements and traditions to decide what to produce. Typically, these economies are focused on some kind of agricultural commodity (like cotton, corn, or cattle) or mineral commodity (like copper). For example, some Native American tribes in the Southwest developed economies based on raising corn and sheep and then using the livestock for mutton and wool.

Traditional systems usually stay fairly small and rural, with economic decisions closely tied to hierarchies. These economies usually have work roles tied to traditional family and gender roles. Boys tend to take up the occupations of their fathers, while girls stay close to home with their mothers.

People make their livings using the same production methods that their families used for generations. Traditional economies often resist change and only slowly adopt new technologies. Resources like land and labor are generally not very specialized, so traditional societies may not produce as much as they could if their resources were used more efficiently.

The economic decision of how to distribute goods and services is also made through tradition. Because these economies develop around hierarchies, what people get is often determined by their place in society. Those with a higher status, like landowners, may fare well, while others may not. However, agrarian societies sometimes have worked to support all members, at least at a subsistence level.

Barter

The direct exchange of goods or services for other goods or services.

People in traditional economies often rely on **barter**—the direct exchange of goods or services for other goods or services—to meet their needs. Barter, by its very nature, is found in simple societies. As people's economic needs become complicated and varied, they inevitably need to create money to facilitate trade. This is one reason that traditional systems evolve into more developed market or planned economies.

Table 2.1 summarizes the strengths and weaknesses of traditional economies. Up for Debate, "Is Western-Style Development Appropriate for Other Cultures?",

UP FOR DEBATE

IS WESTERN-STYLE DEVELOPMENT APPROPRIATE FOR OTHER CULTURES?

Issue   *People living in the United States and Western Europe enjoy high standards of living, especially compared to many other countries. Does this mean that policies that stimulate growth in the West will be just as effective for people living in other nations?*

Yes   Some experts believe the answer to this question is "yes" and recommend Western-style legal systems, political structures, and free markets as the basis for making the three economic choices. Societies that are rooted in individual choice and markets have strong economies, as demonstrated in much of the Western world, including the United States. Proof of this can be found by comparing indicators of economic well-being in Western-type economies with other economies. For example, the life expectancy is over 78 years for a child born in 2008 in the United States, Germany, France, and most other Western European countries. The life expectancy for a child born in Angola, Swaziland, or Zambia is fewer than 39 years. Also, it is estimated that in 2005 there were more than 700 telephone mainlines per thousand people in Sweden and the Netherlands, but fewer than 20 per thousand people in Ghana and Angola.

In many Western nations free-market economic institutions have also helped to lead to political freedoms and democracy. A striking example of this is the conversion of some former Soviet-bloc countries to market capitalism as well as democratic political systems.

No   Other experts argue that "grafting" Western institutions onto other nations, some of which have vastly different histories and cultures, may fail to improve living standards and may conflict with traditional cultural norms. For example, many former Soviet-bloc countries had little experience with political freedom and the institutions of free markets, and transplanting Western-style institutional structures did not result in Western-style growth. Inserting Western institutions into countries may force them to make hard decisions between the familiar social orders of the past and new political and economic freedoms.

Simply inserting Western-style institutions may not be enough to create healthy economic growth. In addition, the desirability of imposing Western values on non-Western nations can be questioned. Even the goal of economic development—with its emphasis on increasing output—can be controversial when it conflicts with very different collectively oriented value systems in many parts of the world. Some of the values that those living in Western-style economies take for granted—for example, the emphasis on consumerism and material progress—are themselves foreign to some other cultures.

Sources: Jasen Castillo, "The Dilemma of Simultaneity: Russia and Georgia in the Midst of Transformation," *World Affairs,* June 22, 1997; Mike Dowling, http://www.Mrdowling.com/8oclife.html; U.S. Central Intelligence Agency, *The World Factbook,* http://www.cia.gov/library/publications/the-world-factbook/fields/2102.html.

discusses whether the Western-style free-market system is the best road to development for these traditional and other nonmarket economies.

MARKET ECONOMIES

Market Economy
An economy in which the basic economic decisions are made by individual buyers and sellers in markets using the language of price.

Price System
A market system; one in which buyers and sellers communicate through prices in markets.

Private Property Rights
Individual rights to possess and dispose of goods, services, and resources.

A **market economy** is rooted in the belief that decisions are best made by individuals, or in a philosophy of individualism. In a market economy, individual buyers and sellers interacting in markets[1] make the basic economic choices. Also called **price systems,** market economies rely on prices as the language through which buyers and sellers communicate their intentions. For example, Starbuck's expresses its intention to sell lattes by making them available at a particular price, and consumers tell Starbuck's that they want lattes by paying the price asked. The exchange of the latte is made because the price is suitable to both buyer and seller.

Essential to this system is **private property rights,** which give individuals and businesses the right to own resources, goods, and services, and to use them as they

[1]A market is defined as a place or situation in which the buyers and sellers of a product interact for the purpose of exchange. Markets are discussed in detail in the next chapter.

FIGURE 2.2	*The Circular Flow of Economic Activity*

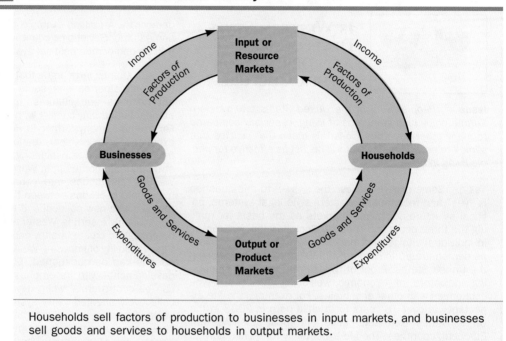

Households sell factors of production to businesses in input markets, and businesses sell goods and services to households in output markets.

choose. In a pure market economy, individuals are free to form businesses, operate with a profit motive, and make their own decisions about price or product-related matters, or to engage in **free enterprise.**

Free Enterprise
The right of a business to make its own decisions and to operate with a profit motive.

Pure market systems, where individual buyers and sellers make *all* economic decisions with no government intervention, have virtually disappeared. But price systems are extremely important for us to understand because they provide the philosophical and operational bases for economies like the U.S. market economy. The United States has kept the key features of a market economy, although it is more of a mixed system because of government's role.

Markets have existed in different types of economies throughout the history of the world. In some instances, markets have served simply as an allocation mechanism to aid people in making the basic economic decisions. For example, ancient Greece at the time of Aristotle featured intense trading despite the fact that the economy was, by current standards, primitive. Even planned economies have used markets in modern times to help allocate goods and services. For example, the former Soviet Union used markets even prior to the economic restructuring of the 1990s.

Capitalism
An economic system with free enterprise and private property rights; economic decision making occurs in a market environment.

Market economies are usually associated with **capitalism,** an economic system in which private individuals own the factors of production and operate on a free-enterprise basis. Pure capitalist economies leave little room for government interference.

Circular Flow Model
A diagram showing the real and money flows between households and businesses in output, or product, markets and input, or resource, markets.

The Operation of a Market Economy

We can best illustrate the operation of a pure market economy with no government intervention by a **circular flow model,** such as that in Figure 2.2. This model shows how businesses and households relate to one another as buyers and sellers. In one part of this relationship, shown in the lower half of Figure 2.2, businesses are the sellers of goods and services and households are the buyers. Here there is a real flow of goods and services from businesses to households and a money flow of dollars from households to businesses. For example, T-shirts, televisions, fajitas, and furniture flow to households, which give businesses dollars for these items.

Output Markets (Product Markets)
Markets in which businesses are sellers and households are buyers; consumer goods and services are exchanged.

Transactions of this type, where businesses sell goods and services and households buy them, occur in **output markets,** or **product markets.** In these markets, buyers and sellers may deal with one another face-to-face, as in automobile showrooms or restaurants, or through more impersonal negotiations, such as catalog orders, Internet purchases, or vending machines.

In the second part of the household–business relationship, businesses are the buyers and households are the sellers. Businesses need resources, or factors of production, which belong to households, to produce goods and services. In the upper half of Figure 2.2, a real flow of labor, capital, land, and entrepreneurship goes from households (sellers) to businesses (buyers). In return for these resources, businesses send a money flow of wages, interest, rents, and profits to households. For example, Ford Motor must hire machinists, design engineers, and line workers to produce vehicles. In return, these employees receive wages. Ford also pays dividends to its stockholders in return for their entrepreneurial role. Transactions involving resource purchases occur in **input markets,** or **resource markets.**

Input Markets (Resource Markets)
Markets in which households are sellers and businesses are buyers; factors of production are bought and sold.

A market economy's basic structure can be fully explained by focusing on the two buyer–seller relationships of businesses and households at the same time, or on Figure 2.2 as a whole. Businesses and households relate to one another through both input markets and output markets. Households sell labor, capital, land, and entrepreneurship to businesses in return for income in input markets. That income is then used to buy goods and services from businesses in output markets.

Economic Decisions in a Market Economy

How are the basic economic choices of what, how, and to whom made in a market system?

What to Produce?   In a market economy, what and how many goods and services are produced is the result of millions of independent decisions by individual households and businesses in the marketplace. A business will produce something if it thinks that enough households will purchase the item at a price that will make its production profitable. If people do not want a good or service or will not pay a price that allows a profit, businesses will not produce that item. This is why some products like calculators and the Ford Mustang continue to appear while some clothing styles and recording artists disappear from the market. New products such as Lego Mindstorms and laptop computers emerge because individuals want them and businesses see profit opportunities in producing and selling them.

In a world of large corporate producers like car and cola companies, can individuals actually bring about product change? A single buyer acting alone may be powerless, but together consumers "vote" for products by virtue of spending or not spending their money on a product. Products disappear from the market when consumers do not buy them.[2] Application 2.1, "Whoops! Missed the Market," describes several cases where consumers decided against a company's product.

[2]An important question must be raised: To what extent are individuals' decisions influenced by advertising and other promotional activities? If businesses exert a strong influence on people's attitudes and tastes, do the dollars consumers spend reflect their independent choices, or do they represent something else? Put differently, do businesses respond to consumers' preferences, do they shape those preferences, or is there some mixture of the two? The independence of consumer economic decision making is a controversial issue. What is your position on this question?

WHOOPS! MISSED THE MARKET

Large corporations can exert great power in the markets for their products, including substantial funding for advertising and promotion. Although it may appear that the individual buyer of these products has little power against a giant corporation, this is not the case when all of the individual buyers' decisions to purchase—or not purchase—a product are tallied. Over the years, buyers have caused sellers to take products off the market or to drastically change them. There are several classic examples of product failure despite the marketing efforts of the seller. Here are a few of those examples.

The Edsel   One of the most legendary misses on the auto market was Ford's Edsel, named after Henry Ford's only child. The Edsel was introduced in 1957 with great expectations for the car and plans to sell more than 200,000 annually. But in 1958, its best year, barely 63,000 were sold. The Edsel had some interesting features, including push buttons on the center of the steering wheel to shift gears and a "horse collar" front grill. It was reported that the Edsel caused Ford Motor Company to lose more than $300,000 per day. In November 1959, Ford announced it would stop production of the Edsel.

New Coke and Crystal Pepsi   Coke drinkers around the country rebelled against the New Coke introduced by Coca-Cola in the mid-1980s. Even marketing campaigns could not assuage the anger of Coca-Cola drinkers who wanted the original taste to return. Less than three months after the introduction of New Coke came the announcement that the original formula would return—as Classic Coke. Crystal Pepsi, a clear cola, was a 1992 failure.

Ford Explorer   For years the Ford Explorer was the top-selling SUV. Then in 2000, news came that more than 100 deaths were linked to Firestone tires, most of which were on Ford Explorers. Sales of the Explorer dropped significantly with questions about whether the tires or the Explorer's design triggered the rollovers. In 2002 Ford introduced a redesigned, more stable Explorer.

Grocery Store Products   The world of food and other grocery-type products provides a plethora of items that consumers have rejected, even when large and multiple companies have introduced a "new" product. Here are a few that disappeared from the market: hot dogs filled with cheese chunks, frozen stuffing, chocolate french fries, garlic cake, aerosol spray toothpaste, monster-buster room freshener, fruit and cream Twinkies, and Dunk-a-Ball Cereal, which was designed to be something kids could play with before eating.

The Yugo   The Yugoslavian subcompact was introduced in the United States in the mid-1980s. Sales peaked at 49,000 in 1987 and fell to about 3,100 in 1991. This subcompact, which was underpowered and prone to breakdowns, was "discussed" in comedy routines and news columns. Plans for a clever marketing campaign in 1992 were scrapped after Yugo America filed for bankruptcy.

Based on: "Firestone Tire Recall Drives Down Sales for Ford Explorers," *Journal Record*, Oklahoma City, OK, November 2, 2000; Joann Muller and Nicole St. Pierre, "Ford vs. Firestone: A Corporate Whodunit; Is It the Tires or Is It the Explorer? Here's the Story So Far," *Business Week*, June 11, 2001; Joann Muller, David Welch, and Jeff Green, "Would You Buy One?; Customers Are Pelting Explorer Dealers with Safety Questions," *Business Week*, September 25, 2000; Rick Popely, "Edsel's Failure a Matter of Timing for Ford," Knight Ridder Tribune Business News, November 17, 2002; Richard Truett, "The Past Ain't What It Used to Be: The Edsel Finally Is Cool," *Automotive News*, June 16, 2003; Martin Friedman, "Broken Promises—Product Launches That Failed—New Food Products Annual, *Prepared Foods*, April 15, 1994; Stuart Elliott, "What Might Have Been: 3 Ad Campaigns for the Yugo," *The New York Times*, May 24, 1992; Ross Bonander, "Top 10: Failed Product Launches," AskMen.com, July 22, 2008.

How to Produce?   In a market economy, businesses decide how to produce goods and services through their choices of production methods. Generally, a business can produce a good or service in more than one way, so businesses must decide which of the available techniques and resources or factors should be used for production. For example, suppose that a company identifies three different methods for producing a type of guitar: by machine, by hand, or by a combination of labor and machinery. The cost for each of the three methods is given in Table 2.2. Which method of production will the company choose in a market economy?

Least-Cost (Efficient) Method of Production
The method of production that allows a good or service of a given quality to be produced at the lowest cost.

The company's owners will choose the **least-cost method of production,** or the most **efficient** method, as we discussed in Chapter 1. Since the owners' profit on the guitars is the difference between the product's price and its production costs, the lower

TABLE 2.2	*Costs of Different Methods for Producing a Guitar*

Method 3 illustrates the least-cost method of production.

Method of Production	Cost to Company per Unit
1. Machine-assembled	$650.00
2. Hand-assembled	900.00
3. Hand-and-machine-assembled	530.00

the cost, the greater the profit. By using both labor and machinery (method 3), the company's owners stand to earn more profit than they would if they chose one of the other methods.

In a market system, factor prices determine the most efficient production method, and are the basis for a firm's decisions about production techniques. In the United States, for example, agriculture is highly mechanized. Given the market prices of farm machinery and labor, and available technology, U.S. farmers find it cheapest to use more machinery and less labor to produce a given output. In other parts of the world, abundant and cheap labor encourages farmers to use production methods that emphasize human effort.

Who Gets Goods and Services?   The price system determines who receives goods and services in a market economy. The circular flow model in Figure 2.2 shows a flow of goods and services going from businesses to households in output markets, matched by a flow of dollars going from households to businesses. In a market economy, people get goods and services only if they can pay for them. In other words, in a market economy goods and services are distributed to those who can afford them.

In market systems, people earn money to buy goods and services by selling factors of production in resource markets. The amount and quality of labor, entrepreneurial skills, capital, or land that people sell determine the amount of income they have to spend on goods and services. People lacking marketable skills are not paid well in resource markets, so they cannot afford many goods and services. People who have many resources, or resources that are highly valued, may enjoy a substantial income, enabling them to buy the items they want in output markets. In a market system, people's abilities to purchase mountain cabins, original artworks, and cellars full of French wine—or peanut butter, one-room apartments, and bus tickets—are determined by the number and value of the resources they offer for sale.

Evaluating Market Economies

Like all economic systems, market economies have both strengths and weaknesses.

Strengths: Efficiency, Consumer Choice, and the Opportunity for Success   On the plus side, market economies tend to produce goods and services efficiently because profit and income act as incentives to guide production. The profit incentive causes businesses to produce goods and services as efficiently as possible, and income rewards provide incentives for households to use their resources effectively and to improve their value. Many students, for example, invest in education to become more productive and obtain higher salaries. (Table 15.5 provides data on the relationship between education and income.)

Market systems also encourage efficiency because the information required for production and distribution decisions passes directly between buyers and sellers via price. In other words, the market coordinates business and household actions, and through prices responds fairly quickly to the decisions of buyers and sellers in production and distribution.

Market systems also provide a wide range of choices in the variety and quality of goods and services for consumers. Market systems sometimes provide goods and services even before consumers realize that they want them. Market economies also offer significant opportunities for growth and change. Stories about the "local boy or girl makes good" abound in market systems. Many immigrants and Americans born into poverty have ascended the economic ladder through talent and hard work.

Weaknesses: Market Power, Equity, and Information   There are several problems inherent in a market economy. Typically these are called **market failures,** a term economists use to describe problems created by a market-based system, or the inability of the system to achieve a society's goals.

The very competition at the foundation of a market economy can be lessened when competition drives out sellers and the market becomes dominated by one or a few sellers. When this happens, the interaction between buyers and sellers becomes lopsided, with undesirable consequences for buyers including higher prices, fewer choices, and less attention to quality. Consider the airport or stadium with just one food concessionaire: here people likely pay a high price and have fewer menu choices.

Another market system weakness is that it provides no protection for those who lack an adequate ability to provide for themselves. In a pure market system, people who cannot contribute to production, such as the disabled, elderly, or children living in poverty, have no provision for support or the acquisition of needed goods and services.

Pure market systems do not protect people who lack the knowledge to make informed decisions about purchases or employment. Few people totally understand the effects of chemicals used in food products or medications, or the design and inner workings of an airplane. Market systems have no organized way to ensure that products offered for sale are safe; the information required to assess every product a person could buy would be expensive, technical, and time consuming to acquire and evaluate.

Market Failure
A market system creates a problem for a society or fails to achieve a society's goals.

Market failure can also occur when age, race, or gender discrimination results in unequal treatment for some workers. Such discrimination leads to the inefficient use of labor resources and undermines the value placed on equal treatment for equal work.

Finally, market failure can result when the profit-driven, cost-minimizing efforts of businesses lead to costs that must be absorbed by all of society, such as the cleanup of pollution or additional health care costs. Hazardous products, poor working conditions, or degradation of the environment could result from the efforts of producers to find less expensive means to operate. A hog farm that lowers its costs by allowing raw sewage to drain into a stream benefits through throwing some of its costs onto society. Table 2.3 summarizes the strengths and weaknesses of a market economy.

Government Intervention in a Market Economy: A Mixed Economy

Not surprisingly, society frequently turns to the government for help when it wants to address its economy's market failures. When government intervenes, the economy moves from its "pure" status to what we call a mixed economy. Figure 2.3 gives some examples of government intervention in the business sector, the household sector, output markets, and input markets when markets fail.

TABLE 2.3	Strengths and Weaknesses of Market Economies

A market economy has both strengths and weaknesses, which are termed market failures.

Strengths	Weaknesses
Strong efficiency incentives	People without marketable skills may
Prices allow direct signals between	not get needed goods and services
buyers and sellers	Market power in hands of few sellers
Economic freedom	No protection for people with
Wide selection of goods and services	inadequate knowledge about products
Incentives for innovation and growth	and jobs
Choices/prices of goods and services	Business cost-minimizing efforts can
reflect buyers' and sellers' values and	lead to social costs
priorities	Age, race, or gender discrimination

There are some general ways in which government influences decision making.

1. Government establishes the legal framework within which businesses and households operate. This involves the definition of property rights, contracts, standards of fair competition, court procedures, and other matters.

FIGURE 2.3	Government Intervention in a Market Economy

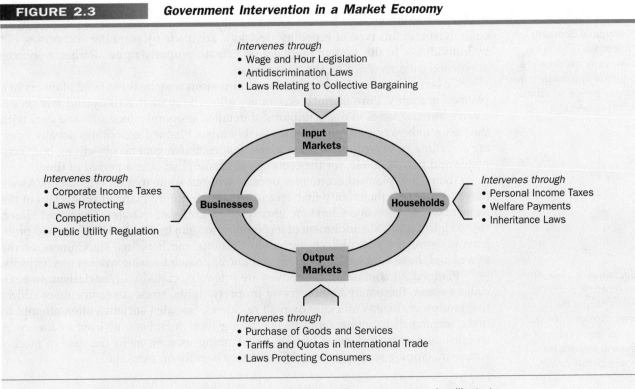

Government can intervene in a market economy in specific ways, as the examples illustrate.

Government Regulation
Government commissions and boards are involved in business decision making.

2. While keeping business ownership in private hands, government sometimes intervenes through **government regulation.** Government commissions may oversee and become involved in managerial decisions that range from pricing, profit, and availability of service in certain industries, such as natural gas, to addressing specific problems, such as pollution and product safety, that cross many industries.

3. Sometimes government intervenes in resource markets to protect workers and wages. In the United States, most businesses must pay workers a minimum wage and obey laws relating to collective bargaining, worker health and safety, and other labor-related issues.

4. Government taxing and spending policies influence economic activity. Because of its sheer size, government spending significantly affects specific industries and markets, such as those related to defense. Taxing and government spending influence employment and inflation conditions, or the overall level of economic activity. For example, Congress engaged in "stimulus" spending in 2009 to reverse a sluggish economy.

5. In the United States, government income support programs range from outright grants of money or goods and services to special programs designed to improve a person's earning potential. Examples include Social Security, job training programs that teach marketable skills, and Medicare payments that help to ensure access to health care for older individuals.

PLANNED ECONOMIES

Planned Economy (Command Economy)
An economy in which the basic economic decisions are made by planners rather than by private individuals and businesses.

A **planned economy,** also termed a **command economy,** is based on a philosophy of collectivism. In this type of economy, decisions are made by planning authorities, not by individuals. In this system there are no private property rights. Rather, resources are owned collectively or by the government.

Government agencies, bureaus, or commissions may be the official planners in a planned economy. Pure planned economies allow no market activity and rely on extensive bureaucracies to make millions of detailed economic decisions and deal with the vast numbers of problems that invariably arise. Planned economies usually operate according to blueprints, termed plans, that establish general objectives, both economic and noneconomic, for the economy to accomplish over a period of time.

Today, few planned economies operate without some market orientation. As we move further into the twenty-first century, the large purely planned economies of the former Soviet Union and China are undergoing significant changes. The Soviet Union rushed into a quick abandonment of its planning system in the late 1980s and had problems adjusting to a new philosophy and institutional mechanisms. The Chinese, on the other hand, have adopted a slower, systematic approach to using market mechanisms.

Socialism
An economic system in which many of the factors of production are collectively owned, and an attempt is made to equalize the distribution of income.

Planned, or command, economies are often associated with **socialism.** In a socialist system, there may be no private property rights, since governments or collective groups of citizens officially own all resources. Socialist societies often attempt to make income distribution more equal among their members, at least in theory. A socialist system may depend heavily on planning or may, as in the case of market socialism, employ some planning but also rely heavily on markets.[3]

---

[3]In market socialism some goods and services (such as those used by households) are allocated through markets while others (such as machinery and equipment used by businesses) are allocated by the planners.

Economic Decisions in a Planned Economy

In planned economies, planning authorities decide what types and amounts of goods and services to produce. Planners use the planning objectives and their value judgments to determine how many buses, submarines, dry-cleaning plants, shoes, and other items the system will produce.

Government planners also decide how to allocate resources to produce goods and services. Here the authority's influence is generally less direct and comes through determining which factors of production and processes will be made available to producers. For example, in printing, design and type can be set by hand or by computer. If planners want to keep typesetters employed, they will not plan to produce computerized printing equipment. In a purely planned economy, a producer cannot order a machine, part, or piece of equipment if the authority has not permitted it to be produced. Planners determine who will work in what jobs; how to use land, buildings, and productive equipment; and where economic opportunities lie.

Predictably enough, planning officials decide who will have access to goods and services. A rationing system may be used to distribute specific items or services, or people in strategic jobs (like defense) may receive more than their equal share as part of efforts to advance a specific goal.

Planners may also give individuals freedom to purchase what has been produced through the plan. If individuals can choose for themselves, then planners face the problem of income determination. That is, planners must decide how much income each production factor should be paid for its services.

Evaluating Planned Economies

What advantages do planned economies offer? These economies may achieve certain societal goals faster than in a less formally organized economy. The development of a high-tech industry or the buildup of the agricultural sector might be accomplished more rapidly when a central authority coordinates efforts. Planned economies should also find it easier to eliminate unemployment when producers can simply be forced to use more labor in their production processes. In addition, the ability to control the distribution of goods and services can alter shares in the economy's output. For example, a planning authority could ensure that the elderly get adequate heating fuel.

Planning Failure
Centralized planning creates a problem for a society or fails to achieve a society's goals.

Just as market economies do not work perfectly, planned economics may experience **planning failures** when they create problems for a society or fail to achieve its goals. It is difficult for planned economies to match consumer wants and needs with production. The value judgments of planners about what to produce may not coincide with consumers' value judgments. Furthermore, the time lapse between a plan's creation and actual production may be so lengthy that items once considered appropriate and desirable are no longer in demand.

The sheer complexity of production where government planners determine which resources, technology, and processes will be used creates issues. Shortages of a key resource can stop production. Mistakes and delays come with a slowed flow of information and decision making. With no incentives for producers or workers, the result can be inferior products and inefficient processes.

The environmental damage that can and has occurred with planning is a serious issue. In Eastern Europe and China, air and water pollution problems are consequences of planners' failures to take the environment into account in many of their decisions. Concerns about polluted air were a serious consideration for athletes who

TABLE 2.4	*Strengths and Weaknesses of Planned Economies*

Planned economies have both strengths and weaknesses, called planning failures.

Strengths	Weaknesses
Ability to accomplish social goals quickly	Creation of production problems due to complexity of planning
Can reduce unemployment by planning for more labor in production	Few incentives to create quality products or services, operate efficiently, or meet consumer demand
Can provide for an equal distribution of income and goods and services	Few incentives to protect the environment
Possible provision for more economic security and safety nets	Few economic choices for most participants

participated in the 2008 Summer Olympics in Beijing. Table 2.4 summarizes the strengths and weaknesses of a planned economy.

MIXED ECONOMIES

Mixed Economy
An economic system with some combination of market and centralized decision making.

Technically, all economies are **mixed economies** because the three basic choices are addressed by some combination of market and centralized decision making. Pure market and pure planned economies are polar cases that help us order our thinking but have no real-world counterparts. An important factor giving the different economies their unique styles is the manner and degree to which individual and collective decision making are combined. As discussed earlier, pure market and pure planned economies are not perfect. Market failures and planning failures cause the movement to mixed economies.

Figure 2.4 provides a helpful way to think about economic systems. With the exception of traditional economies, economic systems can be visualized as lying along a continuum. At one end are pure market economies and at the other end are pure planned economies. The world's economies lie between these extremes and combine elements of market, or individual, decision making and planned, or collective, decision making. Where an economy falls on the continuum depends on its core philosophy about decision making and the degree to which it deviates from this core. For example, the United States lies closer to the market end of the continuum because of

FIGURE 2.4	*Continuum of Economic Decision Making*

United States   Britain   China   Cuba

Pure Market ══════════════════════════════ Pure Planned

Individualism   Collectivism

Economies can be classified according to their dependence on planned versus market decision making.

TEST YOUR UNDERSTANDING

ECONOMIC DECISION MAKING AND THE CIRCULAR FLOW

1. Indicate for each of the following situations whether it would most likely occur in a pure market economy, a pure planned economy, or a mixed economy.

    a. Businesses in a particular industry are free to produce however they want and are constantly on the lookout for new cost-reducing techniques since every dollar saved in cost is an extra dollar of profit.

    b. An economics instructor in a particular country does not bother to explain the circular flow model because it has no relevance to how the basic economic decisions are made in that country.

    c. Union and management representatives submit a deadlocked labor contract negotiation to the government for mediation.

    d. Workers who have lost their jobs and incomes cut back their spending because there is no alternative source of emergency financial support once their savings run out.

    e. Consumers are unable to obtain carburetors and windshield wiper motors for their cars because they are not being produced, yet accordions, which are plentiful and not in demand, continue to be produced.

    f. A catering business goes bankrupt, but its employees receive unemployment compensation while they look for other jobs.

2. Suppose that, because of uncertainty about future jobs and incomes, households decide to increase their savings and reduce their current purchases of goods and services from businesses. With the aid of the circular flow diagram below, answer each of the following.

    a. Identify the flows on the bottom half of the circular flow model and explain what impact these household decisions will have on each of those flows.

    b. Identify the flows on the upper half of the circular flow model and explain what impact the actions taken on the bottom half of the model will have on the flows on the upper half.

    c. Based on the changes in the flows in the entire model, what should be the effect of this decision by households on future jobs and incomes?

Answers can be found at the back of the book.

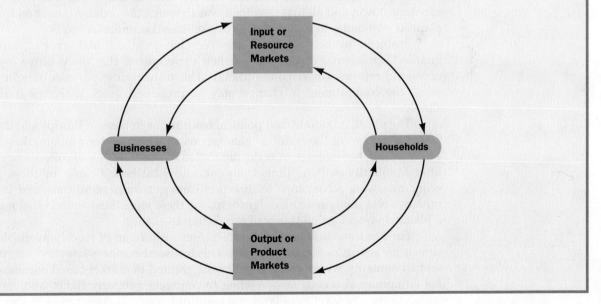

its reliance on markets, and Cuba lies closer to the planned end of the continuum because of its reliance on planning.

Test Your Understanding, "Economic Decision Making and the Circular Flow," allows you to practice distinguishing among the different economic systems and to review the key relationships in a market economy.

CHANGING ECONOMIC SYSTEMS

Since the mid-1980s, dramatic changes have occurred in many of the world's planned economies. The former Soviet Union, Poland, China, and other nations have been moving toward greater use of free markets and individual decision making. Described in terms of Figure 2.4, these and other planned economies have been shifting to the left along the continuum of economic decision making. In several of these countries, economic reform has been accompanied by greater political freedom. Non–Communist Party candidates have been elected to top positions in Russia, Poland, and several of the former Soviet republics, and East and West Germany have reunified.

Privatization
The granting to individuals of property rights to factors of production that were once collectively owned, or owned by the state.

An essential element for planned economies to move toward market economies is **privatization.** Individuals are granted property rights to factors of production that were once collectively owned or owned by the state. Without the protection of private ownership and the right to profit that it secures, individuals have few incentives to carry out the entrepreneurial functions—organizing resources and taking risks—that drive a market economy. Successful privatization is key to the actual transformation of a planned to a market economy.

The Realities of Economic Change

When it first became apparent in the late 1980s that the economic and political changes in Eastern Europe and the Soviet Union were real and that their closely controlled systems were disappearing, many people in the United States and other market-oriented countries felt a sense of unconditional victory. The free-market approach had won the ideological war, and all that remained was to watch the orderly transition from once-planned economies to more efficient market-based economies.

Problems in the transition, however, changed the initial sense of euphoria to guarded optimism. People lowered their expectations that the positive rewards of economic reform would come quickly. The transition experience taught us that, while the commitment to change may be professed quickly, change itself comes slowly.

The social, economic, and political institutions in Eastern Europe and the former Soviet Union were the result of generations of living under a nonmarket ideology. These planned economies were deeply rooted in a philosophy of collectivism and had little familiarity with a philosophy of individualism. People in these planned economies were accustomed to direction from government officials, and individual initiative was rarely rewarded. Furthermore, there were those with vested interests in a planned system. All of this bred opposition to change.

Further transition problems arose from a shortage of readily available professionals to "set up" a market economy. This included business lawyers, entrepreneurs, and accountants, whose roles are taken for granted in market-based economies. Market economies also need laws relating to contracts, property rights, and commercial transactions. These types of laws and institutions simply didn't exist in societies that depend on government planners to carry out their economic affairs.

The rocky start to a market economy in Eastern European countries in the 1990s is evident in data. For example, from 1990 through 1999, prices of consumer goods and services purchased by Russian households increased by more than 1.3 *million* percent and by more than 22.7 *million* percent in Ukraine. In addition, output in Ukraine fell

APPLICATION 2.2

THE PEOPLE'S REPUBLIC OF CHINA

If you put China into your search engine, a huge number of sites for information will be identified. The World Factbook *provides some basic demographic data and information, such as the geography, language, government, religions, and economy of China. Other sites provide historical and cultural information as well as political commentary, since China remains a Communist state.*

For centuries China stood as a leading civilization, outpacing most of the rest of the world in arts and sciences. But in the nineteenth and early twentieth centuries, China experienced civil unrest, major famines, military defeats, and foreign occupation.

This huge country, which borders India, Pakistan, and Vietnam, among others, experienced a serious change in government after World War II. At that time, the Communists, under Mao Zedong, better known as Chairman Mao, established an autocratic socialist system that prevailed until 1978. This Communist regime ensured China's sovereignty but imposed very strict controls over everyday life and took the lives of tens of millions of people in the process.

After 1978, Mao's successor, Deng Xiaoping, and other leaders began moving China from a centrally planned economy to a more market-oriented system. Although a political framework of Communist control has been maintained, there has been an increase in the economic influence of individuals and organizations other than the state. Some of the changes include a movement away from the old collectivization in agriculture to individual and village responsibility, increased authority of local officials and plant managers, the allowing of small-scale enterprises, and increased foreign trade and investment. Since 1978, output has quadrupled and living standards have increased.

But, like other countries, China faces some serious problems. It's one-child policy has left it with an aging population; unemployment persists as state-owned enterprises close and workers are laid off; and there is growing deterioration in the environment, including air pollution, soil erosion, and water shortages.

Over the next decade, China's increase in market-oriented behaviors as it continues to move away from a planned economy and its impact on the world's economies through global trade and finance should be interesting to watch.

Source: United States Central Intelligence Agency, "China," *The World Factbook*, updated April 15, 2008, pp. 1–19.

---

each year of the 1990s: Ukraine's total output in 1999 came to only 30 percent of what was produced in 1990.[4]

Today we watch China, a country of more than 1.3 billion people (the U.S. population is slightly more than 300 million) with a landmass slightly less than that of the United States, experience exceptionally rapid economic growth. Once considered to be a closed planned economy, China has moved slowly and carefully toward a more market-oriented system and has become an important player in world markets. China has quickly become a major consumer of energy and other resources, as well as a supplier of manufactured products. Application 2.2, "The People's Republic of China," gives some background on changes in the economy of China.

THE U.S. ECONOMIC SYSTEM

The U.S. economy has been described as a mixed economic system that largely depends on markets and individual decision making. The government plays a somewhat lesser but vitally important role in the U.S. system. We can trace the evolution of the

---

[4]Data on Russia and Ukraine are from: "Life during Reform: A Portrait in Numbers," *The New York Times,* June 16, 1996, Section 1, p. 6; Ministry of Economy of Ukraine and European Centre for Economic Analysis of Ukraine, *Ukrainian Economic Trends: Monthly Update,* March 1996, pp. 10, 14; Ukrainian–European Policy and Legal Advice Centre, *Ukrainian Economic Trends: Quarterly Issue,* September 2000, pp. 4, 28; Russian European Centre for Economic Policy, *Russian Economic Trends: Monthly Update,* October 11, 2000, p. 3.

U.S. economy into its present form by focusing on two important sets of developments: The first occurred in England and Scotland in the eighteenth and nineteenth centuries, and the second involved major historical events in the United States.

The British Foundations of the U.S. Economy

When the early settlers, primarily from Britain, colonized the North American continent in the 1600s and early 1700s, the American colonies relied largely on agricultural commodities—notably cotton, tobacco, and corn—to trade for European necessities like tea, furniture, medicine, and industrial goods. As the American colonies developed more complex economic relationships, they faced the same dilemma that traditional or agrarian economies face today: how to evolve into a more efficient and effective system.

The colonies relied on their British intellectual heritage for guidance. Two factors helped to transform England and Scotland into the industrial, market economies that served as a model for the U.S. economy long after the colonial relationship with England ended in 1776: the rise of economic individualism in the late 1700s, and the British Industrial Revolution from roughly 1750 to 1850.

Laissez-Faire Capitalism
Capitalism with a strong emphasis on individual decision making; little or no government interference.

Mercantilism
An economic system or philosophy that subordinates individual interests and decisions to those of the state.

Invisible Hand Doctrine
Adam Smith's concept that producers acting in their own self-interest will provide buyers with what they want and thus advance the interests of society.

Industrial Revolution
A time period during which an economy becomes industrialized; characterized by such social and technological changes as the growth and development of factories.

The Rise of Economic Individualism   In 1776 a Scottish philosophy professor named Adam Smith (1723–1790) published a book entitled *The Wealth of Nations*. This book was to have a profound impact on economic thinking in his generation and future generations as well. Even today Adam Smith's book is frequently quoted.

Smith's thesis, put simply, was this: *The best way to increase the wealth of a nation is through individual decision making with minimal government interference.* The system he proposed, called **laissez-faire (let it alone) capitalism,** stood in sharp contrast to **mercantilism,** the then reigning economic philosophy. Mercantilism held that the state is the best judge of what is good for the economy. Mercantilist policies stood for the subordination of individual interests to the collective interests of the state and the belief that economic decisions should not be left to individuals acting in their own interest.

Central to Smith's argument for an economic system based on individual decision making was his **invisible hand doctrine.** According to this doctrine, it is foolish to expect people to base their business dealings with others on altruism or benevolence. Rather, people carry on their business in a way that serves their own best interests. But in a system of free and open competition where buyers have a wide range of businesses with which they can deal, it is in the producer's or seller's best interest to try to give the buyer what he or she wants on terms that are acceptable to both parties. In this way, Smith believed, by pursuing one's own best interest, one is guided "as if by an invisible hand" to advance the interests of all society. Government does not need to closely oversee the operation of the economy, since people working for their personal gain will achieve the most desired results.

Adam Smith's arguments and concepts provided an intellectual justification for an economic system based on individualism. Laissez-faire capitalism challenged both the government's role as economic director and the foundations of mercantilism as an economic philosophy. Both were crumbling in the face of a growing spirit of individualism in Britain and the colonies.

The British Industrial Revolution, 1750–1850   At the same time as the rise of economic individualism, significant technological and social changes were transforming England and Scotland into modern industrial economies. Known as the British **Industrial Revolution,** the British experience with industrialization served as a model for other countries that industrialized later, such as the United States.

APPLICATION 2.3

THE FACTORY GIRL'S LAST DAY

The art and poetry of a particular time period often reflect the social attitudes of the day. Several poems written during the British Industrial Revolution make strong statements about the poor working conditions in factories. Below is an excerpt from "The Factory Girl's Last Day," written in the early 1800s and attributed to various authors.

"'Twas on a winter morning,
    The weather wet and mild,
Two hours before the dawning
    The father roused his child:
Her daily morsel bringing,
    The darksome room he paced,
And cried: 'The bell is ringing;
    My hapless darling, haste!'

"'Dear father, I'm so weary!
    I scarce can reach the door;
And long the way and dreary:
    O, carry me once more!'
Her wasted form seems nothing;
    The load is on his heart:
He soothes the little sufferer,
    Till at the mill they part.

"The overlooker met her
    As to her frame she crept;
And with his thong he beat her,
    And cursed her when she wept.

It seemed, as she grew weaker,
    The threads the oftener broke;
The rapid wheels ran quicker,
    And heavier fell the stroke.

"She thought how her dead mother
    Blessed her with latest breath,
And of her little brother,
    Worked down, like her, to death:
Then told a tiny neighbor
    A half-penny she'd pay
To take her last hour's labor,
    While by her frame she lay.

"The sun had long descended
    Ere she sought that repose:
Her day began and ended
    As cruel tyrants chose.
Then home! but oft she tarried;
    She fell and rose no more;
By pitying comrades carried,
    She reached her father's door.

"At night, with tortured feeling,
    He watched his sleepless child:
Though close beside her kneeling,
    She knew him not, nor smiled.
Again the factory's ringing
    Her last perceptions tried:
Up from her straw bed springing,
    'It's time!' she shrieked, and died!"

Source: Robert Dale Owen, *Threading My Way* (New York: Augustus M. Kelley, 1967), pp. 129–130. Original publication, 1874. Reprinted with permission.

Prior to the mid-1700s, economic activity in Britain was primarily agricultural, and manufacturing processes—like weaving and metalworking—were carried on largely in simple cottage or home industries. Then a series of inventions and innovations began in the textile industry and spread to other industries. Inventions like massive mechanical weaving looms changed the emphasis of economic activity from agriculture and home production to a system fostering the growth of factories. With industrialization came many new and different products (such as the steam engine) as well as new production techniques (such as mass production and the factory system) that increased overall output. Great strides were made in providing goods and services.

Industrialization, however, had its dark side. Factory workers often experienced poor working conditions, low pay, and long hours. Factories often relied on the labor of women and children, who were easier to control than men and who would work for less. Perhaps not coincidentally, in 1818 Mary W. Shelley wrote about the threatening relationship between people and science in a work entitled *Frankenstein*. The poem "The Factory Girl's Last Day," also written in the early 1800s and excerpted in Application 2.3, makes a strong statement about the factory system. What can you learn from the poem about the girl's age and her living and working conditions?

In summary, the British contributed to the U.S. economy in at least two ways. First, Adam Smith introduced a philosophical and intellectual defense of individualism and free enterprise that was to become a cornerstone of the U.S. and many other Western economies. Second, Britain experienced significant economic changes that illustrated both the benefits of capitalism and the problems that this system could create.

Historical Highlights in the Development of the U.S. Economy

In the early history of the United States, the economy was closer to a pure market system, or laissez-faire capitalism, than it is today. Over the years the role and influence of government in the economy have grown, although the economy is still essentially market in nature. Several key events and historical periods are milestones in the movement of the U.S. economy from laissez-faire to its current status. These include the U.S. industrial boom, the New Deal and World War II era, the regulatory and deregulatory waves of the 1960s through 1990s, and recent developments.

The Industrial Boom   Prior to the Civil War, the U.S. economy was primarily agricultural, with production in homes or small workshops and trade in local markets. In this environment laissez-faire was the prevailing system. But after the Civil War, through the early 1900s, significant changes occurred in U.S. economic and social life similar to those during the British Industrial Revolution. Growth in transportation and communications (primarily the railroads and telephone) opened new markets. New energy sources such as oil and electricity permitted mass production and the growth of a factory system. Great numbers of inventions introduced many new goods such as the light bulb, and more efficient farm machinery. People began to move from the farm to the city seeking work and greater opportunities. Immigrants from Europe came to the United States in droves seeking their fortunes in this new country where the rumor was that the "streets were paved with gold."

Two problems developed in the midst of this industrial boom that would bring about government intervention. First, some businesses, such as Andrew Carnegie's U.S. Steel and John D. Rockefeller's Standard Oil, were becoming large and powerful corporations capable of monopolizing an entire market. Other companies were joining together with competitors to form trusts (as in the sugar and tobacco industries). Second, the living and working conditions for many Americans were becoming inordinately harsh. Many labored long hours for low wages in intolerable and dangerous conditions; child labor was permitted; city slums flourished; and attempts to form unions were often met with violence. As a result of these problems, significant legislation was passed that would alter the laissez-faire tradition.

In 1890 Congress, in an attempt to preserve a competitive landscape and prevent monopolies, passed the Sherman Antitrust Act that prohibits businesses from working together to restrain trade and from monopolizing or attempting to monopolize a market. The Sherman Act was followed in 1914 by the Clayton Act, which prohibits certain anticompetitive business practices, and the establishment of the Federal Trade Commission (FTC).

Muckrakers
Authors, journalists, and others who sensationalized American social problems in the early twentieth century.

The living and working conditions experienced by many U.S. laborers were not changed by a single sweeping law; rather, improvement resulted from bits and pieces of new federal and state legislation that began in the early 1900s. The **muckrakers,** a group of authors, journalists, photojournalists, and others, stirred the public through their exposés of the harsh and dispiriting side of the industrial age. For example,

Upton Sinclair, probably the best-known muckraker, wrote of conditions in the meat packing industry in *The Jungle*. The following excerpt shows the sensationalist manner in which Sinclair and other muckrakers wrote. It is no wonder that one response to this book was the Meat Inspection Act of 1907.

> This is no fairy story and no joke; the meat would be shovelled into carts, and the man who did the shoveling would not trouble to lift out a rat even when he saw one—there were things that went into the sausage in comparison with which a poisoned rat was a tidbit. There was no place for the men to wash their hands before they ate their dinner, and so they made a practice of washing them in the water that was to be ladled into the sausage. There were the butt-ends of smoked meat, and the scraps of corned beef, and all the odds and ends of the waste of the plants, that would be dumped into old barrels in the cellar and left there. Under the system of rigid economy which the packers enforced, there were some jobs that it only paid to do once in a long time, and among these was the cleaning out of the waste barrels. Every spring they did it; and . . . cart load after cart load of it would be taken up and dumped into the hoppers with fresh meat, and sent out to the public's breakfast.[5]

Other legislation of this period included the Food and Drug Act of 1906; state legislation limiting the hours and ages of working children; laws setting maximum hours and minimum wages for women; state workers' compensation insurance for injury on the job; and many other laws affecting matters that ranged from fire regulations to mandatory schooling.

Because of the antitrust legislation and consumer and worker regulations, by 1920 the government had established a precedent for intervening in economic activity, and the U.S. economy had moved away from laissez-faire capitalism.

The New Deal and World War II Era   The stock market crash of 1929 signaled the beginning of the Great Depression—a severe economic decline that began in October 1929 and lasted for more than a decade. The Great Depression led to a series of programs and legislative reforms instituted during the presidential administration of Franklin D. Roosevelt and termed the **New Deal.**

New Deal

A series of programs and legislative reforms instituted during the administration of Franklin D. Roosevelt in the Great Depression of the 1930s.

These programs had various objectives. Some were designed to give substantial government aid to specific sectors of the economy. For example, to aid agriculture, farmers for the first time were paid not to grow crops and could seek government help for farm mortgage payments. To help the unemployed, agencies such as the Works Progress Administration (WPA) and the Civilian Conservation Corps (CCC) were established to provide jobs building public infrastructure such as bridges, roads, and schools, as well as in forestry and park work. Also, the Social Security Act was passed in 1935 to provide income for the aged, blind, and others.

Other programs were designed to regulate or bolster business activity and financial markets. The Securities and Exchange Commission (SEC) was created to prevent fraudulent practices and to establish safeguards in securities markets. Banking was affected by several new programs, such as the Federal Deposit Insurance Corporation (FDIC). Also, in 1935 the National Labor Relations Act gave workers the right to bargain collectively.

---

[5]Upton Sinclair, *The Jungle* (New York: Signet Classics, The New American Library), pp. 136–137. Original publication, 1906.

In the Depression years the federal government began to run deficit budgets on a regular basis: It typically spent more than it received from taxes and other revenues. This practice was a break from the past and began a new direction in government budget policy. By the end of the 1930s, widespread government intervention in economic activity was part of U.S. capitalism.

The Great Depression came to an abrupt halt with the entry of the United States into World War II in December 1941. Because of the extent and magnitude of the war effort, many government agencies were instituted to oversee production, human resources, wages, prices, and such. Although most of these agencies were dismantled after the war, they did create a precedent for future reestablishment.

Following World War II, one of the most significant steps toward more government involvement in economic activity occurred with the passage of the **Employment Act of 1946.** This act gave the federal government the right and responsibility to provide an environment in which full employment, full production, and stable prices could be achieved. Under this act, Congress could now manipulate taxes and government spending and run deficit budgets in an effort to bring the economy to a desired level of activity. This meant that rather than influencing some specific part of the circular flow model (such as the input or output markets), government could influence the entire model. Such power had not been legislated before this period.

Employment Act of 1946

Legislation giving the federal government the right and responsibility to provide an environment for the achievement of full employment, full production, and stable prices.

The Regulatory and Deregulatory Waves   Government intervention in the economy increased with a wave of regulatory activity that led to the creation of numerous federal agencies in the 1960s and 1970s. From 1964 through 1977, 25 such agencies were established, compared to only 11 during the Depression years of the 1930s. These agencies include the Environmental Protection Agency, the Equal Employment Opportunity Commission, and the Consumer Product Safety Commission.

The regulatory trend of the 1960s and early 1970s was reversed, however, in the late 1970s and 1980s as the economy went through a wave of deregulation during the Carter and Reagan presidential administrations. Regulatory authority in various industries, such as commercial aviation, trucking, and natural gas, was reduced, and federal regulatory agency staffing began to decline in the early 1980s. Thus, in one sense, the role of government in economic activity was decreasing during this period.

Recent Developments   How can we judge the direction of the government in economic activity in recent years? Are there predictors for future changes?

The deregulatory trend of the Carter and Reagan administrations was reversed during George H. W. Bush's administration with increased support for federal regulatory agencies and increased challenges of business mergers. But, more significantly, the government's impact on the economy increased with a dramatic rise in the federal public debt. During the Reagan years the debt grew from $909 billion in 1980 to $2.6 trillion in 1988. However, by mid-2009, the debt exceeded $11 trillion. Chapter 6 deals with the size and impact of federal deficits and the debt on the economy.[6]

In addition to the rising federal debt, other issues continue to dominate public attention, especially the cost and management of health care, regulation of the financial services industry, the environment, and future funding of Social Security. The pressure for government to tackle and address health care and Social Security began with the Clinton administration as it became clear that a large population of aging

[6]*Economic Report of the President* (Washington, DC: U.S. Government Printing Office, 2008), p. 319. The figure for 2009 is estimated; U.S. National Debt Clock.

boomers would put pressure on these systems. During the presidency of George W. Bush, there was a failed attempt to reform Social Security by moving toward less government control and more individual decision making of investments. In addition, during this Bush administration less government influence was seen in many arenas, from banking to food inspections.

In late 2008 with the election of Barack Obama as president there began a reversal of the Bush administration's moves toward less government intervention as the president and Congress began to tackle a serious economic downturn, failing banks and financial services companies, as well as environmental issues, immigration reform, and education. Bailouts of several companies took place as well as oversight of such industries as banking and automobile manufacturers.

Although generally speaking the economy has moved toward more government intervention, the events of recent years demonstrate that the movement has not been smooth and continuous.

Summary

1. All individuals and economies in the world experience scarcity; no economy can completely satisfy all of its members' wants and needs for goods and services.

2. Because of scarcity, every society must make three basic economic decisions: what goods and services to produce and in what quantities; how to produce goods and services; and who gets the goods and services that are produced.

3. Societies develop economic systems in order to deal with the three basic economic decisions. Societies usually evolve beyond traditional economies as they become more complex and move toward more formal economic systems, which we usually classify as market, planned, or mixed economies.

4. Market economies rely on individual buyers and sellers to make the economic decisions. These systems are rooted in private property rights and free enterprise, and are usually associated with capitalism.

5. In a market economy, buyers and sellers communicate their wants and needs through prices in markets. A market economy produces goods and services if buyers demand them at a price that allows sellers to produce them at a profit.

6 In a market system, businesses produce goods and services efficiently by seeking least-cost production methods to maximize profits. The value of resources—land, labor, capital, and entrepreneurship—that individuals sell determines how many goods and services they can afford to buy.

7. Economists use a circular flow model to illustrate the basic structure of a market economy. This model shows how businesses and households relate to one another as buyers and sellers in output and input markets.

8. Market economies have advantages: They provide incentives to produce and use resources efficiently, allow direct communication between buyers and

sellers, and reflect individual value judgments in production and distribution choices.

9. Market economies have problems called market failures. They may leave the uninformed unprotected, allow discrimination among workers in input markets, not provide goods and services to those unable to contribute to production, foster monopolies, and create environmental problems.

10. In a planned, or command, economy, government planners make the basic economic decisions. These systems are usually rooted in a philosophy of collectivism. Planned economies can allow societies to achieve noneconomic goals more easily, limit unemployment, and provide for a more equal distribution of goods and services. Planning failures may also arise: poor quality products, production stoppages, a lack of worker incentives, problems coordinating production with consumer choices, and pollution problems. Planned economies are often associated with socialism.

11. Mixed economic systems combine elements of market and planned economies. Mixed economies arise in response to planning and market failures. Countries around the world fall on a continuum between pure market and pure planned economies: Pure types no longer exist.

12. Since the late 1980s, the Soviet and other planned economies have moved toward greater dependence on markets and individual decision making. While China has experienced dramatic economic growth, generally the transitions have not been quick or problem free.

13. The U.S. economy can be better understood by examining its British intellectual foundations and key developments in eighteenth- and nineteenth-century British history. These include the rise of a philosophy of individualism, which was advocated in Adam Smith's *The Wealth of Nations,* and the Industrial Revolution.

14. Important events in U.S. history that helped to shape the U.S. economy include the industrial boom following the Civil War, the Great Depression and World War II, the regulatory and deregulatory waves of the 1960s through the 1980s, and recent concerns over health care, Social Security, tax policy, national security, the environment, and other issues.

Key Terms and Concepts

Basic economic decisions	Private property rights
Economic system	Free enterprise
Traditional, or agrarian, economy	Capitalism
Barter	Circular flow model
Market economy	Output markets (product markets)
Price system	Input markets (resource markets)

Least-cost (efficient) method of
production

Market failure

Government regulation

Planned economy (command
economy)

Socialism

Planning failure

Mixed economy

Privatization

Laissez-faire capitalism

Mercantilism

Invisible hand doctrine

Industrial Revolution

Muckrakers

New Deal

Employment Act of 1946

Review Questions

1. What are the three basic decisions every economy must make? Why must these decisions be made?

2. How do traditional, market, planned, and mixed economies make the three basic economic decisions?

3. Draw a simple circular flow diagram to illustrate the structure of a market economy. Include businesses and households, input and output markets, and real and money flows.

4. Below are listed seven activities. Indicate whether each one is: a real flow through a product market; a money flow through a product market; a real flow through a resource market; or a money flow through a resource market.
   a. Receiving a paycheck at the end of each month
   b. Delivering a specially ordered hybrid car to a buyer
   c. Receiving patient care in a hospital
   d. Using a credit card to buy a meal in a restaurant
   e. Earning profit over the summer from your own ice cream stand
   f. Obtaining college credits
   g. Working overtime

5. Identify three strengths of a market economy. Define and give a current example of a market failure.

6. Identify the strengths and weaknesses of a planned economy. Explain what we mean by planning failure.

7. What is the invisible hand doctrine and why is it important for laissez-faire capitalism? How did the British Industrial Revolution affect the way that the U.S. economic system developed?

8. Indicate whether, and explain why, each of the following moved the U.S. economy closer to, or further from, laissez-faire capitalism.
   a. The Sherman Antitrust Act of 1890, the Food and Drug Act of 1906, and the Meat Inspection Act of 1907

b. The New Deal programs of the Roosevelt administration in the 1930s
c. The regulatory reforms of the Carter and Reagan administrations
d. Concern over global warming
e. Privatization of defense functions during the George W. Bush war in Iraq

Discussion Questions

1. Suppose that you have been chosen to be on a blue-ribbon panel of experts to determine how well or poorly the economies of the world are operating. Your task is to come up with a checklist of five criteria by which different economies can be judged. Which five factors would you pick as criteria? Why?

2. What considerations might cause one nation to choose to operate as a market economy and another as a planned economy?

3. Many people today are asking what the U.S. government should do when people who need some type of health care cannot afford it. Is less-than-universal access to health care an example of a market system allocating scarce resources efficiently, or is it an example of market failure?

4. This chapter illustrates how economic systems change over time. What forces might lead to the evolution of an economic system, and how would these forces cause an economy to change?

5. We noted in the text that the movement from a planned to a market economy was not smooth for the nations of Eastern Europe. What, in your opinion, was the biggest obstacle to this change, and why?

6. Would mercantilism, the economic system that was important in Europe in the seventeenth and eighteenth centuries, be most consistent with a market economy, a planned economy, or a mixed economy? Do you know of any economic activity occurring at the present time that reflects a mercantilist philosophy?

7. Based on your general knowledge of U.S. history and current events, how active a role do you think government will be playing in the economy 20 years from now, compared to the role it plays today?

8. Environmental concerns are increasingly global as we realize that the careless use of the world's resources influences the entire globe. The impact of global warming, excessive energy use, and polluting rivers and streams is not confined to any one nation. What type of economic system do you think would best address environmental concerns? Will global concerns push more nations toward similar systems?

9. Chapter 1 introduced the importance of efficiency and equity as they affect economic decisions. Discuss how each of the three basic decisions are related to efficiency and equity.

Critical Thinking Case 2

JUDGING ECONOMIES

Critical Thinking Skills

Arriving at conclusions

Recognizing value judgments in decision making

Economic Concepts

Productivity and stability of an economy

Distribution of income

Transition of economic systems

Perhaps the two words that contributed most to the geopolitical unrest in the last half of the twentieth century are *capitalism* and *communism*. The clash between the meanings people give to these words goes a long way toward explaining why there was the Cuban Missile Crisis in the early 1960s, the Vietnam War in the late 1960s and early 1970s, and concern about North Korea invading South Korea in the late 1990s.

The fact is that people often judge nations' economies by asking questions like "Is it capitalist or is it socialist?" or "Who has property rights?" Based on the answers to these questions, people often decide whether or not they approve of the economy's direction. Certainly these are important questions, especially today when economies in Russia, China, Poland, and elsewhere are transitioning away from communism. But focusing on which "ism" best describes an economy may lead one to overlook other important questions to be answered when judging its performance. Consider the following questions.[a]

♦ What is the current standard of living in the economy?

[a]The six criteria are based on a presentation by economist Martin Bronfenbrenner.

♦ What is the expected future standard of living in the economy?
♦ How sensitive is the economy to downward shocks?
♦ How is income distributed in the economy?
♦ How does the economy affect people's civil rights?
♦ How does the economy affect people's physical and mental health?

Questions

1. Russia's transition from communism to a more capitalist-based system was not smooth. Over the first 10 years, Russia's standard of living fell, expectations for future standards of living declined, and the economy more or less shattered. What would be your reaction to someone insisting that a comparison of the quality of people's lives before and after the collapse of communism is overwhelming proof that communism works better than capitalism?

2. What do you think is more important when judging an economic system—whether it is capitalist or socialist, or how it performs in each of the six questions given in this case? Generally speaking, do you think that one economic system—be it capitalism, socialism, or another system—will always outperform the others on each of these six points?

3. It might seem a bit of a reach to judge economies in terms of their effects on civil rights and people's health. In your opinion, is it appropriate to pay attention to factors like people's rights and health when judging an economic system?

4. In your opinion, which of the six questions listed in this case should be ranked first in terms of importance for judging an economy? What would you rank second, third, and so on? How are your value judgments influencing your rankings?

CHAPTER 3

Demand, Supply, and Price Determination

CHAPTER OBJECTIVES

To explain demand and supply, and show how they work using schedules and graphs.

To show how demand and supply are affected by changes in price and nonprice factors.

To demonstrate how demand and supply interact in markets to determine prices, and to show equilibrium price and quantity, shortages, and surpluses in a market.

To explain how changes in demand and changes in supply affect equilibrium prices and quantities in markets.

To illustrate how government-imposed price ceilings and price floors influence market conditions.

To introduce the concept and calculation of price elasticity, which measures buyers' and sellers' sensitivities to price changes.

As we noted in Chapter 2, one way societies can make the basic economic decisions is through individual buyers' and sellers' actions in markets. Many societies, such as those in the United States, Western Europe, and Japan, base their economic systems on such market decision making. There are two basic economic tools to study buyers and sellers and their behaviors in the marketplace: demand and supply. Together, these tools help us understand the forces at work in a market economy. In this chapter, we explore demand and supply in detail, and then put the two together to see how they interact to determine the prices of goods and services.

DEMAND AND SUPPLY

Demand: The Buyer's Side

Demand, in economic terms, refers to buyers' plans concerning the purchase of a good or service. For example, you might demand an airplane ticket to London, tennis lessons, or a chemistry lab book. A business might demand workers, raw materials, machinery, or any other factor of production. Many considerations go into determining the demand for a good or service. These include the product's price as well as nonprice factors such as the buyer's income and attitude toward the item and available substitute products.

Demand

The different amounts of a product that a buyer would purchase at different prices in a defined time period when all nonprice factors are held constant.

Demand, Defined   In formal terms, we define a buyer's **demand** for a good or service as the different amounts of the good or service that the buyer would be willing and able to purchase at different prices over a given period of time with all nonprice factors held constant. Therefore, when we speak of a buyer's demand for baseball tickets, gasoline, or whatever, we are speaking of the different amounts of the item that the buyer would purchase at different prices over some period of time, such as a day, a week, or a year, with all nonprice factors unchanged. In determining demand, note that only the product's price is allowed to change: All nonprice factors that affect demand, such as the buyer's income, are held constant in order to highlight the relationship between the product's price and the amount of the product a person would be willing and able to buy.

Demand Schedule

A list of the amounts of a product that a buyer would purchase at different prices in a defined time period when all nonprice factors are held constant.

We can illustrate the relationship between the amount of a product that a consumer would buy and the product's price in two ways: through a **demand schedule** (or table) or through a graph (called a demand curve). Table 3.1 is a demand schedule that shows Zach's weekly demand for fresh-baked bagels.[1] Note the relationship between the price per bagel and the number of bagels that Zach is willing and able to buy. As the price per bagel goes up from $0.20 to $0.40, the number of bagels Zach would buy falls from 15 to 12; as the price increases from $0.40 to $0.60, the amount demanded falls from 12 to 10. Each additional $0.20 increment further reduces the number of bagels Zach would buy. In other words, as the price increases, Zach would buy fewer fresh-baked bagels. We could have used any other consumer and any other good or service—restaurant meals, plastic pink flamingos, digital cameras, or jeans— with the same result: The quantity demanded falls as the price rises, and the quantity demanded rises as the price falls.

Law of Demand   Zach's buying behavior, illustrated in Table 3.1, reflects a typical buyer's plan to purchase a good or service. It shows a relationship between price and

[1]Examples in this chapter are hypothetical.

TABLE 3.1	*Zach's Weekly Demand for Fresh-Baked Bagels*

This demand schedule lists different amounts of bagels that Zach would purchase each week at various prices and illustrates the Law of Demand: It shows the inverse relationship between price and quantity demanded.

Price per Bagel	Number of Bagels Demanded Weekly
$0.20	15
0.40	12
0.60	10
0.80	8
1.00	6
1.20	4
1.40	2
1.60	1

Law of Demand

There is an inverse relationship between the price of a product and the quantity demanded.

quantity demanded that we know to be generally true. This relationship is called the **Law of Demand.** It states that, holding all nonprice factors constant, as a product's price increases, the quantity of the product demanded decreases, and as a product's price decreases, the quantity demanded increases. In other words, the Law of Demand states that a product's price is inversely related to the quantity of that product that consumers demand.

Why do consumers react this way to price changes? Behind the Law of Demand is the fundamental problem of economics: scarcity and choice. Consumers purchasing goods and services face a scarcity problem: Their incomes are always limited. Consumers—even very wealthy consumers—can afford only so much. So as the price of an item goes up, buyers may not be able to afford as much of it as they could at the lower price. On the other hand, when the price of a good or service falls, consumers will likely increase their purchases of the item because they can satisfy more wants and needs with their limited incomes.

Choice also influences demand because consumers can always purchase alternative (or substitute) products. As the price of fresh-baked bagels increases, Zach can choose to eat other foods—doughnuts, cereal, or fruit, to name a few—in place of bagels. As the price of bagels decreases, he may choose to eat more of them and less of other items.

Demand Curve

A line on a graph that illustrates a demand schedule; it slopes downward because of the inverse relationship between price and quantity demanded.

Graphing Demand   Typically, economists display demand in graphs rather than in schedules or tables. Figure 3.1 shows Zach's demand for bagels exactly as it appeared in Table 3.1, but presented graphically. On this graph, price appears on the vertical axis (measured in 20-cent intervals) and quantity demanded appears on the horizontal axis (in two-bagel increments). When we plot each price–quantity combination from the demand schedule in Table 3.1 and then connect those points with a line, we call the resulting downward-sloping line a **demand curve.** Recall from Chapter 1 that downward-sloping lines such as this demand curve represent inverse relationships. Since the Law of Demand predicts this type of inverse relationship between price and quantity demanded, we can generalize that demand curves slope downward: Consumers normally demand more at lower prices and less at higher prices.

FIGURE 3.1   *Zach's Weekly Demand for Fresh-Baked Bagels*

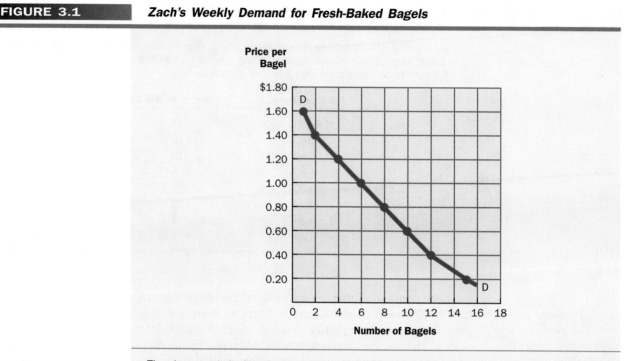

The downward-sloping demand curve illustrates the Law of Demand, showing that Zach demands fewer bagels at higher prices and more bagels at lower prices.

Supply: The Seller's Side

Economists refer to supply as a seller's plan to make a good or service available in the market. Like demand, supply depends on the product's price and any nonprice factors that influence the seller, such as the cost of producing the product and the seller's expectation of future market conditions.

Supply
The different amounts of a product that a seller would offer for sale at different prices in a defined time period when all nonprice factors are held constant.

Supply, Defined   Economists define **supply** as the different amounts of a good or service that a seller would make available for sale at different prices in a given time period, holding constant all nonprice factors that affect the seller's plans for the product. In other words, supply indicates how many hot fudge sundaes, haircuts, tires, or any other product a supplier would be willing to sell at different prices during a week, a month, or a year, with all nonprice factors unchanged. As with demand, we hold all nonprice factors affecting supply constant to highlight the relationship between a product's price and the quantity of the product supplied.

Supply Schedule
A list of the amounts of a product that a seller would offer for sale at different prices in a defined time period when all nonprice factors are held constant.

We can illustrate the relationship between the amount of a product a seller would make available for sale and the product's price in a **supply schedule** (or table). Table 3.2 shows the number of bagels of a particular size and quality that City Bakery is willing to sell each week at various prices. Observe the direct relationship between price and the quantity supplied. At a low price, the bakery would offer no or few bagels for sale, but it is willing to offer more bagels for sale as the price increases. If we were to choose to illustrate the supply of another good or service as an example, the same relationship would appear: The quantity supplied would increase as the price increased, and the quantity supplied would decrease as the price decreased.

TABLE 3.2	*City Bakery's Weekly Supply of Bagels*

The Law of Supply is illustrated in this supply schedule, which shows that more bagels are supplied at higher prices.

Price per Bagel	Quantity Supplied per Week
$0.20	0
0.40	50
0.60	200
0.80	350
1.00	500
1.20	650
1.40	750
1.60	800

Law of Supply

There is a direct relationship between the price of a product and the quantity supplied.

The Law of Supply   The direct relationship between price and quantity supplied illustrates the **Law of Supply.** This law states that, holding nonprice factors constant, the quantity of a good or service that a supplier is willing to offer on the market relates directly to price. Why does the bakery react this way? Seller behavior and the Law of Supply are based on a seller's ability to cover costs and earn a profit. At very low prices, a seller may not be able to cover costs and would likely not be interested in supplying the product. But as the price increased, a supplier could cover costs and perhaps earn a small profit. If a seller produced many products (as does City Bakery), it might produce some of the product for a small profit but concentrate on producing other items that yield more favorable returns. At higher prices, a seller would want to further increase the quantity supplied as it could cover additional costs from producing more and make greater profits.[2] The bakery, for example, might be willing to decrease its production of birthday cakes, danish, eclairs, and other products in order to increase its production of bagels if the price and profit on bagels were extremely high.

We can easily understand the Law of Supply in relationship to our own labor that we supply in labor markets. Take campus tutoring as an example. If you were offered a job in the Economics Tutoring Center for $3 an hour, how many hours a week would you be willing to work? How much would you be willing to work if the wage were $10 an hour? $20 an hour?

Supply Curve

A line on a graph that illustrates a supply schedule; it slopes upward because of the direct relationship between price and quantity supplied.

Graphing Supply   Economists usually present supply, like demand, graphically, with price measured on the vertical axis and the quantity supplied measured on the horizontal axis. Each price–quantity combination from Table 3.2 appears in Figure 3.2, and a **supply curve** is drawn by connecting those points. Note that a supply curve slopes upward, showing that higher prices correlate with larger quantities supplied. Recall that the Law of Supply indicates a direct relationship between price and quantity supplied. Because direct relationships appear in graphs as upward-sloping lines, we can generalize that supply curves slope upward to reflect that direct relationship.

[2]Is it valid to assume that the cost per bagel might increase as the bakery produces more bagels? Yes. For example, the owner might incur extra expenses from additional repairs on equipment because it is used more often, or producing more bagels might require that the employees of the bakery work overtime at a higher wage rate. See Chapter 12 for details on rising costs associated with increased production.

FIGURE 3.2   *City Bakery's Weekly Supply of Bagels*

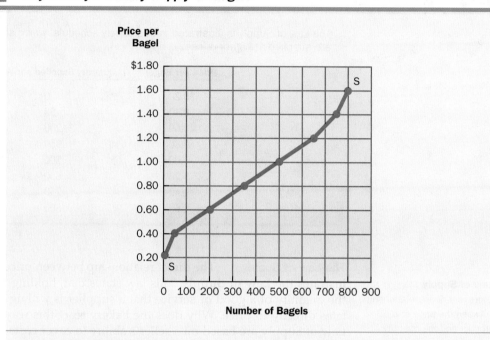

The upward-sloping supply curve illustrates the Law of Supply, showing that more is supplied at higher prices and less is supplied at lower prices.

You might be amazed at how often we are affected by the Laws of Demand and Supply. Application 3.1, "The Laws of Demand and Supply," focuses on travel and organic milk and gives some situations where price had an important impact on the decisions and behaviors of buyers or sellers.

MARKET DEMAND, MARKET SUPPLY, AND PRICE SETTING

Market Demand and Market Supply

Market
A place or situation in which the buyers and sellers of a product interact for the purpose of exchange.

Market Demand and Market Supply
The demand of all buyers and supply of all sellers in a market for a good or service; found by adding together all individual demand or supply schedules.

When buyers and sellers come together to exchange goods or services, they form **markets.** A market can arise anywhere—a store, Internet auction, used-car lot, stock exchange, or vending machine, for example. Once we speak of multiple buyers and sellers, we move from individual demand and supply to **market demand** and **market supply.** Market demand and market supply represent the sum of all individual quantities demanded and supplied of a product at each price in a market. For example, the market demand for an Academy Award–winning motion picture sums up all the individual demands to see the film. When we discuss markets we are concerned with the sum of all buyers' and sellers' actions—rather than individual demand and supply decisions.

Markets and Price Setting

Markets perform the critical function of price setting as buyers and sellers interact and make economic choices. To see how markets operate to set prices, let's return to the bagel example, where we analyzed Zach's individual demand and City Bakery's individual supply of fresh-baked bagels.

APPLICATION 3.1

THE LAWS OF DEMAND AND SUPPLY

Law of Demand

Air Travel   Following the 9/11 terrorist attacks and a weakening of the economy at about the same time, commercial airlines found it increasingly difficult to attract passengers. The attacks on the Twin Towers and the Pentagon raised fears about flying, and the weakened economy led businesses to cut their travel budgets. Not surprisingly, the airlines responded to this emptying of seats by lowering fares to entice travelers.

According to one study there was a 20 percent drop in average one-way airfares from 2000 to mid-2003 and an increase of over 50 percent in the use of cheaper, nonrefundable tickets by business travelers. For example, for a brief time in 2003 you could fly from Boston to Amsterdam on Northwest Airlines for $185, and British Airways would fly you from Boston to London and provide a one-night stay at a hotel for $298. But you had to move fast because the low-fare opportunities did not last that long.

Gasoline   Rapidly rising gasoline prices usually capture headlines, as they did in 2008 when prices went over $4.00 a gallon. And, when they do, people are always quick to express their frustrations and react with altered behaviors.

In response to rising gas prices, people have been known to drive a few miles to wholesale stores for discounted gas, cross a state line to buy gas because of a lower state gas tax, spend a lot of time waiting in line to fill up at a station with lower prices, car pool, and simply drive less. One unfortunate behavior change is the increase in thefts when prices go up, especially by drivers pulling away from a gas pump without paying.

What drives these reactions to higher gas prices? We have limited incomes, and paying more for gas means having less for other things like tuition, restaurant meals, and new shirts. Then there is substitutability. Unlike many other consumer needs, the alternatives to putting gas in the tank aren't easy. Can you just put a tank of corn-based ethanol in your vehicle? Can you just zip over to the car dealership and switch out your car for a hybrid?

Law of Supply

Organic Milk   In the "olden" days, people went to the store and bought milk—milk was milk. Dairy farmers had few alternatives: they milked their cows and sent their product to the market. Today, we have choices about milk: whole, skim, 1 percent, 2 percent, and even chocolate. While these don't have a direct influence on dairy farmers, the latest opportunity for choice in milk selection—organic milk—certainly does.

Organic milk is a major product in the trend toward buying organic foods. To be labeled as organic milk, a set of federal standards must be met. These include guidelines about feed, soil, outdoor access for cows, processing operations, as well as a ban on antibiotics and growth hormones.

While the route to become an organic milk producer cannot be put in place overnight because time is needed to ensure that operations and herds meet the standards set to receive the organic label, dairy farmers now have an alternative to producing "regular" milk. This means that as the price of organic milk rises, farmers have an incentive to switch production from nonorganic to organic.

And, the price of organic milk is certainly higher than nonorganic milk. A visit to the Straub's supermarket in St. Louis in May 2009 revealed that a gallon of nonorganic 2 percent milk averaged $3.07. A gallon of organic 2 percent milk averaged $8.49.

There is evidence that the rise in price in organic milk is increasing the quantity supplied. A few years ago, organic milk could be found only in specialty health-food type stores. Today, supermarkets not only devote much shelf space to organic milk, but like the St. Louis grocery store, typically carry several labels or brands.

Based on: Trebor Banstetter, "Study Finds Demand for Business Travel May Not Rise Soon," *Fort Worth Star-Telegram*, Knight Ridder Tribune Business News, October 7, 2003, p. 1; Keith Reed, "Now Is Time to Take Advantage of Discount Airfares to Europe," *The Boston Globe*, Knight Ridder Tribune Business News, April 16, 2003, p. 1; www.horizonorganic.com.

Table 3.3 shows market demand and market supply schedules for fresh-baked bagels. We can find the market demand for bagels each week by adding together the number of bagels that Zach and all other buyers in this market would purchase at each price. Similarly, we can find market supply by adding together the quantity of bagels that City Bakery and all other sellers in this market would make available at each price. In the analysis of this market and those that follow, we assume that both buyers and sellers compete strongly with one another. No buyer or seller

---

TABLE 3.3   *Weekly Market Demand and Supply of Fresh-Baked Bagels*

Market demand and market supply illustrate the different amounts of a product that all buyers in a market would demand and all sellers in a market would supply at various prices.

Price per Bagel	Quantity Demanded	Quantity Supplied
$0.20	30,000	2,000
0.40	24,000	8,000
0.60	20,000	12,000
0.80	16,000	16,000
1.00	12,000	20,000
1.20	8,000	24,000
1.40	4,000	28,000
1.60	2,000	30,000

exerts any unusual or undue influence, and no price-controlling government regulation occurs.[3]

In the market shown in Table 3.3, the price for a fresh-baked bagel ranges from $0.20 through $1.60. What would happen in this market if the price were $0.20 per bagel? At $0.20, buyers would demand 30,000 bagels, and sellers would offer only 2,000 for sale. Thus, at a price of $0.20 the quantity supplied would fall short of the quantity demanded by 28,000 bagels (30,000 quantity demanded − 2,000 quantity supplied): The market would experience a **shortage** of 28,000 bagels. In response to this shortage, sellers who observed the number of buyers left unsatisfied in the market would raise the price and increase the quantity they would offer on the market (because of the Law of Supply). Once the price rose, the quantity demanded would fall (because of the Law of Demand), and the bagel shortage would shrink.

Shortage

Occurs in a market when the quantity demanded is greater than the quantity supplied, or when the product's price is below the equilibrium price.

So, then, what would happen if the price were $0.40 per bagel? At $0.40, buyers would demand 24,000 bagels and suppliers would offer 8,000 bagels. The market would again experience a shortage, but of only 16,000 bagels (24,000 quantity demanded — 8,000 quantity supplied). Sellers would react to the shortage by raising prices above $0.40. As price increased, suppliers would offer more bagels and buyers would demand fewer bagels: The shortage would again shrink.

What would happen if sellers charged $1.60 per bagel? At $1.60, consumers would want to buy only 2,000 bagels, but sellers would offer 30,000 bagels for sale. The quantity demanded would fall short of the quantity supplied by 28,000 bagels, or there would be a **surplus** of 28,000 bagels on the market. Sellers would react like any other seller with excess merchandise at a price consumers will not pay: They would lower their prices. As the price fell, the Law of Demand would go into operation, and some buyers who would not purchase bagels at $1.60 each would do so at the lower price. At the same time, because of the Law of Supply, the lower price would encourage suppliers to reduce the quantity supplied, and the surplus would diminish. If the price charged were $1.40, a surplus of 24,000 bagels would develop, sellers would again lower their price, and the surplus would again shrink.

Surplus

Occurs in a market when the quantity demanded is less than the quantity supplied, or when the product's price is above the equilibrium price.

[3]A more technical definition of a market appears in Chapter 13. At this point, however, it is sufficient to know that a particular market is made up of a group of sellers that compete with each other for the same group of buyers. In other words, because of geographic distance, many separate markets for fresh-baked bagels arise. For instance, a market in Houston is not the same as a market in Seattle because each is composed of different buyers and sellers.

FIGURE 3.3   *Weekly Market Demand and Supply of Fresh-Baked Bagels*

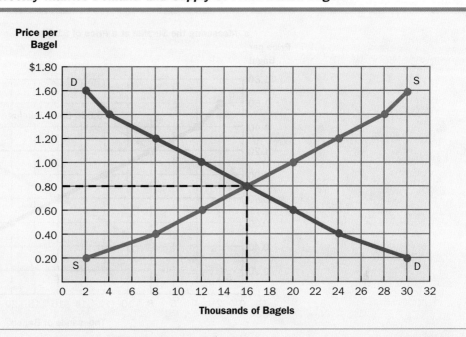

The equilibrium price and quantity in a market occur at the intersection of the market demand and supply curves. At equilibrium, the quantity demanded in a market equals the quantity supplied.

Equilibrium Price and Equilibrium Quantity

The market in Table 3.3 appears to be moving automatically toward a price of $0.80, where the quantity demanded equals the quantity supplied at 16,000 bagels. If sellers charge $0.80 per bagel, no surpluses or shortages will arise and sellers will have no incentive to raise or lower price.

Equilibrium Price and Equilibrium Quantity
The price and quantity where demand equals supply; price and quantity toward which a free market automatically moves.

We call the price that sets buyers' plans equal to sellers' plans ($0.80) the **equilibrium price.** The quantity at which those plans are equal (16,000 bagels) is the **equilibrium quantity.** Thus, equilibrium price and equilibrium quantity are the price and quantity toward which a market will automatically move. At the equilibrium price, quantity demanded equals quantity supplied, and neither sellers nor buyers will want to change the price or the quantity. Economists often refer to the equilibrium price as the **market clearing price,** because at this price the amount that buyers want exactly matches the amount that sellers offer, thereby clearing the market of the good or service.

Market Clearing Price
Equilibrium price; price at which the quantity demanded equals the quantity supplied.

If the price of a good or service is below its equilibrium level, a shortage will develop, and the price will be driven up toward equilibrium. If the price is above equilibrium, a surplus will develop, causing the price to fall toward equilibrium.

The bagel market shown in Table 3.3 is graphed in Figure 3.3. We draw the demand curve from the Price per Bagel and Quantity Demanded columns, and the supply curve from the Price per Bagel and Quantity Supplied columns. From the graph, we can easily see that the equilibrium price and quantity lie at the intersection of the supply and demand curves—in this case, at a price of $0.80 per bagel and a quantity of 16,000 bagels.

Shortages and surpluses can also be illustrated graphically. Figure 3.4a shows that at a price of $1.20 the quantity demanded is 8,000 bagels and the quantity

FIGURE 3.4   *Measuring Surpluses and Shortages on Demand and Supply Curves*

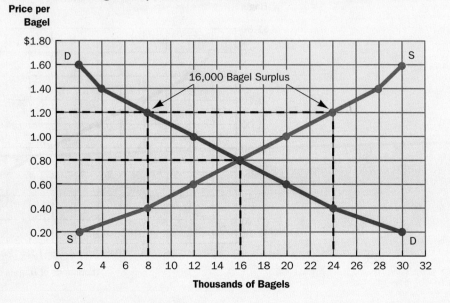

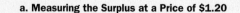

a. Measuring the Surplus at a Price of $1.20

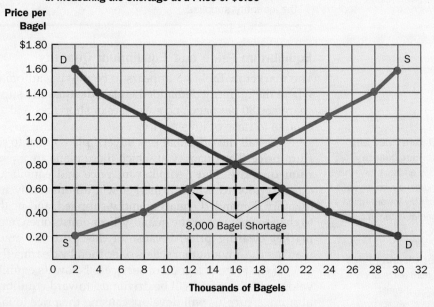

b. Measuring the Shortage at a Price of $0.60

The surplus or shortage at a particular price is equal to the difference between the quantity demanded and the quantity supplied at that price.

supplied is 24,000 bagels, a surplus of 16,000 bagels. The difference between the demand and supply curves at $1.20 equals the amount of the surplus. Notice that as the price comes closer to the equilibrium level, the distance between the demand and supply curves narrows, and the surplus becomes smaller. Figure 3.4b measures the shortage of 8,000 bagels that would occur at a price of $0.60. Can you determine the shortage at a price of $0.20 per bagel?[4]

Changes in Quantity Demanded and Quantity Supplied

Change in Quantity Demanded and Quantity Supplied

A change in the amount of a product demanded or supplied that is caused by a change in its price; represented by a movement along a demand or supply curve from one price–quantity point to another.

When the price of bagels in Table 3.3 and Figure 3.3 changed, the amount that buyers would have purchased also changed. For example, as the price rose from $0.20 to $0.40, the quantity demanded by buyers fell from 30,000 to 24,000 bagels. When a change in a product's price causes a change in the amount that would be purchased, a **change in quantity demanded** occurs. Graphically, a change in quantity demanded appears as a *movement along a demand curve* from one price–quantity point to another, such as from the point representing $0.20 and 30,000 bagels to the point representing $0.40 and 24,000 bagels on the demand curve in Figure 3.3.

Likewise, the amount of bagels that the sellers in Table 3.3 and Figure 3.3 were prepared to sell changed as the price changed. As the price fell from $1.60 to $1.40, the quantity supplied fell from 30,000 to 28,000. When a change in a product's price causes a change in the amount of the product that a seller would supply, a **change in quantity supplied** occurs. A change in quantity supplied appears as a *movement along a supply curve* from one price–quantity point to another, such as from the point representing $1.60 and 30,000 bagels to the point representing $1.40 and 28,000 bagels on the supply curve in Figure 3.3. In the next section, we emphasize the difference between such changes in *quantity* demanded or supplied and changes in demand or supply.

CHANGES IN DEMAND AND SUPPLY

When we introduced demand and supply, we emphasized that the buyers and sellers of a product respond both to the product's price and to nonprice considerations. Then, as we developed demand and supply schedules and curves, we held nonprice factors constant in order to focus on buyer and seller behavior in response to a price change. For example, when we derived Zach's demand for bagels, only the price of bagels was allowed to change. All nonprice factors, such as Zach's income, the popularity of bagels, and the degree of substitutability between bagels and other foods were held constant.

Now it is time to no longer hold nonprice factors constant and to examine how nonprice factors influence buyer and seller behaviors—and ultimately how they influence market equilibrium.

Changes in Demand

Change in Demand

A change in the demand schedule and curve for a product caused by a change in a nonprice factor influencing the product's demand; the demand curve shifts to the right or left.

A change in one or more nonprice factors influencing the demand for a product causes a **change in demand** for the product. Changes in nonprice factors cause demand

---

[4]A shortage of 28,000 bagels would result.

| **TABLE 3.4** | | *Gwen's Weekly Demand Schedule for 12-Ounce Cans of Cola before and after an Increase in Income* | |

A change in a nonprice factor causes a change in the amount of an item demanded at each price. After an increase in Gwen's income, the number of cans of a particular cola she demands each week increases at every price.

BEFORE		AFTER	
Price per Can	Number of Cans Demanded Weekly	Price per Can	Number of Cans Demanded Weekly
$0.20	18	$0.20	24
0.40	16	0.40	22
0.60	14	0.60	20
0.80	12	0.80	18
1.00	10	1.00	16
1.20	8	1.20	14
1.40	6	1.40	12
1.60	4	1.60	10
1.80	2	1.80	8

schedules and curves to change as buyers develop new sets of plans. Someone's weekly demand for, say, a particular brand of cola could change because of a change in a nonprice factor influencing that demand. For example, suppose that Gwen, who has a demand for a particular cola, gets a raise. She might respond to the raise by buying more cola. We can illustrate this increase in Gwen's demand in Table 3.4, which shows Gwen's demand for the cola before and after a change in her income. Notice how the number of cans that Gwen demands in a week increases at each price. For example, at $1.00 a can the amount increases from 10 to 16 after her raise takes effect.

Nonprice Factors That Influence Demand   To help us see the key difference between price and nonprice factors, we can categorize major **nonprice factors that influence demand.**

Nonprice Factors Influencing Demand
Nonprice factors, such as income, taste, and expectations, that help to determine the demand for a product.

- **Taste, fashion, and popularity.** The demand for "in" items typically increases; and when an item is "out," demand decreases. A good, catchy advertising campaign that makes a product popular can increase demand.
- **Buyers' incomes.** Changes in buyer income can encourage people to buy more or less of an item. For example, with more income people may want to buy more new cars, but fewer used cars.
- **Buyers' expectations concerning future income, prices, or availabilities.** What people anticipate for the future affects behavior in the present. For example, if people think a particular toy will someday be a collector's item and worth thousands of dollars, the current demand may increase.
- **Prices of goods related as substitutes and complements.** Buyers' demand for a product can change when the price of an item they regard as a substitute or complement for that product changes. For example, people might buy more peanut butter to make sandwiches when the price of cheese (a substitute for peanut butter) goes up and less peanut butter when the price of jelly (a complement to peanut butter) goes up.

♦ **The number of buyers in the market.** As the number of buyers in a market increases, so does demand. With people moving into newly renovated lofts in city neighborhoods, local restaurants have more customers.

Increases and Decreases in Demand   We can label a change in demand as either an increase in demand or a decrease in demand. An **increase in demand** means that buyers want to purchase more of a product at every price because one or more nonprice factors have changed. Graphically, an increase in demand causes the demand curve for a good or service to shift to the right.

Such a shift is shown in Figure 3.5a, which illustrates Gwen's demand schedules for cola in Table 3.4. Curve D1 shows Gwen's original demand for cola before her change in income. When Gwen's income increases, and she wants to purchase more cola at each price, her demand schedule changes. When this new schedule is graphed in Figure 3.5a, the demand curve shifts to the right, to D2. Observe on the graph that at $0.80 she is now willing to buy 18 rather than 12 cans, and at $1.20 she is now willing to buy 14 rather than 8 cans. Clearly, she demands more at each price, or has experienced an increase in demand.

A **decrease in demand** means that buyers want to purchase less of a product at every price because of a change in a nonprice factor. Graphically, a decrease in demand causes the demand curve to shift to the left. For example, U.S. consumers frequently change their vehicle preferences. At one time the large SUV was the choice of families. But today households are turning toward hybrids and away from large gas-guzzling SUVs. Figure 3.5b shows a change in the demand for large SUVs as consumer tastes change. Where 225,000 were demanded at a sticker price of $34,000 before the change in taste, only 125,000 are demanded after large SUVs become less popular.

In summary, an increase in demand means that more of a product is demanded at each price and the demand curve shifts to the right. A decrease in demand means that less is demanded at each price and the demand curve shifts to the left.

Changes in Supply

Changes in nonprice factors that influence supply cause entire supply schedules and curves to change, or cause **changes in supply.** Changes in these nonprice factors cause the supply curve to shift either to the right (an increase in supply) or to the left (a decrease in supply).

Nonprice Factors That Influence Supply   Just as for demand, we can categorize **nonprice factors that influence supply.**

♦ **The cost of producing an item.** When a seller experiences a decrease in the production costs of a good, perhaps due to technology, more of that good can be made available at each price. Increases in production costs cause less to be made available. For example, when the price of a barrel of crude oil (the basic material for refining gasoline) increases on the market, the supply of gasoline decreases.[5]

♦ **Expectations about future market conditions.** Just as with buyers, sellers can anticipate future conditions that affect their current behavior. When car

---

[5]Take care to distinguish between the terms *price* and *cost*. Price is the amount that an item can be sold for in the market. Cost is the expenditure required to produce the item.

FIGURE 3.5 *Increases and Decreases in Demand*

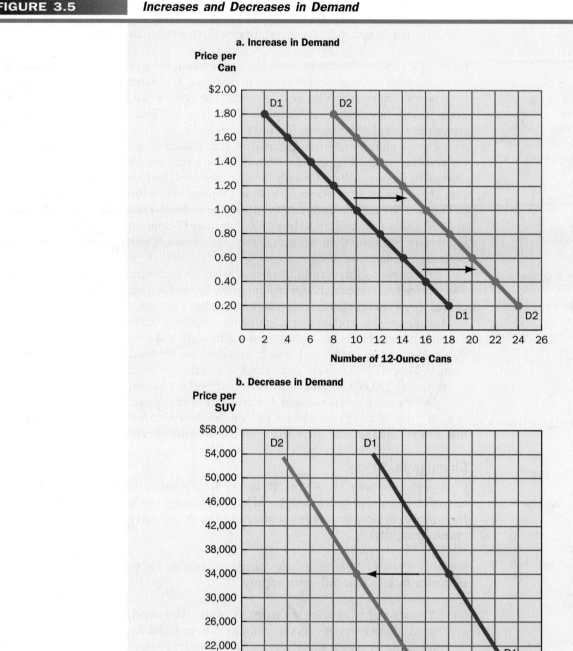

An increase in Gwen's demand for a cola causes the demand curve to shift to the right from D1 to D2, indicating that she now demands more cans of the cola at each price. A decrease in the demand for large SUVs causes the demand curve to shift to the left from D1 to D2, indicating that fewer are demanded at each price.

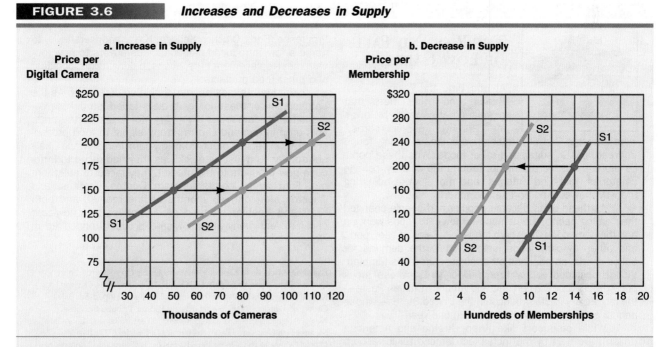

| FIGURE 3.6 | *Increases and Decreases in Supply* |

An increase in the supply of digital cameras causes the supply curve to shift to the right from S1 to S2, indicating that sellers offer more at each price. A decrease in the supply of health club memberships causes the supply curve to shift to the left from S1 to S2, indicating that fewer memberships are supplied at each price.

manufacturers believe that consumer incomes will fall, they may supply fewer cars.

♦ **Other items the seller does, or could, supply.** If a seller finds a profitable alternative item to offer for sale, it could affect the supply of other items. If a discount house finds that buyers really want food and candy items, it may lessen the supply of tires and automotive products to make room for edibles.

♦ **The number of sellers in the market.** As competition increases and more sellers enter a market, the supply increases. When sellers leave a market, supply decreases.

Increase in Supply
A change in a nonprice influence on supply causes more of a product to be supplied at each price; the supply curve shifts to the right.

Decrease in Supply
A change in a nonprice influence on supply causes less of a product to be supplied at each price; the supply curve shifts to the left.

Increases and Decreases in Supply   An **increase in supply** means that sellers want to offer more of a good or service for sale at each price and that the supply curve for the good or service shifts to the right. In Figure 3.6a, assume that S1 is the original supply curve indicating that sellers of digital cameras were willing to sell 50,000 at $150 each or 80,000 at $200 each. After an increase in supply, which causes the supply curve to shift to S2, sellers are willing to offer more cameras at each price: for example, 80,000 at $150 and 110,000 at $200. Sellers could have experienced lower production costs, new production technology, or are trying to increase sales now for fear of a weakening market in the future.

A **decrease in supply** means that sellers are willing to offer less of a product at each price because one or more nonprice factors have changed. Figure 3.6b shows the original supply curve for an area's health club memberships as S1, indicating that clubs were willing to sell 1,400 memberships at a price of $200 each. A decrease in supply, represented by a shift of the supply curve to S2, reveals that clubs are now

THE RISE AND FALL OF LOW CARBS

At one time the Atkins, South Beach, and other diets that promised better health by lowering carbohydrates, or "carbs," were the rage. Carbohydrates are a source of energy found in bread, pasta, sugar, and other foods. With these popular diets, carbs were a no-no. Around the country, college cafeterias, fast-food eateries, and moms were adjusting the way they cooked and served food.

As these diets became popular and people changed their eating habits, the demand for low-carb foods went up and the demand for high-carb foods fell. Sales of beef, pork, and other low-carb foods jumped, while the demand for baked goods, pastas, and other higher-carb foods tumbled. Victims included Krispy Kreme Doughnuts, whose stock price dropped by 62 percent, and American Italian Pasta—the largest dry pasta producer in the United States—whose annual earnings fell by 93 percent in one year!

While producers like Krispy Kreme and American Italian were hurt by the increased demand for lower-carb foods, others saw an opportunity to earn more profit through bringing new products to the market. General Mills, Progresso, Betty Crocker, Kellogg, Kraft, and Hershey's, to name a few, introduced diet-conscious buyers to new low-carb meal-replacement bars, soups, baking mixes, cookies, and other food products.

But just as fads appear, they also disappear. As the enthusiasm for these low-carb diets faded, so did the demand for low-carb foods in grocery stores and restaurants. This drop in demand sent a strong signal to food producers: The expected profit from low-carb items would likely not appear. And just as quickly as they had raced to introduce new products to the market, they raced to pull them out. Frito-Lay pulled its low-carb Doritos, Tostitos, and Cheetos after only six months on the market, and both Kraft and Keebler stopped production of their low-carb cookies. And many other low-carb products ended up in closeout bins.

Based on: Michelle L. Kirsche, "Business Looks Up As Carbs Come Down," *Drug Store News*, July 19, 2004, p. 16; Brian Louis, "Krispy Kreme Doughnuts Investors Get News of Holes in Hoped-For Sales Growth," *Winston-Salem Journal*, Knight Ridder Tribune Business News, August 27, 2004, p. 1; Rob Roberts, "Year in Review: Low-Carb Means High Drama for Food, Restaurant Industries," *The Business Journal* (Kansas City), December 31, 2004, p. 12; Stephanie Thompson, "No-Carb: Sales Fail, Trend Ends," *Advertising Age* (Midwest Regional Edition), April 4, 2005.

willing to sell fewer memberships at each price, for example, only 800 at $200 each. Sellers could have decreased the supply because of increased wage, equipment, or liability insurance costs, or could have switched to the production of another item that is more profitable.

In summary, an increase in supply means that a larger quantity of a product is made available for sale at each price, causing the supply curve to shift to the right. A decrease in supply means that a smaller quantity is made available for sale at each price, causing the supply curve to shift to the left. Application 3.2, "The Rise and Fall of Low Carbs," shows how nonprice factors influenced the demand and supply of some types of foods.

Changes in Quantity Demanded or Supplied and Changes in Demand or Supply: A Crucial Distinction

Be warned: We must maintain clear distinctions between changes in quantity demanded and quantity supplied, and changes in demand and supply. Although the terms are similar, they refer to completely different concepts.

Changes in quantity demanded and quantity supplied arise *only* from changes in a product's price. Quantity is a variable tied to price. We illustrate the responses to price changes by movements along fixed demand or supply curves from one price–quantity combination to another. For example, the movement along the demand curve in Figure 3.7a from $20 and 100 units to $10 and 150 units illustrates an increase in quantity demanded caused by a decrease in price. The movement along the supply curve in Figure 3.7b from $20 and 100 units to $10 and 50 units illustrates a decrease in quantity supplied caused by a decrease in price.

| FIGURE 3.7 | Changes in Quantity Demanded and Quantity Supplied versus Changes in Demand and Supply |

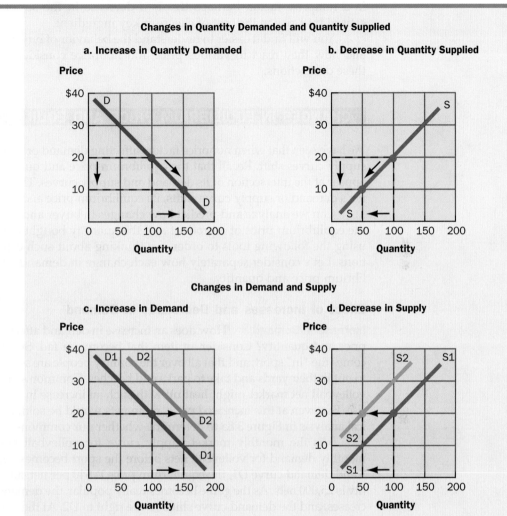

Changes in quantity demanded or quantity supplied are shown by movements along a fixed demand or supply curve, but with changes in demand or supply, the entire curve shifts.

On the other hand, changes in demand and supply do not result from changes in a product's price. Rather, they result from changes in a nonprice determinant of demand or supply. Changes in demand or supply appear as shifts of the demand or supply curve to the right or left.

In Figure 3.7c, the demand curve shifts to the right from D1 to D2, or there is an increase in demand because of a change in a nonprice influence on that demand. For example, at a price of $20, the amount demanded increases from 100 to 150 units. These could be great deep-dish pizzas that people might now order more often because word of their superb taste has gotten around.

The shift of the supply curve in Figure 3.7d from S1 to S2 illustrates a decrease in supply. Fewer items are supplied at $20 and every other price because of a change in a nonprice factor. Perhaps this is a decrease in the supply of deep-dish pizzas caused by a rise in the cost of cheese, a key ingredient.

You will find it easier to understand the behavior of buyers and sellers in markets, and how they react to various price and nonprice considerations, if you remember these distinctions.

CHANGES IN EQUILIBRIUM PRICE AND EQUILIBRIUM QUANTITY

We have seen that when nonprice factors affecting demand or supply change, demand or supply curves shift. Recall that the equilibrium price and quantity of a good or service appear at the intersection of its demand and supply curves. Therefore, whenever a product's demand or supply curve shifts, its equilibrium price and quantity change as well.

Can we analyze and predict how changes in buyer and seller behavior alter both the equilibrium price of a product and the quantity bought and sold? Yes we can, by using the following tools to order our thinking about such changes in market conditions. Let's consider separately how each change in demand and supply affects equilibrium price and quantity.

Effect of Increases and Decreases in Demand

Increase in Demand   How does an increase in demand affect a product's equilibrium price and quantity? Consider an item that becomes a fad. Suppose that volleyball becomes the "in" sport, and that all over the country people are searching for volleyball nets to put in their yards and take to parks and beaches. Common sense would tell us that the volleyball net market might heat up with such an increase in demand, and price would rise. But even at this increased price, more nets would be sold. Let's examine the graphical analysis in Figure 3.8a to determine whether our common-sense analysis is correct.

S is the monthly market supply curve for volleyball nets, and D1 shows the monthly demand for volleyball nets before the sport becomes a fad. With supply curve S and demand curve D1, the equilibrium price is $40 per net, and the equilibrium quantity is 25,000 nets. As the game becomes really popular, the demand for volleyball nets increases, and the demand curve shifts to the right to D2. At the new equilibrium of S and D2, 35,000 nets are sold to buyers at a price of $80 each. Thus, an increase in the demand for a product causes both its equilibrium price and equilibrium quantity to increase.

Decrease in Demand   How does a decrease in demand affect a product's equilibrium price and quantity? Consider the market for mid-sized rental cars in a location popular with tourists during the summer months. Assume that S in Figure 3.8b is the weekly supply curve for mid-sized rental cars in this location and that D1 is the weekly demand curve for these cars during the summer. With S and D1, the equilibrium price is $300 per week and the equilibrium quantity is 1,200 cars.

But during the winter, fewer tourists visit this location and the demand for rental cars decreases. Figure 3.8b shows such a shift of the demand curve to the left from D1 to D2. As a result of this decrease in demand, the equilibrium price falls to $150 and the equilibrium quantity falls to 800. Thus, a decrease in the demand for a product causes both its equilibrium price and equilibrium quantity to fall. Consider the passing of a recent fad, like a singer who loses popularity with the young teen crowd. What happened to the price and quantity sold of that singer's recordings as the singer became less popular?

FIGURE 3.8   *Effect of Increases and Decreases in Demand*

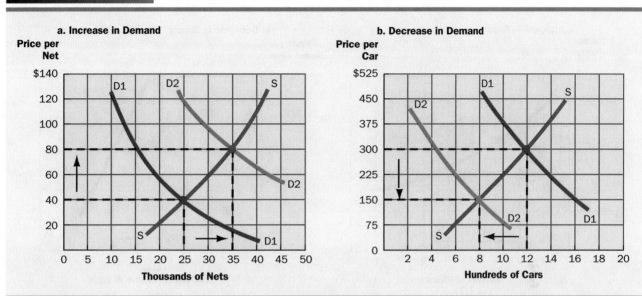

An increase in the demand for a product, such as volleyball nets, causes an increase in the product's equilibrium price and equilibrium quantity. A decrease in the demand for a product, such as rental cars, causes a decrease in the product's equilibrium price and equilibrium quantity.

Effect of Increases and Decreases in Supply

Increase in Supply   What effect does an increase in supply have on the equilibrium price and quantity of a product? We might respond immediately that an increase in the product's supply means that the price will fall and the amount sold will increase. Let's test this response.

Over the years several products, such as cell phones, have become much more plentiful because technology has made them cheaper to produce and, hence, to supply. Many new companies have also entered the market. In Figure 3.9a, S1 and D are the original supply and demand curves for cell phones. With this supply and demand, the equilibrium price is $100 a unit, and the equilibrium quantity is 2 million units. Later, as new technologies and new manufacturers impact the market, the supply curve shifts to S2. Following this increase in supply, the new equilibrium price is $60 per unit, and the equilibrium quantity is 6 million units. Thus, with an increase in supply, the equilibrium price falls and the equilibrium quantity increases.

Decrease in Supply   What will happen to a product's equilibrium price and quantity if supply falls? Assume that a virus is infecting chickens, causing fewer eggs to be produced, so that the supply of eggs decreases, but the demand for eggs does not change. D and S1 in Figure 3.9b are the demand and supply curves for eggs before the available amounts are reduced. With D and S1 the equilibrium price is $1.40 per dozen, and the equilibrium quantity is 12 million dozens. Suppose now that fewer eggs come to the market, causing the supply curve to shift to the left to S2. With this decrease in supply, the new equilibrium price is $2.10 per dozen, and the equilibrium quantity is 10 million dozens. Thus, a decrease in supply leads to an increase in the equilibrium price and a decrease in the equilibrium quantity of a product.

FIGURE 3.9   *Effect of Increases and Decreases in Supply*

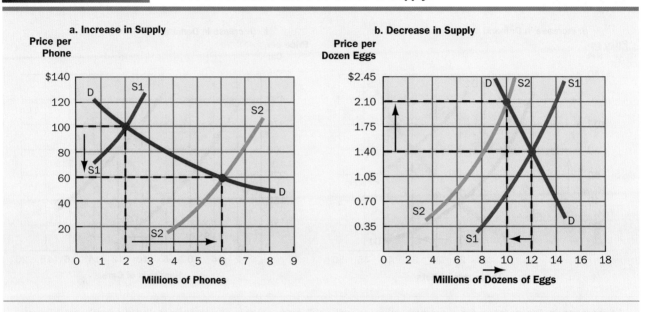

An increase in the supply of a product, such as cell phones, causes a decrease in the product's equilibrium price and an increase in its equilibrium quantity. A decrease in the supply of a product, such as eggs, causes an increase in the product's equilibrium price and a decrease in its equilibrium quantity.

Test Your Understanding, "Changes in Demand and Supply," lets you evaluate your skill at analyzing the factors causing demand and supply curves to shift and the effects of those shifts on equilibrium price and quantity.

Effect of Changes in Both Demand and Supply

In each of the preceding examples, we held constant one side of the market—either demand or supply—to examine the effects of changes in nonprice factors. In reality, both demand and supply might change simultaneously. For example, both the demand and supply of volleyball nets or cell phones might increase at the same time. Although such simultaneous changes are not illustrated here, your graphing skills should enable you to arrive at some conclusions about them.[6]

[6]If you try graphing simultaneous changes in demand and supply, you should get the following results.

Change	Equilibrium Price Will	Equilibrium Quantity Will
Demand and supply both increase	Increase, decrease, or stay the same	Increase
Demand and supply both decrease	Increase, decrease, or stay the same	Decrease
Demand increases and supply decreases	Increase	Increase, decrease, or stay the same
Demand decreases and supply increases	Decrease	Increase, decrease, or stay the same

In the cases where equilibrium price or quantity can increase, decrease, or stay the same, the actual change depends on the size of the changes in supply and demand. For example, an increase in demand that is larger than an increase in supply will result in an increase in price, whereas an increase in demand that is smaller than an increase in supply will result in a decrease in price.

TEST YOUR UNDERSTANDING

CHANGES IN DEMAND AND SUPPLY

Complete the table by determining which of the following each example represents.

a. An increase in demand   d. A decrease in supply
b. A decrease in demand   e. No change in either demand or supply
c. An increase in supply

Example	Result	Graphic Change	Change in Equilibrium Price	Change in Equilibrium Quantity
1. Some sellers drop out of the car wash market.	d.	supply curve shifts to the left	increase	decrease
2. A clothing retailer increases the effectiveness of its advertising campaign without increasing its advertising costs.				
3. A waste hauler finds its costs increasing because of environmental regulations.				
4. Automobile prices increase.				
5. Buyers in the upscale motorcycle market experience a decline in their incomes.				
6. Fans become more supportive of a pro football team because it has a winning season.				
7. A technological advance makes it cheaper to produce HDTVs.				
8. Buyers decide that a product that has been a fad is now out of style.				
9. Buyers expect that antifreeze will be unavailable or in short supply in the future.				
10. Local movie theaters raise their ticket prices.				
11. The number of buyers in the farm implements market decreases.				
12. Several new stores selling mountain bikes open in town.				
13. The price of apples goes down.				
14. A seller of a popular soft drink shifts more resources toward that product after discontinuing production of a less successful beverage.				

Answers can be found at the back of the book.

LIMITING PRICE MOVEMENTS

Up to this point we have dealt with free-market conditions, where buyers and sellers interact independently without any kind of outside intervention. But sometimes governments step into certain markets and interfere with free pricing by setting upper or lower limits on prices. State governments, for example, have limited prices on utilities, home mortgage interest rates, and interest rates on credit cards. The federal government has propped up prices for other goods and services, such as labor (with the minimum wage law) and some farm products. We can use supply and demand analysis to explain how this type of government intervention affects market conditions.

Price Ceilings

**Price Ceiling
(Upper Price Limit)**
A government-set maximum price that can be charged for a good or service; if the equilibrium price is above the price ceiling, a shortage will develop.

Legally imposed **upper price limits,** called **price ceilings,** keep prices from rising above certain levels. Price ceilings have been placed on gas and electricity in some states, rental apartments, and the interest rates people pay to borrow money. If the market goes to equilibrium at a price below the government-established upper legal limit, or ceiling, the ceiling will have no impact on buyers and sellers. In fact, the ceiling will not take effect. But if the market tries to go to an equilibrium price above its upper legal limit, the price ceiling will take effect and a shortage will occur.

For example, suppose that a state law sets the maximum interest rate on student loans at 12 percent. Such laws that set maximum interest rates are called **usury laws.** Figure 3.10a gives the demand for and the supply of loans when the equilibrium interest rate is lower than the ceiling rate—so the ceiling has no impact. Here borrowers' and lenders' plans balance at an interest rate of 10 percent, and $10 million is loaned each month. Do you see that, because the government-imposed ceiling on interest rates lies above the equilibrium rate, the usury law is irrelevant in this case?

Usury Laws
State laws setting maximum interest rates that can be charged for certain types of loans.

Suppose, however, that more students want to borrow money, causing the demand curve to shift to the right. This new situation appears in Figure 3.10b. If the market were free to go to equilibrium after this increase in demand, the new interest rate would be 14 percent. However, the upper legal limit is 12 percent, so lenders may charge no more. Rather than increasing from 10 to 14 percent, the interest rate can rise only to the legal limit of 12 percent. At the 12 percent rate, borrowers would like to have $16 million in loans, but lenders would provide only $12 million in funds. At the 12 percent usury limit there would be a $4 million shortage of funds for borrowing. Thus, when the free-market equilibrium price is above the ceiling, a shortage develops.

Price Floors

**Price Floor
(Lower Price Limit)**
A government-set minimum price that can be charged for a good or service; if the equilibrium price is below the price floor, a surplus will develop.

Legally imposed **lower price limits,** called **price floors,** prevent prices from falling below certain levels. Examples of price floors include the minimum wage law, which sets the minimum hourly payment that many workers can earn, and government-guaranteed agricultural prices, which ensure that farmers will receive at least a set minimum price on particular crops. As long as the equilibrium price of a good or service is above its price floor, the free market will not be affected by the limit. However, if the equilibrium price of a good or service falls below the floor, buyers will be forced to pay the government-set price. Because this legally imposed price is higher than the price the free market would have permitted, sellers offer more than buyers want to buy at the set price, and surpluses develop.

Consider the effect of the minimum wage law as an example. Suppose that the minimum wage is set at $7 per hour. If the supply and demand for a certain type of

FIGURE 3.10   *Effect of a Price Ceiling on a Market*

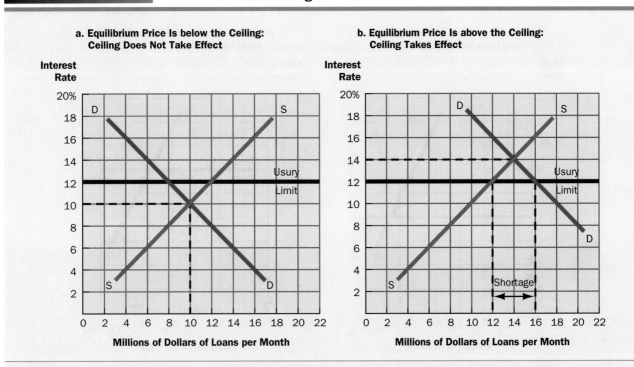

a. Equilibrium Price Is below the Ceiling:
Ceiling Does Not Take Effect

b. Equilibrium Price Is above the Ceiling:
Ceiling Takes Effect

Millions of Dollars of Loans per Month

When the equilibrium price for a product is below its legal upper limit, the price ceiling has no effect on the market. When the equilibrium price is above its legal upper limit, the price ceiling takes effect and a shortage develops.

labor are as shown in Figure 3.11a, the minimum wage will have no impact on the market. The equilibrium wage of $8 per hour is greater than the minimum wage, and the number of available workers equals the number demanded.

Now suppose that the government raises the minimum wage from $7 to $9 per hour, but that neither the supply nor demand for labor changes in this market. Because the equilibrium wage rate is $8, or less than the minimum wage, the $9 minimum wage will take effect. That is, businesses buying this type of labor must pay $9 per hour rather than $8. Figure 3.11b shows the market condition with the new minimum wage rate. At $9 per hour the number of workers demanded falls to 1,000, and the number of willing and able workers rises to 1,200. The price floor has created a surplus of 200 people who cannot obtain a job in this market. Thus, when the free-market equilibrium price is below the government-imposed floor, a surplus develops.

In summary, price ceilings, when they take effect, keep prices lower than they would otherwise be and result in shortages. Price floors, when they take effect, keep prices higher than they would otherwise be and result in surpluses. Price ceilings and price floors benefit some groups and hurt others. Application 3.3, "Is Rent Control a Good Thing or a Bad Thing?", explores some issues around the setting of ceilings on rents for apartments in New York City. Hopefully, the application will help you recognize why it is difficult to arrive at a clear answer to questions like who gains and who loses from rent control.

FIGURE 3.11   *Effect of a Price Floor on a Market*

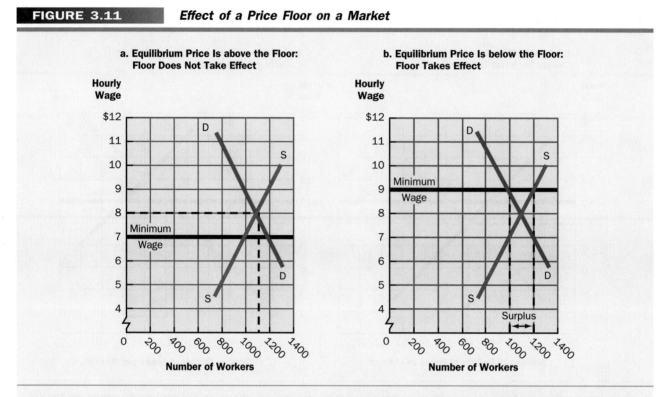

a. Equilibrium Price Is above the Floor:
   Floor Does Not Take Effect

b. Equilibrium Price Is below the Floor:
   Floor Takes Effect

When the equilibrium price for a resource or a product is above its legal lower limit, the price floor has no effect on the market. When the equilibrium price is below its floor, the floor takes effect and a surplus develops.

Up for Debate, "Is It a Mistake to Raise the Minimum Wage?", applies this same question to labor markets. Who gains and who loses from an increase in the minimum wage?

We should note that government can also affect markets by influencing the supply side of the market. For example, local governments can limit the number of trash haulers in an area and the Food and Drug Administration controls the flow of new medications onto the market.

PRICE ELASTICITY OF DEMAND AND SUPPLY

Our message for this chapter should now be clear: The quantity of a good or service that consumers demand relates inversely to its price; the quantity of a good or service that sellers supply relates directly to its price. But we need one last piece of the buyer and seller puzzle: How much will these quantities demanded and supplied change as buyers and sellers respond to a particular price change? If a sporting goods store offered a huge sale—say, 50 percent off—on its finest touring bicycles, would cash-strapped college students line up around the block to buy top-of-the-line bikes for $2,000 (half off of the usual retail price of $4,000)? Would they more likely show up for a 50 percent sale on sturdy, comfortable backpacks? When the price of an item—say peanut butter—increases, do consumers respond weakly, demanding just a little less of the item, or strongly, demanding much less? What about their response when the price of steak or fine wine increases?

APPLICATION 3.3

IS RENT CONTROL A GOOD THING OR A BAD THING?

Want to start an argument in New York City? Just bring up the subject of rent control. Likely, if there are two people within earshot, one will think it's wonderful and the other will think that, short of selling the Yankees, it is the best way to destroy the city. And what can begin as a civil discussion on the topic may well end as an intense battle of words.

Rent control was instituted in New York City in 1943 to help keep local residents from losing their apartments to better-paid transient wartime workers who could afford higher rents. More than 65 years later, many of the city's rental units are still subject to some type of price control.

Part of the argument over rent control comes from the disparity in what people get for what they pay in controlled versus uncontrolled units. Take the woman who lived for over 30 years in a rent-controlled one-bedroom suite with a kitchenette in a hotel overlooking Central Park. She paid just $8 a day, the price of a bowl of soup in a good hotel restaurant, while hotel guests paid up to $1,600 a day. Then there is the student working as a doorman who, along with two of his friends, paid $1,200 a month for a non-rent-controlled apartment so small that one of them slept on the living room floor.

One of the arguments against rent control is that the rents are simply too low. One landlord complained that people in his neighborhood pay more to park than they pay to rent. Landlords often say that it is difficult to survive as their costs rise. Another argument is that rent control has nothing to do with need. Many well-to-do people who can comfortably pay more for their living accommodations live in rent-controlled apartments, keeping poorer families out of low-rent units. Sometimes a lone elderly person lives in a spacious three-bedroom apartment because moving to a smaller non-rent-controlled unit would be more costly. And sometimes families stay in increasingly dangerous neighborhoods because they don't want to pay more for housing. Also, there are the stories about black markets for rent-controlled apartments: "Let me sign a year's sublease and I'll give you $5,000 in cash under the table."

But there are arguments on the other side of the debate. There are renters—like the man on disability who spends $400 of his monthly $600 check on rent—who might be living on the street were it not for the controlled rate. Also, while rent controls can be blamed for reducing people's mobility, they can also be credited for providing people with the stability that comes from being able to remain in one location, raise their families, and develop a network of friends over an extended period of time.

So, is rent control a good thing or a bad thing? Probably the safest answer is "depends on who you talk to."

Based on: "New York City Tenants, Landlords Keep Rent-Control Debate Raging," *Newsday*, Knight Ridder Tribune Business News, June 18, 2003, p. 1; Laurie Cohen, "Some Rich and Famous in New York City Bask in Shelter of Rent Law," *The Wall Street Journal*, March 21, 1994, pp. A1, A8; Nancy Keates, "Only in New York: Luxury at $8 a Day," *The Wall Street Journal* (Eastern Edition), January 23, 1998, p. 1; Eileen Pollock, "Curse of Rent Control," *The New York Times*, June 14, 2000; Daniel Rose, "The Theology of Rent Control: History of Low Income Housing," *Vital Speeches of the Day*, August 15, 2003, p. 670.

Price Elasticity
A measure of the strength of buyers' or sellers' responses to a price change.

Price Elastic
A strong response to a price change; occurs when the percentage change in the quantity demanded or supplied is greater than the percentage change in price.

Price Inelastic
A weak response to a price change; occurs when the percentage change in the quantity demanded or supplied is less than the percentage change in price.

We can ask similar questions about sellers. Would automobile manufacturers respond weakly or strongly if the price of luxury cars dropped by 10 percent? How much corn would farmers plant next year if the price of corn rose 50 percent this year? How would computer hardware and software companies respond to a decrease in the price of their products?

Price elasticity measures the strength of buyers' or sellers' responses to a price change. If buyers or sellers respond strongly to a price change, we say that their demand or supply is price elastic. More specifically, demand or supply is considered to be **price elastic** when a given percentage change in price (say 5 percent) results in a *larger* percentage change in quantity demanded or supplied (say 6 percent or 10 percent). If buyers or sellers are less sensitive to a price change—that is, if their response is weak—we say that their demand or supply is price inelastic. Again, more specifically, demand or supply would be **price inelastic** if a given percentage change in price (say 8 percent) resulted in *a smaller* percentage change in quantity demanded or supplied (say 7 percent or 3 percent). The mechanics of calculating elasticities of demand and supply are explained in the appendix to this chapter.

IS IT A MISTAKE TO RAISE THE MINIMUM WAGE?

Issue   *In 2007 Congress passed a law with phased increases in the minimum wage. The minimum wage would be raised from $5.15 to $5.85 per hour in July 2007, to $6.55 per hour in July 2008, and to $7.25 per hour in July 2009. Congress has raised the minimum wage several times since it was enacted in the 1930s. Clearly, any worker who takes home more money because the minimum wage has gone up is a winner. But some people think that raising the minimum wage is a mistake because some businesses, especially small ones, lose out when such mandated increases take effect. Is raising the minimum wage a mistake?*

Yes   It is a bad idea to raise the minimum wage. The higher wage may help workers who will now take home more income, but it also raises the cost of doing business for a worker's employer. These increased costs may force some small or financially strapped businesses to re-think their workforce needs and hire fewer workers in the future—or even lay workers off now. An increase in the minimum wage might be enough to push an employer to finally buy the machine that will, once and for all, replace workers, or to move its production operations to China, India, or some other country. And if a business cannot absorb the increased costs, it may be forced to close. What good does it do workers to be promised an increase in wages, only to lose their jobs as a result of that increase?

Also, if the new minimum wage falls above the equilibrium wage in a market, it will lead to an increase in the number of available workers at the very time that businesses are cutting back the number of workers demanded. Some people who would have had jobs at the lower equilibrium wage will now find themselves unable to obtain work. This may be a particular problem for college students looking for summer employment.

No   It is not a mistake to raise the minimum wage for several reasons. For one, a scan of job advertisements shows that many people, such as those working in fast-food restaurants and college students seeking summer jobs, are already earning more than the minimum wage. To say these people would have greater difficulty finding or keeping work may overstate the problem created by an increase in the minimum wage.

But perhaps the strongest argument for raising the minimum wage is the inability to subsist on this wage. A person working eight hours a day, five days a week, fifty weeks a year at the minimum wage of $6.55 per hour would earn $13,000 for the year. By comparison, the official poverty-level income in 2008 (when the minimum wage was $6.55) was $14,000 for the average two-person household. This reality is important for the minimum wage earner who is the only, or primary, source of income for a family. Not all minimum wage workers are high school or college students working part-time while living in a higher income household.

Sources: Phased increase data from U.S. Department of Labor, Employment Standards Administration, Wage and Hour Division, http://www.dol.gov/esa/whd/flsa. The 2008 poverty level is from U.S. Department of Health and Human Services, "The 2008 HHS Poverty Guidelines," http://aspe.hhs.gov/poverty/08poverty.shtml. The poverty threshold is calculated for a two-person household with no children in which the wage earner is under age 65 and not living in Alaska or Hawaii.

Price Elasticity of Demand

As we just indicated, demand is price elastic when a given percentage change in price results in a larger percentage change in quantity demanded, and price inelastic when a given percentage change in price results in a smaller percentage change in quantity demanded. Why do consumers respond strongly to some price changes and weakly to others? In other words, what determines whether demand will be relatively price elastic or inelastic?

Factors Affecting Price Elasticity of Demand   Several categories of factors affect price elasticity of demand.

- **Necessities versus luxury goods.** Generally, people respond more strongly when the price of a luxury good changes than they do when the price of a necessity changes. You would expect a fairly strong response by buyers to a price increase on dinners at an upscale restaurant or designer shoes. On the other hand, when a product is absolutely essential, people do not cut back much on their purchases, even when the price rise is substantial. Regardless of how much emergency medical care costs, parents will still generally take their seriously ill children to the ER. Typically, consumers respond weakly to price changes on necessities like water, gasoline, electricity, and prescription drugs. It is a lot easier to cut back on vacation plans than antibiotics.

♦ **Substitutes.** The availability of acceptable substitutes influences consumer responses to product price changes. If buyers can switch to similar or alternative products when prices rise, they will respond more elastically to the price change. If movie theater ticket prices increase, you can go to a concert or rent a DVD instead. On the other hand, if prices increase for a good or service with no or few substitutes, buyers may have little choice but to pay the higher prices: a price-inelastic response. When the price of a required textbook increases, for example, students have little choice but to buy it.

♦ **Proportion of income.** The portion of income that a purchase requires influences buyer responses to price changes. A person with an average income will likely respond weakly to a 20 percent increase in the price of a birthday card but respond strongly to a 20 percent increase in college tuition. The greater the portion of income required for a good or service, the stronger the reaction will be to a price change for that good or service, or the more price elastic will be the response.

Price Elasticity of Demand and Total Revenue   The seller of a product needs to know whether buyers will react strongly or weakly to a price change. Without this information, a seller may be surprised by the impact that a price change has on the total revenue received from selling the product. For example, Maggie owns a successful ice cream shop and has been doing quite well with her smoothies, averaging sales of 900 smoothies a week at a price of $2.50 each for a total revenue of $2,250. (Total revenue is equal to price times the quantity sold, or $2.50 × 900.) With so many customers, Maggie decides to experiment with pricing to increase total revenue above the current $2,250 per week. But how will customers react to any price change?

When customers react strongly, or elastically, to a price change, total revenue moves in the opposite direction from the price change. If price is increased and consumers react strongly by demanding much less, total revenue will fall—the strong quantity response brings total revenue down with it. If price is decreased and consumers react strongly by demanding much more, total revenue will increase. If Maggie raises the price of a smoothie to $3.00 and customers react strongly—causing a drop in sales to 600 per week—total revenue will fall to $1,800.

When buyers react weakly, or inelastically, to a price change, total revenue moves in the same direction as the price change. If price is increased and consumers react weakly by demanding a little less, total revenue will rise with the price increase—the weak quantity response will not be enough to offset the effect of the price increase. If price is decreased and consumers react weakly by demanding just a little more, total revenue will decrease. If Maggie raises the price of a smoothie to $3 and customers don't much care so that sales fall to 850 per week, total revenue will rise to $2,550.

Thus, if Maggie's goal is to raise total revenue, she needs to know whether people will respond weakly or strongly to a price change. If she has loyal customers who think that "there is nothing like a Maggie smoothie," she can raise the price and increase total revenue. If a competitive smoothie shop down the street serves great smoothies, she probably should lower price to increase revenues. Table 3.5 summarizes this information.

TABLE 3.5 *Price Elasticity of Demand and Total Revenue*

Total revenue moves in the opposite direction of the price change when demand is elastic, and total revenue moves in the same direction as the price change when demand is inelastic.

IF THE PRICE CHANGE IS	
Elastic	**Inelastic**
Total revenue and price move in opposite directions	Total revenue and price move in the same direction
$\uparrow P \rightarrow$ strong $\downarrow Qd \rightarrow \downarrow TR$	$\uparrow P \rightarrow$ weak $\downarrow Qd \rightarrow \uparrow TR$
$\downarrow P \rightarrow$ strong $\uparrow Qd \rightarrow \uparrow TR$	$\downarrow P \rightarrow$ weak $\uparrow Qd \rightarrow \downarrow TR$

APPLICATION 3.4

FICKLE MARKETS

Hybrids Over the last few years, the word hybrid has entered the vocabulary of more and more car buyers and sellers. While the term once applied mainly to the cross-breeding of plants and animals, today it also refers to cars like the Toyota Prius (the first of the hybrids) that are powered by both gas and electric systems. While hybrids are not seen on every street today, the growth in the market for these cars has been spectacular. From 2000 through 2004, sales grew by more than 900 percent, and in May 2008, Toyota announced that, cumulatively, more than one million Priuses had been sold worldwide.

When the Prius first came on the market, buyers had to wait six months or more to get the cars they had ordered, and buyers didn't seem to mind paying more for the car than they thought they would have to pay. Some dealers were adding markups of $5,000 or more to the Prius's sticker price.

It's not that Toyota had better things to do than produce the Prius. Rather, it simply did not have enough time to expand its production to meet the demand. With time, Toyota was able to increase its supply of the Prius from 10,000 to 15,000 per month. And with even more time, car companies have been able to adjust their production lines to create additional new hybrids. Buyers are now able to choose hybrids with model names such as the Chevrolet Malibu, Ford Escape, Honda Civic, and many others.

Why are some buyers relatively insensitive to paying more for a hybrid? Clearly the high mileage per gallon is a factor, particularly when consumers consider the long run, when the higher price may pay for itself in lower fuel costs. But concerns about the reduction in environmental damage done by hybrids as opposed to conventional cars may also be a factor. Finally, some people think the hybrid is so unique that it has no reasonable alternatives or substitutes.

Recordings In 2008, the Jonas Brothers—Joe, Nick, and Kevin—were clearly the hot boy band, as they created a frenzied hysteria across the globe with sold out concerts in the United States, Europe, and Latin America. Scalpers were reportedly getting $2,000 a ticket the weekend before the band's August 2008 Madison Square Garden concert.

And, their fans were desperate for a limited recording made earlier by the brothers. In 2006—long before the Jonas Brothers were the heartthrob of the younger set—they recorded "It's About Time." Only 62,000 of this CD were sold.

As the frenzy over Joe, Nick, and Kevin increased to fever pitch in the summer of 2008, the 2006 CD was carrying a huge price tag. It was reported that the CD fetched $160 on Amazon.com and more than $200 on eBay.

As with so many recording stars, popularity comes and goes. Some stay on the charts for years; some have limited star stay. The future of the Jonas Brothers remains to be seen. It will be interesting to see what people will pay for "It's About Time" in 2010 or 2012. Will it be more than $200 or just $5?

Based on: Terry Box, "Demand for Toyota Prius Booming Despite Wait Lists," *The Dallas Morning News*, Knight Ridder Tribune Business News, August 31, 2004, p. 1; Sholnn Freeman, "Auto Watch: Hot for a Hybrid Car? Cool Your Engines," *The Wall Street Journal* (Eastern Edition), June 13, 2004, p. 4; Lillie Guyer, "Hybrids Soar via Word-of-Mouth," *Advertising Age*, February 21, 2005, p. 36; Arlena Sawyers, "Used Prius Costs Same As New One," *Automotive News*, May 23, 2005, p. 44; Serdar Tumgoren, "Hybrid Happy," *The Dispatch*, Knight Ridder Tribune Business News, May 12, 2005, p. 1; Dom Yanchunas, "Dealers and Consumers Can't Get Enough of Hybrids, " *Lancaster New Era*, Knight Ridder Tribune Business News, April 25, 2005, p. 1; "IntelliChoice.com 2008 Annual Hybrid Survey Shows Economic Benefits of Going Green," *Business Wire*, New York: April 22, 2008; Anonymous, "Worldwide Prius Sales Top 1 Million Mark," *JCN Newswire—Japan Corporate News Network*, Tokyo, May 15, 2008; "A Rare CD by Today's Hot Boy Band: Bids Start at $160. Do I Hear $200?" *The New York Times*, August 4, 2008, p. C6; www.Jonasbrothers.com.

Price Elasticity of Supply

Let us look at supply and sellers' responsiveness to price changes: How much more will sellers be willing to supply at a higher price, and how much less at a lower price? If sellers respond strongly to price changes, we say that supply is price elastic. If they respond weakly to changes in price, we say that supply is price inelastic.

Factors Affecting Price Elasticity of Supply   For most sellers, price elasticity of supply is primarily affected by time. The more time sellers have to react to a price change, the greater is the ability to change the quantity supplied, and the more elastic is the response. Suppose that a particular style of jeans becomes very popular and the increase in demand pushes up its price. Sellers of these jeans can initially supply only as many pairs as the inventory on hand allows. Thus, the immediate response to this increase in price is inelastic. But given more time, sellers can order more jeans and respond with a larger increase in the quantity supplied—a more elastic response. Given even more time, other sellers and manufacturers may see how popular this style has become and may offer many more for sale. The jeans supply becomes even more price elastic.

Application 3.4, "Fickle Markets," looks at how supply and demand have played out in two markets: hybrid cars and recordings by a popular band. Can you explain how the relationship between demand and supply has influenced prices in these markets? How have nonprice factors and the elasticities of both demand and supply played a role?

Summary

1. Demand refers to a buyer's willingness and ability to purchase different amounts of a product at different prices in a given period of time when all nonprice factors are held constant. The relationship between a product's price and the quantity buyers plan to purchase at each price is typically shown in a demand schedule or graph called a demand curve, which slopes downward. Demand schedules and curves reflect an inverse relationship between price and quantity demanded, called the Law of Demand. The Law of Demand results from limited buyers' incomes and substitute products.

2. A supply schedule shows the different amounts of a product that a seller would offer in the market at different prices in a given time period when all nonprice factors are held constant. Graphically, a supply schedule appears as an upward-sloping supply curve because of the Law of Supply, which states that there is a direct relationship between price and quantity supplied. The Law of Supply follows from sellers' efforts to cover costs and earn profits.

3. The total amount of a product demanded by all buyers in a market at a particular price is market demand, and the total amount made available by all sellers at that price is market supply.

4. The price that equalizes buyers' and sellers' plans, and toward which a market automatically moves, is called the equilibrium price. Equilibrium price is at the intersection of the product's market demand and supply curves. If the market price of a product is above its equilibrium price, a surplus of the product will appear on the market, and forces will bring the price down to its

equilibrium level. If the market price of a product is below its equilibrium level, a shortage will result, and forces will bring the price up to its equilibrium level.

5. Nonprice factors also influence buyers' and sellers' behaviors. Changes in these nonprice factors lead to shifts in demand and supply curves. An increase in demand or supply means that buyers are demanding or sellers are supplying more of a product at each price, and the demand or supply curve has shifted to the right. When less of a product is demanded or supplied at each price, demand or supply decreases, and the demand or supply curve shifts to the left. Because the equilibrium price and quantity of a product are shown by the intersection of its demand and supply curves, increases or decreases in demand and/or supply cause the product's equilibrium price and quantity to change.

6. It is important to understand the difference between changes in demand and/or supply, shown by shifts in the demand and/or supply curves, and changes in quantity demanded and/or quantity supplied, shown by movements *along* existing demand and/or supply curves. Changes in price cause *movements along* a demand or supply curve from one price–quantity point to another, or cause changes in quantity demanded or quantity supplied. Changes in nonprice influences cause shifts of demand or supply curves, or cause changes in demand or supply.

7. If government sets a price ceiling for a good or service, and the equilibrium price is above the ceiling, the ceiling price takes effect and a shortage develops. If government sets a price floor for a good or service, and the equilibrium price is below the floor, the floor takes effect and a surplus develops.

8. Price elasticity measures buyers' and sellers' sensitivities to changes in the price of a product. Demand or supply is price elastic when the quantity demanded or supplied changes by a greater percentage than the percentage price change. Demand or supply is price inelastic when the quantity demanded or supplied changes by a smaller percentage than the percentage price change. Elasticity of demand is influenced by whether the product is a luxury or a necessity, the availability of substitutes, and the price of the product relative to the buyer's income. Time is the major determinant of a product's price elasticity of supply.

9. When the response by buyers to a price change is inelastic, total revenue moves in the same direction as the price change. When the response by buyers to a price change is elastic, total revenue moves in the opposite direction of the price change.

10. (*From the appendix*) Price elasticity of demand or supply is calculated by dividing the percentage change in quantity demanded or quantity supplied by the percentage change in price. If the resulting number is greater than 1, demand or supply is price elastic. If the resulting number is less than 1, demand or supply is price inelastic. And if the resulting number is exactly 1, demand or supply is unitary elastic.

Key Terms and Concepts

Demand	Nonprice factors influencing demand
Demand schedule	Increase in demand
Law of Demand	Decrease in demand
Demand curve	Change in supply
Supply	Nonprice factors influencing supply
Supply schedule	Increase in supply
Law of Supply	Decrease in supply
Supply curve	Price ceiling (upper price limit)
Market	Usury laws
Market demand and market supply	Price floor (lower price limit)
Shortage	Price elasticity
Surplus	Price elastic
Equilibrium price and equilibrium quantity	Price inelastic
Market clearing price	*From the appendix*
Change in quantity demanded and quantity supplied	Elasticity coefficient
	Unitary price elastic
Change in demand	

Review Questions

1. Define the Law of Demand and Law of Supply. Draw a demand curve and a supply curve and explain how each curve illustrates the related law. Identify the factors underlying these laws.

2. Surpluses and shortages are temporary conditions in freely operating markets. Explain what causes each and how these temporary conditions resolve themselves in free markets.

3. Distinguish between a change in quantity demanded or quantity supplied, and a change in demand or supply. How would you represent each change graphically?

4. Explain how each of the following would cause demand or supply to shift and how the equilibrium price and quantity for the good or service in question would change.
   a. A decrease in the number of builders in a housing market
   b. Expectations by automobile buyers that new, more efficient hybrids will be on the market next year
   c. An increase in the popularity of organic peanut butter
   d. A wage increase paid to a hospital's employees

e. A cost-reducing innovation adopted by the producers of a mobile communication device

f. The identification of a food as high in cholesterol

5. Plot the following demand and supply schedules on the accompanying graph, and answer questions a through e.

a. What is the equilibrium price and equilibrium quantity?

b. How much of a shortage or surplus would occur at $2.50?

c. How much of a shortage or surplus would occur at $7.50?

d. What would happen if the government established a price floor of $8.75 on this item?

e. What would happen if the government established a price ceiling of $8.75 on this item?

Price per Item	Quantity Demanded	Quantity Supplied
$1.25	150	0
2.50	140	50
3.75	125	60
5.00	105	70
6.25	80	80
7.50	50	90
8.75	10	100
10.00	0	110

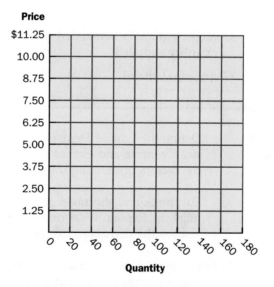

6. What does price elasticity of demand and of supply measure? Identify factors that affect these price elasticities and give examples of each.

7. (*From the appendix*) Calculate the price elasticity coefficient for demand or supply for each of the following. Identify whether the response is elastic, inelastic, or unitary elastic.

a. The number of cans demanded of a soft drink increases by 30 percent after its price decreases by 40 percent.

b. The number of available apartments increases by 8 percent following a 6 percent increase in rents.

c. The number of small Caesar salads demanded at a restaurant increases from 60 to 80 per week when the price falls from $5.00 to $4.50.

d. At a price of $200, 10,000 gas grills were supplied each month. Since the price increased to $250, 14,000 are supplied each month.

e. The number of DVDs demanded each weekend from a movie rental service falls from 500 to 400 following an increase in the rental charge from $2.00 to $2.40.

Discussion Questions

1. People pay attention to political upheavals in foreign countries, local and national elections in the United States, and environmental and other developments around the world because such events can directly affect their lives. But the functioning of markets may go relatively unnoticed because market effects are usually less obvious or dramatic. How does the functioning of markets affect your everyday life? If prices were not set in markets, how else could they be determined? How would this affect your life?

2. We placed great emphasis on the distinction between changes in quantity demanded and quantity supplied and changes in demand and supply. Why would an automobile dealership treat buyers' reactions to price changes differently than it would their reactions to changes in everything else that affects their purchasing decisions? Does that seller have any control over nonprice determinants of demand, such as buyer taste? How and why?

3. Both real and perceived differences arise among the kinds of entertainment, food, and clothing that are popular among buyers in different age groups. Pick one product from each of these three categories that is popular with your age group and explain how its demand and equilibrium price would change if it were marketed to people older than you. How would the cost of this increased marketing affect its equilibrium price and quantity?

4. Minimum wage laws keep many workers' hourly wages above what they would be in the absence of such laws. Do minimum wage laws help or hurt college students looking for summer work?

5. If a government-imposed price ceiling or floor helps some people but hurts others, what factors do you think the government should consider before deciding on such a policy? (You might consider interest rate ceilings on credit cards and student loans, and price supports on milk in answering this question.)

6. Give some examples of goods and services where a consumer's response to a price change might typically be elastic and where it might typically be inelastic. Explain why the response would be elastic or inelastic.

7. How does price elasticity of demand determine whether a seller's revenue will increase or decrease following an increase in the price of its product? What impact might the cost of production have on a seller's decision to change its price?

Critical Thinking Case 3

HOW DO SUPPLY AND DEMAND WORK IN HEALTH CARE?

Critical Thinking Skills

Identifying exceptions to a norm

Comparing applications of a principle in different settings

Economic Concepts

Supply and demand

Pricing

About a year ago John decided that, with 160,000 miles on his 2000 Volvo, the time had come to buy a new car. He was successful in his job and wanted to update his look. Because John knew this would be expensive, he spent a good bit of time reading reports about different models, shopping online, and going from dealer to dealer. Finally, after three weeks of visits to showrooms, John found a car he really liked. Its price tag was $31,000. John wanted the car, but this didn't stop him from trying to talk the dealer down from the $31,000 sticker price because he had done enough research to know this was possible. After a few days of phone calls back and forth, John bought the car for $24,000 plus his 2000 Volvo in trade.

About three weeks later, John called a doctor after having severe knee pain following a fall. The doctor told him to come in for a checkup as soon as possible. After an exam and some tests, John's doctor recommended surgery. With John's agreement, the doctor scheduled all of the routine presurgery testing as well as the surgery at South City Hospital where he is on staff. There are other hospitals closer to John's home, but John didn't bother to ask about going to one of them. He also did not ask about the costs involved with the testing and surgery.

Shortly after arriving at the hospital, John was assigned to a room on the third floor. He was surprised to see how many beds on the floor were empty. After surgery and post-op recovery, John's doctor gave him two prescriptions, released him from the hospital, and set appointments for checkups and physical therapy. John collected his belongings, paid his co-payment for his health insurance, and hobbled out the door. On his way home, he filled and paid for his prescriptions. He didn't bother to ask the pharmacist if there were cheaper generic drugs he could use in place of his prescriptions. He was just happy to be on his way home.

Later in the month John totaled up the bills for his doctor's visits, hospital treatment, medications, and therapy. They came to $31,000.

Based on: Paul Disser, "Whose Ox Is Being Gored?" *Broker World*, February 25, 2005, p. 36; Rashi Fein, *Medical Care, Medical Costs* (Cambridge, MA: Harvard University Press, 1986), p. 131; David Rosenbaum, "America's Economic Outlaw: The U.S. Health Care System," *The New York Times*, October 26, 1993, pp. A1, A11.

Questions

1. Contrary to conventional economics, physicians (the suppliers) typically decide the quantity and type of health care services their patients (the demanders) will purchase. What is it about medical services that usually allows the supplier to determine the demand?

2. Suppose a person who knows nothing about auto maintenance takes a car in for its 30,000-mile checkup. The service manager reads off a list of repairs that need to be done. In your opinion, will this person act like John did on learning the doctor's diagnosis? Does the market for auto repairs behave like the market for medical care? Should it?

3. Many people have a large part of their health care expenses paid by an insurance provider. Explain how this might lead patients to pay little attention to the price of their treatment. Other than insurance coverage, what other factors would cause a patient to pay little attention to the price of a treatment?

4. Conventional economics suggests that a business with unsold, or surplus, merchandise will lower its price to attract buyers. Do you think that a physician would lower the price of a procedure or a hospital would lower its daily bed rate to attract patients?

CHAPTER 3
APPENDIX

MEASURING PRICE ELASTICITY

Elasticity Coefficient
The absolute value of the percentage change in quantity demanded or supplied divided by the absolute value of the percentage change in price; greater or less than 1 when demand or supply is price elastic or inelastic, respectively.

The degree to which demand or supply is price elastic or inelastic can be measured by calculating an **elasticity coefficient** from the formula:

$$\frac{|\% \text{ change in } Q|}{|\% \text{ change in } P|},$$

where Q represents the quantity demanded or supplied of a product, and P represents the product's price. The vertical lines on each side of the numerator and denominator indicate that we are interested in the absolute values of the percentage changes in quantity and price. Absolute value focuses on the size of a change but not its direction. Whether the change in price or quantity is up or down, or has a plus or minus sign in front of it, is not important in calculating elasticity: All changes are treated as though they are preceded by a plus sign.[1]

When demand or supply is price elastic, a given percentage change in price leads to a *greater* percentage change in quantity demanded or quantity supplied. Using the formula, *the elasticity coefficient is greater than 1*. When demand or supply is price inelastic, a given percentage change in price leads to a *smaller* percentage change in quantity demanded or quantity supplied. Using the formula, *the elasticity coefficient is less than 1*.

If the quantity demanded of a particular shoe falls by 20 percent after its price rises by 10 percent, demand is price elastic because the percentage change in quantity demanded is greater than the percentage change in price. Specifically, when the elasticity coefficient is calculated,

$$\frac{|\% \text{ change in } Q|}{|\% \text{ change in } P|} = \frac{20\%}{10\%} = 2,$$

the number is greater than 1, indicating that demand is price elastic. If the quantity demanded of the shoe decreases by 8 percent following a 10 percent price increase, demand is price inelastic because the percentage change in quantity demanded is less than the percentage change in price, and the elasticity coefficient,

$$\frac{|\% \text{ change in } Q|}{|\% \text{ change in } P|} = \frac{8\%}{10\%} = 0.8,$$

is less than 1.

Applying the concept of price elasticity to supply, a 12 percent decrease in quantity supplied following an 8 percent decrease in price results in an elasticity

---

[1]For example, if one item increases by 2 percent and another falls by 2 percent, the direction of the first change is +2 percent and the direction of the second is −2 percent, but the size, or absolute value, of each change is simply 2 percent.

coefficient of 12%/8% = 1.5, indicating that supply is price elastic, or that sellers are responding strongly to the price change. A 6 percent increase in quantity supplied following an 18 percent increase in price means supply is inelastic, or that sellers are responding weakly, as shown by the elasticity coefficient of 6%/18% = 0.33.

Determining Percentage Changes

Often the percentage changes in price and quantity needed to calculate elasticity are not given and simple price and quantity numbers must be converted to percentages. These percentage changes are determined by dividing the change in quantity by the original, or base, quantity and the change in price by the original, or base, price, or

$$|\% \text{ change in } Q| = \frac{|\text{change in } Q|}{|\text{base } Q|},$$

and

$$|\% \text{ change in } P| = \frac{|\text{change in } P|}{|\text{base } P|}.$$

Again, we are interested in the size, and not the direction, of the change.[2]

Suppose that a seller is willing to supply 300 units of a product at a price of $50 each and 390 units when the price is $75, as shown in the following supply schedule.

Price	Quantity Supplied
$50	300
75	390

What is the elasticity of supply coefficient when the price is increased from $50 to $75? How do we calculate the percentage changes? The percentage change in quantity supplied is equal to the change in quantity of 90 units divided by the original quantity of 300 units, or 90/300 = 30%. The percentage change in price equals the change in price of $25 divided by the original price of $50, or $25/$50 = 50%. From this, elasticity can be calculated in the usual way by dividing the percentage change

---

[2]Price elasticity can also be calculated by using a "midpoint," or average, formula. This formula measures the percentage change in quantity and in price by dividing the change in quantity and price by the average quantity and price, rather than the base quantity and price. That is,

$$|\% \text{ change in } Q| = \frac{|\text{change in } Q|}{|\text{average } Q|}$$

and

$$|\% \text{ change in } P| = \frac{|\text{change in } P|}{|\text{average } P|}.$$

Average Q is found by adding both the quantity before and after the price change and dividing by 2, or $(Q_{old} + Q_{new})/2$. Average P is found by adding both the old and new price and dividing by 2, or $(P_{old} + P_{new})/2$.

in quantity supplied by the percentage change in price: 30%/50% = 0.6. The following equation summarizes these calculations:

$$\frac{|\text{change in } Q/\text{base } Q|}{|\text{change in } P/\text{base } P|} = \frac{|\% \text{ change in } Q|}{|\% \text{ change in } P|} = \text{elasticity},$$

or

$$\frac{90/300}{\$25/\$50} = \frac{30\%}{50\%} = 0.6.$$

Can you prove that the price elasticity of demand for a product would be 1.2 if the quantity demanded fell from 500 to 200 units following a price increase from $20 to $30?

Finally, a given percentage change in price could result in an equal percentage change in quantity demanded or quantity supplied. For example, a 4 percent change in price could lead to a 4 percent change in quantity demanded or supplied. When this occurs, the elasticity coefficient is equal to 1, and demand or supply is **unitary price elastic.** Table 3A.1 summarizes the measurement of elasticity using the elasticity coefficient.

Unitary Price Elastic
The percentage change in quantity demanded or supplied equals the percentage change in price; elasticity coefficient equals 1.

TABLE 3A.1	*The Measurement of Elasticity*

When the absolute value of the percentage change in quantity is greater than, less than, or equal to the absolute value of the percentage change in price, demand or supply is elastic, inelastic, or unitary elastic, respectively.

When Demand or Supply Is	The Elasticity Coefficient Is
Elastic	$\frac{|(\text{change in } Q/\text{base } Q)|}{|(\text{change in } P/\text{base } P)|} = \frac{|\% \text{ change in } Q|}{|\% \text{ change in } P|} > 1$
Inelastic	$\frac{|(\text{change in } Q/\text{base } Q)|}{|(\text{change in } P/\text{base } P)|} = \frac{|\% \text{ change in } Q|}{|\% \text{ change in } P|} < 1$
Unitary elastic	$\frac{|(\text{change in } Q/\text{base } Q)|}{|(\text{change in } P/\text{base } P)|} = \frac{|\% \text{ change in } Q|}{|\% \text{ change in } P|} = 1$

PART 2
The Macroeconomy

CHAPTER 4

Goals and Problems of the Macroeconomy: Employment, Prices, and Production

CHAPTER OBJECTIVES

To introduce the three fundamental areas on which macroeconomics focuses: employment, prices, and production.

To introduce unemployment—its causes, consequences, and related data and concepts.

To discuss inflation—its causes, consequences, and measures.

To define full production and economic growth as well as contributing factors and associated costs.

To introduce GDP, the primary measure of production.

To define productivity and discuss changes in U.S. productivity over the years.

Macroeconomics
The study of the operation of the economy as a whole.

This chapter begins the section of the textbook devoted to **macroeconomics,** which is the study of the economy as a whole, or the "big picture." Macroeconomics brings us such topics as aggregate (total) employment and production, unemployment, inflation, economic growth, money, and government stabilization policies. (Microeconomics, which focuses on decision making by individual units in the economy, is covered in Part 3 of this textbook.) The study of macroeconomics will help you to understand the roles the household, business, and government sectors play in the economy, and how the sectors relate to each other. We will also learn about problems that arise in the big picture economy and how those problems can be resolved.

Before we begin any analysis, we must become familiar with some basic terms and concepts involving employment, production, and prices. These three areas are the sources of the major problems of the macroeconomy: unemployment, falling production, and inflation. They are also the basis for the major goals of the macroeconomy: full employment, full production and economic growth, and stable prices. These problems and goals will be explored in this chapter.

In the United States, full employment, full production and economic growth, and stable prices are regarded as important economic goals. As noted in Chapter 2, Congress enacted the **Employment Act of 1946** to permit the government to help in creating an economic environment that would lead to the achievement of these goals. This legislation states that:

Employment Act of 1946
Legislation giving the federal government the right and responsibility to provide an environment for the achievement of full employment, full production, and stable prices.

> *The Congress hereby declares that it is the continuing policy and responsibility of the Federal Government to use all practicable means consistent with its needs and obligations and other essential considerations of national policy . . .* **to promote maximum employment, production, and purchasing power.** *[emphasis added]*[1]

In this act the government does not ensure that these goals will be achieved. Rather, it commits to providing an environment that will lead to their achievement.

UNEMPLOYMENT AND FULL EMPLOYMENT

Unemployment
A resource available for production is not being used.

One of the primary macroeconomic goals in the United States is employment for all available factors of production, or the minimization of unemployment. **Unemployment** means that a resource available for production is not being used. While machines, raw materials, warehouses, and trucks can all be unemployed, our primary concern is the unemployment of people who would like to be working but are not. This concern results because the consequences of unemployment among people are obviously more striking.

The most dramatic siege of unemployment the United States has ever witnessed occurred in the Great Depression of the 1930s. From 1932 through 1935 the unemployment rate stayed at 20 percent or more of the civilian labor force and in 1933 it reached almost 25 percent: Roughly one out of every four people who wanted to work could not.[2]

---

[1]*United States Statutes at Large,* 1946, vol. 60, part 1, *Public Laws and Reorganization Plans* (Washington, DC: U.S. Government Printing Office, 1947), p. 23.
[2]U.S. Bureau of the Census, *Historical Statistics of the United States, Colonial Times to 1957* (Washington, DC: U.S. Government Printing Office, 1960), Series D 46–47, p. 73.

Consequences of Unemployment

Why is there so much concern about unemployment, especially among workers? Unemployment has several undesirable consequences, including economic losses for society and individual hardships for the unemployed.

Economic Loss for Society   Recall that economics is the study of how people use scarce resources to satisfy unlimited material wants and needs. If more resources are available and put into use, a greater number of wants and needs can be satisfied. If resources are unemployed, some wants and needs that might have been satisfied are not. Thus, unemployment intensifies the scarcity problem.

Each year the economy produces a certain amount of goods and services. With unemployment, output is less than it could be and substantial amounts of goods and services that could have been produced are lost.[3]

Individual Hardships   In addition to its effects on society, unemployment causes hardships for people who would like to be working but are not. Unemployment intensifies an individual's struggle with scarcity. When people are out of a job, they are usually forced to alter their spending habits and lifestyles and in some cases make dramatic changes, such as moving into cheaper housing or liquidating assets.

Along with the financial dimension, a person's self-esteem and relationships with others may suffer from unemployment. A number of studies dealing with the psychological and physiological costs of unemployment have shown that the incidence of depression, suicide, mental hospitalization, ulcers, and even the common cold can be affected by being out of work.

Application 4.1, "What's at Stake When a Job Is Lost?", goes into more detail about the adverse economic and social consequences that can befall the unemployed and those around them.

Types of Unemployment

Before unemployment can be remedied, we need to understand its cause. There is no single cause of unemployment; instead there are three main sources: (1) friction in the labor market, (2) cyclical or periodic changes in the demand for goods and services, and (3) changes in the structure of the economy. These three sources provide a framework for us to define the primary types of unemployment:

- ◆ frictional unemployment,
- ◆ cyclical unemployment, and
- ◆ structural unemployment.[4]

---

[3]In 1992, for example, the unemployment rate for the civilian labor force was at 7.5 percent (its highest level for 1985 through 2008), and the economy produced $6.88 trillion of goods and services. It is estimated that if full employment were reached, $7.02 trillion of good and services could have been produced. In other words, about $140 billion of goods and services were lost. (Unemployment figures are from *Economic Report of the President*, 2008, p. 276; output figures are from Michael Pakko, Federal Reserve Bank of St. Louis, and are real chained 1996 dollars.)

[4]A fourth type of unemployment, called seasonal unemployment, is not discussed here. The seasonally unemployed are those who lose their jobs at the same time each year because of weather changes or tradition. Farmworkers unemployed in the winter when land is out of production and teachers unemployed in the summer because of traditional school-year schedules are examples of the seasonally unemployed. Because it occurs predictably each year and can be planned for well in advance, seasonal unemployment need not be a problem.

APPLICATION 4.1

WHAT'S AT STAKE WHEN A JOB IS LOST?

What causes a person to feel good? According to Sigmund Freud, two main anchors of mental health are love and work. The impact of love on mental health should come as no surprise, but work? People like to complain about work: so-and-so at the office, the meeting that refused to end, the surprise "I need it now" visit from the boss, and other annoyances.

All these complaints notwithstanding, work can have a huge positive impact on a person's sense of well-being. Regrettably, this sometimes becomes apparent only after a job has been lost.

What do people lose when their jobs disappear and the world they've taken for granted is replaced by something much less certain? One important dimension of loss and uncertainty is obviously economic. The loss of a job can dramatically heighten a household's economic insecurity. Now that the job is gone, how much will spending need to be cut? Will we be able to meet our rent or mortgage and auto payments? What's going to happen to our credit card debt? Will we be able to afford our daughter's tuition?

And the economic concerns are not just about right now. The loss of a job can make the future very cloudy. The length of unemployment and its impact on a household's savings and borrowing are unknown, as is the income from a future job.

But the impact of job loss can go far beyond economics. The everyday structure and routine provided by going to work is gone. This, in turn, can disrupt and dramatically change household responsibilities, authority, and schedules. Also gone is the status conferred by employment, and along with it may go a person's sense of self-esteem, confidence, and contribution to the household or community. Finally, it can be hard to maintain friendships if they are with people with whom a person *used to* work and no longer frequently sees.

What personal and social consequences can come from job loss? Studies indicate that job loss can cause depression, increased anxiety, and a greater risk for suicide, alcohol abuse, traffic accidents, and criminal or violent behavior. Those close to people who have lost their jobs can suffer as well. Spouses of people who have lost their jobs have been shown to have a higher incidence of psychiatric disorders than do spouses of people who are working. Not surprisingly, unemployment has been linked to spouse and child abuse, and it is a contributing factor to separation and divorce.

Based on: Richard H. Price, Daniel S. Friedland, and Amiram D. Vinokur, "Job Loss: Hard Times and Eroded Identity," in *Perspectives on Loss: A Sourcebook*, ed. John H. Harvey (Philadelphia: Brunner/Mazel, 1998), pp. 303–310.

Frictional Unemployment

Occurs when people are voluntarily out of work for a short period of time while searching for a job.

Full Employment

Occurs when only those voluntarily out of work are unemployed, or the unemployment rate includes only frictional unemployment.

Frictional Unemployment   Some job seekers have voluntarily quit a job to search for another one. Some may be entering the job market for the first time or after a period of not looking for work. These job seekers will likely experience a short period of unemployment while they collect references and credentials, fill out applications, follow up leads, and interview with prospective employers. The inability to make quick and smooth transitions from old employment situations to new jobs comes from "friction" in the labor market. Thus, the **frictionally unemployed** are job seekers voluntarily out of work for a short period of time while they search for new prospects.

In a large, complex economy like the United States, people are always voluntarily unemployed: We always have some frictional unemployment. These job seekers may have quit a job because they were unhappy with it, want to relocate or change their occupation, or have some other reason. Because frictional unemployment always exists, when we say that the economy is at full employment we do *not* mean that 100 percent of the labor force is working. Rather, **full employment** means that everyone in the labor force except the frictionally unemployed is working.

Cyclical Unemployment   Market economies do not produce goods and services at a constant rate over time. Rather, market economies go through upswings and downswings in production called business cycles. Periodically, the economy falls into a downswing, or recession, during which the demand for goods and services decreases. When this happens, workers producing those goods and services may be

Cyclical Unemployment
Involuntary unemployment that results from a downswing in a business cycle, or a recession.

involuntarily laid off. This type of unemployment is termed **cyclical unemployment** because it is the result of a recession, or a downswing in the business cycle.

Cyclical unemployment is a matter of serious concern because, unlike frictional unemployment, it is involuntary and continues until the economy breaks out of the recession. A downturn could be a matter of a few months and involve a relatively small number of workers, or it could last for several years and extend to millions of households. As we noted earlier, the unemployment rate was at 20 percent or more for several years during the Great Depression. More recently, the unemployment rate rose from 4.6 percent in 2007 to 6.7 percent by November 2008 due largely to a cyclical downswing in the economy.[5]

Some industries are more sensitive than others to changes in general economic conditions, and workers in these industries are particularly vulnerable to cyclical unemployment. When a recession is looming, consumers may postpone purchases of durable goods, such as new homes and automobiles, and businesses may postpone, or even cancel, purchases of capital goods, such as heavy machinery and buildings. As sales decline, workers in these industries may be laid off. Auto, heavy manufacturing, and construction workers are among those especially susceptible to cyclical unemployment.

Workers who are young and lack seniority are also vulnerable to cyclical unemployment. When a downswing occurs, young, newly hired workers are usually among the first to be laid off; when the economy improves, they are usually among the last to be rehired.

Structural Unemployment
Involuntary unemployment that results when a worker's job is no longer part of the production structure of the economy.

Structural Unemployment   Like cyclical unemployment, **structural unemployment** is involuntary. It occurs when a worker loses a job because that job is no longer a part of the structure of the economy. The good or service the worker produced may no longer be demanded or may now be made in a way that eliminates that particular job. Unlike cyclical unemployment, structural unemployment offers no prospect for rehire in the future.

Structural unemployment can come from several factors: technological changes in the economy, changes in the types of goods and services people demand, the reorganization of positions and processes as firms downsize or merge, and the closing of domestic manufacturing plants because production has been moved out of the country or because of competition from foreign-produced goods.

In today's fast-paced economy, there are many examples of structural unemployment. Offices used to depend on large numbers of clerical workers to type, file, keep books, and so on. With today's computer-based workstations, networks, and wide-ranging software, fewer people are needed to accomplish these tasks. In mining and manufacturing, workers are being replaced by high-tech, automated equipment; in many businesses and nonprofits, administrators and managers are being eliminated as efficiencies from reorganization are sought; in banks, electronic transactions have lessened the need for tellers; and in the arts, studio musicians and graphic artists are being replaced by sophisticated software.

A structurally unemployed person faces difficult choices: Find a new occupation or go without work. This could mean that time and money are needed to retrain or family and friends are left behind because relocation is necessary. Structural unemployment imposes a real hardship on older workers who might need costly retraining and face competition with younger workers willing to accept a lower salary.

[5]*Economic Report of the President* (Washington, DC: U.S. Government Printing Office, 2009), p. 327.

Continued technological advancements, efforts by firms to operate more efficiently, and foreign competition promise to bring about more structural changes in the U.S. economy and to threaten many types of blue-collar and white-collar jobs. As a result, there is some concern that the middle class is shrinking as semiskilled jobs are eliminated, leaving a workforce of highly paid, highly skilled workers and poorly paid, unskilled workers. Retraining workers and lifelong education are essential to meet changing job requirements in the U.S. economy.

EMPLOYMENT AND UNEMPLOYMENT: MEASURES AND STATISTICS

When we talk about the labor force, the employed, and the unemployed, whom do we include and how do we arrive at the numbers we use?

Labor Force

All persons 16 years of age and older who are working or actively seeking work.

The **labor force** is defined as all persons 16 years of age and older who are working or actively seeking work. If a person is capable of working but is not working and not interested in seeking work, then that person is not included in the labor force. It is the activity directed toward employment, not the capability of holding a job, that determines whether a person is or is not in the labor force.

Table 4.1 gives some frequently reported statistics on the labor force. The second and third columns of the table give, respectively, the number of people eligible for, and the number actually in, the labor force for selected years.[6] It is important to appreciate how many millions of people are in the U.S. labor force: over 154 million in 2008.

Participation Rate

The percentage of some specified group that is in the labor force.

Participation rates for the labor force are given in the fourth column of Table 4.1. The term **participation rate** refers to the percentage of some group that is in the labor force. The group could be the entire eligible population, women, persons in different age groups or of different ethnic backgrounds, and so on. According to Table 4.1, in 2008, 65.8 percent of those eligible for the labor force were in the labor force. That is, approximately 155 million people out of a population group of approximately 235 million were employed or seeking work.

Unemployment Rate

The percentage of the labor force that is unemployed and actively seeking work.

The fifth and sixth columns of Table 4.1 give some data on the unemployed. Column five shows the number of unemployed persons in the labor force, and column six gives the **unemployment rate,** which is the percentage of the labor force that is unemployed and actively seeking work. For example, the unemployment rate of 6.7 percent in 2008 indicates that 10,331,000 persons in a labor force of 154,616,000 were unemployed and actively seeking work.

Along with overall labor force numbers, participation rates and unemployment rates are also calculated for various subgroups. Table 4.2 provides a sample of participation rates for some labor force subgroups for selected years. It shows, for instance, that in 2008, 59.4 percent of all women 16 years of age and older were working or actively seeking work. Participation rates are important because, when examined over time, they show us changes in the composition of the labor force. For example, we can see in Table 4.2 that over the past few decades there has been, in general, an increase in the overall labor force participation rate, with much of this growth due to

---

[6]All figures in this table are for the noninstitutional civilian population, which is all people 16 years of age and older who are living in the United States and are not confined to penal, mental, senior-nursing, or other institutions, and are not on active duty with the armed forces. (http://stats.bls.gov/bls./glossary.htm#c)

| TABLE 4.1 | | *The Labor Force, the Participation Rate, and Unemployment*[a] | | | |

Many labor-related statistics are collected in the United States. Some of the most important are the labor force, the participation rate, and the unemployment rate.

Year	Population Eligible for Labor Force[b]	Civilian Labor Force	Participation Rate	Unemployed Persons	Unemployment Rate
1929	—	49,180,000	—	1,550,000	3.2%
1933	—	51,590,000	—	12,830,000	24.9
1940	99,840,000	55,640,000	55.7%	8,120,000	14.6
1945	94,090,000	53,860,000	57.2	1,040,000	1.9
1950	104,995,000	62,208,000	59.2	3,288,000	5.3
1955	109,683,000	65,023,000	59.3	2,852,000	4.4
1960	117,245,000	69,628,000	59.4	3,852,000	5.5
1965	126,513,000	74,455,000	58.9	3,366,000	4.5
1970	137,085,000	82,771,000	60.4	4,093,000	4.9
1975	153,153,000	93,775,000	61.2	7,929,000	8.5
1980	167,745,000	106,940,000	63.8	7,637,000	7.1
1985	178,206,000	115,461,000	64.8	8,312,000	7.2
1990	189,164,000	125,840,000	66.5	7,047,000	5.6
1991	190,925,000	126,346,000	66.2	8,628,000	6.8
1992	192,805,000	128,105,000	66.4	9,613,000	7.5
1993	194,838,000	129,200,000	66.3	8,940,000	6.9
1994	196,814,000	131,056,000	66.6	7,996,000	6.1
1995	198,584,000	132,304,000	66.6	7,404,000	5.6
1996	200,591,000	133,943,000	66.8	7,236,000	5.4
1997	203,133,000	136,297,000	67.1	6,739,000	4.9
1998	205,220,000	137,673,000	67.1	6,210,000	4.5
1999	207,753,000	139,368,000	67.1	5,880,000	4.2
2000	212,577,000	142,583,000	67.1	5,692,000	4.0
2001	215,092,000	143,734,000	66.8	6,801,000	4.7
2002	217,570,000	144,863,000	66.6	8,378,000	5.8
2003	221,168,000	146,510,000	66.2	8,774,000	6.0
2004	223,357,000	147,401,000	66.0	8,149,000	5.5
2005	226,082,000	149,320,000	66.0	7,591,000	5.1
2006	228,815,000	151,428,000	66.2	7,001,000	4.6
2007	231,867,000	153,124,000	66.0	7,078,000	4.6
2008[c]	234,828,000	154,616,000	65.8	10,331,000	6.7

[a]Some adjustments in the population definitions that affect the year-to-year comparability of the data have been made over time. For additional information concerning these adjustments, see the source for this table.

[b] This and all other columns refer to the noninstitutional civilian population.

[c] Figures for November 2008.

Source: *Economic Report of the President* (Washington, DC: U.S. Government Printing Office, 2009), pp. 326–327.

the increased participation of women. At the same time, the table shows a drop in the participation rate for men. What do you think is causing women to increasingly join—and men to increasingly leave—the labor force? Why do you think the participation rate for teenagers has decreased since 1980?

TABLE 4.2	*Participation Rates: Civilian Labor Force and Subgroups for Selected Years*

Participation rates differ among subgroups in the labor force. Changes in participation rates affect the composition of the labor force over time.

Group[a]	1970	1980	1990	2000	2008[b]
Overall	60.4%	63.8%	66.5%	67.1%	65.8%
Males	79.7	77.4	76.4	74.8	72.7
Females	43.3	51.5	57.5	59.9	59.4
Teenagers (16–19 years old)	49.9	56.7	53.7	52.0	38.3

[a]Includes persons 16 years of age and older in the civilian population.
[b]Numbers are for November 2008.

Source: *Economic Report of the President* (Washington, DC: U.S. Government Printing Office, 2009), p. 331.

Table 4.3 lists unemployment rates for selected labor market subgroups during several different years. We can make some interesting observations. Notice the disparity in the unemployment rates of the various subgroups for any given year. For example, in 2007 the unemployment rate for married men was 2.5 percent, compared to 15.7 percent for teenagers and 4.7 percent for all men. You might also notice that, over time, some groups tend to have higher unemployment rates, and other groups

TABLE 4.3	*Unemployment Rates: All Workers and Labor Force Subgroups for Selected Years*

Over the years, some groups in the labor force, such as teenagers, have faced more severe unemployment problems than other groups.

Group[a]	1985	1990	1995	2000	2007
All workers	7.2%	5.6%	5.6%	4.0%	4.6%
Male	7.0	5.7	5.6	3.9	4.7
Female	7.4	5.5	5.6	4.1	4.5
Married men, spouse present	4.3	3.4	3.3	2.0	2.5
Women who maintain families	10.4	8.3	8.0	5.9	6.5
Teenagers (16–19 years old)	18.6	15.5	17.3	13.1	15.7
Males with less than 4 years of high school[b]	11.2	9.6	10.9	5.4	6.6
Males with 4 or more years of college[b]	2.4	2.1	2.6	1.5	1.9

[a]Includes persons 16 years of age or older in the civilian labor force.

[b]Data for 2000 and 2007 are for males with less than a high school diploma and for those with a bachelor's degree or more.

Sources: *Economic Report of the President* (Washington, DC: U.S. Government Printing Office, 2009), p. 334. 1985–1990 data for male high school dropouts and men with 4 or more years of college are from U.S. Bureau of the Census, *Statistical Abstract of the United States: 1996*, 116th ed. (Washington, DC: U.S. Government Printing Office, 1996), p. 415; 1995 are from *Statistical Abstract: 2001*, 121st ed., p. 389; 2000 and 2007 are from *Statistical Abstract: 2009*, 128th ed., p. 395.

have lower rates. For example, the data in Table 4.3 show a better employment experience for married men (compared to all workers taken as a group), but not for women who maintain families. Also, men with 4 or more years of college have fared relatively well, while male high school dropouts have fared poorly. These statistics raise an important policy question: should government unemployment programs be directed toward the unemployed generally or toward specific groups?

Calculating Unemployment Statistics

The U.S. Department of Labor, Bureau of Labor Statistics (BLS), calculates unemployment rates and other labor force data on a monthly and annual basis.[7] Each month's calculations are published by the BLS, and the overall unemployment rate is given wide coverage by the media. Contrary to what many people think, unemployment statistics are not based on numbers reported to the U.S. government by state employment offices. Rather, they are derived from a survey conducted for the BLS, called the Current Population Survey.

Each month a scientifically developed sample of households from across the United States is surveyed through interviews. On the basis of their responses, persons are classified as employed, unemployed, or not in the labor force.

Many people find the requirements to be classified as employed a surprise. A person is classified as employed if, during the survey week, that person

♦ did *any* work—even just 1 hour—as a paid employee, or in his or her own business, profession, or on his or her own farm,
♦ worked without pay for 15 or more hours in a family-operated business, or
♦ was temporarily away from a job or business due to illness, weather, vacation, labor-management disputes, or personal reasons.

As a result of the way in which we officially classify the employment status of people, many who are seeking to work more hours or full-time while doing limited work for themselves or others (even just 1 hour of work per week) show up as "employed" in government data.

Interpreting Unemployment Statistics

There are some subtle, but important, details we should keep in mind when evaluating unemployment statistics.

Discouraged Workers
Persons who drop out of the labor force because they have been unsuccessful for a long period of time in finding a job.

Sometimes people become **discouraged workers**: They search unsuccessfully for a job for a long time, then lose hope for employment, give up the job search, and drop out of the labor force. Because the unemployment rate measures only those who are unemployed and *actively* seeking work, discouraged workers are excluded from the statistic: They are not counted as unemployed. By excluding discouraged workers, the unemployment rate understates the true level of unemployment in the economy. The number of discouraged workers changes with economic conditions. It is higher when the economy is in a downswing and work is harder to find than when the economy is close to full employment and work is easier to find.

The overall unemployment rate is a national figure and does not tell us the unemployment situation in various parts of the country. With such a diversity of industries

---

[7]The following is based on U.S. Department of Labor, Bureau of Labor Statistics, *BLS Handbook of Methods*, April 1997 Edition (last modified April 17, 2003), Ch. 1, http://www.bls.gov/opub/hom/homch1_b.htm, "Description of the Survey," http://www.bls.gov/opub/hom/homch1_c.htm, "Concepts."

in the United States, it is possible that a slowdown in one of them, such as the auto industry or defense-related airplane manufacturing, will have a regional impact that is greater than the impact on the country as a whole. Today there is growing emphasis on evaluating the impact of regional unemployment. Think about the region in which you live. What industries are at the base of its economy? What impact would a slowdown in one of these have on your region?

The overall unemployment rate provides no information about the jobs held by the employed. It does not indicate how many people classified as employed are working part-time but are seeking permanent full-time work. Recall that even one hour of work can label a person as employed. With the increasing costs of health insurance and other benefits, there has been substantial growth in temporary and part-time employment.

Underemployment

A resource is not used to its fullest productive capability.

The overall unemployment rate does not provide information about those who are underemployed. **Underemployment** occurs when the full capabilities and skills of a resource are not utilized. Many people with valuable skills and good educations will accept unskilled jobs rather than be unemployed. Consider the college graduate who works as a food server.

The Goal of Full Employment

As stated earlier, full employment is a major macroeconomic goal. However, full employment does *not* mean that 100 percent of the labor force is working. It means that only those who are voluntarily out of work are unemployed.

What is the unemployment rate at which full employment occurs? What percentage of the labor force tends to be voluntarily, or frictionally, unemployed? There are no hard-and-fast answers to these questions.

The rate of unemployment that is associated with full employment has changed over time. At one point we associated full employment with a 4 percent rate of unemployment; during the 1970s and 1980s we thought that it was up to 6 percent. In recent years we again believe that full employment may be as low as a 4 to 5 percent rate of unemployment.

Over the years changes in the structure of the economy have occurred that cause us to periodically reevaluate the unemployment rate associated with full employment. Changes in the composition of the labor force brought about by increased participation of women, and changes in government unemployment compensation payments are two factors to consider. Also, evaluating full employment is further complicated by the growth in temporary and part-time work where jobs are plentiful and people are counted as employed, even though they are seeking full-time work.

Conceptually, full employment means that all resources available for production are *fully* utilized. Thus, the statistic called "full employment" may not perfectly represent the economic concept of full employment.

The ultimate test of where the full employment rate is may be inflationary pressure. As you will soon learn in the next section, a market economy that is operating at full employment, or at capacity, has a tendency to experience inflation.

Natural Rate of Unemployment

The unemployment rate that includes the frictionally and structurally unemployed; occurs when cyclical unemployment is eliminated.

The Natural Rate of Unemployment   Some economists believe that achieving the **natural rate of unemployment,** a different measure than full employment, should be the goal of the macroeconomy. The natural rate of unemployment includes the frictionally and structurally unemployed, or is the rate at which there is no cyclical unemployment. Because it includes the structurally unemployed, the natural rate is higher than the full employment rate and can be achieved with more unemployed workers. The natural rate of unemployment has become a popular goal with some policymakers because traditional macroeconomic stabilization tools, which will be introduced in the next few chapters, are more suited to dealing with cyclical than with structural unemployment. Also, cyclical unemployment is typically of shorter duration than structural unemployment.

INFLATION AND STABLE PRICES

Inflation
An increase in the general level of prices.

Another major macroeconomic goal in the United States is to maintain stable prices, or to control inflation. Like unemployment, inflation can have serious consequences. **Inflation** occurs when there is an increase in the general level of prices. It does not mean that prices are high, but rather that they are increasing. For example, assume that over the past two years the price of a certain collection of goods has been stable at $100 in country A and has gone up from $10 to $30 in country B. Country B, not country A, faces a problem with inflation. Inflation refers to price movements, not price levels.

Since inflation refers to an increase in the *general level* of prices, the price of every good and service need not increase. An inflation rate of 7 percent does not mean that all prices are increasing by 7 percent. Rather, it means that, on average, prices are going up by that amount. Also, an increase in the general level of prices is not necessarily a matter of concern. An economy with an inflation rate of 2 or 3 percent a year does not have a problem. But, when prices increase quickly by a large percentage, such as 8 percent to 10 percent or more per year, inflation becomes a serious issue.

Hyperinflation
Extremely rapid increases in the general level of prices.

How serious can inflation become? Some countries in Europe during the 1920s provide a classic example of **hyperinflation,** or rapid price increases. In January 1922, 48 German paper marks were worth 1 German gold mark. By July of that year it took 160 paper marks to buy 1 gold mark, and by November 1923 it took over 1 trillion paper marks to equal 1 gold mark. But perhaps the worst incidence of hyperinflation occurred in Yugoslavia, when prices increased by 5 quadrillion percent (that's 5,000,000,000,000,000%) from October 1, 1993, to January 24, 1995.[8]

Consequences of Inflation

When an economy experiences inflation, several problems emerge. Inflation can

- intensify scarcity when income does not rise as quickly as prices,
- penalize some groups, such as savers and lenders receiving low interest rates,
- change the value of assets, and
- be politically and socially destabilizing.

Money (Nominal) Income
Income measured in terms of current dollars.

Inflation and Income   Unemployment intensifies scarcity by reducing or even terminating the incomes of some people. Inflation can also reduce a person's income—not in the same way as unemployment—but by reducing the purchasing power of money. With inflation, a given amount of **money,** or **nominal, income**—income measured in terms of current dollars—buys fewer goods and services. Expressed

---

[8]Shephard B. Clough, Thomas Moodie, and Carol Moodie, eds., *Economic History of Europe: Twentieth Century* (New York: Harper & Row, 1968), pp. 111, 124; Thayer Watkins, "The Worst Episode of Hyperinflation in History: Yugoslavia 1993–94," http://www.rogershermansociety.org/yugoslavia.

| FIGURE 4.1 | *The Purchasing Power of Income* |

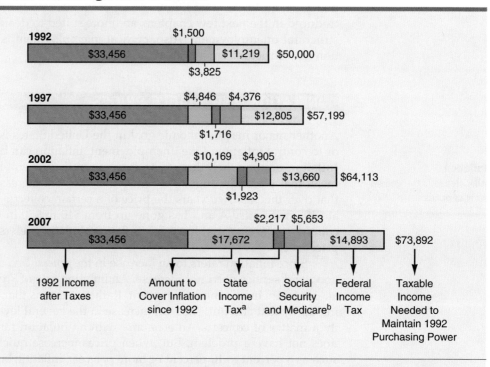

A single person who made a $50,000 taxable income in 1992 would have needed a $73,892 taxable income in 2007 just to maintain the same standard of living or to purchase the same amount of goods and services. This increase was needed to cover inflation and taxes.

[a]State income tax rates vary widely from state to state, so when calculating J.B.'s state income tax payments, a rate of 3% was assumed.
[b]Social Security payments and Medicare are jointly referred to as FICA, or Federal Insurance Contribution Act, taxes.

Sources: U.S. Department of the Treasury, Internal Revenue Service Instructions for Form 1040, 1992, p. 41; 1997, p. 45; 2002, p. 70; 2007, p. 71; US Legal Inc., FICA Taxes Law & Legal Definition, http://definitions.uslegal.com /f/fica-taxes/; *Economic Report of the President* (Washington, D.C.: U.S. Government Printing Office, 2008), p. 295.

Real Income

Income measured in terms of the goods and services that can be purchased with a particular amount of money income.

differently, inflation causes **real income**, or income measured in terms of the goods and services that a sum of money income can purchase, to fall. As a result, people's scarcity problems increase when money incomes do not rise as rapidly as prices.

So, how much must money income increase in the face of inflation to sustain the same purchasing power, or real income, from year to year? Figure 4.1 offers an answer. This figure shows that to maintain the same purchasing power, or real income, with inflation, money income must rise to compensate for both price increases *and* any increases in taxes. For example, Figure 4.1 shows that J.B., a person with a taxable income of $50,000 in 1992, would have been able to purchase $33,456 worth of goods and services after taxes and Social Security contributions. To buy the same amount of goods and services in 2007, J.B. would have needed an income of $73,892. Part of this increase was from the additional $17,672 needed to keep up with inflation, and part was due to J.B.'s tax and Social Security bills of $22,763, which resulted from the larger money income.

Inflation hits some income groups harder than others. People living on a fixed income, such as a pension, are particularly susceptible to inflation. If the size of a pension check remains unchanged while prices keep rising, the purchasing power of that check keeps shrinking. Over time, with serious bouts of inflation, retired persons dependent on fixed incomes may suffer greatly from a declining standard of living.

Contract workers may also be hurt by inflation if their contracted wage increases are less than the inflation rate. For example, the teachers in a school district might sign a contract that provides for an annual wage increase of 4 percent over the next three years, and then encounter inflation rates that range between 6 percent and 9 percent. These teachers will experience a decline in their real standards of living. To avoid this situation, many contracts provide **cost-of-living adjustments (COLAs),** which are automatic wage or payment increases when prices go up.

Inflation and the Interest Rate   Lenders, borrowers, and savers refer to the price of money as an **interest rate.** Interest rates determine how much savers receive for their money, how much borrowers pay for loans, and how much lenders receive for making a loan.

Those who save may be hurt by inflation if the interest rate they receive is less than the rate of inflation. Take the case of Martha and John Quinn, who inherited $100,000 in 1988. They decided to save it for college expenses for their future children and put the money in a bank account, where it earned 3 percent annual interest. In 2008, when the money was needed, the $100,000 had grown to $170,243.

How much better off were the Quinns in 2008 with the additional earned interest? Between the time they put the money in the bank and 2008, prices had risen. What they could have purchased for $100,000 in 1988 cost $181,592 in mid-2008.[9] The additional interest they earned did not keep up with the rate of inflation. Also, the Quinns had to pay income tax on the interest they earned from this money, further reducing its buying power. People who save their money can be penalized by inflation if the after-tax interest they earn on their savings does not keep up with the inflation rate.

Lenders may also be hurt by inflation if the interest rate they charge is less than the rate of inflation and if the terms of the loans are fixed and cannot be altered to allow interest rate increases. This problem sometimes occurs when a lender makes a long-term loan commitment.[10] Experience has taught many lenders to transfer risks to borrowers. Many home mortgages are currently made with variable rates and flexible terms.

On the other hand, borrowers can benefit from low interest rates, especially if inflation occurs. Consider the wave that began about 2002 when large numbers of homeowners sought to refinance their homes at historically low rates. These lower interest rates significantly reduced monthly mortgage payments. When homeowners lock in low mortgage rates or students lock in low rates on student loans, they transfer much of the risk of inflation to the lenders of such loans.

When we evaluate how inflation affects savers and borrowers, we need to consider the real rate of interest. The **real rate of interest** is the nominal, or stated, interest rate minus the inflation rate. For example, if the nominal interest rate on a certificate of deposit (CD) is 6 percent and the inflation rate is 8 percent, the real rate

Cost-of-Living Adjustment (COLA)
An arrangement whereby an individual's wages automatically increase with inflation.

Interest Rate
The price of money; determines the return to savers and lenders of money, and the cost to borrowers.

Real Rate of Interest
The nominal, or stated, rate of interest minus the inflation rate; a nominal interest rate adjusted for inflation.

[9]Based on the Consumer Price Index for all items, *Economic Report of the President* (Washington, DC: U.S.: Government Printing Office, 2008), p. 295; U.S. Department of Labor, Consumer Price Index Summary, May 14, 2008. Price index number for April 2008. http://www.bls.gov/news.release/cpi.nr0.htm.
[10]A fixed rate means that the interest rate does not change during the loan repayment period. A long-term loan means that the borrower has a considerable period of time for repayment, perhaps as much as 30 years.

TABLE 4.4	*Winners and Losers from Inflation*

For some people inflation creates opportunities and for others it creates problems.

Winners	Losers
People with after-tax income rising faster than the rate of inflation	People on fixed incomes or working under contracts with wage increases below the inflation rate
Borrowers paying back loans at an interest rate less than the inflation rate	Savers and lenders earning interest rates below the inflation rate
Owners of assets that increase in value with inflation	People who want to buy assets that are rapidly increasing in price
Politicians gaining support because of their position on inflation	Politicians losing popular support because of their inability to control inflation

of interest on the CD is −2 percent: The saver is hurt by inflation. If the inflation rate is 3 percent during the term of a 6 percent CD, the real rate of interest is 3 percent: The saver has gained by saving.

Inflation and Wealth   Although people may use the terms *income* and *wealth* interchangeably, each has a very different meaning. Income is a flow of earnings from selling factors of production. **Wealth** measures the value of people's tangible assets, or what they own. Wealth includes stocks, bonds, real estate, cash, diamonds, fine art, and such. Someone could have a large income and little wealth, or great wealth and a small income.

During inflation, many assets appreciate, or increase in value, as prices rise. Thus, the wealthy become wealthier. Consider real estate. A home valued at $100,000 in 1995 might well be worth $200,000 today largely as a result of inflation.

While inflation often benefits people who have wealth, it penalizes people who are looking to make asset purchases. Again, consider real estate. As prices rapidly increase, people who want to purchase a home—the largest asset purchase for most people—find it more difficult. Young adults who are trying to purchase that first home pay a high penalty for inflation.

Social and Political Consequences of Inflation   In addition to its economic consequences, inflation may have social and political implications as well. Inflation-related issues often form planks in election campaigns as candidates trade blame and offer solutions.

If prolonged or severe enough, inflation might lead not only to changes in leadership but also to changes in social and political institutions. The eminent British economist John Maynard Keynes wrote, "There is no subtler, no surer means of overturning the existing basis of society than to debauch the currency."[11] The rise of Adolf Hitler and Nazism can be traced in part to the discontent and social disruption caused by the German hyperinflation of the early 1920s.

Table 4.4 summarizes who gains and who loses from inflation.

Wealth
A measure of the value of tangible assets; includes such items as real estate and corporate securities.

---

[11]John Maynard Keynes, *The Economic Consequences of the Peace* (New York: Harcourt, Brace and Howe, 1920), p. 236.

Causes of Inflationary Pressure

Since inflation is an upward movement in the general level of prices, and prices result from the interaction of buyers' and sellers' decisions, economists have created a logical way of classifying the causes of inflation. Inflation that originates from pressure on prices from the buyers' side of the market is termed demand-pull inflation. Inflation that originates from pressure on prices from the sellers' side of the market is called cost-push inflation.

Demand-Pull Inflation When buyers' demands to purchase goods and services outstrip sellers' abilities to supply them, prices on available goods and services rise, and **demand-pull inflation** occurs. When this demand-based spending subsides, so does the pressure on prices.

Demand-pull inflation has a tendency to occur when the economy is close to or at full employment. Recall that at full employment the economy is at full capacity. Since it is producing the maximum amount of goods and services possible, production cannot be easily expanded. At the same time, consumer demand for goods and services is high because more people are working and have money to spend. Businesses may now also find it profitable to expand and begin to spend on investments in new buildings and machinery. This spending pressure by households and businesses, coupled with production at or near capacity, sets off demand-pull inflation.

Demand-pull inflation is also related to the amount of money in the economy. The ability of households and businesses to spend depends in part on the amount of money available for spending. If the supply of money in the economy increases at a faster rate than production, upward pressure on prices can result. If the economy is at full employment and more money is put into the hands of businesses and consumers, the result will be inflationary. Thus, too much money in the economy and in the hands of businesses and consumers can contribute to demand-pull inflation.

Cost-Push Inflation When price pressure comes from the sellers' side of the market, **cost-push inflation** occurs. In this case, increases in sellers' costs are wholly or partially passed on to buyers, who will then face higher prices. Anything that is a cost to a business is a potential source of price increases and, if significant enough, of cost-push inflation. Upward pressure on prices could come from increased costs of labor, raw materials, fuels, machinery, borrowing, and even attempts to increase profit.

Classic examples of cost-push inflation have come from oil price increases. In the 1970s and 1980s, energy prices contributed to serious inflation when a barrel of oil that sold for $3.18 in 1970 jumped to $31.77 in 1981. In 2008, oil-induced inflation again surfaced when the price of a barrel of oil increased from $69.61 in July 2007 to $137.11 in July 2008.[12]

More likely, cost-push inflation results when costs push up the prices of businesses that play a large role in the economy, such as car manufacturers, or when the costs push up the prices of a significant number of firms. Increases in the costs of energy, for example, have an impact on almost every seller, large or small, in the economy. There are also fears that the increasing cost of health insurance covered by employers and the higher costs of health care will contribute to inflation.

Demand-Pull Inflation
Pressure on prices from the buyers' side of the market; tends to occur when spending is greater than the productive capability of the economy.

Cost-Push Inflation
Pressure on prices from the sellers' side of the market, particularly from increases in costs of production.

---

[12]U.S. Bureau of the Census, *Statistical Abstract of the United States: 1990*, 110th ed. (Washington, DC: U.S. Government Printing Office, 1990), p. 692; "All Countries Spot Price FOB Weighted by Estimated Export Volume (Dollars per Barrel)," http://tonto.eia.doe.gov, August 15, 2008.

APPLICATION 4.2

THE $4 SUMMER OF 2008

It seemed that the United States needed to add a $4 bill to its currency during the summer of 2008. Quite suddenly the price of two staples of ordinary life—gas and milk—hit $4 a gallon. The $4 price of these key necessities wrecked family budgets, summer vacation plans, and trips to visit grandma. For some businesses, from pizza delivery to household moving companies, these price increases caused huge havoc. Even cities suffered as they gassed up their three-mile-per gallon fire trucks.

We knew an oil-based energy problem was looming. Americans became used to gas-guzzling SUVs and trucks as these vehicles zoomed in popularity. We neglected to fund good public transportation. China and India were growing quickly and putting huge demands on energy sources. There was disruption in oil supplies with the war in Iraq. But, what we didn't anticipate was the suddenness and severity of the rise in oil and gasoline prices.

We also didn't think that another staple of ordinary life—milk—would take such a large price jump. Yet, it was another consequence of the energy crisis. As alternatives to fueling vehicles with gas were pursued, there was a turn toward ethanol. Ethanol is produced primarily from corn, a key ingredient in the diet of farm animals. Farmers who paid $2.04 for a bushel of corn in 2006 were suddenly faced with prices in excess of $5.70 per bushel in June of 2008 as the demand for corn increased.[a]

There are not many good alternatives to a gallon of gas or a gallon of milk. In the summer of 2008 families were stuck with figuring out how to purchase these necessities and live within their means. But, for many businesses to survive, there was no choice but to raise the price of their products. This included farmers in the dairy business and food suppliers who had to haul goods by truck.

Here is a tale of cost-push inflation. By late summer 2008, the $4 gallon was certainly fueling inflation. CPI data indicated that prices increased over the summer by 7.2% and that energy increased by a whopping 32.9%.[b] Inflation—cost-push inflation—reared its ugly head.

[a]"Monthly Average Corn Farm Price Received in Illinois for the 1960–2008 Calendar Year(s)", www.farmdoc.uiuc.edu, August 14, 2008.
[b]Bureau of Labor Statistics, "Economic News Release, Consumer Price Index Summary," http://www.bls.gov/news.release/cpi.nr0.htm. Figures are percent changes in CPI for all urban consumers (CPI-U) for June, July, and August 2008.

Cost-push and demand-pull inflation can come simultaneously and have a potential to spiral. An increase in overall spending that leads to demand-pull inflation could cause people to negotiate higher wages to compensate for the inflation. Employers who now face increased wage costs may pass them on to buyers through higher prices. It is easy to see the escalating pattern of inflation as rising prices from increased spending can fuel increased wages that can fuel increased prices to cover them. Application 4.2, "The $4 Summer of 2008," focuses on cost-push inflation. Can you see from this application the potential for a spiraling of prices as people seek higher wages to cope with the inflation?

The Role of Expectations   Expectations about inflation can cause inflation to occur. On the demand-pull side, buyers' fears of higher prices in the future may lead them to increase their current spending before the expected higher prices become reality. At full employment, this increased spending puts additional pressure on an economy already operating at productive capacity and results in inflation. On the sellers' side, firms that expect increasing costs might raise prices in anticipation of those higher costs. Thus, a curious situation results in which the expectation of rising prices can trigger inflation.

Measures of Inflation

We measure changes in price levels by using a scale called a price index. Price indexes use percentages and provide an easy method to compare and evaluate price changes. The government maintains three primary price indexes to measure inflation,

TABLE 4.5   *A Price Index*

The annual dollar outlays over time for a market basket of goods and services are converted to a percentage scale called a price index. Year 2 is the base year of this index.

Year	Dollar Outlay for Market Basket	Price Index
1	$475	95.0
2	500	100.0
3	550	110.0
4	600	120.0
5	625	125.0
6	750	150.0

each focusing on the prices of a collection of goods and services important to a particular segment of the economy. These are

♦ the Consumer Price Index (CPI), which focuses on goods and services typically purchased by households;
♦ the Producer Price Index (PPI), which focuses on production inputs purchased by businesses; and
♦ the GDP Price Index, which measures price changes in the economy as a whole.

Before we examine these indexes, we will work through an exercise that will help you understand what a price index is, how it is constructed, and how it is interpreted.

Price Index
Measures changes in the price of an item or a group of items using a percentage scale.

Constructing a Price Index   A **price index** is a measure of price changes using a percentage scale. A price index can be based on the prices of a single item or a selected group of items, called a market basket. For example, several hundred goods and services, such as housing, electricity, and automobiles, are used to calculate the Consumer Price Index. Because a market basket includes a range of goods and services, it is a more comprehensive measure of inflationary pressure than a single item.

Table 4.5 demonstrates how to calculate a simple price index. The column headed Dollar Outlay for Market Basket gives the expenditure required to purchase the same items in years 1 through 6. Notice that this expenditure increases each year: The same goods and services that cost $475 in year 1 cost $600 in year 4.

Actual dollar outlays for the market basket are converted to a percentage scale, the price index, which is shown in the right-hand column of Table 4.5. To create an index, a **base year** is selected to serve as the year against which all other years' prices are compared. The base year is given the number of 100.0, or 100 percent, in the index. In Table 4.5, year 2 is the base year.

Base Year
The year against which prices in other years are compared in a price index; given the index number 100.0.

The index numbers for the other years represent, in percentages, how many more or fewer dollars than base year dollars are needed to buy the same items. The equation for calculating an index number for a given year is

$$\frac{\text{dollar outlay for a given year}}{\text{dollar outlay for the base year}} \times 100 = \text{price index number for a given year.}$$

TABLE 4.6   *Consumer Price Index: All Items and Various Categories for Selected Years*
(1982–1984 = 100.0)

The Consumer Price Index measures changes in the prices of goods and services that
consumers typically purchase. Increases in prices for some components in the index,
such as medical care, have been greater than the increase in the overall index.

Year	All Items	Food	Rent, Residential	Household Energy[a]	Apparel	Medical Care
1970	38.8	39.2	46.5	23.1	59.2	34.0
1975	53.8	59.8	58.0	39.4	72.5	47.5
1980	82.4	86.8	80.9	74.8	90.9	74.9
1985	107.6	105.6	111.8	104.5	105.0	113.5
1990	130.7	132.4	138.4	104.5	124.1	162.8
1995	152.4	148.4	157.8	111.5	132.0	220.5
2000	172.2	167.8	183.9	122.8	129.6	260.8
2001	177.1	173.1	192.1	135.4	127.3	272.8
2002	179.9	176.2	199.7	127.2	124.0	285.6
2003	184.0	180.0	205.5	138.2	120.9	297.1
2004	188.9	186.2	211.0	144.4	120.4	310.1
2005	195.3	190.7	217.3	161.6	119.5	323.2
2006	201.6	195.2	225.1	177.1	119.5	336.2
2007	207.3	202.9	234.7	181.7	119.0	351.1
2008[b]	216.6	218.8	245.9	201.2	122.2	365.7

[a]Includes piped gas, electricity, and other items not shown separately.

[b]Numbers are for October 2008.

Source: *Economic Report of the President* (Washington, DC: U.S. Government Printing Office, 2009), pp. 353–354.

For example, in year 4, $600 is needed to buy what $500 bought in the base year.
Putting these numbers into the equation yields

$$\frac{\$600}{\$500} \times 100 = 120.0.$$

The price index number of 120.0 indicates that prices have gone up by 20 percent
from year 2 to year 4. Expressed differently, a person must spend an additional
$100, or 20 percent more, in year 4 to buy what $500 bought in year 2, the base
year.

   The same goods and services that cost $500 in year 2 cost $475 in year 1. Using the
price index equation, this means that the index number for year 1 is ($475/$500) ×
100 = 95.0. Only 95 percent of the dollars used in year 2 were needed in year 1 to buy
the same basket of goods. Prices were 5 percent lower in year 1 than in the base year.

   We read the index numbers for each of the remaining years in the same way as
years 1 and 4. The index number of 125.0 for year 5 indicates that prices are 25 percent higher in year 5 than in the base year, and the dollar outlay of $750 in year 6 is 50
percent higher than the outlay required in the base year.

The Consumer Price Index   The **Consumer Price Index (CPI)** measures changes in
the prices of goods and services typically bought by consumers. In Table 4.6 we see,

**Consumer Price
Index (CPI)**

Measures changes in the
prices of goods and services
that consumers typically
purchase, such as food,
shelter, clothing, and
medical care.

for selected years, the overall CPI as well as separate indexes for various categories of goods and services within the CPI, such as rent, medical care, and household energy. In this table the base year comes from averaging prices over three years: 1982, 1983, and 1984.[13]

We can make some interesting observations about the CPI from this table. In the All Items column, notice the movement in overall consumer prices over the years. What households could purchase for $100 on average in the base period cost $38.80 in 1970 and $216.60 in 2008. Also observe in Table 4.6 that the prices in some categories of goods and services increased by less than the overall index and some by more. Notice, for example, the Apparel category: Not only are the index numbers less than the overall CPI, but they actually fell for most years listed. On the other hand, the numbers for Medical Care grew much faster than the overall index between the base and 2008 when the number was 365.7 for medical care as compared to 216.6 overall. Given the movement of the Medical Care price numbers, it should come as no surprise that the management of health care costs has been an ongoing concern and political issue.

Because a price index compares price changes between a given year and a base year, rather than year-to-year, annual percentage changes in prices, or inflation rates, are not obvious. As a result, Table 4.6 may mask serious inflationary problems the United States faced in the 1970s and early 1980s. Figure 4.2 traces the annual percentage change in the CPI from 1970 through mid-2008.[14] This figure illustrates that inflation was particularly serious in 1974 and 1975, and from 1979 through 1981. Beginning in the mid-1980s and continuing into the twenty-first century, inflation has been much less of a problem for households. The sudden rise in energy prices in 2008 had some influence on the price increases for that year.

Changes in the Consumer Price Index and other indexes are calculated monthly. Because they show monthly changes, the numbers are usually small. These monthly changes must be compounded to arrive at an annual figure for comparison. That is, if a 1.1 percent monthly change in the prices of all items were to persist throughout the year, it would lead to an annual inflation rate of 14.0 percent.

Producer Price Index (PPI)

Measures changes in the prices of goods and services that businesses buy, either for further processing or for sale to a consumer.

Other Price Indexes   As noted earlier, two other indexes, in addition to the CPI, are watched when measuring inflation in the economy: the Producer Price Index and the GDP Price Index.

The **Producer Price Index (PPI)** measures changes in the prices that businesses pay for materials they consume, such as energy and supplies, and goods and services

---

[13]These numbers are not shown in Table 4.6. This average is calculated by adding the numbers for the three years together, dividing by 3, and then using the average of the three years for the base dollar outlay. This further means that the index numbers for these three years average 100.0. In the 2009 *Economic Report of the President*, the source of Table 4.6, the index numbers are 96.5 for 1982, 99.6 for 1983, and 103.9 for 1984. Adding these three numbers together and then dividing by 3 gives us 100.0.

[14]To determine an annual percentage change in prices between two consecutive years, 1 and 2, in a price index, use the following equation:

$$\frac{\text{year 2 index number } - \text{ year 1 index number}}{\text{year 1 index number}} \times 100 = \text{annual percentage change.}$$

For example, using the numbers in the All Items column in Table 4.6, the price change from 2003 (year 1) to 2004 (year 2) would be:

$$\frac{188.9 - 184.0}{184.0} \times 100 = 2.66\%.$$

FIGURE 4.2   *Annual Percentage Changes in the Overall CPI*

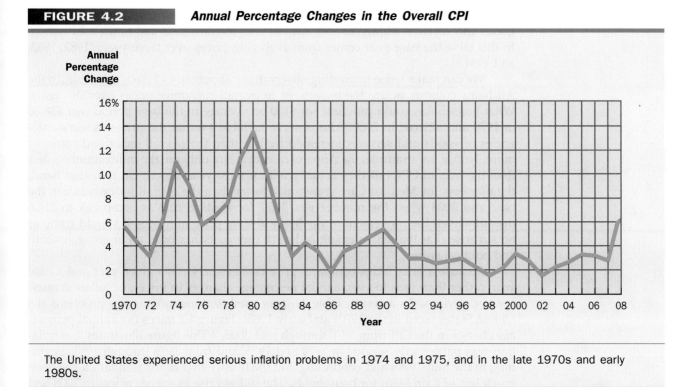

The United States experienced serious inflation problems in 1974 and 1975, and in the late 1970s and early 1980s.

Source: *Economic Report of the President* (Washington, DC: U.S. Government Printing Office, 2009), p. 353, 357. 2008 change is for mid-2008.

they buy for further sale. Just as with the Consumer Price Index, the government calculates and announces the Producer Price Index monthly. The PPI has an important connection to the CPI and is watched carefully. Changes in the prices that businesses pay now often contribute to changes in the prices that consumers pay later. As a result, changes in the PPI may lead to future changes in the CPI.

GDP Price Index
The price index used when calculating price changes for the entire economy.

The **GDP Price Index** is used to measure price changes for the entire economy and is calculated in a slightly different way from the CPI and PPI. The use of this index is discussed later in this chapter.

Importance of Indexes   Academics, businesspeople, and government officials do not study price indexes out of idle curiosity. Rather, they have an important impact on policymakers' decisions and on the operation of the economy. They directly affect wages of union workers who receive cost-of-living adjustments based on the CPI, and they influence the size of many nonunion income payments as well. Employers and employees often look to these indexes in determining fair salary increases. Some government programs, such as Social Security, base changes in monthly checks on a variation of one of these indexes. Private business contracts may provide for price adjustments based on the Producer Price Index and, in some instances, other payments such as child support and rent have been tied to one of these indexes.

Deflation and Disinflation

Deflation
A sustained decrease in the general level of prices.

We must note two important terms before leaving the discussion of inflation: deflation and disinflation. **Deflation** occurs when there is a sustained decrease in the general level of prices. This does not mean that a few items decrease in price or that there is a decrease for a short period of time. In the United States, deflation has not occurred since the 1930s.

Although a sustained decrease in the general level of prices might sound attractive, deflation, like inflation, can create problems for households and businesses. For example, homeowners who want to move could be forced to sell their houses for less than they paid for them, and businesses could suffer losses if their products' prices dropped to a level that did not cover previously incurred production costs. Also, people might be less enthusiastic about deflation when one of the prices that drops is the price they get for their labor.

Disinflation
A slowing of the inflation rate.

We refer to a reduction of the inflation rate as **disinflation.** Disinflation does not mean that prices are falling; rather it refers to a slowing of the inflation rate, or increases in prices. For example, the movement of the CPI in Figure 4.2 from 1990 to 1994 and any other sequence of years when the line is falling illustrates disinflation. When Congress and the Federal Reserve try to slow inflation through their actions, they are pursuing disinflation. Tools available for pursuing disinflation are discussed in Chapters 6 and 8.

PRODUCTION

Production
The creation of goods and services.

Production is the creation of goods and services. Productive activities range from the construction of a piano to the repair of a dented car door. Shipping goods from wholesalers to discount houses constitutes production, as do the grocery store services of renting carpet cleaners and cashing checks. Because production is linked to an economy's standard of living and employment, it is important to measure an economy's overall output and its capacity to produce. Any discussion of setting and reaching macro goals and working through macro problems is based on having data about an economy's production.

Full Production and Economic Growth

Full Production
Occurs when an economy is producing at its maximum capacity, or when it is experiencing full employment.

An economy achieves the macroeconomic goal of **full production** when it produces as much as possible with its available resources, or operates at its maximum capacity. Although the problem of scarcity always exists, full production permits an economy to minimize its impact. Production and employment are interrelated: When an economy reaches full employment, it also reaches full production. When resources are unemployed, full productive capacity is not met.

Economic Growth
An increase in an economy's full production output level over time.

In addition to full production, this macroeconomic goal calls for **economic growth,** which means that the economy's full production–full employment level of output grows over time. In other words, to achieve this goal, the economy must operate at maximum capacity and that capacity must grow over time.

The production possibilities curves for capital and consumer goods in Figure 4.3 illustrate the concept of economic growth. This economy would reach full production in the first year by producing at any point, such as A, on the production possibilities curve for year 1. Economic growth occurs when the production possibilities curve shifts to the right, as is done for the second and third years. This economy

FIGURE 4.3   *Economic Growth*

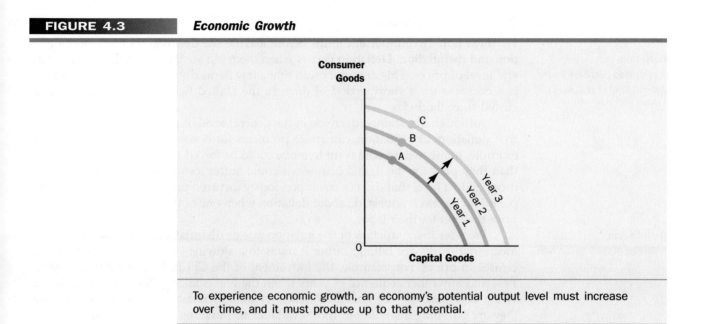

To experience economic growth, an economy's potential output level must increase over time, and it must produce up to that potential.

would achieve the third macroeconomic goal of full production and economic growth if it were to produce at a point such as B along the curve for year 2 and C for year 3.

Economic growth is a goal accomplished over years. It is best understood as a series of small, cumulative advances in full employment output, perhaps in the neighborhood of 2 percent to 5 percent per year, rather than a few large, dramatic leaps from time to time.

Although economic growth is generally defined as an increase in full production output over time, we get a better measure of growth by evaluating full production output per capita over time. If output increases, but population grows more quickly, output per person decreases. Even with more goods and services available, on the average people would be worse off.

The growth of real output per capita in the United States from 1980 through 2008 is illustrated in Figure 4.4. (Real output measures output with the effects of inflation removed and is explained in the next few pages.) Although the figure shows actual production rather than full employment production, it indicates that real output per person has grown substantially over the years. In 1980, when the U.S. population was approximately 228 million, the economy produced $22,666 of real output per person. By 2008, when the population was approximately 300 million, real output per person had grown to $38,362.[15]

Achieving Economic Growth   Simply, an economy's production levels are based on the number of resources available to it and how those resources are used. Thus, economic growth can occur only if more resources are available or resources are used more efficiently. For example, a labor force can be expanded through immigration; new sources of oil and natural gas can be located through drilling; people can

[15]*Economic Report of the President* (Washington, DC: U.S. Government Printing Office, 2009), p. 321. Real output for 2008 is through the third quarter and preliminary.

FIGURE 4.4   *U.S. Economic Growth: Real Output per Capita[a]*

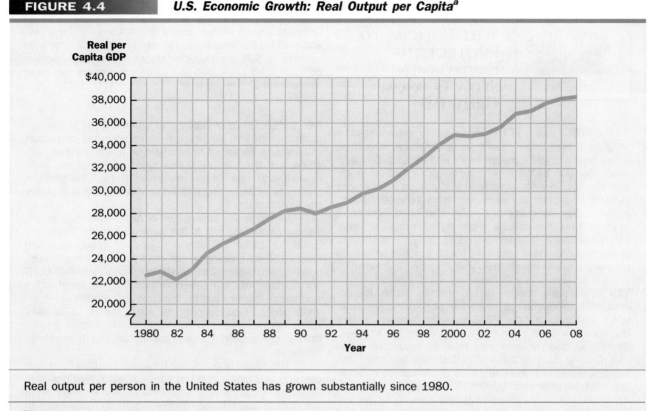

Real output per person in the United States has grown substantially since 1980.

[a]Real output is in chained 2000 dollars.

Source: *Economic Report of the President* (Washington, DC: U.S. Government Printing Office, 2009), p. 321.

become more entrepreneurial; or increases in capital such as machines and buildings can occur. Government can play an important role in encouraging economic growth through policies that impact the availability and use of resources. Changes in the tax code, interest rates, or immigration policy, for example, can foster a change in resources.

Technological change is probably the most important force leading to economic growth. **Technology** is the state of knowledge about production and its processes. In today's world, technology is influencing production in a rapid and dramatic way. Information is immediately available and we can communicate quickly. As a result, everything from the production of this textbook to new medical procedures that have come from breakthroughs in biochemistry or biomedical engineering has been touched by technology.

Sometimes we associate technological change with investments in equipment such as computers. However, investments in people through formal education, training, wellness, and other ways, or **human capital investments,** increase productivity in an important way. When people are better educated and trained, the quality of a workforce is strengthened, individuals are more productive, and the overall level of knowledge in the economy is increased. This knowledge base, in turn, ensures that technological change will continue. An economy of healthy, educated people almost ensures economic growth.

Technology
Increase in knowledge about production and its processes.

Human Capital Investments
Investments, such as formal education, that increase the productivity of people.

WILL POLICIES TO PROTECT THE ENVIRONMENT SLOW ECONOMIC GROWTH?

We are keenly aware of the impact of our current style of living and production on the world's natural resources: global warming, deterioration in air and water quality, and rapid depletion of the limited supply of oil and other energy sources. There is recognition that policies must be put in place to protect the earth for future generations, and global support for doing so. On the other hand, opposition to these protective policies is coming from those who believe that such policies will slow down the world's economies and cause economic stagnation. Will policies to protect the environment actually slow economic growth?

YES   It's really obvious that in order to "clean" the environment, production all over the world must be lessened. Just consider the 2008 summer Olympics in Beijing, China, when in order to clear the air for the athletes, China shut down a large number of its production facilities. Closing many of the world's factories and other polluting facilities will send hundreds of thousands of workers into unemployment. Economies will stagnate.

Cleaner air requires that people drive less. This will have a huge impact on individual lifestyles as they find ways to lessen their discretionary driving. People will patronize restaurants and entertainment venues less and not drive to shopping malls and stores with as much frequency. This has the potential to cause many small businesses and retail outlets to fail.

There are many other negative economic consequences of environmental regulations. As people are forced to lessen the use of resources, there will be an associated loss of jobs from mail carriers to truck drivers to workers in SUV plants. Government entities that provide police and fire protection and code enforcement may have to lessen their service levels to meet environmental regulations.

NO   Policies to protect the environment will encourage economic growth. While there could be some disruption without time to adjust to regulations, a well-planned transition will result in many new types of industries, businesses, and jobs. People are smart and will conquer the challenge of producing and living in a world that protects the environment.

We know the advantages of new technology, accessible information, and better communication. These will move us toward a different kind of production and lifestyle. Take building as an example. Today many businesses and educational institutions are seeking LEED certification[a] of their new construction. This certification promotes efficiencies in the use of resources—from green roofs to solar energy to water runoff. LEED does not bring a decrease in economic growth, rather it is inspiring changes in the way architects and builders do business.

The future is promising for economic growth as life, careers, and production change—not stop. Single-stream recycling, hybrid cars, rainwater reuse, and so much more are already contributing to growth, with so much more to come.

[a]The LEED (Leadership in Energy and Environmental Design) Green Building Rating System is a certification program with nationally accepted benchmarks for the design, construction, and operation of high-performance green buildings. http://www.usgbc.org.

We must also pay attention to maintaining a strong demand for the goods and services the economy produces if we want to achieve economic growth. Insufficient demand could hold back the benefits of growth and result in unemployment or underutilization of resources.

Costs of Economic Growth   Not everyone agrees that a high rate of economic growth is a desirable goal. Today, more than ever, people argue that significant future costs are attached to a push for continually increasing production. The growth of the U.S. economy that has brought its annual output to over $14 trillion has resulted in the creation of billions of tons of garbage, including toxic, nonbiodegradable, and nuclear waste. Now and in the years to come, this waste is becoming costly as landfills close, toxic chemicals seep into the soil, and health problems multiply. We are also aware that the rapid economic growth in countries like China has brought severe air pollution and that global warming is another consequence of rapid growth.

Some people argue that it may be better to produce a smaller output, perhaps with no growth, and deal with the waste and other problems that create future costs. Other people oppose high rates of economic growth because of the dissatisfaction that must be generated about people's possessions to encourage them to continually want new and "better" items. In addition, there is also concern about the depletion of resources that are not easily regenerated and will become a problem of the future.

"Up For Debate: Will Policies to Protect the Environment Slow Economic Growth?" addresses the debate over the relationship between environmental regulatory policies and economic growth.

Measures of Production

Gross Domestic Product (GDP)

A dollar figure that measures the value of all finished goods and services produced in an economy in 1 year.

The United States, as well as most other countries, calculates on a regular basis how much its economy has produced. **Gross domestic product,** or **GDP,** is the dollar figure that measures the value of all the *finished* goods and services produced in an economy in 1 year. GDP counts only finished goods and services, which are those ready for sale to their final users: Products in a stage of production, or not yet completed, are not included. If we included an item in the process of production, say the flour for pasta, and then included it again when the product was completed, say linguini noodles, production would be overstated.

It is also important to understand that GDP measures goods and services produced, not sold. We do not count goods involved in secondhand sales, such as a student's purchase of a 2004 car, because these goods were counted in GDP when they were originally produced. We also do not count purchases of "paper" such as stocks and bonds because they do not represent production, but rather a transfer of assets.

Money GDP (Current, or Nominal, GDP)

Measures the value of production in terms of prices at the time of production.

Real GDP (Constant GDP)

Money GDP adjusted to eliminate inflation; measures real production.

GDP figures are usually given in two forms: money GDP and real GDP. **Money GDP,** sometimes called **current GDP** or **nominal GDP,** measures the value of production in terms of prices at the time of production. Money GDP is affected by both changes in production and changes in prices. **Real,** or **constant, GDP** is money GDP adjusted to eliminate inflation. It measures actual (real) production and shows how actual production, without price increases, has changed. People who "watch the economy" prefer real GDP rather than money GDP figures for gauging the state of the economy.

Calculating Real GDP   Table 4.7 will help you to understand why real GDP is a better measure of production than money GDP. This table presents a hypothetical economy that produces only automobiles. Notice, in the column Output of Autos, that this economy was stagnant from year 1 to year 2, producing 60 cars in each year, had real growth in year 3 when production increased to 65 cars, and experienced a decline in production during year 4 with a drop to 55 cars. During this period, the economy also experienced inflation: The price of autos increased year after year, as shown in the column Price per Auto.

We calculate money GDP, or the current dollar value of production, by multiplying output times price for each year. In year 1, when the 60 cars produced were $16,000 each, money GDP was $960,000, and in year 2 when the 60 cars produced were $18,000 each, money GDP was $1,080,000. This is given in the fourth column.

Notice that the price increases caused money GDP to climb for each of the 4 years. If we relied solely on the money GDP numbers, we could mistakenly believe that production increased from year to year when it did not. Inflation has distorted these production data.

| TABLE 4.7 | | | *Determining Money GDP and Real GDP* | | | |

Money GDP can give a misleading impression of the output of an economy when the level of prices is changing over time.

Year	Output of Autos	Price per Auto	Money GDP	Auto Price Index	Real GDP
1	60	$16,000	$960,000	100.0	$960,000
2	60	18,000	1,080,000	112.5	960,000
3	65	20,000	1,300,000	125.0	1,040,000
4	55	24,000	1,320,000	150.0	880,000

If we want to assess real levels of production, we need to calculate real GDP. To do so, we need a measure of the price changes over the years. In Table 4.7 the prices of the autos over the 4 years are translated to a price index, given in the Auto Price Index column, using year 1 as the base year. This price index provides the mechanism for converting money GDP to real GDP.

The equation for determining real GDP is

$$\frac{\text{money GDP for a given year}}{\text{price index number for that year}} \times 100 = \text{real GDP for the given year.}$$

The real GDP, for example, for year 2 in Table 4.7 is calculated by dividing the money GDP of $1,080,000 by the index number of 112.5, and multiplying that answer by 100.

It is important to notice in Table 4.7 that real GDP did not change from year 1 to year 2, and that it increased in year 3 and decreased in year 4. Real GDP, not money GDP, reflects the actual annual output for this economy.

Assessing U.S. Production   In Table 4.8 we find money GDP and real GDP for the U.S. economy in selected years. Notice the sheer magnitude of the numbers: Money GDP was over $14 trillion in 2008, putting the average daily output of the U.S. economy over $39 billion.

Table 4.8 includes the GDP price index for the entire economy, which was mentioned earlier in this chapter. The government calculates this index as a measure of overall inflation and uses it to convert money GDP to real GDP. Just as we did in the auto example, we find real GDP for a given year by dividing that year's money GDP by that year's GDP price index number, and then multiplying by 100.[16]

In the base year of the price index, money GDP equals real GDP since the price index value is 100.0. In 2000, the base year in Table 4.8, money GDP and real GDP are equal at $9.82 trillion. In years when a dollar buys more than in the base year, the GDP price index number is less than 100.0, and real GDP is greater than money GDP. Observe that in 1995 the real GDP of $8.03 trillion is greater than the money GDP of $7.40 trillion. In years when a dollar buys less than in the base year, the GDP price index number is greater than 100.0, and real GDP is less than money GDP. In 2007, real GDP is less than money GDP.

[16]If you try to check your understanding of the conversion of money GDP to real GDP by applying the conversion formula to the numbers in Table 4.8, some of your real GDP figures may be slightly different than those given there—partly because the numbers in the table have been rounded, and partly because of some properties of the index.

TABLE 4.8	*Money GDP, Real GDP, and the GDP Price Index for Selected Years*

Real GDP is a much more accurate measure of the economy's performance over time than is money GDP.

Year	Money GDP (Trillions)	Real GDP (Trillions)	GDP Price Index (2000 = 100)
1970	$1.04	$3.77	27.54
1975	1.64	4.31	38.01
1980	2.79	5.16	54.06
1985	4.22	6.05	69.72
1990	5.80	7.11	81.61
1995	7.40	8.03	92.12
1996	7.82	8.33	93.86
1997	8.30	8.70	95.42
1998	8.75	9.07	96.48
1999	9.27	9.47	97.87
2000	9.82	9.82	100.00
2001	10.13	9.89	102.40
2002	10.47	10.05	104.19
2003	10.96	10.30	106.41
2004	11.69	10.68	109.46
2005	12.42	10.99	113.04
2006	13.18	11.29	116.68
2007	13.81	11.52	119.82
2008[a]	14.42	11.71	123.21

[a]Figures are for the third quarter and preliminary.

Source: *Economic Report of the President* (Washington, DC: U.S. Government Printing Office, 2009), pp. 282, 284, 286.

In Table 4.8 we find the reason for using real GDP rather than money GDP to evaluate the economy. Look at the GDP data for 2006 through 2008. Changes in money GDP might lead us to conclude that the economy grew by well over $1 trillion from 2006 to 2008 while the real GDP figures indicate that production levels grew by much less: just two-fifths of a trillion. Money GDP can give a false impression of the economy and mislead people who are unaware of how price changes, or inflation, can distort output measures.

The government calculates and publicly announces GDP figures on both a quarterly and an annual basis. Quarterly figures are used to gauge the health of the economy and are usually reported by the media. Concern is generated when little or no growth occurs in GDP from quarter to quarter.

Test Your Understanding, "Calculating Price Indexes and GDP," provides an opportunity to practice calculating and evaluating price indexes and GDP figures.

Does GDP Tell the Whole Story?

Although we rely on GDP data to evaluate production levels in the U.S. economy, we need to realize that those data do not give us a complete picture of production. GDP figures actually understate our output levels because many goods and services that

TEST YOUR UNDERSTANDING

CALCULATING PRICE INDEXES AND GDP

The following problems provide an opportunity to calculate price indexes, money GDP, and real GDP.

1. Calculate two price indexes for the market basket in the following table. Use year 2 as the base year for the index in column 3, and year 4 as the base year for the index in column 4.

Year	Price of Market Basket	Price Index	Price Index
1	$176		
2	220	100.0	
3	242		
4	275		100.0
5	286		
6	330		

2. Assume that a hypothetical economy produces only water slides for small swimming pools, as given in the following table.

Year	Output (Number of Slides)	Price per Slide
1	500	$10,000
2	550	11,000
3	500	12,500
4	450	13,000
5	600	15,000
6	600	15,500

Determine this economy's money GDP, GDP Price Index, and real GDP assuming that year 1 is the base

year. Record these in the appropriate columns of the following table.

Year	Money GDP	GDP Price Index	Real GDP
1			
2			
3			
4			
5			
6			

3. Below are money GDP and GDP Price Index numbers over several years for a hypothetical economy. Calculate real GDP for each of the years given in the table below and record your answers in the appropriate column. Answer the questions following this table.

Year	Money GDP (Billions)	GDP Price Index	Real GDP (Billions)
2003	$900.0	90.0	
2004	1,000.0	100.0	
2005	1,260.0	105.0	
2006	1,500.0	120.0	
2007	1,600.0	128.0	
2008	1,800.0	150.0	
2009	2,000.0	160.0	

a. On the basis of real GDP, how has this economy performed from year to year?
b. Generally, for the entire period, how does the picture of the economy's performance using real GDP compare with the picture using money GDP?

Answers can be found at the back of the book.

are produced are never included in the calculation. In other words, the U.S. economy is more productive than is reported. Activities that are not included are

♦ nonmarket productive activities,
♦ unreported work, and
♦ swapped services.

Some goods and services are not included in GDP because they are not bought and sold in a market. Many people maintain their own cars, paint their own homes, cook meals, volunteer in hospitals and camps, or spend hours a day "working" without

APPLICATION 4.3

THE BALLAD OF JOE AND MARY

Joe and Mary own a small five acre farm. They work hard to be self-reliant. They grow as much of their food as possible and provide for most of their own needs. Their two children chip in and the family has a rich home life. Their family contributes to the health of their community and the nation . . . but they are not good for the nation's business, because they consume so little.

Joe and Mary realize they can no longer make ends meet. Joe finds a job in the city. He borrows $13,000 to buy a new car and drives 35 miles to work every day. The $13,000 and his yearly gas bill are added to the nation's Gross Domestic Product.

Two years later Mary divorces Joe because she can't handle his bad city moods anymore. The lawyer's $11,000 fee for dividing up the farm and assets is added to the nation's GDP. The people who buy the five acres develop it into townhouses at $200,000 a pop. This results in a spectacular jump in the GDP.

Then, after work one day, Joe and Mary accidentally meet in a pub. They decide to give it another go. They give up their city apartments, sell one of their cars and renovate a barn behind Mary's father's farm. They live frugally, watch their pennies and grow together as a family again. Guess what. The nation's GDP registers a fall and the economists tell us we are worse off.

Source: By Kalle Lasn, from *Adbusters*, Vol 1, No 3, Summer 1990. Reprinted by Permission of Adbusters.

being paid. These activities result in the actual production of goods and services and improve the economy's well-being but are not included in GDP because no pay is involved. If someone were paid to do this work, the dollar value of the output would be included in the accounts. For example, if you teach yourself to use Excel, it is not included in GDP, but if you pay for a course and an instructor teaches you Excel, the value of this service is included in GDP.

When people work for cash and do not report this income to the federal government, the work is not included in GDP. Young people often cut grass or sit with children, accept their wages in cash, and either do not fill out a Form 1040 or do not report it on the form. Sometimes, major work is not reported, such as full-time housecleaning, tip income, or moonlighting by plumbers or electricians. On occasion people will swap services: A dentist maintains the teeth of a lawyer in return for legal advice. Also, people who are engaged in illegal activities likely don't report that income, causing illegal production not to be included in GDP.

Underground Economy
Productive activities that are not reported for tax purposes and are not included in GDP.

We use the term **underground economy** to refer to productive activities that are not reported for tax purposes and are, therefore, not included in GDP. While economists care that these goods and services are not included in GDP, most of the concern about the underground economy centers on the lost tax revenue and the social harm resulting from some of these activities.

We must also note that GDP fails to measure the impact of production and consumption on the environment. It also does not account for future costs that may be incurred from current production. And sometimes GDP is not a sure indicator of the quality of people's lives. Application 4.3, "The Ballad of Joe and Mary," shows that we can be led astray by relying solely on high GDP figures as a testament to a good life.

Productivity

In addition to measuring real GDP, we also periodically evaluate the productivity of our resources. The amount of goods and services that an economy produces is influenced by the way in which its resources are used. Is labor efficient? Is technology fostered in production processes? Is adequate and updated capital equipment used?

Productivity
Concept of assessing the amount of output produced by an economy's resources; often measured specifically by output per worker.

The concept of assessing the amount of output produced by an economy's resources is called **productivity.** Basically, productivity measures output per worker. This measure takes labor plus other factors of production into consideration. Productivity does not measure how hard a person works, but rather the output that results when labor is combined with other inputs. For example, the product per hour of someone who is building a wall for a landscape contractor depends not just on the person but also on the equipment that is used. The number of hybrids that roll off an assembly line at an auto plant each day depends on workers, machinery, management style, energy, and other resources. Productivity increases when the equipment used on the job is technologically advanced and efficient.

Not surprisingly, productivity in the U.S. economy has increased dramatically over the past few decades. This increased productivity provides benefits for the economy. Fundamentally, it lessens the scarcity problem when resources are used more efficiently. In short, we get more goods and services from available resources. More immediate to the goals of macroeconomic policy, improved productivity can ease inflationary pressure by allowing firms to meet rising costs through increased output rather than through higher prices. Increased productivity can change employment opportunities: It may stimulate new, higher-skilled jobs, but it may also result in some structural unemployment.

A POSSIBLE POLICY PROBLEM

In the Employment Act of 1946, the federal government officially committed to help create an environment conducive to reaching full employment, full production, and price stability. While each of these goals is desirable, it may be difficult to simultaneously reach them all.

We know that when the U.S. economy reaches full production and full employment, pressures from increased spending power on the buyers' side of the market can combine with the inability of the economy to expand its output to cause demand-pull inflation. We also know that removing the upward pressure on prices by curbing buyers' demands could lead to unemployment and less than full production.

This dilemma sometimes faces policymakers and may force them to choose to seek full employment and full production accompanied by inflation, or stable prices accompanied by unemployment and less than full production. In the next few chapters you will learn about policies that can change economic conditions and who is responsible for pursing these policies. You will learn about Congress and fiscal policy, and the Federal Reserve and monetary policy. While there are disputes about what goals to seek, how to reach them, and who benefits, we are fortunate to have some options available.

Summary

1. The three fundamental goals of the U.S. economy are full employment, stable prices, and full production and economic growth. The three fundamental problems are unemployment, inflation, and falling production. To help create an environment in which these goals can be reached, Congress enacted the Employment Act of 1946.

2. Unemployment intensifies the scarcity problem for society and creates personal hardships for individuals who are out of work. Unemployment can be frictional, cyclical, or structural. Frictional unemployment is voluntary, short term, and primarily due to the time required to locate work. Cyclical unemployment is involuntary and caused by downswings in the general level of economic activity. Structural unemployment is involuntary and occurs when a particular job is no longer in demand in the economy.

3. The labor force includes all persons 16 years of age and older who are employed or actively seeking work. A participation rate measures the percentage of a group that is in the labor force. The overall unemployment rate is the percentage of the labor force that is unemployed and actively seeking work. Unemployment rates and participation rates can be calculated for subgroups within the labor force and differ from group to group.

4. The government calculates unemployment rates from a monthly sample survey. People who work even 1 hour per week while looking for full-time employment are considered to be employed. When people quit looking for work because they have been unsuccessful in their search, they become discouraged workers. Discouraged workers and part-time workers seeking full-time work may cause the unemployment rate to understate the extent to which labor resources are underutilized.

5. Full employment occurs when everyone in the labor force except the frictionally unemployed is working. The unemployment rate associated with full employment is not universally agreed upon and has changed over time. The natural rate of unemployment is the rate that includes the frictionally and structurally unemployed.

6. Inflation refers to an increase in the general level of prices. It reduces the purchasing power of money, hurts some groups in society more than others, and may lead to social and political instability.

7. When inflation is caused by upward pressure on prices from the buyers' side of the market, it is termed demand-pull inflation. When it comes from the sellers' side of the market, it is termed cost-push inflation. Expectations of future economic conditions can influence demand-pull and cost-push inflation.

8. Three widely used indicators of inflation are the Consumer Price Index, Producer Price Index, and GDP Price Index. Price indexes express the prices for a collection of goods and services in different years as a percentage of the prices for those same goods and services in a base year. A price index number of 120.0 means that prices in a certain year are 20 percent higher than prices for the same items in the base year.

9. Deflation occurs when there is a sustained decrease in the general level of prices. Disinflation occurs when there is a slowing of the inflation rate.

10. An economy's levels of production and employment are related. Full production is reached when an economy operates at maximum capacity, or at

full employment. Economic growth is an increase in the full employment level of output over time and is represented by a shift of the production possibilities curve to the right. Economic growth is based on the number and use of resources available to an economy. Technological change and human capital investments are important in achieving growth.

11. Gross domestic product (GDP) is a dollar figure that measures the value of all finished goods and services produced in an economy in 1 year. Money GDP is the value of output in prices at the time production occurs and is affected by changes in both output and price levels. Real GDP is money GDP adjusted to eliminate inflation, and it changes only as the level of output changes. Real GDP is a better measure of production than money GDP. GDP understates actual output because some production is never included in the calculation.

12. It is important to measure the productivity of an economy's resources. Productivity is measured by output per worker, which combines the results of production from labor and other inputs.

13. It may not be possible to reach full employment, full production, and price stability at the same time. As the economy approaches full employment, increased spending causes demand-pull inflationary pressure. The reduction of spending to dampen demand-pull inflationary pressure can cause employment and production to fall.

Key Terms and Concepts

Macroeconomics	Real income
Employment Act of 1946	Cost-of-living adjustment (COLA)
Unemployment	Interest rate
Frictional unemployment	Real rate of interest
Full employment	Wealth
Cyclical unemployment	Demand-pull inflation
Structural unemployment	Cost-push inflation
Labor force	Price index
Participation rate	Base year
Unemployment rate	Consumer Price Index (CPI)
Discouraged workers	Producer Price Index (PPI)
Underemployment	GDP Price Index
Natural rate of unemployment	Deflation
Inflation	Disinflation
Hyperinflation	Production
Money (nominal) income	Full production

Economic growth

Technology

Human capital investments

Gross domestic product (GDP)

Money (current, or nominal) GDP

Real (constant) GDP

Underground economy

Productivity

Review Questions

1. Define the three major goals and the three major problems of the macroeconomy. What is the significance of the Employment Act of 1946 with regard to these goals and problems?

2. Identify which of the following individuals would be classified as unemployed and, if they are, the type of unemployment that each is experiencing.
    a. A student who decides at mid-semester to devote the rest of the term to studying and quits her part-time job
    b. A graphic artist who is out of work because a computer now does her job
    c. A waiter who quits his job and is applying for the same type of work in a restaurant where the working conditions are better
    d. The son of a local farmer who works 20-hour weeks without pay on the farm while waiting for a job at a nearby factory
    e. A travel agent who is laid off because the economy is in a slump and vacation travel is at a minimum
    f. A plumber who works five hours per week for his church (on a paid basis) until he can get a full-time job

3. Define labor force, unemployment rate, participation rate, full employment, and the natural rate of unemployment. Explain what each measure tells us about the economy.

4. What is the difference between demand-pull inflation and cost-push inflation? Must the economy experience only one type of inflation at a time, or can these types occur simultaneously? How might inflation tend to spiral?

5. Calculate price index numbers for the following table assuming that year 3 is the base year, and put your results in the last column.

Year	Market Basket Dollar Outlay	Price Index
1	$170	_____
2	180	_____
3	200	_____
4	200	_____
5	224	_____
6	250	_____
7	280	_____

6. What is the difference between deflation and disinflation? Although the United States has not experienced deflation since the 1930s, what problems could result if deflation occurred over the next 5 years?

7. In each of the following examples, identify whether the person or institution will be penalized by inflation and, if so, why.
   a. Mosie borrows $5,000 for her college expenses at an interest rate of 4 percent to be paid off over 5 years, during which time the inflation rate averages 6 percent.
   b. Oscar invests $3,000 in securities that pay 5.3 percent annually for 10 years, and the inflation rate during that time averages 6.4 percent.
   c. The Lilyton National Bank commits to $10 million in 15-year mortgages at an average mortgage rate of 7.75 percent. The inflation rate averages 8 percent over this 15-year period.
   d. Barney bought a house in 1998 for $100,000 that he is now selling for $200,000. During this time the inflation rate has averaged 3 percent.

8. How is economic growth illustrated using a production possibilities curve, and what are the primary factors responsible for economic growth?

9. Complete the following table for a hypothetical economy assuming that year 1 is the base year for the price index. How does the completed table illustrate that real GDP is a better measure of the performance of an economy over time than is money GDP?

Year	Real Output (units)	Price per Unit	Money GDP	GDP Price Index	Real GDP
1	100	$4.00	____	____	____
2	120	4.40	____	____	____
3	110	5.00	____	____	____
4	110	5.20	____	____	____
5	135	5.20	____	____	____
6	140	5.60	____	____	____

Discussion Questions

1. Suppose that you are a candidate for the U.S. Congress. National Public Radio, which attracts an educated and sophisticated audience, interviews you about the economy. How will you answer each of the following questions?
   a. Since it is fairly apparent that the economy cannot sustain full employment and stable prices at the same time, which of these two goals would you choose?
   b. Do you favor using the full employment rate of unemployment or the natural rate of unemployment as a macro goal?

c. How would you reduce cyclical and structural unemployment? How far would you be willing to intervene in the operations of businesses to control unemployment?

2. Can you identify someone you know who is working part-time but would like to be working full-time, or is working in a job that is not fully using the person's skills? In your opinion, is listing this person as employed a serious flaw in the way unemployment statistics are gathered and reported? What changes, if any, would you make in the way we calculate unemployment?

3. Each of the following allows you to integrate this chapter into your everyday life. Choose one from this list to complete.
a. Interview someone who has been out of work for over a month. Is this person classified as unemployed, and, if so, what type of unemployment is this person experiencing? What are the costs of unemployment to this person?
b. How has inflation affected the tuition you pay at the college or university you are currently attending? What was the tuition in 1995, 2000, 2005, and the current year? How have changes in your school's tuition compared to changes in the overall Consumer Price Index?
c. Compile a list of all the goods and services that you have produced in the last month that would not be counted as part of GDP. Why would they not be counted? Can you estimate the value of this production?

4. What are some economic, social, and political reasons that make economic growth important to a nation? How could a population increase contribute to economic growth, and how could it hinder growth?

5. An argument can be made that the aggressive pursuit of economic growth may impose costs on people today and in future generations. Is growth important enough that these costs should be ignored, or should they be balanced against the gains from economic growth when making decisions about the path the economy should follow in the future?

6. In recent years the annual rate of growth in productivity in the United States has increased. What do you think is most responsible for this increase?

7. Create three separate lists showing the groups that you think are hurt most by unemployment, inflation, and declining production.

Critical Thinking Case 4

STATISTICS AND DECISION MAKING

Critical Thinking Skills

Understanding the statistical concepts of population and sampling

Determining whether data support a generalization

Evaluating the reliability of a statistic used to make a judgment

Economic Concepts

Relationship between statistical measures and economic decision making

Factors underlying the calculation of the unemployment rate

"The average age of smokers has fallen by 3 percent." "Prices are expected to increase by 9.9 percent this year." "The unemployment rate has dropped to 5.8 percent." "Corporate profits rose by 8 percent."[a] We are constantly bombarded with statistics about economic and noneconomic phenomena. Statistics are often used because they add precision to statements that might otherwise be vague and authority to the positions people take. People like to hear and use statistics.

Statistics often provide the incentive for making a decision. For example, many people have chosen to quit smoking because of statistics on the health and longevity of smokers and nonsmokers. And the prediction of a high unemployment rate—say, 10 percent—could induce some households to save more, cause some businesses to spend less on investment, and lead to the enactment of certain government stabilization policies.

Too often, though, numbers are accepted without question. We do not stop to consider where a statistic comes from, how it is calculated, or how accurately it represents the statement it supports. Consider an announcement that the unemployment rate in a large metropolitan area has increased from 5.4 percent to 6.2 percent in the last 3 months. Does this statistic accurately reflect this area's unemployment? What data were collected, how were they collected, and how were they analyzed in order to arrive at this statistic?

The concepts of population and sampling are important in understanding what lies behind a statistic. Population identifies the group from which the statistic is drawn. On learning the unemployment rate for this particular metropolitan area, many questions about the population that statistic represents could be asked. For example, does it have the same characteristics as the population used to determine the national unemployment rate? Does it include the city and all its suburbs, or does it extend to adjacent rural counties?

The sample for the statistic is the group selected from the population for actual measurement. Both the size of the sample and the method of selecting the sample are important because a statistic based on a poorly drawn sample could misrepresent the larger population. If your college makes the statement that graduates earn on average $70,000 the first year after receiving their degrees, you might be curious about how many graduates were sampled and how those sampled were selected. This statistic could be based on a response to a questionnaire by only five graduates, all of whom are proud of their high salaries and who worked for several years before graduating.

Unfortunately, we usually do not have ready access to information on the population and sample from which a statistic is drawn. However, a simple awareness of these concepts reminds us that a statistic is only as good as its population and sample, and that decisions based on faulty statistics can lead to poor results.

[a]The numbers are hypothetical.

Questions

1. The population and sample for deriving the overall unemployment rate in the United States are given in this chapter. What are the population and sample for this statistic?

2. If you could change the current procedures for calculating some key economic statistics, how would you redefine the term unemployed and who would you include in the population and sample for measuring the unemployment rate? What would you include when determining the Consumer Price Index?

3. In the next few days, locate the population and sample for three publicly issued statistics. These could be on the sports page in your local paper, in a news report, or in this textbook.

4. Assume it was reported today that "the interest rate on car loans is expected to jump by 5 percentage points in the next year." What types of economic decisions might be made as a result of this statement? What serious consequences could occur if this statistic were inaccurate?

CHAPTER 5

Foundations of the Macroeconomy

CHAPTER OBJECTIVES

To define and explain business cycles.

To understand how total spending drives the economy's levels of employment and production, and influences prices.

To examine the spending behavior of households, businesses, government units, and the foreign sector.

To identify the macroeconomy's "leakages" and "injections" and show how they affect economic activity.

To introduce the multiplier effect.

To discuss how expectations affect the economy's output and price levels.

To identify the role of total spending in macroeconomic policies.

Part of the daily news coverage by CNN, major television networks, the Internet, and newspapers is devoted to the state of the economy. There are stories on the stock market, jobs, and inflation, forecasts of recovery or recession, updates on the status of foreign trade, and numerous other topics devoted to reporting the pulse of the economy. What should be clear from the media is that the U.S. economy continually changes: It goes through upswings and downswings, or periods of expansion and contraction, and never stays at a particular level of activity. Two data series discussed in Chapter 4 attest to this movement: the unemployment rate and real GDP, both of which change on a regular basis.

This chapter deals with fluctuations in the level of production, or economic activity, in the macroeconomy. It identifies the pattern of these fluctuations and provides a foundation for understanding why they occur.

CHANGES IN MACROECONOMIC ACTIVITY

Generally when people say that the economy is getting better or worse, going into an upswing or downswing, or expanding or contracting, it is because the economy's real GDP is increasing or decreasing. Sometimes, however, people focus on changes in the unemployment rate as their gauge of changes in the economy. Regardless, these two indicators are related: Changes in real GDP cause changes in unemployment. Increases in production bring about reductions in unemployment, and decreases in production increase unemployment.

Figure 5.1 shows changes in real GDP from 1985 through early 2009 in the upper graph and changes in the unemployment rate over the same period in the lower graph. In the top graph, notice that real GDP constantly changes and that it does not change at the same rate from year to year. In some years, growth or decline was more rapid than in other years. In the bottom graph, notice the change in unemployment that results from changes in real GDP. For example, unemployment began to grow when real GDP fell in late 1990, in 2001, and in late 2008.

While the connection between production and employment is fairly straightforward, the connection between production and price levels is not. We learned in the last chapter that when real GDP approaches its full production level and people continue to spend, demand-pull inflation may occur. However, when real GDP increases, but is well below the full-production level, or when real GDP decreases, price levels may remain relatively stable. Since price levels may, or may not, be affected by production levels, we use the expression "changes in economic activity" to refer to changes in production and employment and not prices.

Business Cycles
Recurring periods of growth and decline (or expansion and contraction) in an economy's real output, or real GDP.

Recovery, Peak, Recession, Trough
The phases of the business cycle during which real GDP, or output, increases, reaches its maximum, falls, and reaches its minimum, respectively.

Business Cycles

Changes in economic activity do not occur randomly or haphazardly, but rather in wavelike patterns called business cycles. These patterns provide some degree of predictability that enables us to better use macroeconomic policy tools to address downswings. **Business cycles** are recurring periods of growth and decline in real output, or real GDP. A business cycle goes through four phases: a **recovery,** which is an expansionary phase during which real GDP increases; a **peak,** where maximum output occurs; a **recession,** during which real GDP falls; and a **trough,** where real

FIGURE 5.1   *Real Gross Domestic Product and the Unemployment Rate for 1985 through early 2009[a]*

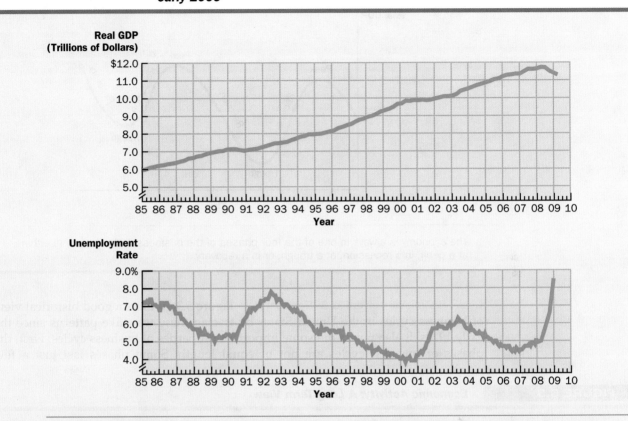

A market economy, such as that of the United States, constantly goes through upswings and downswings in its level of output. There is a generally inverse relationship between the economy's level of output and the rate of unemployment: As output decreases or increases, unemployment tends to rise or fall, respectively.

[a]GDP is given in chained 2000 dollars and the unemployment rate is seasonally adjusted for civilian workers.

Sources: U.S. Department of Commerce, Bureau of Economic Analysis, Gross Domestic Product, http://research.StLouisfed.org/fred2/data/GDPC1.txt; Federal Reserve Bank of St. Louis, "Civilian Unemployment Rate" (from U.S. Department of Labor, Bureau of Labor Statistics), http://research.StLouisfed.org/fred2/data/UNRATE.txt, May 3, 2009.

GDP reaches its minimum.[1] Figure 5.2 illustrates the wavelike movement of business cycles and shows how the phases of the cycle are repeated.

The economy is always in some phase of a business cycle. It does not remain stationary at a particular level of output until some force causes it to increase or decrease. Instead, the economy is always expanding, contracting, or at a turning point in activity.

[1]The terms *recession* and *depression* do not have the same meaning. A recession is a downswing in economic activity. The Great Depression was a historical event in the 1930s when the United States and other economies experienced sharp reductions in output and increases in unemployment.

| FIGURE 5.2 | *Phases of the Business Cycle* |

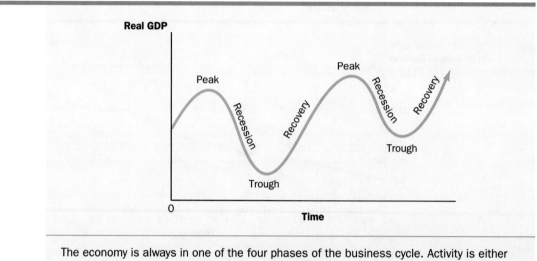

The economy is always in one of the four phases of the business cycle. Activity is either at a peak, in a recession, at a trough, or in a recovery.

Cyclical Behavior of the U.S. Economy   Figure 5.3 gives us a good historical view of business cycles in the United States by tracing these wavelike patterns since the early 1920s. It also points out some important properties of business cycles. First, the phases of business cycles are not of equal length: Some phases last just a few

| FIGURE 5.3 | *Economic Activity: A Long-Term View* |

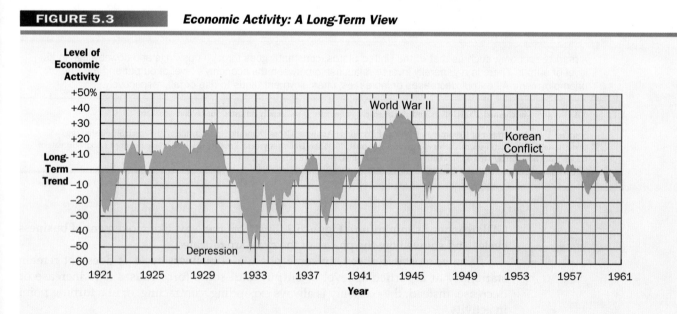

The length of each phase and the intensity of the change in output differ from cycle to cycle.

months, whereas others last for years. Notice also that after the 1940s, periods of expansion outweigh periods of contraction and there is less severity in the cycles. This might be due in part to the Employment Act of 1946, which formalized the federal government's commitment to a healthy economy, a better understanding of the economy, and improved information to make economic decisions. A second important property of business cycles is the unequal intensity, or strength, of expansions and contractions. For example, the output declines from 1929 to 1932 and in 1945 were dramatic, whereas others are not as severe.

Every business cycle is unique in the lengths of its phases and the intensity of its recovery and recession. Regardless of the message of some financial gurus, as you can see, there is no exact rule for determining the duration and magnitude of recessions and recoveries or for defining the exact amount of time required for each business cycle.

Causes of Economic Fluctuations

What causes the economy to expand and contract? This is likely the most important macroeconomic question to be asked: If we understand why we have recessions and recoveries, we can foster the upswings and control the downswings.

For centuries, people have pondered the causes of economic fluctuations. Over the years some theories, like one attributing business cycles to sunspots, have emerged and disappeared while others have been accepted and refined. Even today there are several theories about what causes economic activity to change. When considering the merits of these theories, it is helpful to remember what we learned in Chapter 1: Theories are abstractions that are based on assumptions and focus on the

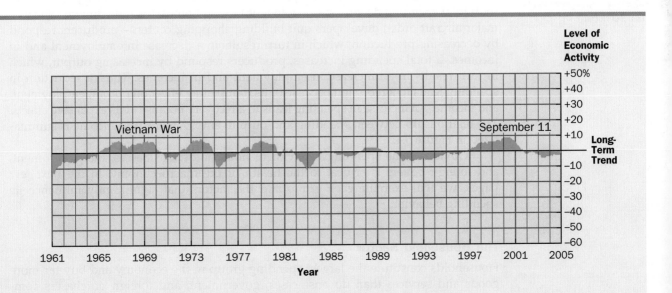

Source: Tom King, "Industrial Production Index, " Board of Governors of the Federal Reserve System, G.17 Industrial Production and Capacity Utilization.

relationship between two variables. That is, different macroeconomic theories use different assumptions and variables, and explain the economy's behavior from different perspectives.

There are several popular theories today that deal with causes of recessions and recoveries. In addition to this chapter, Chapter 9 presents several other generally accepted theories. However, to fully appreciate and understand the working of the macroeconomy, as well as these macroeconomic theories, it is important to have a solid grasp of some basics. That is the goal of this chapter.

TOTAL SPENDING AND MACROECONOMIC ACTIVITY

Analyzing the macroeconomy is not easy: Sometimes it is difficult to bring orderly relationships to such a large picture. To ease our study, economists tend to think of the macroeconomy as having four large groups or sectors: households, businesses, government, and the foreign sector. All macroeconomic activity falls into one of these groups, and each group makes decisions that play an important role in the health of the economy.

Total, or Aggregate, Spending

The total combined spending of all units in the economy (households plus businesses plus government plus foreign) for new goods and services.

Economists have also identified an important macroeconomic relationship that we need to understand: Changes in total (aggregate) spending in the economy cause changes in total (aggregate) production and employment. **Total, or aggregate, spending** is all of the spending for all new goods and services that occurs in the economy, which means that we lump the spending of each of our major groups—households, businesses, government units, and foreign buyers—together.

In a market economy, spending is the driver. As long as buyers spend their money, producers will continue to produce goods and services and hire people to do so. If total spending decreases—people quit buying homes, the government cancels a major aircraft order, developers quit building shopping centers—producers respond by decreasing production, which in turn results in a decrease in employment and in incomes. If total spending increases, producers respond by increasing output, which in turn results in an increase in employment and in incomes. Thus, a reduction in spending leads to a recession because of its dampening effect on output, employment, and income. An increase in spending leads to a recovery because of its expansive effects. The relationship between spending and output, employment, and income is summarized in Figure 5.4.

Obviously the spending behavior of households, businesses, the government, and foreign buyers is critical to the health of the macroeconomy. In the next few pages, we will examine each group and the factors that significantly influence its spending behavior.

The Household Sector

Households constitute the largest spending group in the economy and buy far more goods and services than do businesses, government, and foreign purchasers combined. For example, households purchased about $9.7 trillion of the approximately $13.8 trillion output produced in 2007.[2] Furthermore, individuals do not radically

---

[2]*Economic Report of the President* (Washington, DC: U.S. Government Printing Office, 2009), p. 282.

| FIGURE 5.4 | *Total Spending and the Level of Economic Activity* |

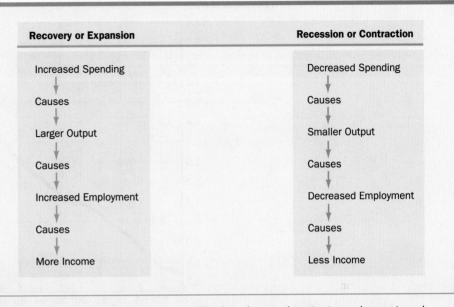

Changes in total, or aggregate, spending lead to changes in output, employment, and income.

alter their spending patterns from year to year, making this spending fairly stable as it generally increases. It is fortunate for the economy that the largest spending group is so steady in its spending patterns.

Technically speaking, we call aggregate household spending on new goods and services **personal consumption expenditures.** Figure 5.5 plots real personal consumption expenditures for 1980 through early 2009.[3] Notice that the line almost always slopes upward with little fluctuation.

Personal Consumption Expenditures
Household spending on new goods and services.

The Household Sector and the Circular Flow   Most of the spending that we do comes from income that we earn. We deliver pizzas, work as CEOs, own and run bed-and-breakfasts, and do a host of other activities to earn money. In the macroeconomy, then, we know that the majority of spending by the household sector on new goods and services comes from the income earned by households, or is **income-determined spending.**

Income-Determined Spending
Household spending on new goods and services that comes from income earned from providing resources to producers.

Figure 5.6 builds on the circular flow model introduced in Chapter 2; it illustrates some of the important factors that influence household spending and how they are related. For now, observe lines 1, 2, 3, and 4. Line 1 shows a flow of earned income from selling factors of production to businesses (line 2), and line 4 shows a flow of personal consumption expenditures for goods and services (line 3). You can see that earned income provides the spending power to purchase goods and services.

While earned income is the major source of household spending, it is not the only source. Households can also spend from funds that they borrow through bank loans, credit card purchases, or such, and from government **transfer payments,**

Transfer Payment
Money from the government for which no direct work is performed in return.

[3]The numbers in Figure 5.5 as well as Figures 5.7, 5.10, and 5.12 are given in real terms. That is, the numbers are adjusted for price increases, or inflation.

FIGURE 5.5

Real Personal Consumption Expenditures for 1980–2009[a]

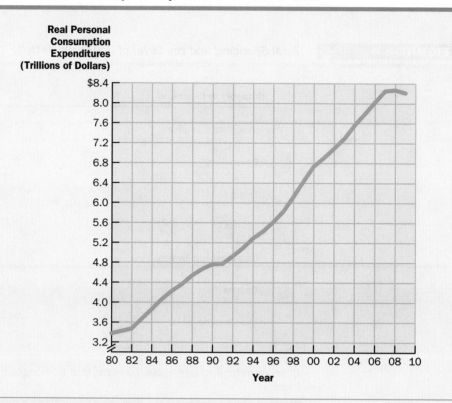

Real Personal Consumption Expenditures (Trillions of Dollars)

Total spending by households does not fluctuate widely from year to year, and the growth of personal consumption expenditures is relatively stable over time.

[a]Given in chained 2000 dollars.

Source: U.S. Department of Commerce, Bureau of Economic Analysis, Table 1.1.6, "Real Gross Domestic Product, Chained Dollars," http://www.bea.gov/national/nipaweb. The data for 2009 are for the first quarter.

FIGURE 5.6

Household Spending, Borrowing, Transfers, Saving, and Taxes

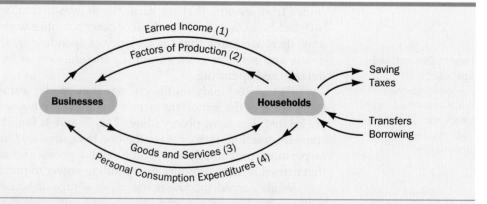

Household spending, which is influenced mainly by the size of earned income, is also affected by transfers and borrowing, which provide injections into the spending stream, and by saving and taxes, which are leakages from the spending stream.

which are payments from the government for which no direct work is performed in return. Social Security payments, unemployment compensation, and agricultural subsidies are examples of transfer payments. Checks from working for a government are not transfer payments.

When households make personal consumption expenditures from money that they borrow or receive in transfers, we call that **nonincome-determined spending.** It is important to separate income- and nonincome-determined spending. Since nonincome-determined expenditures are based on sources other than earned income, they become **injections into the spending stream.** That is, they are expenditures over and above what household earned income alone would allow. Injections into the spending stream are important because they lead to an expansion of output, employment, and income in the economy as businesses produce more to meet this additional demand. In Figure 5.6, transfers and borrowing are shown as injections into the circular model.

We also know that households do not spend all of their income: Some is used to pay taxes and some is saved. Households pay a variety of taxes to various government units. Households also save in a variety of ways through the use of **financial institutions** such as banks, brokerage houses, credit unions, and insurance companies. Both saving and taxes are **leakages from the spending stream** because they are income that households are not spending. Leakages from the spending stream cause output, employment, and income in the economy to shrink as businesses cut back production in response to a reduced demand.

In summary, the amount that households spend is influenced by

- earned income,
- saving,
- taxes,
- borrowing, and
- transfers.

When people earn more or less, change their saving habits, or change any of the other factors just listed, total personal consumption expenditures and the economy as a whole can be affected. For example, fear of a recession could cause people to increase saving, with a resulting decline in spending; or a decrease in interest rates could encourage people to borrow for new cars, home remodeling, and other spending purposes.

Although personal consumption expenditures is the largest component of total spending, the impact on the economy of changes in the household sector is affected by spending in the business, government, and foreign sectors. As a result, we need to examine the other sectors and consider all of them together before drawing any conclusions about the economy.

Up for Debate, "Is Saving a Healthy Habit?", examines conflicting messages about saving. Do you agree with the underlying message that what may be good for the individual may not be good for the group?

The Business Sector

Businesses play an extremely important role in the macroeconomy because of their spending habits. The size of business spending on new goods is huge: Each year they put hundreds of billions of dollars into new machinery and equipment, replacement

Nonincome-Determined Spending
Spending that is generated from sources other than household earned income.

Injections into the Spending Stream
Spending that comes from a source other than household earned income; nonincome-determined spending.

Financial Institutions
Organizations such as banks, credit unions, and insurance companies that provide a means for saving and borrowing.

Leakages from the Spending Stream
Uses for earned income other than spending, such as paying taxes and saving.

Is Saving a Healthy Habit?

Issue   *From the time we are children we are encouraged to save. Grandparents often give savings bonds and accounts to celebrate a birthday; banks frequently provide penny accounts; and parents attempt to encourage savings habits by matching amounts saved or by providing other rewards. By the time a person enters adulthood, regularly saving money may be a lifestyle choice.*

But the argument that it is smart to save seems to contradict a basic economic relationship that we've just explored: Increased spending leads to more output and employment, and decreased spending—or more saving— leads to declines in output and employment. In other words, for the good of the economy, it is healthier to spend than to save. Faced with these contradictory messages, we need to ask: Is saving a healthy habit?

Yes   People should save on a regular basis. Good planning for the future involves good financial planning, and good financial planning encourages saving. The ability to make a down payment on a house, qualify for a mortgage, send kids to college, or retire comfortably is affected by the amount that a person has saved. In addition, the peace of mind afforded by a cushion of certificates of deposit, stocks, bonds, and other assets may lessen the stress that can arise in everyday life.

Saving also provides a means for increasing income through interest and dividends. As one saves more, the income earned from saving increases and affords additional funds for more saving or spending.

It is also important to develop good savings habits and build up a reserve of funds because life throws us curves that can be better negotiated if we have money. Job loss, illness, or an auto accident could be disastrous without money to assist us through such a crisis. Life can also throw us opportunities that can be seized if we have the funds—traveling, an interesting nonpaying internship, a stock tip, and a partnership in a business, to name a few.

No   People need to be careful that they do not save too much because, while saving may be good for the individual, the health of the economy depends on the overall level of spending. And, since ordinary consumers like us are part of the largest spending group, it is important that we buy goods and services and not save too much money.

When we increase our saving, businesses respond by cutting back on production. For example, if we all decided to wait to buy a car until we have saved enough to pay cash, car sales and production would fall dramatically, jobs would be lost in the auto and related industries, and the economy would slow down.

Increases in saving could kick off a downward spiral into a recession, with resulting job losses. Without jobs, there is no income to save. If we all listen to the adages about the value of saving, we can hurt ourselves.

Investment Spending
Business spending on new goods, such as machinery, equipment, buildings, and inventories; nonincome-determined spending.

parts, buildings, inventories, and the like. Technically, we term this **investment spending** and we label it nonincome-determined spending because investment spending does not come from household earned income.

Investment spending is not steady and tends to fluctuate from year to year. Figure 5.7 plots real gross investment for 1980 through early 2009 and shows how this spending fluctuates. This figure gives us an excellent picture of a very important piece of macroeconomic reality: *Changes in investment spending are a primary cause of changes in economic activity.* When business spending declines, it can bring about a slowdown or recession; when it increases, it can help pull the economy into a recovery. Figure 5.7 shows serious declines in investment spending in 1982, 1990 and 1991, 2001 and 2002, and a dramatic decrease in 2008 and 2009. During these years the United States experienced recessions and increasing unemployment rates.

Business Spending and Profit Expectations   Why does business spending fluctuate? Business spending habits in the aggregate are very different from household habits because the motivation for spending is different. Householders look to their earned income as the basis for spending; businesses look for the potential to make a

| FIGURE 5.7 | *Real Gross Investment for 1980–2009[a]* |

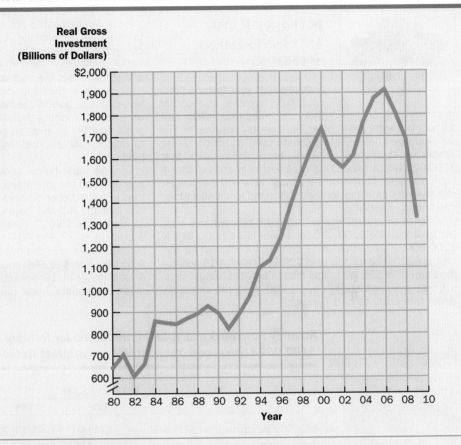

Investment spending can fluctuate widely from year to year and is a major cause of changes in economic activity.

---

[a]Gross investment is outright purchases of investment goods plus a depreciation allowance for capital that was used up during the current year; numbers are in chained 2000 dollars.

Source: U.S. Department of Commerce, Bureau of Economic Analysis, Table 1.1.6, "Real Gross Domestic Product, Chained Dollars," http://www.bea.gov/national/nipaweb. The data for 2009 are for the first quarter.

profit as their basis for spending. Businesses invest in new buildings and equipment if they expect to earn enough profit from the investment to make it worthwhile. The reason Wal-Mart constructs a Sam's Club or Ford retools a truck plant is that these companies expect to increase their profit levels.

Sometimes businesses plan for new investment spending—perhaps a technology upgrade—but "hold on" to those plans and postpone them. Most investment spending is postponable: Building a new strip mall, constructing a new ride at a theme park, and remodeling corporate headquarters are likely not expenditures that must be made for day-to-day operations to continue. Since most businesses can delay major capital expenditures until profit expectations increase, this adds to the reasons for fluctuations in business spending.

APPLICATION 5.1

INTEREST RATES AND INVESTMENT SPENDING

Suppose that your favorite pizza spot has become so popular that customers must often wait an hour or longer for a table. The owners, because of this demand, are contemplating constructing additional dining space in their facility. They have determined that $200,000 will be needed for this investment and are analyzing the cost of borrowing the money. How will the interest rate that they must pay for these borrowed funds affect their decision to remodel?

With an annual interest rate of 6 percent, the interest for borrowing $200,000 for 1 year is $12,000 (6% × $200,000 = $12,000); at 12 percent the interest for borrowing $200,000 for 1 year is $24,000; and at 18 percent the interest is $36,000. This means that the annual interest cost alone will change by $2,000 when the annual interest rate changes by 1 percent.

If interest rates are high, the owners may not want to invest in remodeling: Large interest payments could cause the remodeling project to be unprofitable. The additional profit from serving more customers may not be enough to offset the high cost of interest.

Assume that the owners of the pizza restaurant would like to borrow the necessary $200,000 and pay it off in equal monthly installments over 5 years. Also assume that the interest would be recalculated each month to account for the declining balance of the loan as it is paid off.

The table below summarizes the required monthly payment and the total interest paid for a loan of $200,000 that is retired over 5 years at various interest rates. Notice that the monthly payment for borrowing $200,000 at 18 percent is $5,078.70 and that the monthly payment at 6 percent is $3,866.60—a difference of $1,212.10 per month. Notice also the total interest paid over 5 years. At 6 percent it is $31,996 and at 18 percent it is $104,722. A loan made at 18 percent rather than 6 percent would mean additional forgone profit of $72,726.

Monthly Payments and Total Interest Paid for Retiring a $100,000 Loan over 5 Years at Various Interest Rates

	INTEREST RATE		
	6%	12%	18%
Monthly payment	$3,866.60	$4,448.90	$5,078.70
Total interest paid	$31,996.00	$66,934.00	$104,722.00

An important factor that influences expected profit and investment spending is expectations of future overall levels of economic activity. Fear of a recession can discourage investment spending as businesses speculate that falling demand and growing inventories of unsold goods will make their operations unprofitable. Likewise, expectations of healthy sales and a surge in economic activity can bring about an increase in business spending. Predictions of economic doom-and-gloom coupled with the reality of falling demand and rising unemployment at the end of 2008 and the spring of 2009 helped to scare businesses into postponing investment spending plans. The economy was so skittish that the stock market even reacted to announcements about a possible spread of swine flu.

The price tag on a business's investment plans can be staggering. Imagine the construction costs for a new stadium for one of the major league baseball teams or even for a medical center in your hometown. Since most businesses borrow the funds for their investment spending, the interest rate that they must pay to borrow greatly influences the level of investment spending. If the interest rate is high, businesses may decide that it is best to postpone spending because the high cost of borrowing reduces the expected profitability of the investment. If the interest rate is low, businesses may take advantage of the reduced cost of funds and increase their borrowing.

Application 5.1, "Interest Rates and Investment Spending," provides a very simple example of how an investment decision can be affected by the interest rate. In this

FIGURE 5.8   *Business Investment Spending, Saving, and Taxes*

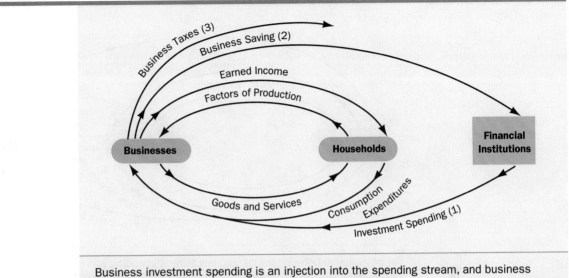

Business investment spending is an injection into the spending stream, and business saving and taxes are leakages from the spending stream.

---

application, a 5-year loan for $200,000 at an 18 percent interest rate would cost a business owner $1,212.10 more in monthly payments, or a total of $72,726 more than would the same loan at a 6 percent interest rate. The importance of the effect of changes in the interest rate on economic activity will be discussed further in Chapter 8.

The Business Sector and the Circular Flow   The circular flow model in Figure 5.8 shows the role of the business sector in economic activity. Line 1 is business investment spending, which is an injection into the spending stream because it is nonincome-determined spending. Line 2 represents business saving, called **retained earnings.** Line 3 represents business taxes: corporate income tax, sales tax, and license fees, to name a few. Both business saving and taxes are leakages from the spending stream.

Notice the addition of financial institutions to Figure 5.8. These are important for business saving and investment borrowing. Businesses use financial institutions to hold their savings through deposits, stocks, bonds, or some other security that earns money until the funds are needed. Financial institutions also provide the means for financing investment spending through loans, new shares of stock, or simply redeeming the retained earnings.

The Saving–Borrowing Relationship   This is a good time to point out a critical flow in the macroeconomy: the **saving–borrowing relationship.** Figure 5.9 adds household saving and borrowing back into the circular flow and allows us to see a fuller picture of saving and borrowing. Through financial institutions, dollars saved by households and businesses—dollars that are leakages from the spending stream—can be borrowed and spent by other households and businesses and thereby returned to the spending stream. In other words, financial institutions are vehicles for changing leakages from the spending stream into injections.

Retained Earnings
The portion of a business's accumulated profits that has been retained for investment or other purposes.

Saving–Borrowing Relationship
The relationship between the amount saved by households and businesses and the amount returned to the spending stream through business and household borrowing.

| FIGURE 5.9 | *Saving, Investing, and Borrowing by Households and Businesses*

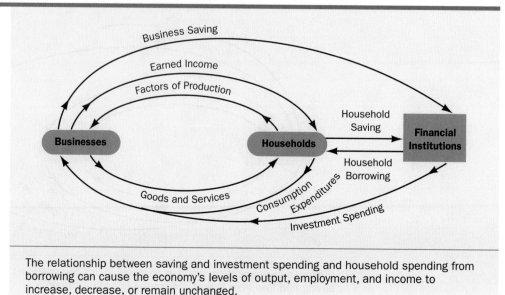

The relationship between saving and investment spending and household spending from borrowing can cause the economy's levels of output, employment, and income to increase, decrease, or remain unchanged.

Since the motivations for saving and for borrowing are not the same, it is important to understand that the amount saved may not equal the amount borrowed. In other words, the economy could experience conditions where savings are greater than borrowing, savings are less than borrowing, or savings equal borrowing.

Because saving is a leakage from the spending stream and spending from borrowing is an injection into the stream, overall spending in the economy and the resulting levels of output and employment are influenced by this relationship. When saving is greater than borrowing, the relationship will foster a decrease in total spending and a downturn in the economy. When saving is less than borrowing, the relationship will foster an increase in total spending and an upturn in the economy. We need to understand that, at this point, we have isolated this saving–borrowing relationship. Before we draw any big picture conclusions, we need to put other relationships into the model.[4]

The Government Sector

Government—federal, state, and local—is another sector that has a major impact on the economy because of its own spending as well as its power to influence spending in the other sectors through the taxes that are imposed. And, as we will soon learn in Chapter 6, the federal government can use its spending and taxing to change the direction of the economy. We classify government spending into two major categories: purchases of goods and services, and transfer payments.

Governments provide us with many needed services and, as a result, make **government purchases of goods and services** to do so: fire trucks, police radar

Government Purchases of Goods and Services
Government spending on new goods and services; nonincome-determined spending.

---

[4]We are simplifying the saving–borrowing relationship by assuming that 100 percent of borrowed funds are spent. While this may not always be true, it does allow us to understand the impact of this important relationship. To be precise, we would compare saving with spending from borrowing.

FIGURE 5.10   *Real Government Purchases of Goods and Services for 1980–2009[a]*

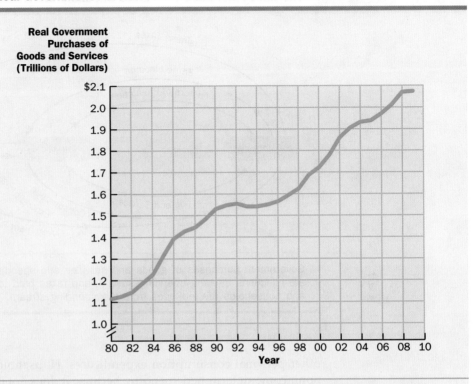

The growth in government purchases of goods and services has been relatively stable.

[a]Numbers are in chained 2000 dollars.

Source: U.S. Department of Commerce, Bureau of Economic Analysis, Table 1.1.6, "Real Gross Domestic Product, Chained Dollars," http://www.bea.gov/national/nipaweb. The data for 2009 are for the first quarter.

detectors, defense systems, park benches, paper, and the services of government employees to fix roads and maintain a court system, to name a few. Technically, we classify government purchases of goods and services as nonincome-determined spending because they do not come directly from household earned income. Government purchases have the same impact on the economy as does other spending: Increases in government purchases can increase economic activity and decreases can decrease output, employment, and income.

In most years, government spending for new goods and services is the second largest component of total spending. Figure 5.10 plots real government purchases of goods and services for 1980 through early 2009. This figure shows that, like household spending and unlike business spending, government purchases tend to be stable and increase over time.

Government also uses a substantial portion of its funds for transfer payments, such as Social Security and unemployment compensation, which go to individuals or households that perform no direct work in return. These transfer payments can then be used to buy groceries, pay for prescriptions or rent, or make

FIGURE 5.11   *The Government Sector and the Circular Flow*

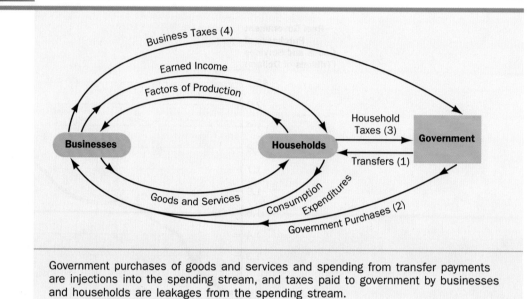

Government purchases of goods and services and spending from transfer payments are injections into the spending stream, and taxes paid to government by businesses and households are leakages from the spending stream.

other personal consumption expenditures. Household spending from transfers is nonincome-determined spending because it does not come from household earned income. In 2008, about $1.8 trillion went from government to households as transfer payments.[5]

We want to point out the importance of thinking of government spending in terms of the two categories just discussed: government purchases and transfer payments. This distinction will help you to better understand the material in this chapter and the following one.

The Government Sector and the Circular Flow   The government sector is added to the basic circular flow model in Figure 5.11. Line 1 shows the flow of transfer payments, which can be used for consumption spending; line 2 represents government purchases of goods and services; and lines 3 and 4 show taxes going from households and businesses to government. This model shows that government purchases are a direct injection into the spending stream, transfers provide an injection through households, and taxes are a leakage.

The Government Taxing–Spending Relationship   There is another relationship like the saving–borrowing one that is important to economic activity: the government taxing–spending relationship. This one, however, is slightly more complicated because while government taxing and spending may be equal, the amount leaked from the spending stream may not equal the amount injected because of saving. That is, taxpayers may pay their taxes using part of their incomes that would have been saved and part that would have been spent, and transfer recipients may save part of their payments. For readers who want to explore the details of this complication, footnote 6 gives that

[5]*Economic Report of the President*, 2009, p. 319. Number is preliminary.

information.[6] For our purposes here we will discuss the amounts leaked from and injected into the spending stream through the government sector, rather than taxes and spending.

Sometimes the amount that flows into the government in taxes does not equal the amount that is returned to the spending stream through government purchases and spending from transfers. When the amount that is leaked through taxes is greater than the amount returned through these injections, a downswing in economic activity is fostered. When the amount that is leaked in taxes is less than the amount returned through these injections, an upswing in economic activity could result. When they off-set each other, there is no change in economic activity from this relationship.

When we complete our discussion of all four economic sectors, we will put the government sector relationships together with the others to get a complete picture.

The Foreign Sector

The fourth major sector that has an impact on the direction of the macroeconomy is the foreign sector. While it is the smallest of the four, it has been growing significantly in importance. Most of us interface daily with some aspect of today's global economy: We buy televisions produced in Asia, work on farms that have corn sold to Mexico, wear shoes from Brazil and China, read foreign papers, go to college credit programs in Europe, and surf for good foreign stock opportunities. In short, the lines between domestic and foreign products and services have become increasingly blurred.

We term goods and services produced in the United States and sold abroad as U.S. **exports,** and goods and services produced in foreign countries and sold in the United States as U.S. **imports.** Generally speaking, exports increase spending in the economy and imports take spending out of the economy. As a result, we tend to think of exports as injections and imports as leakages. In 2008, exports were 13 percent of GDP and imports were equal to 16.3 percent of GDP.[7]

The real values of U.S. exports and imports from 1980 through early 2009 are plotted in Figure 5.12a. Notice that the values of exports and imports have generally grown over the years and that the value of U.S. imports has usually been more than U.S. exports. When we subtract imports from exports, we get the difference between their values, or **net exports.** Net exports is positive when exports are greater than imports and negative when exports are less than imports. Net exports of goods and services for 1980 through early 2009 is plotted in Figure 5.12b. Negative net export years fall below the zero line on the graph. It is easy to observe that for most years net exports is negative—and in recent years exceptionally negative.

Exports
Goods and services that are sold abroad.

Imports
Goods and services purchased from abroad.

Net Exports
Exports minus imports; is positive when exports exceed imports and negative when imports exceed exports.

[6]We are being careful to compare the amount put into the spending stream through government purchases and transfers with the amount taken from the spending stream through taxes. This is because not all transfer payments are used to purchase goods and services, and not all taxes are paid with money that would have been spent. When households receive transfer payments, a portion of what they receive from the government may be saved. When households pay taxes, part of that payment may come from money that would have been used for personal consumption expenditures, and part may come from money that would have been saved. For this reason, assessing the impact of government expenditures and taxes becomes somewhat complex. Let us illustrate with the following example.

Suppose that the government taxes households $100 billion and uses that money to purchase $100 billion of goods and services. Suppose also that $70 billion of that tax is paid with dollars that households would have used for personal consumption expenditures, and $30 billion is paid with dollars they would have saved. Because of this, the tax of $100 billion reduces household spending by only $70 billion. Thus, the net effect of the tax of $100 billion and the expenditure program of $100 billion is to enlarge the spending stream by $30 billion, and the economy grows. In this example, if the government wanted the effect of its spending and taxes to be neutral, it would spend $70 billion and tax $100 billion.

This example could be further complicated by assuming that out of the $100 billion in government expenditures, only $50 billion is spent for the purchase of goods and services and that the other $50 billion goes for transfer payments. The $50 billion spent on goods and services goes directly into the spending stream, but part of the $50 billion in transfers could go into savings. If households saved $15 billion and spent $35 billion, then only $85 billion of the government's total expenditures would go into the spending stream.

[7]U.S. Department of Commerce, Bureau of Economic Analysis, Table 1.1.6, http://www.bea.gov/national/nipaweb.

FIGURE 5.12   *Real U.S. Exports, Imports, and Net Exports of Goods and Services for 1980–2009[a]*

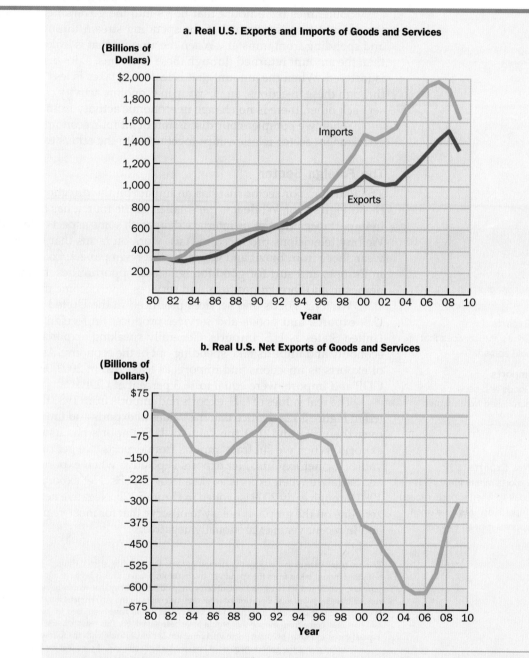

a. Real U.S. Exports and Imports of Goods and Services

(Billions of Dollars)

b. Real U.S. Net Exports of Goods and Services

(Billions of Dollars)

In general, real U.S. exports and imports of goods and services have increased since 1980, and imports have been greater than exports.

[a]Numbers are in chained 2000 dollars.

Source: U.S. Department of Commerce, Bureau of Economic Analysis, Table 1.1.6, "Real Gross Domestic Product, Chained Dollars," http://www.bea.gov/national/nipaweb. The data for 2009 are for the first quarter.

| FIGURE 5.13 | *The Foreign Sector and the Circular Flow* |

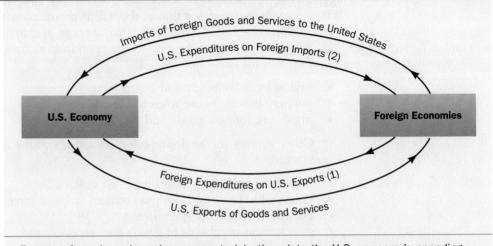

Exports of goods and services generate injections into the U.S. economy's spending stream, and imports cause leakages from the U.S. economy's spending stream.

In addition to the impact on total spending levels from large, consistent negative net export numbers, there are other serious consequences from the substantial flow of dollars to other countries. Chapter 17, International Finance, explores this area in greater detail. It will help you to understand a declining value of the dollar for U.S. citizens traveling abroad as well as the increased purchases of U.S. assets like buildings and stock by foreign dollar holders.

The Foreign Sector and the Circular Flow   Figure 5.13 uses a variation of the circular flow model to show the effect of exports and imports on the U.S. economy. Line 1 represents the injections into the U.S. economy that result from expenditures by foreign buyers on exported goods and services. Line 2 represents the leakages from the U.S. economy that result from expenditures by U.S. buyers on imported goods and services. Imports and exports have the same effect as the other leakages and injections: Purchases of imports deflect spending from the economy and foster a downswing, and purchases of exports by foreign buyers increase spending and foster an upswing. Spending on exports is another example of nonincome-determined spending since it does not come from U.S. household earned income.

Here, once again, is another important relationship—the export–import relationship—to consider. And, again, as with the other sectors, injections and leakages may not be equal. Exports can be greater than imports, which makes net exports positive, causing injections to be greater than leakages and overall spending in this sector to grow. Imports can be greater than exports, which makes net exports negative, causing leakages to be greater than injections and overall spending in this sector to decline. This relationship needs to be considered with the others in evaluating the direction of the overall economy.

Summary of Aggregate Spending, Leakages, and Injections

Let us review. Total, or aggregate, spending drives the economy's production, employment, and income levels. When total spending increases, the economy expands as output, employment, and income increase; when total spending decreases, the economy contracts as output, employment, and income fall. We compute total spending by aggregating the spending of households, businesses, governments, and foreign buyers. It is important to remember that of these four groups, business investment spending, because of its size and instability, is a major cause of changes in economic activity.

Some actions in each of the four spending sectors cause leakages from the spending stream. These include

- saving by households and businesses,
- paying taxes by households and businesses, and
- importing foreign goods and services.

Other actions in the four sectors cause injections into the spending stream. These include

- household spending from borrowed dollars,
- household spending from government transfer payments,
- business investment spending,
- government purchases of goods and services, and
- foreign purchases of exported goods and services.

The relationship between leakages and injections influences aggregate spending and in turn the economy's production and employment levels. Up to this point in our discussion, we have identified three important relationships: the saving–borrowing, the tax–government expenditures, and the import–export relationships. To assess the economy as a whole, we must consider these relationships together. For example, while saving could exceed borrowing, causing a downswing, government expenditures could exceed taxes, causing an upswing.

In looking at the big picture, we know that

- if all leakages from the spending stream are equal to all injections, the economy will not change;
- if leakages are greater than injections, the economy will fall into a recession; and
- if injections are greater than leakages, the economy will expand into a recovery.

These cause-and-effect relationships are summarized in Table 5.1.

Each of the pieces of the macroeconomic puzzle that we have just created is extremely important because of the impact that each can have on the economy. Even a ban on genetically altered grain and seed exports could have macroeconomic implications. As a result, these various pieces are watched closely by those concerned with the state of the economy. And the media are particularly interested in reporting consumer confidence indexes, saving patterns, transfer payment changes, investment declines, and such.

Now that we've covered the basics behind total spending and its role in economic expansions and contractions, you might find Application 5.2, "What's Causing the Economy to Change?", interesting. It presents some brief explanations for economic changes that go beyond what one typically reads or hears.

The Multiplier Effect

In this chapter we have identified spending as either income-determined or nonincome-determined. There is just one example of income-determined spending: the spending on goods and services that comes from people's earned incomes. All of the other spending that we discussed—from borrowing and transfer payments, investment spending, government purchases, and spending on U.S. exports—is nonincome-determined spending because it does not come directly from household earned income.

| TABLE 5.1 | *Leakages, Injections, and Changes in Economic Activity* |

The economy's levels of output, employment, and income depend on the combined impact of all leakages from and all injections into the spending stream.

THE LEVEL OF ECONOMIC ACTIVITY WILL

Expand

When all injections into the spending stream exceed all leakages from the spending stream

Remain Unchanged

When all injections into the spending stream equal all leakages from the spending stream

Contract

When all injections into the spending stream are less than all leakages from the spending stream

Leakages	Injections
Household saving	Household spending from borrowing
Business saving	Household spending from transfer payments
Household taxes	Business investment spending
Business taxes	Government purchases of goods and services
Import expenditures	Export expenditures

Multiplier Effect

The change in total output and income generated by a change in nonincome-determined spending is larger than, or a multiple of, the spending change itself.

It is important to make a distinction between income-determined and nonincome-determined spending. This is because nonincome-determined spending, when it is injected into the economy, is subject to a **multiplier effect.** An increase or decrease in nonincome-determined spending causes changes in output and employment that are far greater than the initial change in spending. An increase, for example, of $100 million in nonincome-determined expenditures will cause the economy to grow by much more than $100 million because of the multiplier effect.

Why is there a multiplier effect? How does it work? Nonincome-determined spending is not part of the "basic circle" of the circular flow model. That is, it is spending that does not come from income earned from production that is taking place. Instead, it comes from outside the core circle of the economy, or is injected into the economy. Once the injection enters the economy, it becomes part of the basic circle and these dollars are spent over and over again.

Let's work through an example. Suppose that a developer borrows $10,000,000 to invest in building some homes. As the homes are constructed, the developer uses the $10,000,000 to hire people and buy materials and other resources. This spending by the developer puts $10,000,000 into the economy that was not previously there. In other words, this investment injection of $10,000,000 initially creates $10,000,000 in output (the homes) and incomes.

People who receive the $10,000,000 in income from this injection will now take part of it and spend it—they can buy cars, go on vacation, eat in trendy restaurants—and use part for saving and taxes. We will assume that they spend $8,000,000. Since this $8,000,000 is "new" to the economy, it will result in $8,000,000 of new production and incomes. The income earners of the $8,000,000 will now take part of that, say $6,400,000, and spend it.

APPLICATION 5.2

WHAT'S CAUSING THE ECONOMY TO CHANGE?

Over the years there have been some interesting explanations for changes in the macroeconomy that are not based on reasons one would describe as "economic." Let's take a brief look at a few of them.

Sunspots   In 1837, 1847, and 1857 the British economy went through a series of downswings. William Stanley Jevons, a highly regarded economist at that time, argued that these downswings may have been caused by sunspots—which show up about every 10 years. Actually, now we know that a connection between sunspots and economic activity is not that far-fetched. Sunspots can adversely affect weather, which in turn can reduce crop yields. The British depended on India to buy exported British products. But since a major source of income for India was its crops, when the crops failed (presumably due to sunspots) India had less income to buy British exports. In turn, the British economy suffered.

Conspirators   During the Great Depression and the administration of President Franklin D. Roosevelt, a theory emerged that downswings are caused by conspirators. Some people said that a group was conspiring to do damage to the economy and that these conspirators were using a popular comic strip to openly communicate with each other. One of the characters in this comic strip was a cigar smoker. According to the conspiracy theorists, smoke coming up from his cigar in a given day's comic signaled one thing to the conspirators and ashes falling from his cigar signaled something else.

Psychology and Theology   Explanations for movements in the economy have also been built on psychological and theological foundations. It has been suggested by some that people go through waves of optimism and pessimism, and that these emotional waves in turn cause the economy to go through waves of expansion and contraction. Others have argued that downswings in the economy are punishment for sins committed while the economy was prospering.

The process does not stop here but continues through the economy in a circular pattern, creating more output and income along the way. In the end, the initial injection of $10,000,000 in the economy creates a substantial amount of output and income. Table 5.2 illustrates this example of the multiplier process through several rounds. When this example is carried through enough successive rounds to approach a zero increase in the last round, and the output and income created in each round are summed, $50,000,000 in total output and income results. This means that the initial injection of $10,000,000 has been multiplied, or magnified, to $50,000,000 of output and income; there has been a multiplier effect equal to five times the initial change in spending.

Calculating the Multiplier Effect   There is an easier way to calculate the multiplier effect than to go through each round of spending, as in Table 5.2. To do so, divide the initial change in nonincome-determined spending by the percentage of the additional income received by households that is *not* spent. Expressed as a formula, the multiplier effect is

$$\frac{\text{initial change in nonincome-determined spending}}{\text{percentage of additional income not spent}} = \text{total change in output and income.}$$

In the preceding example, the initial change in nonincome-determined spending was $10,000,000 and households receiving that $10,000,000 as income spent $8,000,000, or 80 percent, and did not spend $2,000,000, or 20 percent. The households that received $8,000,000 in income spent $6,400,000, or 80 percent, and did not spend $1,600,000, or 20 percent, and so on. Accordingly, in this example, the initial change in nonincome-determined spending of $10,000,000 would be

TABLE 5.2	*Effect on Total Output and Income from a Nonincome-Determined Spending Injection of $10,000,000*

Because of the multiplier effect, an injection of nonincome-determined spending into the spending stream causes total output and income to increase by more than the amount of the nonincome-determined spending itself.

	New Output	New Income	New Personal Consumption Expenditures
Round 1 ($10,000,000 nonincome-determined expenditure)	$10,000,000 →	$10,000,000 →	$8,000,000 ⌐
Round 2	→8,000,000 →	8,000,000 →	6,400,000 ⌐
Round 3	→6,400,000 →	6,400,000 →	5,120,000 ⌐
Round 4	→5,120,000 →	5,120,000 →	4,096,000 ⌐
Round 5	→4,096,000 →	4,096,000 →	3,276,800 ⌐
Rounds 6, 7, and so on	↳ •	•	•
	•	•	•
	•	•	•
	•	•	•
Total	$50,000,000	$50,000,000	

divided by 0.20, the percentage of additional income *not* spent in each round, to result in an answer of $50,000,000, the total change in output and income.[8]

The multiplier effect is dependent on how much is spent and not spent from each successive round of income and output that is created: The more that is spent, the greater the multiplier effect; the less that is spent, the smaller the multiplier effect. If households in the preceding example had spent only 75 percent and not spent 25 percent of each successive round of newly created income, the level of economic activity would have grown by $40,000,000 ($10,000,000/0.25 = $40,000,000) rather than $50,000,000.

The multiplier effect also applies when nonincome-determined expenditures are cut back. For example, a decrease in investment spending of $10,000,000, by the time it works its way through the economy, will cause the level of economic activity to decline by more than the initial $10,000,000 decrease.

The multiplier effect is frequently used in local impact studies. Sometimes colleges and universities, for example, will conduct economic studies and use a local multiplier to show how they bring positive economic benefits to a community. Students can be regarded as bringing injections into a local economy as they buy courses, housing, food, books, and such. In addition, multipliers are used to justify large public projects like stadiums. The case is frequently made that a new stadium brings more fans into an area, becomes a tourist magnet, encourages spending for hotels and food, and thus creates additional employment and income for the area.

In summary, changes in nonincome-determined spending, such as investment spending, government and foreign purchases, and household expenditures from transfer payments or borrowing, will cause changes in economic activity that are a multiple of the initial change in spending.

[8]Be careful when calculating the multiplier effect to always express the percentage of additional income not spent as a decimal. That is, if 20 percent of additional income is not spent, then the multiplier effect is determined by dividing the initial change in nonincome-determined spending by 0.20, not by 20.

APPLICATION 5.3

RIPPLES THROUGH THE ECONOMY

Western Pennsylvania Certainly the older generation in western Pennsylvania, home to coal mining and steel making for over a hundred years, experienced the ripple effect caused by the multiplier principle. Most families in this area knew what it meant when these two industries began to lay off workers.

All one needed was a visit to Pittsburgh or one of the smaller towns like Monesson or Uniontown to see how the slump in steel or coal affected the entire community. As steelworkers or coal miners no longer clocked in to their jobs, the lines formed at the unemployment offices for some relief.

But being out-of-work meant little or no spending at car lots, restaurants, local shops, and even church collections. These establishments then had no choice but to lay off workers, too. As the flower shops, shoe stores, restaurants, remodeling companies, and even churches laid off some of their employees, families had little choice but to cut back on their spending. And you could see it as towns lost their vibrancy. The ripple effect hit almost everyone.

Bring on the Visitors Cities and towns today know the value of attracting tourists, conventions and conferences, and major sporting events. Dynamic communities are funding visitor and convention bureaus, websites, and magazine ads designed to bring people to their towns.

Why are they doing this? It is very simple—the multiplier principle. Consider a major convention. In 2005 Chicago hosted the Rotary International Centennial Convention. More than 60,000 people from all over the globe came to Chicago and rented hotel rooms, ate three meals a day, shopped, visited museums, or, in short spent a lot of money in Chicago. This in turn provided more jobs and income for many Chicagoans, from waitstaff to museum administrators. The ripple effect was felt throughout that economy.

This also explains the competition to attract major sporting events like the Super Bowl and the Final Four, or for cities to cheer their baseball teams on to the World Series. Think about the money that flows into a local economy from four World Series games! Visitors to a city, from the media folks to out-of-town baseball fans, leave the community with millions of dollars that would not have been injected without the event.

The Snowball Effect In the spring of 2009 the economy continued a downward decline that began in the fall of 2008. This downhill spiral was exacerbated by a substantial drop in car sales and uncertainty over the future of General Motors and Chrysler.

When Chrysler announced in May 2009 that it would close a large number of car manufacturing plants in the United States as part of its bankruptcy plan, near panic occurred in cities like Fenton, Missouri, the home of two large Chrysler assembly plants. This would mean a job loss of another 1,000 employees at facilities that just a few years ago employed more than 7,000 people.

Without the plants, suppliers of parts for the Fenton facility—like a nearby car seat company—feared the possibility of going out of business, causing even more workers to be unemployed. And businesses that grew because of the Chrysler plants—from bars and restaurants to grocery stores—worried that their customer base would be gone and they, too, would be forced to shut down.

In addition, the City and the local school district were concerned. How many employees would have to be "let go" because the taxes generated by these facilities would no longer be collected? The plants provided for about 10% of the Fenton city budget and paid $5.7 million annually to the school district.

Fenton officials and business owners were not optimistic about the downward spiral that this old river town could now face. The owner of a local tea house and gift shop was worried about declining customers as spouses of plant workers pinch pennies. "I'm afraid of the snowball effect," she said.

Source: Stephen Deere and Tim O'Neil, "Fenton braces for loss," *St. Louis Post-Dispatch*, May 3, 2009, www.stltoday.com.

Application 5.3, "Ripples through the Economy," provides three examples of the multiplier effect. The first deals with slumps experienced in western Pennsylvania because of coal and steel; the second with rewards from attracting conventions and sporting events to a city; and the third with recent problems in the auto industry. Keep in mind that the multiplier effect applies to both increases and decreases in spending.

A Word about Inflation

We must be careful to understand that it is not always to the benefit of the economy to encourage more spending. When the economy expands, the full production–full employment level of output sets a limit on how far spending can cause production and employment to increase. If spending continues to grow when the economy is at

CHANGES IN ECONOMIC ACTIVITY

In the following examples, explain the effect on output and employment that would result from each action taken alone. Unless specifically indicated, the economy is not at full employment when the action occurs.

1. Businesses install new telecommunications systems.
2. Congress increases personal income tax rates by 5 percent.
3. A decrease in mortgage loan rates and a continued strong demand for housing cause a boom in the home construction business.
4. Overseas buyers purchase a large number of personal computers manufactured in the United States.
5. Newspaper headlines continually carry predictions of a recession in the months to come.
6. Because the economy is at full employment, several major credit card companies successfully campaign to increase the number of, and usage by, cardholders.
7. The interest rates for borrowing money increase.
8. Net exports of goods and services changes from a negative to a positive number.
9. Social Security benefit payments are increased by 2.3 percent.
10. Households, fearing that prices will spiral upward because the economy is at full employment, immediately purchase big-ticket items such as cars and furniture.
11. Businesses postpone their expansion plans while they wait for better economic times.
12. Political pressure prompts Congress to cut its spending on highway projects.
13. Each U.S. taxpayer receives a tax rebate check when the economy is at full employment.
14. A law is passed limiting the number of new foreign automobiles that can enter the country each year.
15. U.S. citizens begin to change their attitudes toward thrift and start to save more.

The following examples relate to the multiplier effect. Determine the direction and size of the change in total output and income that will result from each change in nonincome-determined spending.

16. After several years of drought, farmers in central Illinois spend $50 million on irrigation equipment at a time when households do not spend 25 percent of the additional income they receive.
17. The federal government cuts defense expenditures by $35 billion at a time when households are not spending 40 percent of the additional income they receive.
18. Developers borrow $120 million for new home construction in northern Virginia at a time when households are spending 70 percent of the additional income they receive.
19. Business spending for machinery and equipment falls by $6 billion after predictions of a recession. Households spend only 50 percent of the additional income they receive due to these predictions.
20. Exports increase by $20 million at the same time that imports increase by $25 million. Households spend 60 percent of the additional income they receive.
21. (Be careful!) Government transfer payments increase by $100 million at a time when households spend 80 percent of the additional income they receive.

Answers can be found at the back of the book.

or close to the full production–full employment level of output, demand-pull inflation may result.

Inflation may occur if injections into the spending stream are greater than leakages when the economy is at or near full employment. Too much spending through investment, household borrowing, exporting, and/or government expenditures, or too little saving, importing, and/or taxing could cause prices to rise.

A Word about Expectations

Expectations
Anticipations of future events; can affect current actions by households and businesses and the likelihood that the future events will occur.

Earlier we noted that **expectations** of a recession might induce businesses to cut back investment spending in anticipation of a decline in sales. Expectations of a recession could also cause households to increase their saving because they fear possible job losses. Such actions prompted by the fear of a recession can actually trigger a recession. Fear-induced increases in saving bring about a greater leakage from the spending stream, and a reduction in investment lessens this injection into the spending stream. As saving is increased and investment is reduced, the resulting decrease in spending causes output, employment, and income to fall, and the economy slips into a recession.

Expectations can also cause or worsen inflation. If households and businesses expect prices to rise, they may try to beat the price increases by buying now what they want and need in the future. This surge in spending may serve only to cause or worsen the inflation that is feared.

It is important to maintain good, positive expectations about the economy. Recovery from a recession is more difficult when households and businesses are unwilling to spend because they are pessimistic about the prospects of recovery. Controlling inflation is more difficult if households and businesses believe that prices will continue to go up in the future and that they will be penalized for postponing their expenditures.

You can check your knowledge of the impact of spending, leakages, injections, the multiplier, the full employment ceiling, and expectations on the economy by completing Test Your Understanding, "Changes in Economic Activity."

MACROECONOMIC POLICIES

The goals for a really healthy macroeconomy are full employment, price stability, and full production and economic growth. We have just learned that total spending is the driver of production and employment levels, and sometimes overall price levels. If we want to design policies to reach the healthy macro goals, we need to understand the role of total spending and create policies that affect spending levels.

There are two major types of policies used in the United States to redirect the economy by changing total spending. These policies focus on modifying the leakages and injections that travel through the government sector and through financial institutions.

Fiscal policy modifies spending by changing government taxes, transfer payments, and purchases of goods and services. Fiscal policy can increase spending to redirect the economy into an expansion or decrease spending to slow it down. The workings of this strategy for influencing the economy will be discussed in the next chapter.

Monetary policy focuses on changing borrowing and, to a lesser degree, saving, or the injections and leakages that flow through financial institutions. This policy falls into the domain of the Federal Reserve, whose actions can change interest rates and the amount of funding available for loans. The Federal Reserve can create conditions that encourage borrowing and spending by households and businesses, or tighten credit and discourage borrowing and spending. The Federal Reserve, loan making, interest rates, and monetary policy are covered in Chapters 7 and 8.

Strong opinions and disagreements exist about which policies are best for dealing with problems in the macroeconomy. Various points of view on the proper method for reaching objectives or dealing with problems in the macroeconomy will be covered in the upcoming macroeconomic chapters.

Fiscal Policy
Influencing the levels of aggregate output and employment or prices through changes in federal government purchases, transfer payments, and/or taxes.

Monetary Policy
Influencing the levels of aggregate output and employment or prices through changes in interest rates and the money supply.

Summary

1. Market economies, such as that of the United States, are constantly experiencing expansions and contractions in their levels of real GDP. These recurring upswings and downswings in production are called business cycles. Business cycles affect not only output but also employment and income. Business cycles have four phases: recovery, peak, recession, and trough. The length of time in each phase and its intensity differ from cycle to cycle.

2.   There are several theories about the causes of economic fluctuations. These different theories are based on differing sets of assumptions and variables.

3.   Changes in total, or aggregate, spending on new goods and services cause changes in economic activity. An increase in total spending increases output, employment, and income, and the economy grows until it reaches full employment. A decrease in total spending decreases output, employment, and income, and the economy contracts. Total spending is the spending by the household, business, government, and foreign sectors together.

4.   Household spending on new goods and services, called personal consumption expenditures, is fairly stable as it increases from year to year, and is greater than the combined purchases of businesses, government units, and foreign buyers. Most household spending originates from income earned from producing goods and services. Households can also make purchases from borrowed funds and transfer payments, which are labeled nonincome-determined spending because they do not come from household earned income. These nonincome-determined expenditures are injections into the spending stream. In addition to buying goods and services, households can use income for saving or paying taxes, which are leakages from the spending stream.

5.   The purchase of new goods such as machinery and equipment by businesses is called investment spending and is a form of nonincome-determined spending. Of the major components of total spending, investment is the least stable and a major source of fluctuations in output, employment, and income. Investment spending is influenced by profit expectations that are affected by the outlook for future economic activity and the interest rate for borrowing funds. Investment spending is an injection into the spending stream: Increases in investment spending stimulate the level of economic activity, and reductions in investment spending lead to reductions in output, employment, and income. Business saving and taxes are leakages from the spending stream.

6.   Government can influence spending in three areas: the purchase of goods and services, transfer payments, and taxes on households and businesses. Government purchases of goods and services are a form of nonincome-determined spending and are direct injections into the spending stream. Transfer payments provide injections, and taxes are a leakage.

7.   Expenditures by U.S. buyers on imported goods and services are leakages from the spending stream. Purchases of exported U.S. goods and services by foreign buyers are injections and classified as nonincome-determined expenditures. Net exports is exports minus imports and indicates whether the foreign sector had a net positive or negative impact on total spending. Net exports has tended to be negative over the past few decades.

8.   Leakages from the spending stream include saving and paying taxes by households and businesses as well as purchases of imports. Injections include household spending from borrowing and transfer payments, business investment spending, government purchases of goods and services, and purchases of exports.

9. If all leakages from the spending stream equal all injections, the level of economic activity will continue unchanged. If leakages exceed injections, spending decreases, and the level of economic activity falls. If injections are greater than leakages, the spending stream expands, and the level of economic activity grows.

10. An increase or decrease in nonincome-determined household expenditures, investment spending, government purchases, or foreign spending leads to a multiple increase or decrease in the levels of output, employment, and income. The multiplier effect is calculated by dividing the initial change in nonincome-determined spending by the percentage of additional income received by households that is not spent.

11. If the economy is operating at or near full employment, increases in spending may lead to demand-pull inflation rather than to increases in output and employment. For this reason, increasing total spending does not always cause the economy to expand.

12. Expectations can influence total spending and therefore complicate the job of stabilizing the economy. Because of the effect of expectations on spending, fears can cause self-fulfilling prophecies: The fear of a recession can lead to a recession, and the fear of inflation can lead to inflation.

13. The objectives of full production and economic growth, full employment, and stable prices can be accomplished through increasing or decreasing total spending. Fiscal policy influences total spending through changes in government purchases of goods and services, transfers, and taxes. Monetary policy influences spending through changes in the interest rate and money supply, or changes in lending and borrowing.

Key Terms and Concepts

Business cycles

Recovery

Peak

Recession

Trough

Total, or aggregate, spending

Personal consumption expenditures

Income-determined spending

Transfer payments

Nonincome-determined spending

Injections into the spending stream

Financial institutions

Leakages from the spending stream

Investment spending

Retained earnings

Saving–borrowing relationship

Government purchases of goods and services

Exports

Imports

Net exports

Multiplier effect

Expectations

Fiscal policy

Monetary policy

Review Questions	1. Identify the four phases of a business cycle and describe the changes in economic activity that occur during each phase.

2. What is the basic cause of a recession?

3. What is the difference between income-determined spending and nonincome-determined spending? What are the different types of nonincome-determined spending? Why are all nonincome-determined expenditures injections into the spending stream?

4. Changes in the level of economic activity are related to changes in the spending of households, businesses, government units, and buyers in the foreign sector.
   a. How do personal consumption expenditures, investment spending, government purchases of goods and services, and net exports compare in terms of relative size and stability?
   b. How are personal consumption expenditures affected by taxes, transfer payments, saving, and borrowing?
   c. How is investment spending affected by changes in the interest rate?
   d. Why are government expenditures on goods and services a direct injection and government expenditures on transfer payments not a direct injection into the spending stream?
   e. What effects do transactions in the foreign sector have on domestic levels of output, employment, and income?
   f. Under what circumstances would an increase in total spending lead primarily to an increase in output, and when would it lead primarily to an increase in prices?

5. Identify the various leakages from and injections into the spending stream in a circular flow model of the economy. What is the relationship between leakages and injections when the level of economic activity is expanding, contracting, or remaining unchanged? What role do financial institutions play in the relationship between leakages and injections?

6. What is the multiplier effect, and how is it related to nonincome-determined spending and the circular flow of economic activity? What happens to the multiplier effect when the percentage of additional earned income not spent increases? Why does this happen?

7. In each of the following cases, calculate the change that occurs in the level of output as a result of the multiplier effect.
   a. Government purchases of goods and services increase by $600 million, and 20 percent of additional income received is not spent.
   b. Household spending from borrowing declines by $1 billion, and 30 percent of additional income received is not spent.
   c. Investment spending increases by $800 million, and 75 percent of additional income received is spent.
   d. Investment spending increases by $20 billion at the same time that U.S. net exports decrease by $15 billion, and 60 percent of additional income received is spent.

e. Household purchases from transfer payments increase by $500 million when the economy is at full employment, and two-thirds of additional income received is spent.

8. Take a large sheet of paper and construct a circular flow model that illustrates all of the leakages and injections in the macroeconomy.

---

1. Figure 5.1 shows that since 1985 business cycles in the U.S. economy have had long recovery and relatively short recession phases. Why do you think this has happened? Do you think this pattern is typical of what we can expect from the economy in the future?

2. Suppose the economy were in a recession and someone said to you, "If we simply started producing more, the recession and unemployment problems would go away." How would you evaluate this statement?

3. Personal consumption expenditures grow at a relatively constant rate over time, while investment spending fluctuates widely. What reasons might explain why personal consumption expenditures are more stable than investment spending?

4. Suppose the economy is in a recession and a member of Congress sponsors a bill to limit imports of vehicles, clothing, and other manufactured goods. The bill, if passed into law, would allegedly ensure that some of the dollars currently leaving the spending stream for imports would instead be spent on domestic products, thereby increasing output, employment, and income, and reversing the recession. Is this bill a realistic solution to reversing the recession? How would you vote for this bill if you were in Congress?

5. Expectations play an important role in determining the level of economic activity and how the level of activity will change. What events might cause people to expect a recession? What events might cause people to expect inflation? What could be done to make the economy more predictable and help stabilize expectations?

6. Do you think there will be a positive or negative impact on economic activity as the United States pursues more "green" efforts? Consider a move toward more fuel-efficient vehicles and buildings in your answer.

7. The multiplier effect is larger or smaller depending on whether households spend more or less of their additional income. What effect might the expectation of a recession have on the multiplier? What effect might the expectation of inflation have on the multiplier?

8. Fiscal and monetary policies are designed to influence the level of economic activity through their impacts on total spending. Using the circular flow model, identify the leakages and injections each of these policies affects.

Critical Thinking Case 5

PRESIDENT TRUMAN'S DESPERATE WISH

Critical Thinking Skills

Understanding the value of predictors of future behavior

Determining appropriate data from which to form an opinion

Economic Concepts

Changes in the level of output

Indicators of economic activity

President Harry S. Truman (1945–1953), frustrated with advisers taking one position on the state of the economy and then backing away to another position, finally reached the point of asking if he could find a one-armed economist who wouldn't say, ". . . but on the other hand."

The fact is that how data about changing economic conditions predict the future is not obvious and is often disputed by people observing those data. For example, on June 7, 2008, the *McClatchy–Tribune Business News* published an article headlined, "Oil surge, job losses rip stocks: Combined factors have economists fearing recession." Then, three days later the *Wall Street Journal* published a story headlined "U.S. News: Bernanke Unshaken by Jobless Rise; Fed's Outlook Intact As Other Indicators Ease the Worst Fears." Ben Bernanke is not just another economist; he is the chairman of the Federal Reserve system. What's the likelihood that people reading the *Wall Street Journal* would have come away with more confidence about the state of the economy than those reading the *McClatchy–Tribune Business News?* And if they were more confident, might they have spent more and saved less of their income than the person reading the *Business News?*

To make matters worse, there are a lot of places you can go to get forecasts about the state of the economy. A recent computer search on "U.S. economic forecast" came up with over 3 million hits. Admittedly most of those could be thrown out right away, but the fact is there would be more than a few sites left.

What do people look to when trying to anticipate the future course of the economy? While there is no short list of warning numbers that everyone watches, there are several indicators that are widely reported. One, as noted, is changes in the unemployment rate and, related to this, new applications for unemployment insurance. Another is stock price movements, which hint at people's expectations about business profitability. Many economic analysts also look at the Consumer Confidence Index, which tracks household confidence about the state of the economy. And then there are actions taken by the Federal Reserve to raise or lower interest rates, which affect the ability to borrow of consumers and businesses.

What's a good rule when confronting information on the state of the economy? Think about what you're reading or hearing, and don't be afraid to ask the "why" question.

Sources: Paul Gores, Joel Dresang, "Oil surge, job losses rip stocks: Combined factors have economists fearing recession," *McClatchy–Tribune Business News,* June 7, 2008; Greg Ip, Sudeep Reddy, "U.S. News: Bernanke Unshaken by Jobless Rise; Fed's Outlook Intact As Other Indicators Ease the Worst Fears," *Wall Street Journal* (Eastern edition), June 10, 2008, p. A3.

Questions

1. Why would someone be interested in locating indicators to predict the future behavior of the economy? Why would these indicators of economic activity, rather than data on current changes in total output itself, be useful?

2. How do each of the indicators given in this case—the unemployment rate, new applications for unemployment insurance, stock prices, consumer confidence, and Federal Reserve policies—convey information about changes in total spending and the level of economic activity?

3. In addition to the indicators listed here, what other kinds of data might be used to predict the direction of the economy, and why?

CHAPTER *6*

The Role of Government in the Macroeconomy

CHAPTER OBJECTIVES

To identify the major expenditures and revenues of federal, state, and local governments.

To distinguish among progressive, proportional, and regressive taxes, and discuss recent tax issues and reforms.

To introduce fiscal policy, explain its mechanics, and differentiate between discretionary and automatic fiscal policy.

To define a surplus, balanced, and deficit budget, and identify the economic impact of each.

To explain the relationship between the federal budget and fiscal policy.

To define the national debt, explain its financing, size, and burden on taxpayers, and introduce crowding out.

Let's begin this chapter with a quick civics lesson. As the world becomes more global and we are far more influenced by the activities of other nations and cultures, differences in the types of governments under which people live become more relevant. Global concerns have also fostered an increased awareness of, and interest in, the democratic form in the United States. Here people elect other people to represent them and make decisions on their behalf; decisions are not made by dictators, military or religious leaders, or kings.

The philosophy underlying a representative form of government has fostered multiple political subdivisions in the United States: Authority and functions are dispersed through many government units. There is a federal jurisdiction along with state and local jurisdictions. As a result, we elect and give decision-making authority to a president, congresspersons, a state governor and state legislators, and local mayors, council members, county and township representatives, school board members, and others. Try to fill in Table 6.1 by identifying the elected officials who represent you.

While governments wrestle with everything from national security at airports to summer recreational camps for kids, our focus is on the role of the government sector in the macroeconomy. We know from Chapter 5 that total spending influences the direction of the economy and that government impacts this spending through its purchases of goods and services, transfer payments, and the taxes it collects. This is a sizable role: The sheer magnitude of expenditures and taxes makes government extremely important in the functioning of the economy.

Not surprisingly, the largest single purchaser of goods and services in the United States is the federal government. A decision made at the federal level to initiate or cancel an interstate highway project or defense system, or to increase or decrease taxes, can have a far-reaching impact on the economy. Similar effects are felt when state and local governments change their tax and expenditure patterns. Enacting a local sales tax to fund park trails, building a new high school gym, and buying a street sweeper have an impact on the economy.

TABLE 6.1   *Government Representatives*

Use the following table to identify the persons who represent you.

U.S. CONGRESS

My state senators are _____ and _____.
My congressional district representative is _____.

STATE

My governor is _____.
My district's state senator is _____.
My district's state representative is _____.

LOCAL

My head of county government is _____.
I am represented at the local level (could be a mayor, council member, township representative, school board member) by
_____, who is a _____ (title);
_____, who is a _____ (title); and
_____, who is a _____ (title).

TABLE 6.2

Total, Federal, and State and Local Government Expenditures, and Total Government Expenditures as a Percentage of GDP, Selected Years 1985–2008 (Billions of Dollars)

Over the years, government expenditures have increased in absolute terms and remained relatively stable as a percentage of GDP.

GOVERNMENT EXPENDITURES

Year	Total[a]	Federal	State and Local	Total as a Percentage of GDP
1985	1,366.1	948.2	498.7	32.4%
1990	1,872.6	1,253.5	730.5	32.3
1995	2,397.6	1,603.5	978.2	32.4
2000	2,886.5	1,864.4	1,269.5	29.4
2005	3,882.6	2,558.6	1,684.9	31.3
2008	4,802.5	3,140.2	2,048.8	33.3

[a]Total government expenditures have been adjusted to eliminate the duplication of spending from federal grants-in-aid to state and local governments.

Source: *Economic Report of the President* (Washington, DC: U.S. Government Printing Office, 2009), Tables B-1, B-22. Figures for 2008 are preliminary and through the third quarter.

Since government spending and taxing can affect the economy's levels of output, employment, income, and, sometimes, prices, government can modify the direction of the economy through its impact on total, or aggregate, spending. An important outcome for you from working through the material in this chapter is the foundation that you will gain for critically evaluating government tax and spending policies. These policies constantly receive widespread attention because we are always debating some related issue: the size of the national debt, appropriate government programs, tax cuts, the Social Security system, school funding, and many others. Government taxing and spending issues always play an important role in political campaigns. After learning the material in this chapter, you should be better able to tell whether the 30-second campaign sound bite of a candidate is accurate or even realistic.

GOVERNMENT EXPENDITURES AND REVENUES

Government Expenditures

In 2008, all government units together spent about $4.8 trillion for a huge variety of purposes ranging from military aircraft to the construction of sewage plants to police salaries. Table 6.2 lists the total expenditures of all government units combined as well as the federal government and state and local governments for selected years from 1985 through 2008. In addition to the magnitude of government expenditures, notice that federal expenditures exceed state and local spending by a wide margin.

People frequently express concern over increases in government spending and the size of the government sector. Is this concern justified? One way to evaluate the size of government is to measure total government expenditures as a percentage of GDP. This is done in the last column of Table 6.2. A scan down this column shows that, over the years, government spending as a percentage of GDP has been relatively stable.

TABLE 6.3	*Federal Government Expenditure Categories, Selected Years 1985–2008*

The composition of federal spending has changed over the years. Transfer payments constitute the largest expenditure category, and interest payments have fluctuated.

	PERCENTAGE OF TOTAL EXPENDITURES[a]					
Expenditure Category	**1985**	**1990**	**1995**	**2000**	**2005**	**2008**
Purchases of goods and services	36%	33%	27%	27%	30%	30%
Transfer payments	44	45	52	56	58	57
Interest payments	18	19	18	15	10	11
Financial assistance	2	2	2	2	2	2
Total	100%	100%	100%	100%	100%	100%

[a]Percentages may not add to 100 percent due to rounding.

Source: *Economic Report of the President* (Washington, DC: U.S. Government Printing Office, 2009), Table B-84. Figures for 2008 are preliminary and through the third quarter.

Government Purchases of Goods and Services
Government spending on new goods and services.

Public Good
A good (or service) provided for all of society; no one is excluded from use of a public good.

Quasi-Public Good
A government-provided good that could also be offered in a private market.

Transfer Payments
Money from the government for which no direct work is required in return.

Categories of Government Expenditures   We can classify government expenditures into several categories. Some spending is for **government purchases of goods and services,** such as the services of people who work for the government in many jobs from military careers to public pool lifeguards and goods ranging from limousines for dignitaries to paper clips. Many government purchases are for **public goods,** which are those provided for everyone and which exclude no one from their use. Lighthouses, public parks, and flood control dams are all examples of public goods. When government provides a good or service that could also be offered in a private market, such as education or an ambulance haul, it provides a **quasi-public good.** The provision of public and quasi-public goods is an important function of government.

Another category of government spending is **transfer payments,** which are payments from the government for which nothing is required in return. That is, people who receive monthly Social Security payments, veterans' benefits, unemployment compensation, or public assistance receive transfer payments, unlike people who receive wages for working as government employees.

Interest paid on borrowed funds is another government expenditure category. Since government units sometimes finance some of their spending through borrowed funds, the interest on that money is an expense that the government unit must pay.[1] Finally, the federal government may also incur expenses from financial assistance to state and local governments and others who use the funds for hospitals, additional police, road reconstruction, and such.

Table 6.3 shows how the federal government has allocated money among the various expenditure categories just identified. Notice that the largest percentage of federal expenditures is for transfer payments and that this percentage is growing.

The way state and local governments allocate their spending has not changed significantly over the last few decades. In recent years, over 70 percent of state and

---

[1]Borrowing at the federal level is done through various securities issued by the U.S. Treasury and at the state and local levels with municipal bonds or other instruments.

local expenditures has gone toward the purchase of goods and services. Much of this spending is for salaries of police, fire, hospital, school, and other state and local government employees.

The spending information in Figure 6.1 provides a different way to look at spending by the federal and state and local governments by giving the function or purpose for using the funds. This figure helps us to understand the type of spending and programs that are in the jurisdiction of these government units. Notice that the federal government's major spending is for defense, veterans, Social Security, and Medicare and that education ranks first among the state and local government spending purposes.

Government Revenues

In 2008, governments received over $4.1 trillion in revenue. Every man, woman, and child in the United States contributed, on average, $13,645 to all government units.[2] Most of the revenue that governments receive comes from taxes, and we pay many different kinds: federal and state income taxes; local earnings taxes; sales tax; property tax on a residence; personal property tax; capital gains tax; inheritance and gift taxes; utility tax; gasoline, liquor, and cigarette taxes; tariffs on imports; corporate income tax; various business taxes; and others.

Social Insurance Program

Contributions from an individual's wages are made to a fund from which that individual may draw when eligible for benefits.

Governments also receive revenue from sources other than taxes. For example, the federal government's Social Security program is a **social insurance program.** Although payment is required from participating individuals, the payment is considered to be a contribution to a retirement and welfare fund rather than a tax. Many local governments count on fees for revenue: building permits, rentals for the local ice rink, and fines for speeding, to name a few.

Revenue Sources   Table 6.4 gives the major sources of federal government revenue. The largest source of funds, and a fairly stable source, is the individual income tax; other taxes, such as the corporate income tax and excise taxes, typically provide less than 20 percent of federal revenue. The second largest source of revenue, at about one-third, is social insurance, primarily contributions to Social Security. The federal government's reliance on household income as a source of revenue, through the individual income tax and contributions to social insurance, helps to stir agitation about the tax burden imposed on individuals.

State and local government revenues come from a wider variety of sources than do federal revenues: Taxes, primarily property, sales, and individual income taxes, account for less than 60 percent of the total. Nontax sources include license fees, tuition from public colleges and universities, some recreation and other fees, and interest, as well as funds—typically grants—received from the federal government.

A wide disparity exists in the types of taxes and tax rates (percentages) imposed by different state and local government units. For example, it was recently estimated that a family in Philadelphia, Pennsylvania, earning $50,000 per year pays 13.7 percent of their income to state and local taxes, whereas a family in Jacksonville, Florida, earning $50,000 pays 4.7 percent. In Indianapolis, Indiana, the effective tax on residential property is $3.21 per $100, and in Honolulu, Hawaii, it is $0.38 per $100.[3] Some states

---

[2]*Economic Report of the President* (Washington, DC: U.S. Government Printing Office, 2009), Table B.82. Based on preliminary total government revenue figure for third quarter of 2008. Civilian population for 2007 was used to calculate per capita numbers. U.S. Census Bureau, *The 2009 Statistical Abstract*, Table 2, "Population: 1960 to 2007."

[3]*Statistical Abstract of the United States: 2008*, p. 280. Taxes were estimated for 2005.

FIGURE 6.1   *Federal and State and Local Government Expenditures, by Function*

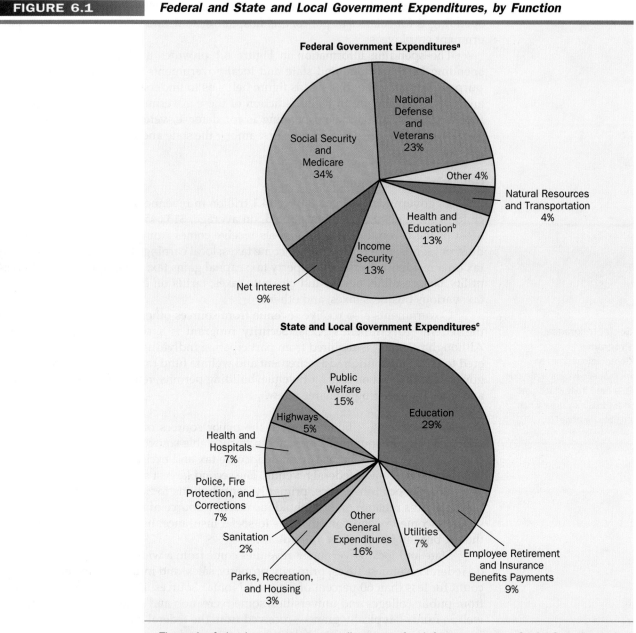

Federal Government Expenditures[a]

- National Defense and Veterans 23%
- Other 4%
- Natural Resources and Transportation 4%
- Health and Education[b] 13%
- Income Security 13%
- Net Interest 9%
- Social Security and Medicare 34%

State and Local Government Expenditures[c]

- Public Welfare 15%
- Education 29%
- Highways 5%
- Health and Hospitals 7%
- Police, Fire Protection, and Corrections 7%
- Sanitation 2%
- Parks, Recreation, and Housing 3%
- Other General Expenditures 16%
- Utilities 7%
- Employee Retirement and Insurance Benefits Payments 9%

The major federal government expenditures are for defense, veterans, Social Security, and Medicare, and the major state and local expenditure is for education.

[a]Estimated 2007.
[b]Includes training, employment, and social services.
[c]Figures are for 2004.

Source: U.S. Bureau of the Census, *Statistical Abstract of the United States: 2008*, 127th ed. (Washington, DC: U.S. Government Printing Office, 2008), pp. 270, 308.

TABLE 6.4						

Sources of Federal Government Revenue, Selected Years 1985–2008[a]

Individual income taxes and social insurance payments are the primary sources of revenue for the federal government.

	PERCENTAGE OF TOTAL REVENUE PER YEAR[b]					
Source	1985	1990	1995	2000	2005	2008
Individual income taxes	46%	45%	44%	50%	43%	45%
Social insurance[c]	36	37	36	32	37	36
Corporation income taxes	8	9	12	10	13	12
Excise taxes	5	3	4	3	3	3
Customs, estate, and gift taxes	3	3	3	2	2	2
Miscellaneous receipts	3	2	2	2	2	2
Total	100%	100%	100%	100%	100%	100%

[a]Fiscal years; 2008 is estimated.
[b]Percentages may not add to 100 percent because of rounding.
[c]Includes social insurance and retirement contributions.

Sources: 1985 from *Statistical Abstract of the United States: 1990*, p. 310; 1990 from *Statistical Abstract of the United States: 1996*, p. 331; 1995 from *Economic Report of the President*, 2001, p. 370; 2000 from *Economic Report of the President*, 2002, p. 416; 2005 from *Economic Report of the President*, 2006, p. 378; 2008 from *Economic Report of the President*, 2009, Table B-81.

have had unusual revenue sources: for example, a tax on income earned by "persons expounding religious doctrines" in Hawaii, a tax on raw fish in Alaska, and a fee for each parachute jump in New Hampshire.

Progressive, Proportional, and Regressive Taxes

There are always issues around the payment of taxes. Even though voters may elect to raise a tax, few people welcome an additional tax burden. The burden of paying a tax is not the same for all individuals. The proportion of one's income that goes to a tax differs with each specific tax and with the level of income. To help us understand how a tax impacts income, we classify taxes as progressive, proportional, or regressive.

Progressive Tax
A tax reflecting a direct relationship between the percentage of income taxed and the size of the income.

With a **progressive tax** there is a direct relationship between the percentage of income taxed and the size of the income: The percentage of income taxed increases as income increases and decreases as income decreases. The federal personal income tax is progressive. For 2008, a single taxpayer had six income steps: 10% on income up to $8,025; 15% on income between $8,025 and $32,550; 25% between $32,550 and $78,850; 28% between $78,850 and $164,550; 33% between $164,550 and $357,700; and 35% on income above $357,700.[4] Some states also have income taxes with progressive rates.

Proportional Tax (Flat Tax)
A tax equal to the same percentage of income regardless of the size of the income.

With a **proportional tax,** or **flat tax,** the percentage of income taxed is the same for any income, large or small. A city wage tax of, say, 1 percent means that an individual earning $10,000 per year would pay 1 percent, or $100, to the city and an individual earning $100,000 would also pay 1 percent, or $1,000. In each case, the same percentage of income is taken as tax. Proposals to change the federal income tax from a progressive to a flat tax often surface in political campaigns. This happened in the 1992 and 1996 presidential campaigns, and there is no doubt that it will happen again. Up for

[4]U.S. Department of the Treasury, Internal Revenue Service, *1040 Instructions for 2008*, p. 92.

SHOULD THE FEDERAL INCOME TAX BE CHANGED TO A FLAT TAX?

Issue   *There have been several proposals to change the U.S. federal personal income tax from its current progressive structure to a flat tax, where everyone pays a tax equal to the same percentage of income regardless of the size of the income. Should we adopt a flat tax?*

Yes   The current federal income tax system should be abandoned in favor of a flat tax because the current system is complicated and not as progressive as it might appear. This system has hundreds of tax forms and schedules, and it is estimated that nearly 5 billion person-hours are required to "do taxes." With these complications, people make mistakes or may not find the tax protection to which they are entitled. With a flat tax, a one-page form may be all that is needed.

Although in principle the current tax system is progressive, it is a system riddled with shelters and exemptions that favor special groups. Once people take advantage of various tax-reducing opportunities, such as home mortgage, business expense, and retirement account reductions, some of the progressiveness of the system may be reduced. In the end, some higher-income earners may

not pay much more than lower-income earners. Also, the federal income tax is only progressive up to a point. While a larger percentage of income will be taxed for a person earning $500,000 than for a person earning $50,000, a person earning $5 million or even $50 million will pay no higher a percentage than the person earning $500,000. Where has the progressiveness gone?

No   The current progressive tax structure should be maintained because of the uncertainty about who actually benefits from a flat tax and the possibility that a greater tax burden will be placed on people with lower incomes. While a flat tax system would be easier to understand and administer, the equalized tax rate could result in lower taxes for those with higher incomes and higher taxes for those with lower incomes. The real issue is whether a flat tax treats everyone the same or whether it puts a greater tax burden on those least able to pay the tax.

At the heart of the issue is whether we want to acknowledge the struggles that come with low incomes and with the misfortunes and crises of life. Do we really want someone who tries to maintain a family on $25,000 a year to pay, say, 20 percent of income in taxes, the same percentage that someone who earns $250,000 or $2,500,000 would pay? Do we really want to eliminate the tax deductions that come from the expenses of a medical crisis or a natural disaster such as a hurricane? At least today's tax system provides an opportunity to reduce the tax bill for those in need.

Debate, "Should the Federal Income Tax Be Changed to a Flat Tax?", raises some interesting points for both sides of this issue. Which position do you favor, and why?

Regressive Tax

A tax reflecting an inverse relationship between the percentage of income taxed and the size of the income.

With a **regressive tax,** the percentage of income taxed varies inversely with the size of the income: The percentage increases as income decreases and decreases as income increases. In other words, a regressive tax hits those with low incomes the hardest. Sales taxes are considered to be regressive, particularly the sales tax on food. On the surface, sales taxes may not appear to be regressive because they are a specified percentage of a product's price or the amount sold. But remember it is the relationship between the tax paid and *income,* not between the tax paid and the purchase, that makes a tax regressive. For example, with a sales tax of 6 percent on food, an annual grocery bill of $8,000 means that a tax of $480 must be paid. For a family earning $24,000 a year, that $480 tax amounts to 2 percent of their income. For a family earning $80,000 a year, it amounts to just 0.6 percent of their income. The person with a low income likely thinks about the $6 that must be paid with every $100 grocery order and what must be given up to pay it.

Tax Reform and Issues

Tax Reform

Changes in tax policies and structures.

Our elected government representatives frequently find themselves in a tug-of-war. On one side are those constituents who want more from government—a larger armed military, prescription drug coverage, more police patrols, local leaf pickup—and on the other side are those who want a reduction in taxes. As a consequence, changes in tax policies and structures, or **tax reform,** is the subject of much discussion and action at all levels of government. Sometimes tax reform reflects a need for more revenues to

---

APPLICATION 6.1

A Chronology of Federal Income Tax Policies

- **1909** A federal corporate income tax of 1 percent with a $5,000 exemption is adopted.
- **1913** A federal individual income tax is enacted; applies mainly to a small number of high incomes—the lowest bracket is 1 percent on taxable income up to $20,000; taxes are paid in quarterly installments in the year following the receipt of the income.
- **World War I Era** The corporate income tax rate is raised to a high of 12 percent in 1918; the individual rate is raised to 6 percent on taxable income up to $4,000; and the top bracket rate is raised to 77 percent on taxable income over $1 million.
- **The 1930s** The corporate tax rate changes several times, ranging between 7 and 27 percent; no significant individual rate changes for most average-size incomes.
- **World War II** The need to raise revenue for the war effort causes significant increases in tax rates and a lowering of brackets and exemptions. Corporate rates reach as high as 25 percent on the first $25,000 of profit, 53 percent on the second $25,000, and 40 percent on profit over $50,000. Individual income tax rates reach as high as

23 percent on taxable income up to $2,000 and 94 percent on taxable income over $200,000.
- **1943** The tax payment system is changed so that individual income taxes are paid when income is earned, rather than in quarterly installments in the following year.
- **1952** The tax on corporate profit over $25,000 is raised to 52 percent and remains at approximately that level until 1974; however, other changes, such as rules for determining depreciation, occur over this same time period.
- **1964** The first significant cut in individual income taxes since the 1940s occurs; rates are cut on lower income brackets and the highest rate is dropped to 77 percent.
- **1968** A 10 percent additional charge is applied to all individual and corporate income taxes to help reduce inflationary pressure caused by spending on the Vietnam War effort.
- **1982** As a result of legislation in 1981, individual income tax rates are significantly lowered; the highest rate drops to 50 percent.
- **1987** Corporate tax rates, which have continuously declined during the 1980s, are lowered to 15 percent for the first $50,000 of profit and 34 percent on profit over $335,000.
- **1988** A new tax law takes effect that lowers the highest marginal rate on individual income to 33 percent.
- **1990–2008** The highest marginal tax rate fluctuates between 31 and 39.6 percent.

---

support the demands for increased spending. For example, at the local level more taxes might be needed to fund the education of increasing numbers of school-age children or to purchase more fire equipment as new homes and apartments are built. But sometimes tax reform is rooted in politics. For example, candidates running for public office often make taxes a campaign issue as they attempt to win voters.

Value judgments and political considerations enter into all discussions of tax reform. If a state, for example, needs more funding for its highways, should it tax everyone equally, should a progressive tax that places a greater burden on people earning higher incomes be imposed, or should the tax be levied on those who directly benefit from using the highways?

Changes in the federal income tax provide good examples of how value judgments and political considerations lead to tax reform. Application 6.1, "A Chronology of Federal Income Tax Policies," highlights some major changes in federal corporate and individual income tax rules that have occurred since the beginning of the twentieth century. What values or political considerations might explain some of the changes recorded in this application? How does armed military conflict tend to affect the structure of taxes?

Tax Bracket Indexation

A policy of adjusting income tax brackets to account for inflation.

Tax reform was particularly vigorous in the 1980s. In 1981 Congress passed the Economic Recovery Tax Act, which, among other changes, introduced the concept of indexing, or adjusting, the federal personal income tax brackets to inflation. **Tax bracket indexation** helps offset "bracket creep," which occurs when taxpayers are

Tax Reform Act of 1986
Major legislation that changed federal income tax exemptions, deductions, brackets, and rates.

pushed into higher tax brackets as their money, or nominal, incomes increase to keep pace with inflation. Another significant overhaul of the federal income tax system occurred with the **Tax Reform Act of 1986.** This brought major changes in the way an individual's federal personal income tax is calculated, including a reduction in the number of tax brackets and rate levels in those brackets. Prior to this act, there were 15 brackets and a maximum tax rate of 50 percent. Today, with amendments to this act, we have six brackets with a maximum rate of 35 percent.

Tax Base
The particular thing on which a tax is levied.

Tax Base   An important decision for those imposing a tax is the **tax base,** or the particular thing on which the tax will be levied. For example, the tax base for an income tax is income, for a sales tax it is the price of the item sold, and for a property tax it is the value of the property. Often the choice of a tax base is determined by legislation, and some government units are limited in the selections they may make. The other important decision concerns the **tax rate,** or the amount that is levied on the base.

Tax Rate
The amount that is levied on the base.

Many local and state governments are facing a declining or changing tax base. As large cities in the United States experience declines in population and the departure of businesses to other locations, local officials become concerned about an eroding ability to raise adequate revenues. In many large cities, taxes are being paid by fewer businesses and the populations that remain tend to be poorer. On the other hand, many suburban communities have benefited from both property and sales taxes because of this migration. The growth in huge suburban malls and big-box stores, and the relocation of corporate headquarters have had positive tax consequences for the tax districts in which they are located.

Tax Abatement
A policy of reducing or eliminating a tax that would normally be charged.

Sometimes state and local governments try to lure large companies, retailers, and manufacturing facilities into their areas by providing substantial financial incentives, including **tax abatement.** For example, in September 2008, the Kokomo, Indiana, Council approved a 10-year, $160 million tax abatement for Delphi Electronics to continue hybrid technology work at a plant that provides about 3,000 jobs, and in August 2008, the Michigan Economic Growth Authority announced that more than $650 million in economic development projects in the state were approved, with many anchored by tax credits including abatement.[5] And at many local levels tax relief is sought to establish larger retailers and office buildings. Although the intent of these incentives is to create jobs and stimulate the economy in a region, many question whether state and local governments can recoup what they have been giving up.

FISCAL POLICY

We know that the amount of money that government spends and taxes affects the economy's levels of output, employment, and income. And, a change in either spending or taxes can cause the economy to move into an expansion, or recovery, or move into a contraction, or recession. When the federal government changes its spending and/or taxing to control unemployment or demand-pull inflation, it is putting **fiscal policy** into play.

Fiscal Policy
Influencing the levels of aggregate output and employment or prices through changes in federal government purchases, transfer payments, and/or taxes.

Fiscal policy has evolved largely from the theories of John Maynard Keynes, who focused on the relationship between aggregate spending and the level of economic activity, and suggested that the government could fill in a spending gap created by a lack

[5]Ken de la Bastide, "Council approves Delphi abatement," Kokomo Tribune.com, http://www.kokomotribune.com; "Granholm announces $658 million in investments," Crain's Detroit Business, http://www.crainsdetroit.com, December 8, 2008.

of private spending. The theories of John Maynard Keynes and other economists are discussed in greater detail in Chapter 9.

The Mechanics of Fiscal Policy

If you remember the material in Chapter 5 (the role of spending, the circular flow, the relationship between leakages and injections), the mechanics of fiscal policy should be easy. Remember the basic principle of that chapter: Increases in spending cause the economy to expand and decreases in spending cause it to contract.

When the economy experiences unemployment because of a decline in spending, Congress could help to reverse that unemployment through fiscal policy actions that increase the level of aggregate spending and, consequently, the level of economic activity. Increased spending could come from

♦ increased government purchases of goods and services, and/or
♦ increased transfer payments, and/or
♦ decreased taxes.

These three actions could be taken separately or in combination.

Although each of these actions can cause economic activity to grow, the expansionary impact of increasing government purchases by a particular amount is greater than the expansionary impact of increasing transfers or decreasing taxes by the same amount. All of the dollars spent on government purchases are injected directly into the spending stream, whereas increased transfers and decreased taxes provide additional income, part of which will be spent but part of which will be saved. In other words, there would be a stronger economic impact from spending $10 million to improve trails in national parks than from giving taxpayers a $10 million tax break.

If the economy is experiencing demand-pull inflation from too much spending, the appropriate fiscal policy action for lowering the inflation rate is to decrease aggregate spending. Excess spending could be removed from the economy by

♦ decreasing government purchases of goods and services, and/or
♦ decreasing transfer payments, and/or
♦ increasing taxes.

Again, a more pronounced decrease in spending results from a decrease in government purchases because some of the reduced transfers and increased taxes would affect saving rather than spending.

Government expenditures and taxes affect nonincome-determined spending, and, as a result, they are subject to a multiplier effect. (Again, review this material in Chapter 5 if you have forgotten it.) This means, for example, if the government injected $50 billion into the spending stream through increased purchases or transfers, or through decreased taxes, the level of economic activity would increase by more than $50 billion. Alternatively, if the government withdrew $50 billion from the spending stream, output, income, and employment would decrease by more than $50 billion.

Discretionary and Automatic Fiscal Policy

Fiscal policy can be either discretionary or automatic.

Discretionary Fiscal Policy   The members of Congress, sometimes with the leadership of the president, exercise **discretionary fiscal policy** when they deliberately adjust

Discretionary Fiscal Policy
Deliberate changes in government expenditures and/or taxes to control unemployment or demand-pull inflation.

government spending or taxing in response to a problem with unemployment or demand-pull inflation. Congress has significant fiscal powers: It can cut or raise taxes, change tax exemptions or deductions, grant tax rebates or credits, initiate or postpone transfer programs, and initiate or eliminate direct spending projects.

Congress has used discretionary fiscal policy several times in recent decades. In 1968 a 10 percent surcharge was levied on income taxes to reduce inflation caused by Vietnam War spending. In 1975 a tax cut was passed to counteract a recession. In 2001 an effort was made for a tax cut to offset a threatening recession. To strengthen the economy in 2008, the U.S. Treasury sent payments of up to $600 per person to more than 130 million people in households that filed a 2007 federal tax return. And, significant amounts of discretionary spending and tax cutting occurred in early 2009.

Automatic Fiscal Policy   At the federal level, we have built-in automatic changes in government spending and taxing that help us to challenge a recession or demand-pull inflation. Without any deliberate action by Congress, **automatic fiscal policy,** or **automatic stabilization,** increases aggregate spending in a recession and dampens aggregate spending when the economy expands. Two automatic fiscal policy stabilizers are important: transfer payments, especially unemployment compensation, and the personal income tax.

Let's consider a recession to understand how automatic stabilization works. During an economic downturn, when people lose their jobs and earned incomes fall, some important changes in government expenditures and taxes occur automatically. Some of the unemployed become eligible for transfer payments, particularly unemployment compensation. In addition, some unemployed people may realize lower tax payments, or even a tax refund. Because the federal personal income tax is structured as a progressive tax with several rate steps, unemployment and the resulting decline in income could drop a person into a lower tax bracket.[6] Both the increased transfer payments and lower tax rates are automatic and provide additional spending dollars. Without these built-in stabilizers, or automatic responses, household spending would drop more dramatically and the economy would likely slide into a deeper recession.

When the economy expands, unemployment falls, and incomes rise, the built-in stabilizers automatically remove spending from the economy to dampen demand-pull inflationary tendencies. As more people are employed, the government provides less in transfer payments, and higher incomes push some individuals into higher tax brackets. Without this automatic removal of spending power as the economy heats up, particularly toward full employment, inflation could be worse.

Automatic stabilizers soften the impact of cyclical expansions and contractions. Without the help of any deliberate legislative action, they pump spending into the economy during a downswing and decrease aggregate spending during an upswing. However, in the face of a severe recession or inflation, automatic stabilizers alone would not be sufficient to correct the problem. The role of fiscal policy in economic stabilization is summarized in Table 6.5.

Economic Stimulus: 2008 and 2009

As noted earlier, Congress passed a bill in February 2008 that provided rebate payments of up to $600 for some individuals who filed a 2007 tax return. This was the first deliberate fiscal policy action to support the economy as it began to slide in 2008 and the first expansionary fiscal action branded as an **economic stimulus** program.

Automatic Fiscal Policy (Automatic Stabilization) Changes in government expenditures and/or taxes that occur automatically as the level of economic activity changes; helps to control unemployment or demand-pull inflation.

Economic Stimulus A term used for fiscal policy actions to counteract a recession by stimulating spending through government purchases of goods and services, increased transfer payments, and/or decreased taxes.

[6]The following example helps to clarify this point. Assume that a person was earning a taxable income of $60,000 in 2007, and that an amount sufficient to pay a total federal income tax of $11,430 for the year was withheld every month from his pay. If this person lost his job and his 2007 taxable income was reduced by one-half to $30,000, his tax bill would have been only $4,113, or less than 36 percent of the tax on $60,000. From Department of the Treasury, Internal Revenue Service, *2007 1040 Instructions,* pp. 66, 70.

TABLE 6.5	*Fiscal Policy Summary*

Discretionary fiscal policy and automatic stabilization can be used to control unemployment or demand-pull inflation by changing the size of the spending stream.

PROBLEM

Unemployment	Demand-pull inflation

REMEDY

Increase total spending	Decrease total spending

FISCAL POLICY RESPONSE

Discretionary

Congress can	Congress can
increase government purchases	decrease government purchases
increase transfer payments	decrease transfer payments
decrease taxes	increase taxes

Automatic Stabilization

Automatic increases in some transfer payments (especially unemployment compensation), decreases in federal personal income taxes	Automatic decreases in some transfer payments (especially unemployment compensation), increases in federal personal income taxes

EFFECT

Puts more dollars into the spending stream	Withdraws dollars from the spending stream

By the fall of 2008, there was sufficient economic evidence to warn of a serious downturn in the economy as unemployment rose and real GDP fell. The situation was complicated by the failure of some huge financial institutions, such as Lehman Brothers. By the presidential election in November 2008, interest turned from the war in Iraq as the major issue between the candidates to the state of the economy.

When Barack Obama was elected president, he began to advocate for a substantial economic stimulus package, one that he and his supporters believed was necessary to pull the economy out of a deepening recession. In February 2009, the **American Recovery and Reinvestment Act (ARRA)** was signed into law. This act provided for about $800 billion in government spending and tax cuts through a variety of programs. This economic stimulus included weekly payroll tax credits, as well as spending for health care, public infrastructure, schools, energy, and other areas. Because part of the intention of this spending was to put people to work immediately, applications for some of the infrastructure funding had a prerequisite that the project be "shovel ready," that is, the project was ready to go and did not need time for right-of-way acquisition, design, or engineering.

It was clear by early 2009 that the federal government was ready to use its fiscal policy tools to an extent not seen for more than 50 years. As you read Chapter 8 and learn about monetary policy, you will see one of the advantages of fiscal policy over monetary policy when an economy is in a serious downturn. Fiscal policy can directly inject spending into the economy, while monetary policy effects interest rates. If interest rates are already low and people are not borrowing to spend, fiscal policy provides an alternative spending mechanism.

American Recovery and Reinvestment Act (ARRA)

Passed in February 2009 to provide about $800 billion for stimulating the economy through government spending and tax cuts.

GOVERNMENT BUDGETS

Every year elected officials who are responsible for determining how a political unit's money is spent—from a trustee of a small village in Illinois to a state legislator in California to your own congressperson—forecast their government's revenues and expenses and lay out a plan for the year ahead. Typically, there is a formal passage of this plan, or budget. Unfortunately, unpredictable events occur that can alter that budget. These range from economic slowdowns that lessen tax collections to disasters of extreme magnitude. Even the $4 per gallon gas in 2008 that wrecked family budgets hurt governments that had to fuel police cars, street sweepers, and trucks.

It is the resulting actual, not planned, year-end budget that is important for assessing how a government unit has influenced economic activity over the year. Here is where actual leakages from and injections into the spending stream are tallied. This figure indicates whether the government spent an amount equal to, less than, or greater than its revenues, or, putting it more technically, whether the government ran a balanced budget, a surplus budget, or a deficit budget.

Types of Budgets

Balanced Budget
A government's total expenditures equal its total revenues.

Surplus Budget
A government's revenues are greater than its expenditures.

Deficit Budget
A government's expenditures are greater than its revenues.

When a government's total expenditures equal its total revenues, it has run a **balanced budget.** A **surplus budget** occurs when a government does not spend all of its revenues, or when total expenditures subtracted from total revenues yields a positive dollar amount. A government with a surplus budget can pay off past loans or save the surplus and earn interest on the funds. A **deficit budget** occurs when a government's total expenditures are greater than total revenues, or when total expenditures subtracted from total revenues yields a negative dollar amount. When a government operates with a deficit budget, it must either borrow and go into debt or use its reserve fund (savings) if one exists.

It is the federal government budget that is of most interest when considering macroeconomic activity because of its size and its relation to fiscal policy. Table 6.6 lists federal government receipts, outlays, and resulting surpluses or deficits for the years 1960 through 2008.

The Surplus or Deficit column of Table 6.6 indicates that the federal government typically operates with a deficit budget. While there were four consecutive years of budget surpluses from 1998 through 2001, those surpluses were preceded by 28 consecutive years of deficits. Table 6.6 also indicates that wartime is particularly hard on the federal budget. The Vietnam War (especially in 1968) and the war in Iraq brought relatively high deficits. Observe the significant growth in the size of the budget deficits that began in the mid-1970s, continued through the 1980s, and led to deficits that approached $300 billion in the early 1990s. Finally, notice that as a result of the weakening economy following late 2001 and again in 2008, the war in Iraq, and tax reductions, annual budget deficits again rose—this time to all-time-high levels of greater than $400 billion. In 2008 the federal deficit was the largest ever: $455 billion.

Beyond the Budget Figures   The "watchdogs" of the federal government budget are keenly aware of issues that are masked by using the basic reported surplus and deficit numbers to evaluate the federal budget, as we have just done. Since 1969 the

TABLE 6.6   *Federal Budget Receipts, Outlays, and Surpluses or Deficits for Fiscal Years 1960–2008 (Billions of Dollars)*

The federal government has operated with a budget deficit for 43 of the 49 years from 1960 through 2008.

Fiscal Year	Receipts	Outlays	Surplus or Deficit (−)	Fiscal Year	Receipts	Outlays	Surplus or Deficit (−)
1960	$92.5	$92.2	$0.3	1985	$734.1	$946.4	$−212.3
1961	94.4	97.7	−3.3	1986	769.2	990.4	−221.2
1962	99.7	106.8	−7.1	1987	854.4	1,004.1	−149.7
1963	106.6	111.3	−4.8	1988	909.3	1,064.5	−155.2
1964	112.6	118.5	−5.9	1989	991.2	1,143.8	−152.6
1965	116.8	118.2	−1.4	1990	1,032.1	1,253.1	−221.0
1966	130.8	134.5	−3.7	1991	1,055.1	1,324.3	−269.2
1967	148.8	157.5	−8.6	1992	1,091.3	1,381.6	−290.3
1968	153.0	178.1	−25.2	1993	1,154.5	1,409.5	−255.1
1969	186.9	183.6	3.2	1994	1,258.7	1,461.9	−203.2
1970	192.8	195.6	−2.8	1995	1,351.9	1,515.9	−164.0
1971	187.1	210.2	−23.0	1996	1,453.2	1,560.6	−107.4
1972	207.3	230.7	−23.4	1997	1,579.4	1,601.3	−21.9
1973	230.8	245.7	−14.9	1998	1,722.0	1,652.7	69.3
1974	263.2	269.4	−6.1	1999	1,827.6	1,702.0	125.6
1975	279.1	332.3	−53.2	2000	2,025.5	1,789.2	236.2
1976	298.1	371.8	−73.7	2001	1,991.4	1,863.2	128.2
1977	355.6	409.2	−53.7	2002	1,853.4	2,011.2	−157.8
1978	399.6	458.7	−59.2	2003	1,782.5	2,160.1	−377.6
1979	463.3	504.0	−40.7	2004	1,880.3	2,293.0	−412.7
1980	517.1	590.9	−73.8	2005	2,153.9	2,472.2	−318.3
1981	599.3	678.2	−79.0	2006	2,407.3	2,665.4	−248.2
1982	617.8	745.7	−128.0	2007	2,568.2	2,730.2	−162.0
1983	600.6	808.4	−207.8	2008[a]	2,523.9	2,978.7	−454.8
1984	666.5	851.9	−185.4				

[a]Estimated.

Source: *Economic Report of the President* (Washington, DC: U.S. Government Printing Office, 2009), Table B-80.

Unified Budget
A budget that assembles all federal government receipts and outlays, and the resulting overall deficit or surplus, in one report.

Trust Fund
A restricted fund; payments from this fund are specified as to recipients and/or uses.

federal government has used a **unified budget** to report its surplus and deficit figures. That is, all federal government transactions for the year are reported in one lump sum. The unified budget figures, those used in Table 6.6, give no details about trust fund balances, the sizes of payments through entitlement programs, and government operations such as the U.S. Postal Service.

The federal government has created several trust funds to administer some of its programs. A **trust fund** is an account earmarked for a specific purpose or program: Contributions to the fund and distributions from it are used solely for the program. Social Security and Medicare are the best-known trust funds. With Social Security, for example, contributions from employers and employees go directly to the fund, and all payments to beneficiaries are made from the fund.

| TABLE 6.7 | Federal Government Unified, On-Budget, and Off-Budget Balances, 1995–2008 (Billions of Dollars) |

In recent years, off-budget surpluses have reduced the size of the unified budget deficit.

Year	Unified Surplus or Deficit	On-Budget Surplus or Deficit	Off-Budget Surplus or Deficit
1995	−164.0	−226.4	62.4
1996	−107.4	−174.0	66.6
1997	−21.9	−103.2	81.4
1998	69.3	−29.9	99.2
1999	125.6	1.9	123.7
2000	236.2	86.4	149.8
2001	128.2	−32.4	160.7
2002	−157.8	−317.4	159.7
2003	−377.6	−538.4	160.8
2004	−412.7	−568.0	155.2
2005	−318.3	−493.6	175.3
2006	−248.2	−434.5	186.3
2007	−162.0	−343.5	181.5
2008[a]	−389.4	−573.7	184.2

[a]Estimated from budget mid-session review.

Source: *Economic Report of the President* (Washington, DC: U.S. Government Printing Office, 2009), Table B-78. Figures are for fiscal years.

Entitlements

Programs set up by the government to pay benefits to people who meet the eligibility requirements of the programs.

The term **entitlements** refers to programs set up by the government to pay benefits to people who meet the eligibility requirements for the programs. Spending for entitlement programs tends to be less controllable than other types, such as funding for airport runways or national parks. Social Security and Medicare are examples of entitlement programs, as are veterans' benefits and the federal government employees' retirement program.

To identify the effects of some of these government programs on the overall budget, the unified budget figures have been broken into two categories: on-budget and off-budget. Although Congress has not been consistent about identifying the types of programs in each category, the general guideline is that **on-budget** figures are for programs, such as interstate highway construction, that are more controllable and can be better used for fiscal policy actions. **Off-budget** figures are for programs, such as Social Security, that are less controllable. Table 6.7 provides the unified, on-budget, and off-budget surplus and deficit figures for 1995 through 2008.

On-Budget/Off-Budget

Categories of the unified budget established by Congress; generally refers to programs that have immediately controllable and noncontrollable receipts and expenses, respectively.

Notice that the off-budget figures have been positive. This has occurred because of annual surpluses in the Social Security trust fund. That is, more Social Security contributions have been taken in each year than have been paid out. Building up the fund has been deliberate, since fewer working adults will support retirees in the years ahead. However, these substantial annual surpluses can lead to a misrepresentation about federal government deficits and surpluses. Without the Social Security surpluses, unified budget deficits would have been much larger and surpluses smaller

APPLICATION 6.2

How Much Do We Love Granny?

Granny loves her grandkids; the grandkids love their grandparents. So, is there any concern about these familial relationships? Why do some people see the possibility of real tension and resentment in the years ahead?

It's the Social Security system. This system is on its way to paying out way more than it takes in and creating a huge financial burden on the younger generation—today's grandkids. Some estimate that the program will start losing money in 2018, and if it continues like it is today, it will lose over $760 billion a year by 2030.

Workers pay into the system when they work and get money from it when they retire. It's a big fund. People do not have individual accounts in their names. Instead, what people pay into the fund is used to help support people receiving payments. So the system needs workers to keep paying into the fund in order to make payments to recipients from the fund. The fund does have a reserve. It is just not enough.

The problem is a demographic one caused largely by the composition of the U.S. population. The number of people approaching retirement age is growing at a faster rate than the number of working people who will be making Social Security contributions. And the fund's reserve is not large enough to compensate.

The number of Americans 65 and older is expected to grow by over 70 percent from 2010 through 2030, while the number of workers 20 through 64 paying into Social Security is expected to grow by less than 5 percent. In 1935 when the Social Security Act was passed, there were 25 workers to support each retiree. Today there are only three, and by 2020 the number is expected to fall to two workers per retiree.

Here is the possible tension. Any suggestion to simply cut Social Security benefits could have dire consequences for all of those grandparents. For about two-thirds of its recipients, Social Security accounts for half of their income. For about 15 percent of the recipients, it is their only source of income. On the other side of the issue, any suggestion to raise the amount withheld from workers' paychecks for Social Security contributions could have a negative impact on many grandkids' incomes, particularly those who live on wages barely above the minimum wage level. In so many cases it is an individual situation: Some older workers live better than their grandkids; some do not.

Almost all of us live in a household where someone is paying into or receiving money from Social Security. Because of this, the coming Social Security crisis will likely affect most of us. What can we expect? You can be sure that we will have a difficult and controversial debate.

Source : John Kiernan, "Commentary: Social Security in Need of Reform," *Long Island Business News,* February 25, 2005, p. 1; Arthur Postal, "House Panel Divided on Social Security," *National Underwriter: Life & Health,* March 14, 2005, p. 10; Elaine Thompson, "Group Wants Change in Social Security//Panelists Agree Crisis Must Be Averted," *Telegram & Gazette* (Worcester, MA), July 22, 1998, p. B1.

each year. In 2007, for example, without the off-budget figures the deficit would have been $343.5 billion rather than $162 billion as reported in the unified budget.

Even with the substantial surplus in the Social Security trust fund, there is concern that the coming retirement of the huge numbers of people in the baby-boom generation will cause an economic crisis. Current entitlement programs—especially Social Security and Medicare—as they now exist, even with a surplus, will not be able to support this large population. Application 6.2, "How Much Do We Love Granny?"offers some background about this predicament. Over the next few years, we can expect proposals for dealing with this impending demographic problem. What would you suggest as a change in public policy to deal with retirement entitlements? The Critical Thinking Case at the end of this chapter, "NIMBY (Not in My Backyard)," presents some interesting thoughts about how well we can face up to this issue as a nation.

The Budget and Fiscal Policy: Tying Them Together

All of our discussions concerning government spending and taxing, budgets, and fiscal policy can be tied together.

A surplus budget occurs when government revenues exceed government expenditures. Generally, a surplus budget will slow the economy as the amount removed from the spending stream is greater than the amount returned.[7] In other words, a surplus budget dampens aggregate spending.

Discretionary fiscal policy suggests that the corrective action for managing demand-pull inflation is a reduction in government spending on its purchases and transfer payments and/or an increase in taxes. Each of these measures leans toward a surplus budget. And, in terms of automatic stabilization, in good times when spending is up, automatically tax collections increase and transfer payments fall. These, again, favor a surplus budget.

With a deficit budget, government expenditures exceed revenues, or more is pumped into the spending stream than is taken out. Unless the economy is at full employment and incapable of expanding, a deficit budget will increase economic activity. In other words, a deficit budget will increase aggregate spending as well as output, employment, and income.

If the economy is in a recession, fiscal policy measures that increase expenditures and/or reduce taxes can be used to aid in reversing the recession. These tools will push the budget toward a deficit position whether they are used deliberately or whether automatic stabilization, which causes tax collections to fall and transfer payments to increase in bad times, kicks in.

A balanced budget, contrary to common belief, does not have a neutral impact on economic activity. In determining the effect of a balanced budget, we must recall that dollars from income that has been taxed would otherwise have been used partly for spending and partly for saving. Thus, when the government spends those tax dollars on goods and services, it is taking some money that would have been saved and is spending it. As a result, a balanced budget has a slightly expansionary impact on the economy.

In summary,

♦ a surplus budget dampens aggregate spending and can aid in managing demand-pull inflation,
♦ a deficit budget increases aggregate spending and can help to reverse a recession, and
♦ a balanced budget can slightly expand the economy.

Test Your Understanding, "Government's Impact on the Macroeconomy," gives you an opportunity to assess how various actions by the federal government influence the economy's output, employment, and price levels.

The Realities of Fiscal Policy and the Federal Budget

Let's lay aside the smooth, simple mechanics of fiscal policy and go to the real world where the federal budget doesn't always perform according to the ideal strategy for keeping the economy on track. There are several points to consider in assessing how well the economic concepts that we have just learned are translated into economic policy.

While economists like to think that full employment and stable prices are the primary goal of congressional tax and spending plans, in reality congresspersons may have other, sometimes more important, goals in mind. For example, even though economic conditions might call for a reduction in spending, concerns about homeland security and global warming could result in additional federal expenditures to address those needs.

---

[7]The expression *generally* is used because the ultimate impact of the budget depends on the types of taxes collected, the percentage of those taxes that would have been saved, the percentage of expenditures that goes directly into purchases of goods and services, the percentage of transfers that is saved, and so forth.

GOVERNMENT'S IMPACT ON THE MACROECONOMY

Indicate the effect of each of the following actions—taken alone—on the macroeconomy. That is, in each case determine the changes that would result in aggregate output, employment, or prices. Unless otherwise specified, in each case the economy is not operating at full employment.

1. The amount that households can deduct from their incomes when calculating their federal personal income tax increases.
2. Payments to Social Security recipients are increased, but there is an equal decrease in government purchases of military vehicles.
3. The federal government balances its budget when the economy is at full employment.
4. Congresspersons vote themselves a 20 percent pay increase.
5. A budget surplus occurs as the economy falls into a recession.
6. Taxes on cigarettes and alcohol are raised by 50 percent.
7. The federal government increases taxes with the intention of paying off its accumulated debt within 10 years.
8. Across-the-board increases are made in defense, highway, and education spending.
9. The economy is at full employment, and the Social Security surplus is so large that social insurance taxes are lowered.
10. The federal government runs a deficit budget while the economy is experiencing demand-pull inflation.
11. The number of people eligible for payments under an entitlement program decreases.
12. Government shuts down for a week because agreement cannot be reached on a new budget and funding authorization has expired under the old budget.

Answers can be found at the back of the book.

Fiscal policy and the federal budget are major components of the work of elected public officials. When a change in spending or taxing is proposed, these officials must consider their constituents and how the change will impact the group that the elected official represents. As a consequence, the broad view of "what is best" for the economy may take a congressional backseat to "what is best" for an electorate. It could be extremely difficult for a congressional representative to vote against expenditures that might provide jobs or other benefits for that person's district in the name of helping the larger economy fight an inflation problem. For example, congressional delegates in Missouri and Illinois would likely support funding for a bridge over the Mississippi River regardless of larger macro problems.

Fiscal policy takes time to enact: The statistical information that identifies the extent of an unemployment or inflation problem takes time to gather, and the political debate and discussion over policy tools and between Congress and the executive branch are again time consuming. Sometimes the problem can self-correct while Congress debates the issue.

There is one additional dimension: Since the government can easily borrow to cover budget deficits, from time to time we have seen examples of wasteful and extravagant expenditures. This has led to growing interest among economists in **public choice,** which is the study of the economic motives and attitudes of voters and public officials, and how those motives and attitudes affect government decision making. Public choice is discussed more fully in Chapter 11.

Public Choice

The study of the economic motives and attitudes of voters and public officials, and how those motives and attitudes affect government decision making.

THE NATIONAL DEBT

In the past few decades, the federal government has had a habit of running deficit budgets: Table 6.6 shows persistent annual deficits from 1970 through 1997 and substantial deficits since 2003. Just like people and businesses that must borrow because they have no savings and are spending more than they earn, the federal government must borrow funds to finance its deficits. And, as more is borrowed each year, the federal government goes deeper and deeper in debt. A surplus budget, which allows some of this debt to be repaid, occurs infrequently. The accumulated total debt of the federal government is called the **national debt.**

National Debt
The accumulated total debt of the federal government due to deficit spending.

U.S. Treasury Security
Issued by the federal government in return for funds lent to it.

Financing the National Debt

When the federal government needs to raise money to finance its spending, it borrows at the lowest interest rate it can negotiate from anyone who is willing to lend it money. In return for funds, the lender receives a **U.S. Treasury security:** a formal IOU stating the federal government's promise to make specified interest payments and to

---

APPLICATION 6.3

U.S. Treasury Securities

The following are some commonly asked questions, and their answers, about buying and holding U.S. Treasury securities as savings.[a]

Q: How much money do I need to purchase U.S. Treasury bills, notes, bonds, or TIPS?
A: Treasury bills, notes, bonds, and TIPS are issued in denominations of $100.
Q: What is a TIPS and how does it work?
A: TIPS securities mature in 5, 10, or 20 years, and their value increases with inflation. For example, suppose in 2009 you bought a $1,000 TIPS paying 4 percent and maturing in 2014. If the economy went through a period of inflation between 2009 and 2014, the 4 percent interest you earn would be based on an amount larger than $1,000, as the face value of your certificate increases with inflation.
Q: Where can I obtain a U.S. Treasury security?
A: A security can be purchased directly from the government only when the government publicly announces its intention to borrow. A lender submits a bid stating the amount the lender will provide directly to the U.S. Treasury, a Federal Reserve bank or branch (see Chapter 7), a financial institution, or a government securities dealer or broker. Once a security has been issued, it can be bought and sold on a secondary market, which is a market for "used" securities. Treasury securities are regularly traded through brokers and some banks, and a fee is charged for this service.
Q: How much interest do I get, when do I receive that interest, and how do I receive it?
A: When a security is issued by the government, it carries both a maturity date and a stated annual rate of interest.

Interest is paid on Treasury bills when they mature, and on Treasury notes, bonds, and TIPS every six months based on that rate. For example, if you have a $1,000 Treasury note with a stated interest rate of 8 percent, then you will receive a check from the Treasury, or a direct deposit in an account you specify, every six months for $40 until the maturity date, when you will receive the last interest payment and can claim the principal.
Q: Tell me more about the secondary market.
A: Previously issued Treasury securities can be bought or sold at any time on the secondary market. For example, if you have a $1,000 Treasury note carrying an 8 percent interest rate and maturing in 2014, and need your money tomorrow, you can go to a broker who will sell this security to someone else.

When you sell your security, you may get more or less than its face value. That is, you could get more or less than $1,000 for your note. How much more or less depends on the current interest rate that can be obtained on comparable securities. If the current rate is less than 8 percent, you could get more than $1,000, and if the rate is more than 8 percent, you could get less than $1,000. The selling price is generally found by dividing the annual dollar interest earned on a security by the current interest rate. For example, if the current interest rate is 10 percent, your $1,000 bond, which is earning $80 (or 8 percent) per year, will be worth about $800 ($80/0.10) on the secondary market. If the current interest rate is 6 percent, your $1,000 bond will be worth about $1,333 ($80/0.06).
Q: How safe are Treasury securities?
A: Because U.S. Treasury securities are backed by the U.S. government, most people consider them to be very safe.

[a] Good sources of further information that were used for some of the information reported here are "Frequently Asked Questions about Treasury Bills, Notes, Bonds, and TIPS," http://www.publicdebt.treas.gov/sec/secfaq.htm; and "Treasury Direct: Treasury Securities & Programs," http://www.treasurydirect.gov/indiv/products/products.htm.

U. S. Treasury Bill, Note, and Bond
U.S. Treasury securities that mature, respectively, in 1 year or less; 2 to 10 years; and 30 years.

Treasury Inflation-Protected Securities (TIPS)
U.S. Treasury securities with face values that rise when the economy experiences inflation.

repay the loaned funds on a particular date. The time span from issuance to the maturity, or repayment, date determines whether the security is a **U.S. Treasury bill** (often called a "T-bill"), which matures in one year or less; a **U.S. Treasury note,** which matures in 2, 5, or 10 years; or a **U.S. Treasury bond,** which matures in 30 years. In 1997, the U.S. Treasury began issuing **TIPS,** or **Treasury inflation-protected securities.** These securities protect investors against inflation by allowing the security's face value to go up when prices rise.

The process for federal government borrowing is very open and public, and investors from the average family to highly sophisticated institutional fund managers participate in this process. When it wants to borrow funds, the government publicly announces the total amount it intends to borrow and the repayment date. A kind of auction occurs and the government borrows from those who offer funds at the lowest interest rates.

Who loans the federal government money or owns Treasury securities? The largest portion of the national debt is held by private investors, domestic and foreign, such as individuals, banks, pension funds, and corporations. The rest of the debt is owned by the Federal Reserve banks and government agencies and trusts. Perhaps the U.S. Treasury is in debt to you or your family. If you own a U.S. Treasury security, you have provided the federal government with borrowed funds. Many people are curious about the process of saving money through Treasury securities. Application 6.3, "U.S. Treasury Securities," answers some frequently asked questions about this process.

Size of the National Debt

The size of the national debt is incomprehensible to most people: By the end of the 2008 fiscal year, it had grown to about $10 trillion. Table 6.8 gives the total national debt and the per capita debt for selected years beginning with 1940. Because the debt is linked to the federal budget, years in which deficit spending occurred were also years of an increase in the national debt. Notice the rapid and substantial increases in the debt since 1990, when the debt reached over $3 trillion, increased to over $5 trillion by 1996, and over $9.6 trillion by 2008.

The share of the national debt for every man, woman, and child in the United States is shown in the Per Capita Debt column of Table 6.8. These figures illustrate startling increases in recent years. To have fully paid off the debt in 2008, a family of four would have needed to contribute over $128,000 as its share.[8]

Assessing the Debt

How does the national debt affect the average person today? What does it mean for future generations? Has the debt become too large? Have the substantial increases in the debt in the past ten years been worth it? Should the debt be paid off as soon as possible? The national debt is frequently a topic of conversations—academic, political, and those around the kitchen table—and questions like these are typically discussed. Let us focus on a few critical issues.

The interest that must be paid to borrow and maintain a debt of the magnitude we have created is a significant burden. The amount of interest paid annually to sustain the national debt is given in Table 6.8 in the column Total Interest Paid. In 2006, for example, $406 billion in interest—over $1.1 billion per day—was paid to the holders of

---

[8]A word of caution is in order regarding comparisons of the burden of the debt from year to year. The figures in Table 6.8 are in current, not real, dollars, so inflation has not been factored into these numbers.

TABLE 6.8   *The National Debt, Selected Years 1940–2008*

Over the years, the national debt, the burden of the debt per person, and the interest the government pays to finance the debt have all grown.

Year	Total Debt (Billions of Dollars)	Per Capita Debt (Dollars)[a]	Total Interest Paid (Billions of Dollars)	Percent of Federal Outlays for Interest
1940	$ 43.0	$ 325	$ 1.0	11.5%
1945	258.7	1,849	3.6	3.7
1950	256.1	1,688	5.7	14.5
1955	272.8	1,651	6.4	9.3
1960	284.1	1,572	9.2	10.0
1965	313.8	1,613	11.3	9.6
1970	370.1	1,814	19.3	9.9
1975	533.2	2,475	32.7	9.8
1980	907.7	3,985	74.9	12.7
1985	1,823.1	7,616	178.9	18.9
1986	2,125.3	8,793	187.1	18.9
1987	2,350.3	9,630	195.4	19.5
1988	2,602.3	10,556	214.1	20.1
1989	2,867.5	11,593	241.0	21.1
1990	3,206.2	12,830	264.7	21.1
1991	3,598.3	14,241	285.5	21.6
1992	4,002.1	15,780	292.3	21.2
1993	4,351.4	16,963	292.5	20.8
1994	4,643.7	17,920	296.3	20.3
1995	4,921.0	18,809	332.4	21.9
1996	5,181.9	19,481	344.0	22.0
1997	5,369.7	20,036	355.8	22.2
1998	5,478.7	20,217	363.8	22.0
1999	5,606.1	20,535	353.5	20.8
2000	5,628.7	19,849	361.9	20.2
2001	5,769.9	20,213	359.5	19.3
2002	6,198.4	21,279	332.5	16.5
2003	6,760.0	23,207	318.1	14.7
2004	7,354.7	25,011	321.7	14.0
2005	7,905.3	26,663	352.3	14.3
2006	8,451.4	28,190	405.9	15.3
2007	8,950.7	29,633	433.0[b]	15.9[b]
2008[b]	9,654.4	32,085	—	—

[a]Revised population data are used for per capita numbers from 2000.
[b]Estimated.

Sources: 1940–1960 from *Statistical Abstract of the United States: 1979*, p. 273; 1965–1988 from *Statistical Abstract: 1990*, p. 309; 1989–1991 from *Economic Report of the President, 1994*, p. 359; *Statistical Abstract: 1992*, pp. 318, 319; and *Statistical Abstract: 1993*, pp. 8, 9, 332, 333; 1992–1995 from *Economic Report of the President, 1997*, p. 389; and *Statistical Abstract: 1996*, pp. 9, 334, 335; 1996–1999 from *Economic Report of the President, 2002*, p. 413; *Statistical Abstract: 1998*, p. 342; and *Statistical Abstract: 2001*, pp. 9, 307; 2000–2008 from *Economic Report of the President, 2008*, pp. 267, 319; *Statistical Abstract: 2008*, pp. 7, 8, 308.

federal debt. These dollars are a significant percentage of the federal government's annual budget, as indicated in the last column of Table 6.8. While the percentage has fallen in more recent years due to lower interest rates, during the decade of the 1990s it was greater than 20 percent each year. There is an opportunity cost of paying this interest; there are many alternative uses, or forgone opportunities, for these dollars. Consider spending for education and the environment: In 2007 federal outlays for these areas together accounted for less than 5 percent of total federal spending.[9] And, there are other needs to consider: the rebuilding of aging bridges and highways, and relief for areas such as New Orleans hit by destructive weather to name just two.

The interest burden of the national debt cumulates as additional debt is incurred each year. Because the debt is not being retired, interest must be paid year after year. The burden of the **debt service,** or the interest cost of maintaining the debt, will be passed on to future generations who will have to pay the interest on the current debt. However, while the interest that must be paid is a burden to current and future taxpayers, we need to realize that many U.S. citizens own government securities and count on the interest payments for income. Treasury securities provide a relatively easy and popular way to save money.

The issue of whether the national debt has become too large is a value judgment. At what point, even in the case of our own finances, do credit obligations become too high? One way to evaluate the size of the national debt is to examine it as a percentage of GDP, as is done in Figure 6.2. Notice that the debt as a percentage of GDP generally rose from the 1980s through the mid-1990s, declined, and then rose again. This way of evaluating the size of the debt is analogous to comparing an individual's debt and income. Obviously a person can sustain more dollars of debt at an annual income of $60,000 than at an annual income of $20,000. The problem is whether or not someone can sustain a debt that takes a rising percentage of income.

Should we, or could we, pay off the debt? It would be a huge, probably impossible, burden, even over several years, to raise through taxes and other revenues the amount needed to pay off the debt. (Recall that every person would need to contribute about $32,000.) With repayment of the debt, a significant income redistribution would occur as the average taxpayer had less income due to the increased tax burden and the holders of government securities had more income from their newly redeemed funds. Also, some portion of the debt is external, or foreign-owned. While normally this is not a serious concern, in a period of accelerated repayment it would mean a sizable flow of dollars out of the United States. Finally, in order to pay off the public debt, a series of surplus budgets would be needed. Recall from earlier in the chapter that a surplus budget has a contractionary impact on the economy: While the debt was being paid off, economic activity would decline. In short, the opportunity cost of paying off the national debt would be a substantial slowdown in the economy.

Crowding Out

One other consideration involving deficit spending and the national debt is the strain that government borrowing puts on funds available for loans. The federal government competes with households and businesses to borrow whatever funds are available for loan making. If government borrowing is sizable, two important effects result in the market for loans. First, because the borrowing and lending of money takes place in markets where the forces of supply and demand determine interest rates (the price of money), increases in government borrowing increase

Debt Service
The cost of maintaining a debt; generally measured in interest costs.

---

[9]*Economic Report of the President* (Washington, DC: U.S. Government Printing Office, 2008), p. 322.

FIGURE 6.2   *National Debt as a Percentage of GDP, 1980–2009*[a]

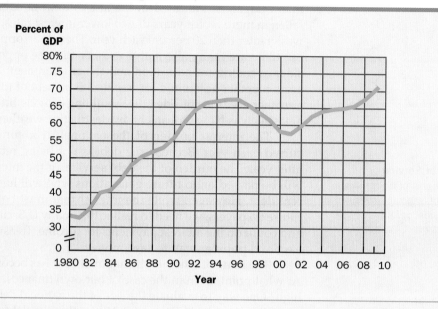

One way to evaluate the size of the national debt is to compare it to GDP. The ratio of debt to GDP has generally been rising.

[a]Figures are for fiscal years; 2008 and 2009 figures are estimated.

Source: *Economic Report of the President* (Washington, DC: U.S. Government Printing Office, 2009), Table B-79.

the demand for loans and cause interest rates to rise. When the federal government borrows substantial amounts, the impact on interest rates can be significant.

A second effect of sizable government borrowing is the **crowding out** of private borrowing. Because households and businesses are sensitive to the interest rate, increases in the interest rate cause them to borrow less. The result is that available funds are soaked up by the federal government, which is not sensitive to the interest rate in its borrowing. Businesses and households borrow less for capital improvements, plant expansion, homes, automobiles, and such. With crowding out, economic growth may be slowed as businesses postpone borrowing to buy the machinery and equipment necessary for growth.

Crowding Out
Occurs when borrowing by the federal government reduces borrowing by households and businesses.

Summary

1.   The two main categories of government expenditures are purchases of goods and services and transfer payments. Some government purchases are for public goods, which are provided for all of society and from which no one can be excluded.

2.   Governments receive revenues from taxes and other sources, such as contributions for social insurance. The primary source of federal government revenue is the individual income tax. Taxes may be classified according to the relationship between the percentage of income taxed and the size of the income: A progressive tax has a direct relationship, a regressive tax has an inverse relationship, and the percentage stays the same for a proportional tax.

3. Tax reform sometimes occurs because of a need for additional government funding or for political reasons. A tax base is the thing on which a tax is levied, and the tax rate is the amount that is levied on the base.

4. Fiscal policy refers to changes in government expenditures and/or taxes for the purpose of influencing the levels of output, employment, or prices in the economy. Fiscal policy can be used to reduce unemployment by injecting more spending into the economy through increased government purchases, increased transfer payments, and/or decreased taxes. Demand-pull inflation is reduced through decreased government purchases, decreased transfer payments, and/or increased taxes.

5. Fiscal policy is either discretionary or automatic. Discretionary fiscal policy is the deliberate adjustment of government purchases, transfers, and/or taxes by Congress to control unemployment or inflation. Automatic stabilization is the automatic change in some government expenditures, like transfer payments, and some taxes, such as the federal personal income tax, that stimulates or dampens aggregate spending as the level of economic activity changes. These changes in spending and taxes automatically help soften the impact of unemployment or inflation.

6. When a government's outlays are less than its revenues, it is operating with a surplus budget; when its outlays exceed revenues, it is operating with a deficit budget; and when its outlays and revenues are equal, it is operating with a balanced budget. Surplus budgets generally cause economic activity to contract, since the government is withdrawing more from the spending stream than it is returning. Deficit and balanced budgets are expansionary because the government is injecting more into the spending stream than is being taken out as taxes. A surplus budget would be proper policy for fighting demand-pull inflation, while a deficit budget would be appropriate for fighting unemployment.

7. There has been a tendency to run annual federal budget deficits. These deficits are generally reported in a unified budget format rather than differentiating between on-budget and off-budget balances. The Social Security trust fund has been operating with annual surpluses that have reduced the size of the unified budget deficit.

8. Fiscal policy considerations compete with other economic and noneconomic objectives in establishing the federal budget. The effectiveness of fiscal policy may be reduced by the time lag from the onset and discovery of a problem to the implementation of a remedy.

9. The national debt is the debt owed by the federal government from the financing of its deficit budgets. In raising funds, the government borrows at the lowest interest rates offered from anyone willing to lend funds and gives U.S. Treasury securities in return. The size of the national debt has grown substantially over the years, as has the interest the government must pay to carry the debt and the debt as a percentage of GDP. In addition, as the federal government borrows more, it can crowd out private borrowing.

Key Terms and Concepts

Government purchases of goods and services

Public good

Quasi-public good

Transfer payments

Social insurance program

Progressive tax

Proportional tax (flat tax)

Regressive tax

Tax reform

Tax bracket indexation

Tax Reform Act of 1986

Tax base

Tax rate

Tax abatement

Fiscal policy

Discretionary fiscal policy

Automatic fiscal policy (automatic stabilization)

Economic Stimulus

American Recovery and Reinvestment Act (ARRA)

Balanced budget

Surplus budget

Deficit budget

Unified budget

Trust fund

Entitlements

On-budget

Off-budget

Public choice

National debt

U.S. Treasury security

U.S. Treasury bill, note, bond

Treasury inflation-protected securities (TIPS)

Debt service

Crowding out

Review Questions

1. Identify the major spending categories and the major revenue sources of the federal government.

2. Determine whether each of the following taxes is progressive, proportional, or regressive.
   a. A sales tax of 7 percent on medicine
   b. A state income tax with three brackets: 3 percent for income under $20,000, 8 percent for income between $20,000 and $100,000, and 15 percent for income over $100,000
   c. A property tax of $2.85 per $100 of assessed property value
   d. A tax of $8 on room occupancy in all hotels in a county
   e. A tax of 3 percent on all wages earned in a city
   f. A sales tax of 5 percent on utilities
   g. A federal tax of $2 per pack of cigarettes

3. Identify the tax base in each of the examples in Question 2.

4. Explain how automatic stabilization stimulates spending in a recession and dampens spending during periods of demand-pull inflation. How does automatic stabilization affect the federal budget?

5. Explain whether the economy will expand, contract, stay the same, or inflate with each of the following fiscal actions taken alone. Assume the economy is not at full employment unless stated otherwise.
   a. Congress votes and sends a $600 tax credit to each taxpayer.
   b. Households are taxed an extra 15 percent, and the government spends the entire amount on purchases of goods and services.
   c. Congress allows many new income tax deductions when the economy is at full employment.
   d. Although Congress intends to balance the budget, a deficit occurs.
   e. At the end of a war, defense expenditures drop dramatically but are replaced by domestic spending programs for health and education.
   f. Congress decides to decrease defense expenditures with no increase in other spending programs.
   g. Congress increases expenditures for transfer payments at the same time it reduces spending on highways and bridges by the same amount.

6. If the U.S. economy fell into a serious recession, what could Congress do to counteract that recession? Specifically, how could it use each of its fiscal policy tools?

7. What effect would each of the following, taken alone, have on a federal budget that is currently balanced? How would the budgetary changes, where they occur, affect the national debt?
   a. An increase in the percentage of income taxed in each of the federal personal income tax brackets
   b. An increase in government expenditures for research on global warming
   c. An equal increase in government expenditures and income tax revenues
   d. An increase in defense expenditures and a decrease in corporate income tax revenues
   e. An increase in Social Security payments by the government matched by a decrease in a subsidy to a particular group in the economy, such as farmers
   f. An exemption from federal income tax for interest earned on small savings accounts in banks

8. Could the national debt be eliminated over the next 10 years? How? What are the opportunity costs of paying off the debt and not paying it off?

Discussion Questions

1. Suppose that the legislators in a particular state are choosing among three strategies to raise revenue: (1) imposing a progressive income tax; (2) imposing a sales tax on food; and (3) imposing a 1 percent tax on all earnings within the state. How do you think residents of the state in the upper, middle, and lower income groups would react to each of these proposals? Which of the three strategies do you favor? Which of the three has the greatest likelihood of being passed?

2. Give some arguments for and against a federal personal income tax that would be proportional rather than progressive. Who stands to win and who stands to lose from a flat tax?

3. Suppose that government policymakers are concerned about a forecasted recession. As a consequence they want to increase spending in the economy by $10 billion and can follow any one of three policies: (1) a $10 billion increase in government purchases of goods and services; (2) a transfer payment increase that would provide funds for households to spend $10 billion; or (3) a reduction in taxes by an amount that would put $10 billion into spending. Does it make any difference which of the three policies is chosen? How would each affect the federal budget? Why might policymakers choose one policy over another?

4. Do you favor legislation requiring the federal government to balance its budget? Why? What are the economic implications of your position?

5. Off-budget entitlement programs such as Medicare have grown in recent years. How could Congress reasonably limit spending for Medicare to bring it under control while maintaining quality health care?

6. You are invited to participate in a commission that is exploring the future of the Social Security system. What recommendations might you make?

7. One area of concern regarding the national debt is the burden it can place on future generations. How might a large national debt burden future generations?

8. Assume that you are a congressperson whose district may be awarded a multimillion-dollar rapid transit project. The economy, however, is in the throes of one of the more severe inflationary periods of the decade. How would you vote on the passage of funds for the project? What would you tell your colleagues? Your constituents?

9. Crowding out, where businesses and households are forced out of the market for borrowed funds by federal government borrowing, occurs because businesses and households are sensitive to interest rate changes while the federal government is not. Why is federal borrowing not sensitive to the interest rate? What would be the effect on federal programs if it were sensitive to the interest rate?

Critical Thinking Case 6

NIMBY (NOT IN MY BACKYARD)

Critical Thinking Skills

Ranking alternatives

Evaluating effects of decisions

Recognizing conflicting objectives

Economic Concepts

Balanced budget

Government expenditures and revenues

Budget determination process

Balancing the federal budget has been one of the most talked about economic agenda items for years. Democratic and Republican lawmakers alike have been on record backing a balanced budget, and, in principle, there is much support for the proposal among U.S. citizens.

But once the discussion moves to deciding what steps must be taken for the balance to occur, the support becomes more guarded and sometimes turns to opposition. This change in position can be traced in part to the NIMBY problem, NIMBY meaning "not in my backyard." People generally support balancing the budget as long as their particular interests are not adversely affected. But once it appears that they personally will be called upon to sacrifice to balance the budget, or that part of the balancing will occur in their "backyard," support evaporates.

Suppose you are a U.S. congressperson who must make the hard decisions required to balance the budget. A list of proposals is put forth to help accomplish that end. You must vote on each. Review these proposals, given below, and answer the following questions.

Proposals

1. Increase all individual and corporate income taxes by 10 percent.
2. Cancel mortgage interest deductions from income taxes for all homeowners and end all agricultural subsidies.
3. Reduce expenditures for military procurement, construction, and operations.
4. Reduce government spending on health care, including Medicare and medical research, by 25 percent.
5. End scholarships, low-interest loans, and other financial support to college and university students.
6. Reduce expenditures on federal law enforcement and correctional facilities.
7. Reduce expenditures for housing, food, and nutritional assistance.

Questions

1. What groups would be most affected by each of these proposals?
2. Rank the proposals according to the likelihood that each would be approved by Congress. Rank the most likely to be approved first and the least likely last. Why did you rank these proposals in this way?
3. Based on these proposals, what conflicts, if any, are there between the goal of a balanced budget and other goals that you as a congressperson might seek?
4. It has been said that it is easier to promise that the budget will be balanced than it is to balance the budget. Based on your experience with these proposals, what do you think is the likelihood that the budget will be balanced?

CHAPTER 7

Money, Financial Institutions, and the Federal Reserve

CHAPTER OBJECTIVES

To define money and explain the functions of money.

To identify the various measures and components of the U.S. money supply and different monetary standards.

To introduce the financial institutions that are important for the maintenance and control of the U.S. money supply, and to highlight commercial banks and commercial bank regulation.

To explain the role of the Federal Reserve system, its organization, and the functions that Federal Reserve banks perform.

To discuss recent legislative and structural changes in the financial institutions system.

We have explored several topics that in one way or another involve money. For example, we learned that economic activity expands or contracts as the size of the spending stream increases or decreases and that with inflation the purchasing power of money deteriorates. Without money, modern economies as we know them could not exist. Even though money does not itself produce goods and services, as do land, labor, capital, and entrepreneurship, it makes large-scale production and distribution possible. If a nation's monetary system becomes unstable, adverse economic consequences can result.

In this chapter we will deal with some basics about money, banks and other financial institutions, and the Federal Reserve, which plays an extremely critical role in the functioning of the economy and is regularly covered in the media. While this chapter provides information that may correct some myths for you (for example, money is backed by gold and silver), more importantly, it lays the groundwork for Chapter 8, where we study how money is actually created and destroyed and the effects of money on economic activity.

MONEY

The Definition and Functions of Money

Money

Anything that is generally accepted as a medium of exchange.

Medium of Exchange

Something that is generally accepted as payment for goods, services, and resources; the primary function of money.

Very simply, **money** is *anything* that is generally accepted as a medium of exchange. A **medium of exchange** is something that people are readily willing to accept in payment for purchases of goods, services, and resources because they know it can be easily used for further transactions. In the United States a $10 bill is a medium of exchange because people are willing to take this bill in payment, knowing that it can be used for other purchases.

Many people believe that money must be made of precious metal or be backed by a tangible asset, such as gold or silver. This is not true. Because a medium of exchange can be anything, possibilities for money include precious metals, stones, beads, coins, cigarettes, pieces of paper, and electronically transferred numbers. The physical form that money takes makes no difference as long as it is the generally accepted means of payment for purchases in an economy. Some unusual types of money that have been used at different times and in different places are listed in Table 7.1.

Value of Money

Measured by the goods, services, and resources that money can purchase.

If anything can serve as money, how is the **value of money** determined? Because money is a medium of exchange, the value of any money—a $20 bill, for example—is measured by the goods, services, and resources that it can purchase. Inflation causes the value of money to decline because fewer goods, services, and resources can be purchased with the same amount of money. Small, incremental increases in the general level of prices or serious bouts of inflation will cause a decline in the value of money: The decline can happen gradually or be a quick, significant deterioration.

Barter System

System in which goods and services are exchanged for each other rather than for money.

What would happen if there were no money—no generally accepted means of payment? In the absence of a medium of exchange, a **barter system** would develop. With barter, a direct exchange of goods and services occurs: A student might exchange some camping gear in return for a psychology textbook. With barter, people have to expend a lot of energy locating someone willing to take what they offer in trade for what they want. In today's world, few people operate on a barter system since it is virtually impossible to have much economic development by trading in this manner. A medium of exchange, or money, removes the problems of barter.

| TABLE 7.1 | *Different Forms of Money* |

Anything can serve as money in a society, provided it is generally accepted as payment for goods, services, and resources.

Form	Location
Cowrie shells	Africa, India, South Seas (perhaps the oldest money in the world)
Snail shells	Queen Charlotte Islands
Porpoise teeth	Malaita (island in the Solomon Group)
Boar tusks	New Guinea
Red woodpecker scalps	Karok Tribe on the west coast of North America
Feathers	South Seas
Beer	English coal mines in the mid-nineteenth century
Bars of crystal salt	Ethiopia
Round stones with centers removed	Yap
Glass	Ancient Egypt
Wampum (polished beads) Animal skins Rice Sugar Rum Molasses Indigo Tobacco	North American settlements and Colonial period
Cowries Tortoise shells Agricultural implements	Ancient China

Source: Norman Angell, *The Story of Money* (Garden City, NY: Garden City Publishing Co., 1929), pp. 73–76, 78–80, 82, 84, 85, 88–90.

Measure of Value
A function of money; the value of every good, service, and resource can be expressed in terms of an economy's base unit of money.

Method for Storing Wealth and Delaying Payments
A function of money; allows for saving, or storing wealth for future use, and permits credit, or delayed payments.

While money serves primarily as a medium of exchange, it also performs two additional functions: It is a **measure of value,** and it provides a **method for storing wealth and delaying payments.** Every nation's money is expressed in terms of a base unit. In the United States, the base unit is the dollar; in Japan, the yen; and in many countries belonging to the European Union, the euro. With a base unit, the value of every resource, good, and service can be expressed in terms of that unit: A house, for example, might be worth 220,000 times a dollar unit ($220,000) and tuition 22,000 times the unit ($22,000). Money's function as a base unit makes it easy to create simple comparisons among the values of goods and services, and the ability to express those values in terms of a common measure greatly reduces the information needed to make economic decisions.

Money also provides a method for storing wealth: It allows us to accumulate wealth or income to use in the future. For example, the $100 bill you have had since 2005 will still add one hundred dollars to your bank account balance when handed to a teller for deposit sometime in the future. With money, we can save from our current income, and a system of lending and borrowing is possible. It is this function that is critical to a stable economy. If there is a question about the future acceptability of what today we call money, people

APPLICATION 7.1

FIXED ASSETS, OR: WHY A LOAN IN YAP IS HARD TO ROLL OVER

Yap, Micronesia—On this tiny South Pacific island, life is easy and the currency is hard.

Elsewhere, the world's troubled monetary system creaks along. . . . But on Yap the currency is as solid as a rock. In fact, it is rock. Limestone to be precise.

For nearly 2,000 years the Yapese have used large stone wheels to pay for major purchases, such as land, canoes and permission to marry. Yap is a U.S. trust territory, and the dollar is used in grocery stores and gas stations. But reliance on stone money . . . continues.[a]

Buying property with stones is "much easier than buying it with U.S. dollars," says John Chodad, who recently purchased a building lot with a 30-inch stone wheel. "We don't know the value of the U.S. dollar." Others on this 37-square-mile island 530 miles southwest of Guam use both dollars and stones. Venito Gurtmag, a builder, recently accepted a four-foot-wide stone disk and $8,700 for a house he built in an outlying village.

Stone wheels don't make good pocket money, so for small transactions, Yapese use other forms of currency, such as beer. Beer is proffered as payment for all sorts of odd jobs, including construction. . . .

Besides stone wheels and beer, the Yapese sometimes spend gaw, consisting of necklaces of stone beads strung together around a whale's tooth. They also can buy things with yar, a currency made from large sea shells. But these are small change.

The people of Yap have been using stone money ever since a Yapese warrior named Anagumang first brought the huge stones over from limestone caverns on neighboring Palau, some 1,500 to 2,000 years ago. Inspired by the moon, he fashioned the stone into large circles. The rest is history.

Yapese lean the stone wheels against their houses or prop up rows of them in village "banks." Most of the stones are 2 1/2 to five feet in diameter, but some are as much as 12 feet across. Each has a hole in the center so it can be slipped onto the trunk of a fallen betel-nut tree and carried. It takes 20 men to lift some wheels.

By custom, the stones are worthless when broken. You never hear people on Yap musing about wanting a piece of the rock. Rather than risk a broken stone—or back—Yapese tend to leave the larger stones where they are and make a mental accounting that the ownership has been transferred. . . .

The worth of stone money doesn't depend on size. Instead, the pieces are valued by how hard it was to get them here. . . .

There are some decided advantages to using massive stones for money. They are immune to black-market trading, for one thing, and they pose formidable obstacles to pickpockets. In addition, there aren't any sterile debates about how to stabilize the Yapese monetary system. With only about 6,600 stone wheels remaining on the island, the money-supply level stays put. "If you have it, you have it," shrugs Andrew Ken, a Yapese monetary thinker.

But stone money has its limits. Linus Ruuamau, the manager of one of the island's few retail stores, won't accept it for general merchandise. And Al Azuma, who manages the local Bank of Hawaii branch, the only conventional financial institution here, isn't interested in limestone deposits or any sort of shell game. So the money, left uninvested, just gathers moss.

But stone money accords well with Yapese traditions. "There are a lot of instances here where you cannot use U.S. money," Mr. Gurtmag says. One is the settling of disputes. Unlike most money, stones sometimes can buy happiness, of a sort; if a Yapese wants to settle an argument, he brings his adversary stone money as a token. "The apology is accepted without question," Mr. Chodad says. "If you used dollars, there'd be an argument over whether it was enough."

might be unwilling to save and institutions unwilling to lend for investment or other purposes. A bank might be reluctant to make a student loan or lend a developer millions of dollars this year if there were questions about the usability of future repayments.

The functions of money, as well as some of the types of money described in this section, are illustrated in Application 7.1, "Fixed Assets, Or: Why a Loan in Yap Is Hard to Roll Over."

The Money Supply

Every economy has a supply of money that is used to carry out transactions. What makes up the money supply of the U.S. economy and how large is this supply? This is a more difficult question than it appears to be since people look at what is actually

TABLE 7.2	*The U.S. Money Supply: M1*

M1 is the narrower definition of the U.S. money supply.

M1
Coins and paper money in circulation
Nonbank-issued traveler's checks
Demand deposits
Other checkable deposits

Source: Federal Reserve, "Money Stock and Debt Measures," http://www.federalreserve.gov/releases/h6/Current/, February 25, 2009.

M1
Narrower definition of the U.S. money supply; includes coins and paper money in circulation, some traveler's checks, most demand deposits, and other checkable deposits.

Token Money
Money with a face value greater than the value of the commodity from which it is made.

Federal Reserve Notes
Paper money issued by the Federal Reserve banks; includes almost all paper money in circulation.

Currency
Coins and paper money.

Demand Deposits
Checking account balances kept primarily at commercial banks.

money in different ways. For example, some people think that a savings account is money while others do not. As a result, we have two different official definitions of the money supply, with one broader than the other because it includes additional components.

The narrower definition of the money supply is called **M1.** The components of this definition are listed in Table 7.2: coins and paper money in circulation, nonbank-issued traveler's checks, almost all demand deposits (checking accounts) at commercial banks, and accounts called other checkable deposits.[1]

Components of M1   In the U.S. economy, coins, which are issued by the U.S. Treasury, are **token money:** The value of the metal in the coin is less than the face value of the coin. If this were not the case, coins might disappear from circulation. For example, in the past, when the price of copper increased to a level where a penny contained almost one cent worth of copper, pennies became short in supply. (Today, pennies are made almost entirely of zinc.)

Paper money constitutes a larger share of our money supply than coins. Almost all U.S. paper money is **Federal Reserve Notes.** (Notice the inscription on the top of a paper bill that states "Federal Reserve Note.") Federal Reserve banks, which will be discussed shortly, issue and back this paper money. Coins and paper money make up **currency.**

Traveler's checks, which can be used in the United States or abroad, are purchased from banking organizations as well as from American Express and other companies. However, only traveler's checks from "nonbank issuers" are categorized separately in M1, and these constitute the smallest component of M1.

The **demand deposit** component of the money supply is checking account balances kept primarily at commercial banks. These deposits include small balances kept by individuals as well as large sums kept by businesses and nonprofit institutions for payroll and other payment purposes. Demand deposits are merely bookkeeping numbers. When a check is deposited or written, numbers are transferred from one set of records or computer entries to another. Because demand deposits are a large portion of the U.S. money supply, we need to realize that much of the

[1]Only coins and paper money in circulation are included in the money supply. Although a large amount of both of these items is "warehoused" in U.S. Treasury, bank, and Federal Reserve vaults for future use, it is not counted as money until it is in the hands of the public. For an explanation of which demand deposits are excluded from the M1 money supply, see the notes accompanying the source for Table 7.2.

TABLE 7.3 *Currency, Traveler's Checks, Demand Deposits, and Other Checkable Deposits (Billions of Dollars)[a]*

Currency has surpassed demand deposits and other checkable deposits as the largest component of the M1 money supply.

Year	Currency (Coins and Paper Money)	Traveler's Checks	Demand Deposits	Other Checkable Deposits	Total (M1)[b]	Total (M1) as a Percentage of GDP	Velocity
1980	$115.3	$3.9	$261.2	$28.1	$408.5	14.6%	6.8
1985	167.7	5.6	266.9	179.5	619.8	14.7	6.8
1990	246.5	7.7	276.8	293.7	824.7	14.2	7.0
1995	372.8	9.0	389.0	356.6	1,127.4	15.2	6.6
2000	531.2	8.3	309.6	238.4	1,087.4	11.1	9.0
2005	723.9	7.2	324.9	318.5	1,374.5	11.1	9.0
2008[c]	795.0	5.8	360.5	311.9	1,473.1	10.2	9.8

[a] Figures are seasonally adjusted.
[b] Components may not sum exactly to total (M1) due to rounding.
[c] Money figures are for October 2008; GDP is preliminary for the third quarter.

Source: *Economic Report of the President* (Washington, DC: U.S. Government Printing Office, 2009), Tables B-1, B-69, B-70.

money supply is simply numbers in accounts. Some people might think that checks themselves are money, but they are not. A check is just a piece of paper that gives a bank the authority to transfer funds in a demand deposit account to someone else or to cash.

Other Checkable Deposits

Interest-bearing accounts similar to demand deposits offered by financial depository institutions.

Other checkable deposits are similar to demand deposits but offer interest on the funds in these accounts. The distinction between these and demand deposits is made for technical reasons. Most of us, including merchants, utility companies, and other payment receivers, pay almost no attention to the distinction among checks, drafts, withdrawal orders, or other technical names given to these accounts. These accounts were introduced in the early 1980s and are provided by banks and other depository institutions.

Table 7.3 gives the amount of each component of the M1 money supply as well as other important money-related information. Notice that until recently checking-type accounts (demand deposits and other checkable deposits together) have typically been the largest part of the money supply. It is easy to understand why this would be the case. Few of us would buy something expensive, like a big-screen TV, or pay for rent or utilities with cash. In addition, businesses and nonprofits make most of their transactions through these deposit accounts rather than cash. And today many bills are paid electronically and paychecks are automatically deposited in accounts.

Closer observation of these data shows that the currency component of M1 has grown significantly since 2000, and in more recent years was larger than demand deposits and other checkable deposits combined. Much of the early impetus for this growth in currency came with the Y2K scare, when people feared that a major computer crash would occur on January 1, 2000, and bank records would be lost. The popularity of ATM machines that make cash easily accessible has also contributed to the rise of paper and coins in circulation.

Notice the column in Table 7.3 that shows the total M1 money supply for each year as a percentage of that year's GDP. Every year the total amount spent on new goods and services exceeds the amount of money in circulation. For example, the money supply in 2008 was equal to only 10.2 percent of the total expenditures made

TABLE 7.4	The U.S. Money Supply: M2

M2 is the broader definition of the U.S. money supply

M2

M1
+

Money market deposit accounts
Savings deposits
Time deposits of less than $100,000
Some money market funds

Source: Federal Reserve Statistical Release, "Money Stock Measures," http://www.federalreserve.gov/releases/h6/ Current/, June 19, 2008.

Velocity of Money
Average number of times the money supply is turned over in a year in relationship to GDP.

on new goods and services that year. Obviously, so much output can be purchased with so few dollars because the same dollars are spent several times over during the course of the year.

The average turnover of the money supply in relationship to annual GDP is termed the **velocity of money.** That is, velocity measures the average number of times a dollar is spent during a year as it is used for the purchase of new goods and services. The far right-hand column of Table 7.3 gives the velocity of M1. Notice that from 1980 through 1995 velocity fluctuated very little: The average dollar was spent about seven times a year. This should be no surprise: We are fairly consistent about the frequency of receiving paychecks and making major payments. However, velocity jumped in 2000 and continues to be higher.[2]

M2: The Broader Definition of the Money Supply   As we said, there are differing opinions as to what constitutes money and because of this two definitions of the money supply are used. M1 is considered by many to be too narrow, especially with the growth of new types of accounts not included in M1 that can be used to buy goods and services or readily converted to payment instruments. Suppose a person receives a paycheck for $1,000 and puts $500 into a demand deposit account, $200 into a savings account, and $300 into a money market deposit account that pays interest and allows limited checking privileges. According to the definition of M1, only the $500 deposited in the checking account would be considered money. Although the funds in the savings account are easily transferable to a checking account or cash and the funds in the money market deposit account can be spent, they are not counted in M1.

M2
M1 plus savings and small-denomination time deposit accounts, money market deposit accounts, and other financial instruments.

The broader definition of the money supply, **M2,** is given in Table 7.4. Notice that it builds on M1, adding money market deposit accounts, savings deposits, certificates of deposit (time deposits) of less than $100,000, and some money market funds. M2 is considered by many observers to be an important measure of the money supply because it includes money market deposit accounts that allow limited checkable transactions and savings and time deposits that can be easily converted to spendable funds.

[2]There is a relationship between velocity and M1 as a percentage of GDP. That is, velocity = 1/M1 as a percentage of GDP. For example, the velocity of 9.8 in 2008 is equal to 1/0.102 = 9.8. (Be careful: The 10.2% is converted to a decimal (0.102) when used in this equation.)

Liquidity
Ease of converting an asset to its value in cash or spendable funds.

Commodity Monetary Standard
An economy's money is backed by something of tangible value, such as gold or silver.

Paper Monetary Standard
An economy's money is not backed by anything of tangible value such as gold or silver.

In other words, many of the components have a high degree of **liquidity**. Not surprisingly, there is a substantial difference in the sizes of M1 and M2. At the beginning of 2009, M1 was $1.6 trillion and M2 was $8.2 trillion.[3]

Monetary Standards   People are often curious and sometimes concerned about what backs our money and that of other countries. Economies have monetary standards, or designations, for the backing of their money supply. An economy in which money is backed by something of tangible value, such as gold or silver, is on a **commodity monetary standard.** If the money is backed by gold, the economy is on a gold standard; if it is backed by silver, the economy is on a silver standard.

For much of its history the U.S. economy was on a commodity standard. Prior to 1933 the United States had a gold-coin standard, where gold not only backed the money supply but also freely circulated in the hands of the public. The use of gold pieces as money was common. Then, U.S. citizens were asked to turn their gold in to the government, and in 1934 the United States went on a gold-bullion standard. This meant that gold backed the money supply but was no longer available to the general public. Under this gold-bullion standard, however, foreign holders of dollars were paid in gold. In the years after 1950, more and more international debts were paid in gold, and the U.S. gold supply gradually diminished. This brought about a reduction in the gold backing of the money supply. By 1971 official U.S. gold reserves had decreased to the point where the gold supply was frozen. U.S. gold was to be made available to no one, and the dollar was no longer to be converted to gold, not even to settle international transactions.

Since 1971 the U.S. economy has been on a **paper monetary standard.** This means that money itself has little or no intrinsic value and that it does not represent a claim to any commodity, such as gold or silver. What backs paper money is the strength of the economy, the willingness of people to accept the money in exchange for goods and services, and faith and trust in the purchasing power of the money.

What is better for an economy, a paper standard or a commodity standard? It is easy to argue that there is more faith in money if it is backed by gold or silver, but history does not bear this out. In the past, panics and monetary crises have occurred even when money was backed by a precious metal. In fact, the knowledge that paper money can be converted into gold or silver can make people act more dramatically on their fears.

But the most important reason that advanced economies turn to a paper standard is that the amount of gold or silver a nation possesses generally has very little to do with its economic needs and potential. It is much more important that the amount of money in an economy be tied to the country's economic conditions rather than the availability of a commodity like gold or silver. But there is always a warning with a paper standard. The administrators of the money supply must be informed and impeccably trustworthy in the decisions they make concerning the money supply and carefully manage it. Without proper controls, serious economic problems can arise.

---

[3] Federal Reserve Statistical Release, "Money Stock Measures," http://www.federalreserve.gov/releases/h6/Current/, February 19, 2009. Figures are preliminary for January 2009. In 2006 the Federal Reserve ceased publishing an even broader definition of the money supply titled M3. M3 was equal to M2 plus time deposits of over $100,000, Eurodollar holdings by U.S. residents, and other components. M3 was discontinued because its data were costly to collect and it was not considered to offer information about the economy beyond what is already provided in M2.

Financial Depository Institution
Institution that accepts and maintains deposits, and makes loans; can create and destroy money.

In the United States, there are organizations called **financial depository institutions** (FDI) that play an extremely important role in the economy because of their association with the money supply. To be classified as an FDI, two functions must be performed: accept and maintain deposits, and make loans. Commercial banks are the most important of the financial depository institutions, but thrifts like savings associations and credit unions are also among these organizations. While they may seem similar to us, they are different in the kinds of deposits and loans they are permitted to offer and the degree of regulation they face.

Financial depository institutions are vital to the economy because they have the ability to create and destroy money. Here is one of our myths to correct. Many people think that money is created only when currency is printed. This is not so. *Money is created when loans are made by financial depository institutions and destroyed when loans are repaid.* The process for doing this will be thoroughly explored in the next chapter. For now we want to let you know that these institutions, with their special abilities to accept deposits and make loans, are central to expanding and contracting the money supply.

Commercial Banks

Commercial Bank
Institution that holds and maintains checking accounts (demand deposits) for its customers, makes commercial (business) and other loans, and performs other functions.

The primary financial depository institution is the **commercial bank**—where most individuals, businesses, and nonprofit organizations do their banking. A commercial bank attracts deposits by offering checking accounts, or demand deposits, as well as other deposit arrangements, makes loans to businesses and individuals, and performs a number of other functions. Banks earn profit for their owners by attracting deposits and converting them to interest-earning assets such as loans. In 2007 there were about 7,300 commercial banks in the United States.[4]

In 1980 Congress passed a significant piece of banking legislation that leveled the playing field for most financial institutions and made them almost indistinguishable: the Monetary Control Act of 1980. Before this act, the ability to make loans to businesses was held almost exclusively by commercial banks.

We saw in Table 7.3 that in 2008 approximately 24 percent of M1 was in demand deposits, or checking accounts, at commercial banks. In addition, commercial banks held some portion of other checkable deposits as well as trillions in savings and time deposits. The huge dollar value of these deposits makes commercial banks the most important of all financial depository institutions.

Commercial Bank Regulation   Commercial banks are unique: They are profit-driven businesses but play an essential role in maintaining and changing the size of the U.S. money supply. Since their actions are key to the economy, we must ensure that commercial banks be sound and secure, and not abuse their money-creating abilities. To accomplish this aim, a number of agencies set standards and regulations for commercial banks that include, for example, the backing needed for deposits, the allowable riskiness of loans, and the money capital necessary to open a bank.

All commercial banks must be incorporated, or have a corporate charter. Because both the federal and state governments have the right to charter banks, the United

---

[4]Number is for FDIC insured commercial banks. FDIC, http://www2.fdic.gov/hsob/hsobRpt.asp.

Dual Banking System
Label given to the U.S. banking system because both the federal and state governments have the right to charter banks.

National Bank
Commercial bank incorporated under a federal rather than a state charter.

State Bank
Commercial bank incorporated under a state charter.

Federal Deposit Insurance Corporation (FDIC)
Government agency established in 1933 to insure deposits in commercial banks up to a specified amount.

Asset
Something that an individual or business owns; can be used to cover liabilities.

Liability
A claim on assets; an obligation or a debt of an individual or a business.

Net Worth
Assets minus liabilities; the monetary value of a business.

States has a **dual banking system:** That is, a bank may be chartered by the federal government or by a state government. Federally chartered banks are called **national banks,** and state-chartered banks are simply called **state banks.**

While bank regulation appears to be scattered among several agencies, there is order among them to prevent duplication of bank-examining tasks and an exacerbation of the disruption that comes with a visit from the examiners. The following gives the various agencies with which a bank may have to deal.

- ◆ *Charter Authority.* The charter sets up the first line of regulation: National banks are regulated by a federal agency and state banks by a state banking agency.
- ◆ *The Federal Reserve.* The Fed, which we will discuss shortly, has various levels of regulatory authority. The Federal Reserve regulates its own members, which include all national banks (they must belong) and state banks that choose to belong, or become "state member banks." The Federal Reserve also imposes some uniform regulations on all commercial banks regardless of whether they belong to the system or not. Today Federal Reserve regulatory authority over all banks is extensive and the distinction between Federal Reserve member and nonmember banks has lessened.
- ◆ *Federal Deposit Insurance Corporation.* Additional regulation comes from the **Federal Deposit Insurance Corporation (FDIC),** which was established in 1933 and insures deposits in commercial banks up to a specified amount. All national and state member banks are insured. Nonmember state banks (those that do not belong to the Federal Reserve) may affiliate with the FDIC and are termed "nonmember state insured banks." Relatively few banks are nonmember noninsured state banks.

Bank Failures   With such extensive regulation, can banks fail? Banks are no different from other businesses that no longer have the assets necessary to pay their debts. Despite regulation, banks and other financial depository institutions have found themselves in this same bankruptcy-prone position.

Bank failure is easy to understand with some basic accounting terminology. Recall that the two functions of a financial depository institution are to make loans and to hold deposits. The loans of a bank are a major **asset** (what the bank owns), and its deposits are a major **liability** (what the bank owes). The **net worth** of a bank is its assets minus its liabilities.

A bank fails when its assets are no longer sufficient to cover liabilities that must be paid. This is usually the result of heavy loan losses combined with deposit withdrawals. For example, if a bank loans a developer $50 million to build a subdivision of homes, the bank has an asset of $50 million. If the developer goes belly up, perhaps unable to sell the homes in various stages of construction, the bank becomes the new owner of those homes. It will likely not receive the full $50 million it loaned as it tries to dispose of this construction project. In short, the bank is "stuck" with an asset of less than $50 million, or has taken a loan loss.

When a bank's assets decline, it has fewer funds available for depositors who want to withdraw their money from the bank; in other words, it cannot meet the demands of the holders of its liabilities. If a bank has made too many bad loans, it may simply not be solvent. With an insured bank in this position, the FDIC steps in and guarantees that depositors with accounts of less than a specified amount will receive their money. With an uninsured bank, depositors have no such promise, and their funds may be lost.

APPLICATION 7.2

AM I COVERED?

Sally took her $1,000 paycheck to her bank, deposited it into her checking account, and went home. Ed took his $1,000 paycheck to his bank, cashed it for ten $100 bills, and took them home and buried them in his backyard. The next day Sally's bank failed and closed, and an earthquake dropped Ed's backyard and stash of hundred-dollar bills into the Pacific Ocean. Ed lost all of his money, but what about Sally? If Sally's account is in a bank insured by the FDIC, she will likely get all her money covered by the insurance back within a few days following the bank's closing. Since the FDIC began in 1933, customers of failed banks have gotten all of their insured money back.

Is everything you put in an insured bank automatically protected by the FDIC? No. There are certain restrictions on what and how much is protected. Funds in checking or savings accounts, certificates of deposit (CDs), money market funds, and some retirement accounts and trusts are insured. But if you use your insured bank to buy U.S. Treasury securities or invest in mutual funds made up of a variety of corporate stocks or other investment products, that money is not insured by the FDIC. Also, and perhaps not surprisingly, the FDIC does not protect the contents of your safe deposit box if it is crushed or burned, or protect you if you are a victim of identity theft.

Also, simply having an account in an FDIC-insured institution does not mean that you will get *all* your money back if something goes wrong: There are limits on the amount insured. If you have one or more insured accounts in only your name at an FDIC-protected bank, the maximum you can recover is $250,000. If you have a checking account with a balance of $50,000, you'll get $50,000 back. But if one or more accounts together have balances over $250,000, when the bank fails you'll only get $250,000.[a]

There is a way to get more than $250,000 in protection from an FDIC-covered bank—put the funds into a joint account where two or more people have equal rights to the funds, such as an account in the name of a husband and wife. In this case, the maximum protection would be $500,000 ($250,000 for each named account holder). There are also some reimbursement rules about retirement accounts, trusts, and such.

What might you want to do if you inherit some money or you cash a hot stock tip that brings the total balance of your accounts in an FDIC-insured bank over the maximum insurable amount? Your best bet might be to open an account for some of your funds at another FDIC-insured bank—and probably not convert the funds into cash that is buried in your yard!

[a]Insurance coverage was raised from $100,000 to $250,000 in 2009 on a temporary basis as part of the federal government bailout of some financial institutions. As of this writing it is not possible to determine whether the raised limit will continue beyond December 31, 2009.

Source: Federal Deposit Insurance Corporation, http://www.fdic.gov/deposit.

In 2008, 25 banks failed. This number of closings comes nowhere near the record number of bank failures during the Great Depression—for example, 4,004 in 1933 alone.[5] Application 7.2, "Am I Covered?", gives some more information on how the FDIC protects people with accounts in banks.

Other Financial Depository Institutions

Other financial depository institutions that play an important role with the money supply are savings institutions, such as savings and loan associations and savings banks, and credit unions. In 2006 there were 1,279 insured savings institutions and 8,362 credit unions. Although the number of these institutions is larger than the number of commercial banks, their total size is smaller. In 2006, assets of all savings institutions and credit unions together were just 25 percent of commercial bank assets.[6]

[5]A bank closing is defined as either a permanent or temporary suspension of operations by order of the bank's supervisory authorities or its directors. 2008 data are from FDIC, "Failed Bank List," http://www.fdic.gov/bank/individual/failed/banklist.html, February 5, 2009. The 1933 bank failure figure is from Bruce R. Dalgaard, *Money, Financial Institutions, and Economic Activity* (Glenview, IL: Scott, Foresman & Company, 1987), p. 103.
[6]*Statistical Abstract of the United States: 2008*, 127th ed., p. 729.

In the early 1980s, significant changes were made in the legislation regulating these institutions to permit them to offer a greater variety of deposit accounts, to make different types of loans, and to bring some aspects of their operations under Federal Reserve control. The deregulation of deposits and loans, however, caused a serious crisis in the savings and loan industry, requiring financial intervention from the government. This crisis will be discussed later in this chapter.

The future of some of these financial depository institutions remains unclear. The number of savings institutions and credit unions has fallen in recent years. The closing and merging of failing savings and loans, switches from a savings to a commercial bank charter, and the acquisition of savings institutions by commercial banks have all contributed to this movement. However, while falling in numbers, credit unions have become stronger as membership, assets, loans, and savings accounts have all increased. The "clublike" appeal of credit unions may make them more viable.[7]

THE FEDERAL RESERVE SYSTEM

While the Federal Reserve is familiar to us through media coverage, many people are unaware of the considerable power and authority that it has over our money and the economy. A paper monetary standard, like the one under which we operate, requires careful control. That job has been given to the Federal Reserve. And, as we will learn in Chapter 8, through its control of the supply of money the Fed has the ability to influence levels of employment and prices and affect unemployment and inflation problems.

Created in 1913, the **Federal Reserve system** has been charged to

Federal Reserve System
Coordinates commercial banking operations, regulates some aspects of all depository institutions, and oversees the U.S. money supply.

♦ oversee the money supply and adjust its size to meet the needs of the economy,
♦ coordinate commercial banking operations, and
♦ regulate some aspects of all depository institutions.

Prior to the creation of the Fed, there was little central organization, a hodgepodge of state and federal banking laws, a history of questionable banking practices, and a recurrence of monetary panics.

Organization of the Federal Reserve System

Board of Governors
Seven-member board heading the Federal Reserve System; develops policies concerning money, banking, and other financial institution practices.

Open Market Committee
Oversees the buying and selling of government securities by the Federal Reserve System.

The Federal Reserve system is organized on both a functional and a geographic basis. Figure 7.1 outlines the important features in the system's functional structure. The system is headed by the seven-member **Board of Governors,** each appointed by the president and confirmed by the Senate for a 14-year term.[8] One member is designated by the president as chairperson and serves as the spokesperson for Federal Reserve policy. (Alan Greenspan, who was the well-known and carefully watched chair of the Board for over 18 years, was replaced in January 2006 by Ben Bernanke.)

The Board of Governors has duties and responsibilities typical of a board of any organization: It sets objectives for carrying out its charge and appropriate policies to meet those objectives. The **Open Market Committee,** which includes the Board of Governors among its members, carries out the most important procedure for money supply control: It authorizes the buying and selling of government securities by the Federal

[7]*Statistical Abstract of the United States: 2008,* 127th ed., pp. 730, 732.
[8]The 14-year term was intended to keep any one president from appointing a majority of the Board of Governors. However, many appointees do not serve for 14 years, thus weakening the original intent of this arrangement.

FIGURE 7.1   *Functional Structure of the Federal Reserve System*

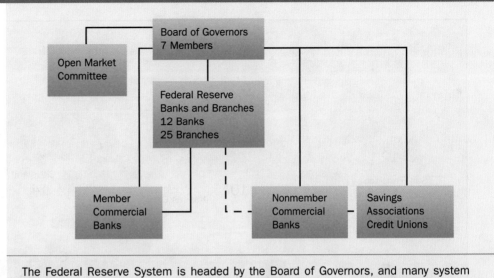

The Federal Reserve System is headed by the Board of Governors, and many system activities are carried out through the Federal Reserve banks and their branches.

Reserve.[9] You can go to the Federal Reserve Web site, www.FederalReserve.gov, for the pictures and biographies of the current members of the Board of Governors.

Federal Reserve Banks
Twelve banks that deal with commercial banks and other financial institutions.

At the center of the Federal Reserve system are 12 **Federal Reserve banks** and their 25 branches, located throughout the country. These are not commercial banks: They deal with commercial banks and other financial depository institutions and perform a variety of functions that will be covered shortly. Each Federal Reserve bank is an independent corporation with its own board of directors, and each bank carries out the same functions. The remainder of the Federal Reserve system is the country's financial depository institutions, which are influenced by Federal Reserve policies, may depend on the Fed for certain services, and differ in their relationship with the Fed based on whether or not they are member banks.

The Fed is also organized geographically. The United States is divided into 12 Federal Reserve districts, each represented by a Federal Reserve bank that is responsible for its own branch banks and the member commercial banks in its geographic area. Figure 7.2 illustrates the 12 Federal Reserve districts. In what district do you live, and how close are you located to one of these banks?

Functions of the Federal Reserve Banks

What do the Federal Reserve banks do? What would I see if I visited one of these locations? The Federal Reserve banks and their branches perform a variety of functions that do not directly involve the typical commercial bank customer. In fact, there is little reason for the average individual or businessperson to ever enter a Federal Reserve bank.

Supervise and Examine Member Banks   One function of each Federal Reserve bank is to supervise and examine member banks within its district. For this purpose,

[9]The operation of the Open Market Committee will be discussed in detail in Chapter 8.

FIGURE 7.2 *Federal Reserve Districts*

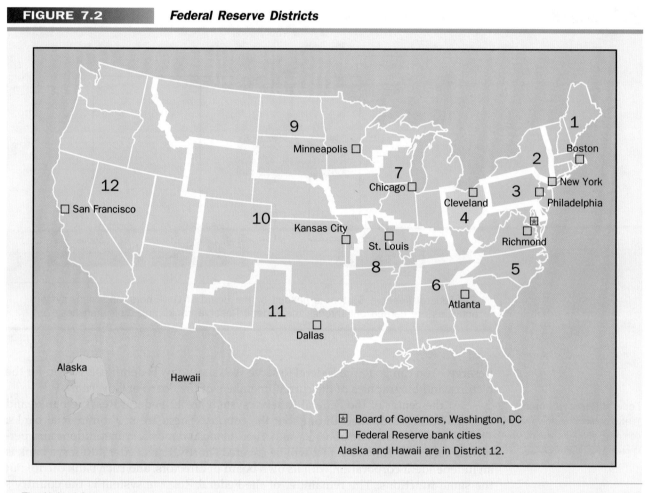

- ⊠ Board of Governors, Washington, DC
- ☐ Federal Reserve bank cities

Alaska and Hawaii are in District 12.

The United States is divided into 12 Federal Reserve districts, each with its own Federal Reserve bank.

Source: *Federal Reserve Bulletin*, Spring 2005, p. 312.

each Federal Reserve bank employs a staff of examiners who periodically check each member bank's financial condition and compliance with system regulations.

Reserve Account
Deposit in the name of a financial institution held at a Federal Reserve bank or other designated place.

Maintain Reserve Accounts Another Federal Reserve bank function is to maintain reserve accounts for financial depository institutions. A **reserve account** is a deposit in the name of a financial institution that is held at a Federal Reserve bank or other approved place. Financial depository institutions must have a reserve account and hold a minimum amount on reserve. However, the actual amount fluctuates daily and may exceed the minimum.

Currency Circulation Federal Reserve banks provide the means for putting coins and paper money into or out of circulation. Each Fed bank maintains a warehouse of used and newly minted coins and paper money in its vaults (obviously with extensive security arrangements). When the public wants to carry more money in the form of coins and paper, as happens, for example, around the Christmas holidays, more checks, drafts, and such are cashed and more visits are made to ATM machines. And as financial institutions require more coins and paper money to convert their customers' deposits to currency, they order what they need from the Fed. When the Fed delivers cash to a financial institution, the cash is paid for out of that institution's reserve account. When less cash is wanted by the public, as happens, for example, after the Christmas holiday season, currency begins to build up at banks and other depository institutions. These institutions will return their cash to the Fed and receive credit in their reserve accounts. Also, when currency is worn out, it is retired by the Fed and, in the case of paper money, destroyed.

Check and Electronic Payment Clearing   The Federal Reserve banks participate in the process of check and payment clearing. Each day the Federal Reserve processes millions of checks and electronic payments as financial institutions use the Fed as a payment clearinghouse. In short, the Fed participates in sorting checks and payments from deposits in financial institutions to be returned to the financial institution from which the deposit or check originated. For example, when you pay your tuition at your college with a check from your bank account, the Fed provides or oversees the means for transferring funds to your college from your bank.

When payment clearing is done within the same Federal Reserve district, the procedure is simple. However, if a check is drawn on an institution in another Federal Reserve district, it is forwarded to that district for further processing, or adds another step to the payments clearing mechanism.

Regardless of whether someone who has an account at a bank uses direct deposits, paper checks, or online banking, deposit and payment clearing causes a financial institution's reserve account to fluctuate. When a deposit is made at a financial institution and sent to the Fed for clearing, the full amount of that deposit is credited (added) to that institution's reserve account. When a check or other payment method is used by a customer with an account at a financial institution and that payment goes through the Fed clearing procedure, the full amount of that payment is subtracted from that institution's reserve account. This process causes a financial institution's reserve account to fluctuate daily, with the size of the fluctuation depending on the value of payments deposited and spent.

It is not necessary that all payments go through the Federal Reserve banks. Other clearinghouse arrangements exist. Regardless of the clearing payments mechanism, the effect on a financial depository institution's reserve account is the same: *Deposits increase a bank's reserves, and payments from an account held by a bank's customers decrease its reserves.*

Figure 7.3 show how a $100 check sent from an aunt in San Francisco to a niece in Atlanta travels through the payments-clearing system. When the niece deposits the check, it increases deposits in her bank by $100. When the check is sent by the niece's bank to the Atlanta Federal Reserve bank for clearing, her bank receives $100 in reserves. From Atlanta the check goes to the San Francisco Federal Reserve bank, where the aunt's bank loses $100 in reserves. Finally, the check goes to the aunt's bank, which lowers the balance in her account by $100.

Technology has created many changes in the payments clearing process. **Check 21** went into law at the end of 2004 and legalizes an electronic picture of a check, allowing banks to use this picture in place of the canceled check. The process described in Figure 7.3 is the same but the electronic picture, rather than the actual check, allows for a quicker movement through the payments clearing process and eliminates shipping

Check 21
Law that allows electronic substitute checks for check-clearing purposes.

FIGURE 7.3   *Check Clearing through the Federal Reserve System*

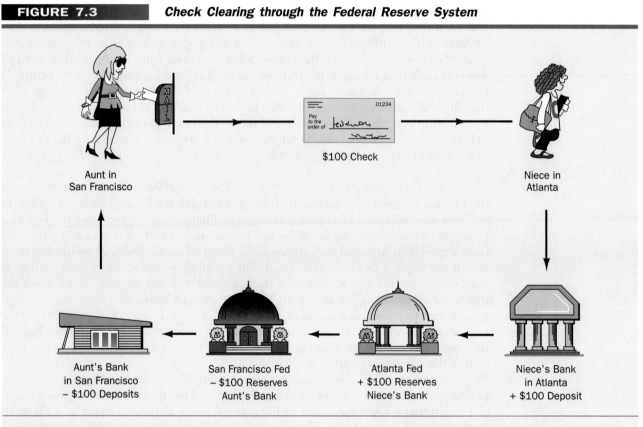

$100 Check

Aunt in
San Francisco

Niece in
Atlanta

Aunt's Bank
in San Francisco
– $100 Deposits

San Francisco Fed
– $100 Reserves
Aunt's Bank

Atlanta Fed
+ $100 Reserves
Niece's Bank

Niece's Bank
in Atlanta
+ $100 Deposit

Depository institution reserve accounts increase or decrease as checks move through the Federal Reserve's clearing system.

Automated Clearing House (ACH) Network
A large electronic payments network that facilitates a reliable, secure, and efficient payments system.

checks. In addition, the growth of the **Automated Clearing House (ACH) Network** has facilitated electronic payments.

Fiscal Agents for the U.S. Government   The Federal Reserve banks act as fiscal agents for the U.S. government by performing a variety of chores, such as servicing the checking accounts of the federal government and handling many of the tasks associated with the maintenance of Treasury securities, or the national debt.

Many of the functions performed by the Federal Reserve banks are necessary for the smooth operation of the banking system. However, sometimes commercial banks depend on each other instead of the Fed for these operational tasks. In this case, banks set up a relationship called **correspondent banking.** Typically, in this arrangement a smaller bank keeps some deposits with a larger bank and receives advice and various services in return.

Be sure at this point that you understand how a reserve account is changed, especially by check clearing. This understanding is key to the material in Chapter 8. You can use the Test Your Understanding, "Changes in a Bank's Reserve Account," questions at the end of this chapter, and exercises in your Study Guide to explore some of the ways a bank's reserve account changes and to calculate reserve positions.

Correspondent Banking
Interbank relationship involving deposits and various services.

TEST YOUR UNDERSTANDING

CHANGES IN A BANK'S RESERVE ACCOUNT[a]

1. The First National Bank of Latrobe starts its day with $18,993,560 in its reserve account. During the day $1,256,780 in checks are deposited and cleared, and $1,379,000 in checks written by the bank's customers are cleared. How much is in First National's reserve account at the end of the day? _____

2. California One begins its day with $35,664,440 in its reserve account at the Fed. During the day it returns $2,350,000 to the Fed in currency that has accumulated in its vaults. What is the bank's reserve account balance after the cash is returned? _____

3. The MBMB Bank of El Campo has $12,450,221 in its reserve account at the beginning of the day.

During the day, $644,970 in deposited checks and $788,450 in checks written by MBMB's customers are cleared. In addition, $350,000 in currency is delivered to the bank by the Fed. What is the bank's reserve account balance at the end of the day? _____

4. Westmoreland Bank ends a Wednesday with $14,544,500 in its reserve account. On Thursday its customers deposit $345,660 in checks, and on Friday they deposit $467,845 in checks, both clearing on the day deposited. On Thursday and Friday, $266,890 and $351,115, respectively, in checks written by the bank's customers are cleared. In addition, the Fed picks up $100,000 in currency on Friday from Westmoreland to return to the Fed's vaults. How much does Westmoreland Bank have in its reserve account at the end of business on Friday? _____

[a]All depository institutions in this exercise are hypothetical. Answers can be found at the back of the book.

RECENT TRENDS IN FINANCIAL INSTITUTIONS

Since the early 1980s, after decades of traditional banking practices and strict government regulatory control over the banking system, U.S. financial institutions have changed significantly. We have seen increased similarities in the roles of financial institutions, consolidations and mergers that have created very large organizations, banks and other financial depository institutions move into new nonbank industries, and the savings and loan industry diminish. Also, in October 2008 the U.S. Congress passed legislation to provide up to $700 billion to bail out troubled financial institutions.

Legislative Changes

Depository Institutions Deregulation and Monetary Control Act (1980)
Legislation that increased the similarity among many financial institutions and increased the control of the Federal Reserve system.

Riegle-Neal Interstate Banking and Branching Efficiency Act (1994)
Allows banking organizations from one state to open or acquire banks, and to open branches, in other states.

Interstate Banking
The performance of services in more than one state by a single banking organization.

In 1980, one of the most significant laws pertaining to money and banking was passed: the **Depository Institutions Deregulation and Monetary Control Act.** This law made financial depository institutions more similar in the deposit accounts they offer and the types of loans they make and eliminated much of the distinction between commercial banks and other financial depository institutions, such as savings and loans and credit unions. The Monetary Control Act also increased the authority of the Federal Reserve and added a new relationship between the Federal Reserve and nonmember depository institutions. In 1982 further legislation strengthened this trend.

In 1994 the **Riegle-Neal Interstate Banking and Branching Efficiency Act** was passed. This act opened the door for widespread **interstate banking,** or the ability for banking organizations to operate in more than one state. Today, we are used to large nationwide banks: Prior to the late 1970s, most banks were limited to operating facilities within a single state.

In 1999 significant new federal legislation was passed: the **Gramm-Leach-Bliley Act.** This act tore down the strong firewall between commercial banking and other financial industries built in 1933 with the Glass-Steagall Act. Glass-Steagall set an environment for control over banking by keeping banking apart from securities, insurance, and other financial industries.

The Gramm-Leach-Bliley Act influenced the activities of some **holding companies,** which are corporations formed for the purpose of owning, or holding, the controlling shares of stock in other corporations. Bank holding companies were permitted to become **financial holding companies,** and financial holding companies were now permitted to engage in a wide range of bank and nonbank activities. More specifically, these financial holding companies could now own corporations that engage in securities underwriting and dealing, and insurance agency and underwriting activities, as well as banking activities. Under Gramm-Leach-Bliley, the Federal Reserve was designated as the "umbrella" supervisor of the financial holding companies. Simply, a bank holding company could now add to its operation a variety of other types of corporations that it was not previously permitted to own.[10]

In October 2008 the **Emergency Economic Stabilization Act** was passed to stem the possible collapse of a large number of banks and financial holding companies that began to fail. Housing was affected with rising numbers of foreclosures, credit was drying up, and there was much uncertainty over the future of the financial markets. This act gave the U.S. Treasury about $350 billion initially, with another $350 billion later. This action by Congress brought controversy over the size of the bailout, continued exorbitant salaries to executives, and a lack of accountability.[11]

Up for Debate, "Should Congress Enact More Stringent Regulations over the Banking System?" looks at both sides of the recent discussion about whether banks need to be subject to more regulation than currently exists or whether the United States should return to earlier standards of regulation.

Structural Changes

All of the legislative changes in regulations concerning branch banking, interstate banking, and the ability to form financial holding companies have changed the face of banking during the past three decades. In addition, advances in technology have altered the way banks do business and made it easier to complete transactions.

The size of a banking organization is largely determined by its ability to attract deposits, which in turn is heavily influenced by location. Even with the growth in technology, people still want easy access to their banks. Banks in large urban areas with a business base and facilities in multiple locations have more potential to be large than banks located in small, rural communities with a few facilities. As a result, **branch banking,** where a bank operates more than one facility, is a significant factor in the size of a bank. In 2007, there were about 79,000 bank branches.[12]

---

[10]The Federal Reserve Bank of San Francisco, "Overview of the Gramm-Leach-Bliley Act, http://www.frbsf.org/publications/banking/gramm/grammmpg1.html.
[11]United States Senate, Committee on Banking, Housing, and Urban Affairs, "Summary of the 'Emergency Economic Stabilization Act of 2008'."
[12]Number of branches is for FDIC-insured commercial banks. FDIC, http://www2.fdic.gov/hsob/hsobRpt.asp.

UP FOR DEBATE

SHOULD CONGRESS ENACT MORE STRINGENT REGULATIONS OVER THE BANKING SYSTEM?

Since 1980 the banking industry has become more deregulated, especially with the Gramm-Leach-Bliley Act in 1999. The near collapse of many large banks in 2008 caused Congress to provide a $700 billion bailout for the financial services industry. One debate that has resulted is over the extent of regulation needed to ensure safety and stability in banking. Should Congress enact more stringent regulations over the banking system?

YES The crisis of 2008 is certainly indicative of the need to return to more stringent banking regulation. From the Depression in the 1930s until more recent years, the United States enjoyed a fairly safe and secure banking industry. During that time, the banking industry was regulated in terms of the activities that banks could undertake, and their size was limited because of various regulations. Banks were more personal places for customers such as business owners, who could turn to their local banker for loans.

While banks are profit-seeking corporations and their stockholders like to see the highest dividends possible, the banking industry is unlike others. Safe and secure banking is essential to a healthy economy. Once the banking system goes, the entire economy becomes dysfunctional. This reality became quite apparent with the quick approval in Congress of a substantial bailout of the financial services industry in the fall of 2008. The collapse of these institutions would have crippled the economy.

It may not be in the best interest of consumers to continue on the road of mergers, consolidations, and adding securities and insurance services to these large banking entities. For one, bank customers may end up with fewer choices, higher prices, and less responsiveness—all results of less competition in markets. In addition, the assumption of less risk with investments because they are bought through a bank, particularly among consumers who mistakenly believe that the FDIC is ensuring these transactions, could hurt the less informed customer.

NO Returning to an era of more stringent banking regulation because of the "sins" of a few is like punishing an entire classroom of children for the actions of one. Just because a few of the financial services holding companies engaged in poor, risky business practices, this is no reason to return to the old style of banking. The action that is needed is better audits and supervision of these financial services companies.

The ability of banks to become financial holding companies has benefits for consumers. Now bank customers can take advantage of a wider array of products in one place to meet their increasingly sophisticated needs. Rather than banking at one location, investing at a second, and taking care of insurance needs at a third, customers can conduct all of these activities at the same place. In addition, with all of these new opportunities, competition in these industries should increase, giving consumers more choices and better prices and services. It also can lead to more efficient operations.

Finally, banks and financial holding companies are profit-seeking corporations that thrive when their owners, the holders of their stock, see a profit from the company's operations. If banks are reregulated, this may come at the disadvantage of their stockholders. In addition, these financial holding companies have provided good jobs with excellent salaries to a large number of people who could now become unemployed.

Today, we are experiencing a growth in large banking organizations. Table 7.5 gives the 10 largest commercial banks as of September 2008. By the time you read this text, this list will have likely changed. Notice the size of the assets of these banks: The largest bank has close to $2 trillion in assets and is almost three times the size of the fourth largest bank. These banks also have rather large numbers of branches, approaching 6,000 in one case.

Mutual Fund
Pool of money from depositors that is used to make investments.

Mutual Fund Growth An additional factor challenging the banking system is the mutual fund industry. A **mutual fund** is a pool of dollars from depositors that is used to make financial investments in corporate stocks or bonds, government securities, or other instruments. Mutual funds now compete with financial depository institutions for household savings and time deposits, and for providing funds for business loans. In 1980 there were $135 billion of assets in mutual funds, and by 2006 that amount was over $10.4 trillion.[13]

[13]U.S. Bureau of the Census, *Statistical Abstract of the United States: 2004–2005*, p. 757; *2008*, p. 745.

TABLE 7.5	*The 10 Largest Commercial Banks*

The 10 largest banks are ranked by assets (September 2008 data).

Rank	Bank Name	Location	Assets (in billions)	Number of Domestic Branches
1	JP Morgan Chase Bank	Columbus, Ohio	$1,769	3,554
2	Bank of America	Charlotte, North Carolina	1,359	5,775
3	Citibank	Las Vegas, Nevada	1,207	1,034
4	Wachovia Bank	Charlotte, North Carolina	664	3,341
5	Wells Fargo Bank	Sioux Falls, South Dakota	515	3,326
6	State Street	Boston, Massachusetts	276	3
7	US Bank	Cincinnati, Ohio	243	2,605
8	Bank of New York Mellon	New York, New York	219	12
9	HSBC Bank	Wilmington, Delaware	182	449
10	Suntrust Bank	Atlanta, Georgia	170	1,766

Source: "Large Commercial Banks," Federal Reserve Statistical Release, September 30, 2008.

Mutual funds appeal to individual savers who want a higher return than they can get from CDs or passbook savings and who are willing to assume some degree of risk. Unlike savings and time deposits in banks, mutual funds are not insured and the return to the owners of these funds fluctuates.

Because financial depository institutions have experienced an outflow of deposits to these funds, banks have responded by providing mutual fund services to maintain customer relationships. Some banks have invited independent major funds to "set up shop" on their premises, while others have offered their own proprietary funds. Competition with mutual funds was one factor prompting support for legislation to allow for a broader range of services by banks.

Savings and Loans   Before the late 1980s, saving and loan associations were a large part of the financial institutions landscape. Since that time most have been merged into other institutions or simply closed. The legislative and structural changes that altered traditional banking roles were the basis for a substantial number of S&L failures in the late 1980s and early 1990s. The failures and insolvencies of these S&Ls caused the federal government to provide significant amounts of financial assistance in what might have been the first Congressional financial bailout.

Deregulation contributed to these failures as many institutions, no longer operating with interest caps, offered unprofitably high interest rates to attract savings and time deposits. Also, with new freedom to provide different types of loans, rather than concentrating on home mortgages, some institutions offered loans with little or no collateral and speculated on risky real estate. In addition, the **Federal Savings and Loan Insurance Corporation (FSLIC)** removed much of the risk because deposits were insured.

Federal Savings and Loan Insurance Corporation (FSLIC)
Federal agency established in 1934 to insure deposits in savings and loan institutions; the FDIC took over many of its functions when the FSLIC was dissolved in 1989.

APPLICATION 7.3

500 BILLION DOLLARS

Some estimates of the cost of the savings and loan bailout range up to $500,000,000,000— five hundred billion dollars—if interest payments are included. There is something engaging about the number five hundred billion, even more so if you put it in perspective.

With $500 billion, the Government could mail a check for $2,000 to every man, woman and child in the United States. If it were in an ecumenical mood and had a global mailing list, it could send $100 to every human being on earth. . . . For the same money, the Government could buy approximately 12 million Mercedes, 20 million Volvos, 30 million Mazdas or 100 million Eastern European cars. . . .

It would take a decade to spend $500 billion at $1,585 a second. . . . Another time analogy is illuminating: A million seconds take approximately 11 days to tick by, whereas a billion seconds require about 32 years. Sixteen thousands years need to pass before 500 billion seconds elapse.

For a more somber equivalence, note that according to UNICEF's 1989 report, millions of children die each year from nothing more serious than measles, tetanus, respiratory infections or diarrhea. These illnesses can be prevented by a $1.50 vaccine, $1 in antibiotics or 10 cents worth of oral rehydration salts. UNICEF estimates that $2.5 billion (most of it going to staff and administrative costs) would be sufficient to keep these children alive and improve the health of countless others. This amount is 1/200th of $500 billion.

It is this last sort of comparison that truly illustrates the enormity of the savings and loan scandal. There are so many other programs that might have been financed.

The tendency we have to be mesmerized by "people" stories and bored by "number" stories should be resisted. Ultimately, however, the distinction between the two is specious. We must find better ways to vivify complex issues. The cost of not doing so will be considerably more than $500 billion.

Resolution Trust Corporation (RTC)
Federal agency created to reorganize troubled savings and loans or to deal with their affairs if they failed and closed.

As Congress dealt with record numbers of failures, it created the **Resolution Trust Corporation (RTC)** to manage the reorganization of troubled S&Ls or to close them and dispose of their holdings. When the Resolution Trust Corporation went out of existence in 1995, it had closed or merged 747 failing thrift institutions. The final price tag for cleaning up the S&L crisis: $480.9 billion.[14]

Application 7.3, "500 Billion Dollars," is excerpted from an article printed at about the time the Resolution Trust Corporation came into existence. The author is amazingly accurate in anticipating the cost of settling the S&L crisis, and puts that cost into terms that are more understandable to most of us. Does viewing the crisis in this way give you a better sense of the enormity of the $700 billion financial bailout of 2008/2009?

Summary

1. Money is a medium of exchange, or something generally accepted as a means of payment for goods, services, and resources. Without money to facilitate transactions, an economy would need to rely on a barter system. Money also serves as a measure of value and as a method for storing wealth and delaying

[14]Robert A. Rosenblatt, "GAO Estimates Final Cost of S&L Bailout at $480.9 Billion," *Los Angeles Times*, July 13, 1996, pp. D1, D2.

payment. The value of money is measured by the goods, services, and resources it can purchase. Inflation causes the value of money to fall.

2. There are two definitions of the U.S. money supply. M1, the narrower definition, includes coins and paper money in circulation, nonbank-issued traveler's checks, demand deposits (checking accounts) at commercial banks, and other checkable deposits. The other definition of the money supply is M2, which is an important measure because it includes M1 plus accounts that have limited checkable features and accounts that are easily convertible to cash.

3. In any year, the economy's money supply is smaller than the value of goods and services produced, or GDP. The velocity of money measures the average annual turnover of the money supply in relation to GDP.

4. When money is backed by something tangible, such as gold or silver, the economy is on a commodity standard. The United States formerly had its money backed by gold but is now on a paper standard, where money is generally backed by people's willingness to accept it and by the strength of the economy. A paper standard has both advantages and disadvantages.

5. Financial depository institutions, such as commercial banks, savings associations, and credit unions, play a critical role in the economy because they can create and destroy money through their loan-making activities. Commercial banks are the most important of these financial institutions. Agencies, such as federal and state banking authorities, the Federal Reserve, and the Federal Deposit Insurance Corporation, regulate commercial banks.

6. The Federal Reserve system coordinates commercial banking operations, regulates other financial depository institutions, and oversees the U.S. money supply. The system, which is organized geographically into 12 districts, is headed by the Board of Governors. The 12 Federal Reserve banks and their branches provide services to financial institutions rather than directly to the general public. The functions of the Federal Reserve banks include supervising and examining the operations of member banks in their districts, maintaining reserve accounts, circulating coins and paper money, clearing checks and some electronic payments, and acting as fiscal agents for the federal government.

7. Significant changes have occurred in the U.S. banking system since the Monetary Control Act of 1980 made financial depository institutions more similar. More recently the Gramm-Leach-Bliley Act permitted the formation of bank and financial holding companies that allow banking organizations to conduct securities and insurance activities.

8. Other significant banking changes include the financial bailout through the Emergency Stabilization Act, the increase in popularity of mutual funds, and the elimination of most savings and loan associations.

Key Terms and Concepts

Money	Asset
Medium of exchange	Liability
Value of money	Net worth
Barter system	Federal Reserve system
Measure of value	Board of Governors
Functions of money	Open Market Committee
Method for storing wealth and delaying payments	Federal Reserve banks
Definitions of the money supply	Organization of the Federal Reserve system
M1	Reserve account
Token money	Check 21
Federal Reserve Notes	Correspondent banking
Currency	Depository Institutions Deregulation and Monetary Control Act (1980)
Demand deposits	
Other checkable deposits	Riegle-Neal Interstate Banking and Branching Efficiency Act (1994)
Velocity of money	
M2	Interstate banking
Liquidity	Gramm-Leach-Bliley Act
Commodity monetary standard	Holding company
Paper monetary standard	Financial holding company
Financial depository institution	Emergency Economic Stabilization Act
Commercial bank	
Dual banking system	Branch banking
National bank	Mutual fund
State bank	Federal Savings and Loan Insurance Corporation (FSLIC)
Federal Deposit Insurance Corporation (FDIC)	Resolution Trust Corporation (RTC)

Review Questions

1. List the basic functions of money and explain how a $20 bill fulfills each of these functions.

2. How much is a $20 bill worth? How is its value measured and what causes that value to change?

3. What are the basic components of M1 and M2? How do these two measures differ? In your opinion, which is a better measure of the money supply? Why?

4. Answer the following questions concerning financial depository institutions.
   a. What distinguishes commercial banks from other financial depository institutions? Why are commercial banks so important?
   b. Give the various classifications of commercial banks and their regulating agencies. Why are commercial banks subject to extensive regulation?
   c. How have financial depository institutions been impacted by federal legislation since 1980?

5. What is the basic purpose of the Federal Reserve system? How is it organized functionally and geographically?

6. List and briefly describe the functions of a Federal Reserve bank.

7. The First National Bank of Anytown had $50,000,000 in its reserve account at the Fed one morning. Later that morning $2,500,000 in checks that had been deposited at the Bank of Anytown were processed at the Fed, and the bank ordered $1,000,000 in currency. Later that day $3,000,000 worth of checks written by the bank's customers cleared through the Fed. How much did the First National Bank of Anytown have in its reserve account at the Fed at the end of the day?

8. Define each of the following terms and explain how each has affected the financial institutions system in recent years.
   a. Branch banking
   b. Interstate banking
   c. Mutual funds
   d. Financial holding company

9. What are the major pieces of legislation that have significantly affected the banking industry since 1980?

Discussion Questions

1. If demand deposits are a medium of exchange, and if a medium of exchange is generally accepted as payment for goods and services, why is it sometimes difficult to pay with a check?

2. Could you make an argument for returning the U.S. economy to a commodity standard based on gold? More generally, are there any circumstances under which a commodity standard might be preferable to a paper standard?

3. "Regulation of financial depository institutions should be eliminated. These institutions should be free to sell their products like any other business in a free-enterprise system. As long as the government continues to insure deposits, regulation is unnecessary." What is your opinion of this statement?

4.   Go to www.FederalReserve.gov and locate the name and a brief biography of each current member of the Board of Governors of the Federal Reserve system.

5.   What is your position on a law that would place the Federal Reserve under the direct control of the president of the United States and that would allow each new president to completely replace the Board of Governors?

6.   What do you think would be the effect of a law that removes all controls over where a bank can open branches and allows a banking organization to engage in whatever financial activities it wants?

7.   Some people believe that taxpayers should not have footed the bill for the savings and loan crisis and that the government should not insure financial depository institutions. Do you think that the government should insure deposits?

8.   Locate information on two or three mutual funds and explain how they differ from one another in terms of what is included in each fund, risk, and income growth potential.

9.   Review the Up for Debate on page 221 and explain your position on this issue.

Critical Thinking Case 7

CIGARETTE MONEY

Critical Thinking Skills

Applying concepts in an unfamiliar setting

Recognizing conventional outcomes in unconventional circumstances

Economic Concepts

The functions of money

Monetary standards

This excerpt is from an article, published shortly after World War II, that describes life in a German prisoner of war camp. It will help in reading this excerpt to know that prisoners received food and cigarettes from German rations and the International Red Cross. Some private parcels of personal items and cigarettes made their way into the camps as well.

Between individuals [prisoners] there was active trading in all consumer goods and in some services. Most trading was for food against cigarettes or other foodstuffs, but cigarettes rose from the status of a normal commodity to that of currency. RMk.s [German Reichsmarks] existed but had no circulation save for gambling debts, as few articles could be purchased with them from the canteen.

[W]hen we reached our permanent camp, there was a lively trade in all commodities and their relative values were well known, and expressed not in terms of one another . . . but in terms of cigarettes. The cigarette became the standard of value. In the permanent camp people started wandering through the bungalows calling their offers—"cheese for seven" (cigarettes). . . .

[E]veryone, including nonsmokers, was willing to sell for cigarettes, using them to buy at another time and place. Cigarettes became the normal currency. . . .

The permanent camps in Germany saw the highest level of commercial organisation. [A] shop was organised. . . . People left their surplus clothing, toilet requisites and food there until they were sold at a fixed price in cigarettes. Only sales in cigarettes were accepted—there was no barter—and there was no higgling. . . .

. . . Laundrymen advertised at two cigarettes a garment. . . . There was a coffee stall owner who sold tea, coffee or cocoa at two cigarettes a cup. . . .

[C]igarettes as currency . . . performed all the functions of a metallic currency as a unit of account, as a measure of value and as a store of value, and shared most of its characteristics. They were homogeneous, reasonably durable, and of convenient size for the smallest or, in packets, for the largest transactions. . . .

Source: Radford, RA. "The Economic Organisation of a POW Camp, *"Economica,"* Blackwell Publishing, November 1945, pp 189–201.

Questions

1. Were cigarettes really money? If so, how did they perform the functions that make something money? What backed the cigarettes used as money?

2. Reichsmarks were the official money of Germany, but they appear not to have been thought of as money by the prisoners in this camp. Why, in this camp, would Reichsmarks have been unable to perform the functions that make something money?

3. How would the homogeneity, durability, and convenient size of cigarettes help them perform the functions of money?

4. Cigarettes may have served as money in this camp, but do you think they could serve as money in a larger, national economy if the official monetary system collapsed due to hyperinflation? Why?

CHAPTER 8

Money Creation, Monetary Theory, and Monetary Policy

CHAPTER OBJECTIVES

To explain the relationship between the economy's money supply and output, employment, and prices.

To explain how money is created and destroyed through the loan-making activities of financial depository institutions.

To explain the role of the interest rate in encouraging or discouraging borrowing from financial depository institutions.

To show how interest rates are affected by changes in financial depository institutions' excess reserves.

To define monetary policy and explain the major tools for carrying out monetary policy by the Federal Reserve.

To show the relationship between government borrowing to cover deficit spending and monetary policy.

For any economy, especially one that is on a paper monetary standard, careful control over the size of the money supply is extremely important. There is a strong relationship between an economy's money supply and the economy's production level, jobs, and overall price changes: Any change in the size of the money supply can change the economy's overall performance. Because of this relationship, changing the money supply is an important way to reach the economy's goals of full production and economic growth, full employment, and price stability. Monetary policy, or changing the money supply to address unemployment and inflation, is in the hands of the Federal Reserve.

You will learn a lot about how money affects the economy in this chapter. You will also learn the processes for creating and destroying money, the tools that the Federal Reserve uses in its role as overseer and controller of the money supply, and how interest rates are determined and influenced through monetary policy. By the end of this chapter you will have a good understanding of an area of the macroeconomy that seems mysterious to many people but is critical to economic stabilization and growth.

THE MONEY SUPPLY AND THE LEVEL OF ECONOMIC ACTIVITY

Let's begin by summarizing some of the key lessons learned in Chapter 5.

- Total, or aggregate, spending drives the economy's levels of production, employment, and income, and sometimes overall prices.
- Total spending is found by adding together the spending of all four major macroeconomic sectors: household, business, government, and foreign.
- Increases in total spending lead to increases in production, employment, and income unless the economy is at full employment.
- At (or near) full employment, increases in spending lead to overall price increases, or demand-pull inflation.
- Decreases in total spending result in a decline in production, employment, and income, and may dampen inflation.

Household and business spending is related to the amount of money in the economy: An increase in the money supply increases spending, and a decrease in the money supply decreases spending. We learned in Chapter 7 that money is created when financial depository institutions, such as commercial banks, make loans. Because households typically borrow to finance the purchase of homes, automobiles, appliances, and other consumer products, and businesses typically borrow to invest in buildings, machinery, equipment, and such, increased loan making results in increased spending.[1] So, increases in loans by financial depository institutions increase the money supply and spending, and when loan making falls, the money supply is decreased and spending declines. This significant relationship among loan making by financial depository institutions, money creation, and the level of spending is explained in detail as the chapter develops.

---

[1]Financial depository institutions also make loans to the government when they purchase government securities for their portfolios.

The Equation of Exchange

The relationship between money and economic activity is laid out in a simple equation called the **equation of exchange:**

Equation of Exchange
$MV = PQ$: illustrates how changes in the supply of money (M) influence the level of prices (P) and/or the total output of goods and services (Q).

$$MV = PQ.$$

On the left-hand side of this equation, M is the supply of money in the economy, and V stands for the velocity of money, or the number of times each dollar is spent for new goods and services in a year. The more frequently the money supply turns over each year, the higher the value of V. On the right-hand side of the equation, P represents the level of prices and Q the actual output of goods and services.

MV, the supply of money multiplied by the number of times it turns over each year, represents total spending on new goods and services in the economy. PQ, the price level multiplied by the actual output of goods and services, can be interpreted as the dollar value of output produced in the economy, or current GDP. Since the circular flow model tells us that a given level of spending brings forth an output of equal value, we know that MV and PQ are equal.[2] Thus, if the supply of money were $1.5 trillion and velocity were 9, MV (or total spending) would equal $13.5 trillion, as would PQ, the value of the economy's output.

Changing the Money Supply   What happens to the level of economic activity when the supply of money changes? The equation of exchange helps answer this question. To keep matters simple, assume that the velocity of money does not change. That is, let V be constant in the equation of exchange.[3]

First, we will deal with expanding the money supply. An increase in M causes the left-hand side of the equation of exchange, or total spending, to increase. Because the two sides of the equation must be equal, the right-hand side of the equation, the dollar value of output, must increase by the same amount. If the economy is not operating at full employment and production, the increase in the value of output comes primarily in the form of an expansion in production and employment. That is, the increase on the right-hand side of the equation of exchange would come mainly in the Q term. However, if the economy were at or near full employment, production and employment would be at or near their upper limits. Under these circumstances, Q in the equation of exchange could go up very little, if at all. At full employment, an increase in the money supply would lead primarily to an increase in the price level, the P term, or to inflation.

A decrease in M decreases total spending, the left-hand side of the equation of exchange. This, in turn, causes a decrease in the dollar value of output, the right-hand side of the equation. A decrease in the money supply typically results in a decrease in Q, or production and employment. P, or the overall price level, usually does not fall with a decrease in total spending. Businesses generally respond to decreases in spending by cutting production rather than by lowering prices. However, if the economy were operating at or near full employment and experiencing inflation, a decrease in the money supply would dampen some of the upward pressure on prices, causing prices to rise less rapidly.

In summary, the relationship between total spending and the economy's production, employment, and price levels is affected by changes in the economy's supply of

[2]Some economists write the equation of exchange as an identity: $MV \equiv PQ$. This equation is so classic that it was for years the license plate of a money and banking professor in St. Louis.
[3]In reality, the velocity of money (M1) does change over time. However, in looking at the effect on the economy of increasing or decreasing the money supply *at a particular moment in time*, the assumption that V is fixed is appropriate.

money. Increasing the money supply facilitates spending and contributes to an expansion of economic activity. Whether this leads to increased production and employment or to inflation depends in large part on how close the economy is to full employment. Decreasing the supply of money inhibits the spending ability of businesses and households and in turn slows the level of economic activity.

MONEY CREATION

We know that money is created when financial depository institutions make loans, and money is destroyed when those loans are repaid. Although these loan-making institutions include savings associations and credit unions, it is the commercial banks that are primarily engaged in money creation and destruction. Because of the huge impact that money supply changes have on the economy, it is important that the capacity of financial institutions to make loans be highly controlled. This is one of the functions of the Federal Reserve. However, in order to understand how the Fed exerts its control over money supply changes, we need to understand under what conditions a financial depository institution can make a loan and how those conditions change.

The Process of Money Creation

Actual Reserves

A financial depository institution's reserve account plus its vault cash.

Every financial depository institution has two assets that it counts as its **actual reserves:** the institution's reserve account and its vault cash. Every institution must have a reserve account, which, as we saw in Chapter 7, can be held at a Federal Reserve bank or at an approved designated institution. Vault cash is all the cash in the depository institution's vault and cash drawers.

Reserve Requirement

Specific percentage of deposits that a financial depository institution must keep as actual reserves.

Depository institutions have a **reserve requirement,** which is a specific percentage of *deposits* that must be kept as actual reserves. For example, a bank with a reserve requirement of 10 percent on demand deposits must have an amount on reserve equal to 10 percent of the value of the demand deposits it is holding. If a bank has $80,000,000 in checking accounts and a 10 percent reserve requirement, it must have at least $8,000,000 (0.10 × $80,000,000) in actual reserves. The amount of actual reserves that a financial depository institution must keep to back its deposits is called its **required reserves.** In this example, the bank's required reserves are $8,000,000.

Required Reserves

The amount of actual reserves that a financial depository institution must keep to back its deposits.

Every day each depository institution makes several calculations pertaining to its deposits and reserves. First, it computes the value of deposits held in the institution that day. Second, it calculates its required reserves. And, third, it determines how much it has in actual reserves. (Remember from Chapter 7: A depository institution's reserve account fluctuates daily due to check—paper or electronic—deposits and clearing and periodically due to currency orders and returns.) In short, the institution determines what it must have and what it actually does have on reserve.

Excess Reserves

Reserves of a financial depository institution over the amount it is required to maintain in actual reserves; actual reserves minus required reserves.

These calculations permit an institution to determine its **excess reserves.** Excess reserves are actual reserves minus required reserves, or reserves over and above those that an institution must maintain. If Hometown Bank has a reserve requirement of 10 percent and demand deposits of $60,000,000, its required reserves are $6,000,000 (0.10 × $60,000,000). If its actual reserves are $10,000,000, then its excess reserves are the actual reserves of $10,000,000 minus the required reserves of $6,000,000, or $4,000,000. In other words, the bank has $4,000,000 on reserve that it doesn't need to have. Table 8.1 summarizes these calculations.

TABLE 8.1	*Hometown Bank's Reserve Calculations*

A financial depository institution's excess reserves are equal to its actual reserves minus its required reserves.

If Hometown Bank's

$$\text{Demand deposits} = \$60,000,000$$
$$\text{Reserve requirement} = 10 \text{ percent, or } 0.10$$
$$\text{Actual reserves} = \$10,000,000,$$

then Hometown Bank's excess reserves are found by the calculation

$$\begin{array}{ll} \text{Actual reserves} & = \$10,000,000 \\ - \text{ Required reserves} & = \$\ \ 6,000,000\ (0.10 \times \$60,000,000) \\ \hline \text{Excess reserves} & = \$\ \ 4,000,000. \end{array}$$

Excess Reserves and Loan Making   Excess reserves are important because they are the foundation for a depository institution's loan-making abilities. Very simply, *a depository institution can make new loans up to the value of its excess reserves.* Why is this so?

When a financial depository institution makes a loan to a business or an individual, it usually gives the borrower those funds in either a cashier's check or through a direct deposit into the borrower's checking account. In either case, when the borrower spends these loaned funds and the payment for this spending is deposited in another institution and cleared through the payment-clearing mechanism, the lending bank loses reserves. For example, if Hometown Bank loans a business owner $40,000 to buy a delivery van, it will lose $40,000 in reserves when the payment for the van is deposited by the van seller in another financial institution and cleared through the payment-clearing mechanism.[4]

Because a depository institution loses reserves when a loan is spent, it must be careful to make loans only up to the value of its excess reserves in order to meet reserve requirements. Return to the example of Hometown Bank, which had $10,000,000 in actual reserves, $6,000,000 in required reserves, and $4,000,000 in excess reserves. Given these figures, Hometown Bank could make new loans of up to $4,000,000. If, however, Hometown Bank made loans of over $4,000,000, say $4,500,000, its $10,000,000 in actual reserves would drop to $5,500,000 when the payments from the loans were cleared. In this case, Hometown Bank would be $500,000 short on its required reserves. It is for this reason that an institution can make new loans only up to an amount equal to its excess reserves.

In making a loan, a depository institution does not take away one customer's money to give to another. Those who hold money at the institution (in demand deposits and other accounts) do not have their deposits altered; they retain all of their account balances and are free to spend their money when they so desire. Instead, in making a loan, a financial depository institution creates new money; that is, it provides dollars for spending that were not in the economy before the loan was made. If a bank maintains $60 million in demand deposits and makes new loans of $4 million, then the $60 million in demand deposits is still money, but it has been supplemented by the creation of an additional $4 million.

---

[4]The effect from lending to households, businesses, or the government is the same. When a financial depository institution lends money to the U.S. government by buying a Treasury security, it pays for that security out of its reserve account, causing the reserve account to decrease.

APPLICATION 8.1

QUESTIONS AND ANSWERS ABOUT RESERVES AND LOANS

Q: Do all financial depository institutions have the same reserve requirement?

A: There are uniform reserve requirements on all financial depository institutions, although the actual percentage requirement differs by type of account (for example, checkable versus time). These requirements are given later in the chapter in Table 8.4.

Q: What happens if an institution does not meet its reserve requirement?

A: Depository institutions are required to compute and report their deposits and reserves over a period of 7 or 14 days, depending on their reporting status. This gives them time to settle their accounts and permits an institution with a reserve deficiency on 1 day to correct it within the next few days and still meet its requirement. If an institution has not met its reserve requirement on the average over its given time period, it will usually borrow the needed reserves rather than pay a fine.

Q: From whom can banks borrow reserves?

A: Banks can borrow reserves from a Federal Reserve bank or from other banks through the Federal Funds market. In the Federal Funds market, banks lend excess reserves to other banks, usually for a period of 1 day. The transfer of funds is completed electronically. Banks borrow in the Federal Funds market to cover reserve deficiencies or to obtain additional reserves with which to make loans.

Q: What is the prime rate, and who determines it?

A: The prime rate is the interest rate banks charge on loans to their lowest-risk customers. It is a benchmark interest rate that a commercial bank sets for loan pricing. A prime rate is determined by each individual bank but is influenced by general credit conditions. The prime rate tends to be a few percentage points above the federal funds rate, a key interest rate discussed on page 245.

Q: How much do financial depository institutions keep in vault cash?

A: Financial depository institutions need enough paper money and coins to service their customers who want to cash a check or redeem savings or time deposits in cash. They do not want to keep excessive amounts of vault cash on hand, however, for security and storage reasons. These institutions also consider the amount of cash that is normally deposited daily by their customers in calculating the level of vault cash to maintain.

Source: Federal Reserve System, *Reserve Maintenance Manual*, April 2008, pp. III-1-7; pp. XVIII-1-6.

When a loan is repaid, money is destroyed. How is money destroyed? Repayment of a loan withdraws money from the economy by returning it to the lending institution, where it becomes reserves. Until the institution makes another loan based on these reserves, this money has disappeared from the system. Application 8.1 gives some typical questions and answers about reserves and loans.

It should be clear by now that excess reserves form the basis for loan making and thus for changing the money supply. The supply of money can be controlled, therefore, by controlling the amount of excess reserves in depository institutions. An increase in excess reserves is appropriate to increase the money supply, and a decrease in excess reserves is appropriate to decrease the money supply.

The Multiple Expansion of Money

So far we have dealt with the money-creating ability of a single depository institution. However, to fully understand the relationship between changes in reserves and money creation and destruction in the economy as a whole, all such institutions must be considered together as a system.

When we make the transition from a single bank's excess reserve loan-making capability to consideration of the system as a whole, there is an interesting and important factor to consider. When excess reserves are changed in the system, a **multiplier effect** occurs: Any change in excess reserves in the system causes a multiple change in loans, or the money supply. That is, a $1 change in excess reserves in the system will create a change in loan making, or the money supply, that is a multiple of that $1. In other words, an initial increase in excess reserves in the system will cause the money

Multiplier Effect (Money)
An initial change in excess reserves in the depository institutions system causes a larger change in the money supply.

TABLE 8.2	*Multiple Expansion of Money (10 Percent Reserve Requirement)*

An initial increase in excess reserves in the system causes the money supply to grow by a multiple of the initial excess reserve change.

	Demand Deposits	Actual Reserves	Required Reserves	Excess Reserves	Loans
Hometown Bank				$10,000.00	$10,000.00
Bank B	$10,000.00	$10,000.00	$1,000.00	9,000.00	9,000.00
Bank C	9,000.00	9,000.00	900.00	8,100.00	8,100.00
Bank D	8,100.00	8,100.00	810.00	7,290.00	7,290.00
Bank E	7,290.00	7,290.00	729.00	6,561.00	6,561.00
Bank F	6,561.00	6,561.00	656.10	5,904.90	5,904.90
Bank G	5,904.90	5,904.90	590.49	5,314.41	5,314.41
Bank H	5,314.41	5,314.41	531.44	4,782.97	4,782.97
Bank I	4,782.97	4,782.97	478.30	4,304.67	4,304.67
Bank J	4,304.67	4,304.67	430.47	3,874.20	3,874.20
Bank K	3,874.20	3,874.20	387.42	3,486.78	3,486.78
Banks L, M, N . . .	. . .	. . .	. . .	. . .	. . .
Total	$100,000.00				$100,000.00

supply to increase by some multiple of that increase in excess reserves, and an initial decrease in excess reserves in the system will cause the money supply to shrink by some multiple of that decrease. The following example illustrates this principle.

Assume that Hometown Bank experiences a $10,000 increase in excess reserves because of a policy change by the Fed. (Different methods for carrying out these policy changes will be discussed shortly.) Because a bank can make new loans up to the amount of its excess reserves, these new excess reserves permit Hometown Bank to make a new loan of $10,000. This is shown in the top row of Table 8.2.

Suppose the bank loans $10,000 to Mid Jones to build a deck on the back of her house. Mid writes out a check in that amount to the contractor for the project, who deposits it in his account at Bank B. If Bank B, as well as each other bank in this example, has a reserve requirement of 10 percent, then that $10,000 deposit gives Bank B actual reserves of $10,000, of which $1,000 are required reserves and $9,000 are excess reserves (remember—check deposits, when cleared, increase a bank's reserves). On the basis of this check, Bank B can now make a new loan of $9,000. Bank B's situation is given in the second row of Table 8.2.

Al Smith, who really wants a sailboat, goes to Bank B and borrows $9,000 for it. The boat dealer takes Al's check for that amount and deposits it in her account at Bank C, where it brings Bank C $9,000 in actual reserves, of which $900 are required reserves and $8,100 are excess reserves. On the basis of this $9,000 deposit, Bank C can now make a new loan of $8,100 that eventually will be deposited by someone in Bank D, and on and on. Table 8.2 carries this example through several more rounds, showing how new loans are made with each round. It is extremely important to realize that none of these loans could have been made without the initial increase in excess reserves at Hometown Bank. It is this initial increase in excess reserves that caused other banks to experience an increase in their excess reserves.[5]

[5]The situation would be the same if any of these banks received multiple deposits: that is, if Hometown Bank or Bank B, C, or so on were repeated on the list in Table 8.2.

When the full effect of this initial change in excess reserves is carried through the system, all the new loans can be added together to determine the total amount of money created. When we do this, it is apparent that the change in the money supply is some multiple of the initial change in excess reserves. In Table 8.2, a $100,000 increase in the money supply has resulted from an initial $10,000 increase in excess reserves. In this case, there has been a **money multiplier** of 10.

Money Multiplier
Multiple by which an initial change in excess reserves in the system can change the money supply.

Calculating the Money Multiplier   The money multiplier is determined by the reserve requirement. In fact, the money multiplier is the reciprocal of the reserve requirement. (The reciprocal of a fraction is the fraction "flipped over": The reciprocal of 1/3 is 3/1, or 3.) A 10 percent (1/10) reserve requirement means a multiplier of 10/1, or 10; a 25 percent (1/4) requirement means a multiplier of 4; and a 15 percent (3/20) requirement yields a multiplier of 20/3, or 6.67.

The initial change in excess reserves times the multiplier gives the total change that could result in the money supply, or stated in equation form:

initial change in excess reserves × money multiplier = total change in money supply.

An initial increase in the banking system of $8 million in excess reserves with a reserve requirement of 20 percent (multiplier of 5) could generate $40 million of new money, and an $8 million decrease in excess reserves with a 10 percent reserve requirement could decrease the money supply by $80 million. The multiplier can work in either direction: Increases or decreases in excess reserves are subject to its effect.[6]

The examples presented here show the maximum by which the money supply can grow or shrink following an initial change in excess reserves. In reality, the expansion of the money supply resulting from an increase in reserves can be dampened by actions such as converting some portion of the deposits to cash, putting some portion into mutual funds, or having institutions lend less than the maximum amount available. For instance, if the sailboat dealer in the example in Table 8.2 deposited $7,000 from Al Smith's $9,000 purchase in the dealership's checking account and took $2,000 in cash, the increase in the other banks' excess reserves and loans, and in the money supply, would have totaled to less than the $100,000 shown at the bottom of Table 8.2. In addition, if any of these banks loaned less than the total amount of their excess reserves, the effect on the money supply would also have been smaller than the $100,000 increase shown in Table 8.2.

It is important to understand that by controlling the amount of excess reserves in the system, the Federal Reserve has significant control over the money supply. It can put

---

[6]Another method for calculating the amount by which the money supply could change following an initial change in excess reserves in the system is to divide the initial change in excess reserves by the reserve requirement, or

$$\frac{\text{initial change in excess reserves}}{\text{reserve requirement}} = \text{total change in money supply.}$$

Thus, if excess reserves increased by $8,000,000 when the reserve requirement was 20 percent (or 0.20), the total change in the money supply could be

$$\frac{\$8,000,000}{0.20} = \$40,000,000.$$

Be careful not to confuse this formula with the multiplier formula in Chapter 5. The formula given here is used to determine how much the *money supply* could change following an initial change in excess reserves in the depository institutions system. The formula in Chapter 5 determines how much *income* and *output* change as a result of an initial change in nonincome-determined spending.

| TABLE 8.3 | Relationship among Loan Making, the Money Supply, Spending, and the Level of Economic Activity |

Changes in loan making lead to changes in spending, which in turn affect the economy's levels of output, employment, and/or prices.

Increases in the Money Supply	Decreases in the Money Supply
Increases in the money supply occur with increases in lending by financial depository institutions.	Decreases in the money supply occur with reductions in lending by financial depository institutions.
↓	↓
Increased loan making leads to increased spending.	Decreased loan making leads to decreased spending.
↓	↓
Increased spending leads to an increase in output and employment if the economy is at less than full employment and/or an increase in the price level if the economy is near or at full employment.	Decreased spending leads to a decrease in output and employment, and a reduction of inflationary pressure if the economy is near or at full employment.

excess reserves into the system, enabling financial depository institutions to expand their loans, and the money supply, by a larger, or multiple, amount, or it can decrease excess reserves, which multiplies the decrease in loans and money in the system.

EXCESS RESERVES, INTEREST RATES, AND THE LEVEL OF SPENDING

Let's summarize a few key points.

- ◆ Changes in the money supply are realized through changes in loan making by financial depository institutions.
- ◆ Increases in loan making lead to increases in spending and, ultimately, to increases in output and employment, or to increases in prices if the economy is at or near full employment.
- ◆ Decreases in loan making lead to decreases in spending and output and employment.

These relationships among lending, the money supply, spending, and economic activity are summarized in Table 8.3.

Businesses and households take out loans with depository institutions because they choose to, not because they have been coerced into doing so. For this reason, simply having excess reserves available in depository institutions does not ensure that loans will be made and money will be created. This leads to two important questions. If borrowing is voluntary, how can businesses and households be stimulated to take out loans when an increase in the money supply and spending would help reduce

Interest Rate

Price paid to borrow money; a percentage of the amount borrowed.

unemployment? And how can businesses and households be encouraged to borrow less when the money supply should be reduced to dampen inflationary pressure?

The answers are found in the role played by the **interest rate,** the price paid to borrow money. If $100,000 were borrowed for 1 year at an annual interest rate of 6 percent, at the end of the year the borrower would have to repay the $100,000 that was loaned plus $6,000 in interest, or $106,000. If the interest rate were 12 percent, at the end of 1 year the borrower would have to repay $112,000. As you can see, as the interest rate increases, so does the price that must be paid to borrow money. Since borrowed money, like any good or service, is subject to the Law of Demand (discussed in Chapter 3), the quantity of funds demanded for borrowing falls as the interest rate rises, and rises as the interest rate falls.

Businesses are particularly sensitive to the interest rate when making decisions about borrowing for investment spending. (Recall this discussion in Chapter 5 on page 152 and Application 5.1.) The cost of borrowing funds to finance equipment, construction, and such must be recovered for any investment to break even, much less earn a profit. As the interest rate goes up, certain investment projects that would have been profitable at lower rates become unprofitable and are dropped from consideration. This in turn leads to a drop in the amount of funds demanded to finance such projects. Households are also sensitive to the interest rate when taking out loans. An increase in the interest rate on mortgages, auto loans, or other consumer loans leads to a decrease in the quantity of borrowed funds demanded by households to purchase homes and other goods.

Determining Interest Rates on Loans

How is the interest rate determined for loans made by financial depository institutions? What causes it to change? The interest rate is determined in the same way other prices are determined—through the interaction of demand and supply.

Recall that demand gives the various amounts of a product that someone will buy at various prices. The demand by businesses and households for loans from financial depository institutions is the different amounts they plan to borrow at different interest rates. A hypothetical demand for loans is given in Figure 8.1 by the demand curve D. As with other demand curves, D slopes downward to indicate an inverse relationship between the amount of planned borrowing and the interest rate.

On the other side of the transaction, the amount of loans that depository institutions are willing to make varies directly with the interest rate. Because a financial depository institution earns its profit from loan making and other sources, it is motivated to use excess reserves in the way that brings the highest return. If the interest rate it can earn on loans is low, a depository institution may likely convert some of its excess reserves to higher-yielding assets. But when it can obtain a high interest rate for loaning funds, it will convert more of its excess reserves to loans. S in Figure 8.1 gives a hypothetical supply curve for loans by depository institutions. Because the base for loan making is excess reserves, there is a fairly steep supply curve: As the interest rate changes, the quantity of loans supplied cannot greatly vary.

Given D and S in Figure 8.1, the interest rate that emerges is 10 percent, with $40 million in loans resulting. This equilibrium condition occurs because at 10 percent, the amount of funds demanded equals the amount supplied. However, this equilibrium position can change. Recall from Chapter 3 that changes in demand and/or supply (shifts in the demand and/or supply curves) cause changes in market equilibrium. In the market for loans, factors that cause demand and/or supply to shift will change the equilibrium interest rate and quantity of loans made. For example, expectations of poor economic conditions could shift the demand curve to the left, causing a decrease

FIGURE 8.1	*Determining the Interest Rate for Loans*

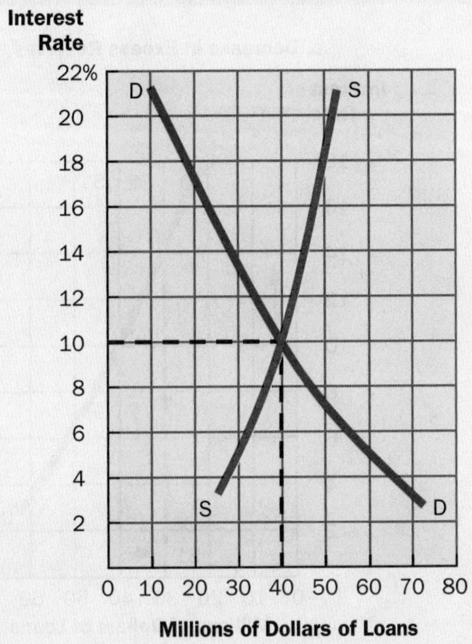

The interest rate for loans is determined by the demand for and supply of funds for loans.

in both the equilibrium interest rate and quantity of loans. When the economy slowed into a serious downturn in 2008 and early 2009, there was much hesitation about borrowing as predictions for the future became more dire. In this case, the demand curve took a noticeable shift to the left.

A change in the excess reserves of depository institutions alters their ability to make loans and shifts the supply curve. If excess reserves are decreased, institutions can make fewer loans, or the supply of loans decreases. This is shown in Figure 8.2a as a shift of the supply curve to the left from S1 to S2. As a result of this decrease in reserves, the equilibrium interest rate rises from 10 percent to 14 percent, and the equilibrium quantity of loans made declines from $40 million to $30 million. In simple terms, a decrease in excess reserves causes interest rates to rise and the amount of loans made to fall.

An increase in excess reserves causes the supply of loans to increase and the supply curve to shift to the right, as shown in Figure 8.2b. When supply shifts from S1 to S2, the equilibrium interest rate falls from 10 percent to 6 percent, and loans increase from $40 million to $50 million. This shows that an increase in excess reserves decreases the interest rate and increases the amount of loans made.

Figure 8.3 extends the relationship among loan making, the money supply, spending, and the level of economic activity summarized in Table 8.3 by including excess reserves and the interest rate.

An additional note of clarification about interest rates is in order. Although we frequently use the expression "the interest rate," in reality no singular interest rate exists. Instead, there are many different markets, each with its own interest rate, in which money is borrowed and lent: markets for home mortgages, secured corporate loans, student loans, and personal auto loans, for example. The interest rates in these markets

FIGURE 8.2   *Effect of Changes in Excess Reserves on the Interest Rate and the Quantity of Loans*

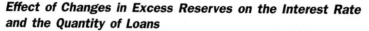

a. Decrease in Excess Reserves

Interest Rate

(Graph: Interest Rate (0–18%) vs. Millions of Dollars of Loans (0–70). Curves labeled D, S2, S1. Dashed lines at 14 and 10, with upward arrow. S2 and S1 labeled at bottom with leftward arrow near 30–40.)

b. Increase in Excess Reserves

Interest Rate

(Graph: Interest Rate (0–18%) vs. Millions of Dollars of Loans (0–70). Curves labeled D, S1, S2. Dashed lines at 10 and 6, with downward arrow. S1 and S2 labeled at bottom with rightward arrow near 40–50.)

Millions of Dollars of Loans

A decrease in excess reserves in the system will cause interest rates to rise and the amount of loans made to fall. An increase in excess reserves will cause interest rates to fall and the amount of loans made to rise.

FIGURE 8.3   *Relationship among Excess Reserves, the Interest Rate, Loan Making, and the Level of Economic Activity*

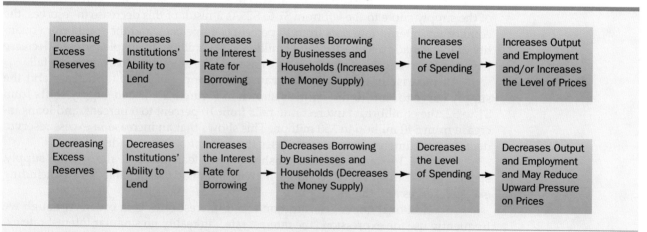

| Increasing Excess Reserves | → | Increases Institutions' Ability to Lend | → | Decreases the Interest Rate for Borrowing | → | Increases Borrowing by Businesses and Households (Increases the Money Supply) | → | Increases the Level of Spending | → | Increases Output and Employment and/or Increases the Level of Prices |

| Decreasing Excess Reserves | → | Decreases Institutions' Ability to Lend | → | Increases the Interest Rate for Borrowing | → | Decreases Borrowing by Businesses and Households (Decreases the Money Supply) | → | Decreases the Level of Spending | → | Decreases Output and Employment and May Reduce Upward Pressure on Prices |

Changes in the level of excess reserves in the system influence institutions' lending abilities, interest rates, the money supply, total spending, and the economy's levels of output, employment, and/or prices.

APPLICATION 8.2

AN INTEREST RATE PRIMER

In the first six months of 2009, the U.S. government auctioned Treasury bonds and notes 33 times to borrow money. The highest interest rate to be paid was 4.25 percent for a 29-year, 11-month bond and a 30-year bond. By the end of 2009 the government was expected to be over $10 trillion in debt to its lenders. In the spring of 2009, a young couple with a household income of $80,000 signed a $175,000, 30-year mortgage to buy their first house. The interest rate on the mortgage was 6 percent. And there was the college student who in the spring got his credit card bill, where he was charged 20 percent interest on the $850 balance he had owed for a few months.

Why is the most deeply in-debt organization in the United States (and perhaps the world) paying the lowest rate on its loans, the couple that borrowed more than they make in two years paying the second lowest rate, and the student who "borrowed" just $850 on his credit card paying far and away the highest rate? There are several reasons, some more obvious than others.

Perhaps the most fundamental explanation for these varying rates is the risk of nonpayment by the borrower; that is, the likelihood that the lender won't get some or all of its money back either because the borrower can't afford to pay or never intended to pay. This is of little concern when lending money to the U.S. government, which is generally recognized as the safest borrower. The feds have an impeccable payback record, and if all else fails, the government can simply borrow more to pay off its debts. In fact, the feds have been considered so safe that people were loaning money to the government at about a 0 percent interest rate in late 2008 and early 2009, when some financial institutions were failing and people acted to ensure that their money was safe.

Lending to homebuyers is riskier than lending to the government, but it is not an excessive risk. Certainly something like the loss of a job or an unexpected medical issue could mean an inability to make mortgage payments, but there are alternatives like refinancing. In the worst case, the lender would end up owning the house. This could turn out well if property values went up between the time the mortgage was signed and the time the house was handed over.

Then there is the student who is paying a high interest rate to borrow just $850 on a credit card—higher than is paid to borrow billions by the U.S. government or tens of thousands by the homeowners. But here the risk is fairly great for the lender. What if the student bought a backpack, some clothes, a DVD, pizza, or other consumables? Would it be possible for the credit card company to locate the student and get back its $850 or the goods that the student bought? Not only is there the risk of not paying back the loan, but here there is no collateral, or something that the lender can get in return for the loan. Collateral is another factor in determining interest rates.

Another consideration—one not often apparent to people who typically don't lend money—is the taxes due on the interest rate received by the lender. If you buy a Treasury security, you will pay tax on your interest income to the federal government, but you may avoid a state tax payment. Because of this, people are sometimes willing to loan money to the U.S. government at a lower rate.

Sources: *Economic Report of the President* (Washington, DC: U. S. Government Printing Office, 2008), p. 319; Treasury Direct, "Recent Note, Bond, and TIPs Auction Results," http://www.treasurydirect.gov/RI/OFNtebnd, July 6, 2009; Federal Reserve Board, "Choosing a Credit Card," http://www.federalreserve.gov/Pubs/shop/.

differ because of differences in risk, loan size, length of repayment, and other factors. Therefore, when we refer to a rise in the interest rate because of declining excess reserves, we mean that interest rates *in general* are rising. Likewise, a fall in the interest rate due to increasing excess reserves in the system means that interest rates *in general* are falling. Application 8.2, "An Interest Rate Primer," provides additional information about how and why interest rates vary in different loan markets. Can you explain, after reading this application, why a medical student taking out a bank loan for 10 years might pay a higher interest rate than a local government taking out a three-year loan to buy an ambulance?

THE FEDERAL RESERVE AND MONETARY POLICY

Several of the relationships we have covered are so important that we will repeat them one more time. The money supply is changed through loan making, and loan making depends on available excess reserves. As a result, control over the money

Monetary Policy

Changing the money supply
to influence the levels of
output, employment, and/or
prices in the economy.

Easy Money Policy

Policy by the Federal
Reserve to increase excess
reserves and decrease
interest rates to increase
spending.

Tight Money Policy

Policy by the Federal Reserve
to reduce excess reserves
and raise interest rates to
reduce spending.

supply comes from control over excess reserves. It is the Federal Reserve in its responsibility to oversee the money supply that influences the level of excess reserves in the economy. When the Fed acts to deliberately change excess reserves and interest rates (and, thus, the money supply) to influence the levels of output, employment, and/or prices in the economy, it is engaging in **monetary policy.**

If the economy has unacceptable rates of unemployment, total spending needs to be stimulated. To do so, the Federal Reserve would act to increase excess reserves in the system, decrease interest rates, and encourage borrowing. When the Fed takes steps to expand the money supply, it is said to be pursuing an **easy money policy.**

If the economy has demand-pull inflation, the appropriate policy prescription is to reduce spending. In this case, the Fed would act to decrease the level of excess reserves in the system, raise interest rates, and dampen borrowing. When the money supply is deliberately reduced, the Fed is said to be pursuing a **tight money policy.**

Monetary Policy Tools

The Federal Reserve has three major tools to change excess reserves in the financial depository institutions system and influence interest rates:

♦   the reserve requirement,
♦   the discount rate, and
♦   open market operations.

The Reserve Requirement   The Federal Reserve could reduce excess reserves and discourage borrowing by increasing the reserve requirement. Suppose that Hometown Bank has $50 million in demand deposits with a 10 percent reserve requirement: Hometown must keep $5 million on reserve. If the reserve requirement were raised to 11 percent, Hometown would need to keep $5.5 million on reserve to back the $50 million in demand deposits. The bank would have $500,000 less in excess reserves and less loan-making ability. On the other hand, a decrease in the reserve requirement would increase excess reserves, giving Hometown the ability to make new loans.

A decrease in the reserve requirement would give institutions in the system more excess reserves and would be appropriate to stimulate the economy. An increase in the reserve requirement would give institutions in the system fewer excess reserves and would be appropriate to fight demand-pull inflation.

Table 8.4 shows the reserve requirements in effect on January 1, 2009. Notice in this table that the only requirement is on transactions, or checkable accounts, and that this requirement is three-tiered, ranging from nothing to 10 percent. The level at which each tier requirement takes effect is adjusted periodically. Notice also that there are no reserve requirements on time deposits. All depository institutions must meet the same reserve requirements.

The Federal Reserve usually does not radically change reserve requirements in carrying out monetary policy. Either an influx or a removal of an extremely large volume of excess reserves could be a shock to the depository institutions system. An increase of 1 or 2 percent in a reserve requirement on checkable accounts could cause banks and other institutions to have to "find" millions of dollars of reserves to meet that requirement.

The Discount Rate   All financial depository institutions may, under certain circumstances, borrow reserves from a Federal Reserve Bank. Typically, when an institution borrows, its reserve account is increased; and when the institution repays the Fed, its

TABLE 8.4   *Reserve Requirements*[a]

All depository institutions are subject to the same reserve requirements.

Type of Account	Reserve Requirement
Transaction or checkable accounts, including demand deposits and other accounts	
Balances up to $10.3 million	0%
Balances between $10.3 million and $44.4 million	3%
Balances over $44.4 million	10%
Time deposits and Eurocurrency liabilities	No reserve requirement

[a]In effect on January 1, 2009.

Source: Federal Reserve Board, "Reserve Requirements," http://www.federalreserve.gov/monetarypolicy/reservereq. htm, February 25, 2009.

Discount Rate
Interest rate that a Federal Reserve bank charges a financial depository institution for borrowing reserves.

reserves are decreased. The interest rate that the Fed charges a depository institution for borrowing reserves is called the **discount rate**.[7] An increase in the discount rate, because it increases the price institutions must pay for reserves, is an attempt by the Federal Reserve to discourage reserve borrowing. A decrease in the discount rate is an attempt to encourage reserve borrowing.

Discount rate changes are always announced publicly and serve as an indicator of the intentions of the Fed. For example, an increase in the discount rate signals an attempt to tighten the money supply, which will probably lead to an increase in the interest rates that depository institutions charge their loan customers. This announcement would indicate that the Fed is pursuing a tight money policy to deal with demand-pull inflationary pressure. A decrease in the discount rate signals an attempt to loosen the money supply and will probably lead to a decrease in interest rates. This measure indicates that the Fed is concerned with a slowing economy and unemployment. Table 8.5 lists the various discount rates charged from mid-2003 through early 2009.

Observe the rise from a discount rate of 2 percent in mid-2003 to a high of 6.25 percent in mid-2006. Then notice that the rate falls with especially low rates in late-2008, when the discount rate fell below 1 percent. These rates reflect a money tightening as the economy grew and there were fears of inflation, followed by an easy money policy to deal with a slowing economy.

The Federal Reserve does not provide a limitless supply of borrowed reserves for depository institutions. It requires the borrowing institution to present a good reason for its loan request, such as an emergency or seasonal problem.

Federal Funds Market
Market in which banks borrow reserves from other banks.

As noted in Application 8.1, banks can also borrow reserves from other banks in the **Federal Funds market.** However, the effect on the system is different when banks borrow reserves from one another rather than from the Fed. When banks borrow from other banks in the Federal Funds market, they are exchanging reserves that are already in the system. Thus, there is no potential for multiplying the money supply. When banks borrow from the Fed, new reserves are created in the system and the money multiplier can take effect.

[7]Be careful to distinguish between the discount rate, which is the interest rate paid by banks to the Fed for borrowing reserves, and the prime rate, which is the benchmark interest rate banks use in setting interest rates on various types of loans.

TABLE 8.5   *Federal Reserve Discount Rates*[a]

Changes in the discount rate influence the borrowing of reserves by financial depository institutions from the Federal Reserve and serve as an indicator of the money supply intentions of the Fed.

Effective Date		Discount Rate[b]	Effective Date		Discount Rate
2003	June 25	2.00%		May 10	6.00
2004	June 30	2.25		June 29	6.25
	Aug. 10	2.50	2007	Aug. 17	5.75
	Sept. 21	2.75		Sept. 18	5.25
	Nov. 10	3.00		Oct. 31	5.00
	Dec. 14	3.25		Dec. 11	4.75
2005	Feb. 2	3.50	2008	Jan. 22	4.00
	Mar. 22	3.75		Jan. 30	3.50
	May 3	4.00		Mar. 17	3.25
	June 30	4.25		Mar. 18	2.50
	Aug. 9	4.50		Apr. 30	2.25
	Sept. 20	4.75		Oct. 8	1.75
	Nov. 1	5.00		Oct. 29	1.25
	Dec. 13	5.25		Dec. 16	0.50
2006	Jan. 31	5.50			
	Mar. 28	5.75			

[a]Each Federal Reserve bank determines the interest rate it will charge. Generally, the rates charged by all 12 banks are the same. However, there may be a lag of a few days when a rate adjustment is made. This table shows the rate charged by the Federal Reserve Bank of New York.

[b]Beginning in January 2003, the Federal Reserve made a distinction between depository institutions eligible for "primary credit" and less financially sound depository institutions eligible for "secondary credit." Higher rates are typically charged on secondary credit loans, and institutions receiving these loans cannot use them to expand their operations. The rates reported here are for primary credit institutions.

Sources: "Historical Discount Rates," The Federal Reserve Bank Discount Window & Payments System Risk Web site, http://www.frbdiscountwindow.org/historicalrates.cfm?hdrID=20&dtID=52, February 25, 2009.

Open Market Operations   Of the three monetary policy tools, open market operations is the one used most often for changing excess reserves in the financial depository institutions system. It is, however, one of the more difficult processes to understand because of the details involved in using this tool. Very simply, **open market operations** is the buying and selling of securities, primarily U.S. government securities, on the open market by the Federal Reserve.[8] The actual physical operation is housed in the Federal Reserve Bank of New York, and buying and selling is carried on each business day. This means that adjustments in reserves can be made quickly. The **Open Market Committee,** consisting of the Board of Governors and five Federal Reserve bank presidents, determines the general direction of open market policy.

When the Fed buys securities on the open market, it can do so from banks or from dealers.[9] If a security is purchased by the Federal Reserve from a bank, the Fed takes the

Open Market Operations
The buying and selling of securities, primarily U.S. government securities, on the open market by the Federal Reserve.

Open Market Committee
Committee that determines the general policy on Federal Reserve open market operations.

[8]Recall that U.S. Treasury securities result from federal government borrowing to finance deficit spending.

[9]The Federal Reserve cannot demand that a bank or dealer sell its securities to, or buy them from, the Fed. Rather, if the Fed intends to buy, it must offer a price high enough to induce a bank or dealer to sell. The reverse holds true if the Fed intends to sell. Most of the buying and selling by the Fed is done through dealers. In fact, many banks work through a dealer rather than directly with the Fed.

security for its own and credits the amount of the security to the selling bank's reserve account. For example, if the Fed wanted to buy government securities and if Hometown Bank were holding $1 million in Treasury notes in its portfolio that it wanted to sell, Hometown could exchange the securities for a $1 million increase in its reserve account.

When the Fed buys securities from a dealer, it pays the dealer. The dealer's proceeds are deposited in a financial institution, where, when they are cleared, the reserve account of the institution is increased by that amount. A $1 million purchase of securities by the Fed from a dealer will increase reserves in the dealer's depository institution by $1 million. Thus, whether the Fed buys securities from a bank or from a dealer, the effect of its buying is an increase in reserves in the system.

When the Fed sells securities, it again trades with banks or dealers. If it sells to a bank, the bank exchanges its reserves for the securities, thus decreasing reserves. For example, if the Fed wants to sell Treasury notes and Hometown Bank wants to buy $2 million worth, Hometown could trade $2 million in its reserve account for these securities.

If the Fed sells to a dealer, the dealer pays for the securities. When the dealer's payment clears, the dealer's depository institution loses reserves. A $2 million sale to a dealer will decrease the reserve account of the dealer's depository institution by $2 million. Thus, when the Fed sells securities, reserves are removed from the system.[10]

It is important to understand that when reserves are increased or decreased because the Fed is buying securities from, or selling them to, banks and dealers on the open market, the Fed is not transferring reserves from one account to another. Rather, the Federal Reserve either creates new reserves for the system or destroys those that already exist.

Open market operations provide a powerful tool for enacting monetary policy for two reasons. First, changes in reserves can be achieved quickly because operations are carried on every business day. Second, the quantity of reserves can be altered slightly or greatly depending on whether government securities are bought or sold in small or large quantities.

Open Market Operations and the Federal Funds Rate   Earlier we mentioned the Federal Funds market, which is the market in which banks lend to one another for a short period of time, usually overnight. This market allows banks that are short on meeting their reserve requirements to borrow from banks that have excess reserves. The interest rate charged in this market is called the **federal funds rate**.

The federal funds rate has become a significant rate to observe because it is a signal of the direction of Federal Reserve policy to change interest rates and the money supply. At each meeting of the Federal Open Market Committee, there is a decision to target the federal funds rate; it could be targeted to increase, decrease, or stay the same. Once this direction is set, open market operations are used to move toward the target federal funds rate. Because interest rates tend to move in the same direction, the federal funds rate changes lead the way in other interest rate changes.

Tools and Policy Objectives   We have just learned how the Federal Reserve can use its major tools to change excess reserves (and the supply of money). If the Fed decided

Federal Funds Rate
The interest rate banks charge to lend reserves to other banks for a short period of time, usually overnight.

---

[10]Securities dealers' banks serve as "pass-throughs" for changes in excess reserves since dealers are buying and selling for clients throughout the country. For example, when a dealer in New York sells a security for a client who banks in Texas, ultimately the proceeds from the security sale pass through the dealer's bank to the client's bank in Texas. Thus, the impact of open market operations is felt throughout the banking system, not just at dealers' depository institutions.

TEST YOUR UNDERSTANDING

FINANCIAL DEPOSITORY INSTITUTION CALCULATIONS[a]

1. Pima Community Bank, which has a reserve requirement of 10 percent on its deposits, has calculated the following numbers as of the end of business today: total deposits = $13,500,000; reserve account = $3,750,000; and vault cash = $2,250,000. Based on this information, determine the following for this bank.
    Required reserves = _____
    Actual reserves = _____
    Excess reserves = _____

2. How much in new loans can ABA National Bank make if its deposits are $45,000,000, vault cash is $5,550,000, and reserve account balance is $7,750,000? ABA's reserve requirement is 8 percent.
    New loans = _____

3. What is the amount that must be borrowed by Fresno Bank to cover its anticipated reserve shortfall if it has a reserve requirement of 12 percent, deposits of $27,500,000, vault cash of $2,500,000, a reserve account of $3,250,000, and it has just made a new loan of $2,500,000 that has not yet cleared?
    New borrowing = _____

4. The Federal Reserve puts $50,000,000 in new excess reserves into the system when the reserve requirement is 8 percent. What is the money multiplier and the maximum amount by which the money supply can increase because of these new reserves?
    Money multiplier = _____
    Money supply increase = _____

5. The Fed decides to raise the reserve requirement from 10 percent to 11 percent. By how much will excess reserves decrease at Nashville Bank if Nashville has $33,500,000 in deposits and $5,750,000 in actual reserves?
    Decrease in excess reserves = _____

6. Lock Haven Bank has a reserve requirement of 6 percent, deposits of $8,500,000, vault cash of $1,255,000, a reserve account of $2,500,000, and $3,000,000 in government securities. How much in new excess reserves will be created at Lock Haven if it sells $2,000,000 of its government securities to the Fed?
    New excess reserves = _____

7. Carolina Coast Bank borrows $3,000,000 from California Coast Bank in the Federal Funds market. Inland Bank borrows $4,000,000 from its Federal Reserve bank. How much in new excess reserves has been put into the system by each transaction?
    New excess reserves by Carolina Coast = _____
    New excess reserves by Inland Bank = _____

8. The Federal Reserve buys $14,000,000 in securities in the open market at a time when the reserve requirement is 5 percent. What is the money supply increase that can result from this purchase?
    Money supply increase = _____

[a]All depository institutions in this exercise are hypothetical and the figures are artificially low to ease calculations.

Answers can be found at the back of the book.

---

that the economy needed to expand, it would pursue lowering interest rates and use its tools to increase reserves in the system by

♦   buying securities from banks and dealers on the open market, and/or
♦   lowering the reserve requirement, and/or
♦   lowering the discount rate.

If the Fed decided to fight demand-pull inflation, it would pursue raising interest rates and use its tools to remove excess reserves from the system and shrink the money supply by

♦   selling securities to banks and dealers on the open market, and/or
♦   increasing the reserve requirement, and/or
♦   increasing the discount rate.

Test Your Understanding, "Financial Depository Institution Calculations," provides an opportunity to practice some computations introduced in this chapter that relate to depository institution reserves and lending, and monetary policy tools.

APPLICATION 8.3

WHO IS THE MOST POWERFUL PERSON IN THE UNITED STATES?

It's a fairly safe guess that if people were asked "Who is the most powerful person in the United States," the largest number of votes would be for the president. But some people would argue that there is someone even more powerful than the president: the chair of the Federal Reserve Board of Governors.

Just examine the records during the tenure of Alan Greenspan, chairman of the Board of Governors from 1987 to 2006, and his successor Ben Bernanke. Greenspan is likely to be remembered for the impact of his every comment, position, and prediction: People around the world paid very close attention to him. For example, in a dinner speech in 1996, Greenspan briefly expressed concern about stock prices being driven up by people's "irrational exuberance" over the state of the stock market. When the New York Stock Exchange opened the next morning, the Dow Jones industrial average dropped by more than 140 points. And Greenspan's comments didn't just affect trading on the New York exchange. Stock prices fell in Australia, Japan, and Europe.

Then there was the dinner speech given by Ben Bernanke on a Monday evening in June 2008, where he raised the issue of high levels of inflation and the Fed's resistance to it. What was the consequence of his comments? Reaction was seen the following morning in financial markets. Perhaps billions of dollars changed hands, stocks were down, and the dollar gained against the euro.

Such an impact also occurs when the chair of the Fed gives the twice-a-year mandatory testimony before Congress. A day or so before the testimony, stock and bond prices around the world may fluctuate widely as people try to anticipate and adjust for what they think will be said at the hearings. Attention is drawn to these public comments because people think they are a signal for policies to come.

Think about this power. Would securities markets around the world have reacted as dramatically if President Bill Clinton or President George W. Bush had commented about irrational exuberance or high levels of inflation? And there was the time that both congressional liberals and conservatives openly voiced their anger at the Open Market Committee for raising some interest rates. Even as angry as they were, the Fed would not reverse its course. Also, when a leading banking magazine wrote about the 10 surprises for 2005, number one on the list was what Greenspan might do to short-term rates.

A well-known relic from President Clinton's first run for the presidency is a sign in a campaign office that said, "It's the Economy, Stupid." The sign was intended to remind campaign workers about what is most important to voters. The hard truth is that people will likely vote for the candidate they think will best strengthen their own economic well-being. But who has the more immediate impact on economic well-being—the chair of the Fed, who can act quickly to change economic conditions and is independent of government control, or a president with an economic agenda that has to be approved through a legislative process that can be slow because of its layers of approval?

Sources: Randall W. Forsyth, "Current Yield: Greenspan's Testimony Has an Ever-More Powerful Effect on the Bond Market; What Can He Possibly Say on Tuesday?", *Barron's*, July 21, 1997, p. MW8; J. W. McLean, "Volatile Rate Spreads Could Put Fed on Hot Seat, "*Journal Record*, Oklahoma City, April 23, 1991, p. NOPGCIT; Howard Schneider, "Ten Surprises for 2005?", *Mortgage Banking*, October 2004, p. 174; Sarah Shemkus, "When Federal Reserve Chairman Ben Bernanke speaks, the markets move," *McClatchy-Tribune Business News*, June 15, 2008, wire feed; Richard W. Stevenson, "A Buried Message Loudly Heard," *The New York Times*, December 7, 1996, pp. 19, 21.

The actions of the Federal Reserve are closely watched because of the impact of policy decisions on interest rates and on economic activity. The public in general has become more aware of monetary terms, such as M1 and M2, and of actions, such as changes in the discount rate, because of the way such matters affect jobs, mortgage rates, automobile loans, and other facets of everyday life. This raised awareness was quite evident in late 2008 and 2009 as the United States struggled with serious economic problems, many of which were related to financial institutions and loan making. Businesses, particularly those in financial areas, hire experts to anticipate Federal Reserve moves because changes in the interest rate by even a small percentage can cost them millions of dollars. The impact—and importance—of Federal Reserve policy can be seen in Application 8.3, "Who Is the Most Powerful Person in the United States?". This application concerns remarks by Alan Greenspan, chairperson of the Board of Governors from 1987 to 2006, and Ben Bernanke, his successor. Among these remarks are several made at dinner meetings that caused shock waves in securities markets around the world.

Government Deficits and Monetary Policy

When the federal government borrows to finance its deficit budgets, it impacts interest rates and the amount that households and businesses borrow. When the federal government enters the market for available loan monies, it puts upward pressure on interest rates and, when they rise, causes households and businesses to borrow less. The consequences of this federal action make it important to understand the relationship between government borrowing and monetary policy.

The downward-sloping demand curve for loans that was illustrated in Figures 8.1 and 8.2 came from the demand for loans by households and businesses, which are sensitive to interest rates. When the government, which is not sensitive to interest rates, plans to borrow to finance its deficit spending, its demand for borrowing is added to that of households and businesses. So, government borrowing shifts the demand curve for loanable funds to the right.

We can see the effect of government borrowing in Figure 8.4a. D1, which represents the demand for loanable funds by households and businesses, shifts to D2 when government borrowing is added to that of households and businesses. As a result of government borrowing, the interest rate rises from 10 percent to 16 percent and the quantity of loans made rises from $250 million to $300 million. The increase in the interest rate that results from government borrowing discourages business and household borrowing, so that the growth in government borrowing is accompanied by a decrease in private borrowing. This is the **crowding out** problem that was introduced in Chapter 6.[11]

Crowding Out

Occurs when borrowing by the federal government increases the interest rate and reduces borrowing by households and businesses.

The rise in the interest rate from government borrowing could be prevented if the Federal Reserve would increase excess reserves in the system by an amount equal to the increase in the demand for funds by the government. Figure 8.4b illustrates a shift in the supply curve for loanable funds to the right, from S1 to S2, which is the amount necessary to compensate for the increase in demand. Notice that the increase in supply to S2 keeps the interest rate at the original level of 10 percent. This increase in excess reserves by the Federal Reserve to accommodate federal government borrowing plans and reduce upward pressure on the interest rate is referred to as **monetizing the debt.** By monetizing the debt, the Fed could hold the interest rate at its pregovernment borrowing level and offset the crowding out effect.

Monetizing the Debt

Increasing the money supply by the Federal Reserve to accommodate federal government borrowing and reduce upward pressure on the interest rate.

Why doesn't the Federal Reserve simply create enough reserves on a regular basis to cover the federal government's demand for funds, thereby eliminating the upward pressure that government borrowing puts on interest rates? The Federal Reserve has generally adhered to a philosophy of controlling the money supply for the benefit of the macroeconomy, rather than accommodating government deficit spending. If it always increased reserves to meet government needs, the money supply could increase by an amount large enough to cause inflation and weaken the value of the dollar. Notice in Figure 8.4b that when the Fed increases excess reserves to meet increased government demand for borrowing, a $150 million increase in loans results. When demand and supply were at D1 and S1, $250 million was loaned, and when demand and supply increased to D2 and S2, $400 million was loaned. As illustrated in Figure 8.4a, were the Fed not to increase excess reserves to accommodate government borrowing, the quantity of loans would increase by only $50 million.

---

[11]The crowding out problem can also be seen in greater detail in Figure 8.4a. Demand curve D1, which represents planned borrowing by households and businesses, indicates that at an interest rate of 10 percent, households and businesses want to borrow $250 million, and at an interest rate of 16 percent, they want to borrow $150 million. Thus, when government borrowing forces the interest rate up from 10 percent to 16 percent, households and businesses borrow $100 million less than they otherwise would borrow.

| FIGURE 8.4 | *Effect of Government Borrowing and Monetizing the Debt on the Interest Rate and Loan Making* |

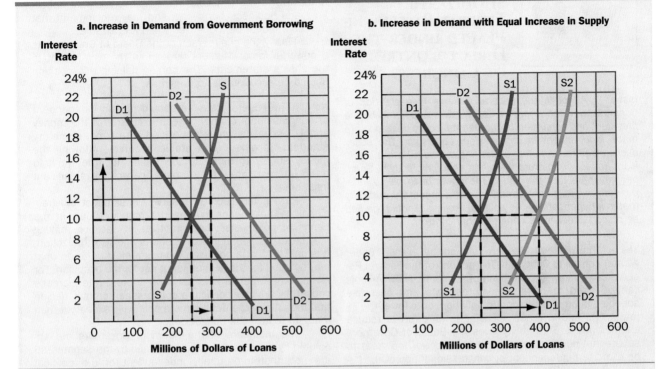

Government borrowing increases the demand for loans and the interest rate. When excess reserves are increased to meet this demand, a larger quantity of loans is made than would otherwise occur.

Advantages and Disadvantages of Monetary Policy

Is monetary policy an effective tool for tackling inflation and unemployment? What are the advantages and disadvantages of using monetary policy? One of the major benefits of monetary policy is the speed with which it can be implemented. Unlike fiscal policy, which could take months to implement, the first steps toward changing the money supply can be taken the day the decision to do so is made. Another major benefit is its size flexibility: Reserves can be increased or decreased in small or large increments.

Monetary policy is also largely removed from politics. The members of the Board of Governors, although appointed by a president, are not as subject to political pressure as are the members of Congress. This may be partially due to the fact that Board members are appointed for lengthy (14-year) terms and are not campaigning for re-election. The Board of Governors' motives in expanding and contracting the money supply are usually economic.

One of the major disadvantages of monetary policy is the loan-making link through which it is carried out. That is, the Fed can increase reserves to stimulate economic activity as much as it wants, but the reserves themselves do not alter the money supply. For the money supply (and spending) to increase, someone must be willing to borrow and a bank must be willing to lend. Because the Fed cannot force the loan-making process, it has only indirect control over increasing the money supply. This

SHOULD THE FEDERAL RESERVE BE PLACED UNDER THE DIRECT CONTROL OF CONGRESS?

Issue   Although the Federal Reserve is a creation of Congress, and the Board of Governors is appointed by the president and confirmed by the Senate, policy decisions are made independent of congressional oversight. The policy decisions pursued by the Board of Governors have a significant impact on interest rates and economic activity. Some people argue that the Fed is too powerful to be so independent, while others strongly favor a monetary authority that is independent of the political process. Should the Fed be placed under more congressional control?

Yes   The Federal Reserve should be placed under greater control of Congress. The actions of the Federal Reserve can change the direction of economic activity: Tools can be used to raise the interest rate and decrease spending in an effort to control inflation, or to lower the interest rate and increase spending in an effort to reduce unemployment. This ability gives the Board of Governors substantial power over the economy—power too great to be exercised independent of congressional approval.

Because Congress is part of the political process, members of Congress may be more responsive to the wishes of the electorate. Congress may prevent interest rates from rising to levels that negatively impact household and business borrowing, and may recommend that the federal debt be monetized when it is sizable.

Finally, the chairperson of the Board of Governors is a powerful force: Markets throughout the world react to the chair's statements. The person holding this position should be accountable to Congress.

No   The Federal Reserve should remain independent of congressional control. Effective control of the money supply, especially when it is based on a paper monetary standard, is a key to a stable economy. Allowing the money supply to increase too rapidly in order to hold down interest rates, for example, can cause significant inflation.

Putting the Federal Reserve under direct congressional control means putting the money supply in the hands of politicians whose motives in decision making may be to support partisan agendas and gain reelection. It is unlikely that a politician will risk reelection to do what may be good for the economy, but not for the politician. For example, in order to hold down an interest rate increase caused by a budget deficit, a congressperson may decide that monetizing the debt is more politically expedient than trying to reduce the budget deficit.

The members of the Board of Governors are appointed by the president and confirmed by the Senate and are not, therefore, totally independent of the political process. The current arrangement provides some limited oversight but permits the Board to put the macroeconomy, not reelection, first in its decision making.

loan-making link may reduce the effectiveness of monetary policy in fighting unemployment during a deep and serious recession. If economic conditions are severe, no expansion of reserves and lowering of the interest rate may be enough to induce borrowers to take out loans.

Another problem with monetary policy occurs during inflation. As the Federal Reserve tightens the money supply and forces the interest rate higher, it raises the price for borrowed money. Businesses that borrow at this high rate may in turn raise prices on their products to compensate. Thus, fighting inflation with monetary policy could worsen it.

Finally, there are those who feel that having the Federal Reserve and monetary policy removed from the political process is a disadvantage. Over the years there have been several proposals to place the Federal Reserve under more congressional control. Proponents of this action do not favor the independence of the Fed and presume that with control it would be more sensitive to public reaction in its policy making. Up for Debate, "Should the Federal Reserve Be Placed under the Direct Control of Congress?", provides arguments on each side of this issue. What is your position on this question?

A Note   Before concluding this chapter, two further considerations merit mention. First, it is possible for unemployment and inflation to occur simultaneously, and when this happens, there is no clearly appropriate monetary policy to follow. In late 1990, for example, this was the policy dilemma faced by the Federal Reserve when the economy was experiencing inflationary pressure while slipping into a recession. In 2008, as gasoline prices rose to extremely high levels and the economy was softening, the fear of simultaneous problems rose again.

Second, there is an economic philosophy called monetarism, and those who adhere to it are termed monetarists. Generally, monetarists believe that controlling the money supply is the main vehicle for controlling economic activity. Some monetarists favor increasing and decreasing the money supply to control unemployment and inflation, while others favor a constant annual increase in the money supply to promote stable growth and prices. Monetarism is discussed in Chapter 9.

Summary

1. Since there is an important relationship between an economy's supply of money and its levels of output, employment, and prices, altering the money supply can help to reach the major macroeconomic goals.

2. The equation of exchange shows how money affects the level of economic activity. It illustrates that, operating through aggregate spending, changes in the supply of money lead to changes in output, employment, and/or prices. Generally, if the economy is at less than full employment, increases in the money supply expand output and employment. If the economy is at or near full employment, increases in the money supply cause increases in prices. A decrease in the money supply decreases output and employment and may dampen upward pressure on prices.

3. Changes in the money supply occur through lending by financial depository institutions: Money is created when loans are made and destroyed when they are repaid. Lending is not accomplished by transferring funds from one account to another. Loans represent newly created money.

4. A financial depository institution can make a loan if it has excess reserves, which is the difference between the institution's actual reserves and its required reserves. Required reserves, which is the amount of reserves that the institution must hold to back its deposits, is found by multiplying the institution's deposits by the reserve requirement. If new loan making exceeds the institution's excess reserves, actual reserves can drop below required reserves.

5. An initial increase or decrease in excess reserves in the depository institutions system will cause total lending and the money supply to change by a larger, or a multiple, amount. The money multiplier itself is the reciprocal of the reserve requirement, and the maximum change in the money supply is equal to the money multiplier times the initial change in excess reserves.

6. Having excess reserves available in financial depository institutions does not ensure that loans will be made by households and businesses. The stimulus for businesses and households to borrow when increased spending is desired, or to reduce borrowing when spending is excessive, is the interest rate,

which is a cost of borrowing money. As the interest rate increases, the amount of borrowing by businesses and households and the amount of total spending based on borrowing decreases. When the interest rate is lowered, the reverse holds true.

7. The rate of interest on loans made by financial depository institutions is determined by the demand for loans and by the supply of available loanable funds, which is based on excess reserves. Increasing excess reserves increases the supply of available loanable funds, lowers the interest rate, and raises the amount of loans made. Decreasing excess reserves increases the interest rate and reduces the amount of loans made.

8. Adjusting the money supply to accomplish macroeconomic goals is a major responsibility of the Federal Reserve. The Fed uses three tools to change excess reserves in the system and influence interest rates: the reserve requirement, the discount rate, and open market operations.

9. Monetary policy to lower interest rates and stimulate spending calls for lowering the reserve requirement, and/or reducing the discount rate, and/or Federal Reserve purchases of securities on the open market. Monetary policy to raise interest rates and dampen spending calls for raising the reserve requirement, and/or raising the discount rate, and/or Federal Reserve sales of securities on the open market. Of the three policy tools, open market operations is the most important and the most frequently used.

10. The Federal Reserve could keep the interest rate stable in the face of government borrowing to finance deficit spending by increasing excess reserves to accommodate the government's demand for funds. However, such actions on a persistent basis, called monetizing the debt, could weaken the value of the dollar.

11. The use of monetary policy to correct unemployment or demand-pull inflation has the advantage of flexibility in timing and size. It has the disadvantages, however, of possible ineffectiveness in a severe recession and of the potential to make inflation worse in a tight money situation. Having the Federal Reserve removed from politics is viewed by some as an advantage and by others as a disadvantage.

Key Terms and Concepts

Equation of exchange

Actual reserves

Reserve requirement

Required reserves

Excess reserves

Creation and destruction of money

Multiplier effect (money)

Money multiplier

Interest rate

Monetary policy

Easy money policy

Tight money policy

Discount rate   Federal funds rate

Federal Funds market   Crowding out

Open market operations   Monetizing the debt

Open Market Committee

Review Questions

1. Assuming that the supply of money in the economy is $3.2 trillion and velocity is 5, answer questions a through d.
   a. What is the dollar value of output produced in the economy?
   b. What would happen to the dollar value of output and the real value of output if $50 billion were added to the money supply when the economy was at full employment?
   c. What would happen to prices and to the level of output produced in the economy if the Fed reduced the supply of money to dampen inflationary pressure when the economy was at full employment?
   d. What would happen to the dollar value of output if people spent money faster (velocity increased) following a reduction in the money supply by the Fed?

2. Assume that Hometown Bank has $30,000,000 in demand deposits, a 15 percent reserve requirement, and $5,200,000 in actual reserves. Based on these figures, what are Hometown Bank's required and excess reserves, and how much in new loans could it make?

3. What is the money multiplier, and how is it related to the reserve requirement? If the Federal Reserve increases excess reserves in the system by $180 million with a reserve requirement of 12 percent, what is the maximum amount by which the money supply can increase as a result of the increased excess reserves?

4. Assume that the reserve requirement is 12.5 percent and that $500,000 is added to Hometown Bank's excess reserves as a result of a change in Federal Reserve policy.
   a. How much in new loans can Hometown Bank make as a result of this increase in excess reserves?
   b. If the entire amount of Hometown Bank's new loans is spent and the funds are deposited in Bank B, by how much can Bank B increase its loan making?
   c. What is the maximum amount by which loan making can be increased in the financial depository institutions system as a result of the increase in Hometown Bank's excess reserves?
   d. What is the maximum amount in new loans that could be made in the financial depository institutions system following the initial increase in Hometown Bank's excess reserves if the reserve requirement were 20 percent?

5. Suppose the Federal Reserve is concerned about demand-pull inflationary pressure that is building in the economy.
   a. What would be the appropriate change in excess reserves to counteract this problem?

b. What would be the appropriate change in the reserve requirement, the discount rate, and open market operations to bring about this change in excess reserves?

6. Use the accompanying supply and demand graphs to explain how each of the following affects the supply of and/or demand for loans, the interest rate, and the actual amount of loans made.
   a. The Federal Reserve sells securities on the open market.
   b. The U.S. government borrows to finance its deficit and the Fed does not monetize the debt.
   c. The U.S. government borrows to finance its deficit and the Fed monetizes the debt.
   d. The Federal Reserve lowers the discount rate.
   e. Private investment spending decreases because of fears of a recession.

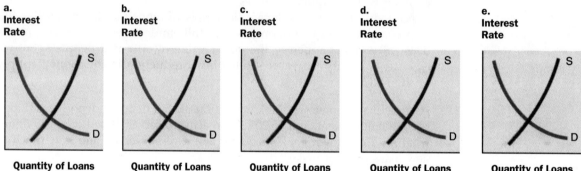

7. What would be the effect of each of the following on Uptown Bank's excess reserves and loan-making ability if the bank had $600 million in deposits, a 5 percent reserve requirement, and actual reserves of $40 million?
   a. The Federal Reserve sells $5 million in government securities to Uptown Bank.
   b. The reserve requirement increases from 5 percent to 6 percent.
   c. The discount rate is increased.
   d. The reserve requirement is lowered from 5 percent to 4 percent, and the Federal Reserve buys $10 million in government securities from the bank.

Discussion Questions

1. It is assumed in the equation of exchange that the velocity of money is fixed, or constant. Is this a safe assumption when applied to your own spending habits over the course of a month or a year? What would erratic and unpredictable velocity do to the usefulness of the equation of exchange?

2. In a discussion with a friend you are told that it makes no difference whether the Federal Reserve uses open market operations, the reserve requirement, or the discount rate to change the supply of money because the impact of each policy is exactly the same. Do you agree or disagree with your friend's position?

3. Control by the Federal Reserve over the money supply and over total spending is weakened by the fact that borrowing by businesses and households is voluntary. How might the power of the Federal Reserve over borrowing be strengthened? Is this method consistent with the philosophy of capitalism?

4. Assume that the economy is at full employment and that the federal government needs to borrow $100 billion to finance a budget deficit. Should the Federal Reserve monetize the debt by putting an extra $100 billion in reserves into the system to finance this borrowing? If not, what action should the Fed take?

5. If you were trying to control inflation, would you depend on fiscal or monetary policy? Why? If you were trying to reduce unemployment, would you depend on fiscal or monetary policy? Why?

6. Suppose the economy is experiencing inflationary pressure because of rising food and energy costs at the same time that it is slipping into a recession because of cutbacks in defense spending. As the chairperson of the Board of Governors, how would you balance the attention you give to these two problems and what recommendations concerning the tools of monetary policy would you make to solve them? Would it make sense to use monetary policy to solve one of the problems while asking Congress to use fiscal policy to solve the other?

7. The tools of monetary policy are used to deal with the problems of unemployment, inflation, and slow economic growth. Could you make an argument that the Federal Reserve should concern itself only with problems relating to inflation and the price level, and that other problems in the macroeconomy should be the responsibility of other policymaking groups?

THE FED AND THE GREAT DEPRESSION

Critical Thinking Skills

Exploring similarities between historical and contemporary events

Identifying cause and effect

Economic Concepts

Monetary policy

The Federal Reserve

What caused the Depression? This question is a difficult one, but answering it is important if we are to draw the right lessons from the experience for economic policy. . . .

During the first decades after the Depression, most economists looked to developments on the real side of the economy for explanations, rather than to monetary factors. . . . However, in 1963, . . . [and in] contradiction to the prevalent view of the time, that money and monetary policy played at most a purely passive role in the Depression, [Milton] Friedman and [Anna] Schwartz argued that "the [economic] contraction is in fact a tragic testimonial to the importance of monetary forces."

. . . Friedman and Schwartz . . . identified a series of errors . . . by the Federal Reserve in the late 1920s and early 1930s [that] led to an undesirable tightening of monetary policy [and] sharp declines in the money supply. [These] could account for the drops in prices and output that subsequently occurred.

[One error] was the tightening of monetary policy that began in the spring of 1928 and continued until the stock market crash of October 1929. This tightening of monetary policy in 1928 did not seem particularly justified by the macroeconomic environment: The economy was only just emerging from a recession . . . and there was little hint of inflation. Why then did the Federal Reserve raise interest rates in 1928? The principal reason was the Fed's ongoing

concern . . . that bank lending to brokers and investors was fueling a speculative wave in the stock market. When the Fed's attempts to persuade banks not to lend for speculative purposes proved ineffective, Fed officials decided to dissuade lending directly by raising the policy interest rate. . . .

According to Friedman and Schwartz, the Fed's tight-money policies led to the onset of a recession in August 1929. . . . The slowdown in economic activity, together with high interest rates, was in all likelihood the most important source of the stock market crash that followed in October. In other words, the market crash, rather than being the cause of the Depression, as popular legend has it, was in fact largely the result of an economic slowdown and the inappropriate monetary policies that preceded it. . . .

[Another] policy action highlighted by Friedman and Schwartz occurred in 1932. By the spring of that year, the Depression was well advanced, and Congress began to place considerable pressure on the Federal Reserve to ease monetary policy. The Board was quite reluctant to comply, but in response to the ongoing pressure the Board conducted open-market operations between April and June of 1932 designed to increase the national money supply and thus ease policy. These policy actions reduced interest rates on government bonds and corporate debt and appeared to arrest the decline in prices and economic activity. [But] Fed officials convinced themselves that the policy ease advocated by the Congress was not appropriate, and so when the Congress adjourned in July 1932, the Fed reversed the policy. By the latter part of the year, the economy had relapsed dramatically.

Source: Excerpted from remarks by Governor Ben S. Bernanke, member of the Fed Board of Governors, at the H. Parker Willis Lecture in Economic Policy, "Money, Gold and the Great Depression," March 2, 2004.

Questions

1. What is the significance of knowledge of Federal Reserve actions during the 1930s for the analysis of contemporary monetary policy?

2. In what ways did Federal Reserve policy in the early 1930s likely affect the U.S. economy?

3. What types of historical information (federal budgets, for example) would you want to know before you determined the extent to which monetary policy contributed to the Great Depression?

CHAPTER 9

Macroeconomic Viewpoints and Models

CHAPTER OBJECTIVES

To understand that there are several major macroeconomic models with different assumptions that focus on different relationships, and to recognize the historical dimension of macroeconomic theory.

To discuss the fundamental relationships of the classical, new classical, Keynesian, new Keynesian, and monetarist schools of thought.

To describe the classical aggregate demand–aggregate supply model and its conclusions.

To understand the basic relationships in the Keynesian model and the policy implications of the model.

To explain the new classical model and its policy implications.

To introduce the Phillips curve, examine U.S. rates of inflation and unemployment, and identify reasons for shifts in the Phillips curve.

In Chapter 5 we discussed macroeconomic fluctuations: The macroeconomy is always expanding or contracting, or in some phase of a business cycle. Production increases and unemployment falls during a recovery, and production decreases and unemployment rises during a recession. The causes of these fluctuations have been pondered for centuries, as have the causes of another major macroeconomic problem: inflation.

The relationship between the amount of total spending in an economy and the economy's levels of production and employment was laid out in Chapter 5. Businesses respond to spending changes by households, other businesses, government, and foreign buyers by increasing or decreasing their levels of production.

The foundation built in Chapter 5 can be used to understand various viewpoints about the macroeconomy and different models that have been developed to explain how it operates. Some important questions can be answered by relying on our Chapter 5 foundation as well as these models. For example, while spending changes may trigger economic fluctuations, what triggers spending changes? Is there a difference in short-run and long-run macroeconomic relationships? Is there a level of activity that an economy automatically seeks?

We begin this chapter with an overview of macroeconomic model building and discuss the components of a model as well as how history has influenced the development of these models. We then introduce some of the major macroeconomic schools of thought—the classical, Keynesian, new classical, new Keynesian, and monetarist schools—and the basic model of each school. The chapter ends with a discussion of the Phillips curve, which is used to show the relationship between inflation and unemployment.

MACROECONOMIC MODEL BUILDING

Much of the work of economists is model building; that is, economists look for explanations for relationships between economic variables or seek answers to why an economic problem or condition occurs. As explained in Chapter 1, model building involves four components: identifying variables, establishing assumptions, collecting and analyzing data, and interpreting conclusions.

Economic theory has an important historical dimension: Searches for explanations of economic problems are often related to historical events. For example, there was significant joblessness during the Great Depression in the 1930s, which gave rise to a need to determine the cause of unemployment and policies to remedy it. One of the great songs of the Depression era, "Brother, Can You Spare a Dime?," captures the extreme distress underlying the need to change the direction of the economy.

"Once I built a railroad, I made it run, made it race against time.
Once I build a railroad; now it's done. Brother, can you spare a dime?
Once I built a tower, up to the sun, brick, and rivet, and lime;
Once I built a tower, now it's done. Brother, can you spare a dime?"[1]

The severe inflations of the mid-to-late 1970s and early 1980s brought serious interest in determining the causes of inflation. In 2008, a deteriorating economy again brought significant interest in economic theory and policy.

[1]Songs of the Great Depression, "Brother, Can You Spare a Dime?," lyrics by Yip Harburg, music by Jay Gorney (1931), http://www.library.csi.cuny.edu/dept/history/lavender/cherries.html.

A Warning

Recall that a model examines the relationship between two variables. It is important to keep this in mind as we study the models in this chapter because not all macroeconomic models attempt to explain the same relationships. Rather, they focus on different problems and variables. In this chapter, one model explores the relationship between prices and output, another the relationship between spending and output, and a third the relationship between money and output.

The assumptions, or conditions held to be true, when building a model are important because they underlie the model and affect its conclusions. Assumptions can be influenced by the values of the model builder, and the role of these values in developing assumptions is often overlooked or difficult to identify. For example, if one values free markets, then free markets can become an underlying assumption of a model and in turn become important to policy recommendations that follow from the model. If one values government intervention, then this value can become important to the assumptions of a model and its resulting policy implications.

It is useful for students to identify the variables, assumptions, and data that go into the construction and presentation of a model. The interpretation of the conclusions of the model as well as its policy implications are affected by the choice of each of these parts of the model. This makes it important for students to be able to put models in their proper context in economics as well as in other classes. For example, in the social sciences, conclusions about people's behavior patterns are often based on research done in a model, so it is useful for students to understand how the model's assumptions and data collection affected those conclusions. Knowledge of the cultural setting of a model in sociology, the values of a teller of history, and the data collection method for a political science survey are all important for a fuller understanding of work in these fields.

Application 9.1, "Paying Close Attention to Models: It's Worth the Effort," provides some additional thoughts about economic model building and the impact of how the story in a model is presented. Can you think of a theory you studied in a social science course, such as psychology, sociology, or political science, that influenced history or the personal beliefs of a large number of people or policymakers?

VIEWPOINTS AND MODELS

Over the years, different models have been developed by economists to explain the operation of the macroeconomy, and different policy prescriptions have been advocated to stabilize the economy. Alternative viewpoints about the macroeconomy often stem from the different assumptions on which the models are formulated. Also, sometimes a viewpoint loses popularity as new data and information provide better explanations of key economic relationships or solutions to problems.

These different macroeconomic theories and the policy prescriptions that follow from them can be better understood by placing them into categories, or "schools of thought." Several schools of thought are significant to the development of macroeconomic theory. These include the classical, Keynesian, new classical, new Keynesian, and monetarist schools.

Classical Economics

Classical Economics
Popularly accepted theory prior to the Great Depression of the 1930s; says the economy will automatically adjust to full employment.

The dominant school of economic thought before the 1930s was **classical economics.** This school, however, was largely rejected during the 1930s because it could not explain the cause of, or offer a successful remedy for, the prolonged and severe unemployment that

APPLICATION 9.1

PAYING CLOSE ATTENTION TO MODELS: IT'S WORTH THE EFFORT

Working your way through an economic model can be difficult, boring, and time consuming. The problem is that economic models have a significant impact on our lives. It is usually the conclusion of a model that is the starting point for policies that affect so many aspects of how we live, from our jobs to the kinds of things we can afford to buy. So, we should pay close attention to what is in a model.

The importance of economic forces is bluntly stated on the first page of a book by Alfred Marshall that played a major role in opening the door to what we think of as modern economics. Marshall wrote: "[M]an's character has been moulded by his every-day work, and the material resources which he thereby procures, more than by any other influence unless it be that of his religious ideals; and the two great forming agencies of the world's history have been the religious and the economic."[a] Stop and think for a moment: These two factors—religion and economics—have played a central role in bringing people together but also in their going to war against each other.

While economic models might be difficult and boring, people (some of whom exert great power) take them very seriously. As John Maynard Keynes, one of the most influential economists of the twentieth century, put it: "[The] ideas of economists and political philosophers, both when they are right and when they are wrong, are more powerful than is commonly understood. Indeed, the world is ruled by little else. Practical men, who believe themselves to be quite exempt from any intellectual influences, are usually the slaves of some defunct economist. Madmen in authority, who hear voices in the air, are distilling their frenzy from some academic scribbler of a few years back."[b]

Sometimes the take on the story a model tells changes after its assumptions and data are explored in detail. For example, you probably know the story of the three little pigs. One lived in a house built of straw, the second in a house built of sticks, and the third in a house built of bricks. When the wolf came along, he blew down the houses of straw and sticks, but not the house of bricks. The usual moral of the story is that the pig in the brick house put in the effort to build a solid house, and the other two pigs were lazy. But how would the moral of the story change if the first pig worked an 80-hour week in the brick factory to get by and feed his kids, the second pig was disabled by an accident in the brick factory and unable to work, and the third pig was the brick factory owner's son?

What is the moral of the story in this application? The influence of economics is not to be taken lightly, and the models used to extend this influence should be thoroughly examined and understood. While we may not tolerate details well, it is those details of our economic models that tell the real story.

[a] Alfred Marshall, *Principles of Economics* (London: Macmillan and Co., 1890), p. 1.
[b] John Maynard Keynes, *The General Theory of Employment, Interest and Money* (New York: Harcourt, Brace and Co., 1936), p. 383.

developed during the Great Depression. The basic premise of the classical school, which dates from Adam Smith and his book *The Wealth of Nations* in the late eighteenth century, is that a free market economy, when left alone, will automatically operate at full employment. And, because a free market economy always automatically corrects itself to full employment, there is no need for government intervention to rectify its problems. Adam Smith is one of the economists featured in Application 9.2, "The Academic Scribblers."

The classical economists arrived at their position about the automatic self-correction to full employment because of several assumptions. First, they assumed that supply creates its own demand in a macroeconomy.[2] In other words, something that is produced will be bought by someone. As a result, there is no need for concern about operating at less than full employment and production: The goods and services that are produced will all be purchased.

[2] "Say's Law," named after the French economist Jean Baptiste Say (1767–1832), states that supply creates its own demand. According to James Mill (1773–1836), one of the important popularizers of this position, whatever individuals produce over and above their own needs is done to exchange for goods and services produced by others. People produce in order to acquire the things that they desire, so what they supply and what they demand are equal. And if each person's supply and demand are equal, it follows that the supply and demand in the entire economy must be equal. Believing that demand and supply are equal for the entire economy, the classical economists saw surpluses in specific markets that would lead to unemployment as being offset by shortages in other markets. The surpluses would be removed by businesses following their own self-interest and guided by the profit motive. See James Mill, *Elements of Political Economy* (London: Baldwin, Cradock, and Joy, 1826), Chapter IV, Section III, especially pp. 228, 232, 234–235.

APPLICATION 9.2

THE ACADEMIC SCRIBBLERS

Adam Smith   Adam Smith, considered by many to be the "father" of market economics, or capitalism, was born in 1723 in Scotland. He lived during a time of tremendous change in Britain: The Industrial Revolution brought inventions allowing for more efficient production, factories, a poor working class, the rise of capitalists, and many other economic and social changes.

Smith was a well-known philosopher in his time. At the age of 28, he was offered the Chair of Logic at the University of Glasgow, and later the Chair of Moral Philosophy. *The Theory of Moral Sentiments,* which he published in 1759, gave Smith recognition as he explored the philosophical question of how people, who are basically motivated by self-interest, consider the moral merits of an action.

Smith's most famous work, *The Wealth of Nations,* was revolutionary for its time because it represented a movement from mercantilist thinking to the idea that individual decision making would best serve a society's interests. In this text, Smith focuses on the market mechanism and shows how individual self-interest operating through markets provides the greatest good for society. He also discusses the importance of competition in a market system and firmly states that government should not intervene in the market mechanism. It is these assertions that strongly connect Smith to classical economics.

No biography of Smith is complete without mention of his absentmindedness; this extended to late-night walks about his village in his nightclothes, an often-mentioned tale about Smith. Smith, who lived peacefully with his mother in his later years, died at 67.

John Maynard Keynes   John Maynard Keynes, probably the most influential economist of the twentieth century, was born in 1883 in England. His father, John Neville Keynes, was an economist and a logician who taught at Cambridge University. John Maynard was well educated, and his first interest was in mathematics. Urging by some distinguished professors sent him in the direction of economics.

Keynes led a full and active life intermingling different careers: a brief stint in the civil service, a lectureship in economics at Cambridge, bursar at Kings College, adviser to various London bankers, and a successful personal financier. His interests were also varied: He had close ties to the colorful Bloomsbury set of intellectuals, married a ballerina, financed a theater group, and had an extensive art collection. An observer of Keynes noted, "He would go out of his way to make something flattering out of what a student had said. . . . On the other hand, when a faculty member got up [he] simply cut their heads off."[a]

Although Keynes is well known for his 1919 book, *The Economic Consequences of the Peace,* which discusses the economics of the Versailles Treaty of World War I, his major work is *The General Theory of Employment, Interest and Money,* published in 1936. This book focuses on Keynes' major contribution—that a market economy's levels of output and employment are the result of the level of aggregate demand. It should be noted that although government interventionist policies are associated with Keynesian economics, Keynes' ideas were rooted in his regard for individualism. The following quote is from *The General Theory.*

> But, above all, individualism, if it can be purged of its defects and its abuses, is the best safeguard of personal liberty in the sense that compared with any other system, it greatly widens the field for the exercise of personal choice. It is also the best safeguard of the variety of life, which emerges precisely from this extended field of personal choice, and the loss of which is the greatest of all losses of the homogeneous or totalitarian state.[b]

Milton Friedman   The face and work of Milton Friedman are familiar to many Americans: He wrote and lectured in a wide variety of places and made appearances on television talk shows. Friedman completed a video series, *Free to Choose,* that has been seen on public television and in many classrooms, and his accompanying book, coauthored with his wife Rose, *Free to Choose: A Personal Statement,* was on *The New York Times* best seller list. In 1976 Milton Friedman received the Nobel Prize in economics.

Friedman was born in 1912 in New York to hardworking immigrants. His father died when Friedman was 15, placing additional financial burdens on his mother and causing Friedman to rely on scholarships to obtain an education. He received his undergraduate degree from Rutgers, went to the University of Chicago for graduate study, and earned his Ph.D. from Columbia University in 1946. Friedman eventually returned to an academic post at the University of Chicago, where he remained until 1977.

Milton Friedman's many contributions to economics focused on the importance of money to the operation of the macroeconomy, and he was associated with renewing interest in money and macroeconomic policy. However, he was also known for strongly embracing a free market philosophy and for espousing the view, associated with the Chicago School, that a market economy works best when left alone. In many cases, such as public education, Friedman believed that a competitive market would do a better job and that the government has done more harm than good. Milton Friedman died in 2006.

[a]William Breit and Roger L. Ransom, *The Academic Scribblers,* rev. ed. (Hinsdale, IL: The Dryden Press, 1982), p. 67.
[b]Breit and Ransom, p. 68. Also see John Maynard Keynes, *The General Theory of Employment, Interest and Money* (New York: Harcourt, Brace and Co., 1936), p. 380.

| FIGURE 9.1 | *Aggregate Supply and Aggregate Demand in Classical Economics* |

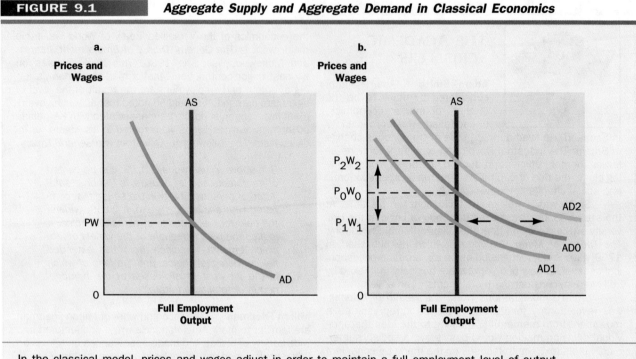

In the classical model, prices and wages adjust in order to maintain a full employment level of output.

A second assumption of the classical economists was that wages and prices are flexible and increase or decrease to ensure that the economy operates at full employment. This assumption is illustrated in Figure 9.1. The perfectly vertical aggregate, or total, supply curve (AS) in Figure 9.1a illustrates an economy producing at the full employment level of output, regardless of whether prices and wages are high or low. The aggregate demand curve (AD) in Figure 9.1a represents the spending plans of households and businesses in the economy. The curve slopes downward to indicate that an inverse relationship exists between prices and wages, and the amount of output demanded. When prices fall (which will also bring wages down in the classical model), households and businesses want to purchase a greater amount of output, and when prices increase, they want to purchase less. In Figure 9.1a, aggregate demand and supply are equal at the full employment level of output with price and wage level PW.

If there is a change in aggregate demand, as illustrated in Figure 9.1b by the decrease or increase in the aggregate demand curve from AD0 to AD1, or AD0 to AD2, respectively, there will be a change in prices and wages that allows the economy to continue to operate at full employment. For example, if initially in Figure 9.1b, aggregate demand were AD0, aggregate supply were AS, and the level of prices and wages were P_0W_0, the economy would be operating at full employment. If aggregate demand were to decrease and the aggregate demand curve shifted to the left to AD1, less would be demanded than supplied at the original price and wage level (P_0W_0), and the economy would experience some temporary unemployment. However, according to the classical assumptions, prices and wages would soon fall to P_1W_1, and the economy would return to full employment. This lower price and wage level would permit full employment at the lower level of demand.

Likewise, if aggregate demand were to increase and the aggregate demand curve shifted to the right from AD0 to AD2 in Figure 9.1b, more would be demanded than could be supplied at the original price and wage level of P_0W_0. Prices and wages would rise to P_2W_2, with the economy continuing to operate at full employment. In the classical model, the adjustment to changes in aggregate demand is through changes in prices and wages, not output and employment. Production will seek the full employment level, regardless of changes in demand.

The classical economists also assumed that savings always equals investment: Everything leaked from the spending stream through savings is returned through the investment injection. This equality always occurs, they reasoned, because changes in the interest rate bring savings and investment into equality.

As indicated earlier, classical theory, with its hands-off attitude toward the economy, was largely abandoned in the 1930s when it could not explain the persistence of the Great Depression or offer a solution to the unemployment problem. In its place came Keynesian theory, which advocated managing total demand to attack the problems of unemployment and inflation. Like classical economics in the 1930s, however, Keynesian theory was not wholly successful in explaining the problems of the 1970s when the economy was experiencing high rates of both unemployment and inflation.

Keynesian Economics

Keynesian Economics
Based on the work of John Maynard Keynes (1883–1946), who focused on the role of aggregate spending in determining the level of macroeconomic activity.

The ideas of the British economist John Maynard Keynes (1883–1946) form the basis for **Keynesian economics.** Keynes, one of the best-known economists of the twentieth century, came to the forefront of economics during the 1930s when prevailing classical theory could not provide a satisfactory explanation for the depression that most industrialized nations in the world faced. Keynes focused on the causes and cures for unemployment and low levels of output. His most famous work, *The General Theory of Employment, Interest and Money,* was published during the Great Depression.[3] Background on Keynes' life and thinking is given in Application 9.2.

Keynes revolutionized economic thinking by focusing on the role of aggregate, or total, spending in the economy. His major contribution was to link increases and decreases in output and employment with increases and decreases in spending. Keynes rejected the classical notion of an automatic adjustment to full employment, reasoning that an economy's output and employment would improve from less than full employment only if aggregate spending increased. Keynes also believed that the spending gap responsible for recessions and unemployment could be filled by the government.

Keynes introduced the idea that a macroeconomy seeks an equilibrium output level, or that there is a level of output toward which an economy moves. Macroequilibrium could be at a low level of output, which results in unemployment and low incomes, or at a high and healthy level of output. During the Great Depression, conditions were such that the economy was moving toward an equilibrium level that was far from full employment.

Macroeconomic Equilibrium
Occurs when the amount of total planned spending on new goods and services equals total output in the economy.

Equilibrium in the Macroeconomy   An economy is in **macroeconomic equilibrium** when the amount that all households, businesses, government units, and foreign buyers plan to spend on new goods and services equals the total amount of output the economy is currently producing. At equilibrium there is no tendency for change in the level of economic activity because the planned spending of all buyers is just sufficient to purchase all the goods and services that are produced.

[3]John Maynard Keynes, *The General Theory of Employment, Interest and Money* (New York: Harcourt, Brace and Co., 1936).

TABLE 9.1	*Total Output and Total Planned Spending (Trillions of Dollars)*

This macroeconomy is in equilibrium at $3.0 trillion, where total output is equal to total planned spending, and injections into the spending stream are equal to leakages.

Total Output	Total Planned Spending	Leakages	Injections	Economic Condition
$0.00	$1.50	$0.00	$1.50	Expansion
0.50	1.75	0.25	1.50	Expansion
1.00	2.00	0.50	1.50	Expansion
1.50	2.25	0.75	1.50	Expansion
2.00	2.50	1.00	1.50	Expansion
2.50	2.75	1.25	1.50	Expansion
3.00	3.00	1.50	1.50	Equilibrium
3.50	3.25	1.75	1.50	Contraction
4.00	3.50	2.00	1.50	Contraction
4.50	3.75	2.25	1.50	Contraction
5.00	4.00	2.50	1.50	Contraction

When the amount that households, businesses, government units, and foreign buyers plan to spend on new goods and services differs from the total output produced, the economy is not in equilibrium, and output, employment, and income will change. If the total planned spending of all buyers is greater than current production, then output, employment, and income will increase, assuming that full employment has not been reached. If the total planned spending is less than current production, then output, employment, and income will fall.

The key to understanding how spending can be more or less than current production is in the role played by **inventories.** Most businesses intentionally maintain an inventory of their products. When total spending in the economy is greater than current production, inventories begin to fall, signaling a need to increase output levels. When total spending is less than current production, unintentional inventories begin to accumulate, causing businesses to cut back on production.

Inventories
Stocks of goods on hand; can be intentional or unintentional.

Illustrating Equilibrium   Table 9.1 illustrates possible levels of total output that a hypothetical economy could produce and the total planned spending of all households, businesses, government units, and foreign buyers that would occur at each level of output at a given point in time. For example, all buyers would purchase $2.5 trillion worth of goods and services at an output level of $2.0 trillion, or $3.5 trillion of goods and services at an output of $4.0 trillion. Total spending increases as output increases because with more output there is more earned income for households to spend.

Notice in Table 9.1 that there is one level of output, $3.0 trillion, where total planned spending equals total output. Here the economy is in equilibrium. At output levels less than $3.0 trillion, planned spending is greater than output; inventories fall, causing businesses to produce more; and the economy expands. At output levels greater than $3.0 trillion, planned spending is less than output; unintentional inventories build up causing businesses to produce less; and the economy contracts toward the equilibrium level of $3.0 trillion.

An important factor determining whether the economy is in equilibrium or expanding or contracting is the relationship between leakages from and injections into the spending stream. (Recall that leakages and injections were discussed in Chapter 5.) When leakages equal injections, the economy is in equilibrium. For example, suppose an economy produces $7 trillion of goods and services, which results in the creation of $7 trillion in income. Assume that from this $7 trillion income, households spend $5 trillion and the rest, $2 trillion, is leaked from the spending stream through saving, taxes, and the purchase of imports. In order to keep the production level unchanged at $7 trillion, or to maintain equilibrium, the entire amount that was leaked must be replaced by injections of an equal amount. That is, $2 trillion in business investment spending, government purchases of goods and services, household spending from transfer payments and borrowing, and/or foreign expenditures on exports must be put into the system.

If the amount that is leaked from the spending stream is greater than the amount injected into the spending stream, the economy will contract. Unintentional inventories will build up, and businesses will respond by cutting back on output and employment. On the other hand, if injections are greater than leakages, the size of the spending stream will increase to a level greater than current output. Intentional inventories will fall and businesses will respond by expanding production, assuming that full employment has not yet been reached.

Observe in Table 9.1 the columns Leakages and Injections. Notice that the economy's injections are $1.5 trillion regardless of the level of output. Because injections are independent of earned income, they do not change as output and income change. Because leakages include saving, taxes, and purchases of imports, leakages are $0 when there is no output or income from which to save, pay taxes, or buy imports, and they increase as output and income increase. Notice in the right-hand column of Table 9.1 that the economy expands when injections are greater than leakages, and it contracts when leakages are greater than injections. At equilibrium they are equal.

Figure 9.2 illustrates the information given in Table 9.1. Total output is measured along the horizontal axis and total planned spending along the vertical axis. A 45-degree line is also plotted on this graph. Every point on this line matches a level of output with exactly the same level of spending. For this reason, the line is named the Spending Equals Output line.

The numbers from Table 9.1 showing total planned spending at each level of total output are illustrated by the Total Spending line in Figure 9.2. Notice that the Total Spending line crosses the Spending Equals Output line at exactly $3.0 trillion of output, which is the equilibrium level in Table 9.1. At output levels less than equilibrium, the Total Spending line is above the Spending Equals Output line. Because spending is greater than output, output will increase toward equilibrium. At output levels greater than $3.0 trillion, the Total Spending line is below the Spending Equals Output line, causing output to fall toward equilibrium.

The difference between the 45-degree line and the Total Spending line at each level of output is equal to the difference between injections and leakages at that output level. When the Total Spending line is above the 45-degree line, injections are greater than leakages; when it is below, leakages are greater than injections. For example, the Total Spending line is $0.5 trillion above the 45-degree line at an output of $2.0 trillion because, at that output, injections exceed leakages by $0.5 trillion.

Keynesian Policy Prescriptions   Based on this model, Keynes pioneered the idea of using government expenditures and taxes to control the level of economic activity. According to Keynes, the appropriate policy prescription for counteracting a recession is to increase aggregate spending. This can be accomplished by increasing government expenditures on goods and services and/or transfer payments, and/or by lowering

| **FIGURE 9.2** | *Equilibrium in the Macroeconomy* |

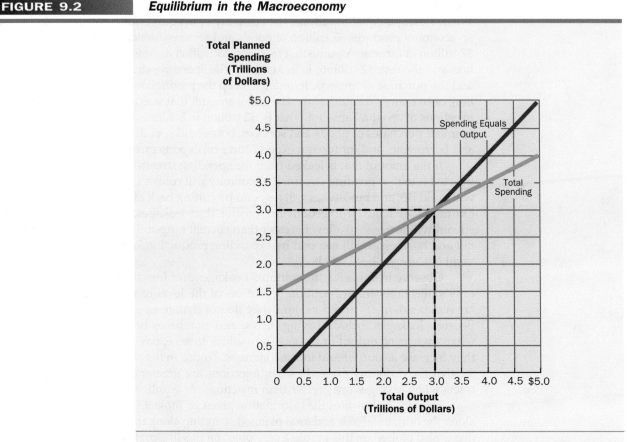

The macroeconomy is in equilibrium at the output level where the Total Spending line crosses the Spending Equals Output line.

taxes. In other words, government can pump in the spending necessary to move the economy out of a recession.

Figure 9.3 illustrates Keynes' ideas about fiscal policy. In the economy in Figure 9.3, full employment would be reached at an output level of $5.0 trillion. Here the Spending Equals Output line becomes vertical to indicate that output cannot exceed $5.0 trillion, even though spending can continue to grow. In Figure 9.3a, the economy is moving toward an equilibrium level of $3.0 trillion, well below the full employment level of $5.0 trillion. In other words, this economy is moving toward an equilibrium with a significant amount of unemployment, or toward a recession.

To reach full employment, additional spending must be injected into the economy. This could be accomplished by increasing government purchases of goods and services, by increasing transfer payments to give households more money to spend, and/or by decreasing taxes, which also gives households more money to spend. Any of these actions could cause total spending to increase, or the Total Spending line to shift upward.

Figure 9.3b shows the result of fiscal policy actions to move the economy to full employment. In this case, government policies have shifted the Total Spending line upward so that the economy will move toward equilibrium at $5.0 trillion rather than $3.0 trillion, and the economy will experience a recovery rather than a recession.

FIGURE 9.3   *Changes in Macroeconomic Equilibrium*

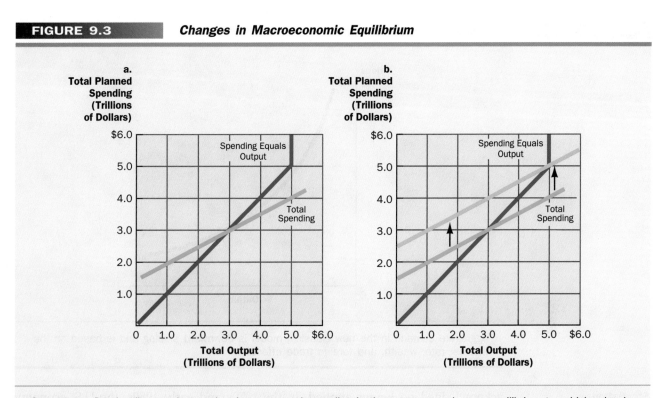

Government fiscal policy can be used to increase total spending in the economy and move equilibrium to a higher level.

Keynes believed that because an economy does not automatically seek a full employment level of output, it is appropriate from time to time for government to provide the spending boost that is needed. In other words, an upward shift of the Total Spending line could be government induced.

Keynesian economics reached its peak of popularity during the 1960s. In the early 1970s, however, it became a target for attack. Some argued that the problems of the 1970s could not be explained or remedied in Keynesian terms and that wasteful spending by government and increasing federal government deficits were linked to the Keynesian approach to economic policy. During the 1980s, the political mood favored a movement away from government intervention in the economy, causing further attacks on Keynesian economics and a renewed interest in other approaches to macroeconomic policy, such as monetarism and new classical economics. In more recent years, there has been increased appreciation for, and application of, the fundamentals of Keynesian economics. In 2008, for example, the federal government sent tax rebate checks to qualifying taxpayers to help ward off a possible recession, and in 2009 an economic stimulus program was enacted.

New Classical Economics

In the mid-1970s, many of the world's economies began to experience serious inflationary problems. A sudden escalation in the price of oil caused a rapid increase in energy costs, which, in turn, kindled cost-push inflation. For example, fuel costing $17 in 1970 more than doubled in price by 1975 to $36.40 and peaked at $104.60 in 1981. In addition, the tradeoff between price changes and unemployment that was traditionally

| FIGURE 9.4 | *Aggregate Demand in the New Classical Model* |

Aggregate demand in the new classical model is downward sloping and is based on the interest rate, wealth, and foreign trade effects.

Stagflation
Occurs when an economy experiences high rates of both inflation and unemployment.

New Classical Economics
A return to the basic classical premise that free markets automatically stabilize themselves and that government intervention in the macroeconomy is not advisable.

Natural Rate of Unemployment
The rate of unemployment at which there is no cyclical unemployment.

acknowledged no longer applied. In the 1970s and early 1980s, the U.S. economy experienced **stagflation,** or high rates of both unemployment and inflation. In 1975, 1980, and 1981, the U.S. economy's rate of unemployment was between 7.1 and 8.5 percent, while the inflation rate was over 9.1 percent.[4]

These economic problems renewed an interest in exploring the relationship between price levels and output, or in returning to the views of the classical school. As a result, **new classical economics** was born.

Many of the basic elements of the classical school can be found in new classical economics. These include an underlying assumption of a free market economy, a model that focuses on output and prices, a downward-sloping aggregate demand curve, and an emphasis on flexible prices. Also, while the classical economists said that the economy tends to operate at full employment, the new classical economists assert that, over the long run, the economy will operate at the **natural rate of unemployment,** or the rate at which there is no cyclical unemployment.[5] Expressed differently, the new classical position maintains there is no tradeoff between unemployment and inflation over the long run.

Aggregate Demand in the New Classical Model   The aggregate demand curve in the new classical model is illustrated in Figure 9.4. Notice that it is basically the same as the aggregate demand curve in the classical model, with its emphasis on an inverse relationship between price levels and the amount of output demanded in the economy as a whole. With the new classical model, however, comes a more sophisticated explanation of the downward-sloping aggregate demand curve that has some important policy implications. The new classical economists provide three reasons for the downward-sloping curve: the interest rate effect, the wealth effect, and the foreign trade effect.

[4]*Economic Report of the President* (Washington, DC: U.S. Government Printing Office, 2008), pp. 276, 300.
[5]Be sure not to confuse the natural rate of unemployment with the full employment rate of unemployment, which includes only the frictionally unemployed. Review Chapter 4 for further information on these concepts.

| FIGURE 9.5 | *Aggregate Supply in the New Classical Model* |

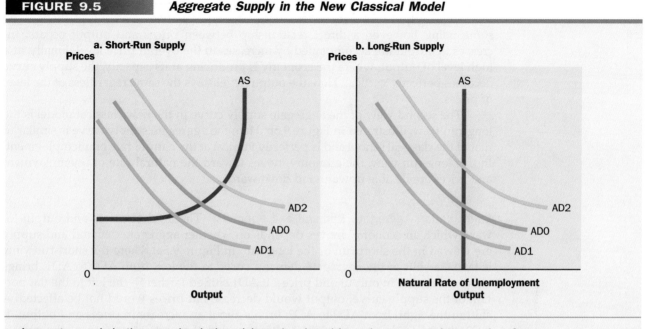

Aggregate supply in the new classical model can be viewed in a short-run or a long-run time frame.

As overall prices change, the price of money, or the interest rate, also changes. When the interest rate increases along with an increase in overall prices, households and businesses borrow less and spend less, causing less output to be demanded. When the interest rate falls along with a decrease in the general level of prices, households and businesses borrow more and spend more, causing more output to be demanded. The downward slope of the aggregate demand curve is, therefore, shaped to a large extent by this relationship between the interest rate and spending, which is called the **interest rate effect** on aggregate demand.

People typically have some level of money wealth that they have accumulated and want to maintain. This includes, for example, cash, bonds, certificates of deposit, and such. When prices increase, the value of this accumulated wealth falls, and as prices decrease, the value of this accumulated wealth increases. In order to maintain the same value of money wealth, people will spend less when prices increase and more when prices fall. Again, the amount of output demanded increases with more spending and falls with less spending. The impact on the aggregate demand curve caused by changes in the value of money wealth is called the **wealth effect.**

As prices rise in the economy, people may turn to lower-priced imports, and, as prices fall, people will likely buy fewer imports. This **foreign trade effect** provides another reason for the downward-sloping aggregate demand curve: As prices rise, spending on the domestic output of goods and services and, therefore, output falls because spending is diverted to imports; and, as prices fall, spending on domestically produced goods and services rises because spending is diverted from imports.

Aggregate Supply in the New Classical Model   The aggregate supply curve in the new classical model can be viewed in two ways: short-run supply with three phases, or long-run supply. Figure 9.5a gives the short-run aggregate supply curve in this

Interest Rate Effect
The interest rate moves with changes in overall prices; there is an inverse relationship between the interest rate and the amount people borrow and spend.

Wealth Effect
In order to maintain the same amount of accumulated wealth, people spend less when prices rise and more when prices fall.

Foreign Trade Effect
There is a direct relationship between changes in overall prices in an economy and spending on imports that diverts spending from domestically produced output.

model. At low levels of output, the aggregate supply curve is perfectly horizontal. In this range, output levels are so low that prices are not affected as output changes. At some point, however, a direct relationship between prices and output occurs: Increases in output are accompanied by increases in the overall price level. Finally, at a high level of output, where the economy is producing at its capacity, the supply curve becomes perfectly vertical. Here the output level stays the same regardless of the level of prices.

The second view of the aggregate supply curve in the new classical model is the long-run view, illustrated in Figure 9.5b. Here the aggregate supply curve is similar to that of the classical school and is perfectly vertical at the natural rate of unemployment. In this long-run view, the economy moves toward the natural rate of unemployment and prices are flexible upward and downward.

Manipulating Aggregate Demand and Supply   The level of prices and output toward which an economy moves depends on whether aggregate demand and supply are viewed in the short run or the long run. In Figure 9.5a, where the short-run view is taken, a shift of the aggregate demand curve to the left, from AD0 to AD1, brings about a decrease in output and prices. If AD1 shifted farther to the left to the flat portion of the supply curve, output would decrease but prices would not be affected. A shift to the right, from AD0 to AD2, brings about an increase in prices and output. If AD2 shifted farther to the right and intersected the vertical portion of the supply curve, price levels would rise but output would not be affected.

In Figure 9.5b, where the long-run view is taken, a shift of the aggregate demand curve in either direction brings a change in the price level but no change in output. In the long-run view, output is at the natural rate of unemployment and prices are flexible in either direction.

The Long Run and Policy Implications   The policy implications of this long-run view are important because they suggest that the government should keep its hands off the economy. Any efforts to manipulate aggregate demand will, over the long run, result in no improvement in the level of unemployment but may cause the price level to rise. The ineffectiveness of government policies in reducing unemployment below its natural rate is called the **natural rate hypothesis.**

This long-run view of the new classical school is supported by the argument that households and businesses have expectations about how the economy should perform—especially with regard to inflation. The expectations may be **adaptive expectations** based on past and current experiences, or they may be **rational expectations** based on an understanding by households and businesses of how they would be affected by proposed government policies. Either way, because of these expectations, households and businesses act in ways that benefit themselves but undermine the intentions of policymakers.

Suppose, for example, that the government follows policies to lower unemployment below its natural rate. In the process of moving toward this goal, more demand is added to the economy, causing the price level to increase. In other words, government policies to shift the aggregate demand curve to the right result in no change in unemployment but increase the price level. This effect, shown in Figure 9.5b by a shift in aggregate demand from AD0 to AD2, results because households and businesses respond to the expectation of rising prices and weakening purchasing power by negotiating higher wages and raising their prices.

Natural Rate Hypothesis
Over the long run, unemployment will tend toward its natural rate, and policies to reduce unemployment below that level will be ineffective.

Adaptive Expectations
Households and businesses base their expectations of the future on past and current experiences.

Rational Expectations
Households and businesses base their expectations of future policies on how they think they will be affected by those policies.

New Keynesian Economics

Keynesians, unlike the classical and new classical economists, saw the economy as not automatically returning to full employment once unemployment occurred. Building on this foundation, and responding to challenges to the Keynesian view that developed after the 1960s, economists known as new Keynesians went about explaining why the economy could persistently operate at less than full employment.

What distinguishes **new Keynesian economics** from its rival schools of macroeconomic thought—especially classical and new classical economics—is how each views the behavior of prices. While classical and new classical economists regard prices and wages as flexible, new Keynesian economists regard them as inflexible, or "sticky," downward. For this reason, new Keynesians do not think prices can be relied on to quickly drop and counter the adverse effects on employment that can result from a decrease in aggregate demand. Rather, because prices and wages are sticky downward, decreases in aggregate demand lead to adjustments on the supply side of the economy in the form of reductions in output and employment. Expressed differently, because prices do not drop, there is no mechanism to ensure that full employment will automatically be restored.

Another distinguishing feature of new Keynesian economics is the attention it pays to decision making by individual firms, or decision making in the microeconomy. One important explanation for the downward inflexibility of prices and wages is that firms set their prices based on what is necessary to maximize their own profits, not on the basis of what is occurring in the economy at large. The fact that individual sellers can resist pressures to lower their prices and may find it most profitable to decrease output when aggregate demand weakens helps explain why unemployment can persist in the economy.

Monetarism

Another school of thought significant to macroeconomic theory is **monetarism.** Those who focus on the money supply and advocate altering it to stabilize the economy are called **monetarists.** Monetarism was a popular viewpoint in the 1970s and early 1980s and challenged Keynesian fiscal policy prescriptions. Monetarism's best-known proponent was Milton Friedman, whose association with the University of Chicago led some to label followers of his thinking as members of the "Chicago School." Application 9.2 provides some background on Friedman.

Monetarists are inclined to favor free markets and advocate limited government intervention in the macroeconomy. In this sense, they tend to align with the classical and new classical schools. Typically, a monetarist would suggest that allowing free markets and maintaining proper control over the money supply is the ideal strategy for reaching full employment or avoiding demand-pull inflation.

Supply-Side Economics

A discussion of alternative macroeconomic viewpoints would not be complete without some mention of **supply-side economics,** which was born in the late 1970s, popularized by its association with President Ronald Reagan and "Reaganomics," briefly rejuvenated during the Dole–Clinton presidential race in 1996, and found support from some individuals in the George W. Bush administration. The basic idea behind supply-side economics is to stimulate the supply side of economic activity by creating government policies that provide incentives for individuals and businesses to increase their productive efforts.

The best-known supply-side proposal is to lower taxes for businesses and individuals. It is argued that lowering the tax burden on businesses would make investments

New Keynesian Economics
Builds on the Keynesian view that the economy does not automatically return to full employment; emphasizes downward sticky prices and individual decision making in the microeconomy.

Monetarism
School of thought that favors stabilizing the economy through controlling the money supply.

Monetarists
Persons who favor the economic policies of monetarism.

Supply-Side Economics
Policies to achieve macroeconomic goals by stimulating the supply side of the market; popular in the 1980s.

UP FOR DEBATE

SHOULD GOVERNMENT'S ROLE IN INFLUENCING ECONOMIC ACTIVITY BE REDUCED?

Issue *One place where classical and new classical economics on the one hand, and Keynesian and new Keynesian economics on the other, part company is the desirability of an active role by government in keeping the economy as close as possible to a noninflationary, full employment level of output. Should the federal government play a less active role in stabilizing the macroeconomy?*

Yes   Government should play a less active role in stabilizing the economy. A major point of classical and new classical economics should be heeded: The economy, if left alone, will tend to operate at its full (or natural) employment output. Overall price and employment levels are of greatest concern in the economy. If government views its primary responsibility as keeping markets as free as

possible, the resulting movement of wages and prices should lead to the adjustments necessary to ensure natural or full employment levels.

A large, interventionist government, rather than solving macroeconomic problems, could add to them because it is reacting in an untimely way, or to the wrong signals, or on behalf of special interests rather than the overall interests of the economy.

No   Government should not play a less active role in stabilizing the economy. According to Keynesian theory, there is no reason to expect an economy, left alone, to automatically reach a full employment level of output. According to Keynes, unemployment, or a recession, arises from a lack of total spending.

Unless total spending increases, or a spending "kick" occurs, the economy can remain stagnant. Since there is nothing inherent in the economy to ensure that this spending increase will occur, government is the logical choice to take the actions necessary to increase spending. It is efficient to give government the authority to lead the way. The wait for millions of decisions by individual households and businesses to spend more could be endless.

in buildings, equipment, and other productive resources more profitable, thereby stimulating growth in the economy. Lowering the tax burden on individuals is said to lead to greater savings (which could be channeled to businesses for investment purposes) and increased personal incentives to work. Government deregulation is also called for to increase productivity.

Supply-side proposals have a political as well as an economic dimension. Reducing taxes and regulatory requirements lessens the presence of government in private economic decision making.

The issue of how much government intervention in the macroeconomy is appropriate is a source of continuous debate. The position taken on this issue is often rooted in one of the theories just discussed. Up for Debate, "Should Government's Role in Influencing Economic Activity Be Reduced?", presents some of the arguments for and against government intervention.

INFLATION AND UNEMPLOYMENT

So far in this chapter we have focused on the several schools of thought that are concerned with understanding the causes of fluctuations in macroeconomic activity. Each of the schools looks at different variables: The classical and new classical economists explore price levels and output levels, Keynesian economists focus on spending and output levels, and monetarists center on the relationship between money and economic activity.

We know that two of the major macroeconomic problems are inflation and unemployment. Inflation is measured by the annual percentage increase in the general

| FIGURE 9.6 | *A Phillips Curve (Hypothetical Data)* |

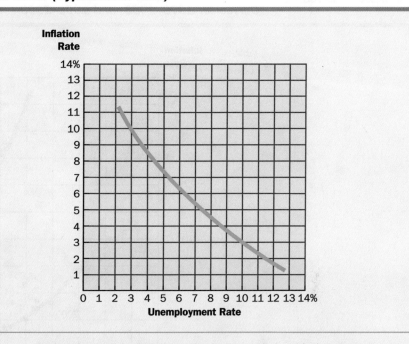

A Phillips curve slopes downward, illustrating the inverse relationship between unemployment and inflation rates.

price level, and unemployment is measured by the percentage of the labor force that is out of work and actively seeking employment. Although the relationship between these two problems has not been the main focus of a school of thought, it is useful to examine that relationship.

The Phillips Curve

Phillips Curve
Curve showing the relationship between an economy's unemployment and inflation rates.

The most popular method for exploring the connection between inflation and unemployment is through a Phillips curve. A **Phillips curve** is based on the assumption that an inverse relationship exists between rates of inflation and rates of unemployment. Figure 9.6 illustrates (using hypothetical data) a downward-sloping Phillips curve with this inverse relationship. Notice that a low inflation rate is associated with a high unemployment rate, and vice versa.

How might a Phillips curve for the U.S. economy look? Data showing the U.S. experience with unemployment and inflation from 1975 through 1985 and 1998 through 2008 are plotted in Figure 9.7. The unemployment and inflation rates for each year are represented by a point on the graph. Notice that both the unemployment and inflation rates were generally higher for 1975 through 1985 than for 1998 through 2008.

We can use these data points to construct representative Phillips curves. The experience of the mid-1970s to mid-1980s provides a clear-cut Phillips curve relationship showing a tradeoff between inflation and unemployment rates. This is shown in Figure 9.7 as PC1. The data also show us that the Phillips curve can shift over time. The line PC2 represents the inflation–unemployment tradeoff from the late-1990s through the

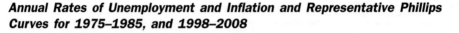

FIGURE 9.7   *Annual Rates of Unemployment and Inflation and Representative Phillips Curves for 1975–1985, and 1998–2008*

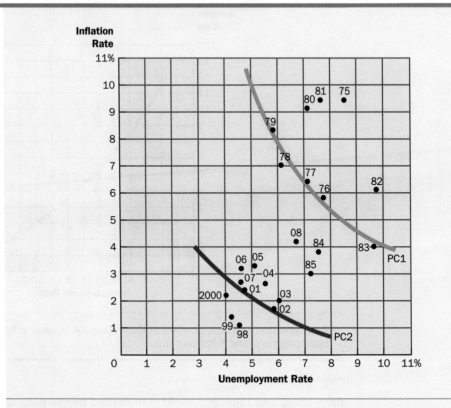

The generally lower unemployment and inflation rates from 1998 through 2008, as compared to 1975 through 1985, caused the Phillips curve to shift to the left, from PC1 to PC2.

Source: *Economic Report of the President* (Washington, DC: U.S. Government Printing Office, 2009), pp. 293, 327. The inflation rate is the annual change in the GDP implicit price deflator. The figures for 2008 are preliminary and not year end.

late-2000s. Here again you see the same inverse tradeoff. These curves also indicate that the tradeoff was much more pronounced in PC1 than in PC2.[6]

Analyzing the Behavior of the Phillips Curve   Several factors help to explain shifts in the Phillips curve: labor force data collection and structural changes, cost-push inflation, and eligibility for government transfer payments.

Participation in the labor force and the calculation of labor force data have an impact on the Phillips curve. During the 1970s the economy experienced increases in the labor force participation rates of women and teenagers, who, at that time, had higher unemployment rates than men. Their increased participation in the labor force could have raised the overall rate of unemployment accompanying any rate of inflation and helped to push the Phillips curve to the right.

[6]The Phillips curve is a general picture of the operation of the economy. It does not require that from each year to the next the inflation rate must go down if the unemployment rate goes up, or vice versa. For example, notice that from 1980 to 1981 both the unemployment and inflation rates went up.

However, by the late 1980s, labor force changes had contributed to the shift of the Phillips curve to the left. The rate of unemployment for women fell below the rate for men, and the movement of teenagers into the labor market began to reverse itself.

Since the late 1980s there has been an increase in the rate of involuntary part-time employment, which has affected the collection of unemployment data. Recall from Chapter 4 that a person who performs any work for pay, even just 1 hour per week, is considered employed, and that involuntary part-time employment has grown substantially. Thus, as more people who wanted full-time jobs settled for part-time jobs, the Phillips curve shifted to the left.

The U.S. experience with cost-push inflation (inflation originating on the sellers' side of the market) and the forces underlying that inflation also impacted the Phillips curve. In the 1970s and early 1980s the United States was plagued with serious cost-push inflation rooted in energy price increases, particularly oil prices. Because cost-push inflation does not respond to changes in aggregate spending (as does demand-pull inflation), it is possible to simultaneously have high unemployment due to a lack of spending and cost-push inflation, or to have stagflation. The stagflation experienced in the United States in the late 1970s and early 1980s is reflected in the PC1 Phillips curve in Figure 9.7.

Another factor that can influence the Phillips curve is the availability of government transfer payments when people become unemployed. Transfer payments, such as unemployment compensation, allow workers to fill in the income gap created by unemployment. Transfers, however, also allow persons who are unemployed to search for jobs with less intensity and willingness to accept a first offer than they would if the transfers were not available. The availability of more generous transfers increases the rate of unemployment associated with any rate of inflation and shifts the Phillips curve to the right. On the other hand, if unemployment compensation eligibility is exhausted or transfer payments are reduced, more people are forced to take jobs they otherwise would not have accepted, and the Phillips curve shifts to the left. Perhaps the inflation–unemployment points around PC2 can be explained in part by the more stringent requirements for receiving government transfers that were introduced in 1996. Test Your Understanding, "Unemployment and Inflation," allows you to draw some Phillips curves from hypothetical data and speculate about the factors causing a Phillips curve to shift.

A FINAL WORD ON MACROECONOMIC VIEWPOINTS

By the end of this chapter you have a good foundation for understanding macroeconomic theories and their relevance for solving macroeconomic problems. You have learned about past and present schools of economic thought that have made significant contributions to our understanding of the operation of the macroeconomy. Ideally, this chapter has provided the groundwork for informed judgments about past, present, and future efforts to understand and stabilize the economy.

It is helpful to keep in mind the discussion at the beginning of this chapter: An economic theory focuses on the relationship between two variables, and assumptions play an important role in the development of an economic theory. No theory is designed to explain all the complex relationships among the players and institutions in a macroeconomy. Furthermore, the economy is not composed of a set of simple relationships that can be easily manipulated to neatly solve various problems as they arise. One can be misled into thinking that a simple policy choice can cure all economic problems. In reality, there are many ramifications to choosing an economic theory as the basis for remedying an economic problem. Accordingly, the assumptions that underlie the theory should

TEST YOUR UNDERSTANDING

UNEMPLOYMENT AND INFLATION

Below are 15 years of unemployment and inflation data for a hypothetical economy. Answer each of the following questions on the basis of these data.

Year	Inflation Rate	Unemployment Rate
1996	2.0%	8.0%
1997	3.0	6.0
1998	3.5	7.0
1999	4.0	5.0
2000	7.5	4.0
2001	5.0	5.0
2002	6.5	4.5
2003	7.0	2.5
2004	5.5	2.0
2005	4.0	3.0
2006	3.0	2.5
2007	2.0	4.0
2008	2.5	3.5
2009	3.5	2.5
2010	1.5	4.5

1. Plot the 15 years of unemployment and inflation data in the accompanying graph and label each year's point, as was done in Figure 9.7.
2. Draw two Phillips curves that you think would accurately summarize the unemployment and inflation experience of this economy from 1996 through 2010. Label the curve for the earlier years PC1 and the curve for the later years PC2.
3. What structural changes in the labor force may have contributed to the shift in the Phillips curve from PC1 to PC2?
4. What changes in cost-push inflationary pressure may have contributed to this shift in the Phillips curve?
5. What changes in government policies on transfer payments may have contributed to this shift in the Phillips curve?

Inflation Rate (y-axis, 1% to 9%)
Unemployment Rate (x-axis, 0 to 9%)

Answers can be found at the back of the book.

---

be known, as should the consequences that could result from implementing policy based on the theory.

Macroeconomic theories and policy instruments must be updated and refined as conditions change and knowledge grows. The environment in which models are built and policy tools are employed is continually changing, and new data, questions, and issues constantly appear. Also, the task of assessing economic theories would be easier if we lived in **closed economies**, where events beyond a country's borders have no effect on its output, employment, prices, or policies. The reality is that we live in **open economies**, which are influenced by actions in countries around the world. Political unrest in the Middle East, reaction to the North American Free Trade Agreement (NAFTA), the development of strong banks and commerce in Asia, and other circumstances outside the United States impact the U.S. economy and policies to stabilize it. As commercial relationships become more global and the economy becomes more open, the need to refine and update our knowledge becomes even greater. It is risky to assume that an understanding of the way things operate today will be sufficient to deal with the problems of the future.

Closed Economy

An economy where foreign influences have no effect on output, employment, and prices.

Open Economy

An economy where foreign influences have an effect on output, employment, and prices.

Summary

1. Economic theory focuses on the relationship between two variables. Economic theories are explored within the context of a model that includes variables, assumptions, data collection and analysis, and conclusions. Because economic theories are often an attempt to identify the cause of an economic problem, macroeconomic theories frequently have an historical dimension.

2. There are several schools of thought important to the development and understanding of macroeconomics. These include classical, Keynesian, new classical, new Keynesian, and monetarism.

3. Classical economics was the prevailing school of thought prior to the 1930s and the Great Depression. The classical aggregate demand–aggregate supply model focuses on the relationship between price and wage levels and output levels. This model concludes that a free market economy's output level always self-corrects to full employment and that prices and wages increase and decrease with changes in aggregate demand. Increases in aggregate demand bring increases in prices and wages, and decreases in aggregate demand bring decreases in prices and wages.

4. Keynesian economics gained prominence during the 1930s when John Maynard Keynes introduced the ideas that a macroeconomy can move toward an equilibrium output level that is less than full employment and that no mechanism is built into the economy to automatically move it toward full employment. Keynes focused on the role of total spending in the economy, indicating that the equilibrium output level of an economy is a direct result of the level of total spending in the economy.

5. Macroequilibrium occurs in the Keynesian model when total spending equals total current output, or when the leakages from and injections into the spending stream are equal. When spending is greater than the current level of output, which is caused by injections exceeding leakages, the economy expands. When spending is less than the current level of output, which is caused by leakages exceeding injections, the economy contracts. Keynes advocated government intervention, or fiscal policy, to move the economy from equilibrium at low levels of output to equilibrium at a higher full employment level of output.

6. New classical economics was born in the 1970s when many of the world's economies experienced stagflation and Keynesian economics could not offer an explanation for the serious inflation. New classical economics focuses on an aggregate demand–aggregate supply model similar to the classical model. Aggregate demand is represented by a downward-sloping curve showing an inverse relationship between price and output demanded levels based on interest rate, wealth, and foreign trade effects.

7. New classical aggregate supply can be viewed in the short run or long run. In the short run, prices do not change at low levels of output, a direct

relationship exists between prices and output in the intermediate range, and at high levels of output prices are flexible upward and downward and output does not change. The long-run view of aggregate supply is based on the natural rate hypothesis: The economy moves toward the natural rate of unemployment as price changes bring aggregate demand into equality with aggregate supply. The new classical school advocates little government intervention in the economy because adaptive and rational expectations by households and businesses undermine the intentions of policymakers.

8. New Keynesian economics builds on the Keynesian view, emphasizes the inflexibility of prices and wages downward, and attempts to better connect macroeconomics to microeconomic decision making. New Keynesians also stress that the macroeconomy does not automatically adjust to full employment.

9. The monetarist school of thought focuses on the role of money in the economy and advocates changing the money supply to stabilize the macroeconomy. Supply-side economics focuses on policies to increase production and productivity.

10. An inverse relationship between rates of inflation and unemployment can be illustrated by a downward-sloping Phillips curve. Data from the U.S. economy show that the Phillips curve can shift. These shifts can result from changes in labor force data and structures, cost-push inflationary pressures, and changes in eligibility for government transfer payments.

11. In evaluating macroeconomic theories and policies, we must continually update our thinking to meet changing conditions. The economy is not composed of simple relationships that allow for neat solutions to economic problems. It must be remembered that individual economic theories focus on specific variables, and that all theories are built on underlying assumptions.

Key Terms and Concepts

Classical economics	Wealth effect
Keynesian economics	Foreign trade effect
Macroeconomic equilibrium	Natural rate hypothesis
Inventories	Adaptive expectations
Stagflation	Rational expectations
New classical economics	New Keynesian economics
Natural rate of unemployment	Monetarism
Interest rate effect	Monetarists

Supply-side economics   Closed economy

Phillips curve   Open economy

Review Questions

1. Identify the four basic components used to develop a model and explain how macroeconomic models can be influenced by history.

2. Using the graph below, draw an aggregate demand curve and an aggregate supply curve that represent the classical model of an economy operating at full employment. Label these as D and S.
    a. Label the price and wage level at which the economy is operating as P_0W_0.
    b. Draw a second aggregate demand curve showing a decrease in demand. Label that curve D1.
    c. Identify the level of output and level of prices and wages that would result when the economy fully adjusted to the decrease in demand. Label the new price and wage level P_1W_1.
    d. Explain how the economy arrived at its new position.

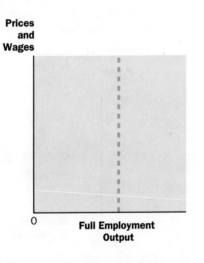

Prices
and
Wages

0   Full Employment
             Output

3. Fill in the table below, indicating where equilibrium output occurs as well as when the economy expands and when it contracts. On the accompanying graph, illustrate two lines. First, draw a "Spending equals Ouput" line and label it. Second, illustrate the relationship between "Total Spending" and "Total Output" in the table. All figures are in billions.

Total Output	Total Spending	Leakages	Injections	Economic Condition
$ 0	$ 240	$ 0	$240	_____
200	360	80	240	_____
400	480	160	240	_____
600	600	240	240	_____
800	720	320	240	_____
1,000	840	400	240	_____

**Total Spending
(Billions of Dollars)**

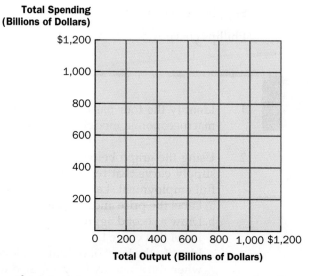

Total Output (Billions of Dollars)

4. Explain how the interest rate, wealth, and foreign trade effects are important to aggregate demand in the new classical model.

5. In the graphs below, illustrate the new classical view of aggregate supply in the short run and in the long run.

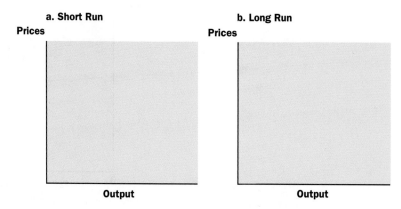

a. Short Run
Prices

Output

b. Long Run
Prices

Output

6. Draw curves in the graph below that illustrate Phillips curves for the United States for 1975–1985 and 1998–2008. Why has the shift occurred?

**Inflation
Rate**

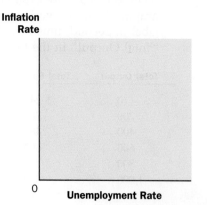

0   **Unemployment Rate**

7. What were the unemployment rate and inflation rate in the United States for each year since 2008? Do these numbers generally fall in line with PC2 in Figure 9.7? Comment on your findings.

8. Fill in the following table by providing, for each listed school of thought, the variables on which the theory is built, the conclusions with regard to the macroeconomy, and the role of government intervention advocated.

School of Thought	Variables	Conclusions	Government Intervention
Classical			
New classical			
Keynesian			

Discussion Questions

1. "When the economy is facing high rates of unemployment and inflation, policymakers must decide which of these problems to curb at the expense of the other." Is this statement accurate? What types of information should policymakers seek before deciding to sacrifice employment for price stability or price stability for employment?

2. Would you consider yourself to be classical, new classical, Keynesian, new Keynesian, monetarist, or other in your attitude toward macroeconomic policies? On what reasoning is your preference based?

3. What is the natural rate hypothesis and what problems does it cause for those wishing to pursue aggressive macroeconomic policies? What problems might adaptive and rational expectations cause for the government in its macroeconomic policymaking?

4. Macroeconomic policy proposals are frequently tied to political agendas. In your opinion, which of the policies that you have studied is politically the most desirable, and which is the least desirable? Explain.

5. Just as macroeconomic problems affect economic theory, they also affect the arts—visual art, music, and literature—of the day. Give an example of how a piece of visual art, a song, a novel, or a poem reflects the state of the macroeconomy at the time it was created.

6. How do the assumptions underlying the various theories you have studied in this chapter help to explain why debates on the proper role of government in macroeconomic activity can become so heated?

7. One lesson from this chapter is that the popularity of an economic theory depends in part on its ability to offer solutions for current, pressing problems. Because economic theories move in and out of fashion as conditions change, does this mean that they are not scientific after all?

Critical Thinking Case 9

DOES ANYONE CARE WHAT ECONOMISTS THINK?

Critical Thinking Skills

Identifying real-world implications from seemingly unreal-world concepts

Recognizing and evaluating values underlying technical arguments

Economic Concepts

Full employment—automatic or not

Government's role in managing the economy

We've just gone through several macroeconomic theories. In exploring these theories you have put up with graphs, theory-makers' assumptions, technical terms such as natural rate of unemployment, and radically differing views on how the world works. These theories are abstract and often contradictory. So much so that George Bernard Shaw said that if you laid all economists end to end you'd never arrive at a conclusion, and John Maynard Keynes hoped for the day when economists would be thought of as humble, competent people—like dentists.[a] Given all this, it is entirely reasonable to ask: "Why would policymakers or others in important decision-making positions pay any attention to what economists say?"

[a]John Maynard Keynes, *Essays in Persuasion* (New York: W.W. Norton, 1963), p. 373.

Questions

1. Do you think policymakers pay attention to ideas like those we have seen in this chapter? Why?

2. Each of the theories in this chapter directly or indirectly takes a position on what public officials should or should not be doing about the macroeconomy. Which of these theories would be supported by an administration wishing to actively manage the economy? Which would be opposed? Why?

3. Is it possible to develop a value-free economic theory? Is it possible to follow a policy that is compatible with all of the theories in this chapter?

4. Do you think policymakers are more likely to stick with long-accepted theories that they know or more likely to readily adopt new theories that address the problem at hand? Why?

PART 3

The Microeconomy

CHAPTER 10

Households and Businesses: An Overview

CHAPTER OBJECTIVES

To provide an overview of households and businesses.

To introduce sources and sizes of household income and types of household expenditures.

To define the basic objective of economic decision making by individuals.

To introduce the balancing process involved in an individual's spending and earning decisions.

To identify the legal forms of business, and to discuss business ownership of other businesses.

To discuss the goal of profit maximization or loss minimization in business decision making, and to explore some questions about this goal.

This chapter begins the study of microeconomics. While microeconomics and macroeconomics are the two major divisions in studying the field and share the common language and model-building techniques of economics, their focus is quite different. Macroeconomics looks at the total economy and how it functions, and studies the economic behavior of groups such as households, businesses, and government units. **Microeconomics** looks at decision making and how it influences the behavior of individuals in households and businesses.

This chapter is designed to give you background information about households and businesses before we do an in-depth study of microeconomic concepts. It is helpful first to know some basic terminology, a few statistics, and something about the economic objectives of decision making within households and businesses.

Microeconomics

The study of individual decision making units and markets within the economy.

OVERVIEW OF HOUSEHOLDS

When economists and others collect and analyze information about the U.S. population they often categorize these data by individuals, families, or households. For example, data tell us that in 2007, the population of the United States was about 302 million persons: 149 million men and 153 million women. The average age was 36 years old and most people lived in urban areas.[1]

People are included in family statistics only when two or more related individuals live together. As a consequence, many people are left out of family data. Household data are more inclusive, and usually preferable, since a **household** is made up of a person living alone or a group of related or unrelated persons who occupy a "housing unit," such as a house or an apartment. (Jails, military barracks, and college dorms do not count.)

In 2007, there were about 116 million households in the United States. The average size was about 2.6 persons (a slight decline in size over the past two decades) and about 27 percent of all households had just one person (a slight increase over the past two decades).[2]

Household

A person living alone or a group of related or unrelated persons who occupy a house, an apartment, or other housing unit.

Household Income and Expenditures

Do you remember the circular flow model in Chapter 2? In this model, households sell factors of production, like labor, for income, and use that income to buy goods and services. Since much economic decision making in household units revolves around these two areas, it is helpful to know something about the sources and sizes of household income and the types of expenditures that households make.

Household Income   Table 10.1 lists the sources of household pretax income, or **personal income,** on a percentage basis for selected years. The figures show that labor income is the primary source of household income and that fluctuations have occurred over the past few decades in the relative importance of all other income sources.

Table 10.1 also shows the importance of transfer payments in providing income: They were over 15 percent of personal income in 2008. Recall from Chapter 5 that **transfer payments** are money received from the government for which no direct work is performed in return. Government transfer payments include Social Security, unemployment, temporary disability, veterans' and public retirement benefits, public

Personal Income

Household gross, or pretax, income; used to pay taxes, spend, and save.

Transfer Payment

Money from the government for which no direct work is performed in return.

---

[1]U.S. Bureau of the Census, *Statistical Abstract of the United States: 2009*, 128th ed. (Washington, DC: U.S. Government Printing Office, 2009), pp. 7, 9, 10.
[2]*Statistical Abstract of the United States: 2009*, 128th ed., p. 52.

TABLE 10.1	*Sources of Personal Income (Percentage Distribution for Selected Years)*

Since 1980 there have been slight changes in the relative importance of income sources. Labor income and transfer payments are the largest.

Source of Income	1980	1990	2000	2008[a]
Earned income				
Wages, salaries, and other labor income	71.6%	68.4%	68.6%	66.5%
Proprietor's income	7.5	7.8	8.6	8.9
Rental income	1.3	1.0	1.8	0.5
Dividends	2.8	3.5	4.5	6.9
Interest	11.9	15.5	12.0	10.0
Unearned income				
Transfer payments	12.1	12.2	12.9	15.4
Personal contributions for social insurance[b]	−7.2	−8.4	−8.3	−8.2
Personal income[c]	100.0	100.0	100.0	100.0

[a]Data are preliminary.
[b]Contributions for social insurance are subtracted from earned income in calculating personal income.
[c]Columns may not total 100.0 because of rounding.

Source: *Economic Report of the President* (Washington, DC: U.S. Government Printing Office, 2009), pp. 318–319.

assistance, and others. Far and away, the largest amount of transfer payments (over 50 percent of total payments in any given year) goes to those covered under the Social Security Act.

How large is average household income? How much does it differ from household to household because of the gender, age, or education of the head of the household? The answers are in Table 10.2. The average income for all households in 2006 was $48,201, and there were significant differences among the average incomes for households when certain characteristics were observed. For example, family households headed by a married couple averaged $69,716, while families headed by a female (with no husband present) averaged $31,818. Not surprisingly, household income was lower for older adults who may be retired from the labor force. It is also important to notice the effect of education on average income. On average, household headed by a person with a bachelor's degree on average earned almost twice as much as a household headed by a high school graduate.

Household Expenditures   Basically, households use their incomes for three purposes: spending, paying taxes, and saving. In 2003, people on average spent about 79 percent of their income, paid about 19 percent in personal tax and nontax payments, and saved about 2 percent. In 2006, they spent about 80 percent of their income, paid about 21 percent in personal taxes and nontax payments, but had to borrow or dip into their savings by an amount equal to about 1 percent of their income to cover what turned out to be overspending.[3] These figures, however, can be misleading because they are averages. For higher incomes, a greater percentage is taxed and saved, and for lower incomes, a smaller percentage is taxed and saved.

[3]*Statistical Abstract of the United States: 2008,* 127th ed., p. 437.

TABLE 10.2	*Average Money Income of Households*[a]

The average income of households differs according to the gender, age, and education of the household head.

Characteristic	Average Income
All households	$48,201
Family headed by a married couple	69,716
Family headed by a female—husband absent	31,818
Household head aged 25–34 years	49,164
Household head aged 65 years or older	27,798
Household head graduated high school	39,426
Household head with bachelor's degree	75,861

[a]The average used is the median.

Source: *Statistical Abstract of the United States: 2009*, 128th ed., p. 443.

When we look at how households spend their money, a popular way to classify expenditures is by whether they are for durable goods, nondurable goods, or services. A **durable good** has a useful lifetime of more than one year—a car, musical instrument, or furniture, for example. A **nondurable good** has a short span of use, such as food or gasoline. In recent years, the largest portion of household expenditures has gone for services—medical care, for example. In 2007, people, on average, used about 56 percent of total expenditures for services, 29 percent for nondurable goods, and 15 percent for durable goods.[4] The percentages in these categories have not stayed constant over time; spending for services has been increasing.

Goals and Decisions of Individuals in Households

Think about all of the economic decisions that you make during a semester. Many of them are minor, like the choices between water and soda or chips and cookies from a vending machine; and many are major, like the choice of coursework, a place to live, or the kind of job to take on. During our lives all of us are constantly faced with decisions about how to use our money and our time. What is it that we are looking for as we make all of these decisions?

At first it might appear that there are a lot of different objectives that individuals could have when making economic decisions. But economists see all these decisions as ultimately coming down to one basic objective: Individuals try to obtain the most satisfaction possible from their decisions. In other words, people are out to maximize their economic well-being.

What do we mean by **maximizing our economic well-being?** Does it mean that we try to acquire all the goods and services that can possibly be obtained or that every waking hour is spent working in order to make lots of money? We derive satisfaction from the things we buy, the things we do, and the decisions we make. Some students really enjoy a cup of coffee in the morning; some dislike coffee. Some people enjoy their work; others find it mildly satisfying. Some students find economics

Durable Good

A good that has a useful lifetime of more than 1 year.

Nondurable Good

A good that has a short useful lifetime.

Maximizing Economic Well-Being

Obtaining the greatest possible satisfaction, or return, from an economic decision.

[4]*Economic Report of the President* (Washington, DC: U.S. Government Printing Office, 2008), p. 226. Data are preliminary.

fascinating; some find communications more attractive. And we can go on with many examples. The point is that everyone has things they enjoy more than others and things they dislike.

Maximizing economic well-being is a balancing process. It involves weighing the advantages, or benefits, and the disadvantages, or costs, of different courses of action and selecting the one that contributes most to economic satisfaction. In other words, people compare the satisfaction they get from various actions with the cost of those actions in making their choices. This notion of balancing costs and benefits in order to maximize economic well-being should become clearer as we apply it to basic spending and earning decisions.

Maximizing Satisfaction from Consuming Goods and Services   With limited incomes, people can't have all of the goods and services they want. This is the individual's own version of the basic economic problem of scarcity: limited resources in comparison to the wants and needs to be satisfied. In Chapter 1 we learned that scarcity imposes decisions and choices: Individuals must choose how to use their limited incomes.

Economists refer to the satisfaction received from consuming a good or service as **utility.** When you buy a lunch or put gas in your car, for example, you receive utility. The goal of an individual in making spending decisions is to choose the combination of goods and services that gives maximum total satisfaction, or maximum **total utility,** for a given amount of income spent. To maximize total utility, a person must, for each good or service that could be purchased, weigh the satisfaction that can be obtained from consuming that good or service against its price. This decision-making process can be illustrated through some simple examples.

Suppose that you are at a sporting event and would like a large, hot pretzel and a soda. All you have is $3, and the pretzel costs $3 and the soda costs $3. What will you buy? Obviously, you will spend your money on the good that adds the greatest amount of satisfaction. If it's the pretzel, you spend $3 for the pretzel; if it's the soda, that is where your money goes. To maximize satisfaction, your $3 will be spent on the thing that adds the most for the money to your total utility.

In this example, the choice is easy because the prices are the same. But what happens when a person is choosing among goods with different prices? Suppose that someone has $100 to spend and would like to get a pizza for $20, go out to dinner for $25, buy $100 worth of hockey tickets, get a new cell phone for $50, and buy a $10 paperback. With so many choices and just $100, what should this person buy?

Before making a decision, this person will weigh the added satisfaction from each item *in comparison to the dollars spent on that item.* If the entire $100 is spent for hockey tickets, satisfaction will be maximized only if those tickets add more than twice the satisfaction from the $50 cell phone, more than five times the satisfaction from the $20 pizza, more than four times the satisfaction from the $25 dinner, and so on.

The Utility–Price Rule   A simple rule emerges from the two preceding examples. To maximize total utility from spending a given income, a buyer must weigh the utility received from each good against the money spent on that good. In deciding between a pretzel and soda, you would have spent your $3 on the item that gave the greatest satisfaction for the money. In allocating $100 among the various alternative goods that could have been purchased in the previous example, the buyer would have weighed the added utility received from each item against its price.

Utility
Satisfaction realized from consuming a good or service.

Total Utility
Total satisfaction from consuming a particular combination of goods and services.

Maximizing utility is not simply a matter of receiving more satisfaction from one item than another: It is a matter of receiving more satisfaction *for the money.* While a person who is car shopping might get a lot of satisfaction from a new hybrid, the price tag is higher than that of a used car. Total satisfaction might be greater by buying a used car plus all of the other goods and services that the lower-priced car allows the person to purchase. Again, in making spending decisions, a maximizing person will consider both the added utility received from the item and the price of the item.[5]

Can this utility–price rule be seen at work in the real world? Do people really use this balancing principle in making purchasing decisions? The answer is yes, they do. The process might not be quite as precise as in the examples presented here, but basically consumers compare the price of an item with the expected addition to satisfaction from acquiring the item. Watch people at a vending machine or in line at a fast-food restaurant trying to choose the items that would give them the most satisfaction for their money. Or think of yourself as you grumble about, but do pay, the electric and other utility bills. Those bills are paid and the services continue because the satisfaction from having light, heat, and water is worth it. Can you see this balancing process at work in Application 10.1, "Family Gossip?"

Maximizing Satisfaction from Earning Income   As with spending decisions, maximizing satisfaction from working involves balancing benefits and costs. There are many considerations that go into the choice of a job: its mental and physical demands, pay, flexibility, availability of overtime work, full-time versus part-time, location, and such. Each of these considerations carries benefits and costs: A flexible-time job that accommodates a decent semester course schedule might pay less than a job with inflexible hours.

Consider the decision to work overtime. Putting in more hours provides additional income that can be spent on goods and services, but extra hours at work mean less time for other activities. The choice that a person makes is this: Is the extra income and satisfaction from working overtime enough to justify the dissatisfaction from forgoing other activities as a result of the extra work? For example, a student who works overtime might afford a better car and get away to Cancun over spring

---

[5]The utility-maximizing rule can be stated more precisely by comparing the added utility from consuming one more unit of each item to the item's price. Economists refer to the additional utility from consuming one more unit of an item as marginal utility. (Marginal utility is discussed more fully in Chapter 11.) If we divide the marginal utility from consuming one more unit of an item by the item's price, we can determine how much is added to total utility *per dollar spent on that item.*

Assume that a person is considering whether to buy Good X or Good Y. The marginal utility from consuming one more unit of Good X is 15 units of satisfaction and the price of Good X is $5.00. If MUx and Px stand for the marginal utility and price of Good X, then $MUx/Px = 15/\$5 = 3$ units of satisfaction for every dollar spent on that unit of Good X. One more unit of Good Y can be purchased for $8.00 and the marginal utility is 16 units of satisfaction. Comparing the marginal utility and price gives us $MUy/Py = 16/\$8 = 2$ units of satisfaction for every dollar spent on that unit of Good Y. Each dollar spent on the last unit of Good Y adds only two units of satisfaction, while every dollar spent on the last unit of Good X adds three. This person would be better off buying one more unit of Good X than Good Y.

When does a person pick exactly the right combination of goods and services to maximize total utility? Maximization occurs when the MU/P ratio is the same for the last unit of each of the items a person buys, or when:

$$MUa/Pa = MUb/Pb = MUc/Pc = \ldots .$$

When all the MU/P ratios are equal for the last unit of each good purchased, the expenditure on the last unit of each item adds as much to total utility as is added by the expenditure on the last unit of each other item. If the MU/P ratio for an item is greater than that of other items, a person should buy more of that item because it adds more *per dollar* to total satisfaction. If the MU/P ratio for an item is less than that of other items, a person should buy less of that item because it adds less *per dollar* to total satisfaction than other items.

APPLICATION 10.1

FAMILY GOSSIP

We all know that collection of assorted relatives—aunts, uncles, grandparents, cousins— who come together for family holidays, birthdays, reunions, and, of course, weddings. Seldom are these events without a good dose of family discussion, or plain and simple family gossip. Take the recent wedding of Jennifer, daughter of Fred and Lynne who spent a year planning the "perfect" day, not to mention the small fortune—almost a year of Lynne's salary—they put out.

At a table of close relatives, enjoying that perfect wedding dinner and reception, the whispering commentary ranged from choices about clothing to food and, of course, the money that was wisely or unwisely (in their opinion) spent. That's the way with family gossip: The genes that make relatives somewhat biologically alike do not necessarily make them alike in their decision making.

"I can't believe that Jen's plain dress cost $4,000! This didn't even include the shopping weekend in New York so that she and Lynne could get a big name designer dress. She could have looked just as beautiful in a dress bought at our local bridal shop for a fraction of that price, and at least it would have had some lace and sequins," reported an observing aunt. "I could have found plenty of uses for that money. Fred and Lynne are always complaining about their old furniture. I say—they should have bought the furniture. It lasts for years. That dress is for one day."

Later the discussion turned to the reception. One cousin commented, "Those big baskets of roses and lilies on every table are a showy waste. Smaller arrangements would have been just as tasteful. It was enough that the church was decked out with enormous vases and sprays and garlands. Such excessiveness." Another cousin said, "I love, love, love the flowers. They have created the most perfect scene for the occasion."

And so it went. One uncle wished for cheaper fried chicken rather than the tenderloin and shrimp; someone else praised the champagne. The wedding cake was too dry but delightfully decorated, a DJ would have worked rather than spending all that money on a live band, ... And everyone noted that when it was all over, the happy couple was moving into a small apartment. The price tag on this wedding was the equivalent of a huge down payment on a home.

The satisfaction we receive from various goods and services drives our spending decisions—and we are all different. Over our lifetime we will go to weddings big and small, some in parks, some in hotels. There will be fancy meal receptions and punch and cake in church halls. Sometimes guests will go home with a remembrance; sometimes with a dizzy head from good champagne. But, for sure, weddings are a great display of how people differ in their satisfaction levels, how they weigh costs and benefits, and how, ultimately, they use their scarce income.

break, but at the cost of a higher GPA. This student must determine whether the extra income is worth the cost. Application 10.2, "You Decide," gives three examples of people doing the cost-benefit balancing act when making career decisions. What is your opinion of each of these choices?

In summary, both spending and earning decisions involve the goal of maximizing economic well-being. The decision maker weighs the advantages, or benefits, and disadvantages, or costs, of different strategies to choose the one that comes closest to accomplishing that objective. This weighing, or balancing, which is at the heart of the individual decision-making process, is covered in detail in the next chapter.

OVERVIEW OF BUSINESS

Business

An organization established to produce and sell goods and services.

Since several of the following chapters focus on business decision making, it is important to have some basic knowledge about the business sector. A **business** is an organization established to produce and sell goods and services. In the United States there are over 28 million legally organized business firms. Many are small operations with annual sales of under $25,000; others are huge enterprises selling billions of dollars worth of goods and services each year.

Business decisions, especially about output and prices, have a powerful influence on the economy. A very large firm, like Wal-Mart, which employed more than

APPLICATION 10.2

YOU DECIDE

Each of the following cases deals with career decision making. You decide: was this a good choice or a bad choice in each example?

Declaring a Major   John is a sophomore majoring in history because he really enjoys it. That changed when he had lunch with his friend Carrie, who is majoring in a technical computer field. John was amazed to learn that one of Carrie's friends with this technical major got a job paying $60,000 a year right after graduating last May. After lunch, John started thinking seriously about changing his major. It's true that he has no interest in computer technology. But who cares if he can get a salary like that. He thought that maybe after a few years on the job he'd find something to like about it. After all, a job is just a job. The next day John went into the student advising office and declared Carrie's field as his new major.

Dealing with a Dreadful Boss   Anna really liked her job. The pay was good, she'd travel to Europe a few times a year on business, and she spent most of her time working on projects that interested her. Then the new boss arrived. It soon became clear that never in his life had he made a mistake (at least in his own mind).

The "Nightmare Boss," as he was quickly nicknamed by Anna's fellow workers, would walk into her office at 4:45 in the afternoon, put something on her desk, and say "Have this ready for me by tomorrow morning." Usually this meant about 5 or 6 hours of work that evening. Finally, Anna had enough. She started looking for other jobs and got some offers. While they paid well, they didn't interest her as much as her current work. After giving it a lot of thought, Anna decided that bosses come and go, and kept her current job.

Making Music   Dan is a pianist who loves music and is very good at it. He typically earns over $40,000 playing jobs about 200 times a year. The thing is, while Dan loves music, his playing keeps him away from his family. The kids are usually asleep when he gets home, and he is usually asleep when they leave for school. And sometimes he and his wife are like two ships passing in the night: She's coming in from work and he's on his way out. Also, while the playing is great, it's unpredictable: Just because he played a lot of jobs this year doesn't mean the jobs will be there next year. Dan decided to make a career change. He was always interested in teaching music and will take coursework to get a teaching certificate. Dan hopes to teach music full time at the local high school and still play jobs—but many fewer times and only when he wants to play.

2 million people in 2008, or one of the other firms listed in Table 10.3, can have a significant impact on employment conditions in an industry or region. A few large firms with a substantial share of a market that accounts for a significant amount of consumer spending could contribute to inflation by raising their prices.

Before we explore the specifics of business decision making, let us examine the legal forms of business and some structural aspects of U.S. businesses.

Legal Forms of Business

A business must take on a legal form before it can operate. It may be a

- proprietorship,
- partnership, or
- corporation.

Proprietorship   A one-owner business that is typically small—such as an antique shop or an independent consultant—is called a **proprietorship.** Usually in a proprietorship the owner is the manager and a jack-of-all-trades, performing the functions of a bookkeeper, financial analyst, and marketing specialist among others. For the owner of the business, this legal form has two advantages: It is relatively easy to start a business that is organized as a proprietorship, and there is independence in decision making. The owner is not responsible or answerable to anyone.

Proprietorship
A one-owner business.

TABLE 10.3	*The 10 Largest U.S. Corporate Employers: 2008*

The decisions of very large corporations that sell billions of dollars of output and employ hundreds of thousands of people can have a major impact on households, other businesses, government, and the economy in general.

Rank	Corporation	Number of Employees
1	Wal-Mart Stores	2,100,000
2	United Parcel Service	426,000
3	McDonald's	400,000
4	IBM	398,455
5	Target	351,000
6	Kroger	326,000
7	Citigroup	324,850
8	Sears Holdings	324,000
9	General Electric	323,000
10	Hewlett-Packard	321,000

Source: "Biggest Companies," *Fortune*, May 4, 2009, F-33.

A proprietorship, however, has several limitations: particularly, difficulty in raising money and unlimited liability. The sole proprietor who wants to raise money for expansion, remodeling, or other purposes can do so only by borrowing from private sources, such as family or friends, or from financial institutions like commercial banks, or through certain government programs. Because proprietorships cannot issue stocks and bonds, a large source of money capital cannot be readily tapped by the single-owner business.

A proprietorship is also subject to **unlimited liability;** that is, the owner's personal assets are subject to use as payment for business debts. If a creditor cannot be fully paid from the assets of the business, the courts may take the owner's personal property to satisfy such debts.

Unlimited Liability
A business owner's personal assets are subject to use as payment for business debts.

Partnership   A business that is similar to a proprietorship but has two or more (perhaps hundreds of) owners is a **partnership.** This arrangement permits the pooling of money, experience, and talent. For example, a person who is skilled in cooking and kitchen administration and a person who is adept at management and finance might create a successful restaurant. Unfortunately, partnerships often lead to dissension between partners and dissolution of the business.

Partnership
The legal organization of a business that is similar to a proprietorship but has two or more owners.

Unless it is legally specified in writing, all owners in a partnership are general partners. A **general partner** is one who has the burden of unlimited liability, and each partnership must have at least one general partner. If misunderstood, unlimited liability can create problems for a partner. In a partnership, each general partner is responsible for 100 percent of the business's debts. In case of default, liability is not necessarily divided in halves, thirds, or other equal amounts. Instead, the debts beyond those covered by the business's assets will be paid through the personal assets of whichever partners possess the means. If one general partner is penniless and the other wealthy, the partner with the assets will pay the debts.

General Partner
An owner in a partnership who is subject to unlimited liability.

Corporation

A legal entity, owned by stockholders; can carry on in its own name business functions normally performed by individuals.

Corporation   A **corporation** is a "legal person" created by law: It can sue or be sued, make contracts, pay fines, and carry on other aspects of business normally performed by individuals. Unlike humans, a corporation can continue indefinitely. To form a corporation, a charter, which involves some cost and red tape to acquire, must be obtained from a state.

As a corporation is established, shares of stock are sold (additional shares may be sold later), and the holders of those shares become the owners of the corporation. One major advantage for corporation owners is limited liability: Personal assets are *not* subject to payment for business debts. In case of bankruptcy, an owner can lose only the money used to purchase the stock. This sum, however, could be considerable.

The owners of a corporation receive profits through quarterly corporate dividend checks. How much profit a stockholder receives depends on the corporation's profitability, the type of stock the owner holds, and the amount of profit that is retained by the business. Corporations can issue both preferred and common stock. **Preferred stock** carries a stated dividend, and preferred stockholders are entitled to their dividends before common stockholders are paid. **Common stock** pays a dividend dependent on the profit position of the firm after creditors and preferred stockholders have been paid. A quarter with healthy sales and sizable profits might yield a healthy return on common stock, and a quarter with no profit will yield no dividend check.[6]

Preferred Stock

Pays a stated dividend to its holder; preferred stockholders are entitled to receive dividends before common stockholders.

Common Stock

Pays a dividend dependent on the profit of a firm after all other financial obligations have been met.

Corporate Board of Directors

Governing body of a corporation; elected by stockholders.

Each share of common stock entitles its owner to one vote on some corporate policies and, most importantly, to elect a board of directors. The **corporate board of directors** is the governing body of a corporation and makes many major decisions, including the selection of the corporation's CEO (chief executive officer) and other top management. These managers run the corporation on a day-to-day basis. Figure 10.1 outlines the structure of a corporation.

With each share of common stock carrying a vote, control of a corporation rests with those who hold a large portion of the stock. These stockholders have the power to elect themselves or their candidates to the board of directors. A person with a few thousand shares in a small corporation might have control over that business, but a few thousand shares in a company like Starbucks would be negligible. Test Your Understanding, "The Price of Stock Shares," discusses how the price of a share of stock is determined by supply and demand, and provides an opportunity to evaluate how changes in supply and demand affect a stock's price.

Bond

A financial instrument through which a corporation can borrow funds and repay them over the long term.

No discussion of a corporation is complete without some mention of **bonds.** Corporations can borrow large amounts of money for building, expansion, and other purposes by selling bonds. Bonds provide a corporation with an avenue other than stocks to tap other corporations, private individuals, and organizations for funds. Corporate bonds are typically sold in $1,000 denominations and have a specified interest rate and maturity date. A bondholder is a creditor of the company and not an owner.

Limited Liability Companies (LLCs)

Businesses that combine the liability protection of corporations with the management flexibility of proprietorships and partnerships.

Since the late 1970s there has been growing interest in the United States in forming **Limited Liability Companies,** or **LLCs,** which combine characteristics of the three legal forms of business we have just discussed. Like corporations, LLCs protect their members with limited liability. But like proprietorships and partnerships, they also allow greater decision-making flexibility than is typically found in corporations. Depending on its legal form and for tax purposes, an LLC can be classified as a proprietorship, partnership, or corporation.

---

[6]Preferred stock does not guarantee a dividend. If the company has not made enough profit for a return to the preferred stockholders, they will not receive a dividend. However, if the preferred stock is cumulative, the stockholders are entitled to receive the return at some future point when profit is made.

| FIGURE 10.1 | *Structure of a Corporation* |

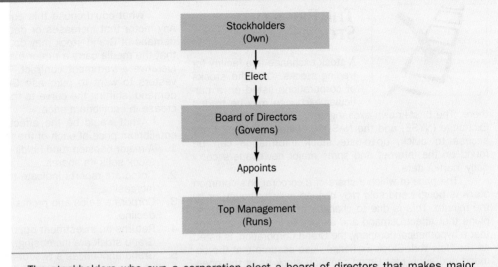

The stockholders who own a corporation elect a board of directors that makes major decisions for the corporation and appoints top management to run the corporation.

Numbers and Sizes of Businesses

How many businesses are there in the United States? How are they organized? Table 10.4 gives the number of legally organized businesses in the United States and the size of business receipts (sales) in 2005. There were about 30 million businesses, with the vast majority, about 72 percent, organized as proprietorships. Only 19 percent were corporations.

Table 10.4 also shows that most of the business receipts went to corporations. Of the $29 trillion in total sales, corporations accounted for about $24 trillion (or about 83 percent). Proprietorships received a little over 4 percent of the total sales. While the vast majority of businesses are proprietorships, they account for only a small percentage of the total sales of the economy. Corporations, which tend to be larger, account for most business sales.

Business Ownership of Business

Not all corporate stock is owned by private individuals. Much stock is owned by funds, such as pension, endowment, and mutual funds, and by other corporations. In fact, in many instances, the controlling shares of stock in one corporation are owned by another corporation. In these cases, the corporation that owns the stock is said to own the other corporation. It is often not readily apparent that one corporation owns another because both may retain separate identities and operate as separate businesses.

Merger (Acquisition)
The acquiring of one company by another; can be accomplished by buying a controlling amount of stock.

The buying of controlling shares of stock in one corporation by another corporation is referred to as a **merger** or **acquisition.** Merger activity in the United States has been high since the 1980s, and the price tags on many corporate acquisitions are in the billions of dollars. For example, in 2008 InBev acquired Anheuser-Busch for

TEST YOUR UNDERSTANDING

THE PRICE OF STOCK SHARES

A stock exchange is a facility for trading stocks. Only the stocks of corporations listed on a particular exchange may be traded there. The best-known exchanges are the New York Stock Exchange (NYSE) and the NASDAQ National Market. Easy access to quick, up-to-date stock information can be found on the Internet and some major newspapers carry daily market data.

The price at which a share of a corporation's common stock is bought and sold may change daily, or hourly, or by the minute. This is due to changes in buyers' and sellers' plans that affect demand and supply. To illustrate, assume that a hypothetical company, the Grand Corporation, is listed on the New York Stock Exchange. Also assume that the demand and supply for Grand common stock as of the opening of trading today is given in the figure shown here.

The downward-sloping demand curve indicates that as the price per share increases, buyers will decrease the quantity of shares demanded. The upward-sloping supply curve shows that as the price per share increases, sellers will be willing to sell more shares. In this market, the equilibrium price is $18.00 per share, and 3,000 shares are bought and sold.

What could cause this equilibrium price to change? Any factor that increases or decreases the supply and/or demand of Grand stock may do so. For example, suppose that the media carry a rumor that Grand is about to sign a lucrative government contract. This rumor can cause investors to want to purchase Grand stock, increasing its demand (shifting the curve to the right) and causing an increase in equilibrium price.

What would be the effect on demand, supply, and equilibrium price of each of the following?

1. A major pension fund holding a large amount of Grand stock sells its shares.
2. Corporate reports indicate that sales and profits are increasing.
3. Corporate sales and profits are on a slow, constant decline.
4. Returns on investment opportunities other than Grand stock are increasing.
5. Grand announces a two-for-one split of its stock in which each outstanding share is now worth two shares.
6. The stock market falls by a record amount, signaling a lack of investor confidence in the economy.
7. The Grand Corporation begins a policy of buying back its own stock on the market.

Answers can be found at the back of the book.

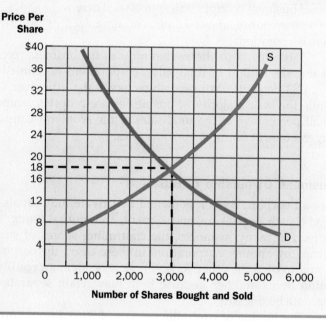

Price Per Share vs. Number of Shares Bought and Sold

| TABLE 10.4 | Number and Receipts of Proprietorships, Partnerships, and Corporations: 2005 |

Although the vast majority of U.S. firms are proprietorships, they account for a small percentage of business receipts. Most receipts go to corporations.

Business Firms	Number	Number as a Percentage of the Total	Receipts	Receipts as a Percentage of the Total
Total	29,903,000	100.0%	$29.0 trillion	100.0%
Proprietorships[a]	21,468,000	71.8	1.2 trillion	4.1
Partnerships	2,764,000	9.2	3.7 trillion	12.8
Corporations	5,671,000	19.0	24.1 trillion	83.1

[a]Includes only nonfarm businesses.

Source: *Statistical Abstract of the United States: 2009*, 128th ed., p. 483.

$52 billion, in 2005 Procter & Gamble acquired Gillette for $57 billion, and in 2000 Time Warner acquired AOL for $126 billion.[7]

When one corporation acquires another corporation and there is no relationship between the goods and services that the two corporations produce, the acquisition is called a **conglomerate merger.** A manufacturer of toys could acquire a carburetor company, or an electronic components producer could acquire a wallpaper firm. General Electric, for example, in addition to manufacturing major household appliances, jet engines, and other products, owns the media giant NBC Universal and GE Commercial Finance, which provides loans, leasing, insurance and other services.[8]

In some cases, a corporation may acquire other corporations that are closely related to it or to each other in some way. Pepsico, for example, owns, or has owned, Pepsi-Cola companies, Tropicana, Frito-Lay, Pizza Hut, Taco Bell, Kentucky Fried Chicken Corporation, and Quaker Foods.[9] When a corporation acquires another corporation that supplies its inputs or distributes its products, such as a supplier-distributor relationship between Pepsi Cola and Pizza Hut, a **vertical merger** has occurred. When a corporation acquires another firm that competes in the same market, as do some Pepsi and Tropicana products, a **horizontal merger** has taken place.

Sometimes a corporation is formed specifically for the purpose of owning or holding stock in other corporations. This type of company, which produces nothing itself, is termed a **holding company.** Figure 10.2 shows a hypothetical example of a bank holding company, Alltown Bank Corporation, which exists only to own controlling shares of stock in Hometown Bank, Downtown Bank, and other banks.

There are many reasons why one firm may seek to merge with another: to fill out a product line or move into a new geographic market, to acquire a company with large amounts of cash, to diversify, to avoid a hostile takeover from yet another company, or some other reason. Mergers and acquisitions are covered in more detail in Chapter 14.

Conglomerate Merger
A corporation acquires another corporation that produces unrelated goods and services.

Vertical Merger
A corporation acquires another corporation that supplies its inputs or distributes its products

Horizontal Merger
A corporation acquires another corporation that competes in the same market.

Holding Company
A corporation formed for the purpose of owning or holding stock in other corporations.

---

[7]Peter J. Howe, "AOL-Time Warner Deal Gets OK, FTC Blesses $126 Billion Merger but Sets Conditions to Ensure Competition," *Boston Globe*, December 15, 2000, p. D1; Robert Barker, "The Barker Portfolio," *Business Week*, July 25, 2005, p. 26; David Nicklaus, "Once-Bold A-B Folds in Face of Bigger Risk Taker," *St. Louis Post-Dispatch*, July 20, 2008, p. E1.

[8]GE Products & Services Overview: Introduction, Businesses, Categories, http://www.ge.com/products_services/index.html.

[9]Mergent FIS, *Moody's Industrial Manual: 2000* (New York: Mergent FIS, Inc., 2000), Vol. 1, p. 2642; Vol. 2, p. 6325; www.pepsico.com. Some of these acquisitions have subsequently been sold.

FIGURE 10.2   *The Alltown Bank Holding Company*

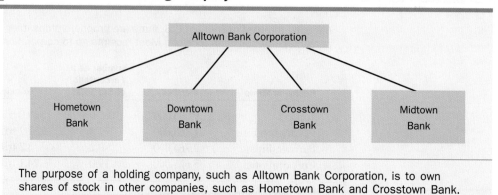

The purpose of a holding company, such as Alltown Bank Corporation, is to own shares of stock in other companies, such as Hometown Bank and Crosstown Bank.

Application 10.3, "Two Profiles: Starbucks and Kraft Foods," provides short profiles of two corporations that all of us know. It is interesting to see how these two companies differ with regard to mergers, ownership, and growth. Notice the holding company arrangement with Kraft Foods and the growth of Starbucks without major acquisitions.

Goals and Decisions of Business Firms

A typical business, large or small, is faced with many decisions about how to legally organize, what products to sell, how to price, whether to expand, and such. What is a business really trying to accomplish? What is the ultimate purpose of its decisions?

In the study of economics, as well as other areas, it is usually assumed that the fundamental objective of business decision making is to maximize a firm's profit or minimize its loss. This doesn't mean just earn any profit or avoid a loss, but rather earn the largest profit possible or take the smallest loss.

How does a firm measure profit or loss? When a business sells a product, the money received from its sales is called **revenue.** For example, when a doughnut shop sells 1,000 dozen of doughnuts a week for $7 per dozen, it receives a revenue of 1,000 times $7, or $7,000. Also, in producing a good or service, a business incurs costs for labor, materials, transportation, insurance, and other inputs. These costs are charged against revenue to determine whether a **profit or loss** has been made. So, for a business firm:

Revenue
Money or income that a company receives from selling its product.

Profit or Loss
What results when a business subtracts its costs from its revenue.

$$\text{profit or loss} = \text{revenue} - \text{costs}.$$

If revenue is $7,000 and costs are $5,000 the business earns a profit of $2,000. If revenue is $7,000 and costs are $7,500, there is a loss of $500.

Profit goes to the owners of a firm who bear the risk of its success or failure. In a proprietorship or partnership, profit goes to the owner(s) who organize and operate the business, and in a corporation it goes to the stockholders.

Profit maximization or loss minimization for a business is a balancing process, just as spending and earning decisions are for individuals. A firm weighs or balances the expected revenue and expected costs of each of the operating strategies from which it can choose, and then picks the one strategy that contributes most to its profitability. This balancing of revenues and costs is covered in detail in the next chapter.

Questions about Profit Maximization   The goal of profit maximization or loss minimization raises some interesting issues and debates. One question is simple: What

APPLICATION 10.3

Two Profiles: Starbucks and Kraft Foods

Starbucks Today Starbucks, named after the first mate in Melville's *Moby Dick*, is a household word and, for some, a necessity in life. While Starbucks began in 1971 in Seattle, it was the mid-1980s before the first Starbucks caffe latte was served and the Starbucks coffeehouse concept was born. And it wasn't until 1992 that common stock in Starbucks was publicly issued and traded.

Starbucks' growth has been huge. This company had just 162 stores in 1992, growing to 1,412 stores by 1997 and over 16,000 worldwide in 2008. Its revenues were $1.0 billion in 1997 and $9.4 billion in 2007—just 10 years later.

Starbucks has not merged with other large companies, although it has purchased a few small companies like Tazo, an Oregon tea company. Starbucks, however, has formed alliances and partnerships, and it has sought accounts that have extended its customer base. These include, for example, an alliance with Dreyer's Ice Cream to produce Starbucks Ice Cream, an agreement with Host Marriott International and Hyatt Hotels corporations, and a relationship with Barnes & Noble.

Starbucks has also built a reputation for social consciousness in doing business. It has partnered with Conservation International, a nonprofit organization, to promote environmentally sound methods of growing coffee, committed to purchase Fair Trade Certified coffee, published a Corporate Social Responsibility Annual Report, and created a foundation that has awarded millions of dollars for programs such as literacy.

Kraft Foods Oreos, Kool-Aid, Planter's Peanuts, Oscar Mayer, DiGiorno Pizza, Velveeta, and Grey Poupon are foodstuffs that we all know. All of these—and more—are products offered for sale by Kraft Foods. Over a century old, Kraft is the largest branded food and beverage company in North America and the second largest in the world. Thirty-five of its brands, including Jello-O and Oscar Mayer, are more than 100 years old.

Started in 1903 when James L. Kraft sold cheese from a horse-drawn wagon, Kraft grew over the next 100 years to a company that had over $37 billion in net revenues in 2007 and earned over $2.5 billion.

The history of the ownership of Kraft over the past few decades is an interesting story. As of April 2007 Kraft became a fully independent company; that is, Kraft is not owned by a holding company or another corporation. Prior to its independence, Kraft was owned by the Altria Group, a holding company formed in 1985 to become the parent company of Philip Morris, the tobacco company. Altria was to produce nothing on its own, but was to hold stock in other companies.

Prior to becoming part of the Altria Group in 2003, Kraft was owned by Philip Morris. In 1998 Philip Morris bought Kraft Foods for $13.1 billion. (Later, in 2000, Philip Morris bought the Nabisco division of RJ Reynolds—another tobacco giant—that had merged with Nabisco in 1985. Perhaps for diversification purposes, Philip Morris branched out into food products.)

In September of 2008 Kraft was named as one of the 30 key U.S. stocks comprising the Dow Jones Industrial Average.

Sources: "Company Profile," "Company Timeline," "Financial Highlights," " Company Fact Sheet," August 2005, Starbucks.com; http://www.starbucks.com/aboutus/pressdesc.asp?id=804, July 25, 2008; Melissa Allison, "Starbucks Shares Continue to Fall," *McClatchy-Tribune Business News*, July 8, 2008, wire feed; Jonathan Birchall, "Kraft Moves to Appease Peltz, *Financial Times* (London), November 8, 2007, p. 27; www.kraft.com; www.altria.com.

---

does profit maximization mean? Does maximizing mean that a business maintains the quality of its product, meets the needs of its workforce, and generally is a good citizen of the community as it seeks the largest profit possible? Or does it imply operating with minimum regard for quality, the environment, working conditions, and wages for the sake of a larger profit?

The relationship between profit-maximizing and socially responsible behavior is of great importance and is addressed in many political and legislative arenas. For example, today there are laws which penalize companies that—in the quest for more profit—destroy the environment, produce unsafe products, give misleading claims about their products, or disregard the rights of their workers.

Another issue centers on whether a business may actually seek some alternative goal other than profit maximization in the short run. For example, a company might sacrifice profits over the short run to introduce a new product into an untapped region of the country, or to get a head start in developing new technology that could

SHOULD PROFITABLE BUSINESSES BE EXPECTED TO ACTIVELY PARTICIPATE IN IMPROVING THEIR COMMUNITIES?

Issue   *Because successful, profitable businesses are part of their local communities, should they be expected to channel some of their resources into projects that benefit their communities?*

Yes   A successful business should be expected to actively participate in its local community. While it is true that businesses bring much to their communities in the form of jobs and in other ways, it is also true that they are given much by their communities in return. When a business considers locating in a community, it evaluates the quality of the schools for its employees' children; the public safety and fire departments that will protect its assets; the recreation, entertainment, and other events available to enrich its employees' lives; and health care services.

Businesses should think of themselves as partners in their communities. Successful businesses have human and financial resources at their disposal to make lasting contributions to the communities that they call home. Sponsoring community events and lending talent to projects and boards are important. In the long run these contributions could have a greater overall impact than that from providing a few extra dollars to each stockholder.

No   A successful business should not be expected to participate in its local community. The primary responsibility of a business is to its owners—not to its community. But even when a business is responsible to its owners, it automatically carries out activities that benefit its community as well. The contribution made by providing jobs for a community's citizens should not be undervalued. This is a contribution to which people give little thought until they learn that a local employer has fallen on hard times and may be forced to close its doors.

Businesses do actively support their communities by contributing tax dollars that are used for education, public safety, and streets, as well as paying off bonds for recreational or other community facilities. The tax revenue provided to a community by its businesses is significant to the financial health of that community. And finally, the question must be asked: Do we really want business managers to take larger social roles when, because of the resources at their disposal, their opinions may carry more weight than the opinions of other groups in the community?

revolutionize its industry. Is sacrificing profit in the short run in order to increase profit in the future inconsistent with the goal of profit maximization?

Debate also occurs over the importance of profit maximization to owners in the different forms of business. It is easy to see how profit maximization can explain the motivation of a sole proprietor or general partner, where the owner is directly involved in decision making. Sometimes it is more difficult to understand profit maximization in a large corporation, where stockholders are typically not directly involved in the decision-making process and where managers who receive fixed salaries run the firm.

Why would the managers of a large corporation be motivated to maximize profit? If the profit performance of a company is unsatisfactory, stockholders can replace the corporation's management. In addition, the fear of a hostile takeover by another corporation could also motivate managers, since a decline in the profitability of a corporation could lead to a drop in the price of its stock, making it cheaper for another firm to acquire shares and gain control. And with new ownership often comes new management of the acquired firm. Finally, in many instances top managers might be motivated to maximize profit because they themselves have significant holdings of the company's stock.

Questions about profit-maximizing behavior are also raised in Up for Debate: "Should Profitable Businesses Be Expected to Actively Participate in Improving Their Communities?". What is your opinion of the arguments on each side, and which side do you think makes the better case?

Summary

1. A household is made up of an individual living alone or several persons living in a group. The majority of household income comes from the sale of resources, particularly labor. Unearned income from government transfer payments is an important source of income. Of the different types of cash benefit transfer payments, Social Security is the largest.

2. The average income of all households taken as a group differs from the average incomes of various subgroups of households. This difference may be related to such factors as the education, age, or gender of the household head. Household income can be saved, used for paying taxes, or spent, with the vast majority going to purchase goods and services. Purchases of goods can be divided between expenditures on durable and nondurable goods.

3. The main economic objective of an individual's spending and earning decisions is to maximize economic well-being. Realizing this objective requires weighing alternatives and choosing the course of action that contributes most to economic satisfaction.

4. The satisfaction from buying a good or service is called utility. To maximize the total utility from spending a given sum of money, a purchaser must weigh the additional satisfaction from each unit of an item consumed against that item's price and compare that to the additional satisfaction and price of alternative goods and services. If one good costs twice as much as another but adds less than twice as much to total utility, a buyer should not purchase the more expensive good.

5. Earning decisions involve weighing and balancing costs and benefits. In the case of working more hours, the added satisfaction from more income is weighed against the added dissatisfaction from forgoing alternatives such as leisure time in order to earn that income.

6. A business is an organization established to produce and sell goods and services. A firm may be legally organized as a proprietorship, partnership, or corporation. Each of these legal forms of organization has certain advantages and disadvantages, such as the ease of starting the business and the nature of the owner's liability. Numerically, there are more proprietorships in the U.S. economy than there are partnerships and corporations, but most receipts go to corporations.

7. Many corporations have a controlling share of their stock owned by another corporation. When a corporation buys the controlling shares of stock in another corporation, a merger, or acquisition, has taken place. Because two firms are related through ownership is no reason to assume that the goods and services they produce are related in any functional way.

8. The basic objective of a business firm is to maximize profit or minimize loss. Profit or loss equals revenue minus costs. As is the case with a household, business profit maximizing requires balancing: in this case, the expected revenues and costs from different operating strategies.

9.   There are some questions concerning the profit-maximizing objective. These include the relationship between profit-maximizing and socially responsible behavior, and the extent to which a firm's other short-term goals are compatible with long-term profit maximization. It is easy to understand why profit maximizing is important to a sole proprietor or general partner, but there are also reasons why it is an important objective for the managers of a corporation.

Key Terms and Concepts

Microeconomics	Corporation
Household	Preferred stock
Personal income	Common stock
Transfer payment	Corporate board of directors
Durable good	Bond
Nondurable good	Limited Liability Companies (LLCs)
Maximizing economic well-being	Merger (acquisition)
Utility	Conglomerate merger
Total utility	Vertical merger
Utility maximization	Horizontal merger
Business	Holding company
Proprietorship	Revenue
Unlimited liability	Profit or loss
Partnership	Profit maximization
General partner	

Review Questions

1.   What are the main sources of household income and the different uses to which household income can be put? How is household income affected by the head of household's age, gender, education, and other factors?

2.   Would a person maximize satisfaction by buying a $15 product that adds twice as much satisfaction as a $5 product? Why? Would the person maximize satisfaction by buying the $15 product if the price of the other product was $10? Why? Explain the utility–price relationship that buyers use in maximizing their economic well-being.

3.   An individual maximizes economic well-being by making spending and earning decisions, and a business maximizes profit by deciding how much of its product to produce and sell. These decisions are similar in that they involve a balancing process.
    a. Generally, what is common to the balancing processes in decisions made by households and businesses?
    b. How do their decisions differ in terms of what is balanced?

4. Explain differences in the three basic forms of business: proprietorship, partnership, and corporation. What are the advantages and disadvantages of each form for the owners?

5. What is the difference between a stock and a bond? Why might it be necessary for a firm to issue bonds in order to acquire another firm?

6. What is the difference among a conglomerate merger, horizontal merger, and vertical merger? Give some examples of each.

7. Suppose a co-worker says: "What's required for a business to maximize profit is very simple: Produce the lowest-quality product you can, don't worry about the environment, and pay the lowest wages you can get away with." Do you think this is what profit maximizing is all about? Why?

Discussion Questions

1. Students who rent apartments close to college campuses often complain that they have to pay a lot for what they get. Explain, in terms of what you have learned in this chapter, why students, despite a limited income, will continue to rent at these high prices.

2. Over the years the amount of income spent on services in the United States has grown to the point where it is larger than the amount spent on both durable goods, such as automobiles, and nondurable goods, such as food, combined. How might this growth in the demand for services be explained by increases in the general standard of living, the movement of homemakers into the labor force, and the aging of the population? What other explanations might there be?

3. Can you explain in economic terms why someone with a so-called sweet tooth might be more than willing to buy an expensive chocolate mousse cake but would not consider buying a high-quality steak?

4. What factors should a person consider when choosing between two job offers?

5. Suppose that you are a business organization consultant, and three people come to you, each wanting to start a business. The first person wants to start a landscape design firm with her sister, the second a music store, and the third a barge line for moving coal on rivers. Each is seeking your advice on whether to organize as a proprietorship, partnership, or corporation. How would you advise each of them? Does it make any difference which form of organization each person chooses?

6. "Paying higher salaries to its workers, or incurring higher costs to increase its share of the market, does not mean that a firm is giving up the objective of maximum profit. Instead, it means that the firm is taking steps now to ensure that it will be able to maximize profit in the future." Do you agree or disagree with this statement? Explain your reasoning.

7. In a proprietorship the owner is often the manager, but in a corporation the owners are often different from the managers. What advantages and disadvantages might there be in having a separation of ownership and management?

Critical Thinking Case 10

TIME TO MAXIMIZE

Critical Thinking Skills

Identifying criteria for decision making

Clarifying frameworks in which decisions are made

Economic Concepts

Maximizing behavior

Costs and benefits

U.S. business managers have been criticized for using a 3-month time frame—the interval between quarterly dividend payments to stockholders—to make decisions that affect corporate profitability. "Stockholders want profit now, so 3 months is the time frame that matters most," goes the argument for looking only this far ahead. A strategy that will dramatically improve profit 5 years down the road may not be seriously considered if it requires stockholders to forgo profit they are expecting today or in the near future. The unavoidable question is: How profitable would a company be today if 5 years ago its management committed to a long-term program of profit enhancement rather than planning from dividend payment to dividend payment?

How far to look into the future when forming plans and making decisions—especially about spend-

ing and earning—is also important to individuals. Author Jeremy Rifkin noted that people with larger incomes tend to have longer time horizons when planning than do people with smaller incomes.[a] A person who is not sure there will be enough income to buy groceries and pay the rent and utility bills this month may find it hard to focus on a plan that will pay off 2 years down the road.

Maximizing behavior involves balancing the costs and benefits of different courses of action in order to identify the one that gives the most desirable result. What is "most desirable" may, however, depend on the time period on which the decision maker is focused. And what is most desirable over one time period may be undesirable over another.

[a]Jeremy Rifkin, *Time Wars* (New York: Simon & Schuster, 1987), pp. 192–194.

Questions

1.   Would a business trying to maximize its profits over 3-month intervals assign the same weights to specific costs and benefits as a business trying to maximize its profit over a 3- or 5-year period? Why?

2.   Would two college juniors make the same spending and earning decisions if one was planning to get a job after graduation and the other was planning to go to medical school? How would the criteria each uses for decision making differ?

3.   If the results of a decision depend on what time frame is considered, how can it be determined which time frame is right for making a decision?

CHAPTER 11

Benefits, Costs, and Maximization

CHAPTER OBJECTIVES

To explain the basic process of balancing costs and benefits in economic decision making.

To introduce marginal analysis, and to define marginal benefit and marginal cost and explain their relationship to total benefit and total cost.

To explain how individuals measure the costs and benefits of actions, and to introduce the Law of Diminishing Marginal Utility.

To explain the measurement of business costs, revenues, and profit, and to differentiate between normal and economic profit.

To identify the rules for maximizing satisfaction by individuals and maximizing profit by businesses.

To introduce the concepts of externalities and social costs and benefits.

To examine how individual costs and benefits form the basis of collective, or public, choices.

As we know, life is all about choices, big and small. Individuals and businesses are constantly making choices while weighing their costs and benefits to try to maximize some result. We choose how to spend our time and money; businesses choose products to sell and how to operate; and as a society we make collective choices that impact our lives.

Whether we are trying to figure out what to do on a Saturday night, or a developer is trying to decide about the best housing options for a project, or government officials are trying to set air quality standards, the thinking process in the decision making is the same. There are some simple thought mechanics used in balancing costs and benefits to find a best strategy. And the same processes are used by everyone: individuals, businesses, and society in general. This chapter introduces those mechanics.

In this chapter, we will learn how individuals, businesses, and society use some specific "rules" for maximizing as they go through the mechanics of weighing costs and benefits. You will also be introduced to marginal analysis, which is the basis of many microeconomic concepts. Marginal analysis will reappear in most of the following chapters.

Cost-Benefit Analysis

Weighing the costs and benefits of an action in order to maximize the net benefit from the action.

The formal study of the process of balancing costs and benefits, referred to as **cost-benefit analysis,** is helpful in evaluating business investment and production decisions, government spending decisions, and individual decisions concerning major purchases. However, the principles of cost-benefit analysis are not limited in their usefulness to evaluating major economic and financial decisions. The principles can be applied to many more areas of human experience than those dealt with in modern economics. The story of Adam and Eve, and the choice to eat the apple in the Garden of Eden, is a lesson in balancing costs and benefits, as is an expression such as:

'Tis better to have loved and lost
Than never to have loved at all.[1]

All rational decision making, be it economic or noneconomic, is based on the balancing of costs and benefits in order to, in the view of the decision maker, maximize something. This is true for the worker trying to maximize well-being by balancing the costs and benefits of working overtime or forgoing more income for the sake of leisure, for the child weighing the costs and benefits of lying to a parent, or for the painter deciding whether to move the ladder or stretch to reach the last few inches on a wall.

BALANCING BENEFITS AND COSTS: THE INDIVIDUAL

Defining Benefits and Costs

When people make decisions, from whether or not to carry an umbrella to class to whether or not to smoke, the goal of this decision making is to maximize, or to get the most from the decision. In doing so, an individual, usually subconsciously, uses a type of mathematical process, or applies certain mathematical rules, to weigh the costs and benefits of different courses of action. (Yes, even when trying to decide what to order at our favorite lunch spot, our brains are engaged in using mathematics to make a decision.) Before we thoroughly discuss this process and these rules, let's understand how an individual measures benefits and costs.

The benefit to a person from any action or purchase is the amount of satisfaction received from that action or purchase. This satisfaction, discussed in Chapter 10,

[1]Alfred Lord Tennyson, "In Memoriam," in *The Poetic and Dramatic Works of Alfred Lord Tennyson*, W. J. Rolfe, ed. (Boston: Houghton Mifflin Co., 1898), p. 170.

| TABLE 11.1 | *Ranking Satisfaction* |

People know what they like and dislike and are able to rank their preferences. The following lists various types of music that you may, or may not, enjoy. Find your favorite and give it 10 points of utility. Now compare all of the other types by giving each one points in comparison to your favorite. For example, if you like a type of music half as much as your favorite, give it 5 points; if you really dislike it, give it 0 points.

Type of Music	Number of Points
Blues	_____
Classical	_____
Country	_____
Jazz	_____
Latin	_____
New Age	_____
Opera	_____
Polka	_____
Rap	_____
Rock	_____

Utility
Satisfaction realized from the consumption of a good or service or taking an action.

is referred to as **utility.** In order to understand the behavior of utility, assume people have a small meter in their heads called a "Util-O-Meter." This meter measures total utility by clicking off points according to the amount of satisfaction received from each additional performance of an action or from the consumption of each additional unit of a good or service.

Any measurement of satisfaction is highly subjective, as are the numbers registered on a Util-O-Meter for the benefits received from any action or purchase. Because of this, it is extremely difficult for two people to compare the degree of satisfaction received by each from taking the same action, such as eating a slice of pizza. However, a person can compare the degree of satisfaction that the person receives from different actions or purchases from which that person can choose. You, for example, know whether you enjoy a popular recording more, much more, or not as much as Mahler's Seventh Symphony. Try the exercise in Table 11.1 to reinforce this point.

An individual usually measures the cost of an item by the dollars paid for it. As discussed in Chapter 1, however, cost can also be measured in terms of the alternative or opportunity forgone to acquire an item or take an action. That is, the cost of something can be measured in terms of its **opportunity cost.** For example, the cost of a $100 textbook could be measured by the dollars required to obtain it or by the football tickets, groceries, shirt, or whatever else would have otherwise been purchased.

Opportunity Cost
The cost of acquiring a good or service or taking an action measured in terms of the value of the opportunity or alternative forgone.

Everything one does has an opportunity cost. The cost of attending a class could be sleep, watching a television program, or working an extra hour at a job. What is your opportunity cost of reading this chapter now?

We can relate opportunity costs to utility, or satisfaction, by measuring the points that would have been added to a Util-O-Meter had another course of action been chosen. For example, if by registering for next term you gave up 1 hour of running, which would have added 125 points to your total utility, then the opportunity cost of registering was 125 points.

Measuring Benefits and Costs

In the example that follows, we will show how individuals measure the benefits and costs of actions and how they apply some simple mathematical maximizing rules to their decision making. This example deals with a student who is planning to spend an evening at a concert on campus. The concert is lengthy and informal: People can come and go as they please. There is no admission charge, but the concert is not free because someone who attends has an opportunity cost in terms of time.

Remember that people try to maximize their satisfaction in taking actions. In this case, the individual going to the concert is attempting to maximize the satisfaction from the time spent during the course of the evening. This means that our concertgoer may spend the entire evening at the concert or may at some point have something else preferable to do and leave the concert. In this example, we will determine whether satisfaction is maximized by attending the entire concert, which lasts for 5 hours, or by leaving after the first, second, third, or fourth hour.

Measuring Benefits   By attending the concert, our student receives satisfaction, or utility: The concert adds points to the individual's Util-O-Meter. Each additional hour spent at the concert adds a certain number of points to total satisfaction. The *change* in total satisfaction from attending each additional hour is called **marginal benefit,** or **marginal utility.** The *total* satisfaction received by attending the concert for a specified number of hours is called **total benefit,** or **total utility.**

Marginal Benefit (Marginal Utility)
The change in total satisfaction from consuming an additional unit of a good, service, or activity.

Total Benefit (Total Utility)
The total amount of satisfaction received from consuming a specified number of units of a good, service, or activity.

Let's assume that our student's Util-O-Meter registers zero before the concert. Let us further assume that by the end of the first hour, 400 points of utility have clicked onto the meter. This means that the total benefit, or utility, from spending 1 hour at the concert is 400 points. At the end of the second hour, 700 points are registered on the meter; or we can say that the total benefit from spending 2 hours at the concert is 700 points. At the end of 3 hours, 900 points are registered; at the end of 4 hours, the total utility received is 1,000 points; and after 5 hours, the meter still registers 1,000 points. This information is given in Table 11.2 in the column labeled Total Benefit (Utility).

Marginal benefit, or utility, is the *change* in total benefit that results from attending the concert for each *additional* hour. Because the Util-O-Meter registered zero before the concert and 400 points at the end of 1 hour, the marginal benefit from the first hour is 400 points. At the end of the second hour, 700 points of total benefit are registered, which means that 300 points of utility are added during the second hour (700 points in total utility at the end of the second hour minus 400 points at the end of the first). Thus, the marginal utility, or benefit, of the second hour is 300 points. During the third hour, 200 points of marginal benefit are added (total benefit increases from 700 to 900 points). The marginal benefit of the fourth hour is 100 points; and the marginal benefit of the fifth hour is zero points because total benefit does not increase from the end of the fourth to the end of the fifth hour. These measures are given in Table 11.2 in the column labeled Marginal Benefit (Utility).

You may have noticed that the marginal benefit points given in Table 11.2 are listed midway between the hours. This is done because marginal values refer to *changes* in total values. When showing a change in total value, or marginal value, in a table like 11.2, the common practice is to place the number for the marginal value between the start point and end point of what is being measured.

Notice that the marginal benefit points decrease with each additional hour spent at the concert. In this example, this individual really enjoys the first hour, finds the second hour slightly less satisfying, and finds each successive hour less enjoyable than

TABLE 11.2	*Utility Points from Attending a Concert*

Total benefit, or utility, is the total satisfaction from consuming a particular amount of a good, service, or activity; marginal benefit, or utility, is the change in total satisfaction from consuming an additional unit of a good, service, or activity.

Number of Hours Attended	Total Benefit (Utility)	Marginal Benefit (Utility)
0	0 points	
		400 points
1	400 points	
		300 points
2	700 points	
		200 points
3	900 points	
		100 points
4	1,000 points	
		0 points
5	1,000 points	

Law of Diminishing Marginal Utility

As additional units of an item are consumed, beyond some point each successive unit of the item consumed will add less to total utility than was added by the unit consumed just before it.

the previous one. By the fifth hour no additional satisfaction is received. This result is consistent with a principle in economics called the **Law of Diminishing Marginal Utility.** This law states that, as additional units of an item are consumed, *beyond some point* each successive unit consumed adds less to total utility than was added by the unit consumed just before it. In other words, as an individual consumes a good or service, there is some point beyond which he or she enjoys each additional unit of the item less.[2] Food is an excellent example of this principle. If you are eating pizza, tacos, doughnuts, or anything else, there is some point beyond which each additional piece of pizza or taco or doughnut gives you less satisfaction than the one before it. Do you generally enjoy the fourth doughnut as much as the first? Would you enjoy a second bike or cell phone as much as the first, and do you find the third hour of a 3-hour lecture class as satisfying and stimulating as the second or first hour?

Measuring Costs   In our concertgoer example, the student faces costs as well as receiving benefits from attending the concert. These costs are opportunity costs based on forgone uses of the student's time, such as studying or watching television, which would have also given the student satisfaction, or would have added points to the student's Util-O-Meter. Thus, the costs of the concert can be measured by the number of forgone utility points from alternative opportunities.

Total Cost

The cost of producing a specified number of units of a good, service, or activity.

Table 11.3 gives the total and marginal costs, measured in forgone satisfaction points, of spending the evening at the concert. **Total cost** is the cost of spending a

---

[2]We are not suggesting that the second unit consumed of an item *will always* add less satisfaction than the first or that the third unit *will always* add less satisfaction than the second. Rather, as successive units of an item are consumed, *eventually* a point will be reached where each additional unit consumed will add less to total satisfaction than was added by the previous unit. This point may arrive early on, as in the case of our concertgoer, or after the consumption of a large amount of an item.

TABLE 11.3	*Total and Marginal Costs of Attending a Concert*

Both the total and marginal costs of an activity, such as attending a concert, can be measured in terms of the utility points that are given up by forgoing an alternative use of time.

Number of Hours Attended	Total Cost	Marginal Cost
0	0 points	
		25 points
1	25 points	
		50 points
2	75 points	
		100 points
3	175 points	
		200 points
4	375 points	
		625 points
5	1,000 points	

Marginal Cost

The change in total cost from each additional unit of a good, service, or activity produced.

specified number of hours at the concert. **Marginal cost** is the change in total cost from each additional hour spent at the concert. As before, the marginal measurements are given at the midpoints between the hours.

Our student has many alternatives to attending the concert. Assume that one alternative to attending the concert for 1 hour is doing laundry. This action would give our concertgoer 25 Util-O-Meter points, thereby making the marginal opportunity cost of the first hour at the concert 25 points. These 25 marginal cost points equal the total cost for attending the concert for 1 hour because no previous total cost points have been accumulated.

To attend the second hour of the concert, assume that the student in our example gives up watching a television program that would have yielded 50 additional points of satisfaction, thereby making the marginal cost of the second hour 50 points. When these 50 marginal points are added to the total cost of 25 points for the first hour, the total cost of 2 hours at the concert becomes 75 points. The marginal cost of the third hour is 100 points of satisfaction that our student would have received from socializing with a friend. When these 100 marginal points are added to the 75 total cost points for 2 hours spent at the concert, the total cost of 3 hours at the concert becomes 175 points.

The alternative to the fourth hour at the concert is studying for an economics quiz that must be taken the following morning. The marginal cost of this hour is the 200 points that would be added to total satisfaction by working for a good grade on the quiz. These points, when added to the 175 points for 3 hours, make the total cost of 4 hours at the concert 375 points. The marginal cost of the fifth hour is 625 points, which is the satisfaction that would be received by putting the finishing touches on an application to a law school that has to go out the following morning. These 625 marginal cost points bring the total cost of attending the entire 5-hour concert to 1,000 points.

Notice that the marginal cost of attending each additional hour of the concert rises with the number of hours attended. The individual first gives up those alternatives that cost the least, and, as the evening goes on, the alternatives become more and more expensive.

TABLE 11.4	Benefits and Costs of Attending a Concert (in Utility Points)

Net benefit is maximized at the point where total benefit exceeds total cost by the greatest amount. Net benefit increases as long as marginal benefit is greater than marginal cost and decreases when marginal cost is greater than marginal benefit.

Number of Hours Attended	Net Benefit	Total Benefit	Total Cost	Marginal Benefit	Marginal Cost
0	0	0	0		
				400	25
1	375	400	25		
				300	50
2	625	700	75		
				200	100
3	725	900	175		
				100	200
4	625	1,000	375		
				0	625
5	0	1,000	1,000		

Maximizing Satisfaction

So far we have measured the benefits and costs for a student spending an evening at a concert. Remembering that the goal of any action is to maximize satisfaction, we will now evaluate these benefits and costs to determine the number of hours that the student would spend at the concert to accomplish this objective.

Table 11.4 lists the concertgoer's total and marginal benefits as well as the total and marginal costs that were given in Tables 11.2 and 11.3. Table 11.4 also includes a measure of the net benefit received from spending a specified number of hours at the concert. Net benefit is what the concertgoer is trying to maximize. Table 11.4 indicates that the net benefit of 1 hour at the concert is 375 points, the net benefit of 2 hours is 625 points, and so on.

The net benefit points given in Table 11.4 show that satisfaction from the concert is maximized by attending for 3 hours. At the end of 3 hours, 725 net benefit points, the most that our student can get from this concert, have been realized. Attending the concert for just 1 or 2 hours or staying for 4 or 5 hours will yield less satisfaction than 725 points.

How is net benefit calculated? The **net benefit** for a specified number of hours at the concert is simply the result when the total cost of those hours is subtracted from the total benefit. For example, as shown in Table 11.4, the total benefit from attending the concert for 1 hour is 400 points and the total cost is 25 points, leaving a net benefit of 375 points; the total benefit from attending for 2 hours is 700 points and the total cost is 75 points, leaving a net benefit of 625 points; and so on.

Net Benefit

The result when total cost is subtracted from total benefit.

Net Benefit Maximizing Rules

Net benefit is maximized where total benefit exceeds total cost by the greatest amount or where marginal benefit equals marginal cost.

Net Benefit Maximizing Rules   There are two **net benefit maximizing rules** with each rule providing the same answer.

♦ Net benefit is maximized where total benefit exceeds total cost by the greatest amount.
♦ Net benefit is maximized where marginal benefit equals marginal cost.

For our student, net benefit is maximized at 3 hours. It is easy to apply the first rule and see this result. But the second rule, the marginal benefit equals marginal cost rule, is not so easy to see. Let's go back to Table 11.4.

For the first hour of the concert, the marginal benefit is 400 points and the marginal cost is 25 points. If you think of marginal benefit as adding points to a Util-O-Meter and marginal cost as subtracting points, then 400 points are added and 25 are subtracted during the first hour, leaving a gain in satisfaction, or gain in net benefit, of 375 points.

During the second hour, 300 more points, the marginal benefit, are added and 50 points, the marginal cost, are subtracted. The result is a gain in net benefit of 250 points to be added to the gain from the first hour. Thus, the net benefit after 2 hours is 625 points (375 points from the first hour plus 250 points from the second hour). During the third hour, 200 marginal benefit points are added and only 100 marginal cost points are subtracted, increasing the net benefit registered by 100 points and bringing it to 725 on the Util-O-Meter.

Notice that for each of these 3 hours, marginal benefit is greater than marginal cost, causing net benefit to increase. But also notice that marginal benefit is shrinking and marginal cost is growing. At some point they will be equal.

During the fourth hour, the marginal benefit is only 100 points, but the marginal cost is 200 points, causing more to be subtracted from total satisfaction than is added. Because of this, net benefit falls from 725 points to 625 points. If our student stayed at the concert for a fourth hour, that fourth hour would cost more satisfaction than it would give. During the fifth hour no points are added, but 625 are subtracted, causing net benefit again to fall.

We can see that our student is increasing satisfaction, or net benefit, by attending the concert as long as more utility points are added from the concert than would be added from the alternatives. Once the alternatives become more attractive, it is to the individual's advantage to switch from the concert to an alternative.

Clearly, using the marginal cost–marginal benefit approach, net benefit is maximized by attending the concert for 3 hours. During the third hour, more marginal benefit points are added than marginal cost points are subtracted, but during the fourth hour more marginal cost points are subtracted than marginal benefit points are added. The concertgoer should leave at the end of 3 hours because at this point marginal cost equals marginal benefit. This equality will be easy to see when this relationship is graphed in the next section.

From this we can conclude that

♦ net benefit increases as long as marginal benefit is greater than marginal cost, no matter how small the difference;
♦ net benefit decreases when marginal cost becomes greater than marginal benefit because more is subtracted than is added to satisfaction; and
♦ net benefit is maximized at the point where marginal cost equals marginal benefit.

In summary, this example illustrates the two rules for maximizing net benefit, both yielding the same result. These rules are so important that we will restate them one more time. Maximization occurs where total benefit exceeds total cost by the greatest amount or where marginal benefit equals marginal cost.

Would you act as the student in our example did? Most likely you would. Have you ever returned early from a date, movie, or shopping because an important test or

APPLICATION 11.1

DO IT YOURSELF

Let's face it—economists generally do not have a reputation for being exciting, wild, and zingy. Perhaps it is their preoccupation with analysis that makes the average person think of adjectives like *staid* and *serious* when generalizing about economists.

So, what about your authors? You will have spent an entire course reading this text, perhaps thinking that the writers are somber individuals who don't think about much except economics. You might be surprised.

Few among us are unaware of the plethora of stores—like Home Depot and Lowe's—catering to "do-it-yourself" projects. Your authors, like "regular" people, think about painting, home repair, the lawn, the falling-in garage, and all the other things that require attention in an 80-year-old house. And they balance off the costs and benefits of getting work done by the local handyman or painter or doing it themselves.

Since the biggest commitment for any do-it-yourself project is time, the authors, like anyone else, figure out whether investing the time is worth it. Some of it comes down to alternatives and some down to sheer satisfaction. Like the student who would like to paint her apartment and can afford the few gallons of paint, but thinks twice about it because of the need to spend some time studying, the authors think about the alternative uses of their time.

In addition to the demands of teaching and writing that are time consuming, there is the sheer satisfaction of doing a job yourself. And that is where the rubber usually hits the road—for any of us. Pat professes there is little time to do home projects and jokes that his favorite tool is the checkbook. While you might think that he is too busy reading and enjoying economics articles, the real reason is his love of music. Playing out with his jazz quartet and taking in a set at a jazz club yield untold utility points or satisfaction for him. Home projects are way down on his list. Gerry, on the other hand, is happiest with a shovel, loads of compost, wallpaper paste, plaster, and frequent visits to Home Depot. She would rather use that checkbook for plants, landscape design projects, and other tools. Home and garden projects are laden with satisfaction for her.

Sooner or later, we all realize that our lives and our decisions are pretty basic and really do come down to a cost-benefit analysis. Understanding that balance between costs and benefits makes us smarter—but, importantly, it also makes us thoughtful in our relationships with family members and friends who may not share our "loves" in life. Understanding this economics stuff actually makes life easier to negotiate.

job interview was scheduled early the next morning? You have applied the maximizing rules in countless situations where you, perhaps subconsciously, weighed the marginal cost and marginal benefit of an action. For example, the decision of whether to eat one more chocolate chip cookie involves balancing the additional cost of the extra calories against the additional enjoyment from the cookie. Other decisions, such as which route to take to work on a snowy day, or whether to access online student tutorials that accompany a textbook, or whether to purchase an expensive or cheap pair of boots, all involve an application of the maximizing rules. What are some of the marginal costs and marginal benefits that might be considered in deciding whether to break the speed limit to arrive at work on time? Application 11.1, "Do It Yourself," gives some additional examples of the application of cost-benefit principles. Do you recognize yourself or someone you know in this application?

Graphing Costs, Benefits, and Net Benefit

The relationships that were just introduced can be illustrated graphically. Our student's total cost and total benefit from attending the concert are shown in the upper graph of Figure 11.1, marginal cost and marginal benefit are given in the middle graph, and net benefit is shown in the lower graph. These figures are plotted from the information in Table 11.4.

As long as total benefit is greater than total cost, there is a positive net benefit. As can be seen in the upper graph of Figure 11.1, net benefit is equal to the vertical

FIGURE 11.1   *Total Cost and Benefit, Marginal Cost and Benefit, and Net Benefit*

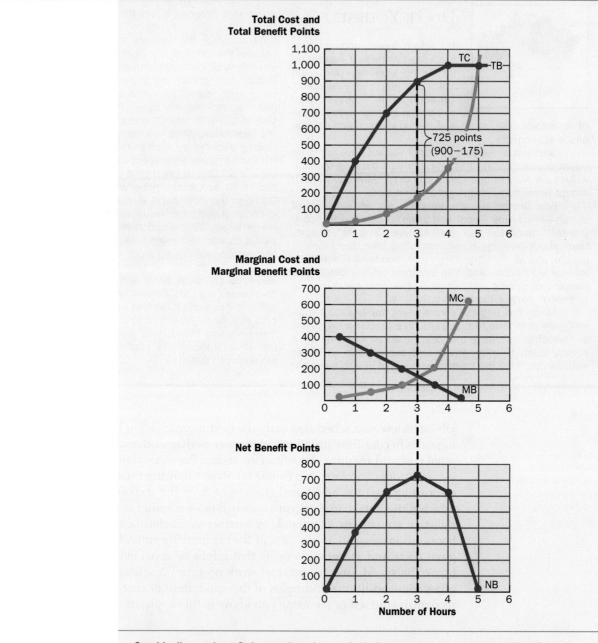

Graphically, net benefit is equal to the vertical distance between the total benefit and total cost curves; it is at its maximum where total benefit exceeds total cost by the greatest amount. Net benefit is increasing when marginal benefit is greater than marginal cost, at its maximum when marginal benefit equals marginal cost, and decreasing when marginal benefit is less than marginal cost.

distance between total benefit and total cost for any given number of hours spent attending the concert. Thus, maximum net benefit occurs where the vertical distance between total benefit and total cost is the greatest in the upper graph or at the highest point on the net benefit curve in the lower graph. This occurs at 3 hours.

Notice also that as long as marginal benefit is greater than marginal cost in the middle graph, net benefit increases in the lower graph, and when marginal cost is greater than marginal benefit, net benefit falls. Net benefit reaches its maximum where marginal cost equals marginal benefit. This again occurs at 3 hours. You might also notice that marginal cost and marginal benefit are plotted at the midpoints, just as they were given at the midpoints in the tables.

BALANCING BENEFITS AND COSTS: THE BUSINESS

Defining Benefits and Costs

Just like individuals, businesses are constantly making decisions. These range from deciding among candidates to fill a part-time job to advertising budgets to possible mergers. While it may appear that business decision making is quite different from individual decision making, it is actually similar in several respects. Like individuals, businesses try to maximize their economic well-being. And, just like individuals, maximizing by a business requires balancing the costs and benefits of different courses of action to find the one most in its interest.

But a business differs from an individual in that its economic well-being is generally measured in terms of profit rather than utility, or satisfaction. So the goal of a business is to weigh its benefits, which are measured by the revenue it receives from selling a product, against its costs of producing the product to find the output level that maximizes its profit.

In economics, we categorize the various costs of producing a firm's good or service into two groups: explicit and implicit costs. **Explicit costs** are direct payments, or actual dollar outlays, made by a business for a workforce, materials, machinery, equipment, and so forth. The monthly paychecks that a company issues to its employees, liability insurance payments, and checks to the local paper for an ad are all examples of explicit costs. Explicit costs are sometimes called accounting costs.

Implicit costs are not direct payments for inputs but are opportunity costs to the owner(s) of a business that must be recovered through profit in order for the business to continue. Implicit costs could be forgone interest from money the owners have invested in the business rather than in securities, rental payments that could have been earned if a building that houses the business were leased to another company, income the owners could have received by using their talents and efforts in an alternative enterprise, or any other returns that have been given up by the owners.

The profit that the owners of a business expect to earn to cover their implicit costs is called **normal profit.** Normal profit is necessary to keep a business in operation because its owners will use their time, money, or talents in an alternative if they cannot receive the gain necessary to compensate for these inputs. In simple terms, normal profit is the profit necessary to keep a business going.

Because a business will shut down if its owners do not earn a normal profit, normal profit is considered to be an economic cost of production. The **economic cost of production** of a good or service is equal to the producer's explicit costs plus its implicit costs, or normal profit to its owners.

Explicit Costs
Payments that a business makes to acquire factors of production, such as labor, raw materials, and machinery.

Implicit Costs
The opportunity costs to business owners from using their resources in the business rather than in an alternative opportunity; must be recovered to keep the business in operation; normal profit.

Normal Profit
Profit necessary to recover implicit costs and keep a business in operation; considered to be an economic cost of production.

Economic Cost of Production
Includes all explicit and implicit costs of producing a good or service.

TABLE 11.5	*Revenues from Selling Chairs*

The total revenue from selling an item is calculated by multiplying the price of the item times the quantity demanded at that price. Marginal revenue is the change in total revenue from selling one more unit of an item.

Price	Quantity Demanded	Total Revenue	Marginal Revenue
$450	0	$ 0	
			$400
400	1	400	
			300
350	2	700	
			200
300	3	900	
			100
250	4	1,000	
			0
200	5	1,000	

Excess Profit (Economic Profit)

Profit beyond normal profit; not considered a cost of production.

Any profit beyond normal profit is called **excess profit,** or **economic profit.** For example, if an owner needed $80,000 of normal profit to remain in business and the actual profit were $92,000, then $12,000 would be economic, or excess, profit. Economic, or excess, profit is not a cost, because the owner would remain with the business if it were not earned. Review Question 5 at the end of this chapter provides a good opportunity for you to test your understanding of normal and economic profits.

Measuring Revenues and Costs

The mechanics for determining profit maximization are the same as those for maximizing satisfaction. The only difference is what is being balanced and what is being maximized. For a business, revenues and costs from operations are being balanced to maximize profit. So the example we are about to work through introduces no new principles. Rather, it shows how the principles already learned for an individual can be applied to a business.

Measuring Revenues   Arts and crafts shows are abundant in communities across the country. Suppose that a metal craftsman who produces all sorts of outdoor work—from yard art to iron gates—has also designed a unique rocking chair. This chair appeals to people looking for a piece of useful art for a porch or patio. The craftsman's problem is to determine how many chairs to produce and haul for sale at each fair. He wants to put just the right number of rockers in his truck for any given fair to maximize his profit.

The solution to how many chairs to haul off to a fair is found by balancing the costs from producing different quantities of the chair against the benefits, which in this example are the revenues, from different levels of sales. The revenues that the craftsperson could earn from selling different quantities of the chair at different prices are shown in Table 11.5.

The first two columns of the table give the demand for this chair by showing quantities of the chair demanded at different prices. At a price of $450, no chairs would be demanded. But if the price were lowered to $400, one chair would be demanded; if it were $350, two chairs would be demanded; and so on. Thus, the first two columns of Table 11.5 show how the Law of Demand operates for potential chair buyers.

Total Revenue
Revenue received from selling a certain quantity of an item; calculated by multiplying the price of an item by the quantity demanded at that price.

The Total Revenue column in Table 11.5 shows how much revenue would be generated at each level of demand. **Total revenue** is calculated by multiplying the price of an item by the quantity demanded at that price. For example, two chairs demanded at $350 each would generate $700 in total revenue.

Marginal Revenue
The change in total revenue when one more (or additional) unit of an item is demanded.

The change in total revenue when one more (or additional) unit of output is demanded is termed **marginal revenue.** In Table 11.5 the Marginal Revenue column gives the change in total revenue with each additional chair demanded. For example, when the number of chairs demanded goes from zero to one, total revenue changes from $0 to $400, making the marginal revenue from the first chair equal to $400; when the number of chairs demanded goes from one to two, total revenue increases from $400 to $700, making the marginal revenue from the second chair $300; and so on. As was done with marginal benefits and marginal costs in the previous example, the marginal revenues in Table 11.5 are listed at the midpoints between the quantities demanded. (If you are interested in understanding why marginal revenue is less than price for the second, third, and fourth chairs sold, see footnote 3.)[3]

Measuring Costs   The craftsperson's costs are shown in Table 11.6. To keep matters simple, let us say that these costs, which include implicit costs, or normal profit, come to $250 for each rocking chair.

Table 11.6 shows the craftsperson's total cost, which is the cost per chair times the quantity of chairs produced, at various levels of output. At a cost of $250 per chair, total cost would be zero if none were produced, $250 if one chair were produced, $500 ($250 × 2) if two were produced, and so on.

Marginal cost measures how much total cost changes as each additional unit of an item is produced. The Marginal Cost column of Table 11.6 shows the additional cost of producing one more chair. For example, when the quantity goes from zero to one, total cost goes from $0 to $250, making the marginal cost of the first chair equal to $250. When the quantity changes from one to two, total cost goes from $250 to $500, and the marginal cost of the second chair is again $250. As was done with the previous marginal values, the marginal costs in Table 11.6 are listed between the quantities produced.

---

[3]You might have noticed that when the quantity demanded is two, three, or four chairs, marginal revenue is less than the price of the chair. For example, when two chairs are demanded at a price of $350, only $300 is added to total revenue by selling the second chair. Why is this so?

If the craftsperson sells only one chair, $400 in revenue is generated. However, in order to sell two chairs, the price must be lowered to $350. This means that the seller is going to charge $350 to the first buyer as well as the second buyer. Rather than receiving $400 from the first buyer, the craftsperson will have to give the first buyer a $50 discount. Because of this, what is added to total revenue from the sale of the second chair is not its price. Rather, the marginal revenue from the second unit sold is the price of the second unit minus the discount given to the first buyer, or $350 − $50 = $300.

Likewise, if the craftsperson wants to sell three chairs, the price must be lowered to $300. But if the third buyer pays only $300, $300 must also be charged to each of the other two buyers who would have otherwise paid $350. Thus, the marginal revenue from the third unit sold is not equal to the $300 price. Instead, it equals the $300 price minus the two $50 discounts given to the other two buyers, or $300 − $100 = $200. To test your understanding of this principle, see if you can explain why the marginal revenue from the fourth unit is $100, while its price is $250.

TABLE 11.6	*Costs of Producing Chairs*

Total cost is the cost of producing a specified number of units of output, and marginal cost measures the change in total cost from producing each additional unit of output.

Quantity	Total Cost	Marginal Cost
0	$ 0	
		$250
1	250	
		250
2	500	
		250
3	750	
		250
4	1,000	
		250
5	1,250	

Maximizing Profit

The number of chairs that the craftsperson should produce and sell to maximize profit can be shown by combining the information from Tables 11.5 and 11.6, as is done in Table 11.7. But before analyzing the numbers in the table, let us review what we should expect to find.

Remember that both the individual at the concert and the craftsperson are trying to maximize net benefit by weighing costs and benefits, and that the only difference between them is how benefits and costs are measured and what they are looking

TABLE 11.7	*Revenues, Costs, and Profit on Chairs*

The maximum profit that can be obtained from producing and selling chairs occurs at two units. At this output level, total revenue exceeds total cost by the greatest amount and marginal revenue equals marginal cost.

Price	Quantity	Profit	Total Revenue	Total Cost	Marginal Revenue	Marginal Cost
$450	0	$ 0	$ 0	$ 0		
					$400	$250
400	1	150	400	250		
					300	250
350	2	200	700	500		
					200	250
300	3	150	900	750		
					100	250
250	4	0	1,000	1,000		
					0	250
200	5	−250	1,000	1,250		

to maximize. Given these similarities, we should expect that the rules for maximizing are the same. So, for the craftsperson, profit should be at a maximum where total revenue exceeds total cost by the greatest amount, or where marginal revenue equals marginal cost. Table 11.7 lets us check this out.

The Profit column in Table 11.7 shows that a maximum profit of $200 occurs at two units of output. How does this relate to total revenue and total cost? **Profit or loss** is found by subtracting total cost from total revenue at each level of output. For example, if the seller were to produce and sell three chairs, total revenue minus total cost would be $900 − $750, or $150. As indicated in this table, maximum profit for a business occurs where total revenue exceeds total cost by the greatest amount.

What is the relationship between marginal revenue and marginal cost where profit is maximized? Reading down the last two columns in Table 11.7, we can see that from zero to one, and from one to two units of output, marginal revenue is greater than marginal cost: Each chair adds more to total revenue than to total cost, causing profit to increase. This can be verified by noticing that the numbers in the Profit column increase as output and sales go from zero to two units.

In Table 11.7 marginal cost is greater than marginal revenue as output goes from two to three, from three to four, and from four to five units. In this case, the third, fourth, and fifth units are adding more to total cost than to total revenue, causing profit to fall. This is confirmed by the figures in the Profit column.

Because marginal revenue is greater than marginal cost up to two units of output, and less than marginal cost beyond two units of output, marginal revenue and marginal cost must be equal at two units. Thus, the two **profit-maximizing rules** are satisfied at an output level of two units. Again, these rules state that profit is maximized at the output level where

♦ total revenue exceeds total cost by the greatest amount, and
♦ marginal revenue equals marginal cost.

Graphing Costs, Revenues, and Profit

The relationships among marginal revenue, marginal cost, and profit as well as among total revenue, total cost, and profit that were set out in Table 11.7 are illustrated in Figure 11.2. The bottom graph in Figure 11.2 shows that profit, or net benefit, is at its maximum where two chairs are produced and sold. The middle graph in Figure 11.2 shows that marginal revenue and marginal cost are equal at exactly two units of output. For smaller output levels, marginal revenue is greater than marginal cost, which causes profit in the lower graph to increase. For output levels larger than two units, marginal revenue is less than marginal cost, causing profit to fall. Finally, in the upper graph in Figure 11.2, the vertical distance by which the total revenue curve exceeds the total cost curve is at its maximum at two units of output, which, of course, is the output level where profit is maximized in the lower graph.

In summary, regardless of whether an individual, business, or government unit is being considered, the net benefit to the decision-making unit from an activity will be maximized if it operates where total benefit exceeds total cost by the greatest amount. This is also where marginal benefit and marginal cost are equal. The main difference between the decision-making units is not that they follow different rules. Rather, the difference is in what is maximized and how costs and benefits are measured. Working through Test Your Understanding, "Maximizing Profit," will allow you to master the maximizing rules.

Profit or Loss
The result when a business subtracts its total cost from its total revenue.

Profit-Maximizing Rules
Profit is maximized at the output level where total revenue exceeds total cost by the greatest amount, or where marginal revenue equals marginal cost.

FIGURE 11.2   *Total Revenue and Cost, Marginal Revenue and Cost, and Profit*

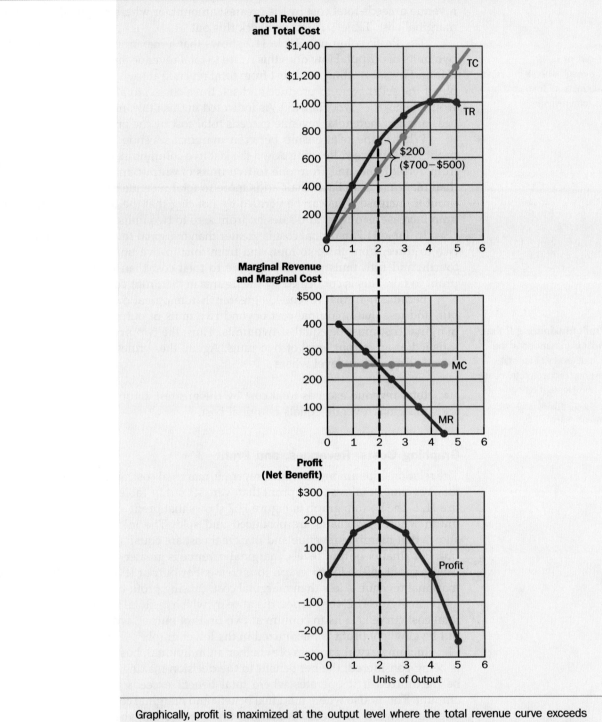

Graphically, profit is maximized at the output level where the total revenue curve exceeds the total cost curve by the greatest amount, or where the marginal revenue curve crosses the marginal cost curve.

TEST YOUR UNDERSTANDING

MAXIMIZING PROFIT

Pete Casso has been invited to exhibit two of his works in the annual student art show and sale. Although those who are invited to participate in the show receive a great deal of personal satisfaction, or "psychic income," from having been selected, the show also presents an opportunity for the exhibitors to earn some money. Pete is concerned about making as much money as he can from this sale to help defray tuition costs for next semester. Because he studied economics last year, he realizes the importance of pricing his works of art correctly in order to maximize profit.

Pete has chosen to include a pen-and-ink drawing of a house and a colorful lithograph in the show because both of these items can bring multiple sales. The house drawing will serve as a sample of Pete's custom work in this area. That is, he produces pen-and-ink drawings of individual homes from photographs and, based on the sample, can take orders for these custom drawings. The lithograph that he has chosen can be easily reproduced many times without losing its design and color, so he can sell multiples of this work.

Table 1 gives the demand schedule that Pete thinks to be true for custom house drawings. He calculates his cost for each house drawing at $50, which accounts for his time and materials. Complete Table 1 to determine the price Pete should charge and the number of drawings he should sell to maximize his profit from the drawings. Why is his roommate not correct in advising him to go for volume and charge $58 per drawing?

Table 2 gives the demand schedule for Pete's lithograph. The cost of producing the first lithograph is high—$200—but the marginal cost for each additional print is only $15. Complete this table and indicate the price Pete should charge for his lithograph. What is the maximum profit that he can expect to make from the sale of his lithograph?

Answers can be found at the back of the book.

TABLE 1 *Demand, Revenue, and Cost Information for Custom-Drawn Houses*

Price per Drawing	Number of Drawings Demanded	Total Revenue	Marginal Revenue	Marginal Cost	Total Cost	Profit
$138	0	____			____	____
128	1	____	____	____	____	____
118	2	____	____	____	____	____
108	3	____	____	____	____	____
98	4	____	____	____	____	____
88	5	____	____	____	____	____
78	6	____	____	____	____	____
68	7	____	____	____	____	____
58	8	____	____	____	____	____

TABLE 2 *Demand, Revenue, and Cost Information for Lithographs*

Price per Lithograph	Number of Lithographs Demanded	Total Revenue	Marginal Revenue	Marginal Cost	Total Cost	Profit or Loss
$180	0	____			____	____
170	1	____	____	$200	$200	____
160	2	____	____	____	____	____
150	3	____	____	____	____	____
140	4	____	____	____	____	____
130	5	____	____	____	____	____
120	6	____	____	____	____	____
110	7	____	____	____	____	____
100	8	____	____	____	____	____
90	9	____	____	____	____	____
80	10	____	____	____	____	____

SOCIAL BENEFITS AND COSTS

In the cases just discussed, any concern over whether, how, or to what extent others might be affected by an individual's or a business's decision was absent. People generally choose courses of action after considering the factors that affect them directly, even though sometimes what they do will benefit or impose a cost on others. Because of this, the costs and benefits to individuals and businesses of their actions may differ from the costs and benefits to society of those same actions.

The effects that decisions and actions have on persons or things that are not involved in the decisions or actions are called **externalities**. Externalities may be either positive and benefit others, or negative and costly to others. For example, getting a flu shot may benefit not only you but also those who could have caught the flu from you. Maintaining your car benefits you and also all the people who could have been delayed if you broke down on the road. In these cases your actions have worked to the advantage of others and have created **positive externalities.**

On the other hand, a factory that pollutes the air or water or individuals who buy alcohol and then drive while intoxicated contribute to the detriment of others and create **negative externalities.** Because of pollution, residents of a community could incur health problems and additional medical bills or have their property values decrease. For example, in one small town in southeastern Missouri, the dust particles from a lead smelter created some health issues for the community's children and left some homes virtually impossible to sell.

Application 11.2, "The Cost of Smoking," deals with recent reports by the Centers for Disease Control and Prevention and others on the costs of smoking, many of which are externalities.

Externality

The effect of an action on a person or thing that was not one of the parties involved in the action.

Positive Externality

An externality that creates a benefit for others.

Negative Externality

An externality that creates a cost for others.

Maximizing Society's Net Benefit

Externalities must be added to individual or business cost-benefit calculations to determine how society is affected by an action. The total effect on society of the private benefits and costs plus the externalities of an action are the action's **social benefits** and **social costs.** So,

Social Benefits and Costs

The total effect on society from the private benefits, private costs, and externalities of an action.

- ♦ private benefits + positive externalities = social benefits;
- ♦ private costs + negative externalities = social costs; and
- ♦ social benefits − social costs = net benefits to society.

Net benefit for society is calculated in exactly the same way as that for businesses and individuals. The only difference is that now we are concerned with social rather than private benefits and costs. Thus, the net benefit to society from an activity is maximized where its total social benefit exceeds its total social cost by the greatest amount, or where marginal social benefit equals marginal social cost.

How do externalities affect the relationship between what is best for the individual or business and what is best for society? If an action of an individual or business has no effect on others, there will be no externalities, and the level of activity that maximizes the net benefit of the individual or business will also maximize the net benefit of society. Where private actions impose costs on others and cause negative externalities, the level of activity that maximizes society's net benefit will be less than the level where private net benefit is maximized. For example, if the profit-maximizing output for a business results in costly pollution problems, society would be better off

APPLICATION 11.2

THE COST OF SMOKING

While the cost of a pack of cigarettes may seem high to many nonsmokers—about $4.50 a pack on average—the external costs can be shocking. There are some interesting findings about the secondary costs of smoking in research done by the Centers for Disease Control and Prevention (CDC) and others.

The CDC has placed some real numbers to the economic cost of smoking in the United States. They have concluded that cigarette smoking has caused annual economic losses for direct medical expenses and lost productivity of about $3,561 per adult smoker; that the economic costs of cigarette smoking are $7.18 per pack sold; and that cigarette smoking robs people of about 5.5 million years of potential life annually.

Data about specific health-related issues linked to cigarette smoking are abundant. The following gives some study conclusions.

- Adverse health effects from smoking account for nearly 1 in 5 deaths each year.
- About 90 percent of lung cancer deaths in men and about 80 percent in women are caused by smoking.
- Cigarette smoking about doubles the risk of a stroke.

- The risk of heart disease, the leading cause of death in the United States, is about 2–4 times more likely to develop in smokers.

Furthermore, people who are exposed to secondhand smoke also experience negative externalities. Their heart disease and lung cancer risks are increased; it causes respiratory problems for children and slows their lung growth; and it has been connected to a host of other problems in children including more frequent and severe asthma attacks.

Another report also identified some interesting costs. In studying term life insurance rates for a $500,000 policy, the lowest rate for a pack-a-day 44-year-old male was $2,571 per year while the lowest rate for the nonsmoker was $1,140. It also found that smokers earn less and have larger bills for dry-cleaning clothing, whitening teeth, preparing cars and houses for resale, and buying mints. But, one of the biggest costs is the lower lifetime retirement benefits received by smokers because of a shorter lifespan caused by a smoking-related illness. "You could be paying into Social Security year after year, and if you die at 66 because you're a smoker, it's money down the drain," says Frank Sloan, author of *The Price of Smoking* and the Director of the Center for Health Policy, Law and Management at Duke University.

Sources: Centers for Disease Control and Prevention, "Economic Facts About U.S. Tobacco Use," "Health Effects of Cigarette Smoking," "Secondhand Smoke," www.cdc.gov; MSN Money, Hilary Smith, "The high cost of smoking," http://articles.moneycentral.msn.com.

if the firm produced a lower level of output and less pollution. And the evidence in Application 11.2 that smoking imposes significant external costs on society strongly suggests that society would be better off with less smoking.

When the actions of an individual or business benefit others and cause positive externalities, the level of activity that maximizes society's net benefit will be greater than the level that maximizes private net benefit. For example, some people maximize private net benefit by not spending money for a college education. But society is clearly better off with an educated population. Cities with a highly educated workforce tend to be more vibrant and economically healthy.

Relationship between Private and Social Net Benefits   The relationship between private and social net benefits is shown in Figure 11.3. Figure 11.3a illustrates production with negative but no positive externalities. Here the private marginal costs and benefits from producing this product are represented by PMC and PMB. Private net benefit (in this case, profit) would be maximized where PMB = PMC, which occurs at the output level shown by point Y on the horizontal axis.

Now let's add negative externalities, or costs to society (such as from air pollution), to determine social costs and, from that, the best output level for society. When the negative externalities are added to the private costs, society's marginal cost is represented by SMC in Figure 11.3a. And since there are no positive externalities, society's marginal benefit, SMB, is the same as private marginal benefit (shown by the line PMB = SMB). Now, from society's perspective, the best level of output is shown

| FIGURE 11.3 | *Maximizing Social Net Benefit with Negative and Positive Externalities* |

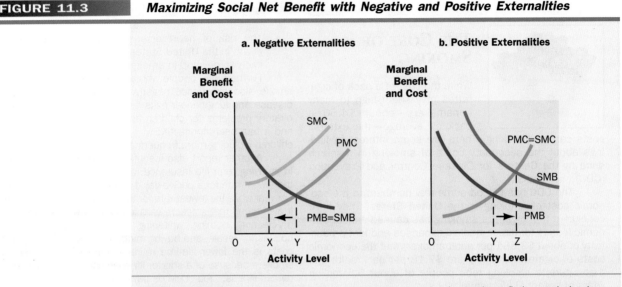

When production generates negative externalities, society's net benefit is maximized by cutting back on the output level. When production generates positive externalities, society's net benefit is maximized by increasing the output level.

by point X on the horizontal axis of Figure 11.3a because here society's marginal benefit, SMB, equals society's marginal cost, SMC. In this case, it would be in the interest of society to cut back production from point Y to point X.

Production that yields positive externalities (such as creating jobs in a depressed area) and no negative externalities is shown in Figure 11.3b. In this case, private net benefit would be maximized by producing where private marginal benefit, PMB, and private marginal cost, PMC, are equal, or at point Y on the horizontal axis. But when the positive externalities are added to the private benefit, social marginal benefit, shown by SMB, results. In this case, where no costs are imposed on society (so that PMC = SMC), the best position for society would be at output level Z, where SMB = SMC. Here it would be in society's interest to increase production from point Y to point Z.

In very simple terms, too many goods and services are produced in markets with negative externalities and too few goods and services are produced in markets with positive externalities. If this is the case, how can society induce individuals and businesses to decrease undesirable and increase desirable activities? Activities that produce negative externalities can be reduced through fines, taxes, outright prohibition, or other penalties. Such methods have been used in the United States to control air and water pollution, drunk driving, and crime. To encourage activities that yield positive externalities, government can provide tax breaks, direct grants of money, subsidies, or other inducements. For example, at times local governments have given tax breaks to businesses for locating in their communities, thereby creating new jobs; and the federal government gives various types of financial assistance to students to help them complete their educations.

Up for Debate, "Should Drivers Be Banned from Using Cell Phones While Operating a Vehicle?," gives two sides of a hotly contested issue. On one side are those who think that the negative externalities created by driving and using a cell phone are so serious that this action should be banned. On the other side are those who think that cell phone usage in cars is part of our lifestyles and that government should not regulate the

SHOULD DRIVERS BE BANNED FROM USING CELL PHONES WHILE OPERATING A VEHICLE?

Issue   *There is an enormous increase in the use of cell phones to communicate: More than 266 million people had wireless communication devices in 2008. With this reliance on cell phones, there is increasing concern about drivers who are distracted using cell phones while driving. While the private benefit of buying and using a cell phone while driving may bring an individual maximum satisfaction, there is concern for the negative externalities that are being generated by this action. There is evidence that accidents, which cause harm to other drivers on the road as well as pedestrians and bicyclists, are the result of cell phone usage while driving. The question that arises is: Should drivers be banned from using cell phones while operating a vehicle?*

Yes   There are many studies which link cell phone usage while driving to accidents. One study at the University of Utah compared driving while drunk (using a simulator of course) and driving while using a cell phone. "We found that people are as impaired when they drive and talk on a cell phone as they are when they drive intoxicated at the legal blood-alcohol limit," said an assistant professor of psychology.

People are inattentive to their surroundings when they are engaged in conversation—sometimes a heated conversation fraught with emotion. When they converse and drive, their concentration on driving is minimal. Recognizing this impairment, several cities and states have passed laws limiting cell phone use. As of 2008, five states prohibit driving while talking on handheld cell phones, and other states ban cell phone use by school bus drivers and novice drivers.

In addition to inattention from conversation, drivers often take their hands off the wheel and eyes off the road to call a phone number, and worse yet, to text message. These behaviors certainly put other drivers, bikers, and pedestrians at risk. Substantial negative externalities are created.

No   Cell phones provide a huge convenience in a hectic world where multitasking has become the expected way of life. Cell phones allow families to keep connected and even travelers to be easily met at an airport. Friendships are extended and enriched by easy and frequent communication. Moreover, in a vehicle, a cell phone can mean security in the event of a car problem or dangerous road condition, and may even calm stressed drivers who can relay that they may be late for an important appointment.

While there are some studies that link cell phone usage to accidents, the real problem is driver inattention. This can occur when reaching for a drink, reading a map, or changing a CD. There are many other reasons for accidents, like driving while intoxicated or while impaired by health or other conditions. If there are such dire consequences from driving and talking on a cell phone, wouldn't there be a national ban against it?

It is a right of individuals to be able to buy and use cell phones when they want. We have enough government regulation and do not need for government to interfere with our right to communicate.

Sources: "Cell Phone Driving Laws," www.ghsa.org/html/stateinfo/laws/cellphone_laws.html; Robert Roy Britt, "Cell Phones Make Drivers as Bad as Drunks," LiveScience, http://www.livescience.com/health/060629_cell_phones.html; "Cellphones and Driving," Insurance Information Institute, http://www.iii.org/media/hottopics/insurance/cellphones/.

use. What is your opinion, and how has your assessment of social costs and benefits led you to this position?

PUBLIC CHOICE

The goal of maximizing economic well-being and the principles of cost-benefit analysis are easily understood in the context of individual and business decision making. In our economic system, however, many important decisions are made collectively—that is, by a group. Collective decision making occurs primarily through the government sector. As a group we make choices about how many municipal police cars and dump trucks to purchase, whether to provide more funds for our schools, how much money to allocate to national defense, and whether to permit budget deficits.

How do individuals participate in collective decision making? In the United States, voting is the root of collective choice. Individuals elect officials at the federal, state, and local government levels who receive the power and authority to act on behalf of the group. Thus, voting provides the link that transforms individual decision making into collective choice.

The term used to describe the set of economic theories that explains the motives and attitudes of voters and public officials in collective decision making is **public choice.** The basic idea behind public choice is that people try to maximize their own well-being in making collective choices. Thus, the fundamental rules of decision making do not change when a group is involved.

Public Choice

The study of the economic motives and attitudes of voters and public officials in collective decision making

Maximizing Behavior and the Voting Process

A look at the voting process helps to illustrate public choice theory. For an election, people make some basic decisions: whether to vote or not; how much information to seek about candidates and issues; and for whom to vote. Each of these choices carries costs and benefits.

The act of voting gives individuals varying degrees of satisfaction: If people believe that their votes make a difference, voting gives them more satisfaction than if they feel that their votes have no effect on the outcome of an election. Voting also imposes costs on individuals, especially the opportunity cost of time. Thus, a person's decision about whether or not to vote in an election depends on his or her marginal benefit and marginal cost of voting. If marginal benefit is greater than marginal cost, the person will vote in an election; if marginal cost is greater than marginal benefit, he or she will not vote.

A second consideration in voting involves the amount of information about candidates and issues that a voter has when making a decision at the polls. Generally, when individuals make private decisions about spending large sums of money, they attempt to gather as much information as possible. Do you, for example, know someone who is about to buy a car? That person is probably visiting websites that rate automobiles, taking test drives, and asking current car owners about how much they like a particular model. Many people will pay as much in taxes this year as they do in car payments or even as much as the cost of a new car. Are those people investing as much time and energy in gathering information about the elected officials to whom they are entrusting these tax dollars? Probably not.

Information seeking about candidates and issues takes time. As a result, the opportunity cost of becoming an informed voter can be high, causing a person to be **rationally ignorant.** That is, a rational voter may perceive that the marginal benefit from becoming better acquainted with a candidate's record and position is less than the marginal cost of becoming enlightened. Because of this, voters often make choices based on limited information that comes from brief advertisements and "sound bites" designed to sell a candidate.

Rational Ignorance

Choosing to remain uninformed because the marginal cost of obtaining the information is higher than the marginal benefit from knowing it.

Which candidate does a voter choose? Again, the principles of cost-benefit analysis apply. A voter will select the candidate perceived to bring the greatest net benefit to the voter. This decision could be based on the candidate's record, the position of the candidate on an issue important to the voter, or any other consideration.

Public choice theory, with its emphasis on self-interest, helps to explain many of the problems that result from collective decision making. For example, **special-interest groups** often cause the will of a minority to be imposed on the majority. Public choice theory explains that members of special-interest groups actively promote their positions through letters, ads, campaign contributions, and other means because of the benefits they expect to receive. The response to these issues from the rest of the population may be weak because of lack of interest or because the opportunity cost of responding is too high. Elected officials are sometimes sensitive to the pleas of special-interest-group members because of the message that they hear or because the group members' support or opposition can impact an official's reelection.

Special-Interest Group

People who share a common position on a particular issue and actively promote that position.

Summary

1. There are general rules for maximizing economic well-being that can be applied to any decision-making unit: an individual, a business, or society. These rules involve the balancing of costs and benefits from different courses of action in order to select the one that contributes most to economic well-being. The formal study of these rules and the balancing of costs and benefits is called cost-benefit analysis. These rules can be applied to many more areas of human endeavor than those traditionally studied in economics courses.

2. For an individual, the benefits of an activity can be measured in terms of the satisfaction, or utility, received from the action. Costs can be measured by the opportunity forgone in accomplishing that action.

3. For a business, benefits are measured by the total revenue received, which is calculated by multiplying the price of an item times the quantity sold. The economic cost of producing a good or service includes explicit costs, which are direct payments for factors of production, and implicit costs, which are returns required by the owner(s) to keep the business in operation. Normal profit is what the owner(s) must earn to recover implicit costs. Economic profit is not a cost of production; it is that profit in excess of normal profit.

4. Total benefit or revenue and total cost are, respectively, the benefit or revenue received and the cost incurred from producing a particular amount of an activity or output. Marginal benefit or revenue is the change in total benefit or revenue resulting from each additional unit of an activity performed or output sold. Marginal cost is the change in total cost from producing one more unit of activity or output.

5. Maximum net benefit (or profit) occurs where total benefit (revenue) exceeds total cost by the greatest amount, or where marginal benefit (revenue) equals marginal cost. Both rules are satisfied at exactly the same level of activity. When marginal benefit (revenue) exceeds marginal cost, net benefit (profit) rises, and when marginal benefit (revenue) is less than marginal cost, net benefit (profit) falls. The main difference in how these rules are applied to various decision-making units is in what is maximized and how benefits and costs are measured.

6. Activities by individuals or businesses may help or hurt others. These effects are called positive and negative externalities. Because of externalities, the level of an activity that maximizes an individual's or a business's net benefit may differ from the level that would maximize society's net benefit.

7. Net benefit is calculated for society in the same way as for individuals and businesses. Society measures its net benefit in terms of social costs and social benefits. Social costs are private costs plus any negative external effects. Social benefits are private benefits plus any positive external effects. When negative externalities are present, society's net benefit is maximized at a lower level of activity than is private net benefit; when positive externalities are present, society's net benefit is maximized at a higher level of activity.

8. Public choice deals with the economic theories behind collective decision making, which is carried out through the voting process. Individuals participate in the

voting process based on the costs and benefits from the acts of voting, information seeking, and candidate selection. Problems that arise from collective decision making, such as the impact of special-interest groups, can be explained using cost-benefit analysis.

Key Terms and Concepts

Cost-benefit analysis	Economic cost of production
Utility	Excess profit (economic profit)
Opportunity cost	Total revenue
Marginal benefit (marginal utility)	Marginal revenue
Total benefit (total utility)	Profit or loss
Law of Diminishing Marginal Utility	Profit-maximizing rules
Total cost	Externality
Marginal cost	Positive externality
Net benefit	Negative externality
Net benefit maximizing rules	Social benefits and costs
Explicit costs	Public choice
Implicit costs	Rational ignorance
Normal profit	Special-interest group

Review Questions

1. In this chapter you have been introduced to marginal benefit, marginal utility, marginal revenue, social marginal benefit, marginal cost, and social marginal cost. To what specifically does each term refer and what concept is common to all of these terms?

2. Explain why: (a) net benefit increases when marginal benefit exceeds marginal cost; (b) net benefit is at a maximum when marginal benefit equals marginal cost; and (c) net benefit falls when marginal benefit is less than marginal cost.

3. In what respects are the following maximizing decisions similar to each other and in what respects are they different?
   a. The decision by a person about how much cake to eat
   b. The decision by a community about how many resources to devote to law enforcement
   c. The decision by a business about how much of its product to produce and sell
   d. The decision by a person about how many hours to work per week

4. The following table gives the utility points received by a person from each additional hour of exercise per week, as well as the points that each additional hour costs. Using this table, answer the questions below.

Hours of Exercise	Marginal Benefit	Total Benefit	Marginal Cost	Total Cost	Net Benefit
0		0		0	____
	60		5		
1		____		____	____
	40		10		
2		____		____	____
	30		20		
3		____		____	____
	20		30		
4		____		____	____
	10		40		
5		____		____	____
	0		55		
6		____		____	____

a. Calculate the total benefit and the total cost of exercising for each of the hours in the table.
b. Calculate the net benefit of exercising for each of the hours in the table.
c. How many hours per week should this person exercise to maximize satisfaction? What is the maximum number of net benefit points that can be earned from exercising?
d. Graph total benefit and total cost, marginal benefit and marginal cost, and net benefit on the graphs below. (Remember to plot marginal benefit and marginal cost at the midpoints between the hours.) Explain how these graphs illustrate the maximizing rules.

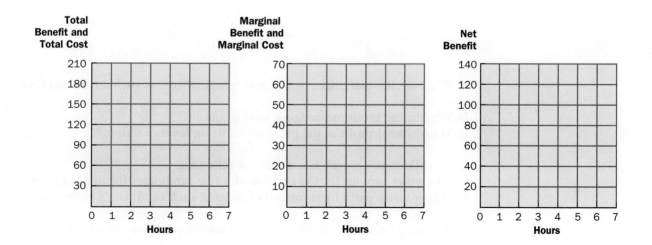

5. Suppose that your neighbor has just closed her books from her first year in the retail flower business and is ecstatic with the profit her accountant says that she has earned. The store grossed $250,000 in sales over the year, and its explicit costs for rent, plants and flowers, electricity, and the like were $150,000. Her husband is not quite as elated but can't figure out exactly why. In discussing the situation with you, he offers the following information. The two of them invested $200,000 of their savings, which was earning an 8 percent return, to go into this business. She gave up her job, which was paying her $64,000 a year, at a local corporation. He worked every evening and most weekends at the store—giving up the opportunity to take on additional clients or to work overtime. In addition to being tired, he figures that he lost $25,000 in additional income. What was their economic cost of production? How much normal profit should they have expected to receive? Have they made any economic profit? What kind of advice would you give them?

6. Using the following cost and revenue information, answer the questions below the table.

Units of Output	Total Revenue	Marginal Revenue	Total Cost	Marginal Cost	Profit
0	$ 0		$ 0		_____
1	50	_____	25	_____	_____
2	90	_____	35	_____	_____
3	120	_____	40	_____	_____
4	140	_____	50	_____	_____
5	150	_____	70	_____	_____
6	150	_____	100	_____	_____
7	140	_____	140	_____	_____
8	120	_____	200	_____	_____

a. What are the marginal revenue and marginal cost of each additional unit of output?
b. What is the profit-maximizing level of output?
c. What is total profit at the profit-maximizing level of output?

7. Use public choice theory to explain the following.
a. Low voter turnout for the election of a few candidates for minor offices
b. Voting along party lines instead of judging each candidate's individual merits
c. A change before an election in an incumbent's position on an issue

d. Voting according to the recommendations given in a local newspaper
e. Low voter turnout when the weather is bad

Discussion Questions

1. In each of the following situations, determine what the decision maker might be seeking to maximize and indicate (1) some factors that should be included in the calculation of costs, and (2) some factors that should be included in the calculation of benefits.
    a. The decision to get a college education
    b. The decision to shoplift a coat
    c. The decision by voters to increase property taxes
    d. The decision by a business to drop a product line
    e. The decision to adopt a child
    f. The decision to lie
    g. The decision to stop smoking cigarettes
    h. The decision to use a cell phone while driving

2. What could be opportunity costs of each of the following actions?
    a. Moving from a smaller home that takes 40 percent of your income to own and maintain to a larger "home of your dreams" that takes 60 percent of your income
    b. Working overtime during the next 2 months in the hope of getting a promotion
    c. Deciding to stop seeing someone because you are not right for each other
    d. Cutting back on certain foods to lose weight

3. Identify some of the negative externalities associated with living in a city that has a high crime rate.

4. The emission of toxins into the air is a well-known example of a negative externality. What are some of the costs imposed on society by these emissions? In answering this question, be sure to consider possible effects from pollution on climate, health, maintenance of buildings and other property, and taxes.

5. Because pesticides and herbicides used by farmers are increasingly poisoning groundwater and streams, would you back a proposal to ban their use? Why?

6. Cost-benefit analysis can be applied to a wide range of economic and noneconomic decisions. Give five examples of noneconomic situations where the cost-benefit analysis developed in this chapter would be useful in arriving at a decision.

7. Although DDT, a pesticide, has been banned in the United States, it is used extensively in many other nations, primarily to curb malaria caused by mosquito bites. In some parts of the world, malaria is a serious health threat. Despite the problems created by extensive use of DDT, many countries find this the least expensive method for attacking malaria and mosquitoes. Using cost-benefit analysis, explain why you would favor or disapprove of the continued use of DDT in some countries.

Critical Thinking Case 11

WATER, WATER EVERYWHERE, BUT NOT ENOUGH TO DRINK

Critical Thinking Skills

Incorporating quantitative and qualitative information into decision making

Comparing alternative strategies

Using costs and benefits to explain and predict decisions

Economic Concepts

Measuring costs and benefits

Externalities

Special-interest groups

About three-quarters of the earth is covered by water, and of all the water consumed each year, only about 8 percent is for drinking water. (The biggest usage is for agriculture.) At first glance it appears that the one area in which people do not face a scarcity problem is the availability of drinking water. As it turns out, nothing could be further from the truth.

There is growing concern that we are on our way to a global health crisis of immense proportion, comparable in some people's minds to the bubonic plague in the 1300s and the HIV pandemic. Driving this crisis are over 1 billion people, mostly in developing countries, who do not have adequate access to clean, safe drinking water.

Virtually the entire population in the United States and other developed countries has access to clean water sources. But in other countries, the numbers drop. A recent survey showed that only 87 percent of the Brazilian population had access to improved drinking water sources. The reported number was 46 percent for Haiti, 39 percent for

Oman, 30 percent for Cambodia, and 13 percent for Afghanistan.

It has been estimated that polluted drinking water causes approximately 5 million deaths each year. Inadequate supplies of safe drinking water cause about one-half of the people in developing countries to experience illness and 20 percent of children below the age of 5 in the poorest countries to die from infectious disease.

The United Nations has set a goal of reducing by one-half the number of people without access to basic water supplies by 2015. But the costs and benefits of this goal are not clear. According to one estimate, the cost of improving water supplies in developing countries would be about $11 billion per year, and the benefit would be about $55 billion per year. According to other estimates, meeting this goal would cost about $44 billion to $60 billion a year.

Concerns over water safety and related issues have been raised at major conferences and meetings for over 25 years. Amazingly, little commitment has been made by countries and international organizations to address the problem.

Based on: "The Right to Water," *Appropriate Technology*, June 2003, p. 4; "Finance and Economics: The Stuff of Life; Economics Focus," *The Economist*, May 15, 2004, p. 87; Rory Clarke, "Introduction: Water Crisis?" The *OECD Observer*, March 2003, p. 8; Brett Parris, "False Economies: A Global Health Crisis," *The OECD Observer*, May 2004, p. 25; United Nations, "Social Indicators, Water Supply and Sanitation," http://unstats.un.org/unsd/demographic/products/socind/watsan.htm, August 18, 2005.

Questions

1. Financial costs and benefits have been estimated for pursuing the U.N. water project. What are some hard-to-measure nonfinancial costs and benefits—such as the effect of bad water on political stability—that should also be considered?

2. What factors should be considered when evaluating the costs and benefits of ignoring the problem? Is ignoring the problem a realistically viable option?

3. A large portion of the costs for the U.N. project would likely be paid by developed countries. What benefits should these countries expect for themselves from the

project, and how would they likely compare in total value to their costs? Which of the benefits would be direct and which would be positive externalities?

4. How might the costs and benefits to the countries that could move the project forward explain the lack of progress over the years? Suppose one special-interest group supports the project and another special-interest group opposes it. Without knowing more, which of the two groups do you think would have more clout with the countries expected to take on the project?

CHAPTER 12

Production and the Costs of Production

CHAPTER OBJECTIVES

To identify the categories into which productive activity in the U.S. economy can be classified.

To explain the nature and importance of production methods.

To explore the relationship between production methods and technology.

To differentiate between short-run and long-run production.

To identify the different types of production costs.

To explain the behavior of production costs as the level of output changes in the short run and the long run.

To provide (in an appendix) a more detailed understanding of short-run average costs.

We engage in many productive activities. Students produce papers and projects; families wash cars and clothes and make meals; businesses produce computers, office buildings, and financial advice; and governments provide police and fire protection. Production is a process: It involves taking resources, like labor and materials, and using them to make goods and services.

This chapter is concerned with the microeconomic aspects of production. While all of the areas of the economy engage in production, the vast majority of measured production is done by businesses. So, while many of the concepts in this chapter can be applied to other areas, the focus is on the production and costs of production of business firms.

There is an important connection between a firm's production, its costs of production, and its objective to maximize profit. Remember from the previous chapters that profit is what remains after costs are subtracted from revenue. All other things remaining unchanged, the lower the cost of producing a product, the greater the firm's profit from selling that product.

PRODUCTION BASICS

In 2008, the U.S. economy produced more than $14 trillion of goods and services.[1] Trying to sort through this huge macroeconomic number in order explore production at a more microeconomic level is a formidable task. Let's look at several ways in which the micro perspective is organized.

Sectors and Industries

To help us in understanding and analyzing production, classification systems have been developed for grouping similar types of goods and services. Two widely used classifications are producing sectors and industries.

Producing Sectors
A broad classification system for grouping goods and services, and the firms that produce them.

Producing Sectors   The broadest classification system for grouping goods and services, and the firms that produce them, is called **producing sectors.** This enables us to lump some production together and be able to track a type of production over time, as well as evaluate a group's size in relationship to other groups. Table 12.1 lists the major producing sectors of the U.S. economy, along with examples of the productive activities included in each sector and the percentage of total output accounted for by each sector in 2007.

While we place different types of productive activities in different sectors, in reality these sectors are closely knit in the production and distribution of goods and services. For example, crops produced in the agricultural sector become food products in the manufacturing sector, and then move to households through the wholesale and retail trade sectors, with the assistance of the transportation sector.

Over time the importance of the different sectors changes. For example, from 1930 through 1988, manufacturing was unchallenged as the dominant producing sector of the economy. For more than 50 years, the U.S. economy provided many jobs in companies that produced chemicals, cars, clothing, and other goods. But in 1989 manufacturing was surpassed by the services sector, which continues to be the largest sector. Today, college graduates are more likely to find employment in health care, law, and other service areas than in manufacturing. Changes have also occurred in the relative importance of other sectors.

[1]*Economic Report of the President* (Washington, DC: U.S. Government Printing Office, 2009), p. 282.

TABLE 12.1	*Major Producing Sectors of the Economy*

Goods and services produced by businesses can be categorized into the various producing sectors of the economy. Services is the largest producing sector.

Sector	Examples of Productive Activities	Percentage of Total Output in 2007
Agriculture, forestry, and fishing	Crops and livestock, agricultural services, forestry, fishing, hunting	1.3%
Mining	Metal and coal mining, oil and gas extraction	2.3
Construction	Building, highway, and heavy construction, general and special trade contracting	4.7
Manufacturing	Apparel, food, fabricated metal, electronic and transportation equipment, chemicals, petroleum refining, printing, and publishing	13.4
Transportation; communications; electric, gas, and sanitary services	Railroad, water, and air transportation, trucking and warehousing; radio and television broadcasting, telephone and telegraph; natural gas transmission and distribution, sewer systems, electric services	11.1
Wholesale trade	Wholesale auto supplies, electrical appliances, sporting goods	6.6
Retail trade	Food and general merchandise stores, restaurants, building material and garden supply stores, auto dealers, gasoline stations	7.3
Finance, insurance, and real estate	Banking, commodity and security brokerage, insurance, real estate	23.6
Services	Personal and business, health, legal, and educational services	29.7

Source: Executive Office of the President, Office of Management and Budget, *Standard Industrial Classification Manual*, 1987 (Washington, DC: U.S. Government Printing Office), pp. 7–8, 40, 43, 45, 55–56, 58, 61, 283–284, 289, 295, 301, 315–317, 319, 321, 328; U.S. Department of Commerce, *Survey of Current Business*, May 2008, p. 43.

Sectors are broadly defined and include activities that, while related, are not always closely related. For example, frog farming and landscape planning are both included in the agriculture, forestry, and fishing sector.[2] For this reason, other narrower types of classifications may be more helpful.

Industry
A group of firms producing similar products or using similar processes.

Industries   A very useful, and narrower, classification is to put firms into industries. An **industry** is a group of firms producing similar products or using similar processes. Examples of industries include aircraft, health care, soft drinks, greeting

[2]Executive Office of the President, Office of Management and Budget, *Standard Industrial Classification Manual, 1987* (Washington, DC: U.S. Government Printing Office), pp. 29, 34.

| TABLE 12.2 | *Sample Industries and Products in the Manufacturing Sector* |

Firms producing similar products or using similar processes are grouped into the same industry.

Industry	Industry Product Examples
Aircraft	Airplanes, helicopters, hang gliders, blimps
Book printing	Printed and bound books and pamphlets
Carpet and rug	Carpets and rugs made from textiles and other materials
Doll and stuffed toy	Dolls, doll clothing, stuffed toys
Fluid milk	Fluid milk, cream, cottage cheese
Mobile home	Mobile homes and nonresidential mobile buildings
Motor and generator	Electric motors, generator sets, power generators, motor housings
Pharmaceuticals	Tablets, capsules, ointments, and other medicinal products for human and veterinary use
Power-driven hand tool	Power-driven drills, grinders, hammers, and others
Steel pipe and tube	Seamless steel pipe, boiler tubes, wrought well casings
Turbines	Solar and wind-powered turbine generators, windmills for generating power

Source: Executive Office of the President, Office of Management and Budget, *Standard Industrial Classification Manual, 1987* (Washington, DC: U.S. Government Printing Office), pp. 71, 90, 111, 127, 138, 175, 199, 207, 222, 236–237, 257.

cards, and food processing. Table 12.2 gives several industries in the manufacturing sector and examples of their products. Although the firms in each of these industries are listed in the manufacturing sector, the products they produce differ significantly from industry to industry.

It is common to find large, multiproduct corporations operating in several industries. Corporate giant General Electric, for example, through its divisions and subsidiaries produces appliances, jet engines, diagnostic medical technologies, media and entertainment through NBC, credit and loan services, and water treatment systems.[3]

The industry classification is sometimes too broad for some purposes. For example, suppose you are interested in finding data about firms that produce windmills for power. In this case, information on the turbine industry, in which windmills are listed, would be too broad. Depending on an information seeker's needs, production in the economy can be viewed from many different levels: producing sectors, industries, narrower parts of industries, or individual firms.

Methods of Production

Whether a huge company such as Boeing is producing commercial jetliners or a small family-owned company is producing carpet-cleaning services, there are usually many different ways, or methods, to choose from to produce the good or service. The method of production actually chosen is dependent on many considerations. It is important, however, to understand that whatever that method is, it underlies the firm's cost of production.

[3]http://www.ge.com.

| **TABLE 12.3** | *A Production Function* |

A recipe is a simple example of a production function because it gives the types and amounts of inputs and the processes needed to produce a particular output.

Banana Pancakes

Young and old visitors, like nephew-in-law Frank Squillace, always request this Sunday brunch favorite on visits to our home. We usually double—and sometimes triple—this recipe.

1 $\frac{1}{4}$ cups flour
2 teaspoons baking powder
$\frac{1}{2}$ teaspoon salt
3 tablespoons brown sugar (packed)
1 egg, beaten
1 cup buttermilk
$\frac{1}{2}$ cup milk
1 tablespoon melted butter (or margarine) plus additional butter for griddle
1–2 large very ripe bananas

Mix all dry ingredients together in large bowl. Stir eggs, milks, and melted butter together and add to dry ingredients. Stir mixture—do not beat. Mash bananas and add to mixture. Stir thoroughly. Melt additional butter or margarine in skillet or on griddle. Put desired-size pancake mixture on griddle and cook. Flip pancakes when bubbles appear. Serve with your favorite syrup and butter. Enjoy!

Production Function

Shows the type and amount of output that results from a particular group of inputs when those inputs are combined in a certain way.

The Production Function   A **production function** shows the type and amount of output that results when a particular group of inputs is processed in a certain way. Production functions exist for every good and service: agricultural products, backhoes, economics courses, rain garden designs, football helmets, hamburgers, and everything else that can be produced. For most types of goods and services, such as gasoline or automobiles, production functions can be clearly defined. But we do find that for some productive activities, such as learning or child rearing, the functions are not as well understood.

A recipe, such as the one in Table 12.3, provides an easy way to understand a production function. In this production function the output is banana pancakes. The inputs include the ingredients listed at the top of the recipe—bananas, eggs, and so forth—as well as kitchen equipment and the labor provided by the person preparing the pancakes. The process for combining these inputs is explained in the text of the recipe and involves such operations as stirring and mashing. All production functions are similar to this recipe in that they specify a type and amount of output, the numbers and types of inputs, and how the inputs are combined.

Usually there are several production functions to choose from when producing a good or service. For example, a painting contractor could paint the exterior of a house with brushes or spraying equipment, someone who is baking pies could make the shell from scratch or frozen crust, and a city could provide for recycling with curbside pickup or a community drop-off facility. Because a business often can choose among several methods to produce an output, it is helpful to understand the factors that underlie this choice.

Efficient Method of Production
The lowest-cost method of production.

Choosing a Production Function   What causes a firm to choose a particular production function? The answer to this question is easy when we recall that the objective of a firm is to maximize profit and that profit is what remains after costs are subtracted from revenue. Every production function has a cost associated with it, and businesses will try to maximize profit by using the production method that produces whatever type and quality of product the business wants at the lowest cost. This is not much different from the way people operate: We look for the least-cost way to accomplish something. Whether our intention is to cook a gourmet meal or a simple supper, we will try to find the production method that produces our intended result at the lowest cost. When someone produces a good or service at the lowest cost, an **efficient method of production** and the efficient use of resources occur.

The choice of the production function that leads to the lowest cost for a business differs from firm to firm, even when the firms are in the same industry. Sometimes the size of an operation influences the way a business produces. Take surveillance in retail stores. It could be more cost effective for a large store to prevent shoplifting by using cameras and for a small store to put its sales personnel through training to spot shoplifters.

Technology
The body of knowledge that exists about production and its processes.

Production Functions and Technology   Technological change has a significant influence on production functions. We can think of **technology** as the knowledge that we possess about production processes. Technology drives how we "do things" and it constantly changes. Technology affects the design of processes and machinery and equipment, and it influences inventory control, packaging, human relations, purchasing, and just about every other part of production. Technological change is leading the way to breakthroughs in the testing and treatment of medical problems, to solving crime through forensics, to advanced information systems that make e-mail and cell phones routine, and to more efficient ways to produce and distribute everything from pickup trucks to fresh herbs.

Technology defines the range of production methods from which a business can choose: from old methods to the latest advances. Even though the most technologically advanced production functions are usually the most efficient, some businesses cannot afford the transition to the latest design. Business profit may be maximized by keeping older equipment and methods. Over time, however, updated processes do become the norm.

Creative Destruction
New, technologically advanced machinery and production methods cause the disappearance of old machinery and methods.

Technology plays a major role in driving growth and change in an economy. As technology grows and new ideas are advanced, some processes and equipment become obsolete. The economist Joseph Schumpeter referred to this as **creative destruction:** New machinery, production processes, and other results of technological change frequently replace the old, causing one area of the economy to grow and prosper and another to shrink and perhaps ultimately disappear. For example, the introduction of robotics into assembly lines has not only affected the demand for labor but has also caused much machinery and equipment in automobile plants to become obsolete.

Creative destruction also occurs at the international level when firms in a country's industry lag because of technological advances adopted by competing firms in another country. For example, the U.S. steel and consumer electronics industries were hurt by the development of advanced production techniques for these products in Japan and elsewhere. Application 12.1, "Learn to Live with It," looks at the positive and negative sides of advances in technology and production that come with creative destruction.

APPLICATION 12.1

LEARN TO LIVE WITH IT

You might say that creative destruction has a bright side and a dark side. On the bright side are updated advances in products and production techniques that we thought were beyond our reach. On the dark side are the losses to businesses and employees that had a major stake in the "old" product and who know that this is the end of the run for them.

While creative destruction often has a dramatic and ongoing impact, it is not something that occurs just once in a while. Creative destruction is ongoing and many instances can be found by looking back over just a short period of time.

Consider Polaroid, which for years was the successful, only producer of instant-developing film cameras. When Kodak introduced its own instant-developing film camera, Polaroid responded by successfully suing Kodak for patent infringement. Kodak stopped its production and many thought that it would be impossible to weaken Polaroid. But, then along came digital cameras—with their creative new technology—that effectively do what Polaroid cameras do. This new technology swept away the demand for instant-developing cameras, which Polaroid subsequently stopped producing.

There are many other current examples of creative destruction. Don't expect your new computer to have a portal for a 3 ½-inch floppy; they have been replaced with CDs and small, convenient flash or thumb drives. If you are flying out of town, you don't need to stand in line to go face-to-face with an agent at the airport. You can now easily get your ticket and boarding pass online. We are saying good-bye to analog televisions which formally began to be creatively destroyed in June 2009 when television went digital with its brighter, clearer picture. And, how often do you get research sources from your campus library quickly via your computer rather than walk into the building and do a physical search like earlier students had to do because there was no other way of getting needed information?

A large part of the dark side of creative destruction is its effect on jobs and incomes. Think about the jobs lost with the introduction of digital cameras, and with all of the online capabilities for travel, research, banking, and shopping.

One widely cited and classic example of creative destruction and its impact is that of the Luddites. The Luddites, a group of early 19th-century English weavers, were losing their jobs to newly designed stocking frames and power looms that were being introduced into clothing factories. This new technology was such a threat to the Luddites that they would storm factories in an effort to destroy the frames and power looms that were jeopardizing their livelihood. Their aggression caused Parliament to pass the Frame Breaking Act in 1812, which allowed the execution of those convicted of breaking weaving machines.

Creative destruction will always be with us. It's a matter of response. Some people fight it and are termed modern-day Luddites. Some are smart and prepare for the impact that it might have on jobs and prepare themselves to move on.

Sources: Federal Communications Commission, "The Digital TV Transition," http://www.dtv.gov/whatisdtv.html; "The Luddites," http://www.spartacus.schoolnet.co.uk/PRluddites.htm; "What is a Luddite?" http://www.usu.edu/sanderso/multinet/lud1.html.

ECONOMIC TIME, PRODUCTION, AND THE COSTS OF PRODUCTION

Short Run
A production time frame in which some factors of production are variable in amount and some are fixed.

Variable Factors
Factors of production that change in amount as the level of output changes.

Variable Costs
Costs of using variable factors.

The production function that a firm chooses is influenced by the time frame in which it views or plans its operations. Generally, production may be regarded as taking place over a short-run or a long-run period of time. These time periods are not defined in terms of hours, months, or years (the usual custom for measuring time). Rather, they are defined in a more abstract way.

The **short run** is the time frame in which production takes place using some factors that can be varied in amount and some that cannot as the level of output increases or decreases. Factors of production that can be varied in amount, such as hourly labor, raw materials, and replacement parts on machinery, are **variable factors**. Because the amount of variable factors used changes as the level of output changes, the costs of these factors to a business also change as the level of output changes. The costs for a business's variable factors are called **variable costs** and include, for example, hourly wages and payments for raw materials and machine parts.

Fixed Factors
Factors of production that do not change in amount as the level of output changes.

Fixed Costs
Costs of using fixed factors.

Long Run
A production time frame in which all factors of production are variable in amount.

Factors of production that cannot be changed in amount as the level of output changes are called **fixed factors.** Fixed factors might include a building, key personnel, some machinery, and insurance. Because the amounts of fixed factors remain unchanged as the level of production increases or decreases, their costs do not change. And, importantly, they must be paid for regardless of whether the firm produces anything or not. The costs of fixed factors are called **fixed costs.** In essence, the short run is the time period in which fixed factors form a boundary within which production takes place.

The **long run** is the time frame in which all factors are regarded as variable: There are no fixed factors to limit production. In the long run, a much wider range of production choices is available because all resources, including buildings and other production facilities, are regarded as alterable.

Suppose that the owners of a restaurant are trying to evaluate the production functions and associated costs of producing meals. If they can alter the number of servers, tables, and menu selections but not the size of the dining or kitchen area, they are planning in the short run. These same owners are planning in the long run when they analyze the methods and costs of producing meals as their facilities are expanded, or as they add new restaurants, or, more generally, when they no longer regard any of their factors as fixed.

This concept of planning in different time frames is easily applied to a student's production of a college education. The long run is the period in which general plans for earning a degree are made. In this long-run period, all factors can be altered: the selection of a college, the course of study to be followed, the number of hours to be taken each semester, and the commitment to a part-time job. Once some of these decisions are made and the student is enrolled in particular courses, producing a college education can be viewed in the short run. Each semester could represent a short-run time frame because the student is producing an education within boundaries set by the school attended, the semester's scheduled classes, and other factors to which the student is obligated.

In order to make production decisions in either the short run or the long run, a business needs to determine the costs associated with producing various amounts of its output. Because production is planned differently in each time frame, we will examine costs in the short run and long run separately.

Short-Run Costs

Again, in the short run all factors used in the production of a good or service can be classified as either variable or fixed. Variable factors and costs change as the level of output changes; fixed factors and costs do not. A hypothetical example follows in which the short-run costs of operating a lawn and grounds maintenance company to service housing complexes are calculated and analyzed. The costs given in this example are those for the weekly maintenance of small apartment and condominium complex lawns and grounds.

Total Fixed Cost (TFC)
The cost of all fixed factors; does not change as the level of output changes and must be paid even when output is zero.

Total Costs   Let's begin the calculation of the costs of operating this service by adding together all bills that must be paid regardless of the number of complex grounds maintained: that is, by determining **total fixed costs (TFC).** These could include payments on a loan for mowers and a truck as well as payments for a storage facility and insurance. Assume that total fixed costs are $400 per week.

Table 12.4, which illustrates the weekly total costs to the business of maintaining from zero through nine complexes, gives the total fixed cost for the firm's operations in the second column. Notice that the $400 fixed cost does not change as more or fewer

TABLE 12.4	*Weekly Total Costs of Maintaining Lawns and Grounds*

Total fixed cost does not change as the level of output changes and must be paid even if nothing is produced. Total variable cost is zero when nothing is produced and increases with the level of output. Because total cost is equal to total fixed plus total variable costs, it also increases as output increases.

Number of Sites Maintained	Total Fixed Cost (TFC)	Total Variable Cost (TVC)	Total Cost (TC)
0	$400	$ 0	$ 400
1	400	200	600
2	400	225	625
3	400	275	675
4	400	350	750
5	400	475	875
6	400	650	1,050
7	400	895	1,295
8	400	1,220	1,620
9	400	1,670	2,070

Total Variable Cost (TVC)

The cost of all variable factors of production; increases as the level of output increases but is zero when output is zero.

Total Cost (TC)

The cost of acquiring and using all factors of production; total fixed cost plus total variable cost.

Average Total Cost (ATC)

The cost per unit of output produced; total cost divided by the number of units produced.

complex grounds are maintained and that it must be paid even if none are serviced. This is because, regardless of how many lawns and grounds are cared for, the fixed factors, and thus the costs of the fixed factors, remain unchanged.

Next, we will calculate the firm's **total variable costs (TVC)**. Because these are costs of variable factors that change in amount as the number of sites maintained changes, variable costs could include expenditures for labor, gasoline, fertilizer and other chemicals, repair of the truck and mowing equipment, small hand tools, and such. The third column of Table 12.4 gives the company's total variable costs for servicing from zero through nine complexes. For example, if this firm were to service four a week, it would face a total variable cost of $350. Notice that the variable costs are zero if the firm services no grounds, they continually increase as more are maintained, and they increase significantly with a large number of complex grounds maintained. An explanation for this pattern of variable cost increases will be given shortly.

The **total cost (TC)** of maintaining from zero through nine sites is given in the last column of Table 12.4. The total cost for a particular level of output is all fixed costs plus all variable costs at that level of production. For example, the total cost of maintaining five lawns and grounds is $875: $400 in fixed costs plus $475 in variable costs.

Unit Costs   In addition to its total costs, a business usually finds it essential to determine per unit costs at each level of output. The cost per unit at a particular level of output is called **average total cost (ATC)**. Average total cost is found by dividing total cost by the number of units produced.

Table 12.5 gives the total cost of maintaining grounds from Table 12.4 and the average total cost for each individual complex when a specified number is maintained. For example, the average total cost of servicing each site when three are maintained is $225. This is found by dividing the total cost of $675 by 3. The average total cost of $185 when seven sites are maintained is found by dividing the total cost of $1,295 by 7.[4]

[4]The average total cost of maintaining zero lawns is not given because any number divided by zero is undefined.

TABLE 12.5   *Weekly Total, Average Total, and Marginal Costs of Maintaining Lawns and Grounds*

Average total cost measures the per unit cost at a specific production level, and marginal cost measures the change in total cost from producing an additional unit of output.

Number of Sites Maintained	Total Cost (TC)	Average Total Cost (ATC)	Marginal Cost (MC)
0	$ 400.00	—	
			$200.00
1	600.00	$600.00	
			25.00
2	625.00	312.50	
			50.00
3	675.00	225.00	
			75.00
4	750.00	187.50	
			125.00
5	875.00	175.00	
			175.00
6	1,050.00	175.00	
			245.00
7	1,295.00	185.00	
			325.00
8	1,620.00	202.50	
			450.00
9	2,070.00	230.00	

Marginal Cost (MC)
The change in total cost when one more unit of output is produced.

Table 12.5 also gives the marginal cost of maintaining lawns and grounds. As explained in the previous chapter, **marginal cost (MC)** is the change in total cost from producing one more unit of output—in this case, caring for one more site. For example, if no sites are maintained, the total cost given in Table 12.5 is $400; if one is maintained, total cost increases to $600. Thus, the marginal cost of the first complex is $200 ($600 − $400). As in the previous chapter, marginal cost is listed midway between the units of output. Table 12.6 summarizes the characteristics of short-run total, average, and marginal costs.

A business could analyze its unit costs in even greater detail. It could, for example, determine its fixed costs per unit (average fixed cost) and variable costs per unit (average variable cost). More detailed cost calculations such as these appear in the appendix to this chapter.

The Pattern of Short-Run Costs

There are patterns to the way total cost, average total cost, and marginal cost behave in the short run. We can observe these patterns in tables of cost figures, such as those listed in Tables 12.4 and 12.5. But they can be more easily observed when the short-run costs are graphed.

Total Cost Pattern   Figure 12.1 plots the total cost, given in Table 12.5, of maintaining from zero through nine sites per week. Notice in Figure 12.1 that total cost is $400 when output is zero. This, of course, is due to the firm's fixed costs, which must be paid regardless of whether or not production occurs. Notice also that total cost continually

TABLE 12.6	Summary of Short-Run Costs

Total, average, and marginal costs are different ways of looking at costs as the level of output changes.

Total Fixed Cost (TFC)

✓ Cost of all fixed factors; does not change as the level of output changes; must be paid if nothing is produced.

Total Variable Cost (TVC)

✓ Cost of all variable factors; varies directly with level of output; zero if nothing is produced.

Total Cost (TC)

✓ Total fixed cost plus total variable cost; equal to TFC at zero production; increases with increases in output.

Average Total Cost (ATC)

✓ Cost per unit of output; total cost divided by the number of units of output; decreases and increases as production increases.

Marginal Cost (MC)

✓ Change in total cost per additional unit of output; decreases then increases as production increases.

increases as more places are serviced. Because the fixed cost of maintaining these grounds never changes, this increase is due solely to the increase in total variable costs.

A closer analysis of total cost shows that in the early stage of production, when few sites are maintained, total cost increases slowly. But in the latter stage of production, when many sites are maintained, total cost increases quickly. Why does total cost follow this pattern?

If this company plans to service just a few places, it might manage by hiring one employee (variable factor) to use the truck and equipment (fixed factors). For each site maintained, the company would also need to provide other variable factors, such as bags for the grass and gasoline for the truck and mowing equipment. However, once labor is hired, the company will not encounter significant increases in the other variable costs to care for each additional site if just a few are maintained. Thus, total cost increases slowly for the first few units of output because the increase in variable factors needed to accompany the fixed factors is small.

After a while, maintaining more sites necessitates more than just an increase in bags and gasoline. Labor costs increase as more workers are needed or as the existing employees are paid overtime. As the truck and mowing equipment are used more often, breakdowns occur, causing the cost of repairs to increase. Also, the owner of the firm may expect a higher normal profit in return for the effort and responsibility of increasing production. At some point, these increases in variable costs cause total cost to increase more quickly as production grows.

As production increases to even higher levels, the number of places serviced will begin to seriously strain the capabilities of the fixed factors, and variable costs will increase substantially as the firm tries to compensate for the limits of the fixed factors. Perhaps, with the existing mowers and truck, the company might reasonably expect to maintain only six or seven sites. If it tries to service eight or nine, many variable factors will be needed to fill in for the limitations of the fixed factors. At this point the

FIGURE 12.1　　*Total Cost of Maintaining Lawns and Grounds*

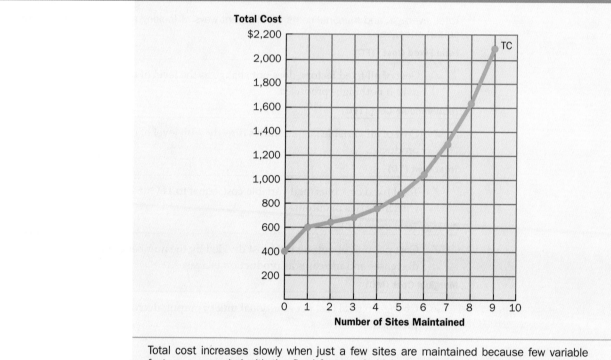

Total cost increases slowly when just a few sites are maintained because few variable factors are needed with the fixed factors. At higher levels of output, total cost increases quickly as more variable factors are needed to compensate for the limitations imposed by the fixed factors.

company may encounter considerably higher variable costs as it rents another truck and more mowers, leases additional storage space, and hires a manager.

In short, total cost increases slowly at first because, with a given amount of fixed factors, few variable factors can increase production significantly. As output levels become larger, total cost increases more rapidly because more variable factors are needed with the fixed factors to increase production. At high levels of production, costs increase very quickly because the fixed factors are approaching the limits of their productivity, and many variable factors are needed to compensate for the fixed factor boundary.

Marginal Cost and Average Total Cost Patterns　　Let us next examine the marginal cost (MC) and average total cost (ATC) patterns as production increases. The marginal cost and average total cost data given in Table 12.5 are graphed in Figure 12.2.

Notice that marginal cost, or the change in total cost from maintaining one more site, decreases at first and then increases. As with total cost, this drop and rise are due to the behavior of the variable factors as reflected in variable costs. With this in mind, the same reasoning that applies to the explanation of the total cost pattern applies to the explanation of the marginal cost pattern.

To service the first site, the marginal cost is $200. If you refer to Table 12.4, you can confirm that this equals the change in variable cost (and total cost) associated with maintaining one rather than no sites. Much of this $200 marginal cost is probably due to the hiring of labor. To maintain a second site, the marginal cost is only $25. This decrease in marginal cost occurs because the additional variable factors needed to maintain the

FIGURE 12.2   *Marginal Cost and Average Total Cost of Maintaining Lawns and Grounds*

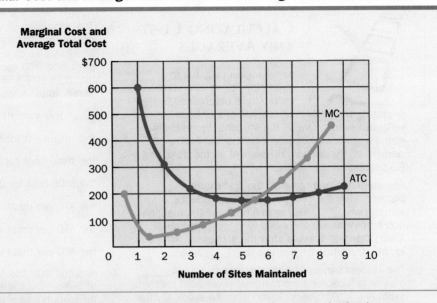

Both marginal cost and average total cost fall and then rise as production increases. When marginal cost is less than average total cost, it pulls average total cost down; when marginal cost is greater than average total cost, it pulls average total cost up.

second site cost the firm only $25. As explained earlier, at this point there will be only a slight increase in the use of some variable inputs, such as gasoline and grass bags.

When a third site is maintained, marginal cost begins to rise because of the increase in variable factors needed to increase production. And as more and more places are cared for, marginal cost rises more rapidly. This more rapid rise is due to the increasing amounts of variable factors that are required to compensate for the limits placed on production by the fixed factors.

Return to Figure 12.2 and observe the average total cost curve. Average total cost decreases and then increases with more production. Why is this so?

The cost per unit falls initially because marginal cost is lower than average total cost. When marginal cost is less than average total cost, it pulls average total cost down. When marginal cost becomes greater than average total cost, it pulls average total cost up. Figure 12.2 also shows that because of these relationships between average and marginal costs, marginal cost must cross, or equal, average total cost at minimum average total cost. Thus, average total cost behaves the way it does because of the behavior of marginal cost.

You encounter this relationship between marginal and average values in determining your average in a course as you take additional exams. If you make a grade on your next exam (remember: each additional exam that you take is a marginal exam) that is lower than your average, that grade will pull your average down. If, on the next exam, you make a grade higher than your average, your average will increase. For example, if you have an average of 93 percent in this economics course and you earn a grade of 70 percent on your next exam, your average will fall; if you earn a grade of 98 percent on your next exam, your average will rise. Test Your Understanding, "Calculating Costs and Averages," gives you an opportunity to further explore the average–marginal relationship and to calculate some short-run costs.

TEST YOUR UNDERSTANDING

CALCULATING COSTS AND AVERAGES

1. A student's grade in a psychology class at a state university is determined by averaging the percentage scores of four equally weighted exams. One of the students in the class earns a grade of 92 percent on the first exam, 79 percent on the second, 80 percent on the third, and 93 percent on the fourth.

The student's average after the first exam is _____ percent. After the second exam, the student's average will _____ (rise or fall) because the marginal score from the second exam is _____ (higher or lower) than the average after the first exam. After two exams, the student's average is _____ percent.

The student's average after the third exam will _____ (rise or fall) because the marginal score from the third exam is _____ (higher or lower) than the average. After three exams, the student's average is _____ percent.

The student's average after the fourth exam will _____ (rise or fall) because the marginal score from the fourth exam is _____ (higher or lower) than the average. After four exams, the student's average for the course is _____ percent.

2. Bert's Trash Company specializes in emptying large commercial recycling containers and delivering the material to a regional single-stream sorting facility. Bert has figured that his total fixed costs per business day are $100. He has also calculated that the total variable cost for one pickup is $250 per day, the total cost for three pickups per day is $400, the marginal cost of the second pickup as well as the fourth pickup is $50, and the average total cost with five pickups is $105. Fill in the following table for Bert's costs.

Pickups per Business Day	Total Fixed Cost	Total Variable Cost	Total Cost	Average Total Cost	Marginal Cost
0	___	___	___	___	___
1	___	___	___	___	___
2	___	___	___	___	___
3	___	___	___	___	___
4	___	___	___	___	___
5	___	___	___	___	___

3. The manager of a college food service has determined that the daily fixed cost of operation is $855. She has also calculated that the total variable cost for preparing 900 meals is $1,170; for preparing 1,800 meals, it is $2,565; and when 2,700 meals are prepared, total variable cost equals $5,328.

Given this information,

the total cost for 900 meals is $_____,

the total cost for 1,800 meals is $_____,

the total cost for 2,700 meals is $_____,

the ATC per meal with 900 meals is $_____,

the ATC per meal with 1,800 meals is $_____, and

the ATC per meal with 2,700 meals is $_____.

4. Assume that the following table applies to the costs of completing the short-form federal income tax return for students by a small accounting service. Fill in this table.

Output	Total Fixed Cost	Total Variable Cost	Total Cost	Average Total Cost	Marginal Cost
0	$ 80	$ 0	$___	–	
					$___
1	___	40	___	$___	
					___
2	___	60	___	___	
					___
3	___	70	___	___	
					___
4	___	100	___	___	
					___
5	___	150	___	___	
					___
6	___	220	___	___	
					___
7	___	340	___	___	
					___
8	___	520	___	___	

Answers can be found at the back of the book.

The Law of Diminishing Returns

Underlying all the short-run cost patterns is a basic principle, which you may likely have heard, called the **Law of Diminishing Returns.** This law states that as additional units of a variable factor are added to a fixed factor, beyond some point (not necessarily right away) the *additional* product from each additional unit of the variable factor decreases. Put another way, the Law of Diminishing Returns says that, after some point, each additional unit of a variable factor used will add less to output than was added by the unit used just before it. This is easily illustrated with an example.

Assume that you own a small restaurant and plan to begin hiring people to prepare and serve meals. The dining room, outfitted with tables and other restaurant furniture, and a fully equipped kitchen are the fixed factors, and the labor used to work in the restaurant is a variable factor.

If one person is hired to work in the restaurant, that person working alone will need to prepare, serve, and clean up after a certain number of meals per day. If a second person is hired, the two together can divide up some of the tasks and work more efficiently. One person can work the kitchen and the other can work the dining room. Together the two will more than double the number of meals that can be prepared and served by one person alone. If you hire a third person, work can be further divided, and the number of meals may again significantly increase. As long as each worker hired adds more to output than was added by the worker hired just before, or as long as diminishing returns don't set in, the marginal cost of each additional meal falls.

At some point, assume when the fourth person is hired, the number of meals that can be prepared and served per day will no longer increase as rapidly with additional workers. That is, the number of *additional* meals prepared and served by hiring the fourth worker will not be as great as the number of *additional* meals prepared and served by hiring the third worker. Four workers cannot operate as efficiently as three because the fixed facility is becoming crowded. In other words, the boundary imposed by the fixed factors begins to limit the productivity of the variable factor. When this occurs, and the additional output from hiring an additional worker begins to fall, diminishing returns have set in. This causes the marginal cost of each additional meal to rise.

Beyond this point, as more (five, six, seven) people are hired, the *additional* work accomplished by each will further diminish. They will become less efficient as the fixed factors more severely limit their full use, and marginal cost will rise at a faster rate. It would, incidentally, be possible to hire so many restaurant workers that they would get in each other's way, causing output to fall.[5]

The Law of Diminishing Returns governs all production in the short run. For example, when a student tries to produce enough knowledge to pass an exam by studying for an extended and uninterrupted period of time, the Law of Diminishing Returns takes effect. During the first few hours of reading and reviewing, each hour will produce more additional knowledge than the hour before it as the material is comprehended. After a while, however, as the student becomes tired and fixed physical and mental factors approach their limit, diminishing returns take effect, and each additional hour of study is less productive than the one before it. Can you use the Law of Diminishing Returns to explain why it is better to study on a consistent basis for shorter periods of time than it is to cram the night before an exam?

While the Law of Diminishing Returns and the resulting pattern of costs given here are common to all production in the short run, the point at which diminishing returns set in differs from product to product. But these differences do not undermine

---

[5]This means that a point can be reached where more would be produced if some of the workers would quit.

the fact that all short-run production can be explained in terms of these patterns: The limitation of the fixed factors, which gives the short run its definition, causes diminishing returns to occur and thus causes marginal, average total, and total costs to rise in the latter stages of production.

Businesses are always trying to find ways to lower their costs, often by making their inputs more productive. Up for Debate, "Do Wellness Programs Lower Costs for Employers?", discusses a controversial expenditure that might lower or raise overall costs for a business, depending on which argument you buy. If wellness programs work, how could they influence the Law of Diminishing Returns?

Long-Run Costs

The long run is the time frame long enough for a business to regard all its factors of production as variable and none as fixed. Calculating the cost of production in the long run means determining the cost of a given level of output when a business can alter the amounts of any and all of its resources. In the long run, production costs are not divided between fixed and variable because all factors, and therefore all costs, are variable.

Table 12.7 gives the long-run costs of constructing from zero through 10 houses by a hypothetical home builder. The second column of Table 12.7 gives the **long-run total cost** of constructing from zero through 10 houses. Notice that long-run total cost increases as more houses are produced and that, because there are no fixed factors or costs, it is zero when no houses are produced.

Long-run total cost is used to calculate **long-run average total cost,** which is determined in the same way as short-run average total cost: Total cost is divided by the quantity of output produced. Long-run average total cost is shown in the third column of Table 12.7. **Long-run marginal cost** can also be calculated from long-run

Long-Run Total Cost, Average Total Cost, and Marginal Cost

Total cost, per unit cost, and cost per additional unit of output, respectively; calculated for production when all inputs are regarded as variable.

TABLE 12.7	*Long-Run Total Cost, Average Total Cost, and Marginal Cost*

Long-run total cost is the total expenditure for each level of output in the long run. Long-run average total cost measures the per unit cost; and long-run marginal cost measures the cost of producing an additional unit of output.

Number of Houses	Long-Run Total Cost (LRTC)	Long-Run Average Total Cost (LRATC)	Long-Run Marginal Cost (LRMC)
0	$ 0	—	
			$400,000
1	400,000	$400,000	
			100,000
2	500,000	250,000	
			100,000
3	600,000	200,000	
			100,000
4	700,000	175,000	
			175,000
5	875,000	175,000	
			175,000
6	1,050,000	175,000	
			350,000
7	1,400,000	200,000	
			600,000
8	2,000,000	250,000	
			700,000
9	2,700,000	300,000	
			800,000
10	3,500,000	350,000	

total cost: It is the change in long-run total cost as one more unit of output is produced.

Economists like to focus on the pattern of long-run average total cost when analyzing the behavior of production and its costs in the long run. Figure 12.3 plots the long-run average total cost from Table 12.7. Notice that, at first, long-run average total cost decreases as the level of output increases. With an ability to vary inputs that were fixed in the short run, the company finds that, initially, the cost per unit of output drops. At some point long-run average total cost reaches a minimum and, in this example, stays at that level for a while as output continues to grow. But at some point, as production increases even further, the cost per unit of output increases. The explanation for this decreasing, constant, and increasing cost pattern, which is typical of the behavior of long-run average total cost, is based on economies of scale, constant returns to scale, and diseconomies of scale.

Economies of Scale

Occur when the increasing size of production in the long run causes the per unit cost of production to fall.

Economies of Scale, Diseconomies of Scale, and Constant Returns to Scale   In the initial stages of long-run production a producer typically experiences **economies of scale** that cause long-run average total cost to decrease. This means that initially as the size, or scale, of the operation becomes larger, the cost per unit of output falls. What causes economies of scale to occur?

| FIGURE 12.3 | *Long-Run Average Total Cost* |

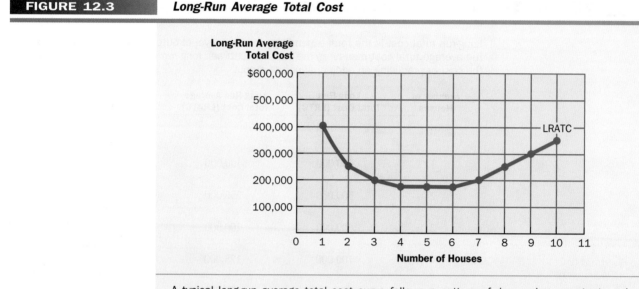

A typical long-run average total cost curve follows a pattern of decreasing, constant, and increasing per unit costs.

With a larger scale and output, a firm can use highly specialized and efficient labor and equipment that might be expensive to obtain, but because of the large output, can actually allow the firm to produce at a lower per unit cost. Economies of scale permit a company to hire more specialized professionals who can apply their expertise to specific areas of the company's operations, such as human resources or finance or supply-chain management. A large company can profitably use more advanced technology and equipment, from bucket trucks to accounting and software systems. Also, as a business becomes large, it may receive quantity discounts on some of its purchases, as well as negotiate lower interest rates on its loans. Think about fast-food restaurants and your local pub. The cost per unit of a burger that is carefully machine-sized, prepackaged, and frozen for instant grilling by an unskilled worker is considerably less than one made by a cook who is starting with fresh ingredients from a local market.

Unit cost savings, or efficiency gains, from economies of scale as a business becomes larger and produces higher levels of output have been a frequent argument in favor of allowing mergers between competing sellers in the same market. Mergers are covered in more detail in Chapter 14.

When cost per unit increases in the latter stages of long-run production, a firm experiences **diseconomies of scale.** In this case, the size or scale of the operation has become so large and unwieldy that the cost per unit of output increases. Diseconomies of scale generally arise because the large size of a company makes control over its operations difficult. As the organization grows and the chain of command lengthens and becomes more complex, it is necessary to hire more managers at all levels, thereby increasing the cost of output. With a longer chain of command, authority and responsibility may become disjointed, causing factors of production to be wasted due to a lack of communication, accountability, or poor control. Costs may also be affected by the amount of time required to pass information and commands through such a large

Diseconomies of Scale
Occur when the increasing size of production in the long run causes the per unit cost of production to rise.

FIGURE 12.4   *The Three Phases of the Long-Run Average Total Cost Curve*

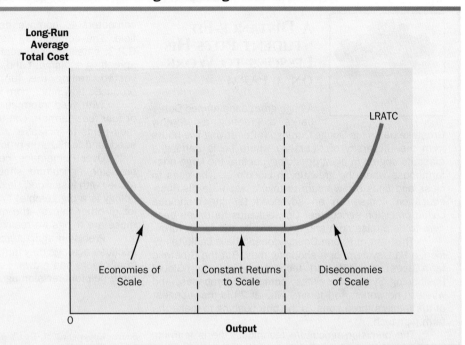

The long-run average total cost curve goes through three phases: a decreasing per unit cost phase caused by economies of scale; a phase of constant returns to scale where per unit costs neither decrease nor increase; and a phase where per unit costs increase due to diseconomies of scale.

organization. Many companies have restructured or reorganized in an effort to reduce diseconomies of scale created by layers of management.

Between economies of scale and diseconomies of scale is a range of production where long-run average total cost neither decreases nor increases. Throughout this output range the firm experiences **constant returns to scale,** or operating levels that have become so large that economies of scale are exhausted but not large enough to encounter diseconomies of scale.

Many real-life examples attest to the existence of economies and diseconomies of scale. This does not mean, however, that every company faces a long-run average total cost curve that looks exactly like that in Figure 12.3. Instead, the long-run average total cost of each firm's product differs in the length and strength of its decreasing, constant, and increasing ranges. A company producing automobiles, for example, will have a different length and strength to its long-run average total cost curve phases than will a fast-food chain producing hamburgers. Figure 12.4 gives the three phases of long-run production costs.

Application 12.2, "A Distance-Ed Student Puts His Lessons to Work on a Farm," provides a real-life application of many of the concepts and terms that you have learned in this chapter. As you read about Jeremy, think about technology and production functions, fixed and variable costs, the short run and long run, and economies of scale.

Constant Returns to Scale

Occur in the range of production levels in which long-run average total cost is constant.

APPLICATION 12.2

A DISTANCE-ED STUDENT PUTS HIS LESSONS TO WORK ON A FARM

A huge great dane named Dottie barks a greeting as Jeremy Groeteke parks his Dodge Durango [after driving two hours from the University of Nebraska where he is earning a master's degree in plant physiology] before the large brick farmhouse where he grew up. In Lincoln . . . he goes to class and finds a few hours to take a separate distance-education course on an advanced farming technique called precision agriculture. On weekends he drives back here to help raise corn and soybeans on the family farm.

This part of Boone County doesn't have cable television, a 911 system, or a shopping mall. But the Groeteke farm uses state-of-the-art technology—including Global Positioning System satellites, computer databases, and wireless networks. And Jeremy, who at 24 is the youngest of the family's three sons, is the one pushing to make the farm high-tech.

The precision-agriculture techniques he is learning through the university's distance-education program use computers to compile detailed information about each field. The computers, installed in tractors and lined to G.P.S. satellites, can control modern seed- and fertilizer-spreading equipment and, later, weigh crops as they're harvested, telling the farmer exactly how much seed produced how much corn in a given location.

With yield information detailed down to every three or four feet, farmers can then customize the treatment of their fields to increase production further, applying water, seed, and fertilizer in precise amounts.

Over homemade peach pie, Jeremy's father says precision agriculture should help the farm make more money with less work. He doesn't believe investing in technology is a big gamble. "We take a lot bigger risks with a lot of other things—the market, the weather,". . . . "And those are things we really can't control."

Precision agriculture is important to the Groetekes because acreage they farm—their own and fields they rent from others has grown. . . . The larger the farm gets, the more helpful precision agriculture becomes. . . .

Source: Copyright 2001, *The Chronicle of Higher Education.* Reprinted with Permission.

Summary

1. The greatest portion of measured output in the U.S. economy comes through the business sector. Categories have been developed for classifying production. Producing sectors is a broad category that includes the services, manufacturing, and other sectors; industry is a narrower category that includes firms producing similar products or using similar processes.

2. A production function shows the output that results when a particular group of inputs is processed in a certain way. Firms have a choice of production functions and seek the least-cost, or efficient, method for producing the desired quantity and quality of output in order to maximize profit.

3. The development of new productive inputs and techniques can come from technological change. Technological change can also lead to creative destruction: New inputs and processes cause those currently in use to become obsolete and some areas of an economy to grow while others decline.

4. The choice of a method of production is influenced by the time frame in which a business plans its operations. The short run is a time period in which some factors of production are variable in amount and some are fixed. The capabilities of the fixed factors, because they cannot be changed, serve as a boundary within which production takes place. The long run is a time period in which all factors are regarded as variable.

5.   In the short run, the total cost of producing a certain level of output is found by adding total fixed cost and total variable cost. Total fixed cost is the same regardless of how much is produced; total variable cost increases as output increases. Average total cost is the cost per unit of output at a given level of production and is found by dividing total cost by the number of units of output produced. Marginal cost is the change in total cost resulting from the production of an additional unit of output.

6.   In the short run, total cost increases slowly at low levels of output and rapidly at high levels of output. Average total cost decreases and then increases, as does marginal cost. These patterns are the result of the way in which variable factor usage increases as production increases. At low levels of output, small amounts of variable factors are needed with the fixed factors, and at high levels of output, large amounts of variable factors are needed to compensate for the limits imposed by the fixed factors.

7.   Underlying the patterns of short-run costs is the Law of Diminishing Returns, which says that as a variable factor of production is added to fixed factors, beyond some point the additional product from each additional unit of the variable factor will decrease.

8.   Long-run average total cost illustrates the pattern of costs in the long run. The shape of the long-run average total cost curve is the result of economies of scale that occur in the early stages of long-run production and cause the cost per unit of output to drop, constant returns to scale where average total cost stays the same, and diseconomies of scale that occur in the late stages of long-run production and cause the cost per unit of output to increase.

Key Terms and Concepts

Producing sectors

Industry

Production function

Efficient method of production

Technology

Creative destruction

Short run

Variable factors

Variable costs

Fixed factors

Fixed costs

Long run

Total fixed cost (TFC)

Total variable cost (TVC)

Total cost (TC)

Average total cost (ATC)

Marginal cost (MC)

Law of Diminishing Returns

Long-run total cost, average total cost, and marginal cost

Economies of scale

Diseconomies of scale

Constant returns to scale

Review Questions

1. A friend has just explained that, as far as the costs of operating a business are concerned, short-run costs are the costs that are incurred within the current year and long-run costs are all costs that are incurred for more than a year. As a student of economics, how would you explain these costs differently to your friend?

2. The short-run average total cost curve and the long-run average total cost curve are similarly shaped. What causes the short-run average total cost curve to slope down and then up? What causes the long-run average total cost curve to slope down and then up?

3. When marginal cost is less than average total cost, average total cost decreases. When marginal cost is greater than average total cost, average total cost increases. Why is this so?

4. Why does a firm incur fixed costs over the short run when its output is zero, and why do fixed costs not change as the level of output changes? Why does a firm's short-run total variable cost increase slowly at smaller levels of output and rapidly at larger levels of output?

5. What is the Law of Diminishing Returns and why does it affect short-run but not long-run production? How will the Law of Diminishing Returns affect the productivity of each additional student who is washing cars at a local church parking lot to raise money for a charity? Why does this effect occur?

6. Complete the following table of short-run costs. From the information in the completed table, plot a total cost curve on the left-hand graph at the top of page 357 and an average total cost curve and a marginal cost curve on the right-hand graph. Remember to plot marginal cost at the midpoint.

Output	Total Fixed Cost	Total Variable Cost	Total Cost	Average Total Cost	Marginal Cost
0	$____	$____	$100	—	
					$____
1	____	____	150	$____	
					____
2	____	____	180	____	
					____
3	____	____	210	____	
					____
4	____	____	280	____	
					____
5	____	____	400	____	
					____
6	____	____	600	____	

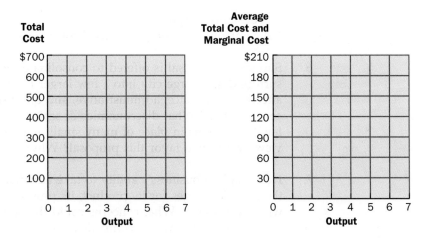

7.   Identify the three phases of a long-run average total cost curve. What is the reason for the behavior of long-run average total cost in each phase?

Review Questions

1.   Can you construct a production function for earning an A in this course?
     a. What are the necessary inputs?
     b. How much of each input is required?
     c. How are the inputs combined?

2.   List some possible explanations for the differences in production techniques used by two pizza restaurants: One is an independent mom-and-pop operation and the other is part of a national chain.

3.   Technological change can cause creative destruction: Because of new technology, one area of an economy expands while another contracts and perhaps disappears. Give some recent examples of the process of creative destruction on the national level and on the international level. What products, industries, and jobs were affected in each of your examples?

4.   The Law of Diminishing Returns was introduced in this chapter and the Law of Diminishing Marginal Utility was introduced in Chapter 11. Are there any similarities between a business using additional units of a variable input to produce a good in the short run in order to maximize profit and an individual consuming additional units of a good in order to maximize utility?

5.   Indicate whether each of the following is probably a fixed factor or a variable factor in the short run.
     a. Raw materials going into a production process
     b. The steam heat required to keep the pipes in a warehouse from freezing
     c. Electricity used to run machinery and equipment
     d. The only person in a company who knows the trade secret formula to a highly profitable product

e. A desktop computer

f. A companywide computer-based software accounting system

6. Suppose a proposal is offered to consolidate the more than 75 towns surrounding a large city into a few larger towns. What economies of scale affecting fire, police, administrative, and other services might result from the consolidation? What diseconomies of scale might result from the creation of a few large towns in place of many small ones? From an economic point of view, would you favor this proposal? Why?

7. How might a business's ability to take advantage of economies of scale affect the price it charges for its product, its profitability, and its competitiveness with rival sellers? What concerns could diseconomies of scale create for pricing, profitability, and competitiveness?

8. We have all been in situations where we see or experience employees standing around and chatting and seemingly not working at their jobs. Discuss an example you have encountered. Do you believe this was due to diseconomies of scale?

Critical Thinking Case 12

THE HUMAN FACTOR

Critical Thinking Skills

Appreciation for a broad perspective

Understanding behavioral considerations

Economic Concepts

The Law of Diminishing Returns

Short- and long-run costs

Creative destruction

Too often there is a sterile, robotic view of factors of production, their costs, and cost-cutting for a business. Workers and managers, while recognized for the important roles they play, can be regarded like machines or buildings or any other resource needed to produce a good or service. But people are complex creatures with personal objectives, needs, and feelings. To neglect this personal side of employees is not smart: It can lead to underutilization of employees, stand in the way of solving problems, and ultimately affect costs.

In a perfect world, a manager would staff an operation with the "right" number of employees; that is, the number that would keep costs down. But a manager could have other objectives, like "empire building." That is, a manager could think that having a large staff moves one up in the ranks and increases power, visibility, and influence. This type of manager might want to increase the size of an operating area for "career" reasons that could be costly to the business.

Or an organization that is struggling with its costs might need to lay off a few employees. In working through a reduction in force, a company could simply let those with the least seniority go—an easy way to address an often-difficult process. But there may be employees with good potential to improve production and increase the profitability of the organization in the future among this group. Again, a sterile view of workers does not recognize the unique abilities of employees who are valuable contributors to an employer.

The human factor is also related to the communication that occurs within an organization. With growth in the ability to rapidly communicate through methods such as text messaging and e-mail, it is easy to be in touch with virtually everyone in an organization and beyond. But how does a person decide what is necessary communication to do an effective job and what is extraneous, time consuming, and unnecessary? Answering those 200 e-mail messages a day takes time away from real production and raises costs.

We might also consider the sense of interconnectedness with one another that seems to be disappearing as, more and more, employees communicate electronically and spend less time meeting face-to-face. Today's workplace puts less emphasis on conversation and collegiality and more on sitting alone behind a desk and looking at a screen. This can lead to an increased sense of isolation and loss of commitment to an organization, which may lead to higher costs.

Questions

1. In addition to empire building and self-promotion, what other managerial traits have you seen that may not necessarily reduce costs?

2. How do today's communication systems lead to cost savings? How do they lead to increased costs? In your opinion, do the savings outweigh the losses?

3. How would you go about measuring whether the decreasing interconnectedness among people at work raises or lowers costs? Are there any strategies to improve this situation?

CHAPTER 12
APPENDIX

A FURTHER LOOK AT SHORT-RUN AVERAGE AND MARGINAL COSTS

A business may want to know more about its per unit costs than can be learned from a calculation of average total cost alone. Just as total cost is made up of total fixed and total variable costs, average total cost is made up of average fixed and average variable costs. A knowledge of how average fixed and average variable costs change as the level of output changes, and how these changes affect average total cost, is useful to a business when making production, pricing, and other decisions that impact its profitability.

Calculating Average Fixed and Average Variable Costs

We have already learned that average total cost is total cost per unit of output and that it is found by dividing total cost by the number of units produced. Similarly, average fixed cost (AFC) and average variable cost (AVC) are the fixed and variable

---

TABLE 12A.1   *Weekly Total, Average, and Marginal Costs of Maintaining Lawns and Grounds*

Average fixed, average variable, and average total costs are calculated by dividing total fixed cost, total variable cost, and total cost, respectively, by the level of output.

Number of Sites	Total Fixed Cost (TFC)	Total Variable Cost (TVC)	Total Cost (TC)	Average Fixed Cost (AFC)	Average Variable Cost (AVC)	Average Total Cost (ATC)	Marginal Cost (MC)
0	$400.00	$0.00	$400.00	—	—	—	
							$200.00
1	400.00	200.00	600.00	$400.00	$200.00	$600.00	
							25.00
2	400.00	225.00	625.00	200.00	112.50	312.50	
							50.00
3	400.00	275.00	675.00	133.33	91.67	225.00	
							75.00
4	400.00	350.00	750.00	100.00	87.50	187.50	
							125.00
5	400.00	475.00	875.00	80.00	95.00	175.00	
							175.00
6	400.00	650.00	1,050.00	66.67	108.33	175.00	
							245.00
7	400.00	895.00	1,295.00	57.14	127.86	185.00	
							325.00
8	400.00	1,220.00	1,620.00	50.00	152.50	202.50	
							450.00
9	400.00	1,670.00	2,070.00	44.44	185.56	230.00	

FIGURE 12A.1   *Marginal and Average Costs of Maintaining Lawns and Grounds*

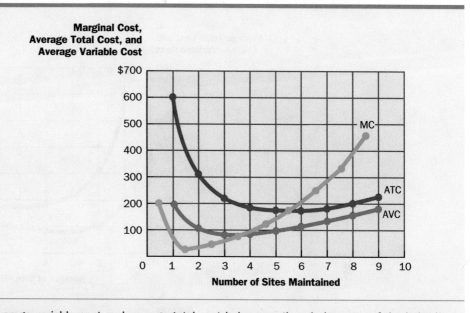

Average variable cost and average total cost behave as they do because of the behavior of marginal cost. Marginal cost behaves as it does because of the Law of Diminishing Returns.

costs per unit of output, and are calculated by dividing total fixed cost and total variable cost, respectively, by the number of units produced.

Table 12A.1 shows the weekly total fixed cost, total variable cost, and total cost numbers from Table 12.4, as well as the average total cost and marginal cost numbers from Table 12.5, for maintaining different numbers of housing complex grounds. Table 12A.1 also gives the average fixed and average variable costs that are calculated from those numbers.

It is easy to see in Table 12A.1 how the different average costs are calculated. For example, for five sites the average fixed cost of $80 is found by dividing the total fixed cost of $400 by 5; the average variable cost of $95 is the $475 total variable cost divided by 5; and the average total cost of $175 is the total cost of $875 divided by 5. The average total cost of $175 can also be found by adding the average fixed cost of $80 to the average variable cost of $95.

Notice in Table 12A.1 how average fixed and average variable costs change as more sites are maintained. Since total fixed cost does not change as the level of output increases, the average fixed cost assignable to each unit produced (in this case, each site maintained) gets smaller and smaller as more is produced. This is sometimes referred to as "spreading the overhead." Average variable cost, on the other hand, decreases at first and then increases at larger levels of output. The explanation for this is the same as the explanation for the behavior of average total cost and is more clearly understood when looking at a graph of average variable cost and marginal cost.

Graphing Average and Marginal Cost Curves

The average total, average variable, and marginal cost information from Table 12A.1 is graphed in Figure 12A.1. Two of the curves in the figure, average total cost (ATC)

Average Fixed, Variable, and Total Costs of Maintaining Lawns and Grounds

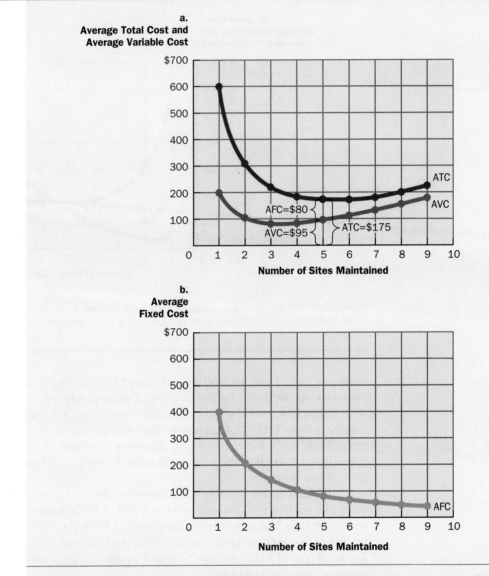

Average fixed cost is shown by the difference between the ATC and the AVC curves. The curves come closer together as the level of output increases because average fixed cost decreases.

and marginal cost (MC), are identical to the average total and marginal cost curves in Figure 12.2.

Notice again that the ATC curve falls when marginal cost is below average total cost, the ATC curve rises when marginal cost is above average total cost, and the ATC curve is at its lowest point when it is equal to marginal cost. Figure 12A.1 also shows exactly this same relationship between marginal cost and average variable cost. Depending on whether it is below, equal to, or above average variable cost, marginal cost pulls the AVC curve down, sets its minimum value, or pulls it up. As was the case with average total cost, this behavior of average variable cost is explained by the mathematical relationship between average and marginal measurements.

The basic economic reality underlying these relationships is, as indicated in the chapter, the Law of Diminishing Returns. Initially, as additional units of a variable factor are employed along with a fixed factor, the fixed factor is utilized more efficiently and marginal cost falls. At larger levels of output, after diminishing returns set in and the limitations of the fixed factor begin to be felt, each additional unit of the variable factor adds less to output than did the previous unit, and marginal cost begins to rise. At very high levels of output, where many additional units of the variable factor are needed to compensate for the now-serious limitations of the fixed factor, marginal cost rises more rapidly. Thus, the Law of Diminishing Returns, which affects how variable and fixed factors interact with one another, causes marginal cost to behave as it does, and the behavior of marginal cost causes average variable and average total costs to behave as they do.

Average Fixed Cost   Average fixed cost is the difference between average total cost and average variable cost; it is shown in Figure 12A.2a by the distance between the ATC and AVC curves. For example, at one site maintained, the ATC curve indicates that average total cost is $600 and the AVC curve indicates that average variable cost is $200. The difference between the two curves is $400, which, as Table 12A.1 shows, is the average fixed cost for maintaining one site. At five sites the ATC curve is at $175 and the AVC curve is at $95. The difference, $80, is equal to average fixed cost at five complexes.

Figure 12A.2a highlights the costs at five sites maintained to strengthen your understanding of how average variable and average fixed costs equal average total cost. Also, it should be clear by now why the distance between the ATC and the AVC curves decreases as the level of output increases: Average fixed cost is decreasing. Decreasing average fixed cost is illustrated in Figure 12A.2b.

CHAPTER 13

Competition and Market Structures

CHAPTER OBJECTIVES

To define a market and explain how its boundaries are determined.

To explain how a firm's pricing and profit behavior are related to the amount of competition it faces in its market.

To give the basic characteristics of the four market structures: pure competition, monopolistic competition, oligopoly, and monopoly.

To describe an individual firm's demand curve, pricing behavior, and nonprice competitive behavior in each of the four market structures.

To explain how a firm's long-run pricing and profit behavior and the degree of efficiency it achieves are affected by the amount of competition it faces in its market.

To evaluate how consumers fare and how efficiency is achieved by firms in each of the four market structures.

To explain (in an appendix) how a firm determines its profit-maximizing price and output level.

We interface with many businesses, ranging from garages that change oil in our cars to discount mall shops to huge insurance companies. Each of these businesses, like the other 28-plus million businesses in the United States, behaves differently. Some businesses have great control over the prices they charge for their products, while others have little or no control. Some spend millions of dollars on TV and print advertising and public relations, while others spend nothing. And the bottom line for some firms yields continuous economic profit, while other firms, no matter how well they are managed, have no such prospect.[1] Think about the different pricing, advertising, and profit behaviors of a farmer, your bank, a sports franchise, a favorite restaurant, a major oil company, and the owner of the concessions at a stadium.

The greatest influence over the price and nonprice decisions of a firm and its ability to earn economic profit over the long run is the competition it faces in its market. All other things being equal, the greater the competition in a market, the less control a business in that market has over the price it charges, and the less likely the firm is to earn economic profit on an ongoing basis. The less the competition in a market, the greater the control a business has over the price it charges, and the more likely the firm is to earn economic profit over the long run. Think again about a business that has the sole rights to concessions at a stadium. With no competition, that business has strong control over the pricing of whatever it sells. People will likely pay more for a drink and burger at a stadium than at one of several local pubs.

Market Structures
A system for grouping and analyzing markets according to the degree and type of competition among sellers.

The amount of competition and the form it takes differ from market to market. We know, however, that patterns can be identified that allow us to group sellers into different classes of markets called **market structures.** To put order into the study of the effects of competition on business decision making and behavior, economists have adopted four market structures to represent different competitive situations: pure competition, monopolistic competition, oligopoly, and monopoly. These four structures encompass a spectrum of competitive conditions. At one end of the spectrum is pure competition, where the competitive pressure is the strongest, and at the other end is monopoly, where there is no direct competition. In between are monopolistic competition, which is closer to pure competition, and oligopoly, which is closer to monopoly.

In this chapter we will analyze each of the four market structures. Particular attention will be paid to the main characteristics that distinguish each type of market and to how those characteristics affect a firm's behavior and profit expectations.

DEFINING A MARKET

Industry
A group of firms producing similar products or using similar processes.

Market
Includes firms that sell similar products and compete for the same buyers.

We know from Chapter 12 that an **industry** is a group of firms that produce similar products or use similar processes. How does this differ from a market where firms sell similar products? Are firms in the same industry necessarily in the same market?

Businesses are in the same **market** when they sell similar products and compete with each other for the same buyers. For example, a movie theater in Chicago and one in Manhattan are in the same industry because they sell similar products, but because they do not compete with each other for the same buyers, they are not in the

---

[1]Remember that there are two types of profit: Normal profit is a return for implicit costs and necessary for a business to continue; economic profit is not a cost of production and is the profit over normal profit.

same market. The movie theater in Chicago and the one in Manhattan are in different markets with different competitors and different customers. In simple terms, a market defines a firm's competitive environment.

Geographic Boundary of a Market
Defined by the geographic area in which sellers compete for buyers.

The boundaries of a market are determined along two lines: geography and product substitutability. The **geographic boundary of a market** depends on the size of the area in which sellers compete for buyers: Markets may be local, regional, national, or international. A bagel shop that competes for customers from a particular neighborhood or town is in a local market, whereas a top-notch university graduate program in business is in an international market because it competes for buyers all over the world. Increasingly, U.S. firms are competing in international markets.

Product Boundary of a Market
Defined by product substitutability among buyers.

The **product boundary of a market** is defined by product substitutability. Sellers are in the same market when buyers view their products as substitutes. If movies are seen as substitutable for live theater, then they compete in the same market. If buyers think that movie rentals and band concerts are substitutes for movies and live theater, then all of these are in the same market.

Trying to identify the boundaries of a market and determine which products and geographic areas are included is important because the size of a market significantly affects the degree of competition that a firm faces: The larger the market, the greater the number of sellers and the greater the competition. However, the definition of a market can be debated because its boundaries are uncertain, and different perspectives yield different opinions as to what constitutes the geographic and product dimensions of a market. For example, if you ask several friends to define the market that your local movie theater is in, you may get several different responses. One person might define the market in a very narrow sense and include only local movie theaters. Another person might regard the relevant market as the market for entertainment and include all theatrical, sporting, musical, and other such events within 50 miles.

One place where the controversy about the boundaries of a market becomes important is in courts of law hearing cases on alleged violations of the antitrust laws. The antitrust laws are designed to protect competition in markets and will be more fully discussed in Chapter 14. For now, however, we can note that one type of antitrust case heard by the courts involves a firm or other organization accused of taking over, or monopolizing, a market. In cases such as this, the definition of the boundaries of the market is of critical importance because, generally, the more broadly the market is defined, the smaller will be the firm's or organization's control, and the easier it will be to argue that the market has not been monopolized.

One problem facing a court hearing an antitrust case is that the accused will likely present one definition of its market's boundaries, and the accuser will likely present another. The court must then determine which definition is correct and, partly on that basis, decide on the guilt or innocence of the accused. An example of this type of market definition problem is given in Application 13.1, "Defining the Boundaries of a Market: The NCAA Case." This excerpt from the court record of that well-known antitrust case shows some of the considerations that were important to the court in determining which definition of the relevant market to accept when deciding on the legality of the National Collegiate Athletic Association's control over televised college football games. The NCAA defined the market as all broadcast programming, and the universities that brought this suit defined the market as live televised college football. How does product substitutability figure into the court's decision?

APPLICATION 13.1

Defining the Boundaries of a Market: The NCAA Case

A suit by the Board of Regents of the University of Oklahoma and the University of Georgia Athletic Association against the National Collegiate Athletic Association went to trial in 1982. The suit was over the NCAA's control of the televising of college football games. In this trial were two definitions of the relevant market: the universities' definition that the market is "televised live college football," and the NCAA's definition that the market is "all broadcast programming." The court's conclusion and some of its reasoning are given below.

The Court concludes that the relevant market for testing whether the NCAA exercises monopoly power is live college football television. This conclusion is based on the following facts. . . .

. . . The vast majority, some 75%, of intercollegiate football games are played on Saturday afternoon. On Saturdays, college football television is free of competition from the programming which logically is the most substitutable; professional football. . . . The games to be broadcast are quite clearly a perishable item. Once the game is over and the score of the game is made known to college football fans, viewers are not nearly so likely to watch the game on a delayed telecast basis. . . . To suggest that college football competes with the complete spectrum of broadcast programming is to ignore the clear fact that Saturday afternoon is the only time at which this perishable product is uniformly available to the broadcaster.

Another factor supporting this conclusion . . . is that on Saturday afternoons the type of programming against which the NCAA football telecasts compete is qualitatively different from that available at other times of the week. . . . It is generally agreed that the quality of Saturday afternoon television, excepting the sports programming, is lower than that offered during other times of the week. . . .

There are also unique characteristics of the product itself. . . . NCAA football is a unique product because of its history and tradition, the color and pageantry of the event, and the interest of college alumni in the football success of their alma mater. . . .

The defendant's theory that the relevant market is all broadcast programming is untenable. College football simply does not compete with shows such as . . . "Saturday Night Live." . . . To accept the defendant's theory of relevant market is to say that every type of programming seen on network television competes with every other type of programming. This is simply not so. Programming patterns vary not only by day of the week, but by the time of day. The audiences for different types of programming have extremely diverse demographic characteristics. The types of advertisers who buy commercial time vary greatly depending on the type of programming. . . .

Source: *Board of Regents of the University of Oklahoma v. National Collegiate Athletic Association*, 546 F. Supp. 1276 (1982), pp. 1297, 1299.

THE MARKET STRUCTURES

We know that the degree of competition that a business faces in a market influences its behavior with regard to the prices it charges, the profit it makes, and the nonprice competition it uses. Economists have created four models of market situations, called market structures, to represent degrees of competition and study their effects: pure competition, monopolistic competition, oligopoly, and monopoly.

Each of these market models has a set of characteristics that differentiates it from the other market models, and is important for determining the type and amount of competition a firm faces. For example, certain features are associated with a monopoly structure and others with oligopoly. The distinguishing characteristics of each of the market models center around three areas.

- ◆ **Number of sellers.** The number of sellers in the market is important to the amount of competition. A market may have one seller, thousands of sellers, or some number in between.
- ◆ **Product type.** The product sold in the market can be identical from seller to seller or be differentiated. If a firm can distinguish its product from those of its competitors through size, color, or any other attribute, then nonprice competition can arise.

♦ **Entry and exit.** The ease or difficulty with which firms can enter or leave the market affects competition. It may be extremely easy for new firms to begin selling in the market, or it may be virtually impossible.

The remainder of this chapter describes the four market structures and analyzes the behavior of firms in each structure. For each structure we will evaluate the control that a business has over the price it charges, the influence and effect of nonprice competition, and whether firms tend to make an economic profit and operate efficiently in the long run.

PURE COMPETITION

Characteristics of Pure Competition

Purely Competitive Market

A market with a large number of independent firms selling identical products, and with easy entry into and exit from the market.

Barriers to Entry

Factors that keep firms from entering a market; can be financial, legal, technical, or other barriers.

The following characteristics define a **purely competitive market.**

♦ There is a very large number of sellers acting independently of each other.
♦ The products offered for sale are identical: Buyers cannot distinguish the product of one seller from that of another.
♦ Entry by business firms into a purely competitive market is easy, as is exit from the market. There are no legal restrictions, fees, impossibly high capital requirements, patents, or other **barriers to entry.**

The markets for crops such as corn, oats, and wheat provide classic examples of pure competition. In each of these markets there are thousands of independent sellers, and the output of any one seller is indistinguishable from the output of any other. Entry into these markets is easy because little is required to grow these crops.

The market in which a corporation's common stock is traded may also provide an example of pure competition. With companies such as Microsoft, Pepsico, and Starbucks, millions of shares of stock are held by thousands of owners. Each share of a company's stock is identical to each other share, and it is easy to enter the market to buy and sell.

Behavior of a Firm in Pure Competition

Pure competition is the market structure to which other markets are compared. As will be shown, it is the ideal from the buyer's point of view because of the prices, costs, profit levels, and efficiency gains that result from the competition.

Price Taker

A seller with no control over the price of its product; takes the market price.

Control over Price One of the most important aspects of the behavior of purely competitive sellers is that the firms are **price takers:** No individual firm has any control over the price it receives for its product. Price is determined solely through the market's competitive forces; that is, price is determined by the interaction of market supply and market demand. The price that a firm charges is a result of the decisions of all buyers and all sellers in the market.

Figure 13.1 illustrates the market for a grain crop (such as wheat) and allows us to review the market price-setting process covered in Chapter 3. D is the market demand curve showing the different amounts of grain that all buyers together plan to purchase at different prices. As expected, the curve is downward sloping, indicating that the

FIGURE 13.1 *Market Demand and Supply for a Grain Crop*

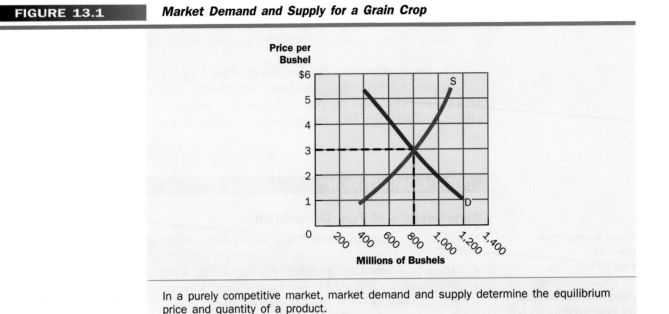

In a purely competitive market, market demand and supply determine the equilibrium price and quantity of a product.

lower the price, the greater the quantity demanded in the market. S is the upward-sloping market supply curve, showing that all sellers (grain farmers) together offer more of the product for sale at a higher price. The actual price that emerges in this market is $3 per bushel. This is the equilibrium price that equates market demand and supply.

In this example, an individual purely competitive firm can sell as much or as little as it wants at the price of $3 per bushel. It cannot charge more than $3 and will not charge less than $3. Why is this so?

Due to the large number of independently acting sellers in the market, the entire output of any one seller represents a "drop in the bucket" compared to the total available output. A seller that would charge a price higher than the market price would sell nothing because buyers can choose from thousands of alternative sellers. Because one seller's product is identical to that of all other sellers, it makes no difference with whom a buyer deals.

It would also be pointless for a single seller to offer output at less than the market price. A grain farmer would not sell grain at $2, $2.50, or even $2.99 per bushel, knowing that the entire crop can be sold at the market price of $3 per bushel. The same pricing behavior exists with regard to common stock. If you own a particular stock and the market price per share is $19.50, you cannot sell your shares for more than $19.50 and have no reason to sell them for less.

Because of large numbers of independent sellers supplying identical products, purely competitive firms have neither the willingness nor the ability to deviate from the price set in the market.

Demand for an Individual Firm's Product   For any product sold, regardless of the market structure, there is a downward-sloping **market demand curve** such as that shown in Figure 13.1. In addition to the market demand curve, each individual seller also has a demand curve for its own product. This represents the amounts of the seller's product that buyers are willing to purchase at certain prices. Thus, an

Market Demand Curve
The demand curve for all buyers in the market together.

| FIGURE 13.2 | *Demand Curve for the Output of a Purely Competitive Seller* |

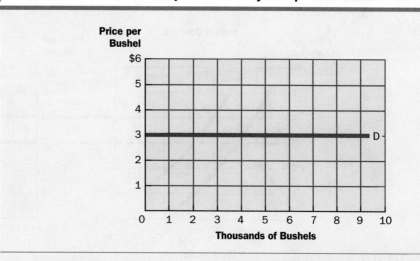

A firm in a purely competitive market can sell as much or as little as it wants at the market price.

Individual Firm's Demand Curve

Shows the amounts of an individual firm's product that buyers are willing to purchase at particular prices.

individual firm's demand curve dictates the price a firm will receive when it chooses an output to sell.

Remember that in pure competition the price an individual firm receives for its product is set by the forces of supply and demand in the market, and each firm supplies a minute fraction of the market. Since the firm's output is negligible when compared to the total, it can offer as much or as little as it chooses *at the market price*. Thus, the demand curve for any single purely competitive seller's product is graphed as a straight, horizontal line at the equilibrium market price.

The grain example in Figure 13.1 can be used to illustrate this concept. At an equilibrium price of $3 in the market, the demand curve for a single seller's grain output would be like that shown in Figure 13.2. At $3 per bushel, buyers are willing to purchase 1,000 bushels, 5,000 bushels, or whatever output the seller wants to offer. If the seller were to charge more, say even $3.01, sales would drop to zero. There would also be no incentive to sell for less than $3 per bushel, since that is the price buyers will pay.

The graphs enable us to better see the relationship between the equilibrium market price and the individual firm's demand curve as well as how changes in the market affect the individual seller. If the equilibrium price in the market increases or decreases, the individual firm's demand curve will also increase (shift upward) or decrease (shift downward). If a large number of new buyers enters the market for the grain in our example, the market demand curve will shift to the right. As a consequence, the equilibrium price in the market rises, and the individual firm's demand curve shifts upward. This is shown in Figure 13.3, where the price increases from $3 to $4 after market demand increases from D1 to D2. What would be the effect on an individual firm's demand curve from an increase in market supply?[2]

[2]An increase in market supply would cause the market supply curve to shift to the right. The resulting fall in equilibrium price would cause the individual seller's demand curve to shift downward.

| FIGURE 13.3 | *Effect on the Individual Firm of an Increase in Market Demand* |

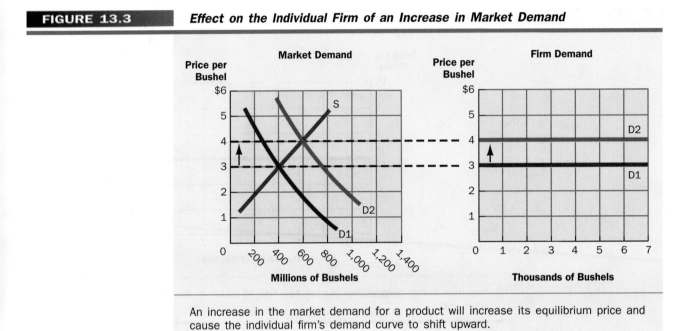

An increase in the market demand for a product will increase its equilibrium price and cause the individual firm's demand curve to shift upward.

Application 13.2, "The Farmers' Almanac: It's a Necessity," takes a closer look at what it is like to be a seller in a purely competitive market. After reading the application, do you think that simply having to accept the price set in the market clears away a large amount of the uncertainty, risk, and complexity that we think accompanies the management of a business?

Pricing, Profit, and Loss   Given that the purely competitive firm has no control over price, can it make a profit? It is possible in the short run that a business could make an economic profit, operate at a loss, or break even with a normal profit. (Remember that normal profit is the profit necessary to stay in business and is included in the economic cost of production. Economic profit is that profit earned beyond normal profit.) To determine its profit or loss position, a firm will compare the price it receives for a product and the cost of producing it.

It is easy to see the profit or loss position of a firm by graphically comparing the firm's demand curve and its average total cost curve. The firm's demand curve gives the price it will receive for each unit of output sold, and the average total cost (ATC) curve gives the cost for producing each unit of output.

Figure 13.4a shows a firm in pure competition that is operating with an **economic profit.** Economic profit results because the firm's demand curve is above the average total cost curve, or price is higher than average total cost. Figure 13.4b illustrates a firm in pure competition operating with a **loss.** This loss occurs because the demand curve is below the average total cost curve, or price is lower than average total cost, regardless of the level of output produced. In Figure 13.4c a firm is just **breaking even** (earning a normal profit) if it produces and sells Qx units of output because price is equal to average total cost at that level of output.

Economic Profit, Loss, or Breaking Even

Occurs when price is greater than, less than, or equal to average total cost, respectively.

FIGURE 13.4   *A Purely Competitive Seller Operating with an Economic Profit, a Loss, or Breaking Even*

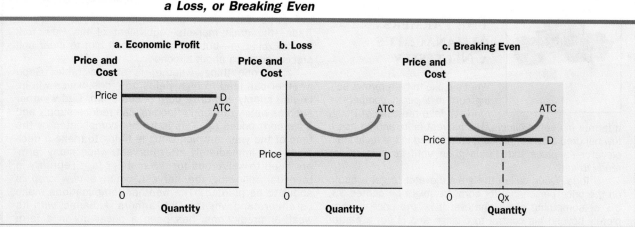

A seller will operate with an economic profit, a loss, or break even, depending on whether price is greater than, less than, or equal to average total cost, respectively.

The appendix at the end of this chapter explains in greater detail how a firm in pure competition determines its profit-maximizing or loss-minimizing level of output.

Nonprice Competition   Firms in pure competition have no need to engage in **nonprice competition.** A purely competitive seller makes no expenditures on advertising, public relations, or other efforts to bring its product to a buyer's attention. The reason for this is obvious: With so many firms selling identical products, efforts at creating buyer awareness of a particular firm's product would be a waste of time and money.[3]

The benefit to consumers from this lack of nonprice competition is that, with no promotional expenditures, firms' costs are lower than they would otherwise be. This in turn means that over the long run, buyers pay less for products.

Long-Run Costs, Profit, and Efficiency   As we examine and evaluate the four market models, one of the most important aspects of our study is the long-run behavior of firms in pure competition. In the long run, purely competitive firms operate at the lowest possible cost, charge the lowest price that they can without going out of business, and earn no economic profit. All of these conditions are ideal for the consumer and result from competition among sellers.

The long-run position of a purely competitive seller is illustrated in Figure 13.5. This figure shows a simple long-run average total cost (LRATC) curve exhibiting economies and diseconomies of scale as well as the firm's demand curve. In the long run, an individual purely competitive seller's position is such that its demand curve just brushes the bottom of its long-run average total cost curve. A firm operating

Nonprice Competition
Firms focus on a feature other than price to attract buyers to their products.

---

[3]Sometimes trade associations to which firms in an industry or market belong will advertise the product itself. Promotions for beef, eggs, and milk are good examples of product—not firm—advertising.

APPLICATION 13.2

THE FARMERS' ALMANAC: IT'S A NECESSITY

What's it like to be a farmer selling corn in a purely competitive market? Take the case of Doug, a farmer in central Illinois. His harvest is in, and he has a few hundred acres of his corn crop stored in the local grain elevator—a place that holds grain until its owners are ready to sell.

Today Doug called the grain elevator to get a quote on the price per bushel for corn. He might be quoted $3, $5, or something else. Whatever it is, the price is completely beyond his control to change and is not a matter for argument. With the quote, Doug is left with a take-it-or-leave-it decision: sell all or some of the corn crop, or not sell anything and continue to pay the storage fee.

Doug's take-it-or-leave-it decision rests largely on two factors: how badly he needs the money, and where he thinks corn prices are heading. Most importantly, there are bills to be paid that can limit Doug's ability to hold out for higher prices. Planting and growing corn requires substantial outlays for seed, chemicals, production equipment, and perhaps an irrigation system. Then there are family expenditures: college tuition, home heating, a mortgage, groceries, and everything else. When bills need to be paid, crops might need to be sold.

The question of where corn prices are headed is not easy to assess. While corn and other grain prices change frequently over the course of a single day, Doug is likely evaluating where they will be in a week, a month, or more. How much higher or lower will they go? Doug can check out some data about corn on the Chicago Board of Trade—the grain markets' equivalent of the New York Stock Exchange—but this will not lead him to clear and precise answers about direction.

For one thing, weather is unpredictable. Good weather can lead to high yields on crops, which will increase supply and drive corn prices down. Bad weather such as heavy rains and flooding can reduce supply and drive corn prices up. This is further complicated by the time of the year in which Doug is trying to make a decision. Is it immediately after harvest, when many farmers need to sell crops for the money? Is it February in the year following the harvest, when a new crop is about to be planted? The weather complications make us understand why the Old Farmers' Almanac, with its weather predictions, has been a necessity in a farm family's home.

There are other price-influencing factors beyond Doug's control. The market for grains is clearly international, causing the price to be influenced by what is produced elsewhere in the world. A bumper crop in Brazil can have a huge impact on farmers in central Illinois.

And then there is the whole debate surrounding ethanol. Certainly the prospect of converting corn into fuel helped to increase prices in 2007 and 2008. But with questions raised about the amount of water required to make ethanol and other issues, what will happen in the market for corn and its price in the future?

Here is the simple fact. While a farmer has no control over the prices for a crop, there are still many price-related decisions to be made. And there just might be more concern over prices in a purely competitive market than in other markets, where businesses can better influence the prices they get.

---

under the conditions given in Figure 13.5 would sell 4,000 units of output at $3 per unit, or would operate at point A. Any other output level would result in a loss because the long-run average total cost curve would be above the demand curve.

Notice that point A is the lowest point on the firm's long-run average total cost curve. This means that the firm is producing at the lowest possible cost per unit of output in the long run, or is operating at the most efficient level of output. **Efficient production** is an important goal for an economy because of the basic problem of scarcity.

Efficient Production
A good or service is produced at the lowest cost possible.

Notice also that at point A price equals average total cost, causing the seller to earn only normal and no excess profit. Also, the $3 price is the lowest price at which the firm can sell and still remain in business. Any price less than $3 would be less than the firm's long-run average total cost, causing it to go out of business.

So, in the long run in pure competition

♦ the cost of production is as low as it can possibly be so firms are operating efficiently;
♦ the price of the product is as low as it can possibly be; and
♦ the consumer pays no economic profit.

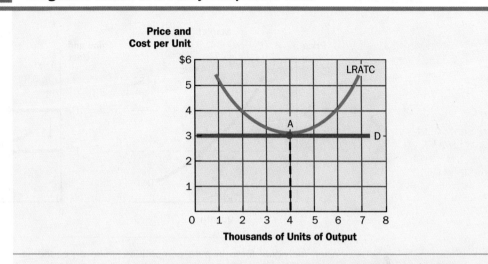

FIGURE 13.5 *Long-Run Position of a Purely Competitive Seller*

In the long run, a purely competitive seller operates where price equals minimum average total cost, which allows just a normal profit.

Why does this long-run condition occur in pure competition? Easy entry into and exit from the market are the basis for the position of the purely competitive firm in the long run. When firms in a purely competitive market earn excess profits, potential sellers recognize the opportunity to also earn such profits and, because of easy entry, come into the market. As additional sellers enter the market, the market supply increases, causing the equilibrium market price to fall. As the equilibrium price falls, each individual seller's excess profit begins to disappear. This process of entry and reduction in both the market price and excess profit continues until each seller operates where price equals minimum long-run average total cost, or with just a normal profit.

The mechanics of this process are illustrated in Figure 13.6. With market price P_1 and the individual firm's demand curve D1 (right-hand graph), the firm is making an economic profit because its long-run average total cost curve lies below D1. As other firms attracted by this economic profit enter the market, the market supply curve (left-hand graph) increases from S1 to S2, market price falls to P_2, and the individual seller's demand curve falls to D2, which allows no economic profit.

If firms are losing money and experiencing less than normal profits, some sellers will close their operations and leave the market. As sellers leave, the market supply decreases, causing the equilibrium price to increase. As the price increases, the losses to remaining sellers get smaller and smaller. This process continues until, again, price equals minimum long-run average total cost.

Figure 13.7 illustrates the effect on an individual firm of an exodus of other firms from the market. At market price P_1, the individual firm is operating at a loss because the cost of producing each unit is greater than the price. As firms leave the market, the market supply curve shifts to the left, from S1 to S2, causing market price and the individual firm's demand curve to rise. When the price rises to P_2, the firm is just breaking even and earning a normal profit.

FIGURE 13.6   *Effect of Entry of Sellers into a Purely Competitive Market*

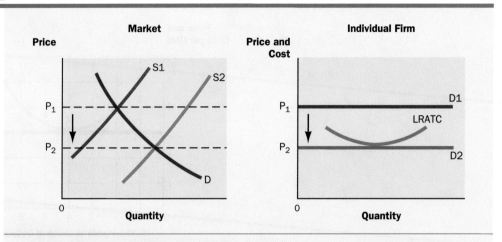

When individual firms in pure competition make an economic profit, new firms are attracted to the market in the long run, causing market supply to increase and equilibrium price to fall. Eventually, the price that each firm receives is equal to the firm's minimum long-run average total cost.

Is There Pure Competition?

The extent to which pure competition is found in the real world can be questioned. The markets for grain and other agricultural products are generally regarded to be close examples of pure competition because these markets have large numbers of independent sellers supplying identical products. However, several factors need to be

FIGURE 13.7   *Effect of Exit of Sellers from a Purely Competitive Market*

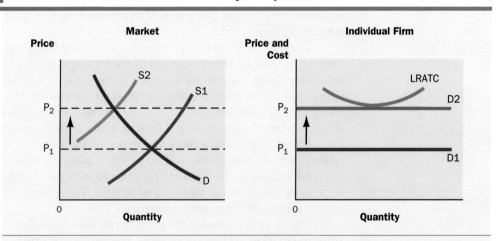

When individual firms in pure competition operate with a loss, some drop out of the market in the long run, causing market supply to decrease and equilibrium price to rise. Price will increase until it equals the minimum long-run average total cost of the remaining firms.

considered in labeling them as purely competitive. For one, various loan, income support, and other assistance programs have been created and are administered by the U.S. Department of Agriculture. These programs influence prices and output decisions, and alter the free operation of supply and demand.

There is also the question of entry into and exit from agricultural markets. Substantial outlays for land, equipment, seed, fertilizer, and other factors may be barriers to entry to anything other than small-scale farming. In some instances, large-scale, efficient operation requires expensive capital for harvesting grain or caring for livestock. (Recall Application 12.2, which dealt with precision agriculture.) Exit from farming can also be difficult; the land or its location may not be well suited for an alternative use, and tax laws may make it difficult to sell a farm or pass it on to other family members.

With considerations such as these, of what value is the study of pure competition? Despite these issues, the purely competitive model does help us better understand the behavior of firms in certain markets. It also provides an ideal against which all real-world markets can be judged. In this regard, pure competition is like human health. There may be no perfectly healthy person, just as there may be no purely competitive market. But we cannot understand the extent of illness or good health without having the ideal of perfect health for comparison. And we cannot understand the extent to which markets are working well or poorly without the ideal of pure competition for comparison.

MONOPOLISTIC COMPETITION

Characteristics of Monopolistic Competition

The market structure closest to pure competition, and where we can find many real-world examples, is **monopolistic competition.** A monopolistically competitive market has

Monopolistic Competition
Market structure characterized by a large number of sellers with differentiated outputs and fairly easy entry and exit.

Differentiated Products
Products of competing firms are different and recognized as such by buyers.

♦ a large number of sellers—not as many as in pure competition, but a large number nonetheless;
♦ **differentiated products**—buyers can distinguish among the products of different sellers; and
♦ fairly easy entry into and exit from the market.

We frequently find ourselves as buyers in stores in monopolistically competitive markets: coffee shops, restaurants, mall clothing shops, and other retailers where a large number of small shops compete with one another. In these markets each seller's product is somewhat different: It might be location, parking, service, image, or a variety of other things. Think about your local coffee shops, where the quality of the coffee used to make a latte, or even the crowd that frequents the shop, differentiates one place from another. It is also relatively easy to open a small store or shop. A place can be leased; no highly trained workers are needed; and there are minimal capital equipment requirements.

Another slightly different example of a monopolistically competitive market is the labor market for college graduates in a particular major, such as communications. Each year a large number of communications majors graduates from colleges and universities. Each of these graduates is unique in terms of grades, background, experience, courses completed, college attended, and initiative. Entry into this market is relatively easy: The major expenditure is the cost of a college degree.

Behavior of a Firm in Monopolistic Competition

Because of differences in the characteristics of monopolistically competitive and purely competitive markets, there are differences in the behavior of firms in these structures. Notably, unlike pure competitors, monopolistic competitors have some control over the prices they receive for their products, and they engage in nonprice competition.

Control over Price   With a large number of firms selling identical products, the individual purely competitive firm has no control over the price it can get for its product. In monopolistic competition there is also a large number of sellers, but because the sellers' products are differentiated, buyers do not view the product of one seller as a perfect substitute for the product of another. For this reason, when a monopolistically competitive firm raises its price, it will lose some, but not all, of its buyers. Some buyers will continue to purchase the product from the firm at a higher price because they see the firm's product as different from and preferable to those of its competitors. Thus, product differentiation allows a firm to carve out a little niche of its own within the larger market.

However, even with product differentiation there is a limit to the amount of control a monopolistically competitive seller has over price. Since many other firms produce similar products, a firm that raises its price too much risks losing many of its buyers. Some buyers may be willing to pay a little extra for better service or a distinctive style, but if they have to pay a lot more, the alternatives become more attractive. For example, you and your friends may continue to eat lunch at a favorite restaurant even if it raises its prices somewhat. However, if the prices are raised too high, you may go somewhere else.

In short, a business selling in a monopolistically competitive market is in an interesting position: It has some control over price because of its ability to differentiate its product, but that control is limited by the presence of many other firms selling similar products.

Demand for an Individual Firm's Product   Because of product differentiation, the demand curve faced by an individual monopolistic competitor is downward sloping, like that in Figure 13.8.[4] This demand curve shows that if the firm raises its price, it will lose some, but not all, of its buyers. For example, in Figure 13.8, when the seller raises the price from $2.50 to $3.00, the quantity demanded falls from 500 to 200 units, not from 500 units to zero as would happen if the seller were a pure competitor.[5]

Pricing, Profit, and Loss   Just like other firms, the profit or loss position of a seller in a monopolistically competitive market can be determined by comparing the demand curve and average total cost curve for its product. If the average total cost curve lies below the demand curve, or the cost per unit of output is less than the price, an economic profit is earned. This is shown in Figure 13.9a. If the average total

[4]Here we need to stress that we are talking about the demand curve for an individual seller's product, not the market demand curve.

[5]Generally, in monopolistic competition the response to a price change is elastic; that is, over the broadest range of the demand curve, buyers respond strongly to price changes. In Figure 13.8, when the price increases from $2.50 to $3.00, or by 20 percent, the quantity demanded decreases from 500 to 200 units, or by 60 percent. Since the percentage change in the quantity demanded is greater than the percentage change in price, the response is characterized as elastic. (The exact price elasticity is 60%/20% = 3. You can refer to Chapter 3 to refresh your memory about elasticity.)

| FIGURE 13.8 | *Demand Curve for the Output of a Monopolistically Competitive Seller* |

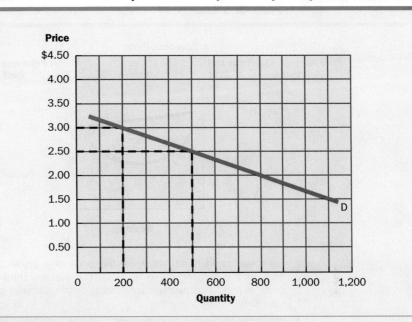

Because of product differentiation, a seller in monopolistic competition will lose some, but not all, of its buyers if it raises its price.

cost curve is above the demand curve, or the cost per unit of output is greater than the price, a loss occurs. This is shown in Figure 13.9b.

Nonprice Competition   Obviously, sellers in monopolistically competitive markets can compete with one another for buyers by lowering prices. But because their products are differentiated, rivalry through nonprice competition is also an option.

Nonprice competition takes all kinds of forms: packaging, parking, facility ambiance, service, location, quality, selection, and guarantees to name a few. A cafe, for example, can attract customers because of its reputation for outstanding soups and sandwiches, hours open, access to parking, or consistent quality service. Think about the places you frequent for coffee, lunch, or to get together with friends. What are the nonprice reasons for supporting these places?

We can gauge the importance of nonprice competition by simply noticing how much advertising is based on nonprice factors. Notice how infrequently advertisements in magazines, on television, or on the Internet stress price as the selling feature.

Business firms are attracted to nonprice competition for two reasons. First, it provides a way for a firm to increase the demand for its product. By increasing buyer interest through service, packaging, and other features, a firm can shift the demand curve for its product to the right—thereby selling more at each price. Second, by highlighting differences and playing down similarities, nonprice competition helps an individual firm make its product appear unique. As this occurs, the seller becomes less sensitive to the presence of rivals. Uniqueness allows a seller to raise prices without losing as many buyers as would otherwise be the case.

A Monopolistically Competitive Seller Operating with an Economic Profit or a Loss

a. Economic Profit

Price and Cost

D

ATC

0

Quantity

b. Loss

Price and Cost

ATC

D

0

Quantity

Economic profit is earned when the price of a product is greater than its average total cost, or the demand curve is above the average total cost curve. A loss occurs when price is less than average total cost, or the demand curve is below the average total cost curve.

Controversy exists over how much nonprice competition is appropriate. Some people argue that nonprice competition raises the cost of doing business and, therefore, brings higher prices for consumers. Others think that nonprice competition benefits consumers with variety and better quality. Up for Debate, "Does Nonprice Competition Waste Resources?," adds an additional twist to this controversy by looking at its potential impact on sustainability of the world's resources.

Long-Run Costs, Profit, and Efficiency   Over the long run, sellers in monopolistically competitive markets earn only normal profits, just like firms in purely competitive markets. This occurs because, like purely competitive markets, monopolistically competitive markets are easy to enter and exit. Easy entry and exit causes the long-run position of a monopolistically competitive seller to look like that in Figure 13.10. The seller in Figure 13.10 can earn a normal profit by selling 500 units of output at $2.50 each. At any smaller or larger output, the long-run average total cost curve is above the demand curve, causing the firm to operate at a loss.

If sellers are earning economic, or excess, profit (like the firm shown in Figure 13.9a), new sellers enter the market and take some demand away from the existing sellers. This causes the demand curves of the existing sellers to shift to the left until they reach a position like that shown in Figure 13.10, where economic profit is competed away and only normal profit remains. If sellers are sustaining losses (like the firm shown in Figure 13.9b), sellers leave the market, causing the demand curves of the remaining sellers to shift to the right until they reach a position like that shown in Figure 13.10, and the remaining firms operate at a normal profit.

While purely competitive and monopolistically competitive sellers both earn only a normal profit over the long run, the two types of sellers differ in an important

DOES NONPRICE COMPETITION WASTE RESOURCES?

Today there is great concern for the sustainability of our world in a time of diminishing nonrenewable resources as well as the inability to keep renewable resources growing at a pace that matches their use. With this concern comes an important question: Does nonprice competition have an impact on sustainability by wasting resources?

Yes There is just one answer to this question, and it is a loud and clear yes. There are several features that come with nonprice competition that certainly foster a waste of our resources.

Consider packaging. One of the popular ways in which producers distinguish their products is through packaging. Think about all of the cardboard boxes with their ads and colors that induce us to buy so many things housed in them—from toothpaste to cake mix to shoes. Not to mention the cardboard in which they are shipped. Then there are individually wrapped items: For example, today there are ever-increasing numbers of snack foods packaged separately in 100-calorie snack bags. And, there are water bottles and hard plastic shells and detergent bottles, to name just a few. Can't we package in a way that requires fewer resources?

Another nonprice competitive feature is parking. Businesses like to have parking close by for their patrons, which can result in more paved surfaces. Increased impervious surfaces affect water runoff and the return of this important resource to the ground.

Finally, there is the expenditure of money for developing marketing strategies that focus on nonprice competition to increase sales. Wouldn't we be better off putting these funds into expenditures that focus on sustainability practices?

No Nonprice competition leads to better products and increases the standard of living for consumers. It better satisfies buyers through closer attention to their wants and needs. Just because resources are diverted to buyer satisfaction is no reason to believe that they are "wasted."

One just needs to think about the areas in which nonprice competition has resulted in better products. Consider food. Today there is a greater abundance of choices, new and different products, and better quality. For example, a cup of good coffee, not just thick-brewed percolator java, is now an essential in many daily lives. Individual foil-wrapped tea bags, small bite-sized candy, and individual pouches of cat and dog food make life better. Even the 100-calorie snack bags have helped countless people keep their weight under control and fight an obesity problem. Plus, so many of these boxes, bottles, and bags can be recycled.

Nonprice competition has made many products more convenient and safer. With durable, small packages and bottled water and soft drinks, life is much easier for the average person to negotiate. And, safety has been increased. The hard shell that encases many products, including medications, ensures a tamper-proof product. Finally, wouldn't it be a really dull world without nonprice competition and the features it brings?

---

way. A firm in a purely competitive market operates at minimum average total cost in the long run and is, therefore, efficient, whereas a firm in a monopolistically competitive market does not operate at minimum average total cost and is, therefore, not as efficient. For the firm in Figure 13.10, the long-run price and per unit cost are $2.50. If the firm were a pure competitor, its price and per unit cost would be about $2.35—the minimum point on the long-run average total cost curve.

It is impossible for a monopolistic competitor to operate in the long run with price equal to minimum long-run average total cost because of product differentiation, which results in a downward-sloping demand curve. This difference gives rise to an important criticism of monopolistic competition: Even though price equals long-run average total cost and the firm is earning only a normal profit, the cost and price are higher than they would be in pure competition, and some efficiency is sacrificed.

OLIGOPOLY

Oligopoly is farther removed from pure competition than is monopolistic competition. In fact, it is so far removed that it makes more sense to discuss how oligopoly and pure competition differ than to discuss what they have in common. While pure competition may be the ideal market structure, oligopoly is the dominant market structure in the U.S. economy. More business is transacted in oligopolistic markets than in any of the three other market structures.

| FIGURE 13.10 | *Long-Run Position of a Monopolistically Competitive Seller* |

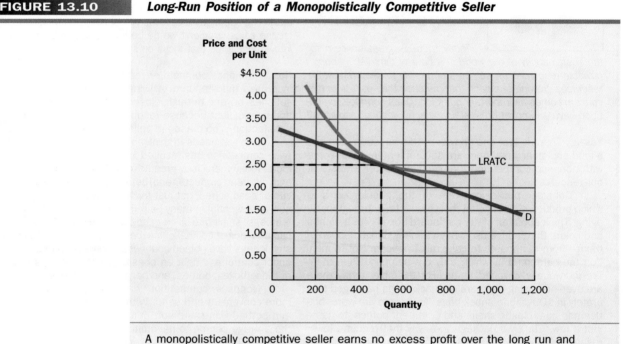

A monopolistically competitive seller earns no excess profit over the long run and operates at a long-run average total cost that is greater than the minimum.

Characteristics of Oligopoly

Oligopoly

A market dominated by a few large sellers; products are differentiated or identical; entry into the market is difficult.

In an **oligopoly**

♦ the market is dominated by a few large sellers, but there may also be small fringe sellers in the market as well;
♦ the products of the sellers may be differentiated or identical; and
♦ entry of firms into the market is quite difficult because of barriers to entry such as the financing needed to enter the market and be large enough to compete.

The supermarket is a good example of an oligopoly with differentiated products. In most cities, there are a few large grocery chains that are differentiated by service, store size, presence of a bakery or prepared foods, location, cleanliness, and other factors. Since new sellers would need to be large enough to establish a presence as a rival, entry into the market would require substantial money and be difficult. The market for aluminum ingot provides an example of an undifferentiated oligopoly. There are a few large firms selling aluminum ingot; ingot produced by one seller is like that produced by the other sellers; and the cost of entering the market is substantial.[6]

Examples of oligopoly are everywhere. The next time you shop for a car, a computer, or even breakfast cereal, notice how few firms are in these markets. Oligopolies are also found in the markets for baseball gloves, gasoline, light bulbs, computer software, credit cards, commercial television broadcasting, and a large number of other products.

---

[6]Some question whether there really are undifferentiated oligopolies. While the physical products of the sellers in the market might be the same, there can be differences among the sellers' delivery systems, financing options, and other arrangements.

Behavior of a Firm in an Oligopolistic Market

Control over Price With few sellers in an oligopoly, each of the dominant firms has a large share of the market. A large market share allows the firm some control over its price—more so than a monopolistic competitor who also has some control because of a differentiated product but faces a large number of rivals.

Having just a few competing sellers introduces an interesting twist to oligopoly that has an important effect on a firm's behavior. With so few rivals, the price, output, advertising, and other policies of one firm can have a significant impact on the other firms in the market, causing, in turn, those other firms to react. For example, if one automobile company offers zero or low interest rates for financing its cars, it may affect the sales of the other automobile companies in the market. These firms may in turn be "forced" to offer their own financing deals or follow other policies that will be detrimental to the sales of the company that initially offered the cheap financing. If a credit card company offers reward points for merchandise or air travel, this may reduce the use of competing credit cards, causing those companies to respond with programs of their own.

In the oligopolistic market structure, sellers are constantly watching and weighing the actions and reactions of their competitors. This phenomenon is called **mutual interdependence.** Because of mutual interdependence, sellers must consider not only the effects of their pricing and other policies on buyers, but the effects on their rivals and their rivals' reactions as well. Mutual interdependence is unique to oligopoly.

Mutual Interdependence
So few sellers exist in the market that each seller weighs the actions and reactions of rivals in its decision making.

Price of an Individual Firm's Product Because mutual interdependence is manifested in so many different ways, there is no single explanation for oligopoly pricing. Rather, several theories have been developed to accommodate different types of interdependence. Two of the best-known theories are leadership pricing and the kinked demand curve model.

Leadership pricing occurs when one firm in a market sets a price that is then adopted by other sellers. The firm that sets the price is called the price leader, and the firms that respond are the followers. Leadership pricing is not uncommon: Often firms in markets such as aluminum, commercial aviation, and banking follow suit when a price change is announced by one of their competitors. The price changes by the followers often come within a few hours or days after the leader's announcement.

Leadership Pricing
One firm in a market sets a price that the other firms in the market then adopt.

A seller may emerge as price leader for several reasons. It could be the largest firm in its market, causing rivals to choose to adopt its price rather than attack it head on and face a possible price war. A price leader might also be the firm that is more sensitive than its rivals to changing market conditions: When the other firms see the leader change its price, they can expect that changing conditions will soon force them to change their prices as well. Banks, for example, experience the same changes in money market conditions, causing a price leadership pattern to emerge with regard to interest rates. Sometimes price leadership is the result of tradition and expectations. Firms respond to a particular seller's price changes because over the years this has become the traditional pattern in the market and firms expect that pattern to continue.

Kinked Demand Curve
Assumes that rivals will not follow price increases but will follow price decreases; illustrates that as a seller's price rises, the amount of its product demanded decreases substantially, but as its price falls, the amount demanded increases only slightly.

The second theory, the **kinked demand curve** model, is based on the assumption that rivals do not follow a seller's price increases but do follow its price decreases. The theory gets its name from the unusual shape of the individual

FIGURE 13.11   *Kinked Demand Curve for the Output of an Oligopolist*

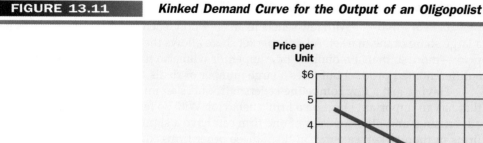

The kinked demand curve of an oligopolist is based on the assumption that the firm's rivals will follow a price decrease but not a price increase.

oligopolist's demand curve under this assumption. A kinked demand curve is illustrated in Figure 13.11.

The price currently charged and the corresponding output sold by the firm are shown at the kink, or bend, in the demand curve. For the firm in Figure 13.11, the current price is $3 and sales are 400,000 units. If the firm raises its price above $3, and its rivals do not follow, it stands to lose a large number of buyers to those other sellers. For example, when it increases its price from $3 to $4, its sales fall by 200,000 units, from 400,000 to 200,000. But, when the firm lowers its price from $3 to $2, its sales increase by only 50,000 units, to 450,000. This is because, when a seller's price is lowered, the seller's rivals also cut their prices to avoid losing buyers. With everyone's price lower, some buyers may be attracted to the market, but there is no reason for many existing buyers to switch to the seller that initiated the price cut.

Thus, the relatively flat portion of the kinked demand curve above the current price shows that a firm increasing its price stands to lose a large number of sales if its rivals do not follow its lead. The steep portion of the curve below the current price illustrates that, with rivals following price cuts, sales increase only slightly. The conclusion to be drawn from this model is that prices are relatively stable in this type of oligopoly market because the fear of rivals' reactions gives little or no incentive to either raise or lower price. In other words, there is not much price competition.

Application 13.3, "Of Course They'll React," briefly describes a highly visible, attention-getting, and ongoing incident of mutually interdependent pricing involving the big-three U.S. auto manufacturers that occurred during the summer of 2005. Given the size and power of these companies, does it surprise you that their pricing strategies played out as they did?

APPLICATION 13.3

OF COURSE THEY'LL REACT

Price competition is standard operating procedure in markets for automobiles, SUVs, mini-vans, and pickup trucks—the mainstays of household transportation. The journey into purchasing one of these vehicles is interesting to potential buyers who enjoy juggling numbers, bargaining, and searching for deals. But there are plenty of buyers who would rather have a tooth pulled than venture into the world of car sales.

In June 2005, General Motors announced a big new price reduction program on its vehicles—the "Employee Discounts for Everyone" program. Buyers could now receive the discount normally offered only to GM employees. Whether or not this was more than a potential buyer could expect to negotiate didn't matter—buyers saw this as a good deal and GM's sales rose by over 40 percent that month. GM saw this as very good news and announced a continuation of the program into July.

With the success of the GM program and its announced extension, Ford and Chrysler had no choice but to respond to this price reduction plan. Ford introduced a "Ford Family Plan" and Chrysler created an "Employee Pricing Plus" program. The Ford Family Plan, for example, provided employee pricing as well as other rebates and promotions. So, for the vehicle shopper in July, there were now multiple car company promotions and deals to consider and weigh.

Were the managers of GM surprised by the responses of Ford and Chrysler, or did they engage in this program knowing that eventually other manufacturers would respond with programs of their own? In a market where rivals continually assess the actions and reactions of each other, GM likely assumed that it had a window of opportunity to attract new buyers before Ford and Chrysler could get their own program up and running. When the June program was extended, GM's rivals could no longer sit back and let GM sales soar. They needed to enter the competition.

What is the lesson to be learned from the actions of these three sellers? The educated consumer can benefit from understanding potential strategies that might be carried out by sellers in an oligopoly market place.

Based on: Rosemary Winters, "Employee Discounts Lure Utah Car Buyers," Knight Ridder Tribune Business News, *The Salt Lake Tribune*, July 14, 2005, p. 1; "Business: Hooked on Discounts; American Carmakers," *The Economist*, London, July 9, 2005, p. 54; Jamie Butters, "Ford, Chrysler Follow GM's Discount Lead," Knight Ridder Tribune Business News, *Detroit Free Press*, July 6, 2005, p. 1.

Nonprice Competition   The degree of nonprice competition found in an oligopoly market depends on the extent to which the products are identical or differentiated. Where competitors sell largely identical products, spending money on product promotion could end up benefiting all firms in the market, rather than just the individual firm that makes the expenditure. On the other hand, a strong promotional campaign emphasizing a seller's product makes sense when the products are clearly differentiable on the basis of quality, style, size, or some other characteristic. Think about all of the beer ads that you have recently seen that want you to buy beer for its taste or its image.

Nonprice competition is important if a seller faces a situation where price cuts do not lead to large increases in sales. In this case, nonprice competition may provide a nice alternative to price competition. However, mutual interdependence also exists with regard to nonprice competition. For example, when one of the frozen meal labels introduced "bowls," the others did the same, and when a textbook company offers a web-based tutorial for students in an introductory course, the other textbook companies do the same.

Long-Run Costs, Profit, and Efficiency   Over the long run, purely competitive and monopolistically competitive sellers earn only normal profit: Easy entry allows new firms to come into the market and compete economic profit away. But with oligopoly, entry is not easy. Therefore, oligopolists can continue to earn economic profit over the long run because new sellers cannot readily enter the market.

The ability to earn economic profit over the long run affects the price buyers pay for a product. With pure competition, easy entry ensures that price is equal to long-run average total cost and is as low as possible. But the ability of an oligopolist to earn economic profit means that the firm's price can be greater than its cost. Thus, over the long run, restricted entry may result in economic profit for the firm and in higher prices for the buyer.

Restricted entry may also allow an oligopolist to operate inefficiently over the long run. The greater the difficulty potential rivals face entering a market, the less the competitive pressure on a firm, and the weaker its incentive to operate at lowest average total cost. Restrictions, or barriers to entry, are more fully explained in our discussion of monopolies.

MONOPOLY

Characteristics of Monopoly

Monopoly
A market with one seller that maintains its position because entry by new sellers is impossible.

Of the four market structures, none is further removed from pure competition than is monopoly. In a **monopoly** market there is

♦ only one seller—the monopolist;
♦ no need to consider the issue of product differentiation since there is just one seller; and
♦ no possibility of entry by new sellers.

There are a number of barriers to entry into a monopolized market. Significant economies of scale in the production of a good or service that cause long-run average total cost to fall as output expands can keep out competitors.[7] In this case, it may be cheaper and more efficient for one large firm to service the entire market by producing all the output at a lower average total cost than to have several firms each produce smaller amounts of output at a higher average total cost. This situation, called a **natural monopoly,** will be further discussed in Chapter 14.

Natural Monopoly
It is more efficient (less costly) to have the entire product in a market come from one large producer rather than from several smaller producers.

If a monopoly is a public utility—the only firm providing natural gas, electricity, or some other essential service to a community—entry of new sellers may be blocked by their inability to receive permission to operate from a regulatory authority. For example, a start-up electric company cannot provide service in an area unless it obtains a license from the state commission that regulates utilities, and usually just one license is granted in an area.

The ownership of a patent on a product or a process may give a firm monopoly power in a market. Anyone who uses the patented process or produces the patented product without the monopolist's permission can be sued. For example, as pointed out in Application 12.1, many years ago Polaroid regained its position as the sole seller of instant cameras and film in the U.S. market after Kodak was ordered out of the market as a result of a patent-related lawsuit.

A firm may be a monopolist because it is the sole owner of a factor necessary for production, such as the franchise for a professional sports team in a city. It may also have gained its monopoly position because it engaged in illegal practices involving prices and contracts that keep potential rivals out of the market.

---

[7]See Chapter 12 for a review of economies of scale.

Whether or not a seller is considered to be a monopoly depends on how the market is defined. Some examples could include a company that owns the only pipeline carrying natural gas into a region, the only newspaper in a city or bookstore on a college campus, the firm that has the food concessions at an airport or a national park, and the only general store near a campground.

Related to monopoly is an arrangement in which several sellers formally join together with the intention of acting as if they were a single-firm monopoly. The organization they form is called a **cartel,** and its purpose is to obtain more profit and other benefits for its members than they would receive if they competed with one another. Although the best-known example of a cartel is the Organization of Petroleum Exporting Countries (OPEC), other organizations have also been found to carry out cartel-type activities. For example, the court in Application 13.1 called NCAA control over college football a classic cartel. Cartels are illegal in the United States.[8]

Cartel
An arrangement whereby sellers formally join together in a market to make decisions as a group on matters such as pricing.

Behavior of a Monopolist

Control over Price   Because it is the only seller in its market, there are two important points to consider about a monopolist's pricing. First, all other things being equal, a monopolist has more control over its price than does a firm in any other market structure. There are no direct competitors to take buyers away when a monopolist raises its price. Second, because the monopolist is the only seller in its market, its demand curve is the market demand curve: All buyers demanding the product demand it from the monopolist.

Demand for a Monopolist's Product   Since market demand curves are downward sloping, and since the monopolist's demand is identical to the market demand, the monopolist's demand curve is the downward-sloping market demand curve.

Unlike the pure competitor, a price taker who must accept the price dictated by market supply and demand, the monopolist is a **price searcher** who will assess the costs and revenues from operating at different levels of output, or different points on the demand curve, and select the one price and output combination that maximizes profit. For example, the monopolist facing the demand curve in Figure 13.12 will assess revenues and costs at different levels of output and apply the profit-maximizing rules to find the one price–quantity combination that yields maximum profit. Depending on the behavior of costs, this combination could be shown by point A, B, C, or any other point on the demand curve in Figure 13.12. The appendix at the end of this chapter fully develops revenue and cost information to show how a monopolist locates the profit-maximizing point on its demand curve.

One of the significant features about pricing in a monopoly market structure is that, since the monopolist's demand and the market demand are the same, the monopolist is establishing the price and output level for the whole market. In other words,

Price Searcher
A firm that searches its downward-sloping demand curve to find the price–output combination that maximizes its profit.

---

[8]Over the years the power of OPEC has diminished due, in part, to two important factors. First, the members of OPEC have had difficulty reaching and maintaining agreements, especially about production levels. As frequently happens in cartels, individual members break the cartel agreement when it is in their own best interest to do so. Second, the power of OPEC has been reduced by new sources of oil, such as the Alaska pipeline, and alternative supplies of energy, such as ethanol and solar energy.

For the court's comment on the NCAA as a classic cartel, see *Board of Regents of the University of Oklahoma v. National Collegiate Athletic Association*, 546 F. Supp. 1276 (1982), pp. 1300–1301.

FIGURE 13.12   *Demand Curve for the Output of a Monopolist*

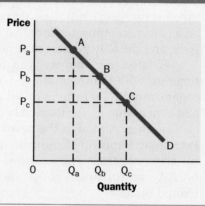

A monopolist will search its downward-sloping demand curve and choose the one price and output combination that will maximize its profit. The monopolist's demand curve and the market demand curve are the same.

one firm makes all the supply decisions. In addition, once the monopolist chooses a price, there are no competitors to force it down. The monopolist also has no immediate threat of entry by new firms.

Table 13.1 gives the 2008 Major League Baseball Fan Cost Index for attending major league games in the league ballparks. If the market is defined as live major league baseball and fans do not regard other forms of sports activities or entertainment as substitutes, then buying a ticket to a major league baseball game could be an example of buying in a monopoly market. It must be noted, however, that this index includes the cost of refreshments, parking, programs, and baseball caps in addition to the tickets—items that may or may not be sold in a monopoly market.

Nonprice Competition   Because monopolists face no direct competitors, they use nonprice competition differently from oligopolists or monopolistic competitors, who use it to attract buyers to a particular brand of a product. For example, in the hybrid market, nonprice competition encourages buyers toward a Ford Escape, Toyota Prius, Chevy Malibu, Lexus RX400, Saturn Aura, or other hybrid. But with monopoly there are no competing brands; there is simply the product. As a result, a monopolist's advertising and other nonprice competition may be designed to make people aware of the good or service itself, not the seller. For example, many people are probably more aware of the advertising slogan "A diamond is forever" than they are of De Beers Consolidated Mines, Ltd., the company with which the slogan is associated. While not having a complete monopoly, De Beers supplies the vast majority of the world's diamonds. If you buy a new diamond, it is very likely to have come from De Beers.

Long-Run Costs, Profit, and Efficiency   The monopolist enjoys its position as sole seller in its market because of barriers to entry that keep potential rivals out. Those

TABLE 13.1	Team Marketing Report's Major League Baseball Fan Cost Index

Buying a ticket to a major league baseball game might be considered a purchase in a monopoly market.

Team	2008 Fan Cost Index[a]
Boston Red Sox	$320.71
New York Yankees	275.10
Chicago Cubs	251.96
New York Mets	251.19
Toronto Blue Jays	230.46
Los Angeles Dodgers	229.14
St. Louis Cardinals	217.28
Houston Astros	215.43
Chicago White Sox	214.61
Oakland Athletics	206.80
San Diego Padres	201.72
Philadelphia Phillies	199.56
Washington Nationals	195.50
Cleveland Indians	192.38
Seattle Mariners	191.16
Detroit Tigers	190.13
San Francisco Giants	183.74
Cincinnati Reds	167.14
Minnesota Twins	165.71
Baltimore Orioles	165.40
Florida Marlins	164.26
Arizona Diamondbacks	162.84
Colorado Rockies	160.00
Atlanta Braves	157.19
Kansas City Royals	151.16
Texas Rangers	148.04
Pittsburgh Pirates	146.32
Milwaukee Brewers	141.52
Los Angeles Angels	140.42
Tampa Bay Rays	136.91

[a]Jon Greenberg, ed., Team Marketing Report, Fan Cost Index 2008

Source: Team Marketing Report, Fan Cost Index 2008, http://www.teammarketing.com/fancost/mlb/.

same barriers allow the monopolist to make an economic profit over the long run. With barriers to entry blocking new competitors, no seller can come into the market, force the monopoly firm to lower its price, and compete economic profit away. The monopolist can protect its economic profit as long as its monopoly position can be maintained. Also, with no competition, the monopolist can operate inefficiently, or at higher than minimum average cost.

However, even with the monopolist's exclusive position in the market, some restraints may exist on its profit-making ability and ability to operate without regard to efficiency. Although it faces no direct competition in its own market, the monopolist must be concerned with competition from products in other, closely related markets. A natural gas distributor may have no direct competition from other gas distributors, but in some respects it faces competition from suppliers of other types of energy. For example, a developer of a subdivision of homes may have the choice of installing gas, electric, oil, or solar heat, and a homeowner always has the option of converting from one type of heat to another. If the gas company's price gets too far out of line, over the long run, as buyers have the opportunity to move into other markets, it could lose business not to other gas distributors but to companies supplying alternative forms of energy.

The monopolist is also restrained in its profit-making ability when it is a public utility. With public utilities, state regulatory commissions or other public authorities oversee the prices they charge. For example, privately held water companies are subject to rates and standards set by a state commission. Typically, prices are set in such a way that the utility's ability to earn excess profit is limited.

MARKET STRUCTURES, THE CONSUMER, AND EFFICIENCY

Let's review what we have learned about competition and the behavior of a business in a market. We are particularly concerned with the effects on consumers of buying from sellers in each of the four market structures and the levels of efficiency achieved by firms in these structures.

Buyers fare best when facing purely competitive sellers since the market, not the individual seller, determines the price. In the long run, price is equal to average total cost and average total cost is as low as possible. This means that over the long run, no economic profit goes to sellers (again, no more profit than is necessary for production to continue), consumers get the good or service at the lowest possible price, and these firms operate efficiently.

In monopolistic competition, price is again equal to average total cost in the long run. But since the demand curve for an individual seller's product is downward sloping, the long-run average total cost of the product is not at its lowest possible level. Thus, even though buyers pay no economic profit to the seller, they do not get the good or service at the minimum possible cost. Since firms do not operate at their lowest average total costs, they are less efficient than purely competitive firms. But, in this structure, consumers enjoy a differentiation in products among sellers.

In oligopoly and monopoly, the price of a product can remain above its average total cost over the long run; that is, in these market structures the prices buyers pay may regularly include an economic profit to the seller. These market structures may also lack the forces that cause firms to produce efficiently. Because of these and other manifestations of the market power of oligopolists and monopolists, the government has taken steps from time to time to modify their behaviors. Some of those measures are taken up in Chapter 14. Table 13.2 summarizes the characteristics and resulting behaviors of firms in each of the four market structures.

TABLE 13.2	*Characteristics and Behavior of Firms in Each of the Four Market Structures*

Consumers fare best in purely competitive markets: Sellers have no control over price, and over the long run, average total cost and price are as low as they can get and sellers earn no economic profit.

Characteristics		**Behavior**
Pure Competition		
Very large number of sellers	→	Price determined by market supply and demand
Identical products	→	No nonprice competition
Easy entry and exit	→	In the long run, price equals minimum ATC and firms operate efficiently with no economic profit
Monopolistic Competition		
Large number of sellers	→	Firms have limited control over price
Differentiated products	→	Firms engage in nonprice competition
Fairly easy entry and exit	→	In the long run, price equals ATC, but not minimum ATC, and firms operate with no economic profit
Oligopoly		
Few sellers	→	Firms have control over price
Mutual interdependence	→	Firms assess rivals' reactions in setting strategies
Barriers to entry	→	In the long run, firms can operate with economic profit, and not at minimum ATC
Monopoly		
One seller	→	Firm has most control over price
Impassable barriers to entry	→	In the long run, seller can operate with economic profit, and not at minimum ATC

Summary

1. A market is composed of firms selling similar products and competing for the same group of buyers. The boundaries of a market are determined by product substitutability and geographic considerations.

2. The degree of competition in a market influences a firm's pricing and nonprice policies as well as its ability to earn economic profit in the long run. To analyze competition and its effects, markets can be classified into four structures: pure competition, monopolistic competition, oligopoly, and monopoly.

3. Pure competition is characterized by a large number of independent firms selling identical products in a market that is easy to enter and exit. Individual purely competitive firms have no control over price, which is set by the forces of supply and demand in the market. An individual firm's demand curve is a straight, horizontal line at the market price, indicating that the

firm can sell as much as it wants at that price but nothing at a higher price. Nonprice competition doesn't occur in purely competitive markets since sellers' products are identical.

4.   Due to easy entry and exit, in the long run a purely competitive seller's price is equal to minimum long-run average total cost. This results in efficient production, the lowest possible price that can be charged in the market, and no economic profit for the firm. From the buyer's point of view this makes pure competition the ideal market structure. In the real world, purely competitive markets are limited in number.

5.   Monopolistic competition is characterized by a large number of sellers with differentiated products in a market that is fairly easy to enter and exit. Because of product differentiation, each seller has a downward-sloping demand curve and exercises some control over its price. This control, however, is limited by the large number of sellers offering buyers similar products. Nonprice competition through packaging, location, and other methods is important in these markets.

6.   Since entry into and exit from the market are fairly easy, over the long run monopolistic competitors operate where price equals long-run average total cost, resulting in no economic profits. However, these firms do not produce at the lowest point on their long-run average total cost curves, so their prices and costs are higher, and the firms are less efficient, than if they were pure competitors.

7.   Oligopoly is characterized by a few sellers producing identical or differentiated products in a market that is difficult to enter. By virtue of their relatively large size in the market, oligopolists have some control over their prices. But large size also causes the competitive decisions of one firm to affect other firms in its market, giving rise to mutual interdependence among the sellers.

8.   Since mutual interdependence can assume different forms, there are several explanations for oligopoly pricing. Two popular explanations are leadership pricing, which occurs when one firm changes its price and others follow, and the kinked demand curve model, which is based on the assumption that rivals follow a firm's price decreases but not price increases. With the entry of potential rivals into the market impeded, oligopolists may be able to charge prices greater than average total cost, earn economic profits over the long run, and not operate efficiently.

9.   Monopoly is characterized by a single seller facing no direct competition in a market that is impossible to enter. All other things being equal, a monopolist has more control over its price than does a firm in any other market structure. Since it is the only seller in its market, the market demand curve is the monopolist's demand curve, and the monopolist searches for the one price and output combination on the demand curve that maximizes its profit. With the entry of new rivals blocked, the monopolist can charge a price greater than its average total cost, earn economic profit over the long run, and not operate efficiently.

Key Terms and Concepts

Market structures

Industry

Market

Geographic boundary of a market

Product boundary of a market

Purely competitive market

Barriers to entry

Price taker

Market demand curve

Individual firm's demand curve

Economic profit, loss, or breaking even

Nonprice competition

Efficient production

Monopolistic competition

Differentiated products

Oligopoly

Mutual interdependence

Leadership pricing

Kinked demand curve

Monopoly

Natural monopoly

Cartel

Price searcher

Review Questions

1. Into which of the four market structures would you place each of the following? Why would you make this classification?
   a. A small organic farm growing herbs and arugula on 5 acres
   b. A large grain farm producing wheat on 2,500 acres
   c. A major airline
   d. A community college
   e. The water company for a region
   f. A small retail shoe store in a large mall
   g. A discount shoe store in a large city
   h. A college food service
   i. The only long-term parking facility at an airport
   j. Passenger travel on Amtrak
   k. The best bakery in town
   l. The local small town newspaper

2. How do firms in each of the four market structures differ in terms of their number of rivals, control over price, product differentiation, ability to earn economic profit over the long run, and efficiency?

3. What is the relationship between price and average total cost when a firm operates with an economic profit, takes a loss, or breaks even? Illustrate, in the accompanying graphs, the relationship between an individual firm's demand curve and average total cost curve in each of the following situations.
   a. A purely competitive firm in the long run
   b. A monopolist earning an economic profit
   c. A purely competitive firm operating with a loss

d. A monopolistically competitive firm in the long run
e. A monopolistically competitive firm operating with a loss
f. An oligopolist pricing at the kink in its demand curve and earning an economic profit

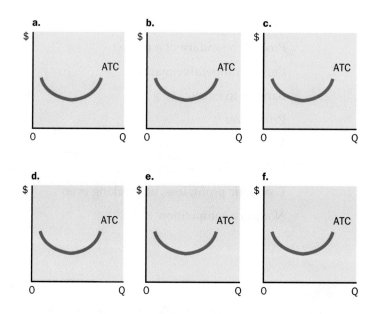

4. Why does a firm in pure competition operate efficiently in the long run while firms in the other three market structures do not? Why is it important to consumers that a firm operate efficiently?

5. Firms in monopoly and oligopoly markets are protected in varying degrees by barriers to entry, and they can earn excess profits in the long run. How do barriers to entry relate to a firm's ability to earn excess profits in the long run?

6. Monopolistically competitive sellers face downward-sloping demand curves, and pure competitors face perfectly horizontal demand curves. What is the difference in the competitive environments of these two market structures that causes this difference in the behavior of the individual firm's demand curve?

7. Explain what is meant by mutual interdependence and how it relates to the price leadership and the kinked demand curve models.

Discussion Questions

1. Pure competition is said to be the most competitive of all the market structures. If this is true, why is it that no one firm is concerned with what any other firm does in a purely competitive market?

2. You have a friend who thinks the market for automobiles should be changed from oligopolistic to monopolistically competitive by breaking the existing firms into a large number of smaller firms. Do you agree or disagree with your friend's proposal? Why?

3. A market is defined according to the geographic area in which sellers compete for buyers and the extent to which buyers view sellers' products as substitutes. What, in your opinion, would be the substitutes and relevant geographic market for each of the following? Be able to defend your answers.
   a. Beer from a small microbrewery in central Pennsylvania
   b. A four-door Swedish automobile for sale at a U.S. dealership
   c. A ski resort in the Rocky Mountains
   d. A major state university
   e. Frozen pizza

4. In the United States, people keep increasing their shopping over the Internet. Does this growth in computer shopping increase competition for retail stores, or are these different markets? Explain your reasoning.

5. Why might a seller in an oligopoly market where mutual interdependence and rivals' responses are important choose to increase its sales through an advertising campaign rather than by lowering the price of its product?

6. Certain vehicles are basically the same but are marketed under different brand names. The cars, sometimes built on the same assembly lines, may have different standard equipment, styling, accessories, and prices. The Ford Expedition and the Lincoln Navigator, for example, are largely the same. It is understandable why one automobile company would want recognizable differences between its cars and those of a rival, but what does the company gain by creating differences among its own products? What costs and benefits do automobile buyers experience from this differentiation strategy?

7. Why are economists so concerned with efficiency? Would the world be a better place to live if all goods and services were produced efficiently and sold in purely competitive markets?

8. Identify a monopoly market in which you participate as a buyer. Can you determine any negative effects on you as a buyer that would not occur if there were more competition in that market?

9. In economics courses students learn that there is value in competition in markets and that competition should be encouraged. In some business courses, students learn strategies for reducing competition. What accounts for the difference in the view of competition in these two areas of study?

Critical Thinking Case 13

THE $800 HAIRCUT

Critical Thinking Skills

Using criteria for grouping

Analyzing the unobvious

Economic Concepts

Market definitions

Market structures

$800 for a haircut! No way!

Well, not so fast. There are stories out there about people paying that much for a haircut. Just go to the Internet and type in $800 haircut, and you might be surprised at the number of hits you get.

It seems unlikely that the average person would pay such an outrageous price for a haircut. Most of us would like to eat a few meals a day, pay the cell phone bill, and put gas in our cars to get to work and the fitness center. But what will people pay for a haircut?

Some folks are willing to "do" the local cheapcuts hair salon. The $10 special on Thursday is okay and serves the purpose. Others search out the best in the area—which might mean a cool $200 rather than $10. In some places, the cheap joints are on almost every corner; in some places, there are independent hairdressers in malls, storefronts, home basements, and garages; and in some places, there are integrated hair salons and spas.

All of this brings us to market structures and pricing. At first glance we might think that haircutting is a good example of a monopolistically competitive market. But spending $800, or even $200, for a haircut when you could spend $10 doesn't seem to conform to what people typically think of when describing monopolistic competition.

So what is the story? Are some of these haircutters monopolists? Have they risen so far above the competition and established such a name for themselves that no one can compete with them? If this is the case, can this happen with chefs? With surgeons? With college professors? With any career or profession?

Questions

1. In what market structure do haircuts generally belong? Does this differ by location?

2. Can a service seemingly in a monopolistically competitive market become so unique that it leaves that market? Could some sellers become oligopolists or monopolists? How do you explain this phenomenon?

3. What other markets can you identify that have behaviors similar to the haircut market described in this case?

4. Do you think a heart surgeon could ever be a monopolist? Why?

CHAPTER 13
APPENDIX

DETERMINING THE PROFIT-MAXIMIZING PRICE AND OUTPUT FOR THE FIRM IN PURE COMPETITION

Profit-Maximizing Behavior

Since a firm in pure competition can sell as much or as little as it chooses at the going market price, how does it determine what quantity it actually will produce and sell?

Remember that the objective of decision making by a purely competitive firm (or a firm in any market structure) is to choose the output level that will maximize profit. In Chapter 11 we learned that a firm will maximize its profit by operating where the additional cost and the additional revenue from the last unit produced and sold are equal. That is, the firm will maximize profit by operating where marginal cost equals marginal revenue. Consider how this rule applies to a purely competitive firm.

Demand, Revenues, and Costs   Table 13A.1 gives price, quantity, and revenue information for a purely competitive grain farmer operating in a market where the equilibrium price is $3 per bushel. The first two columns of the table list the demand schedule for the farmer's grain, which shows that regardless of how much is demanded—be it 3, 1,003, or 8,003 bushels—the farmer receives a price of $3 per bushel. Total revenue, given in the third column, is calculated by multiplying price times quantity demanded at each level of demand. Total revenue with a demand of 3 bushels is $9; with 1,003 bushels it is $3 × 1,003 = $3,009; and so on.

Marginal revenue is the change in total revenue as one more unit of a product (bushel of grain in this example) is demanded. The marginal revenue figures in Table 13A.1 indicate that no matter how much or how little is demanded, the next bushel demanded always adds $3 to the farmer's total revenue. Because $3 is the price at which the farmer can sell each bushel of grain, it can be concluded that in pure competition the firm's marginal revenue is equal to its price.

When graphed, marginal revenue is a straight, horizontal line at the equilibrium market price of $3 per bushel. In other words, in pure competition the individual seller's marginal revenue curve is identical to its demand curve. This is shown in Figure 13A.1 by the line D = MR which illustrates the demand and marginal revenue data for the grain farmer in Table 13A.1.

The marginal cost for a purely competitive seller behaves like the typical marginal cost curve discussed in Chapter 12. Graphically, it is "fishhook" shaped: As output increases, it decreases to a minimum and then increases. The marginal cost for this pure competitor is also illustrated in Figure 13A.1.

Determining the Profit-Maximizing Output   The profit-maximizing output for a firm can be found by examining its marginal cost and marginal revenue curves, as is done in Figure 13A.1. To maximize its profit, a firm should produce where its marginal cost curve intersects its marginal revenue curve. This occurs in Figure 13A.1 at point A. Reading down from point A to the horizontal axis, we can see that the profit-maximizing output is 6,000 bushels of grain.

TABLE 13A.1	*Price, Quantity, and Revenue Information for a Purely Competitive Seller*

Because a seller in pure competition receives the same price for its product regardless of the quantity demanded, the seller's marginal revenue is always equal to the price.

Price	Quantity Demanded	Total Revenue	Marginal Revenue
$3.00	0	$ 0.00	
			$3.00
3.00	1	3.00	
			3.00
3.00	2	6.00	
			3.00
3.00	3	9.00	
•	•	•	•
•	•	•	•
$3.00	1,001	3,003.00	
			$3.00
3.00	1,002	3,006.00	
			3.00
3.00	1,003	3,009.00	
•	•	•	•
•	•	•	•
$3.00	8,001	$24,003.00	
			$3.00
3.00	8,002	24,006.00	
			3.00
3.00	8,003	24,009.00	

An additional note about profit-maximizing behavior is necessary. Up to this point, the marginal cost equals marginal revenue rule has been presented as a guide to lead the firm to maximum profit. But what if a firm is operating at a loss? What if, at every level of output, its costs are greater than its revenues? Here again the marginal cost equals marginal revenue rule leads to the "best" (where best means "least bad") output level.

When a firm is producing at the output where marginal cost equals marginal revenue, it is operating at the strongest net revenue position it can reach. When revenue is greater than costs, this leads to maximum profit, but when revenue falls short of costs, this leads to minimum loss. So, whether a firm is trying to maximize its profit or minimize its loss, the decision-making rule is the same: Operate where marginal cost equals marginal revenue.

We can determine whether a firm is maximizing its profit or minimizing its loss by measuring whether the cost of producing each unit of output is less or more than its price at the best level of output. Graphically, this is indicated by whether the average total cost curve lies below or above the demand curve at the output level where marginal cost equals marginal revenue. Figure 13A.2a shows a grain farmer operating with maximum economic profit where marginal cost equals marginal revenue. At the profit-maximizing output of 6,000 bushels, the price is $3 per bushel, and the average

FIGURE 13A.1   *Profit-Maximizing Output for a Purely Competitive Seller*

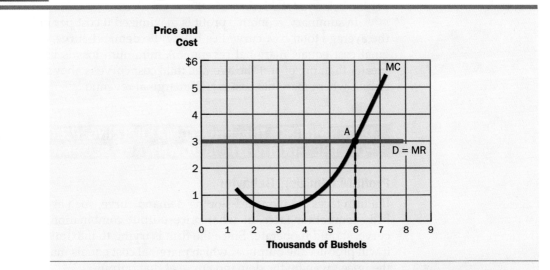

Graphically, a purely competitive seller's marginal revenue curve is identical to its demand curve. Profit is maximized or loss is minimized by operating at the output level where marginal revenue equals marginal cost.

total cost is $2 per bushel. In this case the farmer is earning an economic profit of $1 per bushel, or $6,000 in total economic profit.

Figure 13A.2b shows a grain farmer minimizing a loss by operating where marginal cost equals marginal revenue. At the loss-minimizing output of 6,000 bushels,

FIGURE 13A.2   *A Purely Competitive Seller Maximizing Profit or Minimizing Loss*

If a purely competitive seller's demand curve is above its average total cost curve, it will maximize profit by operating at the output level where marginal revenue equals marginal cost. If its demand curve is below its average total cost curve, it will minimize its loss by operating at the output level where marginal revenue equals marginal cost.

the cost per bushel is $4 and the price received is $3. The farmer is taking a loss of $1 per bushel, or a total loss of $6,000.

In summary, economic profit is maximized if cost per unit is less than price, or if the average total cost curve lies below the demand curve, at the output where marginal cost equals marginal revenue. A minimum loss is incurred if cost per unit is greater than price, or if the average total cost curve is above the demand curve, at the output where marginal cost equals marginal revenue.[1]

DETERMINING THE PROFIT-MAXIMIZING PRICE AND OUTPUT FOR THE FIRM WITH A DOWNWARD-SLOPING DEMAND CURVE

Profit-Maximizing Behavior

If a firm faces a downward-sloping demand curve, such as a monopolist or monopolistic competitor faces, at what price–output combination, or point on its demand curve, should it operate? Since the firm is trying to maximize profit or minimize loss, it will produce the output at which marginal cost equals marginal revenue and charge the price given by the demand curve at that output.

Demand, Revenues, and Costs   A firm with a downward-sloping demand curve, where more can be sold only by lowering price, faces demand conditions identical to those given in the example in Chapter 11 of the craftsperson selling rocking chairs.

---

[1]A firm facing a loss over the short run may minimize its loss by shutting down, rather than producing. Recall from Chapter 12 that a firm has both fixed costs and variable costs in the short run. If it shuts down and produces nothing, it must still pay its fixed costs, but it has no variable costs to pay. Thus, we can say that the "shut-down loss" to a business over the short run is the fixed costs it must continue to pay even though it is not producing.

Whether a firm that is losing money is better off shutting down or producing depends on the relationship between its price and average variable cost. If price is greater than AVC, the firm should continue operating at a loss in the short run: The firm can pay all of its variable costs and contribute something to its fixed costs. Because of this, its operating loss (equal to part of its fixed costs) is less than its shut-down loss (all of its fixed costs). If price is less than AVC, the firm should shut down. In this case the firm cannot cover all of its variable costs. Continuing to operate means that the firm is losing an amount equal to all of its fixed costs *and* some of its variable costs. By shutting down it loses just its fixed costs.

The left-hand figure below shows a firm that should continue to operate. At the loss-minimizing output of 6,000 bushels, the price of $3.00 will cover the average variable cost of $2.50 and contribute $0.50 per bushel to the fixed costs. The right-hand figure shows a firm that should shut down. At the loss-minimizing output of 6,000 bushels, the price of $3.00 will not cover the average variable cost of $3.50. The firm loses all the fixed costs plus $0.50 per bushel for the variable costs.

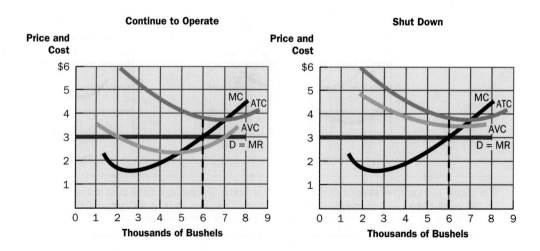

Demand and Marginal Revenue from Selling Chairs

Price	Quantity Demanded	Total Revenue	Marginal Revenue
$450	0	$ 0	
			$400
400	1	400	
			300
350	2	700	
			200
300	3	900	
			100
250	4	1,000	
			0
200	5	1,000	

When price must be lowered to sell a larger quantity, the marginal revenue for each additional unit demanded is less than price. As a result, the marginal revenue curve lies below the demand curve.

Table 11.5 showed that, with demand behaving in this way, the marginal revenue from each additional chair sold was less than its price. Table 11.5 is reproduced in Figure 13A.3.

Since price is shown on the demand curve, and since marginal revenue is less than price when price falls, the marginal revenue curve associated with a downward-sloping demand curve is also downward sloping and lies below that demand curve. To illustrate this principle, the demand and marginal revenue curves for the craftsperson's chairs are also given in Figure 13A.3. Marginal revenue, like all marginal measurements, is plotted midway between the quantities. For example, the marginal revenue of $400 for the first unit is plotted at one-half unit.

The marginal cost curve for a seller with a downward-sloping demand curve is typically like that for any firm: It decreases to a minimum and then increases. Figure 13A.4 illustrates representative demand, marginal revenue, and marginal cost curves for a firm with a downward-sloping demand curve.

Determining the Profit-Maximizing Output   To determine the profit-maximizing position for the seller in Figure 13A.4, the intersection of its marginal cost and marginal revenue curves must be located. To find the profit-maximizing output, one reads down from the point where marginal cost equals marginal revenue to the quantity axis. The profit-maximizing output is 300 units. The profit-maximizing price is found by reading up from the intersection where marginal cost equals marginal revenue to the demand curve, and from the demand curve to the vertical axis. For this seller, the profit-maximizing price is $6 per unit. Thus, point A on the demand curve shows the profit-maximizing price and output position for this seller: This seller should charge $6 and sell 300 units.

As is the case with a purely competitive firm, whether a firm with a downward-sloping demand curve is maximizing economic profit or minimizing loss depends on the relationship between price and average total cost at the output level where marginal cost equals marginal revenue. If the average total cost curve lies below the

FIGURE 13A.4   *Profit-Maximizing Output for a Firm with a Downward-Sloping Demand Curve*

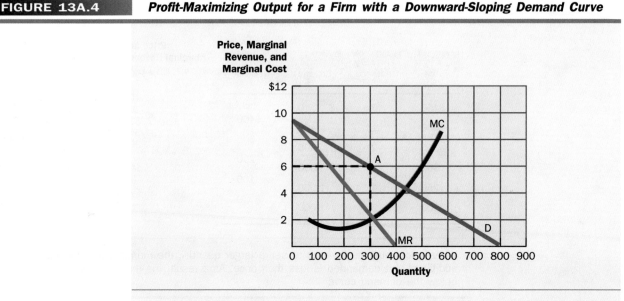

The rule for maximizing profit is the same for all firms: Operate at the output level where marginal revenue equals marginal cost.

FIGURE 13A.5   *A Firm with a Downward-Sloping Demand Curve Maximizing Profit or Minimizing Loss*

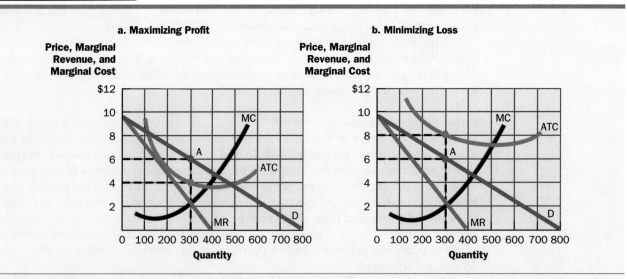

When the average total cost curve lies below the demand curve at the output where marginal revenue equals marginal cost, the firm is maximizing profit by producing that output. When the average total cost curve is above the demand curve, the firm is minimizing its loss by producing where marginal revenue equals marginal cost.

demand curve, economic profit is maximized, and if the average total cost curve lies above the demand curve, the firm is incurring a minimum loss.

Figure 13A.5a shows the firm maximizing profit. At the output level of 300 units, where marginal revenue equals marginal cost, price is $6 per unit and average total cost is $4. Economic profit for this seller is $2 per unit, and total economic profit is $600 ($2 × 300 units).

Figure 13A.5b shows the firm operating with a loss. At the loss-minimizing output of 300 units, price is $6 and the cost per unit is $8, leaving a per unit loss of $2. The total loss for this firm is $600. Test Your Understanding, "Maximizing Profit and Minimizing Loss," lets you check your skill at identifying the best output level at which a firm can operate and the profit or loss it would earn at that output.

TEST YOUR UNDERSTANDING

MAXIMIZING PROFIT AND MINIMIZING LOSS

1. The table to the right shows the market price of corn and the various quantities that a purely competitive farmer could sell at that price. Based on this information, complete the table and answer the following questions about this farmer.

   a. On the basis of your completed table, draw the demand and marginal revenue curves for this farmer's corn on graph A.
   b. To maximize profit or minimize loss, this farmer should sell ____ bushels of corn.
   c. At this quantity the farmer's average total cost is $____ per bushel, profit/loss is $____ per bushel, and total profit/loss is $____.
   d. On the same graph, draw the new demand and marginal revenue curves the farmer would face if the market price were to rise to $3.50 per bushel.
   e. At this price, the farmer should sell ____ bushels of corn to maximize profit or minimize loss.
   f. At this quantity, the farmer's average total cost is $____ per bushel, profit/loss per bushel is $____, and total profit/loss is $____.

2. Given in graph B are the demand and cost conditions faced by a pure monopolist. To maximize profit or minimize loss, this firm should produce and sell ____ units of output and charge a price of $____ per unit. At this level of output the firm's average total cost is $____ per unit, its profit/loss per unit is $____, and its total profit/loss is $____.

Answers can be found at the back of the book.

Price	Quantity Demanded (Bushels)	Total Revenue	Marginal Revenue
$2.00	0	$____	
			$____
2.00	1	____	
			____
2.00	2	____	____
•	•	•	•
•	•	•	•
•	•	•	•
2.00	1,000	____	
			____
2.00	1,001	____	
			____
2.00	1,002	____	
•	•	•	•
•	•	•	•
•	•	•	•
2.00	10,000	____	
			____
2.00	10,001	____	
			____
2.00	10,002	____	

(*Continued*)

Graph A

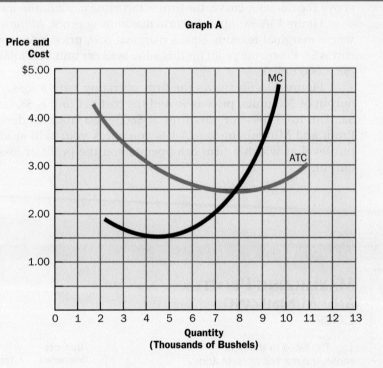

Price and Cost — Quantity (Thousands of Bushels)

Graph B

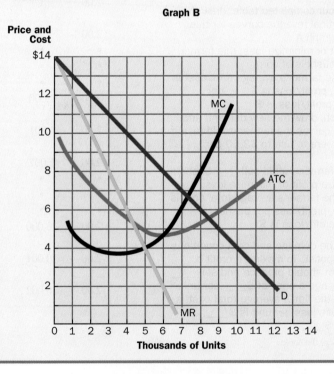

Price and Cost — Thousands of Units

CHAPTER 14

Government and the Markets

CHAPTER OBJECTIVES

To introduce the main forms of government intervention into the operation of markets, and some reasons for this intervention.

To identify the major federal antitrust statutes and the anticompetitive practices they address.

To examine different types of mergers and their possible anticompetitive effects.

To identify the forms and organization of government regulation.

To distinguish between industry regulation and social regulation, and to offer justifications for each.

To introduce issues about the effectiveness of regulation, and policy concerns growing out of the increasing internationalization of economic activity.

In the last chapter we saw that a seller's price, output, promotional strategy, profit, and efficiency are all influenced by the type of market it is in and degree of competition it faces. Obviously, markets and competition play an important role in economic decision making and in determining the well-being of businesses and households.

Economies where decisions are made primarily by individual businesses and households are built on the philosophy that free markets and competition should be at the foundation of economic activity. Although the U.S. economy is based on this philosophy, historically government has intervened in the operation of markets in several important ways. (Recall in Chapter 2 the discussion of market failure and government intervention.) In this chapter we will pick up the discussion of government intervention and focus on the two essential ways government influences competition and market forces in the United States: antitrust enforcement and regulation.

We typically find a wide range of views on the appropriateness of government intervention. Some people feel that current intervention is too extensive; others feel that it is inadequate. Some people hold that government intervention is not achieving its intended results or that it creates an unjustified administrative or financial burden on businesses; others are satisfied with its effects and comfortable with the requirements it imposes.

Why would people who basically favor free markets seek government intervention in the operation of those markets? Government intervention might be sought where the number of firms in a market is so small that strong competition is unlikely or where one firm is so large that it significantly weakens competitive forces. Government intervention might also be sought in the public interest: The public might be better served by a single large, efficient seller that answers to a public body than by several less efficient, smaller sellers competing with one another. This is often the case with the distribution of gas, electric, and water services.

Another reason for seeking government intervention is security. As the economist John Maurice Clark wrote:

> [C]ompetition has two opposites: which we may call monopoly and security. . . .
> Nearly everyone favors competition as against monopoly, and nearly everyone
> wants it limited in the interest of security. And hardly anyone pays much attention
> to the question where one leaves off and the other begins.[1]

Finally, government may be called in to intervene when consumers or workers can be hurt by dangerous products or working conditions. Protection may be sought when people believe that the market does not provide it.

Competition introduces some risks for businesses, and the desire to reduce these risks may inspire support for some government intervention. For example, antitrust laws specifying the ground rules about allowable competitive practices may reduce the risk of failure for smaller or weaker sellers in a market. Laws that regulate monopolies, such as gas or electric suppliers, increase security for consumers by ensuring that these firms continue to supply the market at prices that are regulated.

ANTITRUST ENFORCEMENT

Antitrust Laws
Laws prohibiting certain practices that reduce competition.

Antitrust enforcement centers on a series of laws designed to promote the operation of market forces by limiting certain practices that reduce competition. Specifically, **antitrust laws** are aimed at two broad categories of practices.

[1]John Maurice Clark, *Alternative to Serfdom* (New York: Alfred A. Knopf, 1948), p. 61.

Monopolization and Attempts to Monopolize
A firm acquires or attempts to acquire a monopoly share of its market through unreasonable means.

The first is **monopolization and attempts to monopolize,** which occur when a firm, through unreasonable means, acquires or attempts to acquire such a large share of its market that it does not feel strong competitive pressure from its rivals. The effect that a firm with a great deal of market power can have on competition has been compared by the economist Walter Adams to a poker game where one player brings much more money to the table than the others.

> [I]n a poker game with unlimited stakes, the player who commands disproportionately large funds is likely to emerge victorious. If I have $100 while my opponents have no more than $5 each, I am likely to win regardless of my ability, my virtue, or my luck.[2]

Combinations and Conspiracies in Restraint of Trade
Practices carried out jointly by two or more firms that unreasonably restrict competition.

The second category of practices at which antitrust laws are aimed is **combinations and conspiracies in restraint of trade.** This includes acts carried out jointly by two or more firms that unreasonably limit competition, such as price fixing and the division of sales territories. Monopolization and attempts to monopolize, and combinations and conspiracies in restraint of trade, are explained more fully as we review the major antitrust statutes.

Antitrust enforcement is carried out by both the federal and state governments, with the main responsibility falling on the Department of Justice and the Federal Trade Commission at the federal level. In addition to federal and state enforcement, private parties such as businesses can bring charges that other companies and/or individuals have violated the laws.

Administration of the antitrust laws depends heavily on the courts and is carried out on a case-by-case basis, where each violation is treated separately. In some instances a suit may be dropped because it is judged to have insufficient merit to go to trial, or a pretrial settlement may be reached where the accused firm promises to discontinue a practice or arrives at some other agreement with the opposing side. In other instances a trial may be required before the issue is resolved. Antitrust disputes can become long, costly, and complicated.

The Antitrust Laws

At the federal level, there are five main antitrust laws: the Sherman Act (1890), the Federal Trade Commission Act (1914), the Clayton Act (1914), the Robinson-Patman Act (1936), and the Celler-Kefauver Act (1950). The Robinson-Patman and Celler-Kefauver acts both amend the Clayton Act.

Sherman Act
Original and most broadly worded federal antitrust statute; condemns combinations and conspiracies in restraint of trade, and monopolization and attempts to monopolize.

The Sherman Act (1890)   The original and most broadly worded federal antitrust statute is the **Sherman Act.** When people speak of this act, they tend to refer to it by sections.

- ♦ Section 1 condemns combinations and conspiracies in restraint of trade, and
- ♦ Section 2 attacks monopolization and attempts to monopolize.

Per Se Violations
Anticompetitive agreements between firms where proof of the agreement is sufficient to establish guilt; includes price fixing and division of sales territories.

Combinations and conspiracies condemned by Section 1 of the Sherman Act are either per se or rule of reason violations. **Per se violations** are agreements between firms where proof of the agreement is sufficient to establish guilt: There is no defense

---

[2]Quoted in Estes Kefauver, *In a Few Hands* (New York: Pantheon Books, 1965), p. 196.

for a per se violation. Price fixing and division of sales territories among competitors are included in this category.[3]

Price fixing occurs when sellers take joint action to influence prices. An understanding between competing sellers about the prices they will charge their buyers or the price below which they will not sell would be price fixing, as would an agreement on a system for determining who will submit the lowest offer when pricing is done with sealed bids. With price fixing, competition is diminished and sellers act more like monopolists.

Territorial division occurs when competing firms divide a sales area among themselves. For example, two firms competing in a national market might agree that one takes the territory east, and the other takes the territory west, of the Mississippi River. As with price fixing, territorial division diminishes competition.

Rule of reason violations occur when firms come together in a way that may or may not unreasonably restrain trade. With the rule of reason, there is no blanket condemnation of business practices like there is with price fixing and territorial division. Rather, each challenged practice must be examined to see whether *in this particular case* the restraint is unreasonable.

Activities of industry trade associations and joint ventures fall under the rule of reason umbrella. A **trade association** is an organization of firms in a particular industry, such as construction or furniture manufacturing, that performs certain functions to benefit its members. If a trade association collects data on overall industry trends and general information on supply conditions or buyer behavior and reports it to all its members, the trade association may enhance competition by improving the general state of knowledge in the industry. But if the information gives specific details on the terms of each firm's sales and the names of its buyers, or if the information is not equally available to all interested parties, the trade association's information gathering might help to foster a price-fixing agreement or division of buyers among sellers and would therefore be subject to condemnation under Section 1 of the Sherman Act.

A **joint venture** is a cooperative effort by two or more firms that is limited in scope. The operation of an automobile plant by a U.S. and a Japanese manufacturer or the drilling for oil in a remote part of the world by several firms acting together would be examples of joint ventures. As with trade association activities, the legality of joint ventures must be judged on a case-by-case basis to determine whether competition has been unreasonably restricted.

Cases involving Sherman Act Section 2 violations of monopolization and attempts to monopolize rest largely on two issues:

♦ the specific actions taken by a firm that demonstrate its intent to monopolize its market; and
♦ the firm's share of its market.

Where the firm's market share is small and it is clearly not a monopolist, an attempt to monopolize may be inferred from such actions as pricing below cost to drive rivals out of the market or contracting with critical suppliers or distributors to foreclose their services to the firm's rivals.

Price Fixing
Joint action by sellers to influence their product prices; considered to be highly anticompetitive.

Territorial Division
Joint action by sellers to divide sales territories among themselves; considered to be highly anticompetitive.

Rule of Reason Violations
Actions that may or may not be unreasonable restraints of trade.

Trade Association
An organization representing firms in a particular industry that performs functions to benefit those firms.

Joint Venture
A cooperative effort by two or more firms that is limited in scope.

[3]One explanation for the per se rule is that the court's time is a scarce resource, and the likelihood of society benefiting from acts such as price fixing or territorial division is so remote that it would be a waste of time to require a court to listen to a defense for these acts.

For firms with larger market shares, monopolization may be inferred less from what the firm does and more from its relative size in comparison to its rivals. For example, in *United States v. Aluminum Company of America*, a leading monopolization case, the court enunciated a rough guide for analyzing Sherman Act monopolization questions known as the "30-60-90 rule": "[A greater than ninety per cent share of the market] is enough to constitute a monopoly; it is doubtful whether sixty or sixty-four per cent would be enough; and certainly thirty-three per cent is not."[4]

An extremely important aspect of monopolization cases is the definition of the relevant market, which was discussed in Chapter 13. Ordinarily, the broader a market is defined in terms of its geographic boundaries and/or number of substitute products, the smaller will be the share of that market taken by any one firm. The narrower a market is defined, the larger will be the share taken by the firm. Thus, it may be to the advantage of a firm accused of monopolizing a market to define that market as broadly as possible.

Application 14.1, "Cases Involving the Sherman Act," gives excerpts from the court records of some important and influential antitrust cases dealing with price fixing, territorial division, business associations, and monopolizing behavior that were brought under the Sherman Act. The decision of the court in each case is also provided. Can you explain how competition would have been injured in each case?

We might warn you before reading Applications 14.1 and 14.2, both of which deal with court rulings, that you will be getting a first-hand opportunity to see the complexity in the writing of court documents. They are not always easy to read.

Federal Trade Commission Act
Created the Federal Trade Commission and empowered it to prevent unfair methods of competition, which include antitrust violations.

The Federal Trade Commission Act (1914)   The Federal Trade Commission (FTC) was created by the **Federal Trade Commission Act** and granted power to "prevent persons, partnerships, or corporations, . . . from using unfair methods of competition in commerce."[5] Included among unfair methods of competition are antitrust violations.

When the FTC thinks that a business is engaged in unfair competition, it can issue a complaint and arrange a hearing to determine whether the practice should be prohibited. If it is found that the practice is unfair competition, the FTC can issue a "cease and desist order" requiring the firm to stop the activity. If the firm fails to follow the order, or if it thinks the order is incorrect, either the FTC or the firm can have the order brought before a court for a ruling.[6]

Clayton Act
Federal antitrust statute prohibiting specific activities that substantially reduce competition or tend to create a monopoly.

The Clayton Act (1914)   Unlike the Sherman Act and the Federal Trade Commission Act, which are not specific as to the practices they condemn, the **Clayton Act** is directed toward several particular activities that "substantially lessen competition or tend to create a monopoly."[7] These include exclusionary practices, interlocking directorates, price discrimination, and mergers and acquisitions.

Exclusionary Practices
Practices of a seller to prevent its suppliers or buyers from dealing with a competitor.

Exclusionary practices occur when a seller forecloses its rivals from the market by following policies that make it impossible for the rivals to compete. For example, Company X could agree to sell its product to a buyer only on the condition that it would supply all the buyer's needs for that type of item. Such an agreement would effectively give Company X a monopoly over the buyer's demand for that product.

Tying Contract
A buyer can obtain a good from a seller only by purchasing another good from the same seller.

Another example of an exclusionary practice is a **tying contract,** which occurs when a buyer can obtain one good from a seller only by purchasing another different

[4]*United States v. Aluminum Company of America*, 148 F. 2d 416 (1945), p. 424.
[5]*United States Statutes at Large*, vol. 38, part 1 (Washington, DC: U.S. Government Printing Office, 1915), p. 719.
[6]Ibid., pp. 719, 720.
[7]Ibid., p. 730.

APPLICATION 14.1

CASES INVOLVING THE SHERMAN ACT

Price Fixing: *Monsanto Company v. Spray-Rite Service Corp.* (1984)   From 1957 to 1968, [Spray-Rite Service Corp.], a wholesale distributor of agricultural chemicals that engaged in a discount operation, sold agricultural herbicides manufactured by [Monsanto Co.]. In 1968, [Monsanto] refused to renew [Spray-Rite's] 1-year distributorship term, and thereafter [Spray-Rite] was unable to purchase from other distributors as much of [Monsanto's] products as it desired or as early in the season as it needed them. [Spray-Rite] ultimately brought suit in Federal District Court under §1 of the Sherman Act, alleging that [Monsanto] and some of its distributors conspired to fix the resale prices of [Monsanto's] products and that [Monsanto] had terminated [Spray-Rite's] distributorship in furtherance of the conspiracy. . . . The District Court instructed the jury that [Monsanto's] conduct was per se unlawful if it was in furtherance of a price-fixing conspiracy. . . .

Ruling . . . There was sufficient evidence for the jury reasonably to have concluded that [Monsanto] and some of its distributors were parties to an "agreement" or "conspiracy" to maintain resale prices and terminate price cutters. . . .

Territorial Division: *United States v. Sealy, Inc.* (1967)
The United States brought this civil action for violation of

§1 of the Sherman Act against [Sealy, Inc.], the owner of the trademarks for Sealy branded mattresses and bedding products which it licensed manufacturers in various parts of the country to produce and sell under a territorial allocation system. Sealy agreed with each licensee not to license anyone else to manufacture or sell in a designated area and the licensee agreed not to manufacture or sell Sealy products outside that area. . . . [Sealy] was charged with conspiring with its licensees to fix the prices at which their retail customers might resell Sealy products and to allocate mutually exclusive territories among the licensees. . . .

Ruling . . . The territorial restraints were a part of the unlawful price-fixing and policing activities of Sealy operating as an instrumentality of the licensees and constituted "an aggregation of trade restraints" which was illegal per se.

Business Associations: *Los Angeles Memorial Coliseum Commission v. National Football League et al.* (1984)
In 1978, the owner of the Los Angeles Rams [now the St. Louis Rams] . . . decided to locate his team in a new stadium . . . in Anaheim, California. That left the Los Angeles Coliseum without a major tenant. Officials of the Coliseum then began to search for a new National Football League occupant. . . .

The L.A. Coliseum ran into a major obstacle in its attempts to convince a team to move. That obstacle was Rule 4.3 of Article IV of the NFL Constitution. In 1978, Rule 4.3 required unanimous approval of all the 28

good as well from the same seller. Suppose that many firms, including Company X, sell good A, but that Company X is the only seller of good B. Suppose also that good A's only use is as an input to good B. If Company X "ties" the sale of good B to its brand of good A—that is, it will sell good B only as long as the buyer makes its good A purchases from Company X—it engages in a tying contract. By doing this, Company X is using its monopoly of good B to gain monopoly power over good A.

Interlocking Directorates
The same person sits on the boards of directors of different corporations.

Interlocking directorates occur where the same person sits on the boards of directors of different corporations: for example, the same person is on the boards of a health care group and a banking corporation. Interlocking directorates are not necessarily anticompetitive, but injury to competition could occur if, for example, a person sitting on the boards of two firms competing in the same market enables them to communicate about prices, or a person on the boards of corporations in a buyer–seller relationship gives the seller an unfair advantage over its rivals with regard to major purchases by the buyer.

In each of the activities addressed by the Clayton Act, as well as those included under its amendments, the practices themselves do not automatically constitute violations of the antitrust laws. They become violations only when the activities tend to significantly reduce competition or create a monopoly.

APPLICATION 14.1 (continued)

teams of the League whenever a team . . . seeks to relocate in the home territory of another team. . . . In this case, the L.A. Coliseum was still in the home territory of the Rams. . . .

The Coliseum viewed Rule 4.3 as an unlawful restraint of trade in violation of §1 of the Sherman Act . . . and brought this action in September of 1978. The district court concluded, however, that no . . . controversy existed because no NFL team had committed to moving to Los Angeles. . . .

Soon thereafter, Al Davis, managing general partner of the Oakland Raiders franchise, . . . and the Coliseum signed a "memorandum of agreement" outlining the terms of the Raiders' relocation in Los Angeles. At an NFL meeting on March 3, 1980, Davis announced his intentions. . . .

Over Davis' objection that Rule 4.3 is illegal under the antitrust laws, the NFL teams voted on March 10, 1980, 22–0 against the move, with five teams abstaining. . . .

The Los Angeles Memorial Coliseum Commission then renewed its action against the NFL and each member club. . . .

Ruling [T]he jury returned a verdict in favor of the Los Angeles Memorial Coliseum Commission and the Oakland Raiders on the antitrust claim. . . .

Monopolizing Behavior: *Aspen Skiing Company v. Aspen Highlands Skiing Corporation* (1985) A ski resort operator filed suit in the United States District Court for the District of Colorado against the operator of three other skiing facilities in the area, alleging that the latter had monopolized the local market for downhill ski services, in violation of §2 of the Sherman Act . . . by refusing to continue a long-standing marketing arrangement where-by skiers could purchase 6-day tickets usable on a given day at any of the four facilities . . . and by taking additional actions which made it difficult for the smaller operator to market a multi-area package of its own. The District Court entered judgment on a jury verdict in favor of the smaller operator, after instructing the jury that a firm possessing monopoly power violates §2 of the Sherman Act if it willfully acquires, maintains, or uses that power by anticompetitive or exclusionary means or for anticompetitive or exclusionary purposes, but does not violate the law by refusing to deal with a competitor if there are valid business reasons for that refusal. . . .

Ruling [T]he actions of the larger operator were properly held to violate §2 of the Sherman Act since the evidence was sufficient to support a conclusion that they were not taken for legitimate business reasons, but for the purpose of injuring a competitor.

Sources: *Monsanto Co. v. Spray-Rite Service Corp.*, 465 U.S. 752 (1984), pp. 752–753; *United States v. Sealy, Inc.*, 388 U.S. 350 (1967), p. 350; *Los Angeles Memorial Coliseum Commission v. National Football League et al.*, 726 F. 2d 1381 (1984), pp. 1384–1386; *Aspen Skiing Co. v. Aspen Highlands Skiing Corp.*, 86 L.Ed.2d 467 (1985), pp. 467–468.

Robinson-Patman Act
Federal antitrust statute concerned with anticompetitive price discrimination; amends Section 2 of the Clayton Act.

Price Discrimination
Different buyers acquire the same product from the same seller with the same treatment and service but pay different prices.

The Robinson-Patman Act (1936) Section 2 of the Clayton Act condemns price discrimination when it weakens competition or leads to a monopoly. The **Robinson-Patman Act** elaborates further on that condemnation. **Price discrimination** occurs when a seller charges different buyers different prices for the same product. If a firm sells an item at a particular price to one buyer and sells exactly the same item with exactly the same treatment and service to another buyer at a lower price, price discrimination has occurred.

Price discrimination can injure competition between a seller and its rivals. Through price discrimination, a seller can lower its price to buyers where there is intense competition from a rival, while keeping the price unchanged, or even raising it, for customers where it is not facing competition. If the rival is unable to meet these price cuts, it may lose sales and perhaps be driven from the market.

A buyer's market position, particularly at the wholesale level, can be injured when it pays a higher price than its rivals. The difference in price paid by the discriminated-against firm raises its costs, causing it, in turn, to charge a higher price or absorb the higher cost through forgone profit, either of which damages its competitive position.

The Robinson-Patman Act attacks outright price discrimination as well as several types of "indirect" price discrimination, such as granting quantity discounts on terms that only a few large buyers can meet, paying purchasers for services that have not been rendered, and treating buyers unequally in providing sales facilities.[8]

The Celler-Kefauver Act (1950)   Section 7 of the Clayton Act deals with anticompetitive mergers and acquisitions, and is amended by the **Celler-Kefauver Act.** A business can be acquired or merged with another in two ways: by the purchase of a controlling number of shares of stock or by the outright purchase of assets. The Clayton Act condemned anticompetitive acquisitions through stock purchases but said nothing about the purchase of assets. This loophole was closed by the Celler-Kefauver Act.[9]

As we learned in Chapter 10, there are three main types of mergers: horizontal, vertical, and conglomerate. Each type of merger can have potentially anticompetitive effects. A **horizontal merger** occurs where two sellers competing in the same market join together. When two extremely small sellers in a market merge, the consequence may not be noticeable: A small dairy farmer buying a second farm will have no effect on the dairy market. But where the acquiring and/or acquired firm has a substantial market share, their joining may have an anticompetitive effect by creating a larger organization with an even greater share of the market.

A **vertical merger** involves the joining of a firm with a supplier or a distributor; it may be anticompetitive if it forecloses the firm's rivals from key suppliers or distributors. If a major developer/builder were to acquire both of the existing lumber yards in an area, the local supply of building materials could be foreclosed to rival developers and cause them additional expenses or perhaps even force them out of business. If competition is injured, a vertical merger can also cause antitrust concerns.

A **conglomerate merger** occurs when one firm joins with another that is not a competitor, supplier, or distributor. The joining of a steel wire manufacturer and a large beverage company would be a conglomerate merger, as would be the combining of a publishing company and a chain of retail clothing outlets.

Conglomerate mergers can have anticompetitive effects because of what is known as the "deep pocket." For example, a large, profitable hotel chain might acquire one of several small competing candy companies. As a result of the acquisition, the candy company could receive financial help from the hotel chain's deep pocket full of money for spending on such things as advertising, expansion of facilities, and a larger sales staff. With the help of this money, the candy company could increase its sales and share of the market at the expense of its rivals who do not have comparable financial resources with which to compete.

In the spring of 2002, Sears purchased Lands' End, the mail-order retailer, giving Sears the right to sell Lands' End clothing in its stores. Lands' End had been one of the largest catalog retailers in the country, along with J.C. Penney, Spiegel, and L.L. Bean. In your opinion, was this merger horizontal, vertical, or conglomerate?

Application 14.2, "Cases Involving the Clayton Act and Its Amendments," presents facts and rulings from classic, landmark court cases on tying arrangements, price discrimination, and mergers. Can you explain how competition would have been injured in each of these cases?

Antitrust Penalties   Violations of the antitrust laws can result in one or more of four types of penalties, depending on the offense and who is bringing the suit. The

---

Celler-Kefauver Act
Federal antitrust statute concerned with anticompetitive mergers and acquisitions of firms; amends Section 7 of the Clayton Act.

Horizontal Merger
A merger between two sellers competing in the same market.

Vertical Merger
A merger between a firm and a supplier or distributor.

Conglomerate Merger
A merger between a firm and another firm that is not a competitor, supplier, or distributor.

---

[8]*United States Statutes at Large*, vol. 49, part 1 (Washington, DC: U.S. Government Printing Office, 1936), pp. 1526–1527.
[9]*United States Statutes at Large*, vol. 38, part 1 (1915), pp. 731–732; *United States Statutes at Large*, vol. 64, part 1 (1952), pp. 1125–1126.

APPLICATION 14.2

CASES INVOLVING THE CLAYTON ACT AND ITS AMENDMENTS

Tying Arrangements: *International Business Machines Corp. v. United States* **(1936)**   This is an appeal . . . of a decree of a District Court [enjoining IBM] from leasing its tabulating and other machines upon the condition that the lessees shall use with such machines only tabulating cards manufactured by [IBM], as a violation of §3 of the Clayton Act. . . .

[IBM's] machines and those of Remington Rand, Inc., are now the only ones on the market which perform certain mechanical tabulations and computations . . . by the use in them of cards upon which are recorded data. . . .

To insure satisfactory performance by [IBM's] machines it is necessary that the cards used in them conform to precise specifications as to size and thickness, and that they be free from defects . . . which cause unintended electrical contacts and consequent inaccurate results. The cards manufactured by [IBM] are electrically tested for such defects.

[IBM] leases its machines for a specified rental and period, upon condition that the lease shall terminate in case any cards not manufactured by [IBM] are used in the leased machine. . . .

[IBM's] contentions are that its leases are lawful [partly because their] purpose and effect are only to preserve to [IBM] the good will of its patrons by preventing the use of unsuitable cards which would interfere with the successful performance of its machines. . . .

[It appears] that others are capable of manufacturing cards suitable for use in [IBM's] machines. . . .

Ruling [IBM] is not prevented from proclaiming the virtues of its own cards or warning against the danger of using, in its machines, cards which do not conform to the necessary specifications, or even from making its leases conditional upon the use of cards which conform to them. [S]uch measures would protect its good will, without the creation of monopoly or resort to the suppression of competition. [Case decided against IBM.]

Price Discrimination: *Utah Pie Co. v. Continental Baking Co. et al.* **(1967)** This suit . . . by [Utah Pie Co.], a local bakery company in Salt Lake City, against three large companies each of which is a major factor in the frozen pie market in one or more regions of the country, charged . . . violations by each . . . of §2(a) of the Clayton Act, as amended by the Robinson-Patman Act. The major competitive weapon in the Salt Lake City market was price

and for most of the period [Utah Pie], which had the advantage of a local plant, had the lowest prices. Each [of the other companies] at some time engaged in discriminatory pricing and thereby contributed to a deteriorating price structure during the relevant period. [Pet Milk] sold an economy pie in the Salt Lake City market at a price which was at times lower than that in other markets; and it sold its proprietary label quality pies in Salt Lake City for some months at prices lower than those in California, despite freight charges from its California plant. . . . In June 1961 . . . Continental Baking cut its price in the Utah area to a level well below that applicable elsewhere, and less than its direct cost plus an allocation for overhead. Carnation Co., whose share of the market slipped in 1959, slashed its price in 1960, and for eight months of that year its Salt Lake City price was lower than that in other markets, and that trend continued in 1961. . . .

Ruling . . . There was evidence of predatory intent with respect to each of the respondents and there was other evidence upon which the jury could find the requisite injury to competition.

Horizontal Mergers: *United States v. Philadelphia National Bank et al.* **(1963)**   [The Philadelphia National Bank and Girard Trust Corn Exchange Bank] are the second and third largest of the 42 commercial banks in the metropolitan area consisting of Philadelphia and its three contiguous counties, and they have branches throughout that area. [The banks'] boards of directors approved an agreement for their consolidation. . . . After obtaining reports, as required by the Bank Merger Act of 1960, from the Board of Governors of the Federal Reserve System, the Federal Deposit Insurance Corporation and the Attorney General, all of whom advised that the proposed merger would substantially lessen competition in the area, the Comptroller of the Currency approved it. The United States sued to enjoin consummation of the proposed consolidation, on the ground . . . that it would violate §7 of the Clayton Act.

Ruling . . . The proposed consolidation . . . would violate §7 of the Clayton Act. . . . The consolidated bank would control such an undue percentage share of the relevant market . . . and the consolidation would result in such a significant increase in the concentration of commercial banking facilities in the area . . . that the result would be inherently likely to lessen competition substantially. . . .

Sources: *International Business Machines Corp. v. United States,* 298 U.S. 131 (1936), pp. 132–134, 139, 140; *Utah Pie Co. v. Continental Baking Co. et al.,* 386 U.S. 685 (1967), pp. 685, 686; *United States v. Philadelphia National Bank et al.,* 374 U.S. 321 (1963), pp. 321, 322.

APPLICATION 14.3

ANTITRUST ENFORCEMENT UP CLOSE AND PERSONAL

There's a story told about Bob, a sales representative, who was having dinner at an annual business convention with several friends who work for companies that compete with his company. Shortly into the meal, one of the diners mentioned that his company was about to drop the price on a product that all the companies represented at the table sell. On hearing this, another diner said that her company was also going to drop its price. Discussion about the potential price drop began to lead the conversation to potential "spot" dropping, which is where companies stay away from dropping prices in each other's largest sales territories.

This turn in the conversation is when Bob, reaching for a roll, knocked over his full glass of water—soaking his shirt and pants. Everyone at the table laughed, Bob waved his hands in feigned embarrassment, said good night to everyone as he got up, and left. As it turns out, Bob knocked the water over on purpose because he saw that the conversation at the table was turning to price fixing, which is an unquestionable antitrust violation. Bob wanted it very clear in everyone's memory that he was not there as the conversation went on.

Anyone who has been involved in an antitrust proceeding would likely say that Bob did exactly the right thing because the stress created by an antitrust violation accusation can be personally devastating. First, there is the financial stress: If found guilty, a person could face a fine of $1 million *per offense*—not per suit filed. So if, for example, there were four charges listed in a suit, a person found guilty of each of the charges might face a fine of $4 million. And, we're talking about an individual, not a company. In addition to fines, there is the cost of retaining defense counsel. And, there is reason to expect that an employer might not come to an employee's aid; it might be in the employer's best interest to fire an employee, saying, "Wait, he did this, not us."

Another added stress of an antitrust accusation is the possibility of a prison sentence and all that an incarceration implies. A guilty individual could be looking at up to 10 years in either a minimum or maximum security prison, depending on where the prison system sends you.

Even if a person is not named as a defendant, the mere possibility of being named a defendant in an antitrust suit can take over one's life. The government typically never tells a target when its investigation has concluded, so a person can live under a cloud of stress and suspicion whether or not he or she is actively under investigation.

There is also the reality that once an indictment is issued, the ongoing investigation and litigation can last for years. Over this time, the accused's friends and coworkers might be interviewed, and there may be requests for mountains of documents by, say, the Antitrust Division of the Department of Justice.

The long and short of it is that the antitrust laws should be taken seriously. Violations have the potential to affect personal finances and physical stress with destructive effects on a defendant's family and friends.

---

penalties include imprisonment for up to 10 years, fines as large as $1 million per offense for individuals and $100 million per offense for corporations, structural remedies, and triple damages.

Structural remedies involve preventing two or more firms from merging, or breaking an offending firm into two or more unrelated units. Preventing firms from merging is appropriate where a proposed merger would violate the antitrust laws. In this situation, competition can be promoted by disallowing the merger and requiring the companies to remain separate. Breaking up an offending firm might be used where a single firm has been found guilty of monopolizing a market. Here the monopoly could be ended by separating one or more of the company's divisions into independent units. At one point in the recent highly publicized government's antitrust suit against Microsoft, breaking the company into two separate entities was given serious consideration.

With triple damages, an injured party can, under certain conditions, collect three times its damages from the offending firm. Suppose it was proven in a court suit that over the last 3 years Company B lost $90 million in profit because of an antitrust violation committed by Company A. On the basis of this, the court could require Company A to pay Company B three times $90 million, or $270 million, in damages.

Application 14.3, "Antitrust Enforcement Up Close and Personal," looks at how the possibility of being named a defendant in an antitrust suit can have a significant impact on a person's life.

GOVERNMENT REGULATION

Government Regulation
Government participation, through agencies and commissions, in business decision making; may be industry regulation or social regulation.

In our daily lives, we are much more likely to be affected by government regulation, another way in which government plays a role in the market process, than by the antitrust laws. **Government regulation** refers to participation by the federal and state governments, through agencies and commissions, in business decision making. Actions of the Securities and Exchange Commission (SEC), Federal Communications Commission (FCC), Food and Drug Administration (FDA), and state utility commissions are just a few examples of government regulation.

In some cases, government regulation involves direct participation in specific aspects of a company's operations: The company's product price, the markets it serves, and other decisions must be approved by a regulatory commission before they can be implemented. In other cases, government regulation involves indirect participation in business operations through setting standards for firms to follow. These standards could apply to safety, health, the environment, and other areas. The Food and Drug Administration, for example, sets purity and safety standards for food and drugs, and the Environmental Protection Agency (EPA) sets pollution standards.

While the antitrust laws are directed at the relationships between businesses and the degree of competition in specific markets, regulation is concerned with the interests of particular groups in the economy. For example, some regulation is aimed at protecting the consumer, some at labor, and some at the general public.

Government regulation can be divided into two basic types: industry regulation and social regulation. The first type involves regulation of businesses in a particular industry. In the United States, the railroad, electric power, gas distribution, and other industries have been subject to this type of regulation. Generally, industry regulation is direct: Government plays an important role in determining price, profit, and other aspects of the firms' operations.

With social regulation, a regulatory body deals with a particular problem common to businesses in many different industries. The commissions with authority over job discrimination (Equal Employment Opportunity Commission), consumer product safety (Consumer Product Safety Commission), and unfair business practices (Federal Trade Commission) are examples of agencies that carry out this type of regulation. Much social regulation is indirect and involves setting standards for businesses to follow. Social regulation is often more familiar to us than industry regulation because more resources are devoted by the federal government to social regulation. Estimated federal spending on social regulation in 2009 was $43.5 billion, as compared to $7.6 billion for industry regulation.[10]

Approximately 70 regulatory agencies exist at the federal level. Table 14.1 lists these in chronological order. Notice that a large number of regulatory agencies was created in the early 1970s. Although historically we associate the Great Depression and the New Deal era with the growth of regulation, the number of federal agencies that originated in the 1970s was nearly double the number created during the 1930s.

[10]Veronique de Rügy and Melinda Warren, *Regulatory Agency Spending Reaches New Height: An Analysis of the U.S. Budget for Fiscal Years 2008 and 2009*, Mercatus Center, George Mason University, and Weidenbaum Center, Washington University, 2008, p. 5.

TABLE 14.1   *Chronology of Federal Regulatory Agencies*

Regulatory agencies have been formed throughout the history of the economy, with a large number created in the 1930s and 1970s.

Year	Agency	Department Association[a]
1789	Customs Service	Treasury
1836	Patent and Trademark Office	Commerce
1863	Comptroller of the Currency	Treasury
1870	Copyright Office	Library of Congress
1887	Interstate Commerce Commission *[Transferred to Department of Transportation in 1996]*	
1899	Army Corps of Engineers *[Regulatory duties from this date; established 1824]*	Defense
1903	Antitrust Division	Justice
1913	Federal Reserve System	
1914	Federal Trade Commission	
1915	Coast Guard *[Transferred to Homeland Security in 2002]*	Transportation
1916	Tariff Commission *[Became International Trade Commission in 1974]*	
1920	Federal Power Commission *[Became Federal Energy Regulatory Commission in 1977]*	
1922	Commodity Exchange Authority *[Became Commodity Futures Trading Commission in 1974]*	Agriculture
1927	Bureau of Customs *[Became Customs Service in 1973]*	Treasury
1931	Food and Drug Administration	Health and Human Services
1932	Federal Home Loan Bank Board	
1933	Farm Credit Administration	
1933	Federal Deposit Insurance Corporation	
1934	Federal Savings and Loan Insurance Corporation *[Abolished in 1989]*	
1934	Federal Communications Commission	
1934	National Mediation Board	
1934	Securities and Exchange Commission	
1935	National Labor Relations Board	
1936	Maritime Administration *[Transferred to Federal Maritime Commission in 1961]*	Commerce
1937	Agricultural Marketing Service and Other Agencies *[Transferred to other services in 1972 and 1977]*	Agriculture
1938	Civil Aeronautics Authority *[Became Civil Aeronautics Board in 1940; abolished in 1984]*	
1940	Fish and Wildlife Service *[Established as Bureau of Fisheries in 1871]*	Interior
1946	Atomic Energy Commission *[Transferred to Nuclear Regulatory Commission and Energy Research and Development Administration in 1975]*	
1951	Renegotiation Board *[Abolished in 1979]*	
1953	Foreign Agricultural Service	Agriculture
1953	Small Business Administration	
1958	Federal Aviation Agency *[Became Federal Aviation Administration in 1967]*	Transportation
1961	Agricultural Stabilization and Conservation Service *[Reorganized into the Farm Services Agency in 1994]*	Agriculture
1963	Labor-Management Services Administration	Labor
1964	Equal Employment Opportunity Commission	
1966	Federal Highway Administration	Transportation
1966	National Transportation Safety Board *[Reestablished as independent agency in 1974]*	Transportation
1966	Federal Railroad Administration	Transportation
1969	Council on Environmental Quality	
1970	Cost Accounting Standards Board *[Abolished in 1980]*	
1970	Environmental Protection Agency	
1970	National Credit Union Administration	
1970	National Highway Traffic Safety Administration	Transportation
1970	Occupational Safety and Health Administration	Labor
1971	Employment Standards Administration	Labor

TABLE 14.1   *Continued*

Year	Agency	Department Association[a]
1971	Farm Credit Administration	
1971	Occupational Safety and Health Review Commission	
1972	Bureau of Alcohol, Tobacco, Firearms and Explosives *[Previously part of Internal Revenue Service]*	Justice
1972	Consumer Product Safety Commission	
1972	Domestic and International Business Administration *[Became International Trade Administration in 1980]*	Commerce
1973	Drug Enforcement Administration	Justice
1973	Mining Enforcement and Safety Administration *[Became Mine Safety and Health Administration in 1977, Department of Labor]*	Interior
1973	Architectural and Transportation Barriers Compliance Board	
1974	Federal Energy Administration *[Became Economic Regulatory Administration in 1977, Department of Energy]*	
1974	Council on Wage and Price Stability *[Abolished in 1981]*	
1974	Federal Election Commission	
1975	Materials Transportation Board	Transportation
1976	Federal Grain Inspection Service *[Merged with Packers and Stockyards Administration in 1994 to create the Grain Inspection, Packers, and Stockyards Administration]*	Agriculture
1977	Office of Neighborhoods, Voluntary Associations and Consumer Protection *[Abolished in 1981; functions transferred to HUD]*	Housing and Urban Development
1977	Office of Surface Mining Reclamation and Enforcement	Interior
1979	Office of the Federal Inspector of the Alaska Natural Gas Transportation System	Agriculture
1979	Federal Emergency Management Agency	
1982	Packers and Stockyards Administration	
1985	Office of Environment, Safety and Health *[Renamed Office of Health, Safety and Security in 2006]*	Energy
1986	Pension and Welfare Benefits Administration *[Renamed Employee Benefits and Security Administration in 2003]*	Labor
1987	Bureau of Export Administration *[Renamed Bureau of Industry and Security in 2002]*	Commerce
1989	Office of Environmental Management	Energy
1989	Resolution Trust Corporation *[Terminated in 1995]*	
1989	Office of Thrift Supervision	Treasury
1995	Chemical Safety and Hazard Investigation Board	Treasury
1997	Mine Safety and Health Administration	Labor
2000	Federal Motor Carrier Safety Administration	Transportation
2001	Transportation Security Administration	Transportation
2002	Election Assistance Commission	
2003	Alcohol and Tobacco Tax and Trade Bureau *[Authority previously in Bureau of Alcohol, Tobacco, and Firearms]*	Treasury
2003	Bureau of Customs and Border Protection	Homeland Security
2003	Bureau of U. S. Citizenship and Immigration Security	Homeland Security
2004	Research and Innovation Technology Administration	Transportation
2005	Pipeline and Hazardous Materials Administration	Transportation
2006	Postal Regulatory Commission *[Former Postal Rate Commission]*	

[a]Not all agencies are associated with a department.

Sources: Ronald J. Penoyer, *Directory of Federal Regulatory Agencies—1982 Update*, Center for the Study of American Business, Formal Publication Number 47 (St. Louis: Washington University, June 1982), pp. 43–48; Paul N. Tramontozzi and Kenneth W. Chilton, *U.S. Regulatory Agencies under Reagan: 1980–1988*, Center for the Study of American Business, OP 64 (St. Louis: Washington University, May 1987), pp. 15–24; Melinda Warren and Kenneth W. Chilton, *Regulation's Rebound: Bush Budget Gives Regulation a Boost*, Center for the Study of American Business, OP 81 (St. Louis: Washington University, May 1990), pp. 15–18, 23, 24; Melinda Warren, *Mixed Message: An Analysis of the 1994 Regulatory Budget*, Center for the Study of American Business, OP 128 (St. Louis: Washington University, August 1993), pp. 15–17, 27, 28; Melinda Warren and Barry Jones, *Reinventing the Regulatory System: No Downsizing in Administration Plan*, Center for the Study of American Business, OP 155 (St. Louis: Washington University, July 1995), p. 26; *Federal Regulatory Directory*, 6th ed. (Washington, DC: Congressional Quarterly, 1990), pp. 445, 507; 10th ed., 2001, pp. 7, 137, 141, 311, 320, 339, 369, 392, 423, 446, 483, 669, 674; 11th ed., 2003, pp. 459, 500, 504, 529, 536, 541, 590, 612, 628, 652, 682, 689; 13th ed., 2008, pp. 305, 353, 488, 506, 516, 579, 647; U.S. Department of Labor, http://www.dol.gov/dol/pwba.

The Structure of Regulation

How does regulation come about? First of all, a particular industry or a specific problem is under federal or state regulation depending on whether interstate or intrastate commerce is involved. Federal agencies have jurisdiction over interstate commerce, and state commissions regulate intrastate commerce. For example, the rates charged by utility companies, such as your electric power company, that serve customers within a particular state are under the regulatory jurisdiction of a state public utility commission. Federal regulatory agencies, such as the Occupational Safety and Health Administration (OSHA) and the Interstate Commerce Commission (ICC), are established by Congress to regulate activities that cross state lines.

There are several interesting points to understand about these agencies.

♦ The enabling legislation (legislation that creates the agency) is general. It contains an overall mandate, and specifies the structure of the agency and other important information pertaining to its operation.
♦ When a regulatory agency is established, it is given the power to carry out the general mandates stated in the enabling legislation. To do so, the agency may make detailed rules and regulations that businesses under its jurisdiction must follow. For example, if the mandate is airline safety, the agency can establish detailed rules regarding air personnel qualifications, airplane inspections, equipment, and such.
♦ An agency has the power to enforce its own rules and regulations and to punish those who do not comply. Companies that choose to dispute their treatment by an agency may appeal their case to a court of law.

As Table 14.1 shows, some regulatory agencies are established as independent bodies governed by commissioners who are appointed to oversee the operations of the agency, while others are created as part of an existing department (such as the Department of Commerce) and are headed by an administrator within that department. For example, the Federal Reserve system is an independent body headed by an appointed board of seven governors, whereas the Mine Safety and Health Administration is within the Department of Labor and headed by one of its Administrators. State public utility commissions are usually headed by commissioners who are either elected or appointed by the governor.

Industry Regulation

Industry Regulation
Regulation affecting several aspects (such as pricing, entry of new sellers, and conditions of service) of the operations of firms in a particular industry.

Firms in certain industries, such as the railroad, natural gas, and electric power industries, are subject to **industry regulation.** This type of regulation deals with pricing, entry of new sellers into the market, extension of service by existing sellers, the quality and conditions of service, and other matters. In other words, some of the decision-making ability of a business in a free market does not exist for this type of regulated firm.

In some regulated industries, the firm itself is not free to independently choose or alter the price it charges for its product. Instead, it must seek approval from its regulatory agency to raise or lower its price. For example, privately-owned water companies generally must obtain state government approval before they change their rates. Also, in many regulated industries, new firms cannot begin operation unless they receive permission or a license from that industry's regulatory body. Sewer, water, electric, and other utility companies cannot be initiated at will.

Firms already in existence may need to get permission to abandon service or to extend or alter current services. For years the railroads were not permitted to drop unprofitable passenger routes, and a water company cannot simply cut off service to a university because the company disagrees with political statements made by some students and professors. These firms may also be subject to a host of other regulations, such as on the quality of the product offered for sale (for example, chemicals permitted in the water supply) and safety.

Justifications for Industry Regulation   Two reasons are frequently cited for industry regulation:

♦   an economic justification, and
♦   the public interest.

Efficiency considerations underlie the economic justification for regulation. Quite simply, for some products it is more efficient (less costly) to have the entire output in a market come from one large producer rather than from several smaller producers. In these cases, a **natural monopoly** exists in the market.[11] Water companies are good examples of natural monopolies: It would be quite inefficient and complicated to have several water companies, each with its own pipes and valves running under streets, serving an area.

Natural Monopoly
A market situation where it is more efficient (less costly) to have the entire output of a product come from one large producer rather than from several smaller producers.

Natural monopolies are the result of strong economies of scale in production and distribution. With economies of scale, which were introduced in Chapter 12, a seller's long-run unit or average total cost falls as its output increases. Economies of scale enable a firm to use highly specialized and efficient equipment and personnel and to take advantage of other benefits due to size.

The benefits of a natural monopoly are illustrated in Figure 14.1. Here we have the downward-sloping region of a long-run average total cost (LRATC) curve, which shows that, because of economies of scale, as the level of output increases, the unit or average cost of producing that output falls. Suppose that 10 million units of the output in Figure 14.1 would serve the whole market. If one firm produced the entire amount, the cost per unit would be $1; if two firms each supplied half of the market, or 5 million units, the cost per unit would be $2.25. The total cost to serve the market by one seller is $10 million, considerably less than the total cost of $22.5 million with two sellers sharing the market. Thus, significant economies of scale can lead to a natural monopoly where it is more efficient to have one seller rather than several in a market.

Some industries have significant economies of scale, particularly electric power, water, and others where firms depend on large costly plants and equipment (generators, power plants, water treatment facilities, and so forth) to be efficient. By having one large company that can spread these high capital costs over a larger output, the cost per unit is considerably less. Can you explain how economies of scale might affect production costs for natural gas companies?

Unfortunately, natural monopolies create a dilemma for the consumer. On the one hand, because of economies of scale, buyers benefit from lower unit costs when dealing with one seller. But on the other hand, as the only seller in the market, the

[11]Natural monopoly was introduced in Chapter 13.

FIGURE 14.1   *Economies of Scale and Long-Run Average Total Cost*

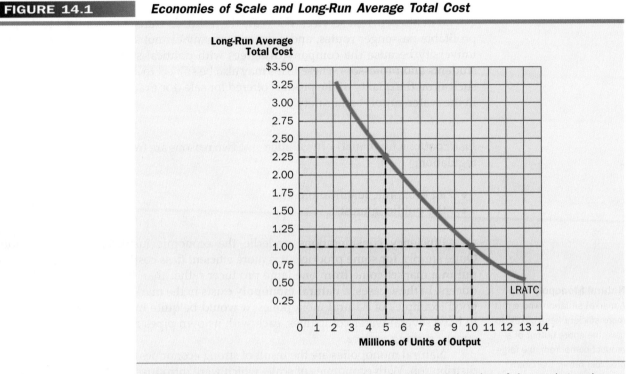

A natural monopoly exists when economies of scale and the size of the market make the long-run average total cost of production lower with one seller in the market than with several.

firm could abuse its monopoly power. Regulation that allows only one firm in the market, while at the same time placing the firm's operations under detailed scrutiny by a public authority so that it cannot unreasonably exploit its monopoly power, resolves this dilemma.

Natural monopoly may explain regulation in certain areas of the economy where there are advantages to having only one seller in a market. But what justifies the regulation of airlines, communications companies, railroads, and other firms that produce in industries where there is more than one seller in a market? This regulation is based on the public interest justification.

According to the **public interest justification,** certain types of businesses provide goods or services so important to the public well-being that the public has a right to be assured of their proper operation through regulation. Examples include radio and television companies, whose programming can influence public opinion, and transportation firms such as railroads, motor and water carriers, and airlines, that are necessary to keep goods, services, and resources moving.

The public interest justification can be applied in many more situations than the natural monopoly justification. If the argument can be made that the welfare of the public is so affected by the operation of a business that it is desirable to regulate that business, then the public interest justification might be used for regulation. The breadth of this justification was defined in 1934 in one of the most important court

Public Interest Justification for Regulation
A good or service is so important to the public well-being that its production and distribution should be regulated.

decisions on regulation, *Nebbia v. New York.* In this case, which dealt with the regulation of milk prices, the Supreme Court stated:

> *It is clear that there is no closed class or category of businesses affected with a public interest. . . . [A] state is free to adopt whatever economic policy may reasonably be deemed to promote public welfare, and to enforce that policy by legislation adapted to its purpose. . . .*[12]

Simply, this case said that states are allowed to regulate a broad range of businesses in a number of ways in the name of the public interest, provided certain conditions of fairness are met.

Price Regulation   One very important aspect of industry regulation is the oversight of the prices, or rates, charged by a regulated company. In many cases a regulated firm, such as a gas or electric or water company, that seeks to raise or lower its rates must appeal to its regulatory commission for permission to do so. And the commission can either approve or deny the request. Typically, rate changes involve formal filings of a request to change a rate, investigations for reasonableness, and hearings before the request is approved or denied.

Regulated firms have two concerns in making rate requests: They must cover their costs, and they must earn enough profit to attract and retain stockholders. Because of these, pricing by regulated firms has traditionally been carried out on a cost-plus basis. With **cost-plus pricing** the rates, or prices, buyers pay are designed to generate revenues sufficient to cover the costs of operation plus a fair return to those who invest in the business.

But cost-plus pricing may not promote economic efficiency. Permission to collect revenues to cover costs plus a fair return to investors may not provide sufficient incentive to keep costs down, as would happen with competition. As a result, there has been a movement toward **incentive regulation,** which allows firms subject to price regulation to profit by improving the efficiency of their operations.

A popular form of incentive regulation is **price caps,** where a maximum is set by a regulatory authority on the price a regulated firm can charge for its product. The company can charge what it wants up to that maximum and, more importantly, retain any additional profit it earns by operating more efficiently. Price caps can lower costs, but firms could also lower their costs by reducing the quality of their services—and not pass those lower costs on to buyers in the form of lower prices.

Social Regulation

The type of regulation that generates the most discussion and controversy because it is closest to our lives is **social regulation.** Social regulation is aimed at correcting a problem, such as pollution, or at protecting a group in the economy, such as workers or consumers. Rather than focusing on a single industry, social regulation applies to all firms that are affected by the mandate of the regulatory body, regardless of the industry.

Social regulation does not directly intervene into a company's price, profit, and other related decisions. (Although complying with social regulation can raise a firm's costs and affect its prices and profit.) Instead, it focuses on setting and enforcing standards concerning products, employees' working conditions, and other matters that could be harmful to the general public. The Occupational Safety and Health

Cost-Plus Pricing
Prices are set to generate enough revenue to cover operating costs plus a fair return to stockholders.

Incentive Regulation
A regulatory philosophy that provides incentives for regulated firms to operate efficiently.

Price Caps
An incentive system allowing regulated firms to price up to a pre-set maximum and retain additional profit from operating more efficiently.

Social Regulation
Regulation aimed at correcting a problem or protecting a group; not limited to a specific industry.

[12]*Nebbia v. New York,* 291 U.S. 502 (1934), pp. 536, 537.

TABLE 14.2	*Some Social Regulatory Agencies*

Much of the effort of agencies concerned with social regulation is directed toward protecting consumers, workers, and the environment.

Protecting Consumers

Consumer Product Safety Commission
Food and Drug Administration
Drug Enforcement Administration
Grain Inspection, Packers, and Stockyards
     Administration
Food Safety and Inspection Service
National Transportation Safety Board
Bureau of Alcohol, Tobacco, Firearms,
     and Explosives
Federal Aviation Administration
National Highway Traffic Safety Administration

Protecting Workers

Mine Safety and Health Administration
National Labor Relations Board
Occupational Safety and Health Administration
Employment Standards Administration
Labor-Management Services Administration
Equal Employment Opportunity Commission

Protecting the Environment

Environmental Protection Agency
Office of Surface Mining
Council on Environmental Quality
Army Corps of Engineers
Fish and Wildlife Service

Source: Melinda Warren and Barry Jones, *Reinventing the Regulatory System: No Downsizing in Administration Plans,* Center for the Study of American Business, OP 155 (St. Louis: Washington University, July 1995), pp. 23–24; *Federal Regulatory Directory,* 11th ed. (Washington, DC: Congressional Quarterly, 2003), pp. 822–858.

Administration (OSHA) is concerned with worker safety and working conditions and is a good example of an agency dealing with social regulation.

Table 14.2 lists some of the federal agencies responsible for social regulation, categorized according to the group each protects (the consumer, the worker, the environment). Notice that some of the agencies listed in the table affect a broader range of firms and industries than do others. For example, how many industries can you name that might be affected by a ruling of the National Highway Traffic Safety Administration? How does this compare with the number that could be affected by a ruling of the Environmental Protection Agency?

It is more difficult to summarize the functions of social regulation than industry regulation because social regulation is so diverse: Consider the differences between the purposes of the Consumer Product Safety Commission and the National Labor Relations Board. However, some generalizations can be made about social regulation. First, as we noted earlier, much more is spent at the federal level on social regulation than on

TEST YOUR UNDERSTANDING

GOVERNMENT AND BUSINESS

Below are 10 hypothetical situations concerning business practices. Determine in each situation whether the practice would likely:

a. violate the antitrust laws, and if so, which one,
b. be subject to industry regulation,
c. call for social regulation, and if so, by which federal agency, or
d. call for no government intervention at all.

1. Several firms located along a major river find that the river provides an easy method for disposing of toxic chemicals from production.
2. The purchaser of a large amount of carpeting that has been specially cut by the seller for installation in an office complex is demanding a refund after the purchaser mistakenly ordered the wrong color.
3. The purchaser of a home appliance is injured when properly using the product because it was poorly designed.
4. Two competing manufacturers of a popular consumer product that currently sells for $14 per unit agree that their prices will never fall below $10.
5. After discussing developments in the world grain market, two small farmers agree that now is the time to sell their corn if they want to get the best price.
6. A regional electric company would like to eliminate its service to a small village of 300 people because the service is losing money.
7. The theater chain showing 60 percent of the films in a major city wants to acquire the second largest chain, which shows 20 percent of the films in the city.
8. A manufacturer charges $30 per unit to buyers who purchase directly from its warehouse and $35 per unit to buyers who want to pay the additional cost of having the product packaged and shipped to them.
9. A local natural gas distribution company decides to double its charge to residential users in order to increase its profits.
10. A major supermarket chain cuts prices below cost in three cities until some of its smaller competitors go out of business.

Answers can be found at the back of the book.

---

industry regulation: Approximately 84 percent of the expenditures of the major federal regulatory agencies in 2006 were expected to go to social regulation. Second, the direction of social regulatory spending has changed over the years. In 2000, 37 percent of all federal social regulatory spending went to homeland security and 29 percent went to the environment. In 2009, 55 percent of social regulatory spending was expected to go to homeland security and 16 percent to the environment.[13]

Test Your Understanding, "Government and Business," lets you practice distinguishing among activities that might call for antitrust enforcement, industry regulation, social regulation, or no government intervention at all.

The Performance of Regulation

The spectacular growth of regulation in the 1970s came to an end toward the end of that decade. Concern over the performance of regulation and its effects on business costs and the economy in general brought about an interest in **deregulation.** Deregulation of the airline, trucking, natural gas, banking, telephone, and other industries came quickly.

Deregulation
A reduction in government regulatory control of the economy.

Proponents of deregulation, then as well as now, believe that in many instances the costs of regulation outweigh its benefits to society. Supporters of regulation hold the opposite view. Up for Debate, "Has Our Enthusiasm for Regulation Gone Too Far?", concerns a case where regulation became more stringent: the tightening of air pollution standards by the Environmental Protection Agency in 1997. What are the costs and benefits of stricter standards, and what is your assessment of the arguments on each side of this issue?

[13]de Rugy and Warren, p. 5.

HAS OUR ENTHUSIASM FOR REGULATION GONE TOO FAR?

Issue   *In 1997 the Environmental Protection Agency (EPA) issued stringent new air quality standards for ground-level ozone (soot and smog). This was the first major revision of the Clean Air Act since 1990. The EPA estimated annual health benefits from the higher standards between $58.1 billion and $120.5 billion, and annual costs of compliance between $6.6 billion and $8.5 billion by the year 2007. Paying the costs to meet these standards places a burden on businesses. Has our enthusiasm for regulation gone too far?*

Yes   Our enthusiasm for regulation has gone too far. The 1997 EPA standards set goals that may be unattainable. With the new standards, over three times as many counties were out of compliance than under the previous standards. Meeting the new standards—even if possible—will cost local governments and businesses tens of billions of dollars and affect the prices consumers pay, jobs, and the viability of small businesses. In setting standards, regulatory agencies should be paying greater attention to the costs those standards will impose on businesses and communities.

Further, the alleged health benefits from the higher standards should be questioned. Ozone may have short-term health effects, but the effects are reversible, and a clear case has not been made about its longer-term effects.

No   Our enthusiasm for regulation has not gone too far. Admittedly, under the new standards many more counties and their businesses were out of compliance, and it is very costly for them to come into compliance. But individuals have long had to incur substantial out-of-pocket and other costs because they live in communities where air pollution is a problem.

The effects of the new standards on prices, jobs, and small businesses are not clear. The standards may simply force businesses in violation to find more efficient ways to operate. Competition may keep prices from rising, more efficient techniques may create new jobs, and typically small businesses are not the principal offenders.

The Clean Air Act requires the EPA to ignore costs when setting standards. When it comes to human health and the quality of life, this is as it should be.

Based on: Kenneth W. Chilton and Stephen R. Huebner, "New Rules Would Be Costly, Have Limited Health Benefits," and Ken Midkiff, "Proposed Standards Are Based on Careful Scientific Study," both in "What Price Clean Air?" *St. Louis Post-Dispatch*, December 8, 1996, p. 3B; John M. Broder, "Deregulation: Crusade Shifts to Compromise," *The New York Times*, January 31, 1997, p. C3; Environmental Protection Agency, "EPA's Decision on New Air Quality Standards," http://www.epa.gov/ttn/oarpg/naaqsfin, September 15, 2005.

The growth in global markets and international economic activity is also an important area of regulatory discomfort. Regulation and antitrust policies tend to be national in scope. Barring a special international agreement, U.S. policies usually will not affect foreign firms doing business in foreign markets. As a result, some believe that U.S. firms are at a disadvantage when competing with foreign firms that face less or little regulation at home or are not subject to the antitrust laws that firms in the United States face. For example, one issue that repeatedly surfaces is the U.S. labor laws that forbid child labor and protect U.S. workers from potential harm at work. These regulations raise costs for U.S. businesses. Countries that permit child labor and have few laws protecting their workers can produce and sell goods at a lower price.

The questions created by nationally focused antitrust and regulatory policies are becoming increasingly important as economic activity becomes more global. And, the debates over the costs and benefits of government intervention are becoming more complicated as a wider array of values and traditions from different cultures are brought forward.

Summary

1.   Government intervenes in the operation of markets in the U.S. economy in two important ways: antitrust enforcement and regulation. This intervention occurs to ensure competition in markets, take advantage of efficiencies resulting from large-scale operations, and provide security to specific groups.

2. Antitrust laws are concerned with the relationships between rival firms and the level of competition in a market. They are designed to promote market forces by attacking monopolization, attempts to monopolize, and combinations and conspiracies in restraint of trade. This type of government intervention is carried out at the federal and state levels, and it depends heavily on the judicial system. Antitrust suits can also be filed by private parties.

3. There are five major federal antitrust laws: the Sherman, Federal Trade Commission, Clayton, Robinson-Patman, and Celler-Kefauver acts. The Sherman Act Section 1 condemns combinations and conspiracies in restraint of trade, and Section 2 condemns monopolization. Combinations and conspiracies in restraint of trade may be either per se or rule of reason violations. Monopolization cases depend largely on the actions and market share of the accused firm.

4. The Federal Trade Commission is empowered to prevent unfair methods of competition, including antitrust violations. The Clayton Act condemns exclusionary practices, interlocking directorates, price discrimination, and mergers, where the effects of these activities are anticompetitive. The price discrimination and merger provisions of the Clayton Act were amended by the Robinson-Patman and Celler-Kefauver acts, respectively.

5. Penalties facing those found guilty of violating the antitrust laws include imprisonment, fines, structural remedies, and triple damages.

6. Regulation is participation by federal and state government agencies and commissions in business decision making. Regulation is aimed at controlling certain industries and problem areas, and at protecting certain groups in the economy. In some instances a regulatory agency directly participates in a company's pricing and other decision making; in others the regulation is indirect and carried out through setting standards.

7. Regulatory authority is under federal jurisdiction for interstate commerce and under a state agency for intrastate commerce. Federal agencies can be independent or attached to departments such as the Department of Labor.

8. Regulation can be divided into industry and social regulation. Industry regulation involves government participation in pricing, output, profit, and other decisions of firms in certain industries, such as the electric and gas distribution industries. Social regulation includes such activities as setting and enforcing standards and is not limited to firms in any single industry.

9. Two frequently cited reasons for industry regulation are the existence of a natural monopoly due to economies of scale and effects on the public interest from the operation of certain businesses. An important aspect of industry regulation is the setting of prices. This has traditionally been done on a cost-plus basis, where prices are designed to generate enough revenue to cover expected costs plus a fair return to investors. More recently, incentive pricing schemes, such as price caps, have been given greater attention.

10. Social regulation focuses mainly on protecting consumers, workers, and the environment. Much more is spent on social regulation than industry regulation.

11. There is an ongoing debate over the optimal levels of regulation and, given the growing globalization of economic activity, concern over the impact of nationally focused antitrust enforcement and regulation.

Key Terms and Concepts

Antitrust laws	Interlocking directorates
Monopolization and attempts to monopolize	Robinson-Patman Act
Combinations and conspiracies in restraint of trade	Price discrimination
	Celler-Kefauver Act
Sherman Act	Horizontal, vertical, and conglomerate mergers
Per se violations	Government regulation
Price fixing	Industry regulation
Territorial division	Natural monopoly
Rule of reason violations	Public interest justification for regulation
Trade association	
Joint venture	Cost-plus pricing
Federal Trade Commission Act	Incentive regulation
Clayton Act	Price caps
Exclusionary practices	Social regulation
Tying contract	Deregulation

Review Questions

1. What do Section 1 and Section 2 of the Sherman Act condemn? What specific acts could be considered violations of Section 1? What are the main factors the courts consider when judging whether a firm has committed a Section 2 violation?

2. What is the difference between a per se violation of the antitrust laws and a rule of reason violation? Why are some business practices considered per se violations while others are not?

3. What activities are prohibited by the Clayton Act, the Robinson-Patman Act, and the Celler-Kefauver Act?

4. In what respects are industry and social regulation similar and in what respects are they different?

5.   What is a natural monopoly and how is it related to economies of scale? What sort of dilemma does the combination of efficiency and monopoly power create for the consumer and the policymaker?

6.   Explain the difference between the natural monopoly justification for regulation and the public interest justification. Why is the public interest justification applicable to a wider range of firms than the natural monopoly justification?

7.   What is cost-plus pricing and how can it lead to inefficient performance by a regulated firm? What are price caps and how can they improve efficiency?

8.   Provide some examples of social regulatory agencies and identify the main groups or areas that each protects.

Discussion Questions

1.   Horizontal mergers, vertical mergers, conglomerate mergers, price discrimination, and interlocking directorates may or may not be anticompetitive. For each of these five activities, describe a set of circumstances where you think the effect would be anticompetitive and where it would not be anticompetitive.

2.   The antitrust laws are designed to control the growth of monopoly power in specific markets. What are some economic reasons for concern over monopoly power? Are there any noneconomic reasons for wanting to control this power?

3.   Antitrust laws reinforce the operation of free markets, while regulation replaces free market forces with an authoritative body. How do you explain that certain economic problems are dealt with by strengthening market forces while others are dealt with by replacing the market mechanism with regulatory authority?

4.   Suppose legislation is passed to repeal the major federal antitrust statutes. How do you think such a repeal would affect competition? Would competition between sellers continue much the same as before the repeal? Would there be a blossoming of monopoly power? Would something else occur?

5.   Assume that the production of a particular good is accompanied by significant economies of scale. Would you recommend vigorous enforcement of the antitrust laws to ensure that no one firm could monopolize the production of this product, or would you allow a monopoly to form and then subject it to industry regulation? Justify your answer.

6.   There is concern about the costs and benefits of regulation. What costs and benefits might be created if the Equal Employment Opportunity Commission were abolished? In your opinion would we be better off without the agency than with it?

7.   What complications are created for businesses and the economy in general as a result of the administration of regulatory and antitrust policies in an increasingly global environment?

Critical Thinking Case 14

EMINENT DOMAIN: IN THE PUBLIC INTEREST OR NOT?

Critical Thinking Skills

Weighing the merits of competing arguments

Identifying consequences of policy choices

Economic Concepts

Social regulation

Public interest justification for regulation

Cost-benefit analysis

In July 2005 the U.S. Supreme Court, in a closely watched 5-to-4 decision, ruled that a local government can condemn and seize someone's property and turn it over to a private contractor to build a development that will strengthen the local economy. The case, *Kelo v. New London*, was brought by a New London, Connecticut, homeowner whose property was to be condemned and transferred by the city to a developer, who would take it and other adjacent properties, tear down the houses and other buildings, and construct a hotel and office complex in their place.

The issue at the foundation of this court decision is a long-standing practice called "eminent domain," where a government unit buys someone's property (often against the seller's wishes) and then uses it in the public interest. Usually, "using property in the public interest" is understood to mean invoking eminent domain for a public project like a highway or flood protection. But in this case, the property was to go to a private developer who would benefit from the project.

The reaction to this court decision was quick and furious. Within a few weeks, bills were introduced in the U.S. House and Senate and over half the state legislatures to limit the use of eminent domain for the benefit of private developers.

Arguments can be made both in support of and opposition to the Supreme Court's decision. In support of the decision, eminent domain might be necessary to encourage private developers to restore declining, at-risk urban areas to healthy, productive places. In addition to the benefit of a revitalized area, construction-related jobs would be created, leading to more spending that benefits everybody. And if handing the property to a private developer leads to more tax revenue for the city than before the property was condemned, then the public interest is further served.

On the other side is the fear that all private property will now be fair game for seizure in behalf of a developer if it can be argued that the developer will contribute more to the area's economic growth than the current owner. There is also the issue of who benefits and who loses from this broader freedom to seize property. Can developers with more money and influence than homeowners of average or lower-than-average income come out on top?

There are other concerns: This expanded power to condemn could be abused by local governments desperate to increase economic development. And, there is concern also that the strong and growing resistance to the Supreme Court's decision could lead to the canceling of projects and losses to contractors.

Based on: "United States: Despotism by Stealth; Eminent Domain," *The Economist*, February 19, 2005, p. 49; Michael Corkery and Ryan Chittum, "Eminent-Domain Uproar Imperils Projects," *The Wall Street Journal* (Eastern edition), August 3, 2005, p. B1; Robin Erb, "Supreme Court Delivers Blow to Property Rights," Knight Ridder Tribune Business News, *The Blade*, Toledo, Ohio, June 24, 2005, p. 1; Scott Hiaasen and Andres Viglucc, "Land Seizures Can Help Developers, Court Says," Knight Ridder Tribune Business News, *The Miami Herald*, June 24, 2005, p. 1; Matt Moroney, "Commentary: Private Property Rights Receive Undeserved Hit," *St. Charles County Business Record*, July 15, 2005, p. 1; Dean Starkman, "Cities Use Eminent Domain to Clear Lots for Big-Box Stores," *The Wall Street Journal* (Eastern Edition), December 8, 2004, p. B1; Sherie Winston, "High Court Ruling May Aid Construction," *Engineering News-Record*, July 4, 2005, p. 9.

Questions

1. The Supreme Court's ruling stretches "improving the public good" to increasing overall economic wealth. Is it appropriate to measure public well-being in terms of overall economic wealth when making a regulatory decision?

2. Suppose a law is passed condemning the use of eminent domain to benefit private developers and contractors. How would this affect the economic renewal of failing urban areas?

3. Because of the reality of scarcity that underlies economics, is it possible to have any social regulation that benefits one group without hurting another? How does this apply to the arguments for and against the Court's decision? What criteria should be used in balancing competing interests?

CHAPTER 15

Labor Markets, Unions, and the Distribution of Income

CHAPTER OBJECTIVES

To understand the behavior of the demand for labor.

To explain, using a basic supply and demand model, how wages are determined.

To introduce some real-world considerations that modify the basic labor supply and demand model.

To describe the types and structure of unions, collective bargaining, and major legislation affecting labor.

To examine the distribution of income in the United States and some explanations for that distribution.

To define poverty, identify the poverty population in the United States, and discuss some government programs for alleviating poverty.

When we think about markets, we frequently think only of the markets in which goods and services are bought and sold: the discount malls we visit, our grocery stores, and the local shops that provide haircuts. But in a market economy, factors of production, like labor and capital equipment, are also bought and sold in markets. There are markets for nurses, book editors, high school math teachers, plumbers, architects, CEOs, and unskilled labor. As in product markets, substitutability and geography play an important role in defining factor markets. For example, an electrician in Denver will likely not compete with one in Houston for a job, but when a large corporation searches for a CEO, it will likely do an international search and consider people with a range of skills and experiences. And prices of factors, such as wages for labor, are the result of the degree of competitiveness in each labor market.

While there are markets for all of the factors of production, we will focus on labor markets in this chapter. The income from the sale of labor—wages, salaries, and such—is the largest single source of income in the U.S. economy: In 2008 labor income accounted for more than 66 percent of all income.[1]

Since most of us will spend a lifetime in labor markets, learning about how they function is useful information. We begin this chapter with a look at a simple demand and supply model for wage determination and then explore the factors that cause many labor markets to deviate from this model. Since labor unions have been an important part of the U.S. economy, we will learn some basics about them as well. At the end of this chapter, we will learn about how income is distributed and how much people earn.

LABOR MARKETS

In a market system, labor is bought and sold in the same way as goods and services: through the interaction of demand and supply. In the case of labor, however, businesses (and governments and nonprofits) are the buyers and individuals are the sellers.

Wage
The price of labor.

The price of labor is called its **wage.** If someone works for a wage of $15 an hour, this is the price of that person's labor as well as the price the buyer is willing to pay.[2]

Figure 15.1 gives a basic supply and demand model for determining the wage in a competitive labor market for workers who produce a particular service. The vertical axis of the figure gives wages, and the horizontal axis gives the quantity of labor demanded and supplied. In this particular market, the equilibrium wage is $12 an hour, and the number of workers employed is 800.

According to Figure 15.1, the demand curve for labor is downward sloping and the supply curve of labor is upward sloping: Buyers are willing to hire more labor as the wage falls, and more labor is offered in the market as the wage increases.

---

[1]See Table 10.1.

[2]Workers often receive a fringe benefit package, which includes such features as health and life insurance, vacation days, and pension contributions, from an employer. These benefits can be a substantial cost for the employer and an important financial consideration for an employee. Although this additional compensation package affects labor demand and supply decisions, we will confine our analysis to money wages for the sake of simplicity. Including fringe benefits would not affect our analysis of labor markets in this chapter in a significant way.

FIGURE 15.1   *A Competitive Labor Market*

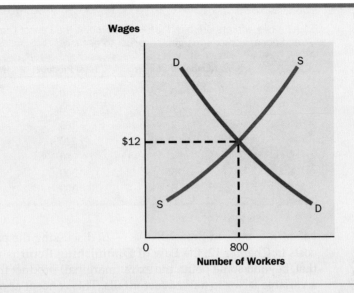

There is a downward-sloping demand curve and an upward-sloping supply curve in a competitive market for labor.

The Demand for Labor

Derived Demand
The demand for a factor of production depends on the demand for the good or service the factor produces.

The demand for labor, or any other factor of production, is a **derived demand:** It is derived from, or depends on, the demand for the good or service the factor produces. Autoworkers have jobs because cars are demanded; grocery clerks are employed because people buy groceries; and the professors who teach your courses do so because students enroll in them.

The wage that a firm is willing to pay for a unit of labor is based on the dollar value of the labor's productivity to the firm. An employee whose daily product is valued at $150 will not be paid $175 per day. In fact, the company will not be willing to pay the employee over $150 a day. No firm can afford to hire at a wage rate greater than the employee's dollar contribution to the company. Baseball players with contracts in the tens of millions of dollars command this kind of money largely because of their expected contributions to their teams' earnings. Outstanding players attract fans who purchase tickets to games and increase revenues for the clubs.

As seen in Figure 15.1, the typical market demand curve for labor is downward sloping. This is because each individual firm's demand curve for labor is downward sloping: A firm is willing to hire more labor when the wage rate falls and less labor when the wage rate increases.[3] If the amount a firm is willing to pay for labor is based on the dollar value of workers' productivity, then the downward-sloping demand curve indicates that the dollar value of labor's productivity falls as more labor is hired.

The declining value of labor's productivity as more labor is hired occurs for two reasons: (1) decreasing marginal productivity and (2) the need to lower product price in order to sell more of a good or service.

[3]Recall from Chapter 3 that market demand curves are found by adding together individual demand curves.

TABLE 15.1	*Total Product and Marginal Product of Labor for a Producer of Good X*

As more workers are hired, after some point the Law of Diminishing Returns causes each additional worker's marginal product to decline.

Number of Workers	Total Product	Marginal Product
0	0	
1	100	100
2	180	80
3	240	60
4	280	40
5	300	20
6	300	0

Law of Diminishing Returns

As additional units of a variable factor are added to a fixed factor, beyond some point the product from each additional unit of the variable factor decreases.

Marginal Product

The change in total product when one more unit of a variable resource, such as labor, is utilized.

Labor Demand and Productivity   In discussing the pattern of short-run production costs in Chapter 12, the **Law of Diminishing Returns** was introduced. This law says that, beyond some point, the extra (marginal) product from adding successive units of a variable factor to a fixed factor falls. This concept applies to labor.

Table 15.1 provides an example of a hypothetical company varying the amount of labor it utilizes to produce good X. The second column of the table shows the total product that results when a specific number of workers is employed: For example, four workers together with the fixed factors produce 280 units of good X. The third column lists **marginal product,** which is the change in total product when one more unit of labor is used. In Table 15.1, for example, the second worker has a marginal product of 80 units of good X (total product goes from 100 to 180 when the second worker is hired), and the fifth worker has a marginal product of 20 units (total product goes from 280 to 300 when the fifth worker is used).

The most important point to observe in Table 15.1 is that marginal product declines as more workers are used.[4] This decline is significant to the company employing the labor because it shows that, due to the Law of Diminishing Returns, each additional unit of labor produces less than the previous unit and is therefore worth less to the firm. This declining marginal productivity is reflected in the downward-sloping demand curve for labor.

Declining marginal productivity can be found in all work situations. Imagine the limited productivity of a baseball team's third, fourth, or fifth catcher. A restaurant will find that at some point the marginal productivity of its additional servers declines as more are employed, and a high school that hires several assistant principals may find each successive one adding less to total product.

Labor Demand and Product Price   The second reason for the declining value of labor's productivity and the resulting downward-sloping labor demand curve is the demand for the good or service the labor is producing. In all market situations except pure competition, firms face downward-sloping demand curves for their products: Consumers will increase their purchases of a company's product only if its price falls. This downward-sloping demand curve for the good or service that labor produces causes the value of labor's productivity to decrease, since the increased output resulting from

---

[4]In this example diminishing returns set in after the first worker. This is not always the case; a firm may employ several workers before diminishing returns set in.

TABLE 15.2	*A Good X Producer's Total Product and Price per Unit*

A firm facing a downward-sloping demand curve for its product can sell the increased output that results from hiring more workers only if it lowers the price.

Number of Workers	Total Product	Price per Unit
0	0	$ 6.25
1	100	6.00
2	180	5.75
3	240	5.50
4	280	5.25
5	300	5.00
6	300	5.00

employing more workers can only be sold at lower prices. Thus, additional units of labor are worth less to the company because the product they produce is sold for less.

To illustrate this point, Table 15.2 gives the total product information from Table 15.1 for the producer of good X and adds a third column listing the prices at which good X can be sold. The price and total product columns reflect the inverse relationship between price and quantity demanded: If the company intends to sell more of its product, it must lower the price. However, lowering the product's price decreases the value of what labor produces.

Combining Declining Marginal Productivity and Declining Product Price   The demand curve for labor is downward sloping because the marginal productivity of additional units of labor decreases and because the value of additional production is lowered by the decline in price necessary to sell the product. In other words, *the Law of Diminishing Returns and the Law of Demand combine to determine the value of labor*.

The effects of declining marginal productivity and decreasing product price can be combined to determine what each unit of labor is worth to a firm. This in turn determines the wage rate a firm is willing to pay. Returning to the good X example, Table 15.3 adds two columns to those given in Table 15.2 in order to determine the wage rate the producer of good X is willing to pay.

The fourth column of Table 15.3 gives the total revenue when various amounts of good X are sold. (Remember: Total revenue is price times quantity.) For example, with a total production of 240 units that can be sold for $5.50 each, total revenue is $1,320 (240 × $5.50).

Marginal Revenue Product

The change in total revenue that results from the sale of output produced when one more unit of a variable factor, such as labor, is utilized.

The last column of Table 15.3 gives **marginal revenue product,** which is the change in total revenue that results from the sale of output produced when one more unit of *labor* is utilized.[5] When one worker is hired, 100 units of good X are produced and sold for $6 each, bringing in $600 for the company. Since the total revenue with no workers is $0, the marginal revenue product of the first worker is $600. When a second worker is employed, 180 units of output are produced and sold for $5.75 each, creating a total revenue of $1,035. Thus, when the second worker is utilized, the company's total revenue increases from $600 to $1,035, or the marginal revenue product of the second worker is $435. For the third unit of labor, the marginal revenue product is

[5]Be careful not to confuse this with marginal revenue, which is the change in total revenue when one more unit of *output* is sold.

| TABLE 15.3 | | *A Good X Producer's Total Product, Price, Total Revenue, and Marginal Revenue Product* | | |

Marginal revenue product is the change in total revenue that results from the sale of output produced when one more unit of a variable factor, such as labor, is utilized.

Number of Workers	Total Product	Price per Unit	Total Revenue	Marginal Revenue Product
0	0	$6.25	$ 0	
1	100	6.00	600	$600
2	180	5.75	1,035	435
3	240	5.50	1,320	285
4	280	5.25	1,470	150
5	300	5.00	1,500	30
6	300	5.00	1,500	0

$285 because total revenue increases from $1,035 to $1,320. The marginal revenue product of the fourth worker is $150 and of the fifth worker is $30.

Marginal revenue product is important because it establishes the firm's demand curve for labor. In the example in Table 15.3, this firm would not hire any labor if the wage rate were above $600. In this case, the wage paid would be greater than the extra revenue created by the production of any worker. The producer would, however, be willing to hire one worker at a wage rate of $600. At $600 the first worker's contribution (marginal revenue product) equals the wage.

The wage would need to fall to $435, the marginal revenue product of the second worker, before the producer would hire two units of labor. At any wage higher than $435, the second worker's contribution to the firm's revenue would be less than the wage. For three units of labor to be employed, the wage would have to fall to $285, the marginal revenue product of the third worker. Four workers would be demanded at a wage of $150 and five at $30.[6]

When the wages and the amount of labor the good X producer is willing to hire at each of those wages are plotted in a graph, the firm's **demand curve for labor** results. This is given in Figure 15.2. Notice that the wage is equal to the marginal revenue product of labor at each point on the demand curve. Test Your Understanding, "A Small Business Determines Its Demand for Employees," provides an opportunity to calculate some of these demand-related numbers and to derive a labor demand curve.

Demand Curve for Labor
Downward-sloping curve showing the amount of labor demanded at different wage rates; based on the marginal revenue product of labor.

The Supply of Labor

In a typical labor market there is a direct relationship between wages and the quantity of labor supplied, causing the **supply curve of labor** to slope upward like that given in Figure 15.3. This relationship implies that less labor will be attracted to a market at a lower wage than at a higher wage. In Figure 15.3, for example, 300 people are willing to work in this labor market for $8.00 per hour, but 700 want to work for $11.50 per hour.

Supply Curve of Labor
Upward-sloping curve showing the amount of labor supplied at different wage rates.

[6]When this firm demands four workers at $150, it does not mean that the firm hires one worker for $600, a second for $435, a third for $285, and a fourth for $150. Instead, the firm pays the same wage rate to all four workers. Since the firm will pay no worker more than the worker is worth and since all workers are paid the same, the wage rate is based on the marginal revenue product of the last worker.

FIGURE 15.2   A Firm's Demand Curve for Good X Workers

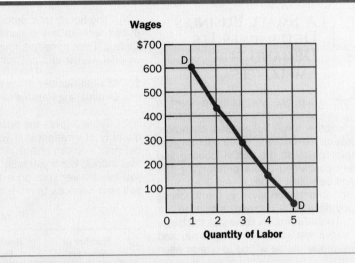

A firm's demand curve for labor is based on the marginal revenue product of labor, which declines as additional workers are hired.

In labor markets, money may be only part of the consideration in seeking a job. Many important factors other than wage or salary influence the supply of labor: location preferences, psychological rewards, long-term work objectives, and other nonwage considerations. Think about your current job or one you have held in the past. What nonwage factors influenced you in taking this job? How do nonwage factors

FIGURE 15.3   Supply Curve of Labor

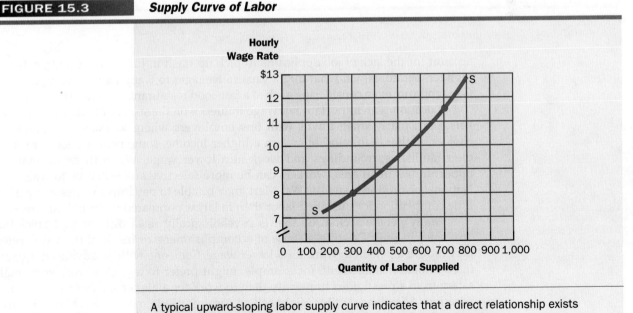

A typical upward-sloping labor supply curve indicates that a direct relationship exists between wage rates and the quantity of labor supplied in a market.

A SMALL BUSINESS DETERMINES ITS DEMAND FOR EMPLOYEES

Suppose you plan to start a small business that will label and stuff envelopes for other small businesses, charitable fund raisers, and political candidates. Since your biggest cost will be for employees to do the actual labeling and stuffing, you are very concerned about determining the hourly wage you would be willing to pay.

Assume that the information given in the following tables is from a study done for a company similar to the one you plan to start. This information serves as the basis for determining the wages you would be willing to pay and how many employees you would be willing to hire at each wage rate.

TABLE 1

Number of Workers	Hourly Total Product	Hourly Marginal Product
0	0	____
1	500	____
2	1,000	____
3	1,500	____
4	1,900	____
5	2,200	____

The hourly total product (envelopes) that can be produced with different numbers of workers is shown in Table 1. Determine the hourly marginal product of each additional worker and answer Question 1.

1. At what number of workers does the Law of Diminishing Returns take effect?_____

Table 2 gives the price for stuffing and labeling each quantity of envelopes: If your output is 1,500 envelopes per hour, you can charge 4¢ ($0.04) per envelope and sell that output. But if you raise your output to 2,250 per hour, you must lower your price to 3¢ ($0.03) per envelope to sell your services to more buyers.

TABLE 2

Number of Workers	Hourly Total Product	Charge per Envelope
0	0	$0.055
1	500	0.05
2	1,000	0.045
3	1,500	0.04
4	1,900	0.035
5	2,250	0.03

Determine the hourly total revenue and the hourly marginal revenue product per worker from the information in Table 2. Put these numbers in Table 3 and answer Questions 2 through 4.

account for the lack of job applicants to pick up trash in July in cities with extremely high temperatures? Or, what might cause a teenager to want a job at Starbucks or the Gap while not even considering a job at a fast-food restaurant that pays the same wage?

Location is an important nonwage influence on the supply of labor in some markets, particularly small towns with few employers where workers face limited job choices. Rather than relocate to earn a higher income, some people choose to stay in their familiar surroundings and work at a lower wage. When there are many job opportunities in an area, workers can be more selective and sensitive to wage rates. National chain stores, such as Wal-Mart, may be able to pay lower wages in areas with little competition for unskilled labor than in large, populated metropolitan areas.

Many people seek a job that is psychologically rewarding or that gives them "psychic" income: Prestige, a sense of accomplishment, or freedom from supervision may induce a person to work for a lower wage. Someone with an advanced degree in international management, for example, might prefer to teach and receive a smaller salary from a prestigious university than to work for a higher salary from a large corporation. A freelance writer might sell an essay for little money to a highly regarded magazine because of the sense of accomplishment from having an article in that particular publication.

TEST YOUR UNDERSTANDING

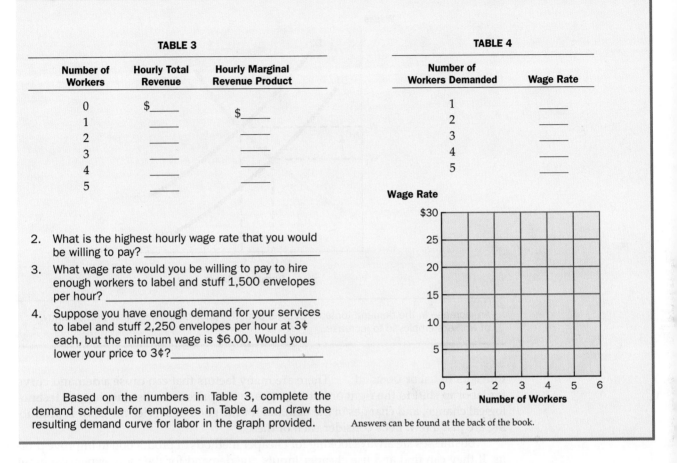

TABLE 3

Number of Workers	Hourly Total Revenue	Hourly Marginal Revenue Product
0	$_____	$_____
1	_____	_____
2	_____	_____
3	_____	_____
4	_____	_____
5	_____	

TABLE 4

Number of Workers Demanded	Wage Rate
1	_____
2	_____
3	_____
4	_____
5	_____

2. What is the highest hourly wage rate that you would be willing to pay? _____

3. What wage rate would you be willing to pay to hire enough workers to label and stuff 1,500 envelopes per hour? _____

4. Suppose you have enough demand for your services to label and stuff 2,250 envelopes per hour at 3¢ each, but the minimum wage is $6.00. Would you lower your price to 3¢? _____

Based on the numbers in Table 3, complete the demand schedule for employees in Table 4 and draw the resulting demand curve for labor in the graph provided.

Answers can be found at the back of the book.

The possibility of long-term gain can also influence the supply of labor. A college graduate may take a position with an employer at a lower salary than that offered by other employers because the potential for future advancement is great or because the job will look good on a resume. Other factors affecting supply include job security; the safety, cleanliness, and working conditions on a job; the degree of skill or formal training required; and flexibility in scheduling work.

Changes in Labor Demand and Supply

In any labor market, changes can occur that will cause labor demand and/or supply to increase or decrease and the demand and/or supply curves for labor to shift to the right or left. When these changes occur, the equilibrium wage and amount of labor hired are affected in the same way that equilibrium price and quantity are affected when demand and/or supply shift in an output market. An increase in the demand for labor, for example, causes the demand curve to shift to the right, resulting in an increase in both the equilibrium wage rate and the number of workers employed. This is illustrated in Figure 15.4, which demonstrates graphically the effect of an increase in the demand for labor from D1 to D2 in a competitive labor market. As demand increases, the equilibrium wage rate rises from W_1 to W_2, and the number of workers employed increases from Q_1 to Q_2.

FIGURE 15.4   *Effect of an Increase in Demand in a Labor Market*

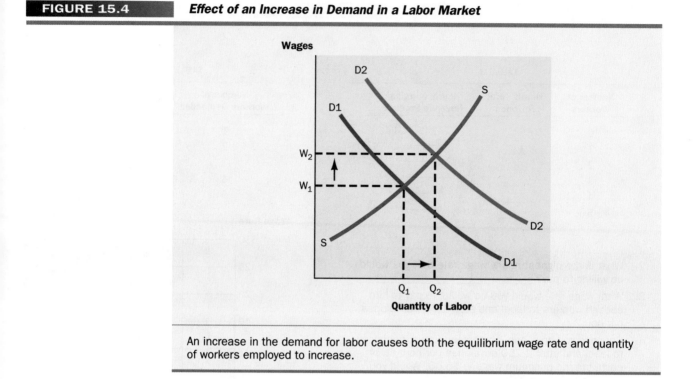

An increase in the demand for labor causes both the equilibrium wage rate and quantity of workers employed to increase.

Changes in Labor Demand   There are many factors that can cause a demand curve for labor to shift to the right or left: changes in the prices of substitute inputs, technological change, and changes in the demand for the good or service the labor is producing are just a few. Let's consider each of these.

Businesses are always looking for cheaper methods of production to improve profits. If they can find and use cheaper inputs, the demand for the more expensive input will decrease and its demand curve will shift to the left while the demand for the cheaper input will increase. The search for cheaper inputs has affected many labor markets. Automobile companies have turned to robotics in their plants, causing the demand for labor to fall; lower labor costs in many foreign countries have led to the closing of U.S. manufacturing plants; and even salad bars and vending machines have influenced labor markets. For example, in September 2008, Hanesbrands, maker of Hanes and Champion apparel, announced that it was closing plants and cutting 8,100 staffers as it consolidates into fewer, larger plants in lower-cost countries, particularly in Asia.[7]

Technological change has an important impact on the demand for labor. The widening use of computer-based information, programs, and storage systems has increased the demand for people with technology-related skills, while at the same time decreasing the demand for many other types of labor. Today most businesses and organizations employ a staff of skilled hardware and software technicians. The emergence of programs such as Turbo Tax, which allows individuals to prepare and file income taxes online, has influenced other fields such as accounting, where fewer "humans" are needed. Even grocery stores are eliminating labor with computerized self-checkouts.

[7]http://www.manufacturing.net/News-Hanesbrand-Cutting-8100-Jobs.aspx?menuid=.

APPLICATION 15.1

AND, WHERE DO I GO?

Moraine, Ohio (AP)—The General Motors Corp. plant in this Dayton suburb is a forest of smokestacks that form the nerve center of this industrial community built along the banks of the Great Miami River. Each day, about 2,400 workers file inside to assemble the GMC Envoy, Chevrolet Trailblazer, Saab 9-7X and Isuzu Ascender sport utility vehicles.

But some time before the summer of 2010, the Moraine plant will be no more. It is one of four that GM announced Tuesday [June 3, 2008] it will close. And there are fears here that the people—and the city's fortunes—will disappear with it.

The loss of the SUV plant will leave behind a bleak landscape for the surrounding community, an area scarred by a dwindling population, high poverty rates and one of the nation's hardest-hit pockets of the housing slump. "It's going to be a ghost town," said [the owner of] a restaurant and bar next to the plant. "There are no jobs here. I don't know what they're going to do."

The plant closings are casualties of surging fuel prices that are hastening a dramatic shift to smaller vehicles. About 8,350 jobs at the four plants [Moraine, Ohio; Janesville, Wisconsin; Canada; and Mexico] will be lost. . . .

Delphi Corp., an auto supplier trying to emerge from Chapter 11 bankruptcy protection, has five plants in the area, all already hit by layoffs or buyouts. GM also operates a separate engine plant here that employs about 1,000 people. . . .

Gaylen Turner, president of [the union] which represents the plant's workers, said he's not giving up on the plant. "It's not optimistic, but I plan on staying around and continuing that fight as best I can," said Turner, who is 53 and has worked at the plant for 28 years. . . .

As for what will become of the remaining workers, [John Heitmann, a history professor at University of Dayton] predicted that they will have few options, all distasteful: Leave town, or accept a lower standard of living. Unless another automaker sweeps in and decides to build a new plant, the jobs simply won't exist. "Many of these workers have extended families here," Heitmann said. "You just can't pack up all of your things in a trailer and drive down to Texas and start over."

Finally, a change in the demand for the good or service that a type of labor is producing may change the demand for that labor. When the demand for new single-family housing increases, developers and construction companies increase their production, causing the demand curve for construction workers to shift to the right. In 2008 and 2009, as the economy fell into a serious recession, the demand for cars and trucks took a serious hit. The decline was so severe that several U.S. auto companies went to Congress seeking a financial bailout to survive. During this period the automobile companies were shutting down production lines as their inventories swelled, and the demand for auto workers clearly went on the decline.

Application 15.1, "And, Where Do I Go?" deals with an auto plant closing in Moraine, Ohio, that leaves thousands of workers without a job. The decrease in demand for labor in this Dayton suburb may have an impact on many other labor markets. Can you identify other labor markets that will be affected?

Changes in Labor Supply   We can identify a number of factors that cause the supply of workers in a labor market to change and the supply curve to shift to the right or left. These include, among others, changes in economic conditions, demographic trends, expectations, and immigration.

Some labor markets are affected by the state of the economy, particularly those for low-paying, unskilled jobs in businesses such as fast-food restaurants, retail stores, and lawn care. With healthy economic conditions, the supply of workers in these labor markets decreases as people find better-paying jobs. When the economy in general or in a region falls into a recession and workers prone to cyclical unemployment are laid off—especially for long periods of time—those laid-off workers, as well as household members who now need to supplement household income, enter these labor markets and increase supply.

Demographic trends also affect labor supply. For example, when the teenage population increases, firms that typically hire from this age group, such as mall shops, experience an increase in labor supply. Also, with the trend toward early retirement there is a drop in supply in some labor markets with full-time jobs and a movement of workers into labor markets where part-time employment is available.

The expectation of future job prospects influences the supply curve in some labor markets. College students, for example, tend to select majors that are perceived as providing good employment opportunities. When the number of teaching positions in secondary and elementary schools increases, for example, the supply curve of new teachers shifts to the right as more students major in education, and when getting a good job in investment banking or other financial services appears less likely, the supply curve of students with majors in finance shifts to the left.

Many other factors cause labor supply to increase or decrease. For example, changes in immigration laws and the extent to which illegal immigrants are returned to their home countries affect several labor markets, and the number of students accepted into medical and law schools influences the supply of labor in those markets.

Changes in Labor Demand and Supply, and Changes in Quantity Demanded and Supplied   The distinction made in Chapter 3 between a change in demand or supply and a change in quantity demanded or supplied applies to labor demand and supply. A **change in labor demand or supply** refers to a *shift* of the entire labor demand or supply curve to the right or left as a result of changes in nonwage factors, such as the prices of substitute inputs, technology, product demand, economic conditions, and expectations about future job prospects. A **change in the quantity of labor demanded or supplied** occurs only as a result of a change in the price (wage) of labor. A change in quantity demanded or supplied is represented by a movement from one wage–quantity combination to another *along* a labor demand or supply curve: The curve itself does not change.

Change in Labor Demand or Supply
A shift in the demand or supply curve for labor caused by changes in nonwage factors.

Change in the Quantity of Labor Demanded or Supplied
A change in the amount of labor demanded or supplied that occurs when wages change; a movement along the demand or supply curve.

Modifications of the Labor Demand and Supply Model

The labor market model introduced in Figure 15.1 at the beginning of the chapter is a useful starting point for analyzing how wages are determined through the forces of supply and demand. But, just as there are imperfections in output markets, there are certain factors at work in real-world labor markets that go beyond what is explained in the simple supply and demand model and that impact the determination of wages and the amount of labor employed. Three of these factors—wage rigidities, legal considerations, and unequal bargaining power—merit special consideration.

Wage Rigidities   In a labor market such as that in Figure 15.1, a decrease in the demand for labor would shift the demand curve to the left, causing fewer workers to be hired and the equilibrium wage to fall. In reality, a decrease in the demand for labor will most likely cause employment to drop, but not money wages.[8] Firms with a need

[8]Notice that the expression *money wages* is used. Money wages are wages stated in current dollars, such as $8 per hour or $35,000 per year. Real wages, a different measure, are money wages adjusted for inflation, or what money wages can buy. In labor markets, money wages tend not to fall, but real wages may fall over time. This occurs when money wage increases do not keep up with inflation or with increases in the general level of prices. The model in this chapter uses money wages, not real wages. Money and real income are explained more fully in Chapter 4.

for fewer workers usually respond by laying off workers rather than by lowering their wages. On the supply side, contrary to the operation of the simple model, an increase in the number of workers in a market (a shift of the supply curve to the right) will also likely not lower the money wage. Thus, money wages tend to adjust upward but not downward to changing labor market conditions.

There are several reasons why money wages tend not to fall: Some workers are earning the minimum wage and by law can be paid no less; an employer may be bound by a labor agreement that sets wages; and it may be in the worker's best interest to be laid off rather than take a cut in pay. A laid-off worker may become eligible for unemployment compensation, can use the idle time to find another job, and will not be acknowledging a willingness to work for less. Also, an employer might believe that better long-term employee relationships can be maintained by laying off workers for a short period of time rather than by asking workers to accept a lower wage.

Minimum Wage Law

Legislation specifying the lowest hourly earnings that an employee can be paid.

Legal Considerations   Labor markets are affected by legislation that influences wages and the demand for and supply of labor. The most obvious legislation is the **minimum wage law.** By setting minimum hourly earnings, this law can override supply and demand by not allowing wages to fall to equilibrium. Figure 15.5 gives the federal minimum wage over time from $0.25 per hour when established in 1938, to $7.25 per hour set in 2009.

| **FIGURE 15.5** | *The Minimum Wage* |

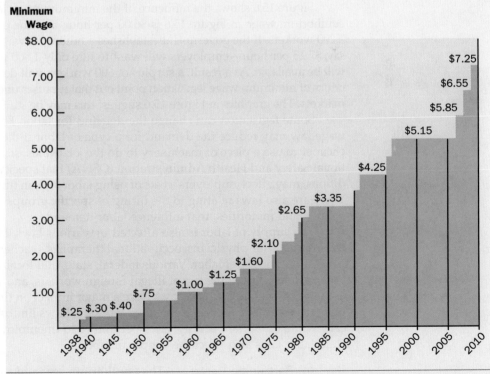

Over the years, the minimum wage has been raised many times from its original $0.25.

FIGURE 15.6   *Effect of a Minimum Wage on a Labor Market*

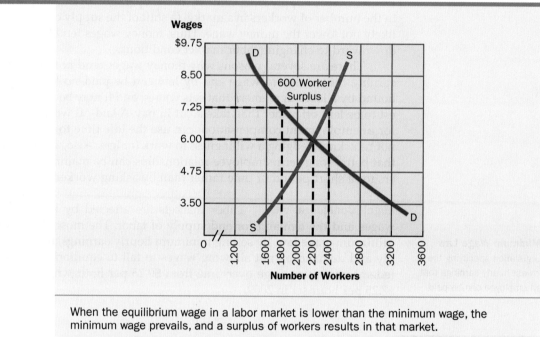

When the equilibrium wage in a labor market is lower than the minimum wage, the minimum wage prevails, and a surplus of workers results in that market.

Figure 15.6 shows the influence of the minimum wage law on a labor market. The equilibrium wage in Figure 15.6 is $6.00 per hour, and the equilibrium employment is 2,200 workers. If the government establishes a minimum wage above the equilibrium—say, $7.25 per hour—employers will want to hire only 1,800 workers, but 2,400 workers will be available. As a result, a surplus of 600 workers will develop in the market. Many critics of minimum wage legislation point out that it causes unemployment in some labor markets. The graphics in Figure 15.6 suggest this may be so.

Some legislation can change the demand for labor. For example, the minimum wage law may reduce the demand for a type of labor if the increased wage makes it cheaper to use a piece of machinery to do the job. Rules, such as those of the Occupational Safety and Health Administration (OSHA) that specify safety and working conditions, may affect employers' costs of using labor and, in turn, their demand for labor. There are also laws relating to the hiring of specific groups in the labor force, such as women and minorities, that influence labor demand.

The supply of labor is also affected by various laws. Licensing and certification requirements for physicians, occupational therapists, teachers, and others have an impact on the supply of labor. Various federal, state, and local laws that influence immigration levels, forbid the use of illegal foreign workers, and impose large penalties on employers who violate these laws have a major impact on the supply of labor in some markets, especially those for unskilled workers. Laws limiting the amount people can earn while on Social Security, laws pertaining to unemployment compensation, and child labor laws also affect the supply of labor.

Unequal Bargaining Power   The equilibrium wage of $12 in the labor market in Figure 15.1 was determined by employers and employees with equal bargaining power. In many markets this is not the case.

If bargaining power is on the side of the employer, the wage will likely be below that set when both parties are of equal strength. For example, workers living in a town with one major employer may be paid a lower wage than if there were several firms competing for their services. And, years ago before free agency status for athletes, studies showed that their salaries were much lower. In general, the fewer the alternative employers from which workers can choose, the weaker the workers' bargaining power.

If bargaining strength is on the side of labor suppliers, the wage will likely be above that set when buyers and sellers have equal power. In general, the greater the suppliers' control over the labor available to a particular employer, the greater their ability to raise wages above the competitive level. A major method used by workers to raise wages has been unionization. In addition, exceptional abilities and skills, such as those of network news anchors or sports personalities, provide greater control over their supply of labor.

LABOR UNIONS

Labor Union
An organization of workers that bargains in its members' behalf with management on wages, working conditions, fringe benefits, and other work-related issues.

A **labor union** is an organization of workers that bargains with management on its members' behalf. Usually unions represent their members in negotiations for wages, working conditions, fringe benefits, rules relating to seniority, layoffs and firings, and other matters. Unions in the United States are primarily economic in their focus, although they may engage in some political activity.

Types of Unions and Union Membership

The percent of the labor force belonging to unions has not been stable over the years. In 1983, 20.1 percent of all wage and salary employees belonged to unions, but since then membership has fallen. By 2008, only 12.4 percent of these workers were unionized. And, perhaps surprisingly, a much larger percentage of public service workers are unionized than are private sector workers: About 37 percent of government workers were unionized in 2008 as compared to 7.6 percent of private sector workers.[9]

The erosion of union membership and power has stemmed from many sources: an antiunion political climate; growth in the relative importance of service sector jobs where unionism has not had a strong presence; the decline in blue-collar manufacturing jobs where unions have been relatively successful in organizing; expanded government regulation of working conditions; and retirements and layoffs of union workers and advocates that are not being replaced.

Craft Union
A union that represents workers with a specific skill or craft.

Labor unions fall into two categories: craft unions and industrial unions. **Craft union** membership is made up of workers who have specific skills, such as bricklaying or plumbing. So, for example, bricklayers on a particular construction job would be represented by one union and plumbers on the same job by another.

A craft union may restrict membership through the completion of an apprenticeship program or some other requirement. Setting such conditions gives the union some control over the supply of workers and can raise its members' wages and fringe benefits. A simple supply and demand model for wage determination indicates that any action that restricts supply (shifts the supply curve to the left) results in a higher wage rate. For example, Figure 15.7 shows that a decrease in the supply of labor from

[9]U.S. Department of Labor, Bureau of Labor Statistics, "Union Members in 2008," http://www.bls.gov/news.release/pdf/union2.pdf, January 28, 2009.

| FIGURE 15.7 | *Restricting Supply in a Labor Market* |

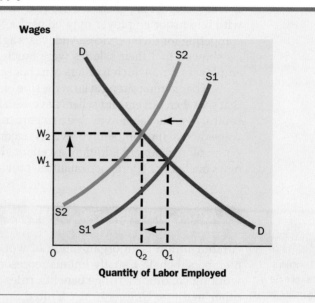

A craft union can obtain higher wages for its members by limiting the supply of labor, which is shown by a shift of the supply curve to the left from S1 to S2.

S1 to S2 leads to an increase in the wage rate from W_1 to W_2. Notice also another important result. This action reduces employment: in this case from Q_1 to Q_2.

Industrial Union

A union that represents all workers in a specific industry, regardless of the type of job performed.

An **industrial union,** rather than limiting itself to workers with a single skill, represents all workers in a specific industry. For example, workers performing different jobs in the automobile industry may be represented by the United Auto Workers, and communications workers performing different jobs may be represented by a single union. When it comes to membership, industrial unions are broader in their focus than craft unions.

A union, whether craft or industrial, is typically headed by a national or international organization that operates on behalf of all the members. Below this headquarters organization are individual "locals" to which the members belong. In some cases, such as the musicians' and other craft unions, members who work for different employers in a particular area belong to the same local. In other cases, such as the autoworkers' and other industrial unions, a local represents members working in a single plant or for a single employer.

Collective Bargaining

With unions, the process of wage determination is more complicated than the simple interaction of market supply and demand, since a union represents the suppliers of labor and management represents the buyer of labor. Here the impersonal forces of the market are replaced by negotiations between union and management representatives seeking to reach an agreement on wages, fringe benefits, and other aspects of a labor contract. This process in which a union negotiates a contract on behalf of its members is referred to as **collective bargaining.**

Collective Bargaining

The process through which a union and management negotiate a labor contract.

Union and management negotiations are primarily about economic issues: wages, job security, payments for insurance, and such. But the actual bargaining process itself is largely political: Negotiation involves a give-and-take process where each side tries to gain the most of what it seeks while giving up the least. The terms of a negotiated contract depend in large part on the relative bargaining ability and strength of the participating parties.

If the parties to a negotiation fail to agree on the terms of a contract, a union may go on strike against the employer. When on **strike,** union members stop working and ordinarily set up a picket line that other workers may refuse to cross. The purpose of the strike is to bring economic pressure on the employer to return to the bargaining table and draft an agreement acceptable to the union. In recent years little labor time has been lost due to strikes. In 2008, for example, less than 0.01 percent of estimated working time was lost because of work stoppages.[10]

Collective Bargaining and the Law

Over the years, we have created a large body of laws concerning the rights and responsibilities of labor unions in collective bargaining and related matters. Two laws have been especially important: the National Labor Relations Act of 1935 and the Labor Management Relations Act, better known as the Taft-Hartley Act, of 1947.

Passed in the depths of the Depression, the **National Labor Relations Act** (also called the **Wagner Act**) specifically gives workers the right to organize and bargain collectively, to choose who will represent them in their collective bargaining, and to carry out "concerted activities" for pro-labor purposes. The law also defines certain actions by employers, such as discrimination against employees because they belong to a union, as unfair labor practices. The **National Labor Relations Board (NLRB),** which hears complaints about unfair labor practices and can order that those practices cease and be remedied, was also created.[11]

The **Taft-Hartley Act** of 1947, which became law in a troublesome year for work stoppages, is generally less supportive of organized labor. Under certain circumstances the Taft-Hartley Act gives workers the right to not join a union or otherwise engage in organized labor activities. Section 14(b) of the law says that union membership cannot be a condition of employment in states that have passed laws to that effect. This is better known as the "right to work" issue, and state laws prohibiting union membership as a condition of employment are called **right to work laws.** With right to work laws, a union's ability to control the supply of labor is diminished, and the union's bargaining strength is weakened. In 2008, 23 states had right to work laws.[12]

The Taft-Hartley Act also allows the president of the United States to impose an 80-day "cooling-off period" during which a particular strike or lockout (where an employer prevents laborers from entering a work site) cannot occur if, in the president's opinion, the work stoppage is a threat to the national interest. If, after 80 days, the situation leading to the strike or lockout is not corrected, the ban is lifted, and the work stoppage can continue.[13]

THE DISTRIBUTION OF INCOME

In any economy, there are always questions about income. How much does the average person make? How is income divided—are there many or a few rich or poor? The **distribution of income** refers to the way income is divided among the

Strike
Work stoppage by union members.

National Labor Relations Act (Wagner Act)
Legislation supportive of unions; permits and strengthens collective bargaining.

National Labor Relations Board (NLRB)
Hears complaints on unfair labor practices and orders remedies where appropriate.

Taft-Hartley Act
Legislation that contains several provisions limiting union activities.

Right to Work Laws
State laws prohibiting union membership as a condition of employment.

Distribution of Income
The way income is divided among the members of society.

[10]U.S. Department of Labor, Bureau of Labor Statistics, "Databases, Tables and Calculators by Subject," http://data.bls.gov/cgi-bin/surveymost, September 12, 2008. 2008 numbers are through July, and from March through July, the percentage was less than 0.005.
[11]*United States Statutes at Large,* vol. 49, part 1 (Washington, DC: U.S. Government Printing Office, 1936), pp. 452–454.
[12]U.S. Department of Labor, Employment Standards Administration Wage and Hour Division, "State Right-to-Work Laws and Constitutional Amendments in Effect as of January 1, 2008 with Year of Passage," www.dol.gov/esa/whd/state/righttowork.htm.
[13]*United States Statutes at Large,* vol. 61, part 1 (1948), pp. 136, 140–142, 151, 155–156.

members of society. If the distribution of income to individuals were perfectly equal, everyone would receive the same amount. But income is not divided equally: Some households are better or worse off than others; and at the extremes, some are very rich and others are very poor.

We can see how income is distributed in the United States in Table 15.4. The left-hand column of the table divides households into five groups—each representing 20 percent of all households—ranked according to the amount of income they received. The lowest group represents the 20 percent of all households that received the lowest incomes, and the highest group is the 20 percent that received the largest incomes. The right-hand column of the table gives the percentage of total income that went to each of the five groups in 2007.

With an equal distribution of income among households, each of the five groups would have received 20 percent of the total. However, in 2007 the lowest 20 percent received 3.4 percent of total income, while the highest 20 percent of households claimed 49.7 percent. Not shown in the table, the top 5 percent received 21.2 percent of total income.[14]

Over the years, journalists and others have watched the release of these annual quintile data to determine whether the rich are getting richer or the poor are getting poorer. Since the mid-1970s, there has been a change. The share going to the poorest 20 percent has generally been falling while the share to the richest 20 percent has generally been rising.[15]

Some members of society are more likely than others to be at the lower or higher end of the distribution of income. In Chapter 10 it was noted that, on average, households with certain characteristics tend to earn more than other households. For example, households headed by a married couple typically earn more than households headed by a single female, and households headed by a college graduate fare better than those headed by an individual with less education.[16]

Differences in Income

Why is income in the United States distributed as it is? Why do some people receive a large annual income while others do not? Several explanations merit discussion.

| TABLE 15.4 | *Income Distribution among Households* |

Income is not distributed evenly among households in the United States. In 2007 the poorest one-fifth of U.S. households received 3.4 percent of total income while the richest one-fifth received 49.7 percent of the total.

Percent of Households	Percent of Total Income In 2007
Lowest 20%	3.4%
Second 20%	8.7
Middle 20%	14.8
Fourth 20%	23.4
Highest 20%	49.7
Total	100.0

Source: U.S. Bureau of the Census, *Historical Income Tables—Household Table* H2, http://www.census.gov/hhes/income/histinc/h02AR.html.

---

[14]See source for Table 15.4.
[15]Ibid.
[16]See Table 10.2.

Resource Ownership   Most income depends on the quality and quantity of productive resources that individuals own and the uses to which those resources are put. People with highly productive or many resources stand to earn more money than those who own less productive or fewer resources. An outstanding athlete or top-rated chef earns more than others with less impressive performances; the owners of fertile farmland in the heart of Illinois earn more income from the production of crops than the owners of less fertile farmland in the hills of western Pennsylvania; and a family with a ranch, an apartment complex, and a fleet of rental trucks is going to have a higher income than one whose sole income source is the labor of an unskilled household head.

Sometimes resource ownership comes from inheritance. Income can be generated from the ownership of real estate, securities, or other assets passed on through a will or trust.

Education and Experience   The case can be made that nothing beats education as a way of improving a person's lifetime earnings. We saw the data in Chapter 10 that show a direct relationship between annual household income and years of education. Table 15.5 provides more detailed information about average weekly incomes for people whose education levels range from less than a high school diploma through a doctorate. The data in the table strikingly demonstrate the importance of education: In 2007 a person with a doctoral degree was earning about 3.5 times as much as a person with less than a high school diploma.

There is also a case to be made for experience, which includes not only work at a job, but training, additional coursework, the reading of work-related articles and books, and other activities over time. It has been shown that the financial benefit of experience is higher for those with more education.[17] Presumably, individuals with jobs that require a higher degree also invest more in additional training. The expenditure of time, effort, and money by a physician who must keep up with licensing requirements, continuing education, and professional readings is typically higher than that by someone in an unskilled labor position.

TABLE 15.5   *Levels of Education and Income*

Education has a strong positive influence on a person's income.

Education Level	Average Weekly Earnings in 2007
Doctoral degree	$1,497
Professional degree	1,427
Master's degree	1,165
Bachelor's degree	987
Associate degree	740
Some college, no degree	683
High school graduate	604
Less than high school diploma	428

Source: U.S. Department of Labor, Bureau of Labor Statistics, Employment Projections, "Education pays . . . ," http://www.bls.gov/emp/emptab7.htm, September 12, 2008.

[17]Federal Reserve Bank of Dallas, "Pulling Ourselves Up by Our Own Bookmarks," 2004 Annual Report, p. 8.

Human Capital Investment
An expenditure to improve a person's productivity.

The expenditures of time, effort, and money to gain an education and improve a person's productivity are called **human capital investments.** Just as a business may invest in machinery and equipment, human beings can and do spend money and time improving their own productive capabilities—both intellectual and physical. Human capital investments include not only learning-related expenditures but also spending on health care, fitness, and other related programs. As the world becomes "flatter" and we compete in a more global environment, there is increased recognition that knowledge-based economies are important for sustained economic growth.

Application 15.2, "Making the Most of Intellectual Capital," discusses the transition in the United States from an economy that was focused on industrial work and skills to a more sophisticated economy dependent on brain power, or intellectual capital.

Discrimination
Unequal treatment in a labor market because of an employer's perception of a category to which a worker belongs.

Discrimination   Workers experience **discrimination** when they are treated unequally in a labor market because they are placed in a category and judged on the basis of the employer's perception of that category, rather than on the basis of their skills or merit. In the United States, concern over discrimination has centered mainly on the labor market experiences of nonwhite as compared to white workers, female as compared to male workers, and older as compared to prime-age workers. But discrimination can be based on any type of categorical distinction, such as religious or political preference or ethnic origin. Typically, the discriminated-against worker receives a lower wage or may have fewer job choices or advancement opportunities.

The effects of discrimination on income can also be indirect. Unequal access to good housing, medical care, or educational opportunities might lead to smaller or less productive human capital investments, which in turn can result in lower incomes.

APPLICATION 15.2

MAKING THE MOST OF INTELLECTUAL CAPITAL

Knowledge didn't fuel America's economy in the past. The Industrial Age thrived on man's mastery over machine. Most work required steady hands to operate factory equipment and minds geared to such repetitive tasks as measuring and counting. . . . Over the course of workers' careers, jobs changed little, so talents acquired in youth often served until retirement. Lifetime learning didn't matter all that much.

America has left the Industrial Age behind. Factory work is increasingly being performed in other countries; much of what remains in the United States is highly technical, relying more on sharp minds than nimble hands.

Postindustrial nations are shifting workers to more sophisticated jobs that require analytical intelligence, imagination and creativity, and the ability to interact with others. The work relies on brains rather than brawn. . . . Equally important, these skills have to be kept sharp in a world of rapidly changing tastes and technology. We can't just get a good education while young and expect it to suffice for an entire career.

The transformation of the way we work gives intellectual capital precedence over the physical capital that once drove the U.S. economy. Both kinds of capital make us richer, but they differ in important ways.

Physical capital grows when businesses invest in buildings, machinery and other productive assets. These are largely management decisions, and the process usually takes just a few months or years. To expand intellectual capital, we invest in human beings over decades—from learning the ABCs in preschool to mastering the latest computer programs at the office.

Companies make important contributions to creating intellectual capital, but workers must assume a large part of the responsibility. No one can learn for us. We have to supply the effort to develop our skills.

Knowledge is ultimately the property of the employee. . . . Workers take it with them when they switch jobs, a factor that limits companies' ability to capture the benefits of investing in human capital. As a result, workers can't count on employers to provide all the training they'll need. They must be active participants in their own education, engaging in lifetime learning on their own.

Source: "Making the Most of Intellectual Capital," Federal Reserve Bank of Dallas, 2004 Annual Report, pp. 13–14.

TABLE 15.6	*Poverty Levels for Families and Individuals*

Poverty levels vary according to family size and age of the head of the household. They indicate the annual money income that must be received to be considered *not* poor by the federal government.

Size of Unit	Income Level in 2008[a]
1 person	
Under 65 years	$ 11,201
65 years and over	10,326
2 persons	
Householder under 65 years	14,417
Householder 65 years and over	13,014
3 persons	16,841
4 persons	22,207
5 persons	26,781
6 persons	30,803
7 persons	35,442
8 persons	39,640
9 persons or more	47,684

[a]Thresholds vary with the number of related children under 18; thresholds given have no related children under 18.
Source: U.S. Census Bureau, *Poverty Thresholds for 2008*, http://www.census.gov/hhes/poverty/threshld/thresh08.html.

Poverty

The income distribution data in Table 15.4 show that, in 2007, the lowest 20 percent of all households received only 3.4 percent of total income, and the next lowest 20 percent received only 8.7 percent. Are these households considered to be the "poor" in our society?

Each of us has a different concept of poverty, or what is meant by poor. What someone living in luxury considers to be poor may be different from what the average income earner thinks is poor. Someone who drives an expensive new car may think a person who drives an old, obviously used car is poor. Someone who drives an old used car may view as poor a person who cannot afford a car at all.

In general, poverty is based on a person's income and level of material well-being: the housing, clothing, food, medical care, and other goods and services that can be afforded.

Government Measures of Poverty   In order to calculate an "official" measure of poverty in the United States, the federal government has created income measures called **poverty levels.** Based primarily on family size, they indicate the amount of annual money income that must be received to be considered *not* poor. Any individual or family receiving an income below its designated level is classified as poor and is included in government poverty statistics.

Poverty Levels
Government-designated levels of income that must be received to be considered *not* poor.

Table 15.6 gives the average poverty levels for families and individuals in 2008. The poverty level increases as the number of persons in a family increases, and the measure varies according to whether or not the head of the household is under 65 years of age.

TABLE 15.7   *Groups Living Below the Poverty Level in 2007*

Many children, elderly, and poorly educated persons, and people in female-headed households live below the poverty levels.

Group	Number of Persons in Group Below the Poverty Level	Percentage of Group Below the Poverty Level
Total population	37.3 million	12.5%
People in female-headed families	13.5 million	30.7%
Children under 18	13.3 million	18.0%
Persons 65 years and older	3.6 million	9.7%
Persons employed full time, year round	2.8 million	2.5%
Persons employed less than full time, year round	6.3 million	12.7%
Persons with no high school diploma	10.1 million	22.4%
Persons with a 4-year college degree or higher	2.4 million	3.9%
Persons living in Mississippi	655 thousand	22.6%
Persons living in New Hampshire	76 thousand	5.8%

Source: U.S. Census Bureau, Current Population Survey (CPS), Annual Social and Economic Supplement, Tables POV01, POV02, POV22, POV29, POV46, http://pubdb3.census.gov/macro/032008/pov.

In 2007, 37.3 million people, or 12.5 percent of the total population, lived in poverty—that is, in households where the money income fell below the poverty levels. Table 15.7 provides information about poverty levels for some groups in 2007. For example, there was a high incidence of poverty among female-headed families: 30.7 percent of persons in female-headed families lived below the poverty levels. Notice that 18 percent of children lived below the poverty levels and that the incidence was higher for high school dropouts—22.4 percent—than for persons with a 4-year college degree or higher—3.9 percent. Many of the poor had jobs, and the incidence of poverty differed among the states.

There has been some disagreement over the official definitions of the poverty levels. Many argue that the levels are too low and do not represent a true measure of poverty. For example, according to Table 15.6, in 2008 the poverty level for a family of three was $16,841—far below the median income of $62,359 for a family household.[18] Also, according to the poverty levels in Table 15.6, a family of four persons earning $22,208 in 2008 would not have been "poor" because its income was $1 above the poverty line.

Some people argue that the plight of the poor is overstated because the income levels used to measure poverty do not account for in-kind benefits, such as government noncash aid for food, housing, and medical care, that improve one's standard of living. If these were added to money incomes, then a smaller percentage of the population would fall below the poverty levels.

---

[18]U.S. Census Bureau, "Income, Poverty, and Health Insurance Coverage in the United States: 2007," Table 1. Income and Earnings Summary Measures by Selected Characteristics: 2006 and 2007, http://www.census.gov/prod/2008pubs/p60-235.pdf. Median income is for 2007.

APPLICATION 15.3

HOMELESS FAMILIES WITH CHILDREN

One of the fastest growing segments of the homeless population is families with children. In 2007, 23% of all homeless people were members of families with children. . . . Homeless families are most commonly headed by single mothers in their late 20s with approximately two children.

Poverty and the lack of affordable housing are the principal causes of family homelessness. . . . Declining wages have put housing out of reach for many families: in every state, metropolitan area, county, and town, more than the minimum wage is required to afford a one- or two-bedroom apartment at [a fair market rent]. In fact, the median wage needed to afford a two-bedroom apartment is more than twice the minimum wage.

Homelessness severely impacts the health and well being of all family members. Children without a home are in fair or poor health twice as often as other children, and have higher rates of asthma, ear infections, stomach problems, and speech problems. Homeless children also experience more mental health problems, such as anxiety, depression, and withdrawal. They are twice as likely to ex-

perience hunger, and four times as likely to have delayed development. These illnesses have potentially devastating consequences if not treated early.

Deep poverty and housing instability are especially harmful during the earliest years of childhood; alarmingly, it is estimated that almost half of children in shelter are under the age of five. School-age homeless children face barriers to enrolling and attending school, including transportation problems, residency requirements, inability to obtain previous school records, and lack of clothing and school supplies.

Parents also suffer the ill effects of homelessness and poverty . . . Homelessness frequently breaks up families. Families may be separated as a result of shelter policies which deny access to older boys or fathers. Separations may also be caused by placement of children into foster care when their parents become homeless. . . . The break-up of families is a well-documented phenomenon: in 56% of the 27 cities surveyed in 2004, homeless families had to break up in order to enter emergency shelters.

Source: National Coalition for the Homeless, NCH Fact Sheet #12, "Homeless Families with Children," June 2008, http://www.nationalhomeless.org/publications/facts/families.html.

The opinion is sometimes expressed that the poor live well on public support and that poverty is largely due to an unwillingness to work. Unfortunately, poverty is a complicated problem that may not be eliminated by simply insisting that people work. In some instances, the poverty we see is a symptom of deeper human suffering. A federal task force study reported that one out of every three of the homeless in the United States suffers serious mental illness.[19] Application 15.3, "Homeless Families with Children," deals with another area of poverty of major concern.

Government Programs and Poverty   There are several government programs that provide cash transfer payments and in-kind benefits. These include Social Security, unemployment compensation, housing assistance, food stamps, medical care, vocational rehabilitation, public assistance, job training, and others. Among these, there is no single program aimed specifically and exclusively at persons living below the poverty levels. Rather, each federal and state program has its own eligibility requirements under which a poor person may qualify. For example, a poverty-level retired couple could be eligible for Social Security if they made payments into the system, or a low income could entitle a household to food stamps.

---

[19]Task Force on Homelessness and Severe Mental Illness, *Outcasts on Main Street: Report of the Federal Task Force on Homelessness and Severe Mental Illness* (Washington, DC: U.S. Department of Health and Human Services, 1992), pp. 1–2.

| TABLE 15.8 | *Average Monthly Payments from Various Government Benefit Programs* |

There are many government cash and in-kind benefit programs. Each program has its own eligibility requirements, and the actual amount of the benefit from some programs can differ significantly from state to state.

Government Program	Average Monthly Payment in 2006
Temporary Assistance for Needy Families	
Per family	$ 525[a]
Food stamps	
Average monthly value per recipient	94
Supplemental Security Income	
For the disabled	471
For the blind	488
For the aged	373
Social Security	
Retired workers	1,044
Disabled workers under age 65	978
Widows and widowers	1,007
Federal civil service retirement	
Age and service	2,363
Disability	1,366
Unemployment compensation	1,200

[a]Figure is for 2005.

Sources: U.S. Bureau of the Census, *Statistical Abstract of the United States: 2008*, 127th ed., p. 359; *2009*, Tables 526, 530, 539, 544, 551.

Many government programs, such as Social Security or unemployment compensation, are closed to those who have no regular employment. As a result, some government benefits may not be available to poverty-level families. In addition, many of the homeless in the United States receive no government aid because they do not qualify for specific programs, have no address, or do not sign up for benefits.

Table 15.8 lists the average monthly payments for various government programs in 2006. The first few listed are those most likely to be received by someone living in poverty. Notice that the average monthly payment for a family under Temporary Assistance to Needy Families (TANF) was $525. In practice this payment varies from state to state, causing considerable deviation from the average.

Sweeping reform of several aid programs, often called welfare reform, occurred in 1996. The maximum time for receipt of certain kinds of aid was limited, and a work activity requirement to qualify for some types of aid was instituted. Welfare reform brings into focus a controversy that has simmered for years: Should there be a limit to how much aid is given to the out-of-work poor? Two opposing views on this question are presented in Up for Debate, "Should There Be a Work Requirement for Those Seeking Public Assistance?."

UP FOR DEBATE

SHOULD THERE BE A WORK REQUIREMENT FOR THOSE SEEKING PUBLIC ASSISTANCE?

Issue *In 1996 the Personal Responsibility and Work Opportunities Reconciliation Act was passed. A new government assistance program with training and work requirements was created—TANF (Temporary Assistance for Needy Families)—and AFDC (Aid to Families with Dependent Children) was eliminated. Since that time, the number of assistance recipients has dropped by more than 60 percent—from about 13 million to 5 million. Many have touted this new program with its work requirement as successful although other programs such as food stamps have increased in participation. Given this apparent success, should we place even more demands on those seeking public assistance by instituting a stronger work requirement?*

Yes We should place more demands on those seeking public assistance. Certainly we have an obligation to those around us who are in need, but at the same time, we are not doing either taxpayers or those receiving assistance a favor by sending the message that public support will always be there for the asking.

Concern is often expressed about creating a permanent underclass of citizens who spend their lives in a culture of poverty with no serious expectation, or attempt, to raise themselves out of poverty. The necessity to work might urge public assistance recipients to attend school and training and to take advantage of other opportunities to improve their economic status.

Responsibility is something we learn, and if the assurance that public assistance will always be available dulls people's sense of responsibility and makes them dependent on others for their day-to-day maintenance, then public assistance is not serving its intended purpose. And, there is a sense of satisfaction from work that people receive: It can be a very positive experience.

No We should not place any more demands on those seeking public assistance. As a society, without a clear picture of how many people really are in a position to work, we could make some serious mistakes by making assistance more difficult to obtain and instituting a stronger work requirement.

By acting on a belief that all adults should work, we neglect to acknowledge the difficult positions of caring for a chronically ill child or of the person with poor health or limited talent.

We must also acknowledge the costs of working. In addition to clothing, transportation costs may be prohibitive, especially if public transportation is not accessible. The cost of a car, insurance, maintenance, and gas may be impossible to pay. Then there is child care, which may not be available or may be too costly. It is possible that the costs of working may be greater than the salary of a low-income earner.

Finally, are the restrictions imposed because of concern that all adults should engage in productive work, or is this group a good target for spending cuts because it is significantly underrepresented in the political process?

Source: Congressional Budget Office, Economic and Budget Issue Brief, April 20, 2005, "Changes in Participation in Means-Tested Programs," http://www.cbo.gov/doc.cfm?index=6302&type=0.

Summary

1. The prices of land, labor, capital, and entrepreneurship are determined basically by the forces of supply and demand. Businesses, governments, and nonprofits are the primary buyers, and their demands for labor and all other inputs are derived from the demands for the goods or services the inputs produce.

2. A demand curve for labor is downward sloping because of diminishing marginal productivity (the Law of Diminishing Returns) and the need to lower output prices to increase sales in all but purely competitive markets (the Law of Demand). A firm's labor demand curve is based on the marginal revenue product of its labor. A market demand curve for labor is the sum of the labor demand curves of all individual firms in the market.

3.   A market supply curve of labor is upward sloping, indicating a direct relationship between the wage rate and the amount of labor offered in the market. The supply of labor is affected by the wage rate and by other factors, such as job satisfaction and locational preference.

4.   A change in labor demand or supply, shown by a shift of the demand or supply curve to the right or left, results from changes in nonwage factors, such as the prices of substitute inputs, technology, and future job prospects. A change in the quantity of labor demanded or supplied results from a change in the wage rate.

5.   The simple supply and demand approach to a market for labor can be modified to account for certain real-world considerations. Wage rigidities, legislation, and unequal bargaining power all influence the determination of wages.

6.   A labor union is a workers' organization that bargains in its members' behalf with management on matters such as wages, fringe benefits, and job security. A craft union represents workers who have a particular skill; an industrial union represents workers who perform different jobs in a particular industry.

7.   The process through which union contracts are negotiated is called collective bargaining. Two important laws affect collective bargaining: the National Labor Relations Act (Wagner Act) of 1935, which is basically supportive of unionism, and the Labor Management Relations Act (Taft-Hartley Act) of 1947, which is a limiting force on unionism.

8.   Income distribution refers to how income is divided among the members of society. In the United States, households with the lowest incomes receive less than a proportional share of the total, while those with the highest incomes receive more. There are several explanations for this income distribution pattern.

9.   The U.S. government has created an official measure of poverty in the United States based on annual money income levels, which vary according to the size of the family. Many of the poor in the United States are children or in a household headed by a woman.

Key Terms and Concepts

Wage

Derived demand

Law of Diminishing Returns

Marginal product

Marginal revenue product

Demand curve for labor

Supply curve of labor

Change in labor demand or supply

Change in the quantity of labor demanded or supplied

Minimum wage law

Labor union

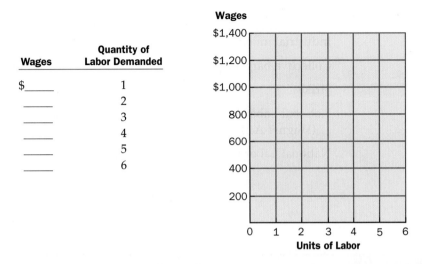

Wages	Quantity of Labor Demanded
$_____	1
_____	2
_____	3
_____	4
_____	5
_____	6

4. Explain how wage rigidities, the minimum wage law, and unequal bargaining power modify the basic labor supply and demand model.

5. What is the difference between a craft union and an industrial union? How can a craft union keep its members' wages high?

6. What was the intent of the National Labor Relations Act and the Taft-Hartley Act? Generally, what is the impact of each act on collective bargaining and organized labor in the United States?

7. What is meant by the expression income distribution? What are some of the explanations as to why incomes are unequally distributed?

8. What groups in society are most likely to be included among the poor, and why is there controversy over the official definition of the poverty levels?

Discussion Questions

1. Match each occupation with what you think is the correct salary, and explain why you think each match is correct. Salaries are averages for 2007. (Answers and source are on page 461.)

Occupation		Salary
1. Air traffic controller	_____ a.	$ 16,860
2. Airline pilot	_____ b.	$ 25,800
3. Chemical engineer	_____ c.	$ 39,360
4. Clinical psychologist	_____ d.	$ 68,150
5. Computer programmer	_____ e.	$ 72,010
6. Court judge	_____ f.	$ 84,090
7. Fast food cook	_____ g.	$ 84,240
8. Petroleum engineer	_____ h.	$ 99,270
9. Preschool teacher	_____ i.	$107,780
10. Radio and television announcer	_____ j.	$113,890
11. Surgeon	_____ k.	$148,810
12. Veterinarian	_____ l.	$191,410

Craft union

Industrial union

Collective bargaining

Strike

National Labor Relations Act
   (Wagner Act)

National Labor Relations Board (NLRB)

Taft-Hartley Act

Right to work laws

Distribution of income

Human capital investment

Discrimination

Poverty levels

Review Questions

1. What would be the effect of each of the following on Company X's demand for labor? (Remember the distinction between a change in demand and a change in quantity demanded.)
   a. An increase in the price of Company X's major competitor's product
   b. A decrease in the price of an input that can be substituted for Company X's workforce
   c. A decrease in the number of buyers in Company X's product market
   d. A decrease in the price of Company X's product
   e. An increase in the wage paid to Company X's workers

2. Explain fully how the Law of Diminishing Returns and the Law of Demand cause a demand curve for labor to be downward sloping.

3. Given the following table for a hypothetical company, fill in the columns for Total Revenue and Marginal Revenue Product. Based on this information, complete the company's demand schedule for labor on page 458 and illustrate the schedule in the accompanying graph.

Units of Labor	Total Product	Price per Unit	Total Revenue	Marginal Revenue Product
0	0	$13	$_____	
				$_____
1	100	12	_____	
				_____
2	170	11	_____	
				_____
3	230	10	_____	
				_____
4	280	9	_____	
				_____
5	320	8	_____	
				_____
6	350	7	_____	

UP FOR DEBATE

SHOULD THERE BE A WORK REQUIREMENT FOR THOSE SEEKING PUBLIC ASSISTANCE?

Issue   In 1996 the Personal Responsibility and Work Opportunities Reconciliation Act was passed. A new government assistance program with training and work requirements was created—TANF (Temporary Assistance for Needy Families)—and AFDC (Aid to Families with Dependent Children) was eliminated. Since that time, the number of assistance recipients has dropped by more than 60 percent—from about 13 million to 5 million. Many have touted this new program with its work requirement as successful although other programs such as food stamps have increased in participation. Given this apparent success, should we place even more demands on those seeking public assistance by instituting a stronger work requirement?

Yes   We should place more demands on those seeking public assistance. Certainly we have an obligation to those around us who are in need, but at the same time, we are not doing either taxpayers or those receiving assistance a favor by sending the message that public support will always be there for the asking.

Concern is often expressed about creating a permanent underclass of citizens who spend their lives in a culture of poverty with no serious expectation, or attempt, to raise themselves out of poverty. The necessity to work might urge public assistance recipients to attend school and training and to take advantage of other opportunities to improve their economic status.

Responsibility is something we learn, and if the assurance that public assistance will always be available dulls people's sense of responsibility and makes them dependent on others for their day-to-day maintenance, then public assistance is not serving its intended purpose. And, there is a sense of satisfaction from work that people receive: It can be a very positive experience.

No   We should not place any more demands on those seeking public assistance. As a society, without a clear picture of how many people really are in a position to work, we could make some serious mistakes by making assistance more difficult to obtain and instituting a stronger work requirement.

By acting on a belief that all adults should work, we neglect to acknowledge the difficult positions of caring for a chronically ill child or of the person with poor health or limited talent.

We must also acknowledge the costs of working. In addition to clothing, transportation costs may be prohibitive, especially if public transportation is not accessible. The cost of a car, insurance, maintenance, and gas may be impossible to pay. Then there is child care, which may not be available or may be too costly. It is possible that the costs of working may be greater than the salary of a low-income earner.

Finally, are the restrictions imposed because of concern that all adults should engage in productive work, or is this group a good target for spending cuts because it is significantly underrepresented in the political process?

Source: Congressional Budget Office, Economic and Budget Issue Brief, April 20, 2005, "Changes in Participation in Means-Tested Programs," http://www.cbo.gov/doc.cfm?index=6302&type=0.

Summary

1. The prices of land, labor, capital, and entrepreneurship are determined basically by the forces of supply and demand. Businesses, governments, and nonprofits are the primary buyers, and their demands for labor and all other inputs are derived from the demands for the goods or services the inputs produce.

2. A demand curve for labor is downward sloping because of diminishing marginal productivity (the Law of Diminishing Returns) and the need to lower output prices to increase sales in all but purely competitive markets (the Law of Demand). A firm's labor demand curve is based on the marginal revenue product of its labor. A market demand curve for labor is the sum of the labor demand curves of all individual firms in the market.

3. A market supply curve of labor is upward sloping, indicating a direct relationship between the wage rate and the amount of labor offered in the market. The supply of labor is affected by the wage rate and by other factors, such as job satisfaction and locational preference.

4. A change in labor demand or supply, shown by a shift of the demand or supply curve to the right or left, results from changes in nonwage factors, such as the prices of substitute inputs, technology, and future job prospects. A change in the quantity of labor demanded or supplied results from a change in the wage rate.

5. The simple supply and demand approach to a market for labor can be modified to account for certain real-world considerations. Wage rigidities, legislation, and unequal bargaining power all influence the determination of wages.

6. A labor union is a workers' organization that bargains in its members' behalf with management on matters such as wages, fringe benefits, and job security. A craft union represents workers who have a particular skill; an industrial union represents workers who perform different jobs in a particular industry.

7. The process through which union contracts are negotiated is called collective bargaining. Two important laws affect collective bargaining: the National Labor Relations Act (Wagner Act) of 1935, which is basically supportive of unionism, and the Labor Management Relations Act (Taft-Hartley Act) of 1947, which is a limiting force on unionism.

8. Income distribution refers to how income is divided among the members of society. In the United States, households with the lowest incomes receive less than a proportional share of the total, while those with the highest incomes receive more. There are several explanations for this income distribution pattern.

9. The U.S. government has created an official measure of poverty in the United States based on annual money income levels, which vary according to the size of the family. Many of the poor in the United States are children or in a household headed by a woman.

Key Terms and Concepts

Wage

Derived demand

Law of Diminishing Returns

Marginal product

Marginal revenue product

Demand curve for labor

Supply curve of labor

Change in labor demand or supply

Change in the quantity of labor demanded or supplied

Minimum wage law

Labor union

2. Assume that the leaders of a local union seek your advice on actions that could be taken to stem the decline of unionism in the United States. What would you suggest to reverse this trend? Do you think that the labor movement will ever return to the status and strength it had during its peak years?

3. Two laws that affect the operations of labor markets are the minimum wage law and the right to work law. Who benefits and who loses from each of these laws?

4. Sometimes a business makes investments in machinery and equipment, and those investments do not pay off—the business does not recover its costs plus something more. Is it possible for an individual to make a human capital investment that does not pay off? In making an informed human capital decision on, say, a college education, what sorts of information would you want to know, and why?

5. You have a friend who argues that poverty is really not a problem in this country because the poor are better off than millions of people in other parts of the world. Evaluate this position.

6. There is much criticism that the poverty levels are not an accurate method for determining who is poor in the United States. Do you think these levels are too high or too low? How would you redefine poverty for statistical purposes?

7. What are the eligibility requirements in your state for a family to receive TANF (Temporary Assistance for Needy Families)? What are the requirements to receive food stamps? What is the monthly TANF benefit? What is the monthly allotment of food stamps? If the qualifications for these two programs are different, explain how and why.

Critical Thinking Case 15

INCOME DISTRIBUTION: ARE THE SHARES OF THE PIE FAIR?

Critical Thinking Skills

Weighing arguments in support of different sides of an issue

Tying philosophy and values to positions on an issue

Economic Concepts

Distribution of income

Equity

The data in Table 15.4, which show the distribution of income among household quintile groups, provides a basis for serious thought and conversation. The table is simple and straightforward: It shows that about 50 percent of income goes to the highest income earners, while 3.4 percent goes to the lowest. Put in plain language, about half the income pie goes to 20 percent of households, and the other half of the pie is shared by about 80 percent of households.

As noted in the text, journalists and others who follow income distribution numbers watch these data closely because of the trend in changes, as well as the social and economic implications, of the numbers. And, the trend has been a general move toward "the rich getting richer" and the "poor getting poorer."

You might want to share this table with your family and friends and provoke some conversation around the data. Here are some questions to guide that discussion.

Questions

1. Is this income distribution pattern "okay"? Is the trend toward richer and poorer "okay"? How do these data fit with the basic philosophy of a market economy where people are rewarded for their contributions to production?

2. What, if any, are the social, economic, cultural, and political implications for an economy that moves in this direction from a more even distribution of income?

3. For people who want to alter the income distribution pattern, what policy recommendations would they make to do so? Would they consider any of the following?

    ♦ Raise taxes on the highest income earners.
    ♦ Raise the minimum wage to a higher level.
    ♦ Increase public assistance to provide every person with a minimum base amount of income on which to live.
    ♦ Cap salaries and earnings at $1 million.
    ♦ Provide free tuition to guarantee that every person can attend college. (Remember: Higher incomes are associated with higher levels of education.)

Answers and Source for Discussion Question 1
Answers: 1. i, 2. k, 3. g, 4. d, 5. e, 6. h, 7. a, 8. j, 9. b, 10. c, 11. l, 12. f.

Source: U.S. Department of Labor, Bureau of Labor Statistics, *Occupational Employment Statistics,*
http://data.bls.gov/cgi-bin/print.pl/oes/current/oes_nat.htm.

PART 4

The International Economy

CHAPTER 16
International Trade

CHAPTER 17
International Finance

International Trade

CHAPTER OBJECTIVES

To present an overview of U.S. international trade by highlighting major U.S. exports and imports as well as countries with which the United States trades.

To explain the principle of comparative advantage.

To define free trade and explore some arguments in its favor.

To define protectionism, explore some arguments in its favor, and introduce the main tools for restricting trade.

To discuss possible trade policies and examine some key trade agreements.

Economic activity is highly globalized. In today's world, it is not unusual to hop a plane to do business in Singapore; for a middle-level corporate manager to work closely with subsidiaries around the world; or to furnish our homes with rugs, art, and furniture from Africa, South America, or Asia. One way to quickly see how globalized economic activity has become is to open your closet and scan the labels on your clothes showing where they were manufactured.

International economics is about the movement of goods and services as well as financial transactions among nations. Medical and disaster aid, military activity, overseas investments, and the import and export of goods such as oil, wine, grain, and automobiles are all relevant to international economics.

This chapter introduces some important topics that relate to international trade, or the movement of goods and services between nations. It begins with an overview of U.S. international trade, including major traded products and important trading partners. Comparative advantage, a basic theory that underlies international trade, the great debate in international economics over free trade versus protectionism, trade policies for stimulating exports, and important agreements affecting trade among nations are then covered. Chapter 17 deals with the financial aspects of international economics.

Trade and financial relationships among nations are growing in importance as the world becomes more globally connected, or "flatter." These relationships affect our national security, international relations, and social understanding. Today we are much more aware of the conditions in which people in many countries work, the use of child labor, and the degree to which AIDS and lack of access to safe drinking water are world problems.

AN OVERVIEW OF U.S. INTERNATIONAL TRADE

International Trade
The buying and selling of goods and services among different countries.

An important aspect of international economics is **international trade**: the buying and selling of goods and services among different countries. International trade affects the availability of goods and services as well as the levels of production, employment, and prices in the trading countries. Sales in overseas markets can increase employment among a nation's workers. But international trade can also bring in strong foreign competitors and lead to a drop in sales, which in turn could lower production and employment for a nation. Also, the presence of foreign goods in a market increases competition, which in turn influences product prices. And for a country that is dependent on a foreign product, increases in the price of that product can influence the country's inflation rate.

The Size and Composition of U.S. Trade

Export
A good or service sold abroad.

Import
A good or service purchased from abroad.

The Size of U.S. Trade   The importance of international trade to the U.S. economy is illustrated in Table 16.1, which lists data on **exports** and **imports** of goods and services for selected years. The middle columns, Exports and Imports, show that in recent years U.S. export and import transactions have resulted in the movement of over a trillion dollars in goods and services annually. For example, in 2008 exports and imports amounted to approximately $2.0 and $2.7 trillion, respectively. Notice also that, not surprisingly, the dollar values of exports and imports have grown over the years.

The last two columns of Table 16.1 list exports and imports of goods and services as percentages of gross domestic product (GDP) for each of the selected years. Notice that both exports and imports have generally grown in relative importance

TABLE 16.1					

U.S. Exports and Imports of Goods and Services (Billions of Dollars)

Both the dollar amount of exports and imports, and exports and imports as a percentage of GDP, have increased over the years.

Year	Gross Domestic Product	Exports	Imports	Exports as a Percentage of GDP	Imports as a Percentage of GDP
1970	$ 1,038.5	$ 59.7	$ 55.8	5.7%	5.4%
1975	1,638.3	138.7	122.7	8.5	7.5
1980	2,789.5	280.8	293.8	10.1	10.5
1985	4,220.3	302.0	417.2	7.2	9.9
1990	5,803.1	552.4	630.3	9.5	10.9
1995	7,397.7	812.2	903.6	11.0	12.2
2000	9,817.0	1,096.3	1,475.8	11.2	15.0
2005	12,421.9	1,311.5	2,025.1	10.6	16.3
2006	13,178.4	1,480.8	2,238.1	11.2	17.0
2007	13,807.5	1,662.4	2,370.2	12.0	17.2
2008	14,420.5	1,971.3	2,677.9	13.7	18.6

Source: *Economic Report of the President* (Washington, DC: U.S. Government Printing Office, 2009), pp. 282, 283. The figures for 2008 are preliminary.

when compared to GDP. In 1970 exports were 5.7 percent and imports were 5.4 percent of GDP. By 2008 exports were 13.7 percent of GDP and imports were 18.6 percent. One can conclude from Table 16.1 that foreign trade has become an increasingly important part of the U.S. economy over the years. Notice also the increasing difference between exports and imports as a percentage of GDP.

The Composition of U.S. Trade   What types of goods and services does the United States export and import? Table 16.2 gives the distribution of U.S. merchandise exports and imports by broad product group for selected years. A broad product group is composed of several related types of goods. For example, the foods, feeds, and beverages group includes grains, meat products, vegetables, fish, and wine.[1]

The upper half of the table shows that the most important class of exports has been capital goods, followed by industrial supplies and materials. The capital goods category includes products ranging from oil drilling and metalworking machinery to hospital equipment and civilian aircraft. Industrial supplies and materials includes such things as iron and steel products, fuels and petroleum products, and building materials.[2]

Imports by broad product group are shown in the lower half of Table 16.2. The table shows that capital goods grew and then declined in importance over the period while industrial supplies and materials decreased and then rose in importance. More specific significant imports to the United States in recent years have been electrical machinery, televisions and VCRs, office and automated data processing

---

[1]U.S. Census Bureau, U.S. Bureau of Economic Analysis, *News*, January 12, 2006, p. 10.
[2]Ibid., pp. 10–11.

| TABLE 16.2 | *Percentage Distribution of U.S. Merchandise Exports and Imports by Broad Product Categories* |

U.S. exporting and importing activity primarily involves capital goods and industrial supplies and materials.

	Exports			
Product Group	**1985**	**1995**	**2005**	**2007**
Foods, feeds, and beverages	11.0%	8.6%	6.5%	7.3%
Industrial supplies and materials	26.7	25.0	25.7	27.2
Capital goods, except automotive	33.8	39.8	40.1	38.5
Automotive vehicles, parts, and engines	10.5	10.6	10.9	10.4
Nonfood consumer goods, except automotive	5.8	11.0	12.7	12.6
Other	12.5	5.0	4.1	4.0

	Imports			
Product Group	**1985**	**1995**	**2005**	**2007**
Foods, feeds, and beverages	6.5%	4.5%	4.1%	4.2%
Industrial supplies and materials	33.8	24.5	31.3	32.4
Capital goods, except automotive	19.3	29.8	22.7	22.7
Automotive vehicles, parts, and engines	19.9	16.7	14.3	13.2
Nonfood consumer goods, except automotive	20.3	21.5	24.3	24.3
Other	0.2	3.0	3.3	3.2

Source: *Economic Report of the President* (Washington, DC: U.S. Government Printing Office, 2009), p. 406.

machines, crude oil, vehicles, and clothing.[3] Notice that capital goods and industrial supplies and materials are important both as exports and imports. Why do you think this is the case? Does it suggest something about what is traded or with whom we trade?

One important fact that Table 16.2 conveys is that the relative importance of goods and services in international trade changes over time. For example, in 1985 exports of foods, feeds, and beverages were about twice as large as exports of non-food consumer goods. In 2005, exports of nonfood consumer goods were about twice as large as exports of foods, feeds, and beverages. Obviously, things change over time.

The Geographic Distribution of U.S. Trade   The percentages of U.S. exports to and imports from major U.S. trading partners in 2007 are given in Table 16.3. The majority of U.S. trade is with developed nations in North America, Europe, and Asia, although trade with less developed nations has grown in relative importance over the years.

In terms of specific countries, Canada, Mexico, China, and Japan are the four most important trading partners of the United States. However, several of the other countries listed in the table are part of the European Union, or EU. The 27 member countries of

---

[3]U.S. Bureau of the Census, *Statistical Abstract of the United States: 2006,* 125th ed. (Washington, DC: U.S. Government Printing Office, 2006), p. 839.

TABLE 16.3	The United States' Fifteen Largest Export and Import Trading Partners in 2007

Most of the largest trading partners with the United States are developed nations in North America, Europe, and Asia.

Exports		Imports	
Country	Percent of Total Exports	Country	Percent of Total Imports
Canada	21.4%	China	16.5%
Mexico	11.7	Canada	16.0
China	5.6	Mexico	10.8
Japan	5.4	Japan	7.4
United Kingdom	4.3	Germany	4.8
Germany	4.3	United Kingdom	2.9
South Korea	3.0	South Korea	2.4
Netherlands	2.8	France	2.1
France	2.4	Venezuela	2.0
Taiwan	2.3	Taiwan	2.0
Singapore	2.3	Saudi Arabia	1.8
Belgium	2.2	Italy	1.8
Brazil	2.1	Malaysia	1.7
Hong Kong	1.7	Nigeria	1.7
Australia	1.7	Ireland	1.6
Total, Top 15 Partners	73.1%	Total, Top 15 Partners	75.6%

Source: U.S. Census Bureau, "Top Trading Partners—Total Trade, Exports, Imports, Year-to-Date December 2007," http://www.census.gov/foreign-trade/statistics/highlights/top/top0712.html.

the EU are joined into a single market area and, in many ways, act like a single trading partner. The United Kingdom, Germany, France, Italy, Netherlands, Ireland, and Belgium—all listed on the table—are part of the EU. As a unit, the EU is a leading exporter and importer. [4]

As the globalization of trade expands, more buyers of shoes, shirts, electronics, vitamins, food, and other products are becoming aware of another side of importing low-cost goods to the United States. It has become clear that safety, quality, and labor standards adopted by the United States are not being applied in many cases by foreign producers. In recent years, we have been faced with a pet food scare due to contaminants in ingredients, lead in toys and other consumer products, impurities in drugs, and the use of child labor in many of the factories that produce these cheap goods. Application 16.1, "A Sad Story," deals with one case where a retailer, Gap, discovered the use of child labor in a factory subcontracted through one of its vendors.

[4] The 27 member countries of the EU in 2008 were Austria, Belgium, Bulgaria, Cyprus, the Czech Republic, Denmark, Estonia, Finland, France, Germany, Greece, Hungary, Ireland, Italy, Latvia, Lithuania, Luxembourg, Malta, Netherlands, Poland, Portugal, Romania, Slovakia, Slovenia, Spain, Sweden, and the United Kingdom. In 1992, 12 of these countries formed the European Community, or EC. The name was later changed to the European Union. See European Union Member State Office in the United States, http://www.eurunion.org/states/offices.htm.

APPLICATION 16.1

A SAD STORY

More and more, goods and services sold by U.S. companies are produced outside of the United States: from Nike shoes produced in factories around the world to help with your computer problems from a technician in India. But as foreign-produced goods account for more of our purchases, there is growing concern over the working conditions endured by many of those producing these goods. When reading about these conditions, one frequently comes across terms such as sweatshop and human trafficking.

In 2007, the clothing retailer Gap found that one of its products—some hand-stitched blouses—was being sewn by child labor in a New Delhi, India, sweatshop with squalid conditions. A British newspaper reported that some of the children were as young as 10, worked for 16 hours a day, and were punished with hits from a rubber pipe or by having oily rags stuffed in their mouths.

One young boy said, "I was bought from my parents' village in [the northern state of] Bihar and taken to New Delhi by train. The men came looking for us in July. They had loudspeakers in the back of a car and told my parents that if they sent me to work in the city, they won't have to work in the farms. My father was paid a fee for me, and I was brought down with 40 other children."

U.S. companies that subcontract work to foreign vendors have tried to monitor operations. In this case, the work was further subcontracted in violation of Gap's policies.

Gap was obviously embarrassed, and its response to this situation was immediate. It promised that none of the garments would ever be sold, ensured that the children were cared for and reunited with their families, reduced the contract of the vendor responsible for the subcontract, made a grant toward improving working conditions in India, and partnered with other organizations to help monitor the kind of work done in more informal settings, such as beadwork.

"We strictly prohibit the use of child labor," said Marka Hansen, Gap North America president. "In 2006, Gap Inc. ceased business with 23 factories due to code violations. We have 90 people located around the world whose job is to ensure compliance with our Code of Vendor Conduct."

In addition to Gap, the company brands include Banana Republic, Old Navy, and Piperlime. Gap Inc. has more than 3,000 retail stores and uses factories in about 50 countries. Gap employs 90 full-time factory inspectors. In 2006 Gap conducted about 4,300 inspections in more than 2,000 garment factories.

Sources: Gap Inc., Update: Combating Child Labor in the Garment Industry, June 12, 2008, www.Gapinc.com; "Gap: Report of kids' sweatshop 'deeply disturbing'," October 29, 2007, http://www.cnn.com/2007/WORLD/asiapcf/10/29/gap.labor/index.html; "The Gap Caps Work With Child Labor Vendor," November, 15, 2007, http://www.cbsnews.com/stories/2007/11/15/business/main3505020.shtml?source=RSSattr . . . ; "The Gap Falls Into Child Labor Controversy," October, 29, 2007, http://www.cbsnews.com/stories/2007/10/29/business/main3422618.shtml?source+RSSattr. . . .

COMPARATIVE ADVANTAGE AND INTERNATIONAL TRADE

Scarcity and Specialization

As we have seen from the very beginning, the study of economics is rooted in scarcity: The resources necessary to produce goods and services are scarce relative to the material wants and needs those goods and services satisfy. One way to lessen the scarcity problem is through increases in production gained by specialization.

Specialization occurs when productive resources concentrate on a narrow range of tasks or on the production of a limited variety of goods and services. The concept applies to all factors of production but is most often associated with individuals and locations. For example, a doctor may specialize in cardiovascular surgery, a student may select economics as her major, and northern California is known for its wine production.

Specialization permits greater levels of production than would be attained without it. By concentrating on one productive activity, a resource can be used more efficiently—and greater efficiency results in greater output without raising costs.

Specialization
Productive resources concentrate on a narrow range of tasks or the production of a limited variety of goods and services.

TABLE 16.4	*Production Possibilities from 1 Unit of Resources*

The United States and Japan have a choice of producing either corn or high-definition television sets when employing 1 unit of resources.

Country	Production Possibilities
United States	10 tons of corn or 1 HDTV
Japan	1 ton of corn or 10 HDTVs

Specialization, however, depends on the ability to sell what one produces and buy what one needs from someone else, or on the ability to trade. Thus, access to appropriate markets where trade can take place is a prerequisite to specialization.

Specialization occurs on an international level when countries concentrate their productive efforts on the goods and services they are best at producing and trade for the goods and services that are most costly to produce. A country that has a relatively inexpensive labor force might specialize in producing goods requiring substantial labor inputs, a country with good agricultural resources might concentrate on growing crops or on livestock, and a country possessing technologically advanced equipment and production methods might use these to its benefit. When each country concentrates on what it does more efficiently than other countries, international specialization increases total production and lessens the scarcity problem on a global level.

The Principle of Comparative Advantage

Comparative Advantage
One country has a lower opportunity cost when producing a good or service than does another country.

International trade can lessen the scarcity problem if each country produces and trades on the basis of its comparative advantage. **Comparative advantage** is practiced when a country produces those goods and services for which it has a cost advantage in comparison to other countries and trades for what it is less adept at producing. If countries produce and trade on the basis of their comparative advantages, the world will have more goods and services than it otherwise would. In essence, the principle of comparative advantage is a restatement of the benefits of international specialization.

A country has a comparative advantage in the production of a good or service when the opportunity cost of producing that item is less in that country than in another country. Fewer goods or services are given up to produce a unit of a particular item in the country with the comparative advantage than in another country.

To illustrate how comparative advantage works, and how it results in overall gains in output, let us examine a simple hypothetical production and trade relationship between the United States and Japan.

Assume that with 1 unit of resources (where 1 unit is equal to a defined combination of land, labor, capital, and entrepreneurship), the United States can produce either 10 tons of corn or 1 high-definition television set. Assume further that with 1 unit of resources Japan can produce either 1 ton of corn or 10 high-definition television sets. Table 16.4 illustrates these production possibilities.

The comparative advantage of each country in this example is obvious: The United States has the advantage in corn, and Japan in television sets. This can be verified by comparing the opportunity costs in each country.

TABLE 16.5	*Production from 2 Units of Resources per Country without Specialization*

When the United States and Japan both produce corn and high-definition television sets with 2 units of resources each, 11 tons of corn and 11 television sets can be produced.

Item	Amount of Production
Corn	10 tons (U.S.) + 1 ton (Japan) = 11 tons total production
Television sets	1 HDTV (U.S.) + 10 HDTVs (Japan) = 11 HDTVs total production

The opportunity cost (measured in forgone television sets) of producing 10 tons of corn in the United States is just 1 television set, while the opportunity cost of producing 10 tons of corn in Japan is 100 television sets. This gives the United States the comparative advantage in corn because its opportunity cost of producing corn is lower. The opportunity cost of producing 1 television set in the United States is 10 tons of corn, whereas in Japan producing 1 television set would mean giving up only one-tenth of a ton of corn. The opportunity cost of producing a television set is lower in Japan, giving Japan the comparative advantage in television sets.

Gains from Specialization and Trade   Let us continue the corn and television example to illustrate why the world would be better off in terms of the amounts of goods and services produced if comparative advantage and trade were exercised. Assume now that the United States has 2 units of resources to employ and uses 1 unit for the production of corn and 1 unit for the production of television sets. In this case, the United States will produce 10 tons of corn and 1 television set. Assume further that Japan also has 2 units of resources to employ and also uses 1 unit for the production of corn and 1 unit for television sets. In this case Japan will produce 1 ton of corn and 10 television sets. With resources employed in this way, total production of these items by these two countries is 11 tons of corn and 11 television sets. This is shown in Table 16.5.

Now assume that Japan and the United States each decides to devote its productive resources to the good in which it has the comparative advantage and to engage in international trade. The United States will now devote its 2 units of resources to corn production, resulting in 20 tons of corn instead of 10 tons of corn and 1 television set. With Japan's 2 units of resources, it will now produce 20 television sets instead of 10 television sets and 1 ton of corn. Table 16.6 summarizes the resulting production when each country specializes its production based on its comparative advantage.

The increased total production registered in Table 16.6 (as compared to the numbers in Table 16.5) demonstrates the benefits of specialization and trade. Without

TABLE 16.6	*Production from 2 Units of Resources per Country with Specialization*

When countries devote their resources to producing goods in which they have a comparative advantage, the total production of these goods increases.

Item	Amount of Production
Corn	20 tons (U.S.) + 0 ton (Japan) = 20 tons total production
Television sets	0 HDTVs (U.S.) + 20 HDTVs (Japan) = 20 HDTVs total production

TEST YOUR UNDERSTANDING

COMPARATIVE ADVANTAGE

1. Assume that Canada can produce 8 tons of wheat or 4 tons of soybeans with 1 unit of resources and that Brazil can produce 4 tons of wheat or 8 tons of soybeans with 1 unit of resources.
    a. The opportunity cost to Canada of producing 1 ton of wheat is _____ tons of soybeans, and the opportunity cost to Brazil of producing 1 ton of wheat is _____ tons of soybeans. The country with the comparative advantage in wheat is _____.
    b. The opportunity cost to Canada of producing 1 ton of soybeans is _____ tons of wheat, and the opportunity cost to Brazil of producing 1 ton of soybeans is _____ tons of wheat. The country with the comparative advantage in soybeans is _____.
    c. If Canada and Brazil each has 2 units of resources, and each uses 1 unit for the production of wheat and the other for the production of soybeans, together they will produce _____ tons of wheat and _____ tons of soybeans.
    d. If each country uses its 2 units of resources to produce the crop in which it has the comparative advantage, Canada will produce _____ tons of _____ and Brazil will produce _____ tons of _____.
    e. If, for political or other reasons, each country uses its 2 units of resources to produce the crop in which it does *not* have the comparative

advantage, together they will produce _____ tons of wheat and _____ tons of soybeans.

2. Assume that Mexico can produce 500 lamps or 100 gallons of gasoline with 1 unit of resources and that Venezuela can produce 25 lamps or 100 gallons of gasoline with 1 unit of resources.
    a. The opportunity cost to Mexico of producing 1 lamp is _____ gallons of gasoline, and the opportunity cost to Venezuela of producing 1 lamp is _____ gallons of gasoline. The country with the comparative advantage in lamps is _____.
    b. The opportunity cost to Mexico of producing 1 gallon of gasoline is _____ lamps, and the opportunity cost to Venezuela of producing 1 gallon of gasoline is _____ lamps. The country with the comparative advantage in gasoline is _____.
    c. If Mexico and Venezuela each has 2 units of resources, and each uses 1 unit for the production of lamps and the other for the production of gasoline, together they will produce _____ lamps and _____ gallons of gasoline.
    d. If each country uses its 2 units of resources to produce the good in which it has the comparative advantage, Mexico will produce _____ (of) _____ and Venezuela will produce _____ (of) _____.
    e. If, for political or other reasons, each country uses its 2 units of resources to produce the good in which it does *not* have the comparative advantage, together they will produce _____ lamps and _____ gallons of gasoline.

Answers can be found at the back of the book.

international specialization, a total of 11 tons of corn and 11 television sets can be produced by both countries together. With production based on comparative advantage, Japan and the United States can together produce a total of 20 tons of corn and 20 television sets using the same amount of resources. Clearly, the scarcity problem can be lessened through the exercise of comparative advantage and trade.

Does the principle of comparative advantage work in the real world? How closely is it followed? In order to fully exercise comparative advantage and reap its benefits, an environment of free trade is necessary. **Free trade** occurs when goods and services can be bought and sold by anyone in any country with no restrictions. Everyone is free to choose with whom he or she deals, regardless of location, and there are no barriers to trade. Import taxes are not imposed to artificially raise prices and discourage purchases, and limits are not set on the amounts that can be bought and sold. This free flow of trade permits specialization to work to its fullest. You can check your grasp of the material in this section by answering the questions in Test Your Understanding, "Comparative Advantage."

Free Trade
Goods and services can be exported and imported by anyone in any country with no restrictions.

FREE TRADE AND PROTECTIONISM

In practice, countries often impose restrictions that impede the international flow of goods and services. Such policies, despite the fact that they may reduce a country's ability to fully exploit its various comparative advantages, are generally justified on the grounds that they are in the best interest of the nation that is imposing them.

Protectionism

The philosophy that it is in the best interest of a country to restrict free trade.

The philosophy that it is in a country's best interest to restrict free trade is known as **protectionism.** According to the protectionist viewpoint, unrestricted importing and/or exporting may lead to economic and noneconomic consequences injurious to the economy as a whole, to certain groups within the economy such as workers in particular industries, and/or to national security. Because of these potentially adverse effects, protectionists argue for restrictions on international trade.

Protectionist policies can be employed in varying degrees: A nation may choose to have detailed regulations or loose restrictions. Also, a nation may alter the degree to which it relies on protectionist policies as economic and noneconomic conditions change.

The merits of free trade and protectionism have been debated for hundreds of years. (See the Critical Thinking Case at the end of this chapter, "A Petition by Frederic Bastiat, 1801–1850," which excerpts a satirical protectionist plea from the early 1800s.) In light of this debate, it is useful to know some arguments on both sides of the issue in order to better form your own opinions. But before introducing the cases for free trade and for protectionism, we will examine the different types of trade-restricting policies that a country may employ.

Trade-Restricting Policies

Three basic policies have traditionally been used to restrict trade: tariffs, quotas, and embargoes. In addition to these, some countries have developed more subtle measures to discourage trade, such as setting very high product standards or an overwhelming number of bureaucratic steps to import a product.

Tariff

A tax on an import.

A **tariff** is a tax placed on an import. Tariffs have the effect of raising import prices to domestic buyers, thereby making foreign goods less attractive. This reduces the quantities of imports demanded and makes it easier for domestic producers to sell their own products.

Examples of tariffs on goods entering the United States are given in Table 16.7. The columns to the right classify nations into three categories for tariff purposes. The column headed General is for nations whose products are not imported under any preferential tariff treatment. Countries such as England, France, and Japan fall into this category. The column headed Special is for nations whose products are imported at reduced tariff rates under special programs, and the rates differ with each program. The rates shown here are for products imported from Mexico under the North American Free Trade Agreement (NAFTA). Other examples of special programs are the Automotive Products Trade Act and the Generalized System of Preferences, which allows developing nations such as Belize and Nepal to sell to the United States at reduced tariff rates or tariff-free. Finally, the column headed Designated Countries is for a short list of nations such as Cuba, Laos, and North Korea.[5]

Table 16.7 illustrates that tariffs can be expressed in dollar terms, as a percentage of the value of the imported product, or as both, and that they differ according to the

---

[5]U.S. International Trade Commission, *Harmonized Tariff Schedule of the United States (2005)* (Washington, DC: U.S. Government Printing Office, 2005), General Notes, pp. GN 6, 7, 11.

TABLE 16.7	*Tariffs for Selected Goods*

Tariffs, which raise the prices of imported goods to domestic buyers, can be expressed in dollar terms, as a percentage of the value of the imported good, or as both a dollar amount and a percentage.

Item	TARIFF General	Special	Designated Countries
Smoked salmon	5.0% of value	Free	25.0% of value
Cheddar cheese	10.0% of value	Free	35.0% of value
Orange juice	$0.045 per liter	$0.0106 per liter	$0.18 per liter
Men's wool suits	$0.388 per kilo + 10% of value	Free	$0.772 per kilo + 54.5% of value
Women's wool dresses	13.6% of value	Free	54.5% of value
Footwear incorporating protective metal toecaps	37.5% of value	7.5% of value	75.0% of value
Upright pianos	4.7% of value	Free	40% of value
Pistols designed to fire only blank ammunition	4.2% of value	Free	105.0% of value
Cotton mattresses	3.0% of value	Free	40.0% of value

Source: U.S. International Trade Commission, *Harmonized Tariff Schedule of the United States (2005)* (Washington, DC: U.S. Government Printing Office, 2005), pp. 1–4, 3–11, 4–28, 22–4, 61–6, 61–26, 64–3, 92–2, 93–3, 94–5.

three country categories. Designated countries pay the highest tariffs, while countries that receive special treatment pay the lowest or, in some cases, no tariff at all.

Quota
A restriction on the quantity of an item that can be imported into a country.

Quotas are restrictions on the quantities of various goods that can be imported into a country. For example, a country may impose a quota allowing only 10 million bushels of wheat to be imported from another country over a 1-year period. Once that amount is reached, no more wheat can flow in from the other country for the remainder of the year. A quota, like a tariff, restricts the ability of foreign goods to compete with domestic goods.

Embargo
A ban on trade in a particular commodity or with a particular country.

An **embargo** is an outright ban on trade in a particular commodity or with a particular nation. For example, the United States and other United Nations member countries imposed embargoes on exports to Iraq in 1990 and to Haiti in 1993 and 1994. These embargoes were imposed for noneconomic reasons: to sanction Iraq in an effort to prompt its withdrawal from Kuwait and to sanction a military government in Haiti in order to restore that country's exiled president. More recently, some trade sanctions have been imposed on Iran and North Korea.[6]

Free Trade Arguments

Arguments favoring unrestricted international trade center on the ability of free trade to increase economic efficiency, provide a source of competition, and increase the availability of goods while lowering their prices.

---

[6]U.S. Department of the Treasury, Office of Foreign Assets Control, "OFAC Country Sanctions Programs," http://www.treas.gov/offices/enforcement/OFAC/programs/.

Trade, Specialization, and Efficiency   Free trade permits the markets in which goods and services are bought and sold to expand, and the possibility of additional sales from expanded markets makes it feasible for resources to specialize in narrower ranges of tasks. In turn, this specialization allows resources to be used more efficiently than would otherwise be the case.

By using resources more efficiently, more goods and services can be produced, lessening the scarcity problem. This was illustrated earlier in the corn and television set example used to explain the principle of comparative advantage.

Increased Competition, Availability of Goods, and Lower Prices   Another argument in favor of free trade is that it increases competition in markets. Competition leads to benefits for consumers: There are larger quantities of goods from which to choose, and prices tend to be lower.

Recall the material in Chapter 3 that deals with supply and demand. An increase in supply will lower prices in a competitive market. And, in Chapter 13 we learned that as the number of sellers increases in a market, the ability of an individual firm to exercise monopoly power over price and output decreases, and price moves more toward cost. Thus, with foreign competitors in a market, domestic sellers are in less of a position to extract monopoly profits.

With free trade, the absence of tariffs benefits the consumer by making foreign goods available at lower prices. In addition, removing quotas has the obvious effect of increasing the amounts of goods available for sale.

In the arguments for free trade, the major beneficiary is the consumer. This is not the case with the arguments for protectionism.

Protectionist Arguments

The main thrust of the protectionist arguments is that, for either economic or noneconomic reasons, it is in the best interest of a nation to place restrictions on imports. The major protectionist arguments center on protection of industries and employment, diversification, and national security.

Infant Industry
An industry in the early stage of its development.

Protection of Infant Industries and Domestic Employment and Output   An **infant industry** is one in the early stage of its development. Technology, new resources, or innovations, for example, can spawn an industry new to an economy. In the early stages of an infant industry, strong competitive pressures from established foreign producers might destroy a prospect for growth. Protectionists argue that it is appropriate to impose trade restrictions to allow the newly forming domestic industry to establish itself.

Protectionists also argue that it is appropriate to protect a domestic industry when the availability of foreign goods would lead to lower domestic output and higher domestic unemployment. In this case, the protectionist point of view is to impose trade restrictions that would make it difficult, or impossible, for foreign goods to compete. Support for this argument frequently comes from both manufacturers and labor organizations in specific industries facing strong foreign competition.

Diversification   The protectionist argument for diversification is based on the potential risks in developing a dependency on foreign-produced goods because changes in the prices or availabilities of those goods could lead to serious economic disruptions at home. A striking example of this problem is the continuing concern over the U.S. dependency on foreign oil. Huge price increases from time to time have caused some issues in the economy.

Protectionists argue that a country should not specialize to the point where it develops critical dependencies on foreign products. Instead, domestic production should be diversified so that there are feasible alternatives to foreign-produced goods.

National Security   For a variety of reasons, arguments have been put forward to impose tariffs, quotas, and embargoes in the name of national security. These reasons include the need to develop strong domestic defense-related industries and the need to diversify in anticipation of interruptions of foreign supplies resulting from military or economic aggression or some other type of international hostility.

It is up to you to decide which of these free-trade and protectionist arguments has greater merit than the others. Application 16.2, "Gloria Flunks the Professor," presents an interesting scenario of the free-trade and protectionism debate. How many of the arguments that were just introduced can you find? How does the application illustrate that a person's position on this issue can be colored by both philosophical commitment and personal interest?

The Real World of International Trade

Most countries do not choose a strict free trade or protectionist philosophy and then adhere only to policies aligned with that philosophy. Instead, these two philosophies are the extremes toward which a country may lean. A country may adopt a comprehensive trade policy based on the principles of free trade or protectionism, or it may adopt more liberal terms of trade with some of its favored trading partners and restrict trade with other countries. Recall from Table 16.7 that the United States gives preferential tariff treatment to goods imported from Mexico and imposes higher-than-average tariffs on goods coming in from Laos.

A country's policies concerning international trade tend to shift with changing political and economic conditions. During a recession or economic downswing, a country's mood tends to become protectionist, resulting in a greater tendency to raise tariff barriers than is the case during a period of economic growth. The Smoot-Hawley Tariff, which was passed in 1930 at the beginning of the Great Depression, raised U.S. tariff rates to some of their highest levels.

Trade Subsidy
A government payment to the domestic producer of an exported good.

Instead of restricting trade, a country will sometimes adopt policies, such as **trade subsidies,** to promote the export of a domestically produced good. For example, if the United States decided that it wanted to encourage foreign purchases of its domestically produced pianos, it could offer domestic piano manufacturers a subsidy, or payment, for each piano sold abroad—which would allow the manufacturers to lower their prices on the pianos and still make a profit. This policy, which might be considered unfair by foreign piano makers, would be useful if the United States wanted to increase its share of the world piano market.

Dumping
Selling a product in a foreign market below cost or below its price in its own domestic market.

On occasion a country has been accused of **dumping** its products in foreign markets. This occurs when a good is sold in a foreign market below its actual cost or below the price at which it is sold in its own domestic market. Countries pursue this policy to eliminate excess production or to gain a greater share of a foreign market.

In the interdependent world of foreign trade, a change in a country's trade philosophy, tariffs, quotas, embargoes, subsidies, or dumping may cause retaliation by a trading partner. And there is always the danger that changing policies and retaliations will result in a trade war. When a trade war breaks out, the benefits of specialization on an international basis are jeopardized. No one seems to benefit.

APPLICATION 16.2

GLORIA FLUNKS THE PROFESSOR

It's not easy to be an economist these days. It used to be enough to have a theory with a good, positive name: like Free Trade. Now people actually expect you to understand the real world. . . .

Take last night. I'm having a quiet drink with Professor Dyzmil. He teaches economics at our local university. In sails Larry [who] announces that he just bought a new Honda—top of the line, all the extras. People around the bar mutter, "Wow," "Great," and so forth. Gloria [the bartender] just keeps pouring drinks.

Finally she says: "I think it's a shame to buy a foreign car when there's so much unemployment in our own auto industry."

"Hey," says Larry, "What am I supposed to buy? . . . Anyway, one car isn't going to make all that much difference to Detroit."

"I know" Gloria sighs, "but it seems like somebody ought to be doing something to protect our people from all these imports."

"Protect *our* people? *Your* people maybe," says Larry. "I think it's awfully nationalistic to worry about protecting American autoworkers. My lifestyle is international. Whoever makes the most interesting, least expensive products gets my business." . . .

["Besides,] protectionism is bad for the economy. Isn't that right, professor?"

"Absolutely," says Dyzmil, solemnly. "Quotas and tariffs and other devices to keep out foreign goods raise domestic prices. As a result, the consumer pays more."

"So what?" says Gloria. "Wouldn't it be worth it if it saved jobs here? . . . "

Seems like a good point, but the professor isn't impressed. "Very superficial analysis," he says sternly. "The real problem is that protecting U.S. industries will make them less competitive. Having to compete with foreign goods keeps you on your toes, makes you more conscious of quality and price, more responsive to the needs of the customer. Protectionism makes an industry lazy and inefficient." . . .

"By that logic," muses Gloria, "the answer to Japanese imports is to open up our markets to even more imports so our industries will be more efficient. That doesn't make sense."

"It's true that the U.S. is already pretty much of an open market," says the professor. "What we need to do is to get other countries to open their economies to free trade."

"Like?"

"Like Japan," the professor replies. "Japan is notoriously protectionist. They have an intricate system of rules and regulations and quotas that keep foreign goods out." . . .

"But if free trade makes a country more competitive and protectionism makes a country less competitive . . . "

"Yes," he nods encouragingly.

"And the Japanese markets are protected and ours are open. . . . Then how come the Japanese are so competitive and we're so uncompetitive?"

"Well . . . uh . . .," stammers Dyzmil, "it's very complicated. For one thing, there are cultural differences. . . . [T]he Japanese work together better. They work more as a unit, as a community. . . ."

"Doesn't sound bad," says Gloria. "Maybe we ought to try some of that here."

"No, my dear," Dyzmil says, shaking his head. "Americans don't like to do things collectively. We thrive on the excitement of competition between individuals."

"Real exciting to be out of work," says Gloria, dryly. "A lot of people *aren't* exactly thriving."

"Not to worry," the professor says. "Our old industries are adjusting. And free trade is helping. . . . Old jobs have to die, Gloria. Just like old people. It's a law of economic nature. Jobs will open up in new industries."

"But aren't imports also taking over the new industries? VCRs are the hottest new item around. I read somewhere that the Japanese made 27 million last year and we made zero."

"Not to worry," Dyzmil assures her. "Even if they do take our manufacturing, Americans excel at services."

"Like laundry?"

"No. Like banking, advertising, computer software."

"But it stands to reason that Japanese businesses will use *Japanese* banks and advertising agencies. So as they expand their industry, they'll expand their services too. If they make the computers, won't they eventually make the software?". . . "Anyway," she continues, "how many laid off autoworkers are going to get a job in a bank or advertising?". . .

I can see that the professor is getting annoyed at having to defend free trade. . . . After all, in the hierarchy of economic principles, free trade ranks above the law of gravity.

"Look, Gloria," says the exasperated scholar, "there are plenty of other places Americans can work. In bars and restaurants, for example. Granted, the jobs pay less.". . .

"Ok," says Gloria suddenly, "You've convinced me, but I don't think you've gone far enough with your free trade idea."

"How's that?"

"Why not extend free trade to economics professors? Maybe the reason that the Japanese economy is better is because Japanese *economists* are better. So if we got rid of tenure in our universities, we might import some Japanese economists who could show us how to create more jobs by working together."

"My dear Gloria," says the stunned professor, . . . "if America exported its economists, who would be left to defend free trade?"

Source: Jeff Faux, "Gloria Flunks the Professor," *Mother Jones* (October, 1985), pp. 50–51, © 1985, Foundation for National Progress.

Trade Agreements among Nations   Since World War II, world trade has been carried out in a relatively liberal environment, thanks to greater international cooperation to reduce tariffs and the work of organizations that facilitate the trading process. For example, the **International Monetary Fund (IMF)** provides loans and other financial assistance to nations seeking to improve their competitiveness in world trade. Tariff reductions have occurred in large part as a result of the **General Agreement on Tariffs and Trade (GATT),** under which countries held their first round of talks in 1947. Since then, there have been several rounds of negotiations, each leading to lower tariff rates.

Three landmark trade agreements were negotiated in the early 1990s. In 1992, 12 Western European nations formally joined together as the European Community, or EC. This alliance now includes 27 members with others seeking admission and is called the **European Union, or EU,** which was introduced earlier in the chapter. The goal of the EU is to create a trading area within which no national barriers slow the movement of people, capital, or goods and services. The EU represents a major world trading power: While less than one-half the size of the United States, in 2008 the combined population of its member countries was larger than the population of the United States.[7]

In 1994, the **North American Free Trade Agreement, or NAFTA,** was put in place. This trade agreement among the United States, Canada, and Mexico removed many barriers to trade and investment in these three countries. One of the effects of NAFTA has been the establishment of businesses in Mexico along the border with the United States that tend to import inputs from the United States, process them with cheaper labor, and return the finished products to the United States as exports. While there is evidence that the Mexican economy has benefited from this trade agreement, NAFTA continues to be a source of debate over many issues such as labor conditions and rights, the environment, and unions in the United States.[8]

The third important agreement was the approval in 1993 of the Uruguay Round of GATT negotiations. This treaty reduced tariff and other trade barriers, involved more than 100 nations, and took years to complete. The trade rules agreed to at the Uruguay Round are implemented by the **World Trade Organization (WTO),** which was founded in 1995 to take over the responsibilities of GATT.

The WTO is a forum for countries to sort out trade issues and negotiate trade rules. These trade rules, or WTO agreements, provide some legal ground rules for international commerce. The WTO also works to settle trade disputes. In 2008, there were more than 150 members of the WTO. In addition to trade in goods, the WTO covers trade in services, inventions, and designs.[9]

In 2004, another regional trade agreement, the Central America–Dominican Republic–United States Free Trade Agreement, or CAFTA, was signed. The six CAFTA partners have worked to eliminate trade barriers and expand trade opportunities among themselves. By 2006, there was increased trade with the United States and within the Central American countries.[10]

International Monetary Fund (IMF)
An international organization that provides loans and other financial assistance to countries.

General Agreement on Tariffs and Trade (GATT)
An international forum for negotiating tariffs.

European Union (EU)
The single unified market formed by the majority of Western European nations; a major trading power.

North American Free Trade Agreement (NAFTA)
The treaty creating a unified market involving the United States, Canada, and Mexico.

World Trade Organization (WTO)
An organization founded in 1995 to take over the responsibilities of GATT.

[7]U.S. Central Intelligence Agency, *CIA—The World Factbook–European Union,* http://www.cia.gov/cia/publications/the-world-factbook/geos/ee.html.
[8]Jeff Fugate, "A Recipe for Success," *Yale Economic Review,* http://www.yaleeconomicreview.com/spring2005/nafta.php.
[9]World Trade Organization, "Understanding the WTO—What Is the World Trade Organization ?," http://www.wto.org/english/thewto_e/whatis_e/tif_e/fact1_e.htm.
[10]Office of the United States Trade Representative, "CAFTA—DR Final Text," and CAFTA Policy Brief, July 2007, "U.S. Trade with the CAFTA-DR Countries,"www.ustr.gov.

UP FOR DEBATE

SHOULD TRADE BE RESTRICTED IF IT RESULTS IN ENVIRONMENTAL DAMAGE?

Issue   *During the past few decades, we have become quite aware of the impact on the global environment from the production and consumption of goods and services by people throughout the world. We know that overharvesting trees, emitting carbon in the air and toxins in streams, and even pursuing some fishing practices can destroy air and water quality, tilt our delicate ecological balance, and ruin habitats and species. Global warming, a serious environmental concern, is a relatively new phrase in our vocabulary.*

It is apparent that some environmental destruction occurs because of international trade: The ability to participate in a large global market can spur on production habits that are unfriendly to the environment. The capacity to sell cheap wood, clothing, and food all over the globe, rather than solely in home markets, contributes to these destructive practices. So, the question to ponder is: Should trade in a particular product be banned if its production causes environmental damage?

Yes   We are more aware than ever that responsibility for the environment is a global concern that takes global action. Air and water quality destruction isn't isolated to a country: The practices of one country can affect another a half a globe away. It is appropriate and necessary that sustainability of the planet be a key component of international trading relationships.

International trade agreements can be vehicles for creating environmental standards of production. They are powerful tools to mandate countries to adopt environmentally safe production practices. If countries like China had to cut toxic air emissions or had to find production methods that ensure safe water quality to be able to trade globally, you can be sure that this would get done.

Furthermore, economic development can be an additional positive impact from agreements that force countries to adopt "green" practices. New technology, industries, and jobs can and do come with new environmental practices.

NO   Banning trade because of environmental issues would be just another excuse to move toward protectionism. Banning trade hurts consumers because of less competition, fewer products, and higher prices. Just think about the higher prices on clothing in the United States that would result if some of the global factories that produce it were closed.

There are already about 200 international agreements dealing with environmental issues—called multilateral environmental agreements (MEAs)—now in place.[a] These are more effective and expedient for nations to deal with each other than to create a wholesale ban on a product.

Trade agreements can be difficult to create and enforce. The environment is just another feature to add to the difficulty. And, countries differ in their standards. The United States, for example, might want to set standards so high that it hurts employment and production in another country. Can countries really dictate environmental standards for other countries?

[a]World Trade Organization, "Understanding the WTO—The environment: a new high profile," http://www.wto.org/english/thewto_e/whatis_e/tif_e/bey2_e.htm.

Gaining consensus on a unified trading program like the EU, NAFTA, or WTO is not easy. Controversy is to be expected when a new treaty changes the economic relations among countries and the economic security of individuals and groups within those countries. In addition, as the world becomes more aware of threats to the environment from the production and consumption of goods and services, there is an added dimension to trade relationships: the issue of whether environmental protection should become part of future trade negotiations. Up for Debate, "Should Trade Be Restricted if It Results in Environmental Damage?", briefly tackles this thorny and complicated issue. What is your position in this debate?

Summary

1. International economics deals with the economic relationships among countries. International trade is concerned with the exporting and importing of goods and services and is important because it affects production, employment, and prices in the trading countries.

2. In the United States, international trade has grown over the years. The largest classes of U.S. exports and imports are capital goods, and industrial supplies and materials. Most U.S. trade is with developed countries in Asia, Europe, and North America, particularly China, Japan, Canada, Mexico, and the European Union.

3. Specialization occurs when resources concentrate on a narrow range of tasks or on the production of a limited variety of goods and services. It permits greater efficiency and larger levels of output than would otherwise be the case.

4. Specialization on an international scale is based on the principle of comparative advantage. A country has a comparative advantage when the opportunity cost of producing a good or service is less in that country than in another. Specialization based on comparative advantage and international trade can increase overall production levels and lessen the scarcity problem. An environment of free trade is necessary for comparative advantage to be fully exercised.

5. Free trade occurs when there are no restrictions on the flow of international trade. The alternative to free trade is protectionism, which is based on the argument that restricted trade is in the best interest of a country. Protectionist policies include tariffs, which are taxes on imports; quotas, which are quantity limits on imports; and embargoes, which are outright bans on trading a product or on trade in general.

6. The arguments for free trade center on the production gains and efficiencies to be obtained from comparative advantage, the increased availability of goods and services for consumers, and the lower prices and other benefits resulting from more competition in markets.

7. The protectionist arguments for trade restrictions include the need to protect infant industries and domestic output and employment, to diversify in case of economic disruptions, and to protect national security. The United States has reverted to protectionist policies at different times in its history.

8. In addition to trade-restricting policies, a nation can seek to increase its foreign sales through the use of subsidies and dumping. International agreements, such as the General Agreement on Tariffs and Trade, the agreements creating the European Union, and the North American Free Trade Agreement, have a significant effect on world trade.

Key Terms and Concepts

International trade	Free trade arguments
Export	Protectionist arguments
Import	Infant industry
U.S. trading partners	Trade subsidy
Specialization	Dumping
Comparative advantage	International Monetary Fund (IMF)
Free trade	General Agreement on Tariffs and Trade (GATT)
Protectionism	European Union (EU)
Tariff	North American Free Trade Agreement (NAFTA)
Quota	
Embargo	World Trade Organization (WTO)

Review Questions

1. Explain how international trade can affect a country's levels of production, employment, and prices.

2. What have been the main export and import categories for the United States in recent years, and who are the primary trading partners of the United States?

3. "Comparative advantage is the application of specialization on an international level." What is meant by this statement? Define comparative advantage and explain how it lessens the basic scarcity problem.

4. With 1 unit of resources, China could produce either 2 tons of wheat or 4 tons of rice, and Hungary could produce either 4 tons of wheat or 4 tons of rice. What is China's opportunity cost of 1 ton of wheat and of 1 ton of rice? What is Hungary's opportunity cost of 1 ton of wheat and of 1 ton of rice? Which country has the comparative advantage in wheat? Which country has the advantage in rice?

5. Given the information in Question 4, how much wheat and rice would be produced if each country had 2 units of resources and devoted 1 unit to the production of wheat and 1 unit to the production of rice? If each country used both units to produce the item in which it has a comparative advantage, how much wheat and rice would be produced?

6. Differentiate among a tariff, a quota, an embargo, a subsidy, and dumping. Explain how each affects trade.

7. Summarize the arguments for free trade and for protectionism.

8. What are the International Monetary Fund (IMF), General Agreement on Tariffs and Trade (GATT), European Union (EU), North American Free Trade Agreement (NAFTA), and World Trade Organization (WTO)? What are the EU and NAFTA countries trying to accomplish?

Discussion Questions

1. Over the past few decades, both exports and imports have grown as a percentage of GDP in the United States.
   a. What effect would an increase in exports have on the level of unemployment and the level of prices in the United States if the economy were operating far below full employment?
   b. What effect would an increase in imports have on the level of unemployment and the level of prices in the United States if the economy were operating at full employment?
   c. What effect would dumping a U.S.-produced good in a foreign country have on employment in the United States if that country responded by dumping one of its goods in U.S. markets?

2. International trade must occur in free markets if countries' comparative advantages are to be fully exploited. Why is this so? If the United States produced according to its comparative advantage, in what goods and services do you think it would specialize?

3. The level of tariffs on foreign-produced cars is a source of continual debate in the United States. What is the current tariff status of automobiles imported from Japan, Germany, and South Korea? Would you favor increasing or decreasing these tariffs? Why?

4. Some people favor free trade while others favor protectionism. This suggests that some groups gain from free trade while others gain from protectionism. Who gains and who loses from free trade and from protectionism? What is your position on free trade and protectionism, and why do you hold this point of view?

5. Protectionists argue that putting a tariff on a good protects a domestic industry's output and employment. Others argue that the country hurt by the tariff may retaliate by restricting trade from the country imposing the tariff. The result could be a loss of output and employment in an exporting industry of the country that initiated the tariff action. Comment.

6. There were strong opinions supporting and opposing the passage of NAFTA. What groups would you expect to favor an agreement such as this, and what groups would you expect to oppose it?

7. The EU, NAFTA, and CAFTA have eased trade among European countries; among the United States, Mexico, and Canada; and among the United States and Central American countries, respectively. Do you see these developments easing trade worldwide or leading to the growth of "trade blocs" that are virtually impossible for traders from other countries to enter?

Critical Thinking Case 16

A PETITION (BY FREDERIC BASTIAT, 1801–1850)

Critical Thinking Skills

Using satire to make a point

Identifying flaws in arguments

Evaluating the impacts of decisions on different groups

Economic Concepts

Free trade

Protectionism

Protectionist arguments

From the Manufacturers of Candles, Tapers, Lanterns, Candlesticks, Street Lamps, Snuffers, and Extinguishers, and from the Producers of Tallow, Oil, Resin, Alcohol, and Generally of Everything Connected with Lighting.

To the Honorable Members of the Chamber of Deputies.

Gentlemen: . . .

We are suffering from the ruinous competition of a foreign rival who apparently works under conditions so far superior to our own for the production of light that he is *flooding* the *domestic market* with it at an incredibly low price; for the moment he appears, our sales cease, all the consumers turn to him, and a branch of French industry whose ramifications are innumerable is all at once reduced to complete stagnation. This rival, which is none other than the sun, is waging war on us . . . mercilessly . . . .

We ask you to be so good as to pass a law requiring the closing of all windows, dormers, skylights, inside and outside shutters, curtains . . . and blinds—in short,

all openings, holes, chinks, and fissures through which the light of the sun is wont to enter houses . . . .

Be good enough, honorable deputies, to take our request seriously, and do not reject it without at least hearing the reasons that we have to advance in its support.

First, if you shut off as much as possible all access to natural light, and thereby create a need for artificial light, what industry in France will not ultimately be encouraged?

If France consumes more tallow, there will have to be more cattle and sheep, and consequently, we shall see an increase in cleared fields, meat, wool, [and] leather . . . .

If France consumes more oil, we shall see an expansion in the cultivation of the poppy, the olive, and rapeseed . . . .

Our moors will be covered with resinous trees . . . . Thus, there is not one branch of agriculture that would not undergo a great expansion . . . .

It needs but a little reflection, gentlemen, to be convinced that there is perhaps not one Frenchman, from the wealthy stockholder . . . to the humblest vendor of matches, whose condition would not be improved by the success of our petition.

We anticipate your objections, gentlemen, but there is not a single one of them that you have not picked up from the musty old books of the advocates of free trade . . . .

Will you tell us that, though we may gain by this protection, France will not gain at all, because the consumer will bear the expense?

We have our answer ready:

You no longer have the right to invoke the interests of the consumer. You have sacrificed him whenever you have found his interests opposed to those of the producer. You have done so in order *to encourage industry and to increase employment*. For the same reason you ought to do so this time too . . . .

Questions

1. What protectionist arguments are presented by the petitioners?
2. Why is this petition absurd? From this, should you conclude that all protectionist arguments are absurd?

3. Based on this petition and what you read earlier in the chapter, how confident are you in a country's ability to develop a trade policy that simultaneously benefits domestic producers and consumers?

4. Can you create a satire that does to free trade what this does to protectionism?

Source: Frederic Bastiat, "A Petition," Arthur Goddard, trans. and ed., *Economic Sophisms* (Irvington-on-Hudson, NY: The Foundation for Economic Education, Inc., 1964), pp. 57–60.

CHAPTER 17

International Finance

CHAPTER OBJECTIVES

To define exchange rates and explain how they are determined.

To introduce foreign exchange markets, and to identify some factors that cause exchange rates to fluctuate.

To identify the major categories into which international financial transactions can be placed, and to understand their interrelationships.

To define balance of trade, and to discuss its performance over the past few decades.

To introduce the debt problem faced by some countries and issues in unifying monetary systems.

Chapter 16 focused primarily on the exporting and importing of goods and services. But many other types of international transactions are important to an economy: the buying and selling of foreign stocks, bonds, and other assets; foreign assistance; and private gifts to foreigners.

Most international transactions involve payment flows between countries, making it necessary to have a mechanism for determining the values of foreign currencies and for exchanging domestic money for foreign money. The value of an economy's currency in foreign exchange markets is especially important because it affects the prices of the country's exports, imports, and foreign investments. The value of the dollar in relation to the yen, euro, and other foreign currencies is so important to U.S. international transactions and to the economy that it is quoted daily in many news broadcasts, in most major newspapers, and easily found on the Internet.

The first part of this chapter deals with exchange rates between countries' currencies, how exchange rates are determined, and how foreign exchange markets operate. The second section of the chapter explains how different types of international financial transactions affect payment flows between countries and how these transactions are classified in the United States for analysis purposes. A discussion of the balance of trade, an important and often-referred-to transactions classification, is included in this section. The chapter closes with a discussion of two current problems in international finance: the external debt crisis caused by the inability of some countries that have borrowed heavily from foreign lenders to repay their loans, and issues encountered in forming a unified monetary system.

EXCHANGING CURRENCIES

Exchange Rates

U.S. goods, services, and investment opportunities—such as stocks, bonds, and real estate—carry price tags that are expressed in dollars. You can buy a particular car for, say, $30,000, or invest in a piece of farmland for, say, $4,000 per acre. Regardless of whether the individual who buys U.S. goods, services, or assets is from the United States, Poland, Indonesia, or some other nation, payment for these items is usually made in dollars. Similarly, buyers and investors, regardless of their nationality, typically pay pounds for British goods and yen for Japanese goods. Thus, importing from or investing in another country requires converting one's money into the money of the nation with which one is dealing. An importer in the United States who buys Japanese cars will need to convert dollars to yen to transact business with the Japanese auto manufacturer, and an Israeli student with shekels from home will need to convert them to dollars before paying U.S. tuition.

Importers and investors need to know how much foreign goods, services, and investment opportunities cost in terms of their own money. The U.S. importer of Japanese automobiles must know not only how many yen each car will cost, but also, and perhaps more importantly, how many *dollars* that price represents. To determine the dollar cost of a car purchased from Japan, the U.S. importer must know the exchange rate between the U.S. dollar and the Japanese yen.

The **exchange rate** between two nations' currencies is the number of units of one nation's currency that is equal to one unit of the other nation's currency. For example, the exchange rate between the Swedish krona and the dollar might be 10 krona to $1, or 1 krona to $0.10. At this exchange rate, a product selling for 400 krona in Stockholm could be purchased by a U.S. tourist for the equivalent of $40. If the exchange rate were 5 krona to the dollar, then each krona would be

Exchange Rate
The number of units of a nation's currency that is equal to one unit of another nation's currency.

TABLE 17.1 *Exchange Rates between the U.S. Dollar and Selected Foreign Currencies (January 27, 2009)*

The exchange rates between nations' currencies are constantly changing as economic and noneconomic conditions change.

Nation	Amount of Dollars Equal to One Unit of Foreign Money	Amount of Foreign Money Equal to One Dollar
Brazil	$0.43131 = 1 real	2.3185 reals = $1
Britain	$1.42146 = 1 pound	0.7035 pounds = $1
Canada	$0.81493 = 1 dollar	1.2271 dollars = $1
China	$0.14629 = 1 yuan	6.8357 yuans = $1
European Union	$1.32468 = 1 euro	0.7549 euros = $1
Japan	$0.01122 = 1 yen	89.1 yen = $1
Korea	$0.00072 = 1 won	1,388.74999 won = $1
Mexico	$0.07028 = 1 peso	14.2299 pesos = $1
Russia	$0.03033 = 1 rouble	32.9738 roubles = $1

Source: Currency Rates, http://moneycentral.msn.com/investor/market/exchangerates.aspx? pkw=PI&vendor=Paid+ . . . , January 27, 2009.

equal in value to $0.20, and the same 400-krona product would now cost the tourist the equivalent of $80.

Exchange rates between the U.S. dollar and several foreign currencies are given in Table 17.1. Using the Brazilian real as an example, Table 17.1 shows that on January 27, 2009, one real was worth 43.1 cents, or 2.32 reals would have exchanged for $1 ($1/0.43131 = 2.3185).

Notice in Table 17.1 that there is a listing for the European Union. This is because EU member countries, such as France and Germany, went to a common currency called the euro. Notice also the differences in the exchange rates between different countries' currencies and the dollar. For example, about 14 Mexican pesos were needed to exchange for one dollar, while more than 1,300 Korean won were needed to exchange for one dollar. Put differently, one peso was worth about 7 cents while a Korean won was worth about 7 one-hundredths of a penny.

The exchange rate quotations in Table 17.1 are for one day only. This is because exchange rates between nations' monies are continually changing in response to economic and noneconomic factors. How and why these rates change will be discussed shortly.

The Determination of Exchange Rates

Today most nations are on a flexible, or floating, exchange rate system. In the past, however, many countries, such as the United States, operated under a system of fixed exchange rates. While the United States abandoned this system in late 1971, the terms and mechanics associated with a fixed system are worth understanding. From time to time, the topic of fixing rates resurfaces.

Fixed Exchange Rates   Before adoption of a flexible exchange rate system, exchange rates between the dollar and many other currencies were based primarily on gold; that is, the value of the dollar and other currencies was expressed in terms of the amount of gold one unit of each country's currency would command. For example, if $1 was worth 1/35 of an ounce of gold, and if 4 German marks were worth 1/35 of an ounce of gold, then the exchange rate between the dollar and the mark would have been $1 equals 4 marks, or 1 mark equals $0.25.

Because the values of their currencies were based on gold, nations were on a **fixed exchange rate** system. As a result, the exchange rates between their monies generally did not change or changed through a very narrow range. The only way a major change could occur in exchange rates was if one nation redefined the value of its money in terms of gold: for example, if the United States were to have declared that $1 would be worth 1/40 rather than 1/35 of an ounce of gold.

When a country declared that its monetary unit would be backed by less gold than previously, that country devalued its money. **Devaluation** of a nation's money constituted an important international economic policy tool because it changed all exchange rates between the devaluing nation's money and all other monies. This in turn had an effect on international trade, investments, and other transactions. For example, when the United States devalued the dollar prior to 1971, it made the U.S. dollar worth less in international transactions and other countries' monies that were backed by gold worth more. This would then require more U.S. money to buy one unit of foreign currency and less foreign money to buy one U.S. dollar. The result was to encourage foreign purchases of U.S. items because U.S. items became cheaper to foreigners, and to discourage purchases of foreign items by those in the United States because foreign items became more expensive.

Flexible Exchange Rates   Today, economies are typically on a system of **flexible,** or **floating, exchange rates,** where the rates at which nations' monies exchange are determined by the forces of demand and supply. As demand and supply conditions change, exchange rates change. In the United States as elsewhere, people who are planning trips to another country or planning to make foreign investments watch the movement of exchange rates as they make decisions. When supply and demand result in a strong dollar, for example, people in the United States take more trips to Europe to shop and sightsee.

The process of determining exchange rates under this system can be illustrated with a hypothetical example involving the U.S. dollar and the Brazilian real. A hypothetical demand curve for Brazilian reals by those with U.S. dollars who want to import Brazilian goods, take advantage of Brazilian investment opportunities, or travel to Brazil on vacation is illustrated in Figure 17.1. The horizontal axis indicates the quantity of reals demanded, while the vertical axis shows the price *in U.S. dollars* that must be paid per real. As expected, the demand curve is downward sloping: At a price of $0.75 per real, 200 million reals are demanded, while at a price of $0.15 per real, 700 million are demanded.

The reason for the inverse relationship between the price and quantity demanded of Brazilian reals is that as the dollar price of reals goes up, the prices of Brazilian goods, services, and investment opportunities also increase for buyers wanting to convert their dollars to reals. With Brazilian goods, services, and investment opportunities becoming more expensive for these buyers, they want to purchase less, causing the quantity of reals demanded to be lower.

For example, suppose that a Brazilian travel agency has a vacation package with a price tag of 8,000 reals. At an exchange rate of $0.30 = 1 real, the cost of the vacation would be $2,400. If the price of reals to U.S. buyers were to rise to $0.45 each, the same 8,000-real vacation would cost $3,600. This higher dollar price would cause fewer U.S. buyers to want to purchase this package, which in turn would lower the quantity of reals demanded.

The supply curve for Brazilian reals is given in Figure 17.2. This curve shows the amount of reals available at various dollar prices in this foreign exchange market. The

Fixed Exchange Rates
Exchange rates fluctuate little, if at all, because the values of nations' monies are defined in terms of gold.

Devaluation
The amount of gold backing a nation's monetary unit is reduced.

Flexible (Floating) Exchange Rates
Exchange rates that fluctuate because they are determined by the forces of demand and supply.

FIGURE 17.1   *Demand Curve for Brazilian Reals by Those with U.S. Dollars*

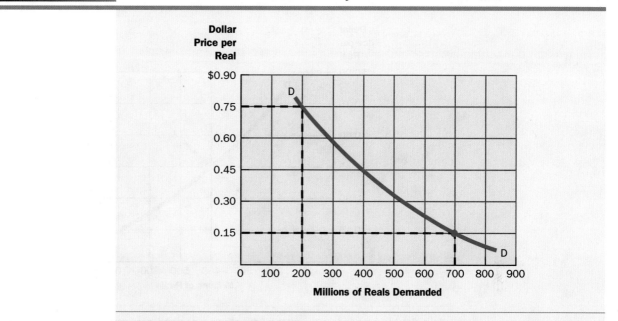

A demand curve for foreign money is downward sloping, indicating that less of the money is demanded as its price increases.

FIGURE 17.2   *Supply Curve of Brazilian Reals by Those Wanting U.S. Dollars*

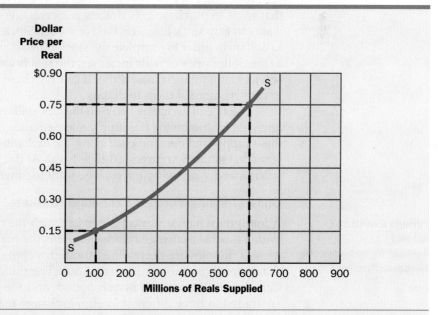

A supply curve for foreign money is upward sloping, indicating that more of the money is made available as its price increases.

FIGURE 17.3

FIGURE 17.3   *Supply of and Demand for Brazilian Reals*

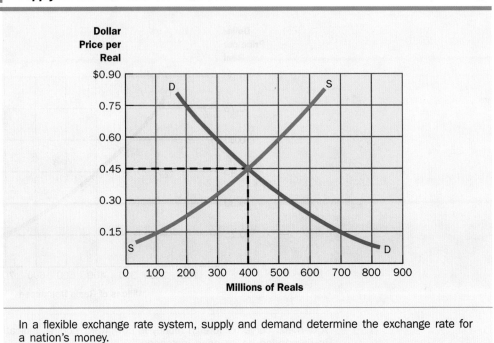

In a flexible exchange rate system, supply and demand determine the exchange rate for a nation's money.

supply curve is upward sloping: At a price of $0.15 per real, 100 million reals would be supplied, and at a price of $0.75 per real, 600 million reals would be supplied. The supply of reals in this market comes from individuals, businesses, and governments that want to purchase U.S. dollars with reals. For example, a Brazilian investor who wants to buy stock listed on the New York Stock Exchange will need to convert reals to dollars in order to complete the stock transaction. The curve slopes upward because as the dollar price of reals increases, the real is worth more in terms of the U.S. goods, services, and financial assets that it can purchase, causing those holding reals to want to convert more of them to dollars.

The rate of exchange between the U.S. dollar and the Brazilian real can now be determined by combining the supply and demand curves, as is done in Figure 17.3. Given these supply and demand conditions, the exchange rate that emerges is shown at the intersection of the two curves: $0.45 = 1 real. At this rate, the number of reals supplied by sellers and demanded by buyers who want to convert U.S. dollars and reals is 400 million.

Understanding Foreign Exchange Markets

Foreign Exchange Market

A market for the trading of two nations' monies.

A **foreign exchange market** is one in which the currencies of two nations are traded. With a flexible exchange rate system, it is the mechanism by which the values of two nations' monies are determined through supply and demand and by which the exchange of those monies is carried out. The Canadian dollar and the U.S. dollar, the Canadian dollar and the British pound, and the Japanese yen and the British pound are traded in three different foreign exchange markets. Foreign exchange markets involve buyers and sellers all over the world who are linked together by sophisticated communications networks. Application 17.1, "Foreign Exchange Markets," provides some detail about these markets.

APPLICATION 17.1

FOREIGN EXCHANGE MARKETS

Foreign exchange markets (known also as forex markets) and the amounts of nations' currencies traded in these markets do not get nearly the media attention that is given to the New York Stock Exchange and stock price movements. This is something of a surprise since, in the aggregate, the market for foreign currencies is the largest in the world. On average, about $2 trillion in trades are made every day. To put the amount spent on foreign currencies in perspective consider this: In 2008 every person in the world would have had to spend more than $300 per day to match what is spent on trades in foreign exchange markets on a typical day. One reason the daily dollar figures are so big is that in many cases hundreds of millions of dollars are spent on a single trade.

In addition to being big, the markets for foreign currencies are very active. Price quotes on a single currency can change every few seconds. And if the currency is actively traded, the quoted rate might change more than 15,000 times over the course of a day.

Not all currencies are actively traded because there is not as much demand for some currencies as there is for others. In fact, a distinction is made between "hard" and "soft" currencies. Hard currencies are from advanced industrialized countries like the United States, England, European Union members, and Japan. These currencies are widely demanded and easily converted to other currencies. A very large percentage of foreign exchange trades involves the dollar, pound, euro, or yen. Soft currencies are typically from less developed countries. There is not a strong demand for these currencies, partly because various controls might make it difficult to trade them for other currencies.

Foreign exchange markets are best understood as networks of traders. Unlike the New York Stock Exchange, which is a hub through which listed stock transactions flow, there is no central or base location through which foreign currency transactions are made. Rather, trades are done largely—but not only—in the United States, United Kingdom, and Japan.

Because primary trading locations are spread around the world, trade goes on 24 hours a day. A New York trader coming to work in the morning can contact a trader in London, where it is early afternoon, and late in the day a trader in Los Angeles can contact a trader in Japan, where it is early the next day.

Who are the main participants in foreign exchange markets? The largest group is banks and other financial institutions. About two out of three transactions are between banks. There are also intermediaries, called brokers, who conduct trades for banks. While banks can directly deal with one another, sometimes there is a preference to remain anonymous. Going through a broker allows the buyer or seller to keep its identity a secret. Nations' central banks also participate in foreign exchange markets. In the case of these banks, participation might be to support a national economic policy objective. Finally, private businesses and individuals might trade one currency for another in order to expand sales, make an investment, travel, or simply make a purchase.

Based on: "Foreign Currency Exchange," Federal Reserve Bank of New York, 2001, http://www.ny.frb.org/education/fx/foreign.html; Sam Y. Cross, "All about . . . the Foreign Exchange Market in the United States," Federal Reserve Bank of New York, 1998, http://www.ny.frb.org/education/addpub/usfxm; http://www.gocurrency.com/articles/stories-fx-market.htm.

Changes in Exchange Rates   Since exchange rates are determined by the forces of supply and demand in foreign exchange markets, any factor that causes a change in the supply and/or demand of a nation's currency in one of these markets will cause a change in the currency's exchange rate and the amount traded. For example, referring to Figure 17.3, if the demand for Brazilian reals by those with U.S. dollars increases, the demand curve for reals will shift to the right, causing the dollar price of reals as well as the amount exchanged to increase. At an exchange rate of $0.45 = 1 real in Figure 17.3, $4.50 will buy 10 reals. If, because of an increase in the demand for reals, the exchange rate becomes $0.60 = 1 real, the dollar is worth less compared to the real, and $4.50 will buy only 7.5 reals. Can you graphically determine the results of an increase in supply?[1]

When an exchange rate changes, the value of one nation's money changes compared to the value of the other nation's money. One becomes worth more compared to the other, and one becomes worth less. Expressions that are heard in the media such as "the declining value of the dollar in world trade" refer to the fact that the exchange rate is changing in favor of other nations' currencies and against the U.S. dollar.

[1]The supply curve of reals will shift to the right, causing the dollar price of reals to fall and the amount exchanged to rise.

APPLICATION 17.2

DOES A LOWER-VALUED DOLLAR HELP THE ECONOMY?

Suppose that over the course of a year the value of the U.S. dollar falls by over 15 percent in relation to the Japanese yen and the Canadian dollar. Since a drop in the value of the dollar on foreign exchange markets effectively puts the U.S. economy on sale, this would make purchases of U.S. goods and services cheaper for these foreign buyers. People with yen or Canadian dollars would be able to buy tuition at U.S. colleges and universities, a trip to Disney World, and even U.S.-manufactured jeans for less of their own money.

At first glance this looks like a good deal for the U.S. economy because a drop in the dollar's value should lead to more spending on U.S.-produced goods and services, which in turn should increase U.S. production and employment. But it just isn't that simple. There are some downsides to a devalued dollar.

While a lower-valued dollar makes U.S. goods cheaper to foreign buyers, it makes imports more expensive for U.S. consumers. A drop in the value of the dollar on foreign exchange markets forces U.S. consumers to pay more for the lumber, automobiles, metals, electronics, and other products they purchase from Canada and Japan, as well as the coffee, bananas, gloves, violins, and other items purchased from other countries.

These changes in the price of exports and imports give rise to important questions that come with the lower-valued dollar. Will we face a problem with demand-pull inflation from more foreign purchases of U.S. goods as well as increased spending on U.S. goods by U.S. consumers who want to avoid the rise in prices of foreign goods? Could there be a problem with cost-push inflation if U.S. firms, having to pay more for imported inputs, are forced to raise prices on their finished products?

We should also consider that a devaluation of the dollar can hurt a vulnerable part of the U.S. population: immigrants who come to the United States to work and support their families living in poverty in their home countries. When the value of the dollar drops, $1,000 sent home exchanges for fewer units of the home money—which means less food, shelter, and other needs for the family.

Based on: Roberto Perez Betancourt, "Devaluation of Dollar Hurts U.S. Consumers," Radio Habana Cuba, May 4, 2005, http://www.radiohc.cu/ingles/especiales/abril05/especiales05abril.htm.

It is important to understand some of the major factors that cause supply and demand to change and exchange rates to fluctuate in foreign exchange markets, because a change in the value of a nation's currency in international exchange markets can have serious economic consequences. As exchange rates rise and fall, the international prices of a country's goods and services rise and fall as well. For example, when the value of the dollar drops in foreign exchange markets, goods produced in the United States become cheaper for foreign buyers and foreign-made products become more expensive for U.S. buyers. In addition, an increase or decrease in the value of a country's money may discourage or encourage foreign ownership of real assets in the country.

Application 17.2, "Does a Lower-Valued Dollar Help the Economy?", explores the effect on the U.S. economy when the value of the dollar falls in foreign exchange markets. Because a lower-valued dollar makes U.S. exports cheaper to foreign buyers and foreign imports to the United States more expensive, it is entirely reasonable to presume that it helps the U.S. economy while hurting foreign economies. But Application 17.2 points out that a drop in the dollar's value can, in fact, hurt the U.S. economy.

Factors Influencing Demand and Supply in Foreign Exchange Markets   Several factors can cause a change in the demand and/or supply of a nation's money in foreign exchange markets. One important factor that causes the demand for foreign currencies to shift is a change in the taste for foreign products: As a country's products become more popular, demand for that country's money increases, and as they become less popular, demand falls. The demand for foreign-made goods has increased in the United States in recent years. This may be due to real or imagined perceptions of the quality of foreign products, a larger array of foreign goods that are now available, or other factors. Consider, for example, the increased popularity of Australian wines, bike trips through France and Vietnam, and Belgian chocolates.

FIGURE 17.4   *Changes in the Demand for and Supply of a Foreign Currency*

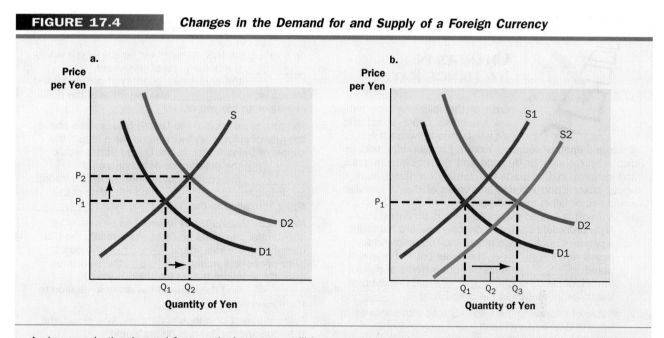

An increase in the demand for a nation's currency will increase the price of its currency. If an increase in the demand for the currency is matched by an increase in supply, the exchange rate will remain unchanged.

Figure 17.4a illustrates the impact on exchange rates of an increase in the demand for a nation's currency caused by an increase in the demand for its products. Using the U.S. dollar and the Japanese yen as an example, an increase in the U.S. demand for Japanese products will increase the demand for yen and shift the demand curve to the right from D1 to D2. This causes the price of yen to rise from P_1 to P_2 and the value of the dollar to decline. Can this decline in the value of the dollar be stopped?

An increase in the supply of yen could cause the exchange rate to return to its original level. This is shown in Figure 17.4b, where the supply curve shifts to the right from S1 to S2 following the shift in demand from D1 to D2. This increase in the supply of yen could occur if there were an increase in the Japanese demand for U.S. products or investment opportunities: A larger quantity of yen would appear on the market as the Japanese sought dollars to buy U.S. products or invest in U.S. assets.

A second factor that can cause a change in the demand or supply of a nation's currency and its exchange rate is a change in economic conditions in either the demanding or supplying country. Consider the effect of inflation on the demand for Canadian dollars by U.S. importers and investors. If the inflation occurs in the United States, it will make the price tags on Canadian goods relatively lower for U.S. importers and investors, thereby causing the U.S. demand curve for Canadian dollars to increase, or shift to the right. As a result, the price of Canadian dollars will rise, as will the number of Canadian dollars exchanged. If the inflation occurs in Canada, it will make the cost of Canadian goods relatively higher for U.S. investors and importers and lead to a decrease, or leftward shift, in the demand curve for Canadian dollars. As a result, the price of Canadian dollars will fall and so will the amount exchanged.

A third factor that influences exchange rates is the rate of interest that can be earned on securities issued by private and government borrowers in different countries. If investment opportunities in another country yield a higher return than is available domestically, some individuals and corporations with global investment strategies will

TEST YOUR UNDERSTANDING

CHANGES IN EXCHANGE RATES

Each of the following hypothetical situations could affect the exchange rate between the U.S. dollar and another country's money. For each situation, indicate how supply or demand and the equilibrium price and quantity in that particular foreign exchange market would change and whether the value of the U.S. dollar would rise or fall in that market.

1. A report is issued that certain wines produced in Argentina could contain chemicals that are harmful to a person's health. As a result, the U.S. demand for pesos would _____, the dollar price of pesos would _____, the equilibrium quantity of dollars traded for pesos would _____, and the value of the dollar in relation to the peso would _____.

2. Rates of interest in the United States move above rates in Britain. As a result, the supply of British pounds to the United States would _____, the dollar price of pounds would _____, the equilibrium quantity of pounds traded for dollars would _____, and the value of the dollar in relation to the pound would _____.

3. Japan introduces a newly designed sports car that is an immediate hit with U.S. automobile enthusiasts.

As a result, the U.S. demand for Japanese yen would _____, the dollar price of yen would _____, the equilibrium quantity of dollars traded for yen would _____, and the value of the dollar in relation to the yen would _____.

4. The rate of inflation in the United States rises above the rate of inflation in Switzerland. As a result, the supply of Swiss francs to the United States would _____, the dollar price of francs would _____, the equilibrium quantity of francs traded for dollars would _____, and the value of the dollar in relation to the Swiss franc would _____.

5. More U.S. citizens travel to Israel as airlines offer substantial discounts on fares. As a result, the U.S. demand for shekels would _____, the dollar price of shekels would _____, the equilibrium quantity of dollars traded for shekels would _____, and the value of the dollar in relation to the shekel would _____.

6. Political unrest develops in Bahrain. As a result, the U.S. demand for Bahrain dinars would _____, the supply of dinars to the United States would _____, the dollar price of dinars would _____, the equilibrium quantity of dinars traded for dollars would _____, and the value of the dollar in relation to the dinar would _____.

Answers can be found at the back of the book.

want to purchase the higher-yielding foreign securities. To do so increases the demand for the currency of the nation with the higher interest rates, thereby causing a change in its exchange rate. The increased buying and selling of financial instruments on a global level in recent years has had an important effect on exchange rate determination.

Fourth, the supply and demand of a nation's money in foreign exchange markets may be influenced by government and central bank policies. For example, in an effort to keep the value of a country's money from falling, its government or central bank might intervene in a foreign exchange market to restrict the supply of its currency. Government intervention in foreign exchange markets occurs from time to time, despite the fact that they are considered to be basically free markets.

Changes in exchange rates will also cause buyers and sellers of foreign currencies to enter or leave the market if they regard foreign goods, services, and assets as substitutes for domestic items. For example, when the value of the peso falls, travel to Mexico by residents of the United States becomes a desirable alternative to travel at home. This increase in foreign travel, considered by itself, would cause the demand curve for pesos to shift to the right and the value of the peso to increase. Finally, other factors such as political climates, expectations, and trade restrictions can cause the demand and/or supply curves for a nation's money to shift and the exchange rate to change. Test Your Understanding, "Changes in Exchange Rates," lets you practice evaluating how changes in economic and noneconomic conditions in two countries would affect exchange rates between their monies.

TABLE 17.2	U.S. International Financial Transactions

The current account records payment flows for goods, services, gifts, and the like; the capital account records payments for financial and real assets.

Type of Transaction		Amount in 2007 (Billions of Dollars)
Current Account		
Balance of trade		−$819.4
Exports of merchandise	$ 1,148.5	
Imports of merchandise	−1,967.9	
Plus: Net services		119.1
Equals: Net exports of goods and services	−700.3	
Plus: Net income		81.7
Plus: Net unilateral transfers		−112.7
Equals: **Current Account Balance**		−731.2
Capital Account		
U.S. assets abroad, net		−$1,289.9
Foreign assets in the United States, net		2,057.7
Equals: **Capital Account Balance**[a]		$774.3
Statistical Discrepancy		41.3
Total		$ 00.0[b]

[a]Includes net capital account transactions and derivatives netting.
[b]May not equal $0 because of rounding.
Source: *Economic Report of the President* (Washington, DC: U.S. Government Printing Office, 2009), pp. 402, 403.

INTERNATIONAL FINANCIAL TRANSACTIONS AND BALANCES

A wide variety of international transactions requires payment flows from one country to another. These include importing and exporting goods and services, buying and selling foreign financial instruments and real assets, military and foreign assistance, gifts, grants, and travel. Some of these transactions involve major outlays for real estate, production equipment, and corporate stock; some involve small sums for gifts to relatives back home.

To analyze the many and varied types of financial transactions that occur between the United States and other nations, these transactions are grouped into major categories. Through the use of these categories, the accounting process for international transactions is simplified and, more importantly, transactions that could cause problems for the economy can be more readily identified. The two major transactions categories are the current account and the capital account.

The Current Account

Current Account
A category of international transactions that records figures for exports and imports of merchandise, services, unilateral transfers, and other foreign dealings.

The **current account** records payments for exports and imports of goods; payments for military transactions, foreign travel, transportation, and other services; income from investments; and unilateral transfers (gifts). The major components of the current account and their dollar values for 2007 are shown at the top of Table 17.2. In

| FIGURE 17.5 | *U.S. Balance of Trade: 1970–2007* |

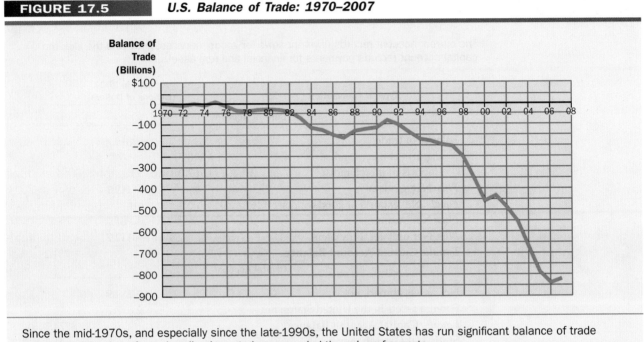

Since the mid-1970s, and especially since the late-1990s, the United States has run significant balance of trade deficits as the value of merchandise imports has exceeded the value of exports.

Source: *Economic Report of the President* (Washington, DC: U.S. Government Printing Office, 2009), p. 402.

Balance of Trade

The figure that results when merchandise imports are subtracted from exports.

presenting these figures, dollar payment outflows to other countries are indicated by negative numbers and dollar payment inflows from other countries by positive numbers. For example, the value of U.S. exports of merchandise (goods) in 2007 was more than $1.1 trillion, a positive number because exports bring payment inflows, while the value of imports of merchandise in 2007 was −$1.97 trillion, a negative number because dollars flow out when foreign goods are purchased. When merchandise imports are subtracted from exports, a net figure called the **balance of trade** results. In 2007 the balance of trade was −$819.4 billion, indicating that U.S. buyers purchased $819.4 billion more foreign goods than foreign buyers bought U.S. goods.[2]

Balance of Trade Surplus (Deficit)

The value of a country's merchandise exports is greater (less) than the value of its imports.

The balance of trade is significant because it involves a large flow of money, reflects the results of a nation's international trade activity, and is frequently cited in studies and discussions of international transactions. When the value of a country's exports of goods is greater than the value of its imports, a **balance of trade surplus** occurs; when the value of a country's imports of goods is greater than the value of its exports, a **balance of trade deficit** arises.

Figure 17.5 charts the annual balance of trade for the United States from 1970 through 2007. There were small trade surpluses in the 1970s, but since then sizable trade deficits have occurred, especially after the late-1990s. The trade deficit has become so large that it is a matter of concern. Factors such as the popularity of foreign

[2]Be careful to notice that the term *balance of trade* is different from the term *net exports*, which was discussed in Chapter 5. The balance of trade is calculated on the basis of exports and imports of goods, whereas net exports uses both goods and services. Net exports of goods and services is given as a separate component in Table 17.2.

goods like automobiles and home electronics equipment, strong foreign rivals in markets for U.S. export products, the rise in the price of oil, and changes in the value of the dollar have contributed to the significant deficits of recent years.

The dollar figures for the other current account classifications in Table 17.2 are given as net amounts; that is, unlike merchandise exports and imports, the payment outflows have already been subtracted from the inflows and are not given separately. For example, on net services, more payment inflows than outflows occurred, resulting in a net figure of $119.1 billion. On the other hand, the unilateral transfer number of −$112.7 billion indicates that, for that category, more payments flowed out of than into the United States.

The balance of trade, net services, net income, and unilateral transfers are added together to arrive at the current account balance, which was −$731.2 billion in 2007. This figure means that transactions from the current account components caused 731.2 billion more U.S. dollars to flow out for payments than the value of money that flowed in. This is referred to as a **current account deficit.** Had the figure been a positive number, there would have been a **current account surplus.**

Current Account Deficit (Surplus)
A negative (positive) figure results when all current account transactions are added together.

Capital Account
A category of international transactions that records the purchase and sale of financial and real assets between the United States and other nations.

The Capital Account

The **capital account,** which is listed in the lower part of Table 17.2, records payment flows for investment purchases such as stocks, bonds, government securities, and real estate. When U.S. individuals, businesses, and governments buy foreign-owned financial or real assets, there are payment flows from the United States. These flows are recorded in the capital account component "U.S. assets abroad, net" as negative numbers since payments are flowing out of the country. When corporate financial instruments, government securities, and real estate owned by U.S. entities are purchased by foreign buyers, there are payment flows to the United States. These are recorded in the capital account component "Foreign assets in the United States, net" as positive numbers, indicating payment inflows.

In Table 17.2, the capital account balance for 2007 is $774.3 billion, a positive number indicating that there was more foreign investment in U.S. assets than U.S. investment in foreign assets during that year. This positive number in the capital account makes sense in light of the large negative current account balance listed in Table 17.2. The large demand by U.S. buyers for imports was not offset by an equal foreign demand for U.S. exports, causing the value of the dollar to drop. As the dollar became cheaper for foreigners to purchase, U.S. financial and real assets became less expensive and more attractive to these buyers.

Balancing the Accounts

In recording these payment inflows and outflows, there should be a balance: The dollars used to purchase foreign goods, assets, and the like should be matched by an equal amount of foreign currency flowing into the dollar exchange markets to accommodate those purchases. As a result, the current account balance and the capital account balance together should total zero. However, because of the volume of money traded and the diversity of locations and customs in foreign exchange markets, the accounting for these transactions may not be completely accurate. To make payment inflows and outflows equal, the government adds an amount for statistical discrepancies to its accounting process. This is given at the bottom of Table 17.2 and, when added to the balances for the two major transactions categories, results in a zero balance in the very last line.

| TABLE 17.3 | *External Debt of Selected Highly Indebted Developing Countries, 2000 and 2005* |

Some countries have an external debt that is much greater than the country's national income.

Country	External Debt as a Percentage of GNI		Dollar Size of External Debt (Billions)	
	2000	2005	2000	2005
Samoa	743%	496%	$ 0.3	$ 0.3
Lesotho	523	591	2.0	2.6
Guinea	396	240	0.8	0.7
Congo, Democratic Republic	298	156	11.7	10.6
Mali	218	119	2.4	2.3
Zambia	186	83	5.7	5.7
Romania	63	31	160.0	229.0
Brazil	42	24	243.7	188.0
Mauritius	27	22	150.3	167.2
China	12	13	145.7	281.6

Source: World Bank, *Global Development Finance* (Washington, DC: The World Bank, 2007), Vol. II, pp. xxxiii-xxxv.

CHALLENGES TO THE INTERNATIONAL FINANCIAL SYSTEM

The globalization of economic activity has created both opportunities and challenges for the international financial system. Two challenges have been particularly important: the debt issues faced by a number of countries as a result of large-scale borrowing from foreign lenders, and efforts to integrate the monetary systems of the countries in the European Union.

External Debt Issues

External Debt

Money owed by borrowers in one country to lenders in other countries.

One important type of international financial transaction included in the capital account is loan making. Many governments and businesses, including those in developing nations, borrow from lenders, such as banks, governments, and individuals, in other countries to help finance investments and other activities. For example, a U.S. bank could lend money to the government of Brazil, a South African could buy U.S. Treasury bonds, or Canadian and U.S. investors could buy corporate bonds in companies of each other's countries. This type of borrowing results in **external debt** because it is owed to lenders outside of, or external to, the borrowing country.

External debt has been a mounting problem for some developing countries. In 2005, the total external debt outstanding in developing countries exceeded $2.7 trillion.[3] The external debt of some developing nations has become so large that they are unable to repay the interest on their loans, much less the loans themselves.

The magnitude of the external debt problem is illustrated in Table 17.3, which ranks several highly indebted developing countries according to the amount each owed to foreign lenders as a percentage of that country's gross national income (GNI)

[3]The World Bank, *Global Development Finance* (Washington, DC: The World Bank, 2007), Vol. II, p. xxxv.

in 2000 and 2005.[4] Also shown is the size of each country's external debt, measured in U.S. dollars. While Samoa and Lesotho are among those with the highest debt as a percentage of GNI, the dollar size of their external debts was relatively small. China, on the other hand, had the smallest external debt when compared to GNI in 2005, but in dollar terms it was the most indebted country in the table.

The Opportunity Cost of External Debt   There are substantial opportunity costs for borrowing nations that seek to service and repay their large external debts and substantial opportunity costs for lending nations if they do not.

To honor their financial obligations to foreign lenders, borrowing nations must cut back on spending by their households, businesses, and governments in order to send money to their debt holders. (This is the same situation that a family faces when it falls deeply into debt: It must cut back on current consumption in order to pay lenders.) In developing nations where incomes are low, the harsh austerity measures needed to cut back spending to repay the debt may not be tolerable or even possible. In addition, payment of a debt of this magnitude causes the postponement of spending on investment goods, which hampers future economic growth. In short, the opportunity cost of repayment is substantial: The decline in current spending could send the economy into a recession, making payments even more difficult and sacrificing future economic growth. To these economic costs can be added the political unrest that could well result from such serious economic disruptions.

Failure by developing countries to meet external debt interest payments or repay loan principals in a timely manner creates problems for lending institutions, especially commercial banks. When countries can no longer meet their loan obligations, millions of dollars of interest income are at risk for these banks, in addition to possible default on the principal. The unacceptably high risk associated with loan making to developing countries has reduced the flow of funds from banks to these countries. In 1980, before the external debt crisis, commercial banks accounted for about 30 percent of the debt to developing countries. By 2005 those same banks accounted for about 7.6 percent of that debt to developing countries.[5]

Dealing with External Debt Issues   An early attempt to alleviate an external debt crisis was the **Brady Plan.** This 1989 proposal, which was used in several countries, aimed to restructure and reduce the debts owed to commercial banks by developing countries, provided the countries implemented policies to strengthen their economies.[6] In 1996 the World Bank and International Monetary Fund, in conjunction with several governments and international financial organizations, launched the **Heavily Indebted Poor Countries (HIPC) Initiative** to ease the external debt burden of highly indebted developing countries that carried out economic reforms to improve educational attainment, health care, and other social conditions. Prior to the Initiative, eligible countries were spending more on debt service than on health and education. By 2004 they were spending almost four times as much on health, education, and other social services than on debt service. By 2008, 33 countries had been approved for debt reduction under the HIPC Initiative.[7]

Brady Plan
A proposal to restructure and reduce developing country indebtedness to commercial banks.

Heavily Indebted Poor Countries (HIPC) Initiative
A joint initiative by the World Bank and International Monetary Fund to help heavily indebted developing countries manage their external debts.

---

[4]Gross national income (GNI) is equal to the total value added by all producers in the country, product taxes that were not included in output evaluation, and primary income to the country from abroad.

[5]The World Bank, *Global Development Finance* (Washington, DC: The World Bank, 2004), Vol. II, p. 3; (2007), vol. II, p. 3.

[6]See John Clark and Elliot Kalter, "Recent Innovations in Debt Restructuring," *Finance & Development*, September 1992, p. 6; William R. Rhodes, "The Disaster That Didn't Happen," *The Economist*, September 12, 1992, pp. 22–23.

[7]International Monetary Fund, "Debt Relief under the Heavily Indebted Poor Countries (HIPC) Initiative," October 2008, http://www.imf.org/external/np/exr/facts/hipc.htm.

Table 7.3 shows that there have been some successes in dealing with the debt crisis. The Democratic Republic of the Congo's external debt dropped from 298 percent to 156 percent of GNI from 2000 through 2005. Other countries, such as Zambia, experienced significant decreases in debt as a percentage of GNI as well. But Table 17.3 also shows that the debt crisis is far from solved for countries like Samoa.

Monetary Integration in Europe

As indicated in Chapter 16, an important development in the 1980s and 1990s was the formation of the European Community (EC), which later became the European Union (EU), a single trading entity larger in population and economic size than the United States. Most of the countries that comprise this large and closely knit trading bloc integrated their monetary systems in 2002.

The first step toward monetary integration occurred in 1979, when the **European Monetary System, or EMS,** was formed to limit the variability of exchange rates between European nations' currencies. Rates were aligned using a mechanism that allowed exchange rates to fluctuate by only a small percentage around a central value. The German mark was the keystone currency on which the EMS was built.

The next major step toward monetary unification was the **Maastricht Treaty** of 1991, which was ratified by the EC members in 1993. Under the terms of the treaty the EMS would be replaced by an Economic and Monetary Union, or EMU, and there would be a common currency and a European Central Bank to oversee a single monetary policy for the member countries. The Maastricht Treaty, in effect, called for a fixed exchange rate system to apply to member countries' currencies.[8]

In 1999 a monetary union of 11 countries occurred, and the euro, a common European currency, was launched. By 2002 the euro replaced the currencies of most EU member countries, and this became the world's largest currency transformation. With time, new countries have joined the EU, and some have adopted the euro. In countries that held out on adopting the euro, like Poland, the financial crisis of late 2008 and 2009 prompted a new look.[9]

From the beginning there were supporters and skeptics of this union, and many concerns—either real or perceived. One concern has been that as the member countries experience different economic problems, a single monetary policy may not be able to address all of their needs at one time. One country might face inflation while another faces unemployment, leading to advocacy for different types of economic policies to follow. Furthermore, some of the smaller countries in the EU may have less capacity to strengthen their economies in a time of severe economic conditions, and they may feel that their economies are of less concern than those of the larger, more powerful members.

The mobility of resources and protection of tradition are other issues. Because of differences in language and tradition, Europeans are less mobile than individuals in the United States. It may be more difficult to relocate from Copenhagen with its Danish language to Madrid with its Spanish language than it would be from Seattle to Boston. The strong attachment to culture and tradition can also be extended to the currency in many countries. There are stories of small towns and villages that have clung to their native currency rather than adopt the Euro.

With just a decade or so of experience with the euro, time will tell whether the original intentions of the EU and the euro, such as improved trade among euro countries,

European Monetary System (EMS)
An agreement to limit the variability of exchange rates between European nations' currencies.

Maastricht Treaty
Called for a common currency and central bank to oversee a single monetary policy for countries belonging to Europe's Economic and Monetary Union.

---

[8]Craig R. Whitney, "Worry over the Euro Sweeps Europe," *The New York Times*, April 19, 1997, p. 4.
[9]Carter Dougherty, "Some Nations That Spurned the Euro Reconsider," *The New York Times*, December 2, 2008, http://www.nytimes.com; Jeffrey Frankel, Harvard Kennedy School Fellow, "The Euro at Ten: Time to Assess," *The New York Times*, Times Topics, January 22, 2009, http://topics.blogs.nytimes.com.

UP FOR DEBATE

EURO-DREAMS

Issue   *Imagine the place in history that awaits the person who persuaded the leaders of nations whose past relations were largely uneasy alliances or hostilities that sometimes degenerated into all-out war to come together, abandon their sovereign currencies and the autonomy of their central banks, and accept a common currency called the euro. Is the dream of a single currency circulating among the member countries of the European Union realistic in the long term?*

Yes   It is realistic to expect the countries of the European Union to accept the euro. The world that European nations face today is vastly different from the world where European relations were marked by distrust and highly focused nationalism. With economic activity crossing national borders on a huge scale, countries that want to be an "island fortress" insulated against all outside interests are painfully out-of-step with the times. By acting as one economic unit rather than separately, European nations will be better able to specialize and flex their muscle in the global arena. Surely it is obvious to the leaders in Europe's capitals that if they are to join together and seek a common outcome, their solidarity will be enhanced by adopting a common currency.

No   It is not realistic to expect the countries of the European Union to wholeheartedly accept the euro. Centuries of deep and abiding nationalism cannot be erased with the stroke of a pen. The unified monetary system may well surpass expectations—until a serious crisis occurs. When this happens, member countries may be slow to support policies that benefit the EU and stabilize the euro at the expense of national objectives. Further, even if the countries are willing to act as one and put EU interests above national interests, the fact is they face different problems that may require conflicting responses, not a single central bank policy. Finally, should we really expect member countries to always be willing and able to follow stringent government tax and expenditure policies in order to stabilize the euro?

are successful. Up for Debate, "Euro-Dreams," takes a look at some of the arguments for and against the continued success of the euro. What do you think will be the long-term reality of the euro?

Summary

1. An exchange rate is the number of units of one country's money that is equal to one unit of another country's money. In the past, exchange rates were often fixed, or tied to the value of the gold backing a country's money. When the gold backing was reduced, devaluation occurred.

2. Most exchange rates are flexible and continually changing because they are determined by supply and demand. The demand curve for a country's money by those holding another country's money is downward sloping, and the supply curve for a country's money is upward sloping.

3. Foreign exchange markets are the mechanisms through which the monies of different nations are traded and exchange rates are determined. When an exchange rate between two nations' monies changes, one nation's money becomes worth more in terms of the other nation's money. Changes in exchange rates affect economic conditions through their effects on the prices of exports, imports, and financial and real assets.

4. Any factor that causes demand and/or supply in a foreign exchange market to change will alter the exchange rate, as well as the amount of money traded. Some important factors affecting the demand for and/or supply of a foreign money include the popularity of imports and exports, economic conditions in either the importing or exporting nation, interest rates that can

be earned on investments in other countries, and intervention in foreign exchange markets by governments or central banks.

5. All international transactions that cause payment outflows or inflows are of economic importance. For accounting and analysis purposes, these transactions are placed into different categories, the most important of which are the current account and the capital account.

6. The current account includes the balance of trade, as well as figures for investment income, unilateral transfers, and the like. When the U.S. current account balance is a negative number, more dollars have flowed out of the United States than foreign payments have flowed in, and a current account deficit exists. When the current account balance is a positive number, more foreign payments have flowed in than dollars have flowed out, resulting in a current account surplus. In recent years, substantial balance of trade deficits have contributed to negative current account balances and caused serious concern in the United States.

7. The capital account records payment flows for financial and real assets. It has a positive balance when more money flows into the United States for stocks, bonds, real estate, and other assets than flows out for foreign assets. A positive capital account balance may be the result of a negative current account balance. The categorizing of international payments also includes a figure for statistical discrepancy that allows all payments to balance.

8. Several nations have accumulated large external debts that may be beyond their abilities to repay. External debt presents problems for both lending and borrowing countries. Significant opportunity costs exist whether the debt is repaid or not, and actions have been taken to reduce many developing countries' external debts.

9. Most nations in the European Union have integrated their currencies. There are ongoing questions about the costs and benefits of having several nations use a single, common currency.

Key Terms and Concepts

Exchange rate	Current account deficit (surplus)
Fixed exchange rates	Capital account
Devaluation	External debt
Flexible (floating) exchange rates	Brady Plan
Foreign exchange market	Highly Indebted Poor Countries (HIPC) Initiative
Exchange rate determination	European Monetary System (EMS)
Current account	Maastricht Treaty
Balance of trade	
Balance of trade surplus (deficit)	

1. Would the value of the dollar, compared to the Swiss franc, increase or decrease if the exchange rate went from 1.3 francs = $1.00 to 1.2 francs = $1.00? Why?

2. Explain why devaluation of a nation's currency could increase the demand for that nation's exports and decrease the demand by that nation for imports.

3. Why is the demand curve for a nation's money in a foreign exchange market downward sloping, and why is the supply curve upward sloping?

4. Illustrate graphically how the exchange rate for a nation's money is determined in a flexible exchange rate system, and show how the rate would be affected by an increase and a decrease in demand and by an increase and a decrease in supply.

5. How would each of the following transactions affect payment flows into or out of the United States, and into which major transactions category would each transaction be classified?
   a. The purchase of U.S. Treasury securities by a Canadian bank
   b. The sale of U.S. grain to Russia
   c. A gift of cash from a family in Pennsylvania to relatives in Poland
   d. The purchase of a condo in Paris by a family in New York
   e. The purchase of stock in an Indonesian company by an economics professor in Chicago

6. What are the major components of the current account, and what is the capital account? Give some examples of international transactions that would cause positive and negative dollar amounts to register in the current account.

7. What is an external debt and what opportunity costs does its repayment impose on a highly indebted country?

8. Summarize the steps Europeans have taken toward a monetary union. What problems could stand in the way of sustaining that union in the long run?

1. Locate a recent listing of foreign exchange rates. (These are given in *The Wall Street Journal*, in other major newspapers, and on the Internet.) Compare the recent rates with those given in Table 17.1. Are there any instances in which the rate has changed substantially? If so, give your opinion as to what factors might have caused such a change.

2. Answer each of the following.
   a. How many Japanese yen would have to be converted to dollars for a person in Japan to purchase a $40,000 U.S. SUV if the exchange rate were 125 yen = $1.00?
   b. How many yen would have to be converted to dollars to purchase the $40,000 SUV after the exchange rate changed to 110 yen = $1.00?

     c. How many dollars would have to be converted to yen for a person in Los Angeles to purchase a 4,000,000-yen Japanese automobile if the exchange rate were 125 yen = $1.00?

     d. How many dollars would have to be converted to yen to purchase the 4,000,000-yen auto after the exchange rate changed to 110 yen = $1.00?

3. What are some advantages and disadvantages of a fixed exchange rate system and of a flexible exchange rate system?

4. Explain how each of the following developments, taken alone, would affect the value of the dollar. Use supply and demand analysis in your answer.

     a. The perception in other countries that the quality of goods produced in the United States is improving

     b. A large federal government budget deficit that raises interest rates in the United States

     c. Intervention by the Federal Reserve in foreign exchange markets that results in dollars moving into those markets

     d. A poor harvest in most of the grain-producing countries of the world except the United States

     e. The expectation of war among several African countries

5. The United States has primarily experienced balance of trade deficits since the late 1970s and serious deficits since the late 1990s. What could be the short-term and long-term effects if this condition persists? What policy actions would you recommend to reverse this trend?

6. Why would a current account deficit lead to a capital account surplus?

7. What problems would arise if a developing country defaulted on its external debt? Who would be hurt? What policies would you recommend to ease external debt problems, and what would be the effects of these policies on borrowing countries?

8. Do you expect that in the long term the euro will be successful as a currency?

Critical Thinking Case 17

HELPING POOR COUNTRIES

Critical Thinking Skills

Examining cause-and-effect relationships

Identifying criteria for appropriate policies

Economic Concepts

External debt

Balance of payments

The IMF provides low-income countries with policy advice, technical assistance, and financial support. Low-income countries receive more than half of the technical assistance provided by the Fund, and financial support is extended at low interest rates and over relatively long time horizons. Low-income countries with high external debt burdens are also eligible for debt relief.

Despite progress in recent decades, the extreme poverty prevalent in low-income countries is a critical problem facing the global community. At present, more than a billion people are living on less than $1 a day. More than three-quarters of a billion people are malnourished—about a fifth of them children. One-hundred and sixteen of every 1,000 children born in low-income countries die before reaching the age of five, the majority from malnutrition or disease that is readily preventable in high-income countries.

[The United Nations has set goals] centered on halving poverty between 1990 and 2015. There is little dispute that a sustained, rapid rate of growth in average per capita incomes is essential for meaningful poverty reduction. The factors that have been shown to promote such growth include openness to international trade, sound economic policies, strong institutions and legal frameworks, and good governance.

[In March 2002 strategies were adopted to meet the United Nations' goals.] The first is the pursuit of sound policies and good governance by the low-income countries themselves. The second is larger and more effective international support, including official development assistance and opening markets to developing country exports.

The IMF is helping low-income countries make progress [toward these goals] through each of the Fund's three key functions—lending, technical assistance, and surveillance.

Questions

1. How might a loan by the IMF to help a developing country meet its obligations to foreign lenders reduce malnutrition, illness, and premature death among its population?

2. The IMF requires that in order to get IMF aid, developing countries accept technical assistance to help manage their economic affairs and surveillance of some policies. Is this an appropriate intrusion into how those countries manage their affairs?

3. What criteria would you recommend for determining whether a country qualifies for financial support by the IMF?

Source: International Monetary Fund, "How the IMF Helps Poor Countries," October 2007, http://www.imf.org/External/np/exr/facts/poor.htm.

Glossary

Actual reserves A financial depository institution's reserve account plus its vault cash.

Adaptive expectations Households and businesses base their expectations of the future on past and current experiences.

AFL-CIO An organization for furthering the common interests of labor unions; does not engage in bargaining with management.

Antitrust laws Laws prohibiting certain practices that reduce competition.

Asset Something that an individual or business owns; can be used to cover liabilities.

Assumptions Conditions held to be true within a model.

Automated Clearing House (ACH) network A large electronic payments network that facilitates a reliable, secure, and efficient payments system.

Automatic fiscal policy (automatic stabilization) Changes in government expenditures and/or taxes that occur automatically as the level of economic activity changes; helps to control unemployment or demand-pull inflation.

Average fixed cost Fixed cost per unit produced; total fixed cost divided by the number of units produced.

Average total cost The cost per unit of output produced; total cost divided by the number of units produced.

Average variable cost Variable cost per unit produced; total variable cost divided by the number of units produced.

Balance of trade The figure that results when merchandise imports are subtracted from exports.

Balance of trade surplus (deficit) The value of a countrys' merchandise exports is greater (less) than the value of its imports.

Balanced budget A government's total expenditures equal its total revenues.

Bank holding company Corporation formed for the purpose of owning, or holding, the controlling shares of stock in a bank or banks.

Barriers to entry Factors that keep firms from entering a market; can be financial, legal, technical, or other barriers.

Barter (barter system) Goods and services are exchanged for each other rather than for money.

Base year The year against which prices in other years are compared in a price index; given the index number 100.0.

Basic economic decisions The choices that must be made in any society regarding what to produce, how to produce, and to whom production is distributed.

Board of Governors Seven-member board heading the Federal Reserve System; develops policies concerning money, banking, and other financial institution practices.

Bond A financial instrument through which a corporation can borrow funds and repay them over the long run.

Brady Plan A proposal to restructure and reduce developing country indebtedness to commercial banks.

Branch banking Operation of more than one facility by a bank to perform its functions.

Business An organization established to produce and sell goods and services.

Business cycles Recurring periods of growth and decline (or expansion and contraction) in an economy's real output, or real GDP.

Capital (goods) Goods, such as machinery and equipment, used in the production of other goods and services.

Capital account A category of international transactions that records the purchase and sale of financial and real assets between the United States and other nations.

Capitalism An economic system with free enterprise and private property rights; economic decision making occurs in a market environment.

Cartel An arrangement whereby sellers formally join together in a market to make decisions as a group on matters such as pricing.

Celler-Kefauver Act (1950) Federal antitrust statute concerned with anticompetitive mergers and acquisitions of firms; amends Section Seven of the Clayton Act.

Change in demand A change in the demand schedule and curve for a product caused by a change in a nonprice factor influencing the product's demand; the demand curve shifts to the right or left.

Change in labor demand or supply A shift in the demand or supply curve for labor caused by changes in nonwage factors.

Change in quantity demanded and quantity supplied A change in the amount of a product demanded or supplied that is caused by a change in its price; represented by a movement along a demand or supply curve from one price-quantity point to another.

Change in supply A change in the supply schedule and curve for a product caused by a change in a nonprice factor influencing the product's supply; the supply curve shifts to the right or left.

Change in the quantity of labor demanded or supplied A change in the amount of labor demanded or supplied that occurs when wages change; a movement along the demand or supply curve.

Check 21 Law that allows electronic substitute checks for check clearing purposes.

Circular flow model A diagram showing the real and money flows between households and businesses in output, or product, markets and input, or resource, markets.

Classical economics Popularly accepted theory prior to the Great Depression of the 1930s; says the economy will automatically adjust to full employment.

Clayton Act (1914) Federal antitrust statute prohibiting specific activities that substantially reduce competition or tend to create a monopoly.

Closed economy An economy where foreign influences have no effect on output, employment, and prices.

Collective bargaining The process through which a union and management negotiate a labor contract.

Combinations and conspiracies in restraint of trade Practices carried out jointly by two or more firms that unreasonably restrict competition.

Commercial bank Institution that holds and maintains checking accounts (demand deposits) for its customers, makes commercial (business) and other loans, and performs other functions.

Commodity monetary standard An economy's money is backed by something of tangible value such as gold or silver.

Common stock Pays a dividend dependent on the profit of a firm after all other financial obligations have been met.

Comparative advantage One country has a lower opportunity cost when producing a good or service than does another country.

Conglomerate merger A merger between firms that are not competitors, suppliers, or distributors.

Constant returns to scale Occur in the range of production levels in which long-run average total cost is constant.

Consumer goods Goods, such as food and household furniture, that are produced for final buyers.

Consumer price index (CPI) Measures changes in the prices of goods and services that consumers typically purchase, such as food, shelter, clothing, and medical care.

Corporate board of directors Governing body of a corporation; elected by stockholders.

Corporation A legal entity, owned by stockholders; can carry on in its own name business functions normally performed by individuals.

Correspondent banking Interbank relationship involving deposits and various services.

Cost of living adjustment (COLA) An arrangement whereby an individual's wages automatically increase with inflation.

Cost-benefit analysis Weighing the costs and benefits of an action in order to maximize the net benefit from the action.

Cost-plus pricing Prices are set to generate enough revenue to cover operating costs plus a fair return to stockholders.

Cost-push inflation Pressure on prices from the sellers' side of the market, particularly from increases in costs of production.

Craft union A union that represents workers with a specific skill or craft.

Creative destruction New, technologically advanced machinery and production methods cause the disappearance of old machinery and methods.

Crowding out Occurs when borrowing by the federal government increases the interest rate and reduces borrowing by households and businesses.

Currency Coins and paper money.

Current account A category of international transactions that records figures for imports and exports of merchandise, unilateral transfers, and other foreign dealings.

Current account deficit (surplus) A negative (positive) figure results when all current account transactions are added together.

Cyclical unemployment Involuntary unemployment that results from a downswing in a business cycle, or a recession.

Debt service The cost of maintaining a debt; generally measured in interest costs.

Decrease in demand A change in a nonprice influence on demand causes less of a product to be demanded at each price; the demand curve shifts to the left.

Decrease in supply A change in a nonprice influence on supply causes less of a product to be supplied at each price; the supply curve shifts to the left.

Deficit budget A government's expenditures are greater than its revenues.

Deflation A sustained decrease in the general level of prices.

Demand The different amounts of a product that a buyer would purchase at different prices in a defined time period when all nonprice factors are held constant.

Demand curve A line on a graph that illustrates a demand schedule; slopes downward because of the inverse relationship between price and quantity demanded.

Demand curve for labor Downward-sloping curve showing the amount of labor demanded at different wage rates; based on the marginal revenue product of labor.

Demand deposits Checking account balances kept primarily at commercial banks.

Demand-pull inflation Pressure on prices from the buyers' side of the market; tends to occur when buyers' demands (or spending) are greater than the productive capability of the economy.

Demand schedule A list of the amounts of a product that a buyer would purchase at different prices in a defined time period when all nonprice factors are held constant.

Depository Institutions Deregulation and Monetary Control Act (1980) Legislation that increased the similarity among many financial institutions and increased the control of the Federal Reserve system.

Deregulation A reduction in government regulatory control of the economy.

Derived demand The demand for a factor of production depends on the demand for the good or service the factor produces.

Devaluation The amount of gold backing a nation's monetary unit is reduced.

Differentiated products Products of competing firms are different and recognized as such by buyers.

Direct relationship Two variables move in the same direction: when one increases, so does the other; graphs as an upward-sloping line.

Discount rate Interest rate that a Federal Reserve bank charges a financial depository institution for borrowing reserves.

Discouraged workers Persons who drop out of the labor force because they have been unsuccessful for a long period of time in finding a job.

Discretionary fiscal policy Deliberate changes in government expenditures and/or taxes to control unemployment or demand-pull inflation.

Discrimination Unequal treatment in a labor market because of an employer's perception of a category to which a worker belongs.

Diseconomies of scale Occur when the increasing size of production in the long run causes the per unit cost of production to rise.

Disinflation A slowing of the inflation rate.

Distribution of income The way income is divided among the members of society.

Dual banking system Label given to the U.S. banking system because both the federal and state governments have the right to charter banks.

Dumping Selling a product in a foreign market below cost or below its price in its own domestic market.

Durable good A good that has a useful lifetime of more than one year.

Easy money policy Policy by the Federal Reserve to increase excess reserves and decrease interest rates to increase spending.

Econometrics The use of statistical techniques to describe the relationships between economic variables.

Economic cost of production Includes all explicit and implicit costs of producing a good or service.

Economic growth An increase in an economy's full production (full employment) output level over time.

Economic policy A guide for a course of action.

Economic profit (excess profit) Profit beyond normal profit; not considered a cost of production.

Economic profit, loss, breaking even Occurs when price is greater than, less than, or equal to average total cost, respectively.

Economic system The way in which an economy is organized to make the basic economic decisions.

Economic theory A formal explanation of the relationship between economic variables.

Economics The study of how scarce, or limited, resources are used to satisfy unlimited material wants and needs; the study of decision making in a world of scarcity.

Economies of scale Occur when the increasing size of production in the long run causes the per unit cost of production to fall.

Efficiency Producing the largest attainable output of a desired quality with a given set of resources; producing at the lowest possible cost.

Efficient method of production The least-cost method of production.

Efficient production A good or service is produced at the lowest cost possible.

Elasticity coefficient The absolute value of the percentage change in quantity demanded or supplied divided by the absolute value of the percentage change in price; greater or less than one when demand or supply is price elastic or inelastic, respectively.

Embargo A ban on trade in a particular commodity or with a particular country.

Emergency Economic Stabilization Act Passed in 2008 to provide $700 billion to the U.S. Treasury for assistance in keeping financial companies from failing.

Employment Act of 1946 Legislation giving the federal government the right and responsibility to provide an environment for the achievement of full employment, full production, and stable prices.

Entitlements Programs set up by the government to pay benefits to people who meet the eligibility requirements of the programs.

Entrepreneurship The function of organizing resources for production and taking the risk of success or failure in a productive enterprise.

Equation of exchange $MV = PQ$; illustrates how changes in the supply of money (M) influence the level of prices (P) and/or the total output of goods and services (Q).

Equilibrium price and equilibrium quantity The price and quantity where demand equals supply; price and quantity toward which a free market automatically moves.

Equity Justice or fairness in the distribution of goods and services.

European Monetary System (EMS) An agreement to limit the variability of exchange rates between European nations' currencies.

European Union (EU) The single unified market formed by the majority of Western European nations; a major trading power.

Excess profit (economic profit) Profit beyond normal profit; not considered a cost of production.

Excess reserves Reserves of a financial depository institution over the amount it is required to maintain in actual reserves; actual reserves minus required reserves.

Exchange rate The number of units of a nation's currency that is equal to one unit of another nations' currency.

Exclusionary practices Practices of a seller to prevent its suppliers or buyers from dealing with a competitor.

Expectations Anticipations of future events; can affect current actions by households and businesses and the likelihood that the future events will occur.

Explicit costs Payments that a business makes to acquire factors of production, such as labor, raw materials, and machinery.

Exports Goods and services that are sold abroad.

External debt Money owed by borrowers in one country to lenders in other countries.

Externality The effect of an action on a person or thing that was not one of the parties involved in the action.

Federal Deposit Insurance Corporation (FDIC) Government agency established in 1933 to insure deposits in commercial banks up to a specified amount.

Federal Funds market Market in which banks borrow reserves from other banks.

Federal Funds rate The interest rate banks charge to lend reserves to other banks for a short period of time, usually overnight.

Federal Reserve banks Twelve banks that deal with commercial banks and other financial institutions.

Federal Reserve Notes Paper money issued by the Federal Reserve banks; includes almost all paper money in circulation.

Federal Reserve system Coordinates commercial banking operations, regulates some aspects of all depository institutions, and oversees the U.S. money supply.

Federal Savings and Loan Insurance Corporation (FSLIC) Federal agency established in 1934 to insure deposits in savings and loan institutions; the FDIC took over many of its functions when the FSLIC was dissolved in 1989.

Federal Trade Commission Act (1914) Created the Federal Trade Commission and empowered it to prevent unfair methods of competition, which include antitrust violations.

Financial depository institution Institution that accepts and maintains deposits, and makes loans; can create and destroy money.

Financial holding company A holding company that can engage in banking, securities, insurance, and other financial activities.

Financial institutions Organizations such as banks, savings associations, and insurance companies that provide a means for saving and borrowing.

Fiscal policy Influencing the levels of aggregate output and employment or prices through changes in federal government purchases, transfer payments, and/or taxes.

Fixed costs Costs of using fixed factors.

Fixed exchange rates Exchange rates fluctuate little, if at all, because the values of nations' monies are defined in terms of gold.

Fixed factors Factors of production that do not change in amount as the level of output changes.

Flexible (floating) exchange rates Exchange rates that fluctuate because they are determined by the forces of demand and supply.

Foreign exchange market A market for the trading of two nations' monies.

Foreign trade effect A direct relationship between changes in overall prices in an economy and spending on imports diverts spending from domestically produced output; influences aggregate demand in the new classical model.

Free enterprise The right of a business to make its own decisions and to operate with a profit motive.

Free trade Goods and services can be exported and imported by anyone in any country with no restrictions.

Frictional unemployment Occurs when people are voluntarily out of work for a short period of time while searching for a job.

Full employment Occurs when only those voluntarily out of work are unemployed, or the unemployment rate includes only frictional unemployment.

Full production Occurs when an economy is producing at its maximum capacity, or at full employment.

GDP price index The price index used when calculating price changes for the entire economy.

General Agreement on Tariffs and Trade (GATT) An international forum for negotiating tariffs.

General partner An owner in a partnership who is subject to unlimited liability.

Geographic boundary of a market Defined by the geographic area in which sellers compete for buyers.

Government purchases of goods and services Government spending on new goods and services; nonincome-determined spending.

Government regulation Government participation, through agencies and commissions, in business decision making; may be industry regulation or social regulation.

Gramm-Leach-Bliley Act Passed in 1999 to allow bank holding companies to become financial holding companies and engage in securities and insurance activities.

Graph An illustration showing the relationship between two variables that are measured on the vertical and horizontal axes.

Gross domestic product (GDP) A dollar figure that measures the value of all finished goods and services produced in an economy in one year.

Heavily Indebted Poor Countries (HIPC) Initiative A joint initiative by the World Bank and International Monetary Fund to help heavily indebted developing countries manage their external debt.

Holding company A corporation formed for the purpose of owning or holding stock in other corporations.

Horizontal merger A merger between two sellers competing in the same market.

Household A person living alone or a group of related or unrelated persons who occupy a house, an apartment, or other housing unit.

Human capital investments Investments, such as formal education, that increase the productivity of people.

Hyperinflation Extremely rapid increases in the general level of prices.

Implicit costs The opportunity costs to business owners from using their resources in the business rather than in an alternative opportunity; must be recovered to keep a business in operation; normal profit.

Imports Goods and services purchased from abroad.

Incentive regulation A regulatory philosophy that provides incentives for regulated firms to operate efficiently.

Income-determined spending Household spending on new goods and services that comes from income earned from providing resources to producers.

Increase in demand A change in a nonprice influence on demand causes more of a product to be demanded at each price; the demand curve shifts to the right.

Increase in supply A change in a nonprice influence on supply causes more of a product to be supplied at each price; the supply curve shifts to the right.

Individual firm's demand curve Shows the amounts of an individual firm's product that buyers are willing to purchase at particular prices.

Industrial Revolution A time period during which an economy becomes industrialized; characterized by such social and technological changes as the growth and development of factories.

Industrial union A union that represents all workers in a specific industry, regardless of the type of job performed.

Industry regulation Regulation affecting several aspects (such as pricing, entry of new sellers, and conditions of service) of the operations of firms in a particular industry.

Industry A group of firms producing similar products or using similar processes.

Infant industry An industry in the early stage of its development.

Inflation An increase in the general level of prices.

Injections into the spending stream Spending that comes from a source other than household earned income; nonincome-determined spending.

Input markets (resource markets) Markets in which households are sellers and businesses are buyers; factors of production are bought and sold.

Interest Income return to owners of capital.

Interest rate The price of money; determines the return to savers and lenders of money, and the cost to borrowers; a percentage of the amount borrowed.

Interest rate effect The interest rate moves with changes in overall prices; there is an inverse relationship between the interest rate and the amount people borrow and spend.

Interlocking directorates The same person sits on the boards of directors of different corporations.

International Monetary Fund (IMF) An international organization that provides loans and other financial assistance to countries.

International trade The buying and selling of goods and services among different countries.

Interstate banking The performance of services in more than one state by a single banking organization.

Inventories Stocks of goods on hand; can be intentional or unintentional.

Inverse relationship Two variables move in opposite directions: when one increases, the other decreases; graphs as a downward-sloping line.

Investment spending Business spending on new goods, such as machinery, equipment, buildings, and inventories; nonincome-determined spending.

Invisible hand doctrine Adam Smith's concept that producers acting in their own self-interest will provide buyers with what they want and thus advance the interests of society.

Joint venture A cooperative effort by two or more firms that is limited in scope.

Keynesian economics Based on the work of John Maynard Keynes (1883–1946), who focused on the role of aggregate spending in determining the level of macroeconomic activity.

Kinked demand curve Assumes that rivals will not follow price increases but will follow price decreases; illustrates that as a seller's price rises, the amount of its product demanded decreases substantially, but as its price falls, the amount demanded increases only slightly.

Labor Physical and mental human effort used to produce goods and services.

Labor force All persons 16 years of age and older who are working or actively seeking work.

Labor union An organization of workers that bargains in its members' behalf with management on wages, working conditions, fringe benefits, and other work-related issues.

Laissez-faire capitalism Capitalism with a strong emphasis on individual decision making; little or no government interference.

Land Productive inputs that originate in nature, such as coal and fertile soil.

Law of Demand There is an inverse relationship between the price of a product and the quantity demanded.

Law of Diminishing Marginal Utility As additional units of an item are consumed, beyond some point each successive unit of the item consumed will add less to total utility than was added by the unit consumed just before it.

Law of Diminishing Returns As additional units of a variable factor are added to a fixed factor, beyond some point the product from each additional unit of the variable factor decreases.

Law of Supply There is a direct relationship between the price of a product and the quantity supplied.

Leadership pricing One firm in a market sets a price that the other firms in the market then adopt.

Leakages from the spending stream Uses for earned income other than spending, such as paying taxes and saving.

Least-cost (efficient) method of production The method of production that allows a good or service of a given quality to be produced at the lowest cost.

Liability A claim on assets; an obligation or a debt of an individual or a business.

Limited Liability Companies (LLCs) Businesses that combine the liability

protection of corporations with the management flexibility of proprietorships and partnerships.

Liquidity Ease of converting an asset to its value in cash or spendable funds.

Long run A production time frame in which all factors of production are variable in amount.

Long-run total cost, average total cost, and marginal cost Total cost, per unit cost, and cost per additional unit of output, respectively; calculated for production when all inputs are regarded as variable.

M1 Narrower definition of the U.S. money supply; includes coins and paper money in circulation, some traveler's checks, most demand deposits, and other checkable deposits.

M2 M1 plus savings and small-denomination time deposit accounts, and other financial instruments.

Maastricht Treaty Called for a common currency and central bank to oversee a single monetary policy for countries belonging to Europe's Economic and Monetary Union.

Macroeconomics The study of the operation of the economy as a whole.

Macroeconomic equilibrium Occurs when the amount of total planned spending on new goods and services equals total output in the economy.

Marginal benefit (marginal utility) The change in total satisfaction from consuming each additional unit of a good, service, or activity.

Marginal cost The change in total cost when one more unit of output is produced.

Marginal product The change in total product when one more unit of a variable resource, such as labor, is utilized.

Marginal revenue The change in total revenue when one more (or additional) unit of an item is demanded.

Marginal revenue product The change in total revenue that results from the sale of output produced when one more unit of a variable resource, such as labor, is utilized.

Market Place or situation in which the buyers and sellers of a product interact for the purpose of exchange; includes firms that sell similar products and compete for the same buyers.

Market clearing price Equilibrium price; price at which the quantity demanded equals the quantity supplied.

Market demand and market supply The demand of all buyers and supply of all sellers in a market for a good or service; found by adding together all individual demand or supply schedules.

Market demand curve The demand curve for all buyers in the market together.

Market economy An economy in which the basic economic decisions are made by individual buyers and sellers in markets using the language of price.

Market failure A market system creates a problem for a society or fails to achieve a society's goals.

Market structures A classification system for grouping markets according to the degree and type of competition among sellers.

Maximizing economic well-being Obtaining the greatest possible satisfaction, or return, from an economic decision.

Measure of value A function of money; the value of every good, service, and resource can be expressed in terms of an economy's base unit of money.

Medium of exchange Something that is generally accepted as payment for goods, services, and resources; the primary function of money.

Mercantilism An economic system or philosophy that subordinates individual interests and decisions to those of the state.

Merger (acquisition) The acquiring of one company by another; can be accomplished by buying a controlling amount of stock.

Method for storing wealth and delaying payments A function of money; allows for saving, or storing wealth for future use, and permits credit, or delayed payments.

Microeconomics The study of individual decision-making units and markets within the economy.

Minimum wage law Legislation specifying the lowest hourly earnings that an employee can be paid.

Mixed economy An economy in which the basic economic choices are made through a combination of market and centralized decision making.

Model The setting within which an economic theory is presented; includes variables, assumptions, data collection, and conclusions.

Monetarism School of thought that favors stabilizing the economy through controlling the money supply.

Monetarists Persons who favor the economic policies of monetarism.

Monetary policy Influencing the levels of aggregate output and employment or prices through changes in interest rates and the money supply.

Monetizing the debt Increasing the money supply by the Federal Reserve to accommodate federal government borrowing and reduce upward pressure on the interest rate.

Money Anything that is generally accepted as a medium of exchange.

Money (nominal) income Income measured in terms of current dollars.

Money GDP (current, or nominal, GDP) Measures the value of production in terms of prices at the time of production.

Money multiplier Multiple by which an initial change in excess reserves in the system can change the money supply.

Monopolistic competition Market structure characterized by a large number of sellers with differentiated outputs and fairly easy entry and exit.

Monopolization and attempts to monopolize A firm acquires or attempts to acquire a monopoly share of its market through unreasonable means.

Monopoly market A market with one seller that maintains its position because entry by new sellers is impossible.

Muckrakers Authors, journalists, and others who sensationalized American social problems in the early twentieth century.

Multiplier effect The change in total output and income generated by a change in nonincome-determined spending is larger than, or a multiple of, the spending change itself.

Multiplier effect (money) An initial change in excess reserves in the depository institutions system causes a larger change in the money supply.

Mutual fund Pool of money from depositors that is used to make investments.

Mutual interdependence So few sellers exist in the market that each seller weighs the actions and reactions of rivals in its decision making.

National bank Commercial bank incorporated under a federal rather than a state charter.

National debt The accumulated total debt of the federal government due to deficit spending.

National Labor Relations Act (Wagner Act) Legislation supportive of unions; permits and strengthens collective bargaining.

National Labor Relations Board (NLRB) Hears complaints on unfair labor practices and orders remedies where appropriate.

Natural monopoly A market situation where it is more efficient (less costly) to have the entire output of a product come from one large producer rather than from several smaller producers.

Natural rate hypothesis Over the long run, unemployment will tend toward its natural rate, and policies to reduce unemployment below that level will be ineffective.

Natural rate of unemployment The unemployment rate that includes the frictionally and structurally unemployed; occurs when cyclical unemployment is eliminated.

Negative externality An externality that creates a cost for others.

Net benefit The result when total cost is subtracted from total benefit.

Net benefit maximizing rules Net benefit is maximized where total benefit exceeds total cost by the greatest amount, or where marginal benefit equals marginal cost.

Net exports Exports minus imports; is positive when exports exceed imports and negative when imports exceed exports.

Net worth Assets minus liabilities; the monetary value of a business.

New classical economics A return to the basic classical premise that free markets automatically stabilize themselves and that government intervention in the macroeconomy is not advisable.

New Deal A series of programs and legislative reforms instituted during the administration of Franklin D. Roosevelt in the Great Depression of the 1930s.

New Keynesian economics Builds on the Keynesian view that the economy does not automatically return to full employment; emphasizes downward sticky prices and individual decision making in the microeconomy.

Nondurable good A good that has a short useful lifetime.

Nonincome-determined spending Spending that is generated from sources other than household earned income.

Nonmember state insured bank Bank that does not belong to the Federal Reserve system but is insured by the FDIC.

Nonprice competition Firms focus on a feature other than price to attract buyers to their products.

Nonprice factors influencing demand Nonprice factors such as income, taste, and expectations that help to determine the demand for a product.

Nonprice factors influencing supply Nonprice factors such as the cost of production and the number of sellers that help to determine the supply of a product.

Normal profit Profit necessary to recover implicit costs and keep a business in operation; considered to be an economic cost of production.

North American Free Trade Agreement (NAFTA) Treaty creating a unified market involving the United States, Canada, and Mexico.

Oligopolistic markets Markets dominated by a few large sellers; products are differentiated or identical; entry into the market is difficult.

On-budget/Off-budget Categories of the unified budget established by Congress; generally refers to programs that have immediately controllable and noncontrollable receipts and expenses, respectively.

Open economy An economy where foreign influences have an effect on output, employment, and prices.

Open Market Committee Determines the general policy on the buying and selling of government securities by the Federal Reserve.

Open market operations The buying and selling of securities, primarily U.S. government securities, on the open market by the Federal Reserve.

Opportunity cost The cost of acquiring a good or service or taking an action measured in terms of the value of the opportunity or alternative forgone.

Other checkable deposits Interest-bearing accounts similar to demand deposits offered by financial depository institutions.

Output markets (product markets) Markets in which businesses are sellers and households are buyers; consumer goods and services are exchanged.

Paper monetary standard An economy's money is not backed by anything of tangible value such as gold or silver.

Participation rate The percentage of some specified group that is in the labor force.

Partnership The legal organization of a business that is similar to a proprietorship but has two or more owners.

Per se violations Anticompetitive agreements between firms where proof of the agreement is sufficient to establish guilt; includes price fixing and division of sales territories.

Personal consumption expenditures Household spending on new goods and services.

Personal income Household gross, or pretax, income; used to pay taxes, spend, and save.

Phillips curve Curve showing the relationship between an economy's unemployment and inflation rates.

Planned economy (command economy) An economy in which the basic economic decisions are made by planners rather than by private individuals and businesses.

Planning failure Centralized planning creates a problem for a society or fails to achieve a society's goals.

Positive externality An externality that creates a benefit for others.

Poverty levels Government-designated levels of income that must be received to be considered *not* poor.

Preferred stock Pays a stated dividend to its holder; preferred stockholders are entitled to receive dividends before common stockholders.

Price caps An incentive system allowing regulated firms to price up to a pre-set maximum and retain additional profit from operating more efficiently.

Price ceiling (upper price limit) A government-set maximum price that can be charged for a good or service; if the equilibrium price is above the price ceiling, a shortage will develop.

Price discrimination Different buyers acquire the same product from the same seller with the same treatment and service but pay different prices.

Price elastic A strong response to a price change; occurs when the percentage change in the quantity demanded or supplied is greater than the percentage change in price.

Price elasticity A measure of the strength of a buyer's or seller's response to a price change.

Price fixing Joint action by sellers to influence their product prices; considered to be highly anticompetitive.

Price floor (lower price limit) A government-set minimum price that can be charged for a good or service; if the equilibrium price is below the price floor, a surplus will develop.

Price index Measures changes in the price of an item or a group of items using a percentage scale.

Price inelastic A weak response to a price change; occurs when the percentage change in the quantity demanded or supplied is less than the percentage change in price.

Price searcher A firm that searches its downward-sloping demand curve to find the price-output combination that maximizes its profit.

Price system A market system; one in which buyers and sellers communicate through prices in markets.

Price taker A seller with no control over the price of its product; takes the market price.

Private property rights Rights given to individuals and businesses to own resources, goods, and services, and to use them as they choose.

Privatization The granting to individuals of property rights to factors of production that were once collectively owned, or owned by the state.

Producer price index (PPI) Measures changes in the prices of goods and services that businesses buy, either for further processing or for sale to a consumer.

Producing sectors A broad classification system for grouping goods and services, and the firms that produce them.

Product boundary of a market Defined by product substitutability among buyers.

Production The creation of goods and services.

Production function Shows the type and amount of output that results from a particular group of inputs when those inputs are combined in a certain way.

Production possibilities table (or curve) Gives the various amounts of two goods that an economy can produce with full employment and fixed resources and technology.

Productivity Concept of assessing the amount of output produced by an economy's resources; often measured specifically by output per worker.

Profit maximizing rules Profit is maximized at the output level where total revenue exceeds total cost by the greatest amount, or where marginal revenue equals marginal cost.

Profit Income return to those performing the entrepreneurial function.

Profit or loss What results when a business subtracts its total costs from its total revenue.

Progressive tax A tax reflecting a direct relationship between the percentage of income taxed and the size of the income.

Proportional tax (flat tax) A tax equal to the same percentage of income regardless of the size of the income.

Proprietorship A one-owner business.

Protectionism The philosophy that it is in the best interest of a country to restrict free trade.

Public choice The study of the economic motives and attitudes of voters and public officials in collective decision making.

Public good A good (or service) provided for all of society; no one is excluded from use of a public good.

Public interest justification for regulation A good or service is so important to the public well-being that its production and distribution should be regulated.

Purely competitive market A market with a large number of independent firms selling identical products, and with easy entry into and exit from the market.

Quasi-public good A government-provided good that could be offered in a private market.

Quota A restriction on the quantity of an item that can be imported into a country.

Rational expectations Households and businesses base their expectations of future policies on how they think they will be affected by those policies.

Rational ignorance Choosing to remain uninformed because the marginal cost of obtaining the information is higher than the marginal benefit from knowing it.

Real GDP (constant GDP) Money GDP adjusted to eliminate inflation; measures real production.

Real income Income measured in terms of the goods and services that can be purchased with a particular amount of money income.

Real rate of interest The nominal, or stated, rate of interest minus the inflation rate; a nominal interest rate adjusted for inflation.

Recovery, peak, recession, trough The phases of the business cycle during which real GDP, or output, increases, reaches its maximum, falls, and reaches its minimum, respectively.

Regressive tax A tax reflecting an inverse relationship between the percentage of income taxed and the size of the income.

Rent Income return to owners of land resources.

Required reserves The amount of actual reserves that a financial depository institution must keep to back its deposits.

Reserve account Deposit in the name of a financial institution held at a Federal Reserve bank or other designated place.

Reserve requirement Specific percentage of deposits that a financial depository institution must keep as actual reserves.

Resolution Trust Corporation (RTC) Federal agency created to reorganize troubled savings and loans or to deal with their affairs if they failed and closed.

Resources (factors of production) Persons and things used to produce goods and services; limited in amount; categorized as labor, capital, land, and entrepreneurship.

Retained earnings The portion of a business's accumulated profits that has been retained for investment or other purposes.

Revenue Money or income that a company receives from selling its product.

Riegle-Neal Interstate Banking and Branching Efficiency Act (1994) Legislation allowing banking organizations from one state to open or acquire banks, and to open branches, in other states.

Right to work laws State laws prohibiting union membership as a condition of employment.

Robinson-Patman Act (1936) Federal antitrust statute concerned with anticompetitive price discrimination; amends Section Two of the Clayton Act.

Rule of Reason violations Actions that may or may not be unreasonable restraints of trade.

Saving-borrowing relationship The relationship between the amount saved by households and businesses and the amount returned to the spending stream through investment and household borrowing.

Scarcity Too few goods and services to satisfy all wants and needs.

Sherman Act (1890) Original and most broadly worded federal antitrust statute; condemns combinations and conspiracies in restraint of trade, and monopolization and attempts to monopolize.

Short run A production time frame in which some factors of production are variable in amount and some are fixed.

Shortage Occurs in a market when the quantity demanded is greater than the quantity supplied, or when the product's price is below the equilibrium price.

Social benefits and costs The total effect on society from the private benefits, private costs, and externalities of an action.

Social insurance program Contributions from an individual's earnings are made to a fund from which that individual may draw when eligible for benefits.

Social regulation Regulation aimed at correcting a problem or protecting a group; not limited to a specific industry.

Socialism An economic system in which many of the factors of production are collectively owned, and an attempt is made to equalize the distribution of income.

Special-interest group People who share a common position on a particular issue and actively promote that position.

Specialization Productive resources concentrate on a narrow range of tasks or the production of a limited variety of goods and services.

Stagflation Occurs when an economy experiences high rates of both inflation and unemployment.

State bank Commercial bank incorporated under a state charter.

Strike Work stoppage by union members.

Structural unemployment Involuntary unemployment that results when a worker's job is no longer part of the production structure of the economy.

Supply The different amounts of a product that a seller would make available for sale at different prices in a defined time period when all nonprice factors are held constant.

Supply curve A line on a graph that illustrates a supply schedule; slopes upward because of the direct relationship between price and quantity supplied.

Supply curve of labor Upward-sloping curve showing the amount of labor supplied at different wage rates.

Supply schedule A list of the amounts of a product that a seller would offer for sale at different prices in a defined time period when all nonprice factors are held constant.

Supply-side economics Policies to achieve macroeconomic goals by stimulating the supply side of the market; popular in the 1980s.

Surplus Occurs in a market when the quantity demanded is less than the quantity supplied, or when the product's price is above the equilibrium price.

Surplus budget A government's revenues are greater than its expenditures.

Taft-Hartley Act Legislation that contains several provisions limiting union activities.

Tariff A tax on an import.

Tax abatement A policy of reducing or eliminating a tax that would normally be charged.

Tax base The particular thing on which a tax is levied.

Tax bracket indexation A policy of adjusting income tax brackets to account for inflation.

Tax rate The amount that is levied on a tax base.

Tax reform Changes in tax policies and structures.

Tax Reform Act of 1986 Major legislation that changed federal income tax exemptions, deductions, brackets, and rates.

Technology The body of knowledge that exists about production and its processes.

Territorial division Joint action by sellers to divide sales territories among themselves; considered to be highly anticompetitive.

Tight money policy Policy by the Federal Reserve to reduce excess reserves and raise interest rates to reduce spending.

Token money Money with a face value greater than the value of the commodity from which it is made.

Total benefit (total utility) The total amount of satisfaction received from consuming a specified number of units of a good, service, or activity.

Total cost The cost of producing a specified number of units of a good, service, or activity; total fixed cost plus total variable cost.

Total fixed cost The cost of all fixed factors; does not change as the level of output changes and must be paid even when output is zero.

Total revenue Revenue received from selling a certain quantity of an item;

calculated by multiplying the price of an item by the quantity demanded at that price.

Total, or aggregate, spending The total combined spending of all units in the economy (households plus businesses plus government plus foreign) for new goods and services.

Total utility Total satisfaction from consuming a particular combination of goods and services.

Total variable cost The cost of all variable factors of production; increases as the level of output increases, but is zero when output is zero.

Trade association An organization representing firms in a particular industry that performs functions to benefit those firms.

Trade subsidy A government payment to the domestic producer of an exported good.

Tradeoff Giving up one thing for something else.

Traditional, or agrarian, economy An economy that relies on tradition, custom, or ritual to decide what to produce, how to produce it, and to whom to distribute the results.

Transfer payments Money from the government for which no direct work is performed in return.

Treasury inflation-protected securities (TIPS) U.S. Treasury securities with face values that rise when the economy experiences inflation.

Trust fund A restricted fund; payments from this fund are specified as to recipients and/or uses.

Tying contract A buyer can obtain a good from a seller only by purchasing another good from the same seller.

U.S. Treasury bill, note, and bond U.S. Treasury securities that mature, respectively, in 1 year or less; 1 to 10 years; and 10 or more years.

U.S. Treasury security Issued by the federal government in return for funds lent to it.

Underemployment A resource is employed in a way that does not fully use its capabilities; intensifies the scarcity problem.

Underground economy Productive activities that are not reported for tax purposes and are not included in GDP.

Unemployment Resources available for production are not being used.

Unemployment rate The percentage of the labor force that is unemployed and actively seeking work.

Unified budget A budget that assembles all federal government receipts and outlays, and the resulting overall deficit or surplus, in one report.

Unitary price elastic The percentage change in quantity demanded or supplied equals the percentage change in price; elasticity coefficient equals one.

Unlimited liability A business owner's personal assets are subject to use as payment for business debts.

Usury laws State laws setting maximum interest rates that can be charged for certain types of loans.

Utility Satisfaction realized from consuming a good or service, or taking an action.

Value judgment The relative importance one assigns to an action or alternative.

Value of money Measured by the goods, services, and resources that money can purchase.

Variable costs Costs of using variable factors.

Variable factors Factors of production that change in amount as the level of output changes.

Velocity of money Average number of times the money supply is turned over in a year in relationship to GDP.

Vertical merger A merger between a firm and a supplier or distributor.

Wage The price of labor; income return to labor.

Wealth A measure of the value of tangible assets; includes such items as real estate and corporate securities.

Wealth effect In order to maintain the same amount of accumulated wealth, people spend less when prices rise and more when prices fall.

World Trade Organization (WTO) An organization founded in 1995 to take over responsibilities of GATT.

Chapter 1

The economy's production possibilities curve is shown by the solid line in the figure accompanying these answers.

1. Twelve million units of capital goods (capital goods decreased from 32 to 20 million units); 10 million units of consumer goods (consumer goods decreased from 10 million units to zero).
2. Point A is slightly to the left of the production possibilities curve, and point B is further to the left than point A.
3. The location of point C depends on how one views the relative importance of capital goods and consumer goods. Point C will be closer to the horizontal axis if capital goods are considered to be relatively more important, and closer to the vertical axis if consumer goods are considered to be relatively more important. Students put point C on the curve based on their opinions about the relative importance of capital goods and consumer goods.
4. If only consumer goods were produced, no machinery or equipment would be produced to replace what is currently being used, and future production would be adversely affected. If only capital goods were produced, there would be nothing to sustain people currently.
5. The production possibilities curve would shift to the right as illustrated by the lighter line in the accompanying figure.

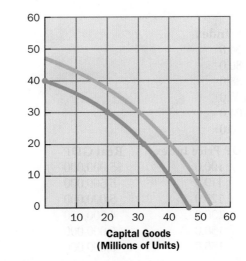

Chapter 2

1. a. pure market
   b. pure planned
   c. mixed
   d. pure market
   e. pure planned
   f. mixed

2. a. Flow of money from households to businesses and flow of goods and services from businesses to households; saving more and spending less reduces the money flow and the goods and services flow.
    b. Flow of factors of production from households to businesses and flow of income from businesses to households; reducing the flows on the bottom half reduces the flows on the top half.
    c. Saving more and spending less decreases the production of goods and services which, in turn, decreases employment of resources and income.

Chapter 3

1. d; supply curve shifts to the left; increase; decrease
2. a; demand curve shifts to the right; increase; increase
3. d; supply curve shifts to the left; increase; decrease
4. e; no shifts; none; none (changes price, not a nonprice factor)
5. b; demand curve shifts to the left; decrease; decrease
6. a; demand curve shifts to the right; increase; increase
7. c; supply curve shifts to the right; decrease; increase
8. b; demand curve shifts to the left; decrease; decrease
9. a; demand curve shifts to the right; increase; increase
10. e; no shifts; none; none (changes price, not a nonprice factor)
11. b; demand curve shifts to the left; decrease; decrease
12. c; supply curve shifts to the right; decrease; increase
13. e; no shifts; none; none (changes price, not a nonprice factor)
14. c; supply curve shifts to the right; decrease; increase

Chapter 4

1.

Price Index	Price Index
80.0	64.0
100.0	80.0
110.0	88.0
125.0	100.0
130.0	104.0
150.0	120.0

2.

Money GDP	GDP Price Index	Real GDP
$5,000,000	100.0	$5,000,000
6,050,000	110.0	5,500,000
6,250,000	125.0	5,000,000
5,850,000	130.0	4,500,000
9,000,000	150.0	6,000,000
9,300,000	155.0	6,000,000

3. Real GDP 2003: $1,000; 2004: $1,000; 2005: $1,200; 2006: $1,250; 2007: $1,250; 2008: $1,200; 2009: $1,250
    a. The economy's output did not grow from 2003 to 2004, grew from 2004 through 2006, did not grow in 2007, decreased in 2008, and grew again in 2009.
    b. Unlike the impression given by money GDP, the economy's real GDP, or output, did not grow every year, and in 2008 it actually declined. Also, the overall growth rate in output from 2003 through 2009 was not nearly as great as money GDP would lead one to believe.

Chapter 5

From each action taken alone, output and employment would change as follows.

1. increase
2. decrease
3. increase
4. increase
5. decrease
6. no change (demand-pull inflation would result)
7. decrease
8. increase
9. increase
10. no change (demand-pull inflation would result)
11. decrease
12. decrease
13. no change (demand-pull inflation would result)
14. increase
15. decrease

From each of these actions, total output and income would change as follows.

16. increase by $200 million
17. decrease by $87.5 billion
18. increase by $400 million
19. decrease by $12 billion
20. decrease by $12.5 million ($20 million export injection – $25 million import leakage ÷ 40.40 = –$12.5 million)
21. increase by $400 million (80 percent of $100 million transfer payment = $80 million in spending; $80 million ÷ 0.20 = $400 million)

Chapter 6

1. output and employment increase
2. output and employment will decrease (some portion of the Social Security will be saved and not spent while all of the government purchases amount will be a decrease in spending)
3. price levels increase
4. output and employment increase
5. output and employment decrease
6. output and employment decrease
7. output and employment decrease
8. output and employment increase
9. price levels increase
10. price levels increase
11. output and employment decrease
12. output and employment decrease

Chapter 7

1. $18,871,340
2. $38,014,440
3. $11,956,741
4. $14,840,000

Chapter 8

1. required reserves = $1,350,000; actual reserves = $6,000,000; excess reserves = $4,650,000
2. new loans = $9,700,000
3. new borrowing = $50,000
4. money multiplier = 12.5
   money supply increase = $625,000,000
5. decrease in excess reserves = $335,000
6. new excess reserves = $2,000,000
7. new excess reserves by Carolina Coast = $0;
   new excess reserves by Inland Bank = $4,000,000
8. money supply increase = $280,000,000

Chapter 9

1 and 2.

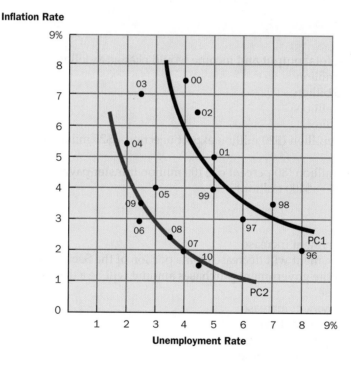

3. Unemployment rate for women fell while participation rates increased; teenage participation decreased; involuntary unemployment decreased.
4. Cost-push inflationary pressure decreased. With less pressure on prices from the seller's side of the market, any rate of unemployment would be associated with a lower rate of inflation.
5. Government becomes less generous in its transfer payment policies. With less transfer income, any rate of inflation would be associated with a lower rate of unemployment.

Chapter 10

1. increase in supply causing equilibrium price to fall
2. increase in demand and a possible decrease in supply causing equilibrium price to rise
3. decrease in demand and a possible increase in supply causing equilibrium price to fall
4. decrease in demand and increase in supply causing equilibrium price to fall

5. increase in supply causing equilibrium price to fall
6. decrease in demand and increase in supply causing equilibrium price to fall
7. increase in demand causing equilibrium price to rise

Chapter 11

According to Table 1, Pete should charge $98 and complete 4 drawings to maximize his profit from the drawings. In going for volume, as suggested by his roommate, his total profit would be $128 less than that received from producing and selling 4 drawings.

As for the lithographs, Pete should charge $100 each and sell 8, earning a total profit of $495. This is indicated in Table 2.

TABLE 1   *Custom-Drawn Houses*

Price per Drawing	Number of Drawings Demanded	Total Revenue	Marginal Revenue	Marginal Cost	Total Cost	Profit
$138	0	$ 0			$ 0	$ 0
128	1	128	$128	$50	50	78
118	2	236	108	50	100	136
108	3	324	88	50	150	174
98	4	392	68	50	200	192
88	5	440	48	50	250	190
78	6	468	28	50	300	168
68	7	476	8	50	350	126
58	8	464	−12	50	400	64

TABLE 2   *Lithographs*

Price per Lithograph	Number of Lithographs Demanded	Total Revenue	Marginal Revenue	Marginal Cost	Total Cost	Profit or Loss
$180	0	$ 0			$ 0	$ 0
170	1	170	$ 170	$200	200	−30
160	2	320	150	15	215	105
150	3	450	130	15	230	220
140	4	560	110	15	245	315
130	5	650	90	15	260	390
120	6	720	70	15	275	445
110	7	770	50	15	290	480
100	8	800	30	15	305	495
90	9	810	10	15	320	490
80	10	800	−10	15	335	465

Chapter 12

1. 92%, fall, lower, 85.5%
    fall, lower, 83.7%
    rise, higher, 86%

2.
Pickups per Business Day	TFC	TVC	TC	ATC	MC
0	$100	$0	$100		—
					$250
1	$100	$250	$350	$350	
					$50
2	$100	$300	$400	$200	
					$0
3	$100	$300	$400	$133.33	
					$50
4	$100	$350	$450	$112.50	
					$75
5	$100	$425	$525	$105	

3. $2,025; $3,042; $6,183; $2.25; $1.90; $2.29

4.
Output	TFC	TVC	TC	ATC	MC
0	$80	$ 0	$ 80	—	
1	80	40	120	$120	$ 40
2	80	60	140	70	20
3	80	70	150	50	10
4	80	100	180	45	30
5	80	150	230	46	50
6	80	220	300	50	70
7	80	340	420	60	120
8	80	520	600	75	180

Chapter 13

1. The total revenue values in the table are: $0, $2, $4, $2,000, $2,002, $2,004, $20,000, $20,002, $20,004. All marginal revenue values are $2.00.
    a. Draw a perfectly horizontal line at $2.00 and mark it D = MR.
    b. 7,000 bushels
    c. $2.50; loss $0.50; loss $3,500
    d. Draw a perfectly horizontal line at $3.50 and mark it D = MR.
    e. 9,000 bushels
    f. $2.50; profit $1.00; profit $9,000
2. 5,000 units; $9.00; $5.00; profit $4.00; profit $20,000

Chapter 14

1. social regulation—Environmental Protection Agency
2. no government intervention
3. social regulation—Consumer Product Safety Commission
4. antitrust enforcement—Sherman Act Section 1 price fixing violation
5. no government intervention—the sellers are pure competitors responding to the price rather than fixing it

6. industry regulation
7. antitrust enforcement—Celler-Kefauver Act
8. no government intervention
9. industry regulation
10. antitrust enforcement—Sherman Act Section 2 monopolization violation

Chapter 15

In Table 1, marginal product is 500, 500, 500, 400, 300.
1. the fourth worker

In Table 3, total revenue is $0, $25, $45, $60, $66.50, $67.50. Marginal revenue product is $25, $20, $15, $6.50, $1.00.
2. $25 per hour
3. $15 per hour
4. no, the MRP of the fifth worker is just $1

In Table 4, the quantity of workers demanded with each wage rate is 1—$25; 2—$20; 3—$15; 4—$6.50; 5—$1.00. These numbers are used to plot the demand curve in the figure.

Chapter 16

1.
   a. 1/2, 2, Canada
   b. 2, 1/2, Brazil
   c. 12, 12
   d. 16 of wheat, 16 of soybeans
   e. 8, 8

2.
   a. 1/5, 4, Mexico
   b. 5, 1/4, Venezuela
   c. 525, 200
   d. 1,000 lamps, 200 gallons of gasoline
   e. 50, 200

Chapter 17

1. decrease, decrease, decrease, increase
2. increase, decrease, increase, increase
3. increase, increase, increase, decrease
4. decrease, increase, decrease, decrease
5. increase, increase, increase, decrease
6. decrease, increase, decrease, decrease or increase depending on whether the effect of the change in demand was greater or less than the effect of the change in supply, increase